LAST IN THEIR CLASS

LAST IN THEIR CLASS

*Custer, Pickett
and the Goats of West Point*

James S. Robbins

ENCOUNTER BOOKS
NEW YORK

First edition published in 2006 by Encounter Books, an activity of Encounter for Culture and Education, Inc., a nonprofit, tax exempt corporation.

Encounter Books website address: www.encounterbooks.com

Manufactured in the United States and printed on acid-free paper.

The paper used in this publication meets the minimum requirements of ANSI/NISO Z39.48-1992 (R 1997)(*Permanence of Paper*).

FIRST EDITION

Library of Congress Cataloging-in-Publication Data

Robbins, James S., 1962
    Last in Their Class: Custer, Pickett and the Goats of West Point/James S. Robbins.
      p. cm.
      ISBN 1-59403-142-8 (alk. paper)
      1. United States Army—Biography.   2. United States Military Academy—Alumni and alumnae—Biography.   3. Soldiers—United States—Biography.   4. Military education—United States—History—19th century.   5. United States—History, Military—19th century.
    E181.R63 2006
    355.0092/273 B 22

                              2005036764

10 9 8 7 6 5 4 3 2 1

To E.L.R., USMA 1992
"Not the Goat"

CONTENTS

INTRODUCTION

THE SPIRIT OF THE GOAT

"My career as a cadet had but little to commend it to the study of
those who came after me, unless as an example to be carefully avoided."
—*George Armstrong Custer*
United States Military Academy, Class of June 1861

THE UNITED STATES MILITARY ACADEMY at West Point is an
institution committed to excellence, which strives to equip each
cadet with the knowledge and the leadership skills they will need
to be Army officers and to fight and win our nation's wars. Yet at West
Point graduation ceremonies, no cadet is applauded louder than the
graduate with the lowest grades, the Goat.

Graduating last at West Point is not a badge of shame but a mark
of achievement. "I'd rather be last man on a first-rate team," said one
Academy graduate, "than first man on any other." Particularly in the
nineteenth century, when graduating classes were smaller and attrition
rates were much higher, the Goat was seen as a survivor. No Goats
stayed at the bottom of their classes for four years straight—most of
those who had stood below them flunked out by graduation. As well,
given the subjectivity of grading and the caprice of circumstance, being
the Goat was as much a function of luck as one of ability. Coming in
last in the class was thus something earned, but also fated. The same is
true in war: bad breaks can disrupt the best plans, while good luck and
individual effort can bring unexpected victory. Ill fortune can make a
Goat, but a Goat can make himself a hero.

The Goat of the Class of 1862, Charles Nelson Warner, was simply glad to have the chance to serve. He had failed an exam in 1861 (due
in part to one of George Custer's stunts) and had been sent home to
Pennsylvania. But at the onset of the Civil War, he was given a second

chance. "If I conduct myself properly," Warner wrote his sister, "I have a chance yet to outstrip those who have excelled me here. I mean to be temperate, prompt, faithful, persevering, never shirking from my duty." After he graduated, Warner had his baptism of fire at the Battle of Antietam, and then proved his devotion to duty with a heroic stand at Chancellorsville.

Warner was the type of Goat who struggles with his studies, finds himself in over his head, but hangs on to graduate at the very bottom. Discipline and hard work are as important as intelligence at West Point, maybe more so. James E. B. Stuart, the Confederate cavalry general who graduated thirteenth in the Class of 1854, noted that success at West Point was not guaranteed by high intellect, nor denied those who were not so gifted. "For one to succeed here," he wrote on Christmas Day of 1851, "all that is required is an ordinary mind and application; the latter is by far the most important and desirable of the two. For men of rather obtuse intellect, by indomitable perseverance, have been known to graduate with honor; while some of the greatest geniuses of the country have been found deficient, for want of application, Edgar A. Poe for instance."[1]

Poe could have excelled academically at West Point if he had cared to, but he was not interested in adopting the Academy's monastic way of life and was forced to leave after half a year. James McNeill Whistler, another great American artist and a second-generation West Pointer, made it until his third year before washing out. Both were of a different type than Warner, intelligent and talented cadets to whom grades and class rank were less important than pranks, socializing and other pursuits. The 1909 *Howitzer* yearbook, for example, defined the Goat as "a man who would have stood first if he had boned" (i.e., studied). George C. Strong, USMA 1857, who graduated fifth in his class, said, "It is a favorite idea among many here that it requires an abler man to stand at the foot of his class throughout the course than at the head of it." The Goat will study only enough to get by day to day, and then before exams will spend "one or two days or nights of intense application," cramming just enough to ensure success. Strong added, "these are some of the symptoms of that epidemic which is called Genius."

These were men like George Custer, George Pickett and Henry Heth, who might well have excelled at their studies had the pursuit of knowledge been more compelling than the lure of good times. They and their comrades lived on the edge, seeking new and inventive ways of skirting the rules, and rising to the occasion only when the situation absolutely demanded it. They were cut from the same cloth as Cadet

William A. Beach of Indiana, of the Class of 1910, whom the *Howitzer* described as "an 'Immortal' of the old school; he is a goat from choice to be sure, and never bones because he thinks it is vulgar to work. . . . Many of his 'goaty' companions have had grave fear for his welfare during exams, but on such occasions his true immortal characteristics loom up and he passes the cleanest exam in the class."[2]

The term "the Immortals" originated in the early nineteenth century and referred to any cadets in the lowest academic section. Brigadier General John C. Tidball, USMA 1848, who was Commandant of Cadets in 1864, noted that the Immortal section "contains those who are hanging on at the ragged edge of deficiency." The derivation of the term is obscure; it may rest with Herodotus, who wrote of a 10,000-man bodyguard of the ancient Persian kings called the Immortals because their numbers never diminished. Likewise, the number in the last section was constant; when those at the bottom failed, those who remained at the tail end of the class became the new last section.

Goats and Immortals were originally synonymous, referring to anyone close to the bottom of the academic rankings.[3] Like "the Immortals," there is no known record of the origin of the term "the Goat," but it is most likely a later invention. The earliest written reference is in the booklet for the Hundredth Night entertainment of February 20, 1886, a celebration traditionally held one hundred days before graduation. One of the jokes reads, "What feature of the instructor of the Immortals in Spanish resembles his section? His beard; it is a goatee, and so is his section." Thus while George Custer and George Pickett are the most famous "Last Men" in the history of the Academy, it is unlikely they were ever referred to as Goats while they were cadets.

The term "goat" connotes many things—stubbornness, persistence, but also mischievousness and playfulness. The Goats were by and large charismatic, adventuresome, with a youthful bonhomie that generally made them very popular with their classmates. "Goat" is also slang for someone who fails at an important task or takes blame, especially in the context of "scapegoat." In Biblical times, the scapegoat was brought to the door of the tabernacle, where a high priest would place his hands upon it and lay the sins of the people on the animal. The goat would then be banished to the wilderness—as the majority of nineteenth-century cadets were, particularly the lower-ranking graduates. A more pointed Biblical reference is in Matthew 25, which tells that God will separate the righteous from the unrighteous "as a shepherd divideth his sheep from the goats." The former are granted life eternal; the latter "go away into everlasting punishment." The expression "to play the goat" referred to someone who acted silly in order to make others laugh, and the goat was also a classical symbol of lust and excess. Both fit the pattern, since the Goats of West Point have always been noted both for frivolity and for their way with the opposite sex.[4]

While intellect alone did not determine class rank, neither did ranking at graduation determine career success. Poring through the academic records and biographies of Academy graduates, one finds that class rank is not a certain predictor of achievement; that the crucible of West Point produced men of many and varied abilities, which were then tested in the arena of life, always at the whim of luck and circumstance. West Point Superintendent Major General Thomas H. Barry, in his address to the graduating Class of 1912, said, "You all begin on a fair field. You change the sleeve stripe for the chevron. The race begins, and the goats will continue to plug along, and they will put some of the stars off the track, and in doing so they have for some reason or other, more or less of my personal sympathy." Barry had graduated in the middle of the Class of 1877 and was awarded the Silver Star in the Spanish-American War. The only Medal of Honor recipient in his class was Matthias W. Day, who showed distinction fighting the Apaches in 1879 and ranked 70th of 76 cadets.[5] Powhatan Clarke, the Goat of 1884, received the Medal of Honor for saving a wounded soldier under fire during the Geronimo campaign—the only Last Man to date so honored.

The tension between the qualities that made for a good cadet as opposed to a good officer were reflected in the way branch assignments were allocated. The top Academy graduates were selected for the most elite branches, the Topographical Engineers and Engineers, and the next tier went into the demanding technical branches of Artillery and Ordnance. Infantry officers came from the middle of each class, while the bottom were made horse soldiers: Dragoons, Cavalry and Mounted Riflemen. Thus the worse one performed at West Point, the more likely one would be assigned to the combat arms. Those who graduated at the top received plaudits, a star by their name, the respect of the faculty and the institution. But those at the bottom were also part of the Long Gray Line; they were entitled to wear the class ring and would be commissioned as officers. They brought to the experience their own special talents, whether innovation, doggedness or bravado. They struggled, adapted and overcame, often showing remarkable courage. The same spirit of adventure that led Custer to sneak out of the barracks in the middle of the night to engage in off-post revelries motivated his dramatic cavalry attacks in the Civil War and afterward. It was the same bravery in the face of adversity that sent George Pickett storming the battlements of the Mexican fortress of Chapultepec and riding confidently across the field at Gettysburg into the teeth of the Union guns.

Telling the story of the Goats is necessarily telling West Point's story—the history of the Academy that shaped them as young men, of the values they learned and the friendships they made that influenced them for the rest of their lives. It is a glimpse of the less-known side of West Point, of the mischief, the fraternization and other unofficial activities at which the Goats excelled. Some of these events, notorious in their day, are now revered as folklore exemplifying the Academy's golden age.

This is also the story of the Army that the Goats served in as officers, both in war and in peace. These nineteenth-century Goats tell us something about the soul of the American solider, his daring, imagination and spirit. The Goats went everywhere the Army went, fought in all its battles, and occasionally changed the course of history.

Above all, it is the story of the men themselves, their character, their fate—who they were, what they aspired to, and what they achieved. It is about Goats such as Custer, Pickett, Henry Heth, Charles N. Warner, Laurence Simmons Baker and James M. McIntosh, who all challenged fate on the battlefields of the Civil War; or Zeb Inge and Ephraim Kirby Smith, who found glory in Mexico; Immortals such as James Longstreet, Philip Sheridan, Fitzhugh Lee and Winfield Scott Hancock; washouts like Poe, Whistler and Lewis Armistead; and the men who helped shape their lives, such as Sylvanus Thayer, the father of the Military Academy, and legendary saloonkeeper Benny Havens. We see them as cadets at the Academy and as Army officers, in life and in death.

These three strands—the Goats, the Academy and the Army—weave together across the formative years of the Academy, when its customs were born. They run through the two great wars of the nineteenth century fought by its graduates, which set in stone the traditions that still largely define West Point today. From the "rockbound highland home" above the Hudson to the swamps of Florida, from the Halls of Montezuma to the blood-soaked battlefields of the Civil War, and ultimately to the Last Stand at Little Bighorn, this is their story.

NATHANIEL WYCHE HUNTER

FRANCIS HENNEY SMITH, United States Military Academy Class of 1833 and founder of the Virginia Military Institute, said that his class "always prided themselves in the opinion that this was the golden era of West Point." Smith was looking back through a tumultuous half century of war and reconstruction at the idealized Academy of his youth. It was a time when the Long Gray Line had not yet grown long, and had only recently turned gray, before the Mexican War made heroes of many West Point graduates and before the Civil War turned them from classmates to enemies. West Point, like the nation it served, was young, growing, and still finding its way. Smith's classmate Nathaniel Wyche Hunter was perhaps more typical in the perspective he had after his first month at the Academy: "I never hated a place so bad in all my life."[1]

Coming to West Point was a culture shock for many cadets, particularly those from the South. Hunter—or "Wyche," as he was known to the Corps of Cadets—came from a well-to-do family in the town of Powelton, Hancock County, Georgia. He arrived at the West Point public landing in June 1829, to no particular fanfare. He was met by the post porter, a former soldier whose missing right arm had been replaced by a hook. The Corps had entered its summer encampment, and Wyche was immediately assigned a small dirt-floored tent on the Plain, where he would remain until the academic year began in August. Encampment was a rude introduction to life at the Academy. "It is a time of joy and merriment to the old cadets," Wyche wrote his father, "but a time of trouble and fatigue to the new ones. The new cadets are compelled to clean the parade ground, before the tents, in the tent, make the beds, clean the ditches, bring water, while the old cadets fiddle, dance, sing, get drunk and be merry."

The daily schedule was punishing: up by four in the morning, if not earlier, with drill until breakfast at seven. Cadets studied until

1 P.M., took an hour for lunch, continued studying until four, and then drilled until seven o'clock and dinner. In addition to the continuous schedule of study and drill, cadets had to stand their daily share of sentry duty. "Our duties while sentinel are enough to kill any man from the South in four years," Wyche wrote. They stood watch for four hours during the day and another four at night; "It matters not if it is raining fire, we have to stand and carry our guns upon our arms. I've nearly worn out my coat sleeve." When he did have time to study, there was so much noise he found it difficult to concentrate, and night-time storytelling lubricated by drink was endemic (if against regulations) among the cadets. "Not a day has passed since I've been here but someone had been drunk." They slept on the ground inside their tents, with no mattresses or cushions. "I have slept upon a blanket and covered with my cloak every night since I've been here," Wyche wrote. "What sleeping!"

Albert E. Church, who graduated first in his class in 1828, wrote fifty years later that the food at the time was "excellent plain fare … surely we never had on West Point so excellent bread and butter." It lacked variety, but "everything was neat, wholesome and well cooked." Wyche had a much different take: "rye bread, rancid butter and oak leaf tea" for breakfast; dinner was "boiled beef (such as you never heard of in your life), Irish potatoes, the meanest I ever saw," and a pudding made from the leftover breakfast bread.

Encampment lasted from June until the end of August. Cadets who had completed two years at West Point were granted a furlough for the summer, but in those days traveling home was so expensive that many remained at the Academy for the entire four years. At the end of his first encampment, Wyche wrote to his brother (addressed from "West Point—Hog Hole"): "Fatigued and disgusted beyond conception with the noise of camp I can with difficulty compose myself sufficiently to enable me to write. Could you but for one day see with your own eyes the labour and fatigue we have to undergo you would exclaim with me there is no place like home."

Wyche's first summer at West Point was difficult, but it was all according to plan. The trials the cadets faced were part of the vision of the Superintendent, Sylvanus Thayer.[2] Thayer had been appointed to the Academy as a cadet by its founder, Thomas Jefferson, in 1807, having recently graduated from Dartmouth at the top of his class. He completed his course of studies the next year and returned in 1809 for a brief tour as a junior instructor. Thayer came to the Academy at a time when it was still struggling to establish its identity, and failing badly.

There was no set curriculum, no age limits (cadets ranged in age from preteen to forty-one), and few rules, infrequently enforced. "All order and regulation, either moral or religious, gave way to idleness, dissipation and irreligion . . . ," wrote John Lillie, a cadet who had entered at the age of ten and a half but departed after several years of fruitless effort. "[It was] well that I left that place of ruin."[3] Congress considered reforms in 1812, but with the onset of the war with Britain, its attention was diverted and the Academy almost expired.

Thayer served as a staff officer during the war and witnessed severe deficiencies throughout the military establishment that contributed to the poor performance of American arms. In 1815, then a brevet major, he was chosen to travel to Europe along with Colonel William McRee, a hero of the late war, to study military education in the more advanced nations. The French in particular had a long academic legacy: King Henry IV established a military prep school at La Fleche in 1604, and the Ecole Polytechnique was regarded as the leading center of scientific and military learning in the world. Thayer was an admirer of Napoleon, and given the recent war between the United States and Britain, he and McRee were not disposed to take lessons from the Royal Military College at Sandhurst. Passage to France was difficult; conflict was winding down on the Continent, and the officers were in port in England when word came of Waterloo. Nevertheless, Thayer and McRee managed to maneuver successfully through the postwar chaos. They learned a great deal about the French system and used this knowledge to devise a plan for reforming West Point.

President James Monroe ordered Thayer to the Academy in 1817 to assume the superintendency from Alden Partridge. Known as "Old Pewt" for the pewter gray uniforms he introduced, which have become emblematic of West Point, Partridge had been a disaster as Superintendent, but he was popular with the cadets because he resisted all attempts at imposing discipline. Partridge had not been informed of the change of command. He countermanded Thayer's orders, and a controversy erupted that led to Partridge's court martial. Though acquitted of serious wrongdoing, Partridge resigned his commission and moved to Vermont, where he founded the American Literary, Scientific and Military Academy, later renamed Norwich University.

Thayer's mission was to bring order and intellectual rigor to the Academy, and he set about it with enthusiasm. He announced that henceforth cadets would be judged by merit alone, and subordination to the code of discipline was to be a defining value. Thayer devised entrance exams, established age limits and enforced the rules of behavior.

Favoritism was dead. The worst disciplinary cases were hauled before courts of inquiry and expelled. Periodic and largely unaccounted-for vacations were replaced by strict leave requirements—no furlough for two years, and none after that until graduation. Recreational reading and board games were banned. Free time vanished. Days were filled with instruction, exercises and drill; evenings were given over to study. Thayer made West Point a difficult school to get into and a tougher place to remain.

Many cadets did not welcome Thayer's reforms, particularly those who were asked to leave. Those who longed for a return to the laxity of the Partridge years attempted to sidestep the chain of command and brought various complaints against Thayer to higher authorities. However, the new Superintendent had the strong backing of former Superintendent General Joseph G. Swift (one of two USMA graduates in 1802), as well as the president and the secretary of war, and the initial complaints were rebuffed. In November 1818, a petition signed by 180 cadets was brought before Congress in an attempt to implicate Thayer and others on his staff in various forms of malfeasance and abuse.[4] Congress, while noting some excesses in the manner the reforms were carried out, reaffirmed the authority of the executive branch to manage the affairs of the Academy and asked the cadets to withdraw their petition.[5] Thayer was given full freedom to craft his system. His leadership soon showed its product. Cadet morale began to rise, a spirit born of ability and pride in the effort required to prevail. West Point no longer had a problem attracting talent—young men in the hundreds from all over the country competed to go there.

Thayer required cadets to demonstrate mastery of each lesson every day by "taking boards," writing answers to problems on chalkboards that ringed the classrooms and briefing the answers to the rest of the class. In the "Thayer System," every cadet would recite in every subject every day. Since the West Point curriculum was dominated by mathematics and the sciences (history, for example, was first eliminated from study in 1825, as was geography, and both had to stage several comebacks), the system was easily implemented. Sections were kept small, no more than twenty, to facilitate the individual attention required for every cadet. It was not an educational environment that favored slackers, and Cadet Hunter quickly developed the habits necessary to survive. "I have never in my life studied half so attentively (so hard as we would say in Georgia) as I have for the last week. I can hardly see my eyes are so weak and sore. . . . I think very probably I shall hold a very respectable standing in my class if I apply myself as I ought."

Plebes studied two subjects, French and mathematics. Knowledge of French was critical since many of the most advanced treatises in the sciences and in military thought were written in that language. As one period report noted, it was a "universal opinion" that the French "have been much more successful and happy in their investigations and explanations of the sciences generally, and of that of war in particular, than those of any other nation."[6] Thayer also had assigned some of the same books he had studied in France, such as Devernon's *Treatise on the Science of War,* written in 1805. Members of the first class had to buy copies for $20, a huge sum at the time for the cadets, whose monthly pay was $16. By Wyche's time, the Academy library had over ten thousand volumes, many in French, and was then the finest technical library in the country. Wyche lamented, "Had I studied French and mathematics I should have been enabled to stand near the head but as it is I shall stand near the foot. You have no idea what smart fellows we have here." The cadets were taught technical, not conversational French, with an emphasis on practicality. Mr. Molinard, one of the instructors, gave a characteristically simple rule for the usage of the articles *de* and *du.* " 'Why gentlemen this is very easy. I will give you a rule by which you can *always* tell when to use *de* and when to use *du.*' He paused. 'Sometimes we use *de* and sometimes we use *du.*' "

In the second or "yearling" year, cadets continued studying math and French and added drawing. It was imperative for officers to be able to draw well in order to make their own maps and tactical plans in the field. Thomas Gimbrede, the professor of drawing, was "an amiable old gentleman" whose "fundamental proposition was in these words: *Every one can learn to draw.* His proof: there are only two lines in drawing, the *straight* line and the *curve* line. Everyone can draw a straight line—and everyone can drawn a curve line—therefore everyone can draw."[7] The third or "cow" year curriculum included experimental philosophy (today called physics), electricity, optics, astronomy, chemistry and topographical drawing. "Firsties" studied engineering, the science of war, rhetoric and grammar, moral philosophy and national law. Throughout their four years, cadets also received instruction in infantry tactics, ordnance and gunnery, cavalry, marksmanship, swordplay, strategy and, of course, drill.

Cadets were ranked in order of merit, and the standings, while not public information, always became known. The section groupings in each class gave much of the list away, and cadet competitiveness filled in the rest. Despite the rivalry implicit in academic ranking, teamwork was an important part of the cadet survival system. Lessons were divided up and answers copied and memorized. Drawings were traced using a system of candles and glass plates, over which the original and a blank sheet were laid. Cadets also came to know the habits of professors, specifically the order in which they would call upon certain cadets to answer questions, and were frequently successful in gaming which problem they might be asked to diagram. If it was generally known that an instructor was tolerably predictable, Thayer might suddenly appear during class and change the sequence of questions, causing a degree of mental panic in the classroom.

The January examination in the plebe year was the first academic winnowing the cadets faced. They were grilled by instructors in front of the faculty, in a process that was intended to intimidate, and did. As he prepared for his first January exam, Wyche wrote: "Should a Professor moved by motive of ill will or any thing of the kind give you the examination such demonstrates as he knows from your former recitations that you have paid no attention to or are too trivial to be noticed, what will hinder you from appearing in the estimation of those who have never heard you before as a numskull?" Those who were deficient ("found," in cadet parlance) were dismissed. They were loaded into sleighs and taken over the hills away from the Academy, past a point of no return known as Goshen. The June exams were even more rigorous, held before the entire Board of Visitors, the assistant professors and the Superintendent, who scrupulously inspected every cadet. Those who ranked at the head of the class were questioned for ninety minutes or so; those with lower rankings were examined for as long as it took to remove all doubt. Final cadet rankings were the result of long deliberations. The top five in each class were given the honorific "distinguished cadet," and were frequently called upon to serve as instructors, which, since it was added to their normal cadet duties, was a mixed honor. Those who failed were either turned back to repeat a year, or dismissed. The casualty rates were high. Of the 100 cadets admitted to the Class of 1828, for example, 93 were left to take the January examination; 73 passed, and of them 51 made it through the end of plebe year.

The Academy's first Goat was John Taylor Pratt of the Class of 1818, which was the first class with academic rankings.[8] Pratt came to West Point in 1814, after already achieving distinction with the Kentucky Cavalry at the Battle of the Thames in Ontario, Canada, under William Henry Harrison. He arrived out of the West on horseback with fellow cadets Billy Johnson, who was Harrison's nephew, and John Payne. The three rustic westerners excited much comment and wonder among the cadets, Kentucky at the time being regarded by most in the East as an untamed wilderness. Johnson later left West Point, and Payne was sent home after a twelve-pounder gun he was manning during a salute went off prematurely, taking his arm in the process. Pratt remained, and became romantically involved with Eliza Kinsley, sister of fellow cadet Zebina J. D. Kinsley, whose family lived on a rocky hill near the Academy still known as "Stoneylonesome." He had a formidable rival for her affections in Lieutenant George W. Gardiner, the Commandant of Cadets, who for his small stature and martial spirit was known as "the Little God of War." The competition eventually came to a head when Pratt confronted Gardiner in his office. The infuriated Commandant grabbed a pair of fire tongs, wrapped them around Pratt's neck and twisted them to the point where he could not remove them. Neither man was punished for the altercation, and in the end Eliza went back to Kentucky with Pratt.

Academic excellence was one pillar of Thayer's system; discipline was another. Thayer was a strict though not harsh disciplinarian who led by example. He pursued an orderly life and his behavior was impeccable. He was an early riser, and cadets frequently saw him on his morning walk as reveille was blowing, properly attired and soberly comported. He took an active interest in the moral development of every cadet and would occasionally meet with them privately if he felt they needed additional guidance. Though personally warm and engaging, he was very strict in his dealings with cadets and showed no preference. Smith said, "It was useless to attempt to awaken tender emotions in him. He was not without feeling but he never displayed it in his office. . . . No cadet entered without a sentiment of awe, or left without a feeling of relief."

The practical expression of Thayer's emphasis on discipline was the famous West Point demerit system. It arose from necessity; before demerits, politically well-connected cadets whom Thayer tried to expel for disciplinary violations were sometimes able to win reinstatement on appeal. The demerit system was instituted to establish a paper trail. Originally, violations did not carry specific penalties, but in September 1825, a point system was devised to reflect the "degree of criminality" of the offense. For example, a disorderly room or oversleeping would be worth one demerit. Visiting after hours carried a three-point penalty. Missing a class or being absent from chapel or reveille rated four to five points. Being discovered absent from the barracks at night was a very serious offense, worth nine points, and the most serious of all, mutinous conduct, carried the maximum ten-point penalty. After 1831, extra points were added to the cadet's annual total depending on his rank.

For example, a firstie would face an additional half-point penalty for having been at the Academy long enough to know better.

Many cadets are listed in the delinquency rolls with no demerits, though most had earned some strikes during the year but had cleansed their record by "walking off" the points on punishment tours. A cadet could erase one demerit for every extra hour marching a post. Robert E. Lee, who graduated second in the Class of 1829, was a rare case of a cadet who was never cited once for a demerit in four years at the Academy. (Half of Lee's assigned page in the Record of Delinquencies was given to his less-disciplined classmate Pleaides Orion Lumpkin from Georgia, who made good use of the space by amassing an impressive 303 demerits in 1827.[9] He left West Point before graduating and served in the revolutionary army of Texas.) Some say that Lee's achievement has never been equaled, but in fact it has been more than once; for example, Lee's classmate Charles Mason not only had an equally pristine disciplinary record, but graduated first in their class.[10] Despite the examples of cadets like Lee and Mason, academic standing and demerit totals were not necessarily related. Frederick A. Smith, first in the Class of 1833, ranked 138th in the Corps in discipline with 81 demerits in his final year. George Washington Cullum, third in the same class, had no demerits, but likewise George Herbert Pegram, who ranked 31st. Roswell W. Lee had the worst disciplinary record of the class, ranking 195th in the Corps with 172 demerits, but he graduated eighth.

Some demerit totals in this period were extraordinary. In 1827, yearling Albert Gallatin Blanchard piled up 489 points but nevertheless managed to graduate two years later, 26th out of 46 in his class, with a more reasonable 301 demerits. Though hailing from Massachusetts, Blanchard went on to become a Confederate brigadier general. George Washington Patten graduated 36th of 42 in the Class of 1830, and in discipline was fourth from the bottom of the Corps that year with 538 demerits. He was the author of many well-known military manuals and later became a noted San Francisco poet. Charles H. Larnard of Rhode Island compiled a record-setting 729 demerits in his yearling year of 1829, which he brought down to 190 by the time he graduated in 1831, when he ranked 16th of 33 in his class.[11] But Larnard's sudden outbreak of relatively good behavior probably had less to do with his developing maturity than the 200-point limit that was instituted in 1831. Any cadet who ended the year beyond that limit was dismissed. Once the 200-point "line of death" was established, the average total demerits declined radically, and the number of cadets walking post correspondingly increased. Thayer saw to it that there would be no more Larnards.

While the point system appeared objective, it could be arbitrary. Frequently the question was not what one did, but who was watching, whether they wanted to report or not, and how many points would be assessed. Cadet Henry D. Bird of the Class of 1829 was for some reason regularly given higher penalties than other cadets for the same offenses (seven points instead of one for a disorderly room, for example), and he left before graduation. Tactical officers ("Tacs") were the source of most reports, but worse were the cadets who reported on their classmates. Wyche noted in a letter to his mother, "I do all in my power to keep from getting reported, but it is impossible. . . . There are officers, I mean Cadet officers, who *seek* to report their fellow Cadets. They are universally despised by the Corps and should be by everybody."[12] Wyche's relatively modest demerit totals ranged from 106 to 139 over his years at West Point, though they could have been much higher. "It is something very remarkable that I have not been caught yet in my many and flagrant violations of the regulations," he wrote his sister. "I have been in an ace of it a hundred times. When others in the commission of the same act have been detected and dismissed—without the hope of being reinstated."

One day in his final year at the Academy it seemed as though Cadet Hunter's luck had run out. Without warning or explanation, he was ordered to the Superintendent's office. He feared the worst. He stood at attention while Thayer looked at him impassively.

"I have understood from various sources and know from personal observation that you are guilty of many little irregularities which you should be particularly careful to avoid," Thayer began. "It becomes you to do so not only as a Cadet disobeying the regulations of the institution but as a gentleman engaged in the ordinary business of life." Was it significant that Thayer had not mentioned that it was also the duty of an officer? Wyche was sweating at this point, wondering which of his hundreds of overlooked transgressions was about to come back to haunt him.

"Do you chew tobacco Mr. Hunter?" Thayer asked.

Wyche calculated—he did not think the Supe had a right to ask him about his infractions; he could only report them and let the punishment system take it from there. Since Thayer was showing such candor, he probably already knew the answer, and if he had wanted to impose punishment, he would not talk about it, he would just do it. Wyche decided that honesty might be the best approach.

"Yes sir I do," he replied.

Thayer, who had expected either a negative answer or an evasion, was visibly surprised. His attitude softened slightly, as much as he would allow, and he spent several minutes giving Wyche some almost fatherly advice, encouraging him to improve his behavior and throw off his bad habits, for his own good. Wyche emerged from the meeting shaken, but unscathed. He later wrote that Thayer showed "so much of interest in my welfare and condescension on his part that I came away with a better opinion than I ever had of the old fox."[13]

The Corps, which in this era numbered around 215 cadets, was divided into two companies, and cadet officers and NCOs were selected from the top three classes. Cadets were housed in two barracks, with a Tac in each to keep order. Rooms were assigned by lot, meaning every cadet had an equal chance of getting choice quarters or one of the less desirable rooms. Three to five roommates, who might be from any class, shared the space. Each room had a fireplace, and fire prevention was a priority concern. "Neglect of fender" carried a three- to five-point demerit penalty. There were no beds; cadets slept on the floor on bedrolls, or on cots. They drew water from springs or cisterns, and there were no indoor bathrooms until the Civil War period. Despite (or perhaps because of) these hardships, life in the barracks was close and convivial. To supplement their bland diet, cadets would hold secret banquets in their rooms, which required some degree of planning and teamwork, particularly if alcohol was involved. Wyche wrote his sister about an eggnog party he attended:

> I assure you the materials for preparing it were procured at the risk of the procuror's reputation and life. If he had been detected he would certainly been dismissed—in skating on the rotten ice down the river he broke through twice and with great difficulty extricated himself. . . . We enjoyed ourselves heartily regardless of the danger attending it and for some time we thought ourselves elsewhere than W. Point. Last night we had a couple of chickens and a large beefsteak cooked in splendid style before and on the coals. The best Parisian cook could not have prepared them better.

A dozen cadets were allowed to board with Mrs. Thompson, widow of a Revolutionary War officer who lived on the post with her three gregarious daughters. "The places were much sought after," Church wrote, "a fact due not only to the excellent fare provided, but, doubtless, in a great degree, to the fondness of the young soldier for female society."[14] John De Witt, the post sutler, also had several daughters, two of whom married officers. The post barber, named Spencer, had two young and pretty daughters, "much admired and visited by some of the cadets," according to Church.[15] This perhaps ameliorated the impact of the grooming regulations introduced in the early 1830s. Cadets were required to have their hair cut once a month on a strict alphabetical schedule. When the policy was introduced, some cadets, who had hair down past their shoulders, ruefully joked that it was a signal day for the New York wigmakers. Cadets of this period had few opportunities to fraternize, but they began to increase in the 1830s. Wyche wrote optimistically to his sister in 1832, "Probably when you see me again I may have been married myself—there is some chance of it—who knows? We Cadets are held in high repute by the ladies."

Cadets looking for recreation could attend meetings of the Dialectic Society, at which the young men would debate important questions of the day, sometimes heatedly, depending on the issue. Hiking and hunting in the surrounding hills were permitted, particularly on weekends. Attendance at Sunday chapel was mandatory. In the early 1820s, cadets were treated to lectures from Reverend Charles P. McIlvaine, who served as chaplain and professor of ethics from 1824 to 1828. His sermons were nationally renowned and they sparked a religious revival on the post. Not everyone was captivated, however. Cadet Church later wrote, "I listened to a dull sermon, one hour and a quarter long, the only lasting effect of which was to lay the foundation of that dislike, which I have ever since entertained, for long sermons."[16] McIlvaine was eventually ordained a bishop and served as chaplain of the United States Senate. He was succeeded at the Academy by the Reverend Thomas Warner, whom Smith said "had a most intellectual face, was a good scholar and a good talker." Warner was not as inspiring as his predecessor, but his ten-minute sermons met with general approval by the Corps. For Wyche's part, he was unimpressed. "I do not like the way they preach here at all," he wrote. "They are all Episcopalians."

Cadets also enjoyed concerts by the West Point Band, led by its chief bugler, an Irish immigrant named Richard Willis who had been recruited by Thayer in 1817 to help maintain cadet morale. Willis was a celebrated artist of the Kent bugle, and his brass-heavy musical arrangements revolutionized American military bands. "For the first time," Thayer wrote, "musical affairs took on an increased stature, not only on the post, but for many miles around. Crowded packets from New York to Poughkeepsie used to drop anchor off West Point to give their passengers an opportunity to listen to Willis and his band as they played evening concerts from a prominent position overlooking the river."

Willis died in 1830, but he established the tradition of riverfront public concerts that continue to draw audiences of hundreds. Knowing
proper dance steps was a necessary part of the training of officers and
gentlemen, and cadets were given lessons by a renowned Bostonian
dancing master named Lorenzo Papanti. His wife, a famous singer of
the day, performed in the chapel when Lorenzo was on post. Papanti
created a sensation when he introduced the waltz to America in 1834;
this European import entwined dancers in ways considered highly
improper. Perhaps not coincidentally, the first cadet hops began that
same year.

   In the winter, cadets would ice-skate on a pond in the Superintendent's yard, and for those wily enough to sneak off post there were
other diversions. "I have been sleigh riding this week for the first time
in my life," Wyche wrote home to Georgia in February 1833. "I am very
much pleased with that diversion and particularly so on account of my
long and constant confinement. I succeeded very fortunately in elud-
ing the vigilance of the *Spies* and officers though they extend all their
endeavors to catch me."

   Hazing was virtually unknown at this time, at least to the degree
it would later develop. Church wrote that "such was the 'esprit de corps'
that an individual treating a fellow cadet as cadets are now treated every
year, would have been expelled from the corps without the aid of military authority or presidential orders."[17] Nevertheless, cadets did not
lack a sense of humor. Once at the beginning of the school year a firstie,
looking very official with sash and sword, stopped by plebe rooms and
solemnly informed them that since tobacco was banned, they were
required to turn over whatever they had. By the end of the day, he had
picked up a year's supply. But of all the diversions at West Point, none
were as valued as letters. They connected the cadets to their loved ones
and events back home, and writing and receiving letters reduced the
sense of isolation. Wyche wrote his parents, "The pleasure I enjoy in
[receiving letters] is the only real pleasure I ever enjoyed at this place."
Of course, he was exaggerating. There were other pleasures to be had.
Like scores of West Pointers before and after him, Cadet Hunter found
succor at an off-limits tavern called Benny Havens'.

BENNY HAVENS'

B ENJAMIN J. HAVENS WAS BORN in Orange, New York, on January 6, 1787.[1] Though he has gone down in history as an Irish-American folk hero, he was actually a fifth-generation American whose great-great-great-grandfather William Havens immigrated to Rhode Island around 1635. Furthermore, the founder of the Havens line came not from Ireland, but from Aberystwyth, Cardiganshire, Wales. Benny first began providing solace to cadets shortly after the Academy's founding, as an assistant to the West Point sutler. He was fired when he was discovered selling rum to a cadet, and he took the opportunity to join the New York militia, serving as a first lieutenant during the War of 1812. After the war, he ran a delicatessen with his wife, located just off the post on property owned by Mr. Gridley, over the boundary known as the "Gridley line." Gridley's hotel was generally off limits to cadets, but the chance to add variety to their menu proved an irresistible temptation.

The passage to Gridley's was through the border fence, an eight-foot-high flat-panel barrier, difficult to scale but with a hidden passage. Cadets had rigged some boards "hung by a single nail at the top with a secret fastening at the bottom . . . so innocently and smoothly as to defy the eyes of the most cute inspector ignorant of their secret."[2] Consequently, there were parties from West Point at Gridley's nearly every night. Old Grid's selections of food and especially drink were popular with cadets, but less so with the Academy. Rather than reinforce the perimeter, Thayer sought to remove the cause of the problem. In the winter of 1824–25, Congress appropriated $10,000 to purchase the property, and "Old Grid" moved to Newburgh. The hotel became the post hospital. Unemployed but still undeterred, Benny relocated further south, to a two-story tavern about two miles from the gate, in the town of Highland Falls, situated on a bluff above the Hudson below Buttermilk Falls. Thus the legend of Benny Havens' began.

Passage to the tavern was difficult. Heavy woods lay between the Point and Highland Falls, which was little more than a flour mill and a few houses. There was an unimproved wood road south and a rough footpath down to Benny's. It was hard going in the dark or in bad weather, but the regulars soon learned the way. Others traveled down the Hudson, either by boat when available or over the ice in winter.

Those who braved the journey were amply rewarded. The specialty drink of the house was the "hot flip," made of rum or cider, beaten eggs, sugar and spices. It was heated by dousing a red-hot poker or "flip dog" into an enormous flagon from which the drinks were served. The key to the "flip" was knowing when to remove the "dog" to produce the distinctive caramel-like flavor, a skill that Old Ben had perfected. However, while Benny Havens was most notorious for serving alcohol, his tavern was truly a haven in many respects. Cadets enjoyed home-cooked meals and were able to relax, unwind and spend a few hours free of the demands of the Academy. Wyche, in the following letter to his sister, captures the mood of the cadets for whom Benny Havens' was a cherished sanctuary:

> There are about a dozen of us in the Corps who have of our weekly suppers [together] (you must not infer that we get drunk—make beasts of ourselves etc.). We eat and drink (wine) moderately, talk of home of graduating and politics toast the *girls* and return to barrack about 3 A.M. This helps very much to pass away the time until June or May when I intend to commence studying. I have told you of Benny's and of the many pleasant hours I have spent there. I hope yet to spend many more before I take my final adieus. However anxious I am to leave this place there are many things from which it will almost rend my heart to be separated forever and among these Benny's holds a very conspicuous place. The old man and his wife, and the chimney corner in which I have smoked many a pipe, and the blazing log fire, and the clean table and tablecloth, and buckwheats and butter cakes, and beef steaks, ham and eggs, all so much remind me of bygone and happier days that I would willingly cling to that forever.[3]

When too few cadets were venturous enough to make the expedition southward, Old Ben would come to them. He would load a small boat with provisions and row upriver, making landfall at a quiet spot beneath the Academy. If no cadets were waiting along the shore, he would pack his wares uphill to a gathering place near the North Barracks called Rinsler's Rock, a granite outcropping that had been the scene of late-night happenings since before the Academy existed, when Native Americans gathered there to dance and tell stories by firelight.

These activities did not go unnoticed. The cadets' primary nemesis was Quartermaster Sergeant Owens, or as they called him, "Bum." He was a "bombardier," a member of the artillery company posted at West Point, whose nightly duty was to watch the South Gate and generally to make life miserable for the more enterprising souls in the Corps. He spent decades at the task and came to know all the cadet haunts and escape routes. Owens kept at his task stubbornly, and sometimes he "skinned" the cadets with a sense of humor. On one occasion he fashioned a dummy to look like the Superintendent and placed it at a landing spot on the river where he knew a large group of cadets would be returning from Benny Havens'. The sixteen shipmates panicked when they saw what they thought was the Supe and rowed quickly away, switching to a route up the cliffs and overland to the barracks, where they were met by Tacs whom Owens had alerted.

"Bum" was responsible for having Benny Havens banned from the post after reporting several of his riverborne excursions. Old Ben accepted his banishment; but Owens went too far when Mrs. Havens, who was traveling up the Hudson by riverboat, landed at West Point and attempted to cross the post to get home. Owens detained her and had his men row her across the river to Constitution Island, over her strong protests. She was later rescued by friends, but a few days later Benny ran across Owens in Cold Spring and beat him severely. Owens sued and was awarded five hundred dollars, which nearly drove Benny Havens out of business. Naturally, the cadets did not approve of Bum's efforts. If they spotted him at a distance in the moonlight nearing their position, they would pelt him with rocks. When Owens interrupted a group of masked cadets who had hoisted the reveille cannon to the roof of one of the barracks as a joke, the malefactors grabbed Bum, bound and gagged him, and left him on the roof with the gun. He was also the object of more serious schemes; Cadet Henry Clay Jr., son of the famous politician, was suspended from West Point for, among other things, firing a pistol at Bum Owens.[4]

The Court Martial of Jefferson Davis

ON THE EVENING OF JULY 31, 1825, during encampment, a massive downpour flooded the Plain. Unable to sleep, their tents a muddy mess, cadets began to wander the post, and a small group made their way south to Benny Havens'. There they dried off and enjoyed the specialties of the house. Meanwhile a formation had been called, and a tactical officer, Captain Ethan Allen Hitchcock, noted their absence. As a former cadet (Class of 1817), he may have had an idea what the group was up to, and he headed for Buttermilk Falls. Hitchcock caught the five wanderers in the act, and Theophilus Mead, James Allison, James F. Swift, Samuel J. Hays and the future Confederate president Jefferson Davis became the first cadets ever to be court-martialed for carousing at Benny Havens'.[5]

The five cadets were victims of bad timing. Spirits had only recently been banned at West Point, the result of a raucous Independence Day celebration that same year. There was a cadet tradition to host a July Fourth dinner for the officers and faculty. Alcohol flowed, and the feasts usually degenerated into some form of excitement. In 1825, the dinner was "more than usually joyous" and late in the evening the cadets carried Major William J. "Haughty Bill" Worth, the Commandant of Cadets, to camp on their shoulders. Thayer, who made it a point to be absent on July 4 to maintain plausible deniability, finally put his foot down and banned the dinners, and also the consumption of intoxicating beverages on the post. Cadet Davis and the others were charged with two specifications of the new regulation, namely, "drinking spirituous and intoxicating liquor" and "going to a public house or place where spirituous liquors are sold," as well as leaving post without permission.

Davis, who was then eighteen years old and had just completed his plebe year, defended himself with the skill of a natural legal mind. He first questioned the legitimacy of the charges, since the new regulations had not been communicated to the Corps, and "isolated as we are from the rest of the world," such orders could not be considered valid. Nor, he said, were they even given a chance to obey them, in their ignorance. He pleaded guilty to the charge of leaving the post, which was a well-known provision of regulations, but noted the special circumstances—the flooding rain, the sounding of the dispersion bugle, and general confusion over what was required. In seeking shelter, he and his comrades "thus urged by circumstances without premeditation wandered too far."

Davis decried the "weak evidence" that had been put before the court, especially on a charge "so contrary to the principles of a soldier and man of honor." He pointed out that Hitchcock had not witnessed him in the act of drinking—and if he was behaving like a man who was intoxicated, it was due to the embarrassment of being caught, "which was certainly enough to have confused any cadet." Davis denied that the regulation even covered Benny Havens', saying that it depends on what the definition of "public house" is. Furthermore, he questioned the logic of a literal interpretation of the rule against being where spirits are sold, since, as he pointed out, the stores on post sold liquors and the cadets were clearly permitted there. He also argued that wine and beer could not rightly be called "spirituous liquors," just to be on the safe side.

Davis's clever wordplay did not impress the court. He was found guilty of all charges and specifications, and sentenced to be dismissed. However, the court added "in consideration of his former good conduct [it] respectfully recommend the remission of said sentence." Hays was also recommended for clemency, and both he and Davis were pardoned and reinstated. Mead and Allison were dismissed. Swift was acquitted outright. He was the son of General Joseph G. Swift, the first graduate of the Military Academy, former Commandant of the Corps of Engineers, former Superintendent, and at the time the chief revenue officer for the Port of New York. Cadet Swift might have learned a lesson from his near escape, but instead he was emboldened, and after another court martial in September he was expelled. Hays may have owed his lenient treatment to the fact that he was the nephew and ward of Andrew Jackson. He too had difficulties adjusting to cadet life, and in the spring of 1826 he went AWOL. Of all the Benny Havens' Five, only Jefferson Davis graduated.

In January and February 1826, and again in September and October, Davis was "distinguished for correct conduct," a recognition given to cadets who had no disciplinary infractions for a given month. Davis's disciplinary record in general was above average. He was promoted to sergeant of the Color Guard, and was for the most part behaving himself. But he soon became involved in one of the most notorious episodes in West Point history, the Eggnog Mutiny of 1826.

Christmas Eve had traditionally been a time when cadets would gather for festivities, usually involving alcohol and frequently overlooked by the authorities, if done in moderation. Even given the climate of Thayer's anti-alcohol crackdown, some cadets planned an evening of frolic. On the nights leading up to the party, emissaries were sent to Benny Havens' to provision, acquiring perhaps a gallon of spirits or more. One cadet, allegedly William Burmley, bribed a sentinel at the public wharf for the use of a boat to fetch the necessary supplies. Eggnog was prepared, and on the 24th, the cadets gathered to greet the Christmas holiday in the traditional way.

The celebration commenced in the evening and gathered steam as it went. Eventually the revelry attracted the attention of Captain Hitchcock, who went to room number 5 in North Barracks and listened at the door for a few minutes before bursting in on the party in progress.

The two candles in the room were quickly extinguished and some cadets ducked out in the darkness. Hitchcock was about to break up the crowd when Davis, who had gotten wind of the Tac's interest but did not know he was already there, rushed into the room saying, "Put away the grog boys, Old Hitch is coming!" Hitchcock immediately placed Davis under arrest and confined him to his room. Davis complied, and Hitchcock ordered the revelers to disperse. The partygoers wandered off, and after inspecting the room, Hitchcock returned to his quarters.

A few minutes later there was shouting in the barracks. Pieces of wood were thrown against Hitchcock's door and stones rained against his windows, breaking most of the panes. A drum started beating in the guardroom, where Hitchcock found Cadet Lucien Bibb, one of the cadets from number 5, who had just broken the drumhead. He ordered Bibb to go to his room under arrest. Hitchcock went back out into the hallway and was met with a fusillade of firewood. He took cover in his room, barring the door and abandoning the barracks to the mutineers. Someone shouted, "The bombardiers are coming! Turn out the Corps! Turn out the Guard!" Cadets milled about in the hallways, shouting and demonstrating, waving swords and clubs, and calling Hitchcock out with threats. It was a night of uninterrupted bedlam. The rioters shattered windows, smashed furniture, broke off the stairway banisters and discharged firearms. Cadet Richard B. Screven was particularly wild, shouting, breaking tables and brandishing a musket.

Seventy cadets were arrested for the mutiny, and detailed proceedings were held from January to March 1827. For his part, Davis was never brought up on serious charges. He had obeyed Captain Hitchcock's order to repair to his room, and he remained there under arrest throughout the night. He testified during the trials, but as in the previous case, he worded his responses carefully to protect his friends. He was released from arrest on February 8, 1827. Scores of cadets were called as witnesses, including Davis's friend Robert E. Lee, who of course was uninvolved. Of the seventy originally arrested, nineteen were sentenced to be expelled. Richard Screven was found guilty of disorderly but not mutinous conduct, and was likewise sentenced to dismissal, but because of his excellent character and "frank admission of his errors," the court recommended remission of the sentence, and Screven was allowed to stay at West Point. President John Quincy Adams, who had followed the case, noted the painful duty of dismissing so many young men "from whom their country had a right to expect better things." He hoped that the example would "not be lost upon the youths remaining at the Academy," and that they would be "admonished to the observance of all their duties," lest they bring similar shame onto themselves, their virtuous parents and their dearest friends.

Despite these brushes with authority and President Adams' entreaties, Davis continued his forays to Benny Havens', and one such outing almost cost him his life. He was at the tavern when someone warned that an officer was coming. Davis and Cadet Emile Laserre quickly ducked out a back way and scrambled back to the Academy along the cliffs above the river.[6] At some point, Davis slipped and fell sixty feet towards the rocks below, but his fall was broken by a stunted tree, and he lay on the ground semiparalyzed. Laserre looked down over the embankment and called out, "Jeff, are you dead?" Davis wanted to laugh but was suffering too much to say much of anything. They made it back to post, Davis stumbling and with his hands cut severely. He was ill for weeks—close to death, his wife later wrote—and he acquired a limp that was with him for months after.

"The sole congenial soul in this God-forsaken place"

ANOTHER REGULAR DENIZEN OF Benny Havens' who would also one day rise to prominence was Cadet Edgar Allan Poe.[7] Compared with the average cadet, Poe was a remarkable oddity. He entered West Point a former sergeant major of artillery. He was a published though as yet little known poet, grandson of Quartermaster General Poe who fought in the Revolution, and a relative of General Winfield Scott's, whom he claimed helped secure his appointment. Poe told his fellows romantic tales of his past: of running away from home and sailing to Europe in a coal ship on a Byronic quest to fight for the Greeks in their continuing war of independence from the Turks; being detained in St. Petersburg, Russia, for passport irregularities but being rescued by the American consul; spending time as a crewman on a whaling vessel; signing on to a merchantman and sailing to the Mediterranean; debarking in the East and touring Egypt and Arabia; living in London as a writer; being wounded in a sword duel over a lady's honor in France; and publishing a fictionalized account of his adventures in French under the pseudonym Eugene Sue.

It would have been a marvelous story, if true. But Poe's autobiography was largely a work of fiction. He had lived in England for five years as a boy, and the events in Russia may have happened to his brother, but the rest of his travels were pure invention. He had lied about his age to secure his appointment to the Academy—he was in fact almost twenty-two and beyond the legal age of admission. General

Scott, whom Poe had never met before going to West Point, was uncle to the second wife of Poe's adopted father, John Allan, a wealthy Richmond tobacco trader, and had no role in his appointment.

Poe did, however, serve in the Army from 1827 to 1829, and rose in rank from private to sergeant major in nineteen months. He was a disciplined worker and respected by his superiors. His immediate commander, Lieutenant John Howard, wrote favorably of Poe, stating that "his habits are good, and intirely free of drinking." Armed with this and other recommendations, Poe sought an appointment to West Point shortly after the death of his stepmother Fanny in February 1829. His initial attempts met with failure, perhaps due to a particularly frosty testimonial from his stepfather, who mentioned Poe's gambling habit at the University of Virginia—the debts he had accrued there having become a matter of some contention between them. A year later Poe came to the attention of Senator Powhatan Ellis of Mississippi, who was Mr. Allan's business partner's younger brother. Ellis wrote a letter of inquiry to Secretary of War John Eaton in March 1830, and Poe received his appointment within a few weeks. He was admitted as a member of the Class of 1834 on July 1, 1830.

When Poe arrived at West Point, he wrote his stepfather hopefully that while the discipline was strict and many new cadets failed, "I find that I will possess many advantages & shall endeavor to improve them." After camp he was assigned to Old Barracks, room 28, with Thomas W. Gibson and one other roommate. Gibson wrote that "Poe at that time, though only about twenty years of age, had the appearance of being much older. He had a worn, weary, discontented look, not easily forgotten by those who were intimate with him." One joke had it that Poe was actually the father of a cadet who had died and he had taken the appointment in his son's stead; another, that he was a descendant of Benedict Arnold.

At USMA he was a popular composer of japes and songs, and was soon well known as a wit with an edge. Many of his verses made fun of faculty and students, and George W. Cullum wrote that "these verses were the sources of great merriment with us boys, who considered the author cracked, and the verses ridiculous doggerel." One example skewered Lieutenant Joseph Locke, an 1828 grad and Tac who showed an inordinate interest in inspecting barracks for cadet misconduct:

> John Locke was a very great name;
> Joe Locke was a greater in short;
> The former was well known to Fame,
> The latter well known to Report.

Locke spent a great deal of time looking in on the irrepressible residents of Number 28. Poe had quickly discovered Benny Havens' and by the fall of 1830 was a regular visitor. He described Old Ben as "the sole congenial soul in this God-forsaken place." Poe and Gibson had established a contraband commissary of sorts, and their room became a storehouse for supplies procured at Benny's, including food, spirits, and other necessaries. Gibson tells that "many a thirsty soul, with not enough of pluck to run the blockade himself, would steal into our room between tatoo and taps to try the merits of the last importation."

On one such occasion, Poe showed that his sense of the macabre was not limited to his literary pursuits. One cold, wet November night, the brandy bottle empty, Poe and Gibson drew straws to see who would make the run to Benny's. Gibson lost and loaded up with four pounds of candles and Poe's last Mackinaw blanket for barter. He set out to the sound of the bugle calling to quarters. "It was a rough road to travel, but I knew every foot of it by night or day, and reached my place of destination in safety, but drenched to the skin." Benny was in a bad mood for bargaining—he had accepted far too many barter items already and was overstocked with cadet candles and blankets. Gibson finally made a deal for a bottle of brandy and an old gander, which Benny obligingly decapitated for the journey back, a squawking fowl being an unacceptable security risk.

Gibson made it to post by nine o'clock, having sampled the brandy en route. His shirt, hands and face were streaked with blood from the bird, which he had carried slung over his shoulders. Poe met him outside, and upon seeing his friend's grisly condition formulated a plan. They tied the bird up in a ball with feathers bristling, and Poe returned to the room, taking the brandy for safekeeping. Back in Number 28, Poe's other roommate was sitting in a corner trying to study, and another cadet awaited Gibson's return to share in the bounty. Poe said nothing but sat down and pretended to read. Moments later Gibson staggered into the room, covered in blood, empty-handed, seemingly drunk.

"My God! What has happened?" Poe exclaimed, feigning horror.

"Old K! Old K!" Gibson said, calling out the nickname of Lieutenant Zebina J. D. Kinsley (USMA 1819), then an artillery instructor who was notorious for reporting cadets, and who was active in the temperance movement, which was perhaps a greater sin.

"Well, what of him?" asked Poe.

"He won't stop me on the road any more!" Gibson growled, brandishing a large, bloodstained knife. "I have killed him!"

"Nonsense!" Poe retorted. "You are only trying one of your tricks on us."

"I didn't suppose you would believe me," Gibson said, "so I cut off his head and brought it—here it is!" He reached out the door, grabbed the gander by the legs and swung it into the room over his head, knocking out the only candle and scuttling it across the floor. The room instantly went dark. Gibson was barely visible, holding aloft his ghastly prize. The visiting cadet panicked, leapt out the window into the slop tub below, and ran to North Barracks screaming that Kinsley was dead and his head was in Number 28. A general excitement began to spread outside, but soon subsided. After a few moments Poe relit the candle. He and Gibson found their roommate sitting in the corner, staring blankly, paralyzed in utter horror. "It was some time before we could restore him to reason," Gibson said.

Poe's humorous rhymes, mischievous nature and access to contraband made him a favorite among the Corps, but few took him very seriously as a student. David E. Hale, a yearling, wrote that Poe "is thought a fellow of talent here but he is too mad a poet to like mathematics." Gibson recorded that Poe "utterly ignored" his studies. Cullum called Poe a "slovenly, heedless boy, very erratic, inclined to dissipation," who "of course, preferred making verses to solving equations." But Poe's peers underrated him. He may have been eccentric, whimsical, and ill disciplined, but academically Poe was in the first section. At the board meeting of January 4, 1831, he placed 17th out of 87 cadets in mathematics, and third in his class in French. By contrast, twenty-seven plebes were "found" that January and sent home. Poe might have looked forward to a successful stay at the Academy. Yet one month later, he was brought up on multiple charges of "gross neglect of all duty" and "disobedience of orders." He pleaded guilty to most of them and was dismissed. Poe left West Point on February 19 and headed for New York with a terrible cold, no overcoat, and twelve cents in his pocket.

The reason Poe departed remains a mystery. He later claimed to have left because his stepfather had died and not given him an inheritance. "The army does not suit a poor man," he wrote, "so I left W. Point abruptly, and threw myself upon literature as a resource." This was a fabrication. John Allan lived until March 1834, though it was true that Poe received no portion of Allan's $750,000 estate and should not have expected any of it. Money had been an enduring source of friction between them, and Allan had grown to despise his ward. Poe sent an angry, self-pitying letter to Allan the day before his Academic Boards, asking for money and complaining about his poor treatment. "You sent me to W. Point like a beggar," he wrote. "The same difficulties are threatening me as before at Charlottesville—and I must resign." He pleaded with Allan to send a permission letter to the Superintendent. Allan wrote on the back of Poe's missive, "I do not think the Boy has one good quality," and he did nothing. Ironically, Poe could easily have attained separation from the Corps by purposely failing the first examination and confirming everyone's expectations that he was a "January colt."

Poe seems to have decided to leave West Point the previous October, when Allan remarried and dashed whatever lingering hopes Poe might have had of becoming his heir. He began to amass demerits and commit acts intended to court official retribution. One legend has it that he reported for drill by the letter of the regulation, "with cross belts and under arms," wearing only white gloves and bandoliers, but not his uniform. The story is not true; but Poe did rack up an impressively poor disciplinary record in a brief time. The final blow was when he simply stopped reporting for formations for the whole month of January 1831. He skipped parades, reveille, classes, chapel and other mandatory gatherings. This brought on his court martial. Two days after he left the Academy, Poe sent a very bitter letter from New York to his stepfather, claiming that he had been dismissed because of illness. Allan described it as "a relic of the Blackest Heart & deepest ingratitude alike, destitute of honour & principle every day of his life." The two never reconciled. Given the conflicting evidence, most of it from Poe himself, the truth behind why he sabotaged his West Point career may never be known.

That spring a second edition of Poe's *Al Aaraaf, Tamerlane, and Minor Poems* was published in New York, dedicated "To the U.S. Corps of Cadets." Colonel Thayer allowed the Corps to make an advance purchase at $1.25 per copy, and 135 cadets signed up. They expected to receive a collection of the satirical and humorous poems that Poe had issued in streams from Number 28 during his brief tenure at the Academy. When the books arrived, they were found to be poorly bound, crudely printed on cheap paper, and, to the disappointment and disgust of the Corps, filled with serious poetry. "For months afterward quotations from Poe formed the standing material for jests in the Corps, and his reputation for genius went down at once to zero," Gibson wrote. "I doubt if even the 'Raven' of his after-years ever entirely effaced from the minds of his class the impression received from that volume." This offense more than anything—willfully inflicting literature on his classmates—forever stained Edgar Allan Poe's memory at the Academy.[8]

Years later, General Scott, who had met Poe at West Point and been favorably impressed, contributed to a collection for the poet, who was then very ill and in the care of a benefactress, Marie Louise Shew. Scott gave five dollars and stated that he wished he could make it five hundred. He dismissed Poe's peculiar public persona, observing that he had "noble and generous traits that belonged to the old and better school. True-hearted America," he added, "ought to take care of her poets as well as her soldiers."

Noble Hearted Hunter

THE NOTORIETY OF BENNY HAVENS' notwithstanding, by the 1830s West Point's reputation as an academic institution was firmly established, particularly in engineering and mathematics. West Point graduates were building the nation's infrastructure, overseeing the construction of roads, bridges, canals, railroads, lighthouses and harbors. They were surveying and mapping uncharted territories and opening the West to settlement. Graduates of West Point, as serving Army officers or civilians, were making a positive impact on the development of the United States in ways far greater than their numbers would suggest. But criticism of West Point had never abated. Opponents repeated the same arguments made since the Academy's founding—that it was elitist, antidemocratic, and the potential source of a military class that could threaten constitutional government. Populist congressman Davy Crockett denounced the Academy as a haven for the "sons of the rich." Alden Partridge, still nursing his grudge against Thayer, wrote an inflammatory pamphlet under the pseudonym "Americanus," bluntly entitled, *The Military Academy at West Point Unmasked: or, Corruption and Military Despotism Exposed.*

Criticism coalesced when Andrew Jackson was elected president in 1828. Jackson's election was a watershed in American politics. "Jacksonian Democracy" was the crystallization of the anti-elite sentiment and radical egalitarianism that typified popular conceptions of government on the frontier. Jackson himself was the embodiment of the idealized citizen-soldier, a Tennessee militia officer who rose to public prominence and the rank of major general by defeating the Creek Indians in 1814, and achieved bona fide hero status by defeating British regulars in the Battle of New Orleans the next year. His outnumbered and decidedly mixed band of western militiamen, Choctaw Indians, pirates, freedmen and local citizens, bested elite British forces led by the brother-in-law of the duke of Wellington, Lord Parkenham, who fell in the battle. To the proponents of militia forces this confirmed the superiority of the doughty backwoodsman over the trained professional. "Old Hickory's" triumph reinvigorated the American martial myth that had its origins at Lexington and Concord, and capped the unfortunate conflict with an exceptional, if immaterial, U.S. victory.

Jackson had mixed opinions about West Point, and he disliked Thayer particularly. He had something of an expert on Academy life close at hand; his presidential private secretary and nephew, Andrew Jackson Donelson, had nearly been dismissed in the first wave of Thayer reforms. He graduated second in the Class of 1820, and resigned his commission after two years to work with his uncle. Another Jackson nephew, Samuel J. Hays, was granted clemency as one of the Benny Havens' Five but later fled the Academy. Jackson did not attempt to close the school, despite the political support he might have been able to muster for the move. West Point was useful, and America needed engineers. But he did begin to insinuate himself into the Academy's administration, and Thayer soon found himself being frequently second-guessed by the president. Jackson was particularly active in over-turning the Superintendent's disciplinary decisions, which had the effect of humiliating Thayer and emboldening the cadets. As Wyche explained, "Servility is not a principle of their nature."[9]

Thomas Gibson, Edgar Allan Poe's former roommate, was a case in point. After the poet left West Point, his comrade's pranks became less imaginative and more destructive. Gibson was a serial arsonist and managed to burn down a small building near the barracks. Thayer twice expelled Gibson, but both times Jackson overruled him and reinstated the cadet. After a third court martial, for attempted desertion, Jackson finally let the sentence stand. There were many other instances of con-flict. During the 1832 election, for example, Jackson partisans encour-aged supporters to plant hickory trees as a sign of support for the president. Thayer awoke one morning to find a pro-Jackson tree planted in the middle of the Plain. An investigation laid the blame on Cadet Ariel Norris, whom Thayer dismissed. Jackson overruled the decision. Norris, thinking himself untouchable, next came to Thayer's attention by fashioning a makeshift scatter gun out of a candlestick and some brass buttons, and firing it at a Tac. Thayer expelled Norris, this time for good. After Jackson was elected to a second term in November, many in the Corps believed that drastic changes were soon coming. Wyche wrote his sister in December that Jackson "has long thought that the Cadets have been persecuted by the Superintendent and his tyrannical martinets and he is determined on effecting a radical reformation in the Institution or abolishing it altogether. The Superintendent has already the hatred of the Pres. for his conduct during the [Blackhawk] war and it is presumed that he will shortly feel the effects . . . a step which would meet with the unanimous approbation of the Corps."[10]

. Some cadets were bold enough to try to take their cases directly to the president. Francis Henney Smith and a group of a dozen prepared an appeal on behalf of one of their fellows who had been expelled for drinking at Benny Havens'. They wrote a letter to the president, "an earnest appeal to the old hero in behalf of a son of a gallant soldier of the war of 1812," Smith said, "adroitly framed to touch the tender feelings of this great man." Cadet Robert McLane, who had been appointed to West Point by Jackson personally, arranged for an audience with the president through his father, Louis McLane, who was the secretary of state at the time. Cadet Willoughby Anderson delivered the letter to the president at the White House. Jackson perused the appeal and then turned to the waiting cadet.[11]

"Who wrote this letter?" he asked.

"I don't know sir," Anderson said.

"Have you read it?"

"No sir."

"Go back to West Point and report for duty," Jackson said, "and tell the young man who wrote this letter, if he don't look out, I will have his ears cut off."[12] The cadets had courted *lèse majesté*, and Old Hickory was not to be manipulated.

As the close of the 1833 academic year neared, Wyche remained characteristically pessimistic. He had survived four years of exams, maintained a reasonable disciplinary standing (far higher than he deserved, he admitted), and had only the final examination standing between him and his commission. Nevertheless, he feared the worst. He had become something of a procrastinator, a fact that he freely admitted. When his brother wrote him helpfully suggesting he could use his time better, Wyche wrote back, "As regards a misapplication of my time I admit the fact; and will only say that *I cannot be compelled to study*."[13] He also had an enduring suspicion that the "Yankee" faculty was out to get him. "Nearly all the instructors here are Yankees," he had written, "and their so partial to the Yankees that it is almost impossible for a Southerner to stay here; if should he happen to stay it is almost impossible for him to have any standing."[14]

When the exam was finally held, the entire class performed extremely well, and Wyche, to his amazement, passed. However, the fates had a final twist for Cadet Hunter. That evening at dinner, Joel

Poinsett, the president of the Board of Visitors, a former congressman who would served as secretary of war under Martin Van Buren (and after whom the poinsettia is named) commented that the exams he observed were the best he had ever heard, and added innocently that he did not see how the class could have done so well without knowing the answers beforehand. Poinsett meant this as a compliment to the class, but Colonel Thayer took it as an indictment of the examination. Thayer suggested canceling the results of the exam and testing the cadets again. Poinsett said he did not think that was necessary, that he was really only trying to commend the cadets, not accuse them of cheating.[15] However, Thayer was adamant. Wyche, despairing, faced the Yankee examiners a second time. But luck was with him. He passed, albeit barely, and in the final academic rankings he stood as the Goat of his class. "Noble hearted Hunter," as Francis H. Smith later described him, had made a lasting impression on his classmates, and they called on him to give a valedictory oration on their leaving West Point. This honor, the recognition of his peers, was a greater tribute than any the institution could bestow. "I had much rather have this expression of their confidence in my ability to perform such a task," Wyche wrote, "than to be head of the class."[16]

For the Class of 1833, the years of preparation for their careers as officers were over. The night before graduation they went to an outcropping on the Plain known as "cremation rock" and built the traditional bonfire of every article they owned that could be consumed—drawing boards, books, furniture—anything they were not taking with them or handing down. They sang and danced around the fire until retreat, and secret celebrations continued long into the night. The next day they wore cadet gray for the last time. Of the 43 graduates that year, 8 were turnbacks from the previous year's class, and 12 others graduated the following year. Of the original 120 hopefuls who came in with Cadet Hunter, only 47 received Army commissions, a graduation rate of 39 percent.

Neither Wyche, who disliked Colonel Thayer, nor Smith, who admired and would later emulate him, could have known four years earlier that theirs would be the last class of the Thayer era. Thayer had notified the faculty the previous February that this would be his final term as Superintendent. The political pressures had become too great for him. He had submitted his resignation, which had been accepted. The faculty were stunned. They suggested a ceremony, something to commemorate his leave-taking, but Thayer demurred. Partridge had been sent off to great demonstrations by the cadets; Thayer chose to leave in a more dignified fashion. The evening after commencement, he took his usual walk down to the dock to watch the last ship of the day depart, accompanied by several officers and a few cadets. Just before the gangplank was raised, Thayer turned. "Good-bye, gentlemen," he said, and as the surprised men on the dock watched silently, Thayer boarded the ship and left West Point.[17] He never returned. The golden age extolled by Smith—the years that had established West Point as an institution on par with any military academy in the world, and had produced Dennis Hart Mahan, who would become Thayer's intellectual successor; Robert Parker Parrot, inventor of the Parrot Gun, the most effective cannon used in the Civil War; Henry DuPont, who would found an empire in munitions; and the Confederate trinity of Jefferson Davis, Joseph E. Johnston and Robert E. Lee—this age came abruptly to a close.

Ephraim Kirby Smith

T HE TACTICAL CURRICULUM AT WEST POINT was designed to produce Napoleonic warriors equipped to fight traditional, European-style wars. Critics of the Academy noted the unlikelihood of such conventional conflict and stated that what the country really needed were Indian fighters. Two decades of relative calm, however, made the debate academic. Most graduates of Thayer's time saw neither conventional conflict nor frontier war, but instead applied their training to peacetime pursuits.

The most important effect of class rank was its impact on branch assignments. The top few cadets were made engineers, the most challenging and most prestigious branch. They designed America's forts, major roads, canals, railroads, harbors and lighthouses, carving a growing nation out of the wilderness. The next most distinctive branch was Ordnance, followed by Artillery. Those further down the list would be sent to the Infantry or the Dragoons. Cadets from the Immortal sections were unlikely to spend the early years of their Army careers supervising large-scale building projects, attending conferences or pursuing post-Academy education in Europe. They were much more apt to find themselves in distant frontier garrisons, with little prospect of adventure or advancement. The spartan conditions at West Point in the Thayer era were good moral and physical preparation for Army life in the 1820s and 1830s. Even in peacetime, it was a difficult and dangerous occupation. Of the thirty-three graduates in Jefferson Davis's Class of 1828, fourteen died within ten years of graduation. Three of these were civilians; ten were on active duty and fell to accident or disease. Only one of them, James F. Izard, was killed in battle, by the Seminoles.

If a newly commissioned officer was looking for a remote posting in those days, he could not go much farther than Fort Mackinac, on tiny Mackinac Island at the northern tip of Lake Huron. It was one of dozens of such forts along the northwest frontier, erected as border

defenses against incursions from Canada. It had been seized by the
British in a surprise attack in July 1812, and transferred back in September 1815 per the terms of the Treaty of Ghent.[1] Since then the area
had seen no action, nor was it likely to.

In 1829, Fort Mackinac became the home of Ephraim Kirby
Smith, the Goat of the Class of 1826.[2] He had spent the previous three
years at the equally remote Fort Howard, fourteen miles up the Fox
River from Green Bay. Kirby, as he was known, was born in 1807 in
Lichtfield, Connecticut, to a distinguished military family. His mater-
nal grandfather, Ephraim Kirby, was an officer in the Continental Army
who fought at Bunker Hill. His father, Colonel Joseph Lee Smith, fought
in the War of 1812 and was a hero at the 1814 Battle of Lundy's Lane.[3]
Colonel Smith was appointed federal judge for the eastern district of
the Florida Territory in 1821, whence Kirby was appointed to West
Point in 1822, the first (though nominal) Floridian to attend.

Kirby was a quixotic, proud and willful young man, and his strong
views on personal honor often led him into difficult situations. He had
a poor disciplinary record at USMA, and if the point system had been
in use when he was a cadet, he would have had a hard time avoiding
expulsion. He was frequently found visiting or absent during study
hours. He was cited for neglect of fender, oversleeping, being late, sitting down on sentry duty, and being AWOL for a week in August 1824,
though this was probably due to travel difficulties returning from furlough. Kirby missed classes and sometimes slept through those he did
attend. In March 1823 he spent twelve days in the stockade for disorderly conduct. Clearly he had become such a lightning rod for quill
(i.e., reports) that he was reported even for trivial misbehavior such as
"candlestick out of place" (on September 7, 1825) and "playing with
football near the barracks" (on April 10, 1826).

After graduation, Kirby traveled to St. Augustine to visit his family before departing for his first assignment. At a local tavern he was
introduced to Edgar Macon, a former U.S. district attorney who had
been openly slanderous against Kirby's father for convincing President
John Quincy Adams to fire him. Kirby would not shake Macon's hand,
which led to an exchange of words, the young officer slinging "epithets
suited to [Macon's] malignity." Macon challenged Kirby to a duel, and
he accepted. Dueling was a federal crime, and military law provided
that no commissioned officer could either send or accept a challenge
to fight a duel, "upon pain of being cashiered."[4] Kirby thought better
of it later, but explained that "as a man and a soldier, my word, without
regard to consequences, must through life be sacred." They agreed to

meet on an isolated shore. Kirby showed up with his second, Captain Wood, and they waited alone for the other pair.

When Macon arrived, he was accompanied by his second, Dr. Richard Weightman, an Army officer and according to Kirby a well-known "scandalous calumniator of a brother officer." They also brought along five other men, a group of women and servants, and even the soldiers who rowed the boat that carried them there. Kirby said that this was "in violation of every honorable pledge by which all persons are bound in affairs of this nature," in particular because it increased the chances that the duelists might be arrested. In the end, the fight never took place; Macon prompted delay after delay, claiming sickness and making other technical objections. Kirby stated that "mattresses and morning gowns had been provided for him, yet his brandy bottle, and all the other ammunition he had brought to the field, were exhausted without effect." But the event drew the attention of the authorities and the pair were thrown in jail. Macon and Weightman, who knew the local magistrates well, cooperated in the subsequent trial, which Kirby found even greater proof of their perfidy. Kirby was convicted, though under the circumstances, and given his father's position, the court recommended leniency. Kirby released a transcript of his impassioned speech before the court as an appeal to his brother officers, and was spared a court martial.[5]

Life in the Michigan Territory did not offer Kirby the adventure he might have craved. The last serious Indian disturbances had ended with the death of Tecumseh at the Battle of the Thames in 1813. In the late 1820s, the only Indians likely to be seen were in fleets of canoes on the lakes, going to outposts for their annual emoluments, occasionally stopping by to sell fish or game or to get rations. Samuel P. Heintzelman, a classmate of Kirby's who served at Mackinac and kept detailed diaries of his days at West Point and afterwards, one day noted "eleven canoes of Saginacs and Ottowas," a splendid sight.[6]

The duties at the remote posts were rudimentary, and the biggest challenge was staying motivated. Jefferson Davis, then a second lieutenant of the First Infantry stationed at Fort Winnebago, in the area later to become Wisconsin, wrote his sister that "the officers of the Post are like those of the Army generally, men of light habits both of thinking and acting, having little to care about and less to anticipate."[7] Officers would keep themselves and their men busy improving local roads, building and repairing bridges, traveling the countryside assessing the timber and natural resources (particularly those of military significance such as sulfur), surveying, making maps, and undertaking construction projects on their posts, not so much to make them more defensible as to make them more comfortable. The forts were sometimes thrown up as temporary expedients that gradually became permanent, and they often needed work. Heintzelman wrote of Fort Gratiat, "Thursday the 2nd of November [1830] made two years since my arrival at this detestable place. I hoped when I arrived that we would have left long ere this; but our prospect is more distant still."[8]

A frontier posting allowed a great deal of time for disconsolate introspection. Heintzelman wrote to his diary, "I completed my twenty fifth year yesterday. It is melancholy to think how I am spending my best days, in this out of the way place, without society, amusement, or improvement."[9] In a similar vein, Jefferson Davis wrote to his sister, "Today I am 22 years old. When I was a boy and dreamed with my eyes open as most do, I thought of ripening fame at this age of wealth and power. As I grew older I saw the folly but still thought that at the age of 22 I should be on the highway to all ambition desired, and lo: I am 22 and the same obscure poor being that I was at fifteen, with the exception of a petty appointment which may long remain as small as it is at present.—and yet," he added, "I am not dissatisfied for I behold myself a member though an humble one of an honorable profession." Davis believed that given his experiences, he had few alternatives. "I cannot say that I like the Army, but I know of nothing else that I could do which I would like better." He said that had he returned home directly from Transylvania College in Lexington, Kentucky, where he attended briefly before going to the Academy, he might have been able to become a respectable citizen, but he did not think he could do so anymore because "the four years I remained at West Point made me a different creature from that which nature designed me to be."[10]

For the enlisted soldiers, frontier life was more difficult. Soldiers signed up for five years, drawing five dollars a month. Morale was the biggest problem. Their duties kept the men busy, but in their free time they had little to do. They had less freedom of movement than the officers did, and no chance to enjoy high society in the cities. On the other hand, they were probably less self-pitying. Cards were a diversion for officer and enlisted alike, though not always approved because card games led to disputes, which were sometimes violent. Drinking was also a popular pastime, mostly whiskey and brandy. Until 1830, troops were issued a whiskey ration, and afterwards were given the cash equivalent. Sutlers sometimes sold whiskey beyond the ration as well, and there were taverns near the forts where soldiers could visit for libations. Revelries ("frolicking") could last until dawn and become quite clamorous. Camp followers constituted another amusement, and women would pitch their tents outside the garrisons with no need for advertisement. Some officers tried to combat this by inviting them to make camp inside the fort, where they could be watched, but most simply ran the women off.

Desertion was a perennial problem. On average there were around 620 desertions per year in these days, which was about 12 percent of the enlisted strength, and the number rose to over 900 in 1829.[11] In some parts of the country a soldier could make a dollar per day as a laborer, which was six times his Army pay and a tremendous inducement. The Army paid a bounty to civilians who returned deserters, which led some enterprising soldiers to go over the hill and have a friend turn them in, with whom they would split the reward.[12] Congress outlawed the death penalty for desertion in May 1830, and the spring of that year was rife with flight. "If matters go on in this way much longer we shall be left without any men," Heintzelman remarked. "All a man has to do is to make the attempt, he is almost certain to succeed."[13] It was almost impossible to apprehend a clever fugitive, who had only to wait in the woods for a chance to cross over to Canada. Sometimes deserters would send letters explaining themselves, seeking assurances that they would not be punished if they returned. Other times they would wander back after a few days on their own, to be disciplined at the discretion of the commanding officer. Some left and came back many times. Hunting down the runaways became another amusement, and was enjoyed particularly by the other enlisted men. President Jackson signed an order giving free pardon to all deserters, releasing all those confined for desertion, and discharging those who so desired, with the provision that they could not rejoin the Army again. This did not solve the problem.

Yet desertion, for all its stigma, was a useful safety valve. It removed the soldiers most dissatisfied with Army life, usually in their first year of enlistment, and left behind those better able to adapt. In the winter, however—with fewer distractions, the stresses of cold weather, claustrophobic conditions, and no possibility of flight—the atmosphere at a frontier post could get vicious. The period of isolation at West Point in the winter months was good training for the frontier, but did not fully replicate the brutality of the cold, or the depth and persistence of the snow. Furthermore, when the cadets "mutinied" at West Point, it was something of a game. On the frontier, mutiny was played for keeps.

On Christmas Day 1829, the Fort Mackinac post commander, Colonel Cutler, took two of his senior officers to dine in the nearby village. Ten minutes after they left, a group of two dozen men gathered on the parade ground. Kirby, the officer of the day, ordered them to disperse. As he gave the order, three soldiers rushed him, falling onto the lieutenant with murderous force. Other officers ran out of their quarters and came to Kirby's relief, whereupon the assembled men retired to their quarters. After an investigation, the ringleaders, nine members of Smith's company, were confined. Kirby was outraged. On his own initiative, he had four men flogged that very day and two others whipped later. Inflicting corporal punishment on soldiers was risky. Aside from being painful, it was humiliating, and it courted retribution. An English visitor to the United States observed at the time that "the American peasant, though a brave and hardy man, and expert in the use of the rifle and musket, is naturally the worst soldier in the world as regards obedience and discipline. He has been brought up to believe himself equal to the officers who command him."[14] Soldiers were not above leveling the field; for example, in June 1830 an officer was shot and killed at Green Bay by a soldier after minor punishment for neglect of duty.

Beyond the humiliation, flogging was illegal and had been since 1812. Kirby was brought before a court martial in Detroit in July, presided over by Colonel Cutler. He was found guilty and sentenced to dismissal, but the court recommended that the president remit the sentence given the circumstances. After all, the soldiers tried to kill him. Kirby was ordered to New York to report to General Scott and await disposition. President Jackson, who had protested against the 1812 law and been infamous for harsh discipline while a commander, had changed his views on corporal punishment by the time he reached the White House. In General Order 28 of 1829 he cautioned against mistreatment of soldiers, who feel protected by the law, and "still less [punishments] should be suffered to be inflicted by an officer, whose duty it is to be the soldier's protector."[15] Jackson did not sympathize with the young officer and he let the sentence stand. Kirby was dismissed from the Army on October 6, 1830.[16]

THE SEMINOLE WAR

NEAR THE ENTRANCE TO THE West Point cemetery, on an empty stretch of grass behind a tall hedge, stands a solitary monument of white Italian marble. Four upright cannon decorate the corners of an oblong square stone, supporting a platform adorned with stars, on which stands a wreathed fasces with an eagle perched on top. On the southward face of the stone are carved eight names. The inscription reads:

TO COMMEMORATE
THE BATTLE OF THE 28TH DEC
1835
BETWEEN A DETACHMENT OF
108 U.S. TROOPS
AND
THE SEMINOLE INDIANS
OF FLORIDA
IN WHICH
ALL OF THE DETACHMENT
SAVE THREE
FELL WITHOUT AN ATTEMPT
TO RETREAT

The monument was erected in 1845 and originally stood prominently on the banks of the Hudson, clearly visible from the Academy across the Plain and from any vessels passing on the river, a mute and graceful reminder of the opening shots of a seven-year conflict that today rarely makes the list of America's forgotten wars.

Captain Ethan Allen Hitchcock was with the first column to arrive at the battlefield, weeks after the action had taken place. He described it as "one of the most appalling scenes that can be imagined." Clusters of bodies, "mostly mere skeletons but with much of the clothing left on them," lay at the ambush site, along the road, and in a nearby redoubt

35

the men had fashioned for their last stand. They lay "in precisely the same position they must have occupied during the fight, their heads next to the logs over which they had delivered their fire, their bodies stretched, with striking regularity, parallel to each other."[1] Hitchcock, like many others present, had friends among the dead, and the skin had dried hard and smooth like parchment, easing the process of identification. They buried their comrades in mass graves, marking that of the officers with an upturned cannon the Seminoles had thrown into a swamp.

The massacre stunned the nation. Two companies of soldiers, well armed, with artillery support, were cut off and annihilated by tribesmen whom most people considered half naked savages. The Army had never suffered so serious a defeat in any previous encounter with Indians. Memorial poems were written in honor of the fallen, and volunteer militia companies formed and moved south.[2] When news of the massacre reached New York in January, diarist and former New York City mayor Philip Hone noted that the Seminole victory would not have the effect that the Indians anticipated. "This very battle in which temporary success has been won by their savage arms will be the ultimate cause of their destruction," he wrote. "Humanity may deplore the fate of the red men, philanthropists talk as they will about equal rights and the oppression of power, but it is inevitable. . . . After some hard service and destruction of the lives and properties of the whites, the Indians will be exterminated."[3]

★ ★ ★

THE SECOND SEMINOLE WAR was the result of an attempt to move the Indians of Florida west to live alongside the Creeks and other eastern tribes, who were being resettled to the Oklahoma Territory. The resistance was led by chiefs and warlords such as Micanopy, Billy Bowlegs, Coacoochee, Alligator, Halleck Tustenuggee, and a dynamic young half-white named Billy Powell, whom the Indians called Osceola. He was not a chief, but his intelligence, charisma and resolve, not to mention hatred of the whites, made Osceola a natural leader. He was opposed on principle to the negotiations, and legend has it that at an 1834 council with General Wiley Thompson, the Indian agent for Florida, Osceola declared, "the only treaty I will execute is with this," driving a knife through a copy of the treaty and leaving it sticking in the table.

Osceola was set on war, and according to Alligator, they had been planning the opening moves for over a year.[4] Their first step was to send a message to the moderates that divisions within the tribe were not to be tolerated. They chose for their example Charley Emathla, a well-known and loved chief who was a proponent of emigration. Osceola and his band openly shot Charley down on November 26, 1835, as he was walking with his two young daughters. This bald act of savagery had its intended effect—none raised a hand against Osceola afterwards.[5] The next stage was to demonstrate to the whites that the Seminoles were serious about remaining in Florida by undertaking a shocking major attack that would leave the Americans reeling. They planned a two-part strike, a coordinated blow led personally by Osceola to take place on December 28, 1835.

The first phase of the attack was targeted at General Thompson, who had recently put Osceola in chains for six days for protesting when the gunpowder supply was cut off. Osceola had won release by agreeing to be shipped west, but he had no such intention and bore a deep grudge. Early on December 28, Thompson and Lieutenant Constantine Smith were strolling and smoking cigars near Fort King when a sudden volley of musket fire from the bushes tore them apart. Osceola's war party ran forward and scalped and mutilated the two officers. Sutler Erastus Rogers and his assistants, whose cabin was outside the walls, were also killed, and the Indians retreated into the wilderness, heading south.

Fifty miles away, Major Francis L. Dade led his column north towards Fort King, oblivious to the threat. His mission was to reinforce the isolated outpost, either to deter Indian attack or to defend against it. Dade was not an Academy graduate, but he knew West Point well, having been commander of the "bombardier" company for several years. He had with him eight officers and one hundred men, led by a local guide named Luis, a slave owned by a sutler named Antonio Pacheco.[6] Luis spoke the local Indian dialects, as well as Spanish, French and English, and was acquainted with the route to the interior. Command of the column had originally fallen to Captain George W. Gardiner, former Commandant of the Academy, "the Little God of War" who had wrapped fire tongs around Cadet Pratt's neck in a fit of jealousy over Eliza Kinsley. Gardiner had since married, and his wife, Frances, had accompanied him to Fort Brooke on Tampa Bay. When Frances fell ill, Dade volunteered to take Gardiner's place so he could remain behind to attend to her. The column set off on Christmas Day, 1835. A short time after the troops had departed, Frances Gardiner was given an opportunity to accompany some friends to Key West and thence to New York, where she might get medical attention. George insisted she go, and after the ship left he mounted his horse and dashed after the column, followed by his dog.

The Seminoles, led by Micanopy, Jumper and Alligator, had planned their ambush well. They waited in concealed positions, in a crescent-shaped formation with interlocking fields of fire. They had taken other means to ensure success—unbeknownst to Dade, his guide, Luis, was working with the enemy.[7] The original plan was to wait for Osceola to join them from Fort King before starting the attack, but as the column neared and Osceola had not arrived, Alligator overruled the older and more cautious Micanopy, and the attack went ahead.

Dade and half his men went down in the first volley. Gardiner, farther back in the column, quickly took command and began organizing a defense. He, Lieutenant W. E. Basinger, second in the Class of 1830, and Assistant Surgeon J. S. Gatlin were the only officers who had not been hit. Basinger and a crew unlimbered the sole artillery piece and fired grapeshot to keep the Seminoles at bay, but being dispersed they did not present a favorable target. Other troops under Gardiner's direction fired their muskets, and during a lull, the thirty or so survivors fashioned a triangular breastwork with pine logs. They brought in as many wounded as they could, and Gatlin patched their wounds. Luis, meanwhile, had feigned death, then took refuge with the Seminoles. When the Indians returned, the soldiers mounted a fierce defense, repulsing at least one rush, Gardiner coolly coordinating the action from the center of the small redoubt. Alligator later described "a little man, a great brave, who shook his sword at the soldiers and said 'God damn!' No rifle ball could hit him."[8] Nevertheless, attrition took its toll on the desperate defenders, who soon found themselves kneeling in a pond of their comrades' blood.

Gardiner eventually went down after taking five wounds. When the firing stopped, the Indians rushed the position and began killing the wounded. Basinger, the only officer left, attempted to surrender his sword, and the Seminoles paused a moment before one of them shot him down. The Indians took most of the scalps, but otherwise left the bodies unmolested.

The Seminoles were jubilant. Osceola's plan had succeeded beyond their expectations. They had annihilated the American force and taken only a few losses. They held a wild celebration at their encampment in Great Wahoo Swamp, at which the scalps of the dead were mounted on poles and addressed as though their original owners were present. Osceola took particular pleasure in renegotiating the emigration treaty with pieces of General Thompson.

Three wounded enlisted men survived the carnage, and after the attackers left they tried to make it back to Fort Brooke. Two of them completed the journey, one of whom later succumbed to his wounds. The only other survivor of the doomed column to return to Tampa was Captain Gardiner's dog.

FLORIDA WAS SOON ENGULFED in violence. By February 1, most of the territory south of St. Augustine was abandoned by settlers. The violence unleashed by the Seminoles was unprecedented in its scope and effectiveness, and it took the country completely by surprise. As one writer observed later in the war, "no nation or tribe, however insignificant, should be unnecessarily provoked to hostility, lest a power of vengeance be imparted to them beyond all foresight or calculation."[9]

Reinforcements were sent to Florida, and volunteer militia units, particularly from Tennessee, rushed to the seat of war. General Winfield Scott was called in to be the field commander. He expected it to be a quick action, similar to one fought by Andrew Jackson twenty years earlier. He confidently laid out his terms—"unconditional surrender." But Scott had poorly estimated the challenge he faced. Florida had some small cities on the periphery, but was largely unexplored in the interior. There were no good maps, which made campaign planning and coordination difficult. There were few roads and fewer bridges. The terrain was hostile: swampland with low hills called "hummocks," lagoons, and pine forests in the higher elevations. Beyond the operational issues, there was no good intelligence on exactly how many Seminole warriors were in the field. President Jackson believed they numbered no more than 400. His secretary of war, Lewis Cass, felt the number to be closer to 750. Jackson's estimate prevailed, not only because he was president, but also because he had fought and defeated these same Indians two decades prior, creating an assumption that he must know what he was talking about.[10]

The conflict quickly fell into a pattern. Columns would march into the wilderness in search of the enemy, without a good idea where they were going. They thus presented an ideal target for the Seminoles, who usually had set up ambushes. Fortunately for the soldiers, the Seminoles lacked training and discipline, and after the first volley they did not exploit their advantage. Seminoles also did not use enough powder per round (powder being a scarce commodity) and the balls that hit their mark did not always have the energy to kill or even wound severely. The Indians would hold their position for as long as they could, and if pressed would scatter. Because the Indians were unencumbered and could retreat in several directions at once, and Army columns were limited by their baggage trains and supply lines, there was no way to exploit a victory. This type of fighting did not result in many Indian deaths, nor did it gain ground, which there was no point in holding anyway.

"Look! There's the Indian!"

AT THE TIME OF THE DADE MASSACRE, Lieutenant William W. Morris of the Fourth Artillery was helping escort emigrant Indians to the Trans-Mississippi. Morris was born in Ballston Springs, New York, in 1801. His grandfather, Lewis, was a member of the Continental Congress and a signer of the Declaration of Independence. His great-uncle Gouverneur Morris also served in the Continental Congress and later helped draft the U.S. Constitution. William Morris entered West Point in 1815 and graduated in 1820, the Goat of his class. He then served in a variety of posts, notably being promoted for bravery at a battle with Arikara Indians in August 1823, serving in garrison in Charleston Harbor during South Carolina's nullification crisis, and most recently escorting emigrant Indians to the Trans-Mississippi. The duty was difficult and required moving bands numbering in some cases thousands of people over hundreds of miles on foot. Roads were poor, locals hostile, supplies uncertain, and the Indians totally unprepared for the trials they faced. Lieutenant John T. Sprague described the group he was taking west: "They were poor, wretchedly, and depravedly poor, many of them without a garment to cover their nakedness.... They left their country at a warm season of the year, thinly clad, and characteristically indifferent to their rapid approach to the rigors of a climate to which they were unaccustomed, they expended what little they had for intoxicating drinks or for some gaudy article of jewelry."[11]

In August of 1836, Morris joined the newly authorized regiment of Mounted Creek Volunteers, which was being formed at Fort Mitchell, at the rank of brevet major. The use of Indian troops was not only viewed as practical (the Seminole/Creek rivalry worked both ways), it had become necessary because white volunteers were growing scarce. The first wave of excitement following the Dade Massacre had come and gone. With most of the original militiamen back on their farms, 759 Creeks joined up for one year and were "to receive the pay and emoluments and equipment of soldiers in the Army of the U.S. and such plunder as they may take from the Seminoles." The regiment was led by Regular Army officers, and even though it was an Indian unit, competition for the officer billets was intense. Service in the volunteer regiment would give the men a chance to assume higher rank than they might otherwise enjoy, and also the opportunity to prove themselves in combat, since it was assumed that this regiment was going straight into action. The coveted colonelcy was given to John F. Lane of Kentucky, a captain in the Second Dragoons.[12] Several other West Pointers joined the unit, as well as Navy Lieutenant William M. Piercy and Lieutenant Andrew Ross of the Marine Corps.

When Morris joined the regiment at Fort Mitchell, he saw a familiar face among the Creeks. It was David Moniac, the first Indian, first minority and first Alabaman graduate of the Military Academy. Moniac was appointed to West Point under the provisions of a 1791 treaty between the United States and the Creek Nation that provided for education for a limited number of Creek children at public expense.[13] His father, half-Dutch Sam Manac, had been on the delegation that had met with George Washington and negotiated the treaty.[14] A clerical error gave David the name "Moniac" when he entered West Point in September 1817 at age fifteen, and he kept it. He was a determined if not brilliant student (he had only recently learned to read when he arrived at the Academy), who repeated his plebe year at his own request. His name appears among the list of cadets who had complained to Congress about Sylvanus Thayer in 1819, when he stated that "my rank in class, as given by my professor, has been lowered arbitrarily and unjustly" by the Superintendent.[15]

Moniac's disciplinary record showed no serious violations, mainly absences and visiting after hours. He served briefly as a cadet NCO in his cow year, but voluntarily returned to ranks as a firstie. Above all he was famous simply for being "the Indian at West Point." When the Corps marched to Boston in the summer of 1821 and did a pass in review for former president John Adams, Moniac was a public sensation. The aged Founding Father was not the sole center of attention for the crowd in Quincy—all along the road, people said, "Look there! There's the Indian!" Adams gave a brief address on the topic "What Is Glory?" after which Moniac was given the opportunity to be introduced to the former president. He demurred, staying instead among the Corps, and a sympathetic Major Worth explained that Moniac was too bashful.[16]

Moniac graduated next to last in the Class of 1822. He went on leave of absence in Alabama for six months, then resigned to tend to his father's failing business. Moniac ran a farm in Baldwin County, planting cotton and raising thoroughbred racehorses. In 1828 he married Mary Powell, whose half-white cousin Billy was at the time yet to find fame as Osceola, and they had two children. In 1835, Moniac served in a regiment raised by Creek chief Opothleyahola to assist General Thomas S. Jesup in putting down resistance to the forced migration policy. Because of his background as a West Point graduate, he was made a captain in the Mounted Creek Volunteers, initially the only Indian officer.[17]

In September the Creek Volunteers steamed across the Gulf to Fort Brooke, and in October they proceeded into the wilderness. The Seminoles harassed the column a few times, but the regiment did not see major action, and it linked up with General Richard K. Call's main force on October 19. Call, the territorial governor of Florida, had taken over command in the theater after a frustrated General Scott sought transfer. That night, Lieutenant Colonel Lane visited his friend Captain Galt in his tent, chatting away cheerily and toying with his saber. He mentioned something about the heat and Galt went out to raise the tent flap. Hearing a groan, he ducked back in to discover that Lane had driven his sword through his right eye into his brain, killing himself. It was unclear whether this was a ghastly accident or Lane had committed suicide, and if the latter, why.[18] The official report termed it a "melancholy death," meaning suicide, and explained that Lane had been suffering from fever and fatigue. Lieutenant Colonel Harvey Brown, sixth in the Class of 1818, took over command.

General Call's approach to fighting the war was no more innovative than Scott's. He knew there were Indian camps out in the wilderness, but did not really know where. So he sent columns into the brush with vague objectives on search-and-destroy missions, failing to find major concentrations of Indians but nevertheless scouting the terrain and at least knowing where they were not. He fought several small engagements that scattered the enemy in the usual way, and perhaps by accident began to close in on the major Seminole settlement in Wahoo Swamp. The Indians took a stand in a blocking position on the edge of dense woods, with a wide cleared field of fire. General Call set off to meet them on November 21, 1836, from a rendezvous point at Dade's battlefield, an ominous locale but one of the few points of reference in the area. He deployed a mile-wide line of battle, with Tennessee militia on his right, regulars and Florida militia in the center. The Mounted Creek Volunteers, who had donned white turbans to distinguish themselves from the other Indians, took the left. The troops being disposed, and with no particular tactical plan other than moving forward, the line began to advance, led by Colonel B. K. Pierce.

"We marched through the open field," Jo Guild of the Tennessee Volunteers later wrote. "The hostile Indians were seen coming out of the edge of a large hammock, half naked, jumping and turning about, accompanied with yelling and the war-whoop."[19] The line advanced to within fifty yards of the Indian position, opened fire and charged. The Indians fired a volley in response, then fell back. The attackers pushed forward through the trees and into another open field. As the troops advanced, the ground grew muddier and the long battle line became disorganized. The Seminoles quickly regrouped at a second position behind a ten-yard-wide stream of black water and began pouring fire into the disordered American troops.

David Moniac, who had been promoted to brevet major for bravery in a skirmish the week before, rallied the Creeks. He charged forward to try to ford the stream and outflank the Seminoles, his men following. As he entered the water, Moniac was drilled by a fusillade of musket balls. He dropped into the murky stream and sank, killed instantly. The Seminoles, seeing whom they believed to be the chief of the Creeks fall, whooped with delight. Morris and the other officers rallied the troops and a sharp contest continued at the stream bank, at point-blank range. Other forces came up some time later and the battle continued until mid-afternoon, when Seminole fire slackened. General Call chose to withdraw rather than attempt to force a crossing, since his men were tired and hungry, and darkness would come in a few hours. A party retrieved Major Moniac's body from the dark water, and in so doing found that the stream was only three feet deep. Had the rest of the troops charged ahead after Moniac, they would have burst across into a lightly defended Seminole flank, no doubt broken through and descended on the Indian settlement they had been seeking.

The Battle of Wahoo Swamp ended inconclusively, as many other such battles had. Seven of the forty-nine graduates of the USMA Class of 1836 were at this battle, and in all there were about sixteen West Pointers on the field. Lieutenant Colonel Brown was brevetted for gallant conduct.[20] Morris would receive a brevet a few months later for Wahoo and other services. There were nineteen American casualties. Seven enlisted men were killed in action. David Moniac was the only officer to die on the field. Marine Lieutenant Ross, mortally wounded, died that evening. In his report to General Call, Colonel Pierce wrote, "I think it a brilliant day, redounding to the honor of our arms, and calculated to bring the war to a speedy termination."[21]

★ ★ ★

IN THE FIRST YEAR OF THE Seminole conflict, the War Department claimed to have killed only 131 Indians and captured 15.[22] Estimates of total enemy forces were still uncertain, but a field intelligence report from July 1837 calculated 1,513 Seminole warriors in the theater of conflict, double Secretary Cass's high estimate at the outbreak of war and almost four times Jackson's estimate.[23] Failure to pacify the territory incited further political squabbles in Washington. There were rivalries between generals and other officers, political interference and sniping at the president and the secretary of war, congressional hearings, debates in the press, and backroom deals with contractors seeking to benefit from the newly doubled War Department budget. In Florida, commander followed commander as battles were fought to inconsequential and expensive victories.

One bright spot in the conflict was the capture of Osceola in October 1837. He had been taken without bloodshed during a parlay, a controversial but effective subterfuge ordered by the new field commander, Major General Thomas S. Jesup. For security reasons, Osceola was removed to Fort Moultrie in Charleston Harbor, where he was treated as a celebrity. Portraitists flocked to the city to capture the image of the terror of the swamps. He graciously sat for them in full panoply: white smock, red bandanna over his cropped black hair, topped with a black-and-white feather. The portraits showed a strong face, stately and confident, in some pictures looking benevolent, but never warlike or fierce. He had expressive eyes and a Roman nose, and the paintings very much conveyed the image of an aboriginal sovereign that the romantics made of him.[24]

Osceola would not long enjoy this renown. He had been suffering from an unknown sickness since the time of his capture, and at the end of January 1838 he died, surrounded by his family. By then Osceola was well on his way to becoming a folk hero, in part because of the idealization of his struggle, and also because the way he was captured was seen as unfair. Many outside of Florida condemned Jesup's move. Lucy Hooper, a young poet who wrote a lengthy paean to Osceola, said that Jesup's stratagem was "a transaction which should ever cover the officer's name with lasting infamy." Another poet, the Reverend John Pierpoint, said that Jesup had dishonored "a flag that [even] Tartar hordes respect."[25] As late as 1858, Jesup was called upon publicly to defend his actions.[26] Meanwhile Osceola, in death, had become the epitome of the noble savage. Counties, towns and ships were named after him, poems and memorials written in his honor. The men he had killed and his role in planning the Dade Massacre and other atrocities were forgotten, but the war he had incited ground on.

★ ★ ★

LIEUTENANT RICHARD B. SCREVEN served in Florida with the Fourth Infantry. He had continued his studies at West Point after his reprieve in the Eggnog Mutiny and graduated last in the Class of 1829. Like William W. Morris he had been escorting Indians west when the war broke out; his unit moved south and got into the action within weeks. Screven had fought in several heavy skirmishes, and in December 1837 the Fourth Infantry moved into the interior for what he hoped would be the final battle.

Screven was part of a column of 1,350 troops, four-fifths of whom were regulars, heading south into the heart of the Seminole stronghold, led by Colonel Zachary Taylor. Over 400 Seminoles awaited Taylor's force in a prepared position near Lake Okeechobee, led by Alligator, Coacoochee (also known as Wild Cat) and Halleck Tustenuggee, a six foot two inch Mickasukie warlord with a fanatical following. Their defensive bastion was in a broad hummock fronted by a half-mile-deep swampy glacis, with waist-deep water and five-foot saw grass. The Indians were deployed in three groups; they had fixed their fields of fire, cut corridors in the tall grass, and rested their rifles in notches cut into the cypress trees. Lake Okeechobee was to their rear, with escape routes to the right and left. They had planned to meet a frontal assault, and Taylor did not disappoint them.

Taylor deployed a regiment of Missouri Volunteers as a skirmish line, followed by the Fourth and Sixth Infantry regiments, with the First Infantry in reserve. The Missourians moved forward at 12:30 P.M. into the teeth of the Seminole fire, and their commander, Colonel Gentry, went down at once, mortally wounded. The militiamen ducked, seeking shelter, and the troops behind them opened up on the Indians. Some of the Missourians were wounded in the crossfire and many fell back. The Seminoles kept up their accurate fire, raking the two regular infantry regiments. Almost every officer and noncom was wounded. Colonel Alexander Ramsey Thompson, Class of 1812 and son of Mrs. Thompson whose rooms were so much in demand at West Point, was struck down leading the Sixth Infantry. He exhorted his men to "Remember the regiment to which you belong!" before succumbing.

After two and a half hours of bloody stalemate, Taylor attempted a flanking maneuver.[27] He sent the reserve force to hit the Indians on their right. The enemy flank buckled, and the main body of the Seminole force scattered back towards the lake. Screven and some elements of the Fourth gave chase until nightfall. Taylor was left holding the field, but there was no chance to exploit the victory, if it could be called that. The Indians took 25 casualties, 11 of them killed. Taylor's force suffered 138 casualties, 26 killed. William H. T. Walker of the Sixth Infantry, a Georgian who had graduated from West Point that spring close to the bottom of the Class of 1837, was "literally shot to pieces" by one account, having four balls pass through his body and being grazed by several more. Remarkably, he survived.[28] Colonel Gentry, in his last minutes, made a final request to Taylor: "be as easy on [the Missouri militia] as you can in your report."[29] But Taylor did not honor the request; his account as much as accused the Missourians of cowardice, leading to another political row in Washington. Despite angry calls for his resignation, Taylor was promoted to brigadier general.

Taylor took over command in Florida the next spring. Jesup, shot through the cheek leading troops at the Battle of Lockahatchee, had grown weary of the conflict. During his tenure in Florida, 2,400 enemy had been captured or killed, 700 of whom were warriors.[30] These numbers were greater than the initial estimates of total Seminole strength, and yet the conflict continued. In the spring of 1838, Jesup wrote to the War Department questioning the wisdom of continuing the costly war against such an elusive enemy, fighting over ground that white farmers would never settle even if it were secured. But his views were not shared by the secretary of war, and in May 1838 he was transferred.

Taylor too had been frustrated by the conduct of the war, and wrote his friend Senator John J. Crittenden of Kentucky that were he a member of Congress, he "would never vote to appropriate a dollar to carry it out under present circumstances."[31] Like Jesup, he believed that if the remaining few Seminoles were left confined to their wilderness refuges they would pose no particular threat, certainly not one worth the effort currently being undertaken. Taylor's innovation was the system of "squares," twenty miles on a side, that he mapped out in the spring of 1839. His idea was to establish a grid in the area of resistance, with a garrison in the middle of each square connected by roads. Each garrison commander would have the responsibility to send out regular mounted patrols and gradually take control of the whole area.

Lieutenant Nathaniel Wyche Hunter, commanding F Troop, Second Dragoons, was sent to establish a post on the bank of the St. Johns River, with few supplies, no guide, no map, and "wholly ignorant of the country in which I am expected to operate."[32] Wyche had been in Florida for several years and had not seen major action. At "Fort Hunter" he sent out periodic patrols but did not encounter any Seminoles. Most of the battles he fought were against the Quartermaster Corps, which would not provide him with lumber or other supplies he needed to establish his post. He poured out his scorn in his diary in pages of invective. "A dolt, dunce, dullard, anything could be a Q. Master now-a-days. . . . The first official act of the Q. Master is to make himself comfortable—the second more comfortable—the third most comfortable—the last to make everyone else as uncomfortable as the licenses of the services will permit. . . . 'Tis a villainous trade."[33] His rudimentary defenses would be insufficient to ward off a Seminole assault, and he noted that he would be "extremely obliged if the Indians would give me a wide berth in their various excursions through the country."[34] It was a sore point for Wyche, who had previously served at a post the Seminoles had infiltrated and burned. He was forced to overwork his troops, with whom he empathized because they reminded him of "some galley slave chained to the bench."[35] Many fell sick, others "chop their feet or do something else (accidentally of course) to excuse them from duty." By the end of his first month in the field, Wyche was finally sent some nails for construction, but unfortunately no hammers. He noted, "I'm most essentially disgusted."[36]

Despite Hunter's assessment, the squares had some impact. Few Indians were apprehended, but the system of outposts began to corral the Seminoles, and more bands made peace and were moved west. So much progress had been made that General Macomb himself came to Fort King to parley with the Seminoles over ending the war. He reached an agreement with several of the remaining chiefs, represented by Halleck Tustenuggee, in which the Indians were to move south of Pease Creek and Lake Okeechobee, to live unmolested until other arrangements could be made. On May 20, 1839, with great ceremony, General Macomb declared the cessation of hostilities. "The Major General commanding in chief has the satisfaction of announcing to the Army in Florida, to the authorities of the Territory, and to the citizens generally, that he has this day terminated the war with the Seminole Indians." The Indians withdrew south, Macomb returned to Washington, settlers began to return to the land, and politicians and the public focused on other matters.

One of the provisions of the peace agreement was that a trading post be established in the Seminole lands, and oversight of the task fell to Lieutenant Colonel William Selby Harney of the Second Dragoons. Harney was thirty-nine years old, six foot three, physically commanding, handsome, confident, and suspicious of the Seminoles. He was from a well-to-do Tennessee family, a neighbor and friend to Andrew

Jackson, who employed Harney's brother James as his personal lawyer. The site chosen for the trading post was Charlotte Harbor, a riverside pine barren twelve miles from the mouth of the Caloosahatchee. Twenty-six men, a storekeeper and clerks were building the post. The truce was holding, and Indians peacefully came and went, expressing satisfaction with the pact.

On the night of July 22, 1839, Harney sacked out half clothed after a boar hunt. At daylight the next morning, 160 Indians led by a chief named Chakaika mounted a surprise attack. Many of the attackers had been to the post many times and knew exactly where to strike. They had surrounded the large hospital tent being used as quarters for most of the men and tore into it simultaneously. Eighteen were killed, most of them in their beds, some pursued to the river and shot, others led to safety by supposedly friendly Indians and then struck down. Seminoles looted the stores, taking thousands in silver coins and materiel. Fourteen men escaped, including Harney, who ran to the river in his underwear and swam for it, then floated downstream in an Indian dugout. Other survivors were forced to hide for days, evading roving Indians and eating raw oysters and fiddler crabs.

The attack sundered the truce. A new wave of Indian violence followed, and public confidence plummeted. Secretary of War Joel Poinsett came under fire by the president's political opponents for his conduct of the hostilities. He was accused of lying to the public and to Congress about the progress of the war and about its costs. The budget was a particularly sensitive issue. Martin Van Buren had inherited a growing economy and the only Treasury surplus in United States history.[37] However, he stepped immediately into a recession, the Panic of 1837, and the public account went back into debt. The economy failed to recover and the president was tagged with the nickname "Martin Van Ruin." War expenses were so great that some critics argued it would be cheaper just to pay the Seminoles to behave. Northerners saw the war as a means of gathering slaves or guaranteeing Florida's admission as a slave state. But the most celebrated dispute arose over bloodhounds.

On his own initiative Governor Call imported thirty-three bloodhounds from Havana, where they had been trained to track runaway slaves, to be used for locating Indians. Taylor, highly skeptical of the efficacy of the dogs, allowed two to be used on a test basis. The experiment was a failure; Wyche, who observed the use of the bloodhounds, wrote, "Dogs of no value whatever . . . the last hope of terminating the war has proved a chimera—a humbug—a hoax."[38] In the Washington echo chamber, the bloodhounds became a national issue far out of proportion to their importance. Many believed the purpose of the dogs was to run down and maul the Indians. Petitions from all parts of the country were laid before Congress to protest this inhumane method of war. The War Department denied responsibility for the move and sent firm instructions to the field that the dogs be muzzled and kept on leashes to ensure that they could only track and did not actually bite the Seminoles. An editorial cartoon showed dogs receiving brevet promotions, and congressman and former president John Quincy Adams submitted a taunting resolution that "the Secretary of War be directed to report to this House the natural, political and martial history of the bloodhounds, showing the peculiar fitness of the class of warriors to be the associates of the gallant Army of the United States . . . and whether he deems it expedient to extend to the said bloodhounds and their posterity the benefits of the pension laws."[39] The issue was a symptom of an administration that had lost its direction. The futile war that Van Buren had inherited from Andrew Jackson helped end his chances at reelection. He lost to William Henry Harrison, famous for defeating the Indians at Tippecanoe, who died after a month in office, leaving the war to President John Tyler.

War Without End

THE SEMINOLE WAR WAS HAVING a devastating effect on the Army. Morale was poor in both officer and enlisted ranks. Where enlisted men chose to escape by desertion, officers resorted to resignation. In the first year of the war, 117 Regular Army officers had resigned, with an average of thirty per year thereafter leaving the colors. Some were frustrated at their inability to find or engage the enemy, others by the seeming ineptitude of their commanders; still others were fed up with life in the Florida wilds. Above all, they were perturbed by a war that refused to come to a close. As an Army camp song put it,

> Ever since creation,
> The best calculation,
> The Florida war has been raging;
>
> And 'tis our expectation
> That the last conflagration
> Will find us the same contest waging.

There was some sympathy for the Indians, even among the soldiers, that echoed the thoughts of the admirers of Osceola. Captain Hitchcock stated that the Seminoles have "nobly defended their country against our attempt to enforce a fraudulent treaty."[40] Lieutenant John T. Sprague wrote that "Their sin is patriotism, as true as ever burned in the hearts of the most civilized."[41] The Indians were compared to the Founding Fathers, fighting for "their homes, their property, their families, and their rights."[42] Wyche, upon receiving a "no prisoners" order from Colonel Taylor, wondered why he would issue such an inhumane directive and vowed to his diary that "No Indian prisoner while under my command shall suffer a premeditated death. I should be proud of an opportunity of showing my utter disrespect for such an order."[43] His experiences in the war had convinced him that there was something fundamentally unjust about the conflict. "I've tried every argument to still my conscience," he wrote, "but this restless imp will not be quiet. . . . Have God and justice no claims upon you prior and paramount to a government, that incites you to the commission of a crime? . . . Is not every act of the Indians sanctioned by the practices of civilized nations?"[44] The Army began to adapt to Indian warfare, developing guerilla-style units and tactics. Though these irregular methods were controversial, they were effective; but for every success against the Seminoles, there were cruel reminders that the war was not yet over.

Lieutenant Alexander Montgomery came to Florida in 1839. He was a classmate of Edgar Allan Poe's and graduated the Goat of the Class of 1834. While stationed at Newport, Kentucky, he won the hand of Miss Sarah Taylor, a local belle and member of the wealthy Taylor family that founded the town, and distantly related to Zachary Taylor.[45] He convinced her to accompany him to Florida, and she soon found herself at Fort Wheelock, one of the interior posts, far from the comforts of the family home and with few of the diversions to which she was accustomed. In December 1840, a friend of hers, wife of Kentucky native Lieutenant Nevil Hopson, an Immortal of the Class of 1837, invited her to visit Fort King. Sarah Montgomery set off on a pleasant morning, dressed in a stylish riding habit, accompanied by Lieutenant Hopson, his classmate Lieutenant Walter Sherwood, Sergeant Major Carroll, and ten privates. Alexander Montgomery, who was not feeling well, stayed behind.

Three miles from the fort, at a creek crossing called Martin's Point, a volley of fire from the bushes took down the mounted men in front of the wagon. The ambush party was led by Halleck Tustenuggee, who had fought Taylor at Okeechobee and had made peace with General Macomb in May of 1839. Lieutenant Sherwood dismounted, began organizing a defense, and ordered Mrs. Montgomery into a covered wagon for safety. He sent Hopson back to Fort Wheelock for reinforcements. Hopson raced back to the fort, preceded by Sarah's horse, which reached the fort before he did, alerting the troops that something was wrong.

Meanwhile the defenders had formed around the wagon and were being picked off one by one. Sherwood went down, shot in the chest, but still living. Sergeant Major Carroll stood over him, defending the wounded officer until he was cut down in hand-to-hand struggle. As the defensive cordon collapsed, the driver and Sarah knew they had to make a break for it if they hoped to survive. They leapt from the wagon and dashed down the road. But Sarah tripped over her long riding dress. The driver tried to help her, and she stood, ran a few more steps, fell, rose, ran, and fell again. Meanwhile the Indians had spotted the pair and were pursuing, laughing as they came. The driver decided that discretion was the better part of valor and saved himself. Sarah, confused in her terror, rose and ran towards the Indians, who quickly killed her.[46] It was exactly five years to the day of the Dade Massacre.

The Martin's Point incident intensified the lingering sense of futility. Taylor gave up command in 1841 and was replaced by Colonel William "Haughty Bill" Worth. The former USMA Commandant was handsome, a good fighter, yet rash and vain. Ordered to end the war, he settled on a strategy of vigorous military action coupled with negotiations and resettlement. His operations order was simple and straightforward: "Find the enemy, capture or exterminate." A bounty of $100 was placed on every warrior killed or captured. Worth pressed a joint Army-Navy-Marine incursion into the Everglades, rooting out Seminole sanctuaries and isolated croplands on small islands, showing the Indians they had nowhere to hide.[47] Elsewhere he kept troops in motion, pushing them into the field even through the summer, forcing the Seminole bands to keep moving too. Some small indecisive actions were fought, but Worth was not seeking decisive engagement. His plan was to wear the enemy down through continual pressure. He brought emigrant chiefs such as Billy Bowlegs back to convince others that life in Oklahoma Territory was a better option than slow, inevitable destruction in Florida.

In the spring of 1841, Worth captured Coacoochee, a respected and eloquent leader who had commanded at Okeechobee, whose band numbered 189 men, women and children. Coacoochee had come to Worth with a small delegation, dressed in the costume of Hamlet he had taken from a theatrical troop his men had waylaid on the road a short time before.[48] Worth made an impassioned plea to the chief to have his people surrender (threatening to hang him if they did not). Eventually they all came in and the group emigrated.

During his captivity, Coacoochee made an enduring contribution to U.S. military culture. At a banquet, he noticed that the soldiers would raise their drinks and make brief toasts before drinking. Toasting was not a Seminole custom, and he asked the interpreter, Gopher John, what the soldiers were saying. Gopher John said that toasting was a form of greeting. Coacoochee, with great dignity, then raised his cup high and said to the assembled in a great deep voice, "Hoo-ah!"[49] The toast was echoed by the soldiers around the table, and was before long adopted across the Army, being immortalized in the chorus of a contemporary drinking song:

> Hoo-ah! boys, hoo-ah—hoo-ah! boys, hoo-ah.
> Let the soldiers' toast be ever, Hoo-ah![50]

Years later, Coacoochee became an officer in the Mexican Army, fighting Comanches in New Mexico. One night he got into a drunken brawl with Gopher John, who caved in the old chief's head with a whiskey bottle, killing him.

By February of 1842, Worth estimated that there were approximately 300 Indians left in Florida, including 112 warriors.[51] Among the holdouts was Halleck Tustenuggee, who with his band of 114 followers resisted to the very end. He participated in the last significant action of the war in April and was taken captive with his band shortly thereafter. When he was finally shipped west on July 14, the bitter chief said, "I have been hunted like a wolf, and now I am sent away like a dog."[52] Worth declared the war over on August 14, 1842.

In the seven years of the Second Seminole War, the Army lost 1,446 dead, 328 of them killed in action, most of the rest to disease. With 10,169 soldiers serving in Florida, the death rate was 14 percent, making it by far the deadliest of any of America's wars. The losses included 74 officers dead and 20 killed in action; 13 of the dead were Academy graduates. The conflict cost between $10 and $40 million, depending on who was doing the estimate.[53]

In addition to the mortal and monetary costs, there were also the intangibles—the suffering, fear, and hollow sense of accomplishment. The Second Seminole War was a brutal, difficult pacification in which progress was measured by inches, and success by the gradual diminishing of Indian attacks. A period observer said it was "indeed, a most remarkable war, and will hereafter be regarded as one of the most successful struggles which history exhibits, of a barbarous, weak, and almost destitute people, with a civilized, strong, and abundantly provided nation."[54] Of the Seminoles, 3,800 were shipped west, an unknown number killed or dying of wounds, starvation or disease in the trackless wilderness. For the troops who fought the Second Seminole War, even for those who later saw action in Mexico and the Civil War, it was universally regarded as the worst service they had ever known. Nathaniel Wyche Hunter likened the sight of the ship coming to take him from Florida to the vista of the Promised Land when the Children of Israel first gazed upon it.

Henry Heth

ABNEY MAURY, A VIRGINIAN who graduated near the middle of the Class of 1846 and who later served as a Confederate major general, said that the four years he spent at West Point were "the only unhappy years of a very happy life."[1] Maury's friend Henry Heth, fellow Virginian and Goat of the Class of 1847, had a much different experience. "Dabney was a good boy at West Point," Heth observed, "but he was not happy; I was not good, I was happy, and had a good time."[2] It was clear from the very beginning that Heth would enjoy his stay at West Point—he chalked up his first two of many demerits for "Laughing in ranks at morning parade."[3]

Henry Heth was born in 1825, the fourth of eleven children of John and Margaret Pickett Heth of Blackheath, Chesterfield County, Virginia. John had served in the Navy under Decatur in the War of 1812, and later was a successful plantation owner who, as head of the Heth Manufacturing Company, also ran lucrative coal and iron concerns. Henry had been well prepared for the academic rigors of West Point. He had matriculated at Georgetown College, which was then a prep school, at the age of twelve, moved on to the Muhlenburg School on Long Island, and finally attended the Peugnet Freres School for Boys in New York. The Peugnet brothers were former French officers who had fought under Napoleon, and they thrilled their charges with tales of the great European battles of the past. The Peugnets specialized in preparing candidates for the Military Academy, and in his two years there Henry grew proficient in French and mathematics, still mainstays of the West Point curriculum.[4] Henry's father died while he was at Peugnet's, and family friend President John Tyler, in sympathy, offered Henry a commission as a midshipman. Margaret Heth turned down her son's appointment, and Tyler countered with a presidential appointment to West Point, which Henry accepted.

Heth sailed north to West Point in 1843. Like Nathaniel Wyche

Hunter and most other cadets, he arrived during the summer encampment. Unlike Wyche, he was protected from most of the indignities inflicted on new cadets by his cousin George Pickett, who was then a yearling and described by William M. Gardner, Class of 1846 and later a Confederate brigadier general, as "a jolly good fellow with fine natural gifts sadly neglected. He was a devoted and constant patron of Benny Haven, [a man] of ability, but belonging to a cadet set that appeared to have no ambition for class standing and wanted to do only enough study to secure their graduation."[5] The two cousins became boon companions, the core of a cadet clique that did not have the patience to wait until after graduation to seek adventures.

George Pickett would make his mark as one of history's most famous Virginians, but he was appointed to West Point from Illinois. After his death, the general's widow, LaSalle "Sallie" Pickett, wove an intriguing story around Pickett's appointment, which over the years grew in the telling. The tale goes that in the early 1840s, when young George was studying law in Illinois, he occasioned to meet Congressman Abraham Lincoln. Pickett, who did not know Lincoln's identity, spoke to him of his secret ambition to become a soldier. Lincoln took note of the young man's aspiration, and soon afterwards, to his surprise, Pickett was notified that he had been appointed a cadet at West Point. This inspired a lifelong loyalty, and during the Civil War, Pickett would rise to the defense of Lincoln if anyone said anything negative about the president in his presence. One of Sallie's stories has it that when Lincoln visited Richmond after its fall in April 1865, he stopped by the Pickett home and was met by Mrs. Pickett, holding her infant son, George Pickett Jr.

"Is this George Pickett's house?" Lincoln asked.

"Yes, but he's not at home."

"I know that Ma'am, but I just wanted to see the place. I am Abraham Lincoln."

"The President!" she gasped.

"No Ma'am! No Ma'am, just Abraham Lincoln, George's old friend."

"I am George Pickett's wife," she said, "and this is his baby." George Jr. reached out to Lincoln, who took the baby in his arms and kissed him.

"Tell your father, the rascal, that I forgive him for the sake of that kiss and those bright eyes." He then handed little George back to his mother and left.[6] The tale of Lincoln's visit is a compelling story of irony and forgiveness, and would be extraordinary if true. Sadly, no other witnesses attest to the story, and it was probably the product of Mrs. Pickett's hagiographic impulses. An 1842 letter from Lincoln to Pickett on his appointment, full of fatherly advice and homespun wisdom, discovered in the early twentieth century, turned out to be a forgery. Furthermore, Lincoln served only one term in Congress, 1847–49, by which time Pickett had already graduated.

But while the particulars of the myth are easily disproved, there is at least a tincture of truth in it. Pickett did go to Quincy, Illinois, in the early 1840s to study law with his uncle Andrew Johnston. Pickett was appointed to West Point through the office of Johnston's friend John Todd Stuart, a congressman from Illinois. Stuart had previously served as a volunteer major in the Blackhawk War, where he had met Lincoln, then captain of a volunteer company. (Both had been mustered into service by Regular Army Lieutenant Jefferson Davis.)[7] Stuart and Lincoln served in the state legislature together and became law partners. Lincoln later married Stuart's cousin, Mary Todd. Andrew Johnston and Lincoln were also close friends, and Johnston was responsible for the only known publication of a Lincoln poem, when he had some verse Lincoln had written him in a letter published in the Quincy Whig, May 5, 1847.[8] Thus while the tale of the Lincoln-Pickett connection has been exaggerated, it is not a complete fantasy. It would be more difficult to believe that Johnston never bothered to introduce his nephew the prospective lawyer to his two successful friends in the west Illinois legal fraternity. Ironically, the only cadet that Lincoln nominated while in Congress was Hezekiah H. Garber of the Class of 1852, who like Pickett graduated as the Goat.[9]

The West Point that Pickett and Heth attended was subtly different from the institution Thayer had created. Major Rene DeRussy of the Class of 1812 followed Thayer as Superintendent and retained all the academic aspects of the Thayer system, which established it beyond question.[10] DeRussy, however, was not the disciplinarian that Thayer had been, and he relaxed some of the stricter standards on cadet behavior. He allowed alcohol to be served again at the Fourth of July dinners, and unlike Thayer, who kept his distance from these festivities, DeRussy joined in. His easygoing approach was popular with cadets, and punishments grew so lax that even Thayer's *bête noire* President Jackson mandated that West Point be "more rigorous in enforcing its discipline."[11]

DeRussy served five years as Superintendent and was succeeded in 1838 by Major Richard Delafield, known as "Old Dickey." Delafield had graduated first in the Class of 1818, the first class of the Thayer era. He thus may have felt a special responsibility to preserve the Thayer legacy. Like DeRussy, he maintained the continuity of the system, but he was much stricter than his predecessor, and so was not liked by cadets. They showed their disregard for him in various harmless ways; for example, two of Delafield's pet ducks were caught and eaten, and cadets would occasionally corral his cow, which was accustomed to grazing on the Plain, to exploit the supply of fresh milk. In 1843 when Delafield banned the traditional cadet practice of having Christmas Eve suppers in their rooms, the Corps boycotted the elaborate catered feast and dance he had arranged in the drill hall. A cadet officer looked in on the desolate scene, and later noted in a letter home, "I really pitied the old gent, after all the pains he had taken—however it will learn him that he can't control a body of men in their amusements or at any rate that he can't make a man enjoy himself if he don't wish to."[12]

Delafield was assisted in his tasks by Commandant John Addison Thomas, Class of 1833, a strict disciplinarian who also was not loved by the cadets. He had been at USMA almost his entire career, as a Tac and professor before becoming Commandant. Since he had formerly taught ethics, his cadet nickname was "Ethical Tom," though he insisted on signing his name "J. Addison Thomas." He was vainglorious and affected a martial bearing, which was not out of place at the Academy but was noteworthy because it was so obviously artificial. He was fond of his full-dress uniform as an officer of artillery, with its towering hat and red plume. A cadet described him during parade: "This resplendent being appeared before us as a radiant vision, and with clanking saber and whiskers of most precise military cut, strode like a field marshal along our ranks, transfixing each of us in turn with the fierceness of his eagle eye."[13] Thomas too was the object of occasional expressions of discontent, such as the time his office was flooded by some cadets he had given Saturday punishment. Thomas's wealthy wife eventually convinced him to leave the Army and become a lawyer, and when his departure was announced to the Corps in late October 1845, after ranks were broken the cadets raised their hats and spontaneously gave three cheers, three times. "This was insubordinate conduct," Cadet George H. Derby explained, "but it could not be punished for there were no ringleaders, and all they could have done would have been to dismiss the whole corps."[14] Later that evening the cadets celebrated with an illumination of the barracks and a serenade of drums, and those who were caught were punished.

In addition to the efforts of DeRussy and Delafield, the Thayer system persisted because of the continuity in curriculum and faculty, particularly in the person of Dennis Hart Mahan. Boy genius of the

Class of 1824, Mahan was chosen by Thayer as his intellectual successor. He spent four years in Europe studying modern methods of war,
and attended the French Military School of Engineers and Artillerists
at Metz. In 1832, at age twenty-nine, he became the head professor of
engineering at the Academy, a post he retained for almost forty years.
He was the author of numerous books, and his textbook on tactics was
highly influential and reprinted without permission by the Confederate government during the Civil War. Mahan was also a deft and able
public defender of the Military Academy against its critics. He paid special tribute to the father of the Academy in 1840 when he named his
newborn son Alfred Thayer Mahan.[15]

Dennis Mahan was brilliant, cold and sarcastic, not a favorite
among the cadets, who respected and feared him. He brooked no dis-
agreement from his students (or anyone else, for that matter), but those
whom he taught learned their subjects well. Due to a slight speech
impediment, Mahan spoke as though he had a head cold, and "as he
was constantly telling his pupils to use a little *cobben sense* he at length
got to be known—such is the irreverence of cadets—as 'Old Cobben
Sense.'"[16] One piece of advice he doled out concerned marriage. Mahan's
wife, Mary Helena, was a beauty whom he had met at a cadet hop in
1830. Their courtship lasted nine years, and Mahan later told cadets
that nothing was more foolish than for a young officer to get married,
and a wife was a luxury that should not be thought of until one reached
the rank of captain.[17] The question of whether it would be beneficial to
forbid officers under the rank of captain from marrying was debated
by the Dialectic Society in September 1840, and the resolution was
defeated 11 to 4. Cadets were forbidden to marry while at the Academy, but many found themselves in wedlock soon after graduation
despite Mahan's sagacious advice.

Completing the course of studies and graduating from West Point
did not get any easier in the post-Thayer years. In Pickett's class, 133
young men were appointed, of whom 122 actually made it to the Academy. At the first January examination, 30 were found deficient and had
to "take the Canterbury Road," i.e., go back home; 56 of the remaining 92 would go on to graduate, but only 47 of them graduated in four
years; the other 9 completed in 1847. So Pickett, even as the Goat, was
like the other Immortals a survivor.

During the period before the Mexican War, the Corps saw pass
through its ranks cadets who would later win fame on the battlefields
of the Civil War. The class rosters of those days read like a Who's
Who of the War Between the States. Yet none at the time knew the

struggles they were preparing for, or which among them were marked for greatness. Class rank was not a good predictor. During his commencement speech for the Class of 1886, Brigadier General John Gibbon, Class of 1847, noted, "one cannot help being struck with the remarkable, sometimes whimsical, way in which the dice-box of Fate has apparently belied all prognostications formed here.... Who cannot recall instances of boys whose future the most exalted estimates were made, and who, when the great test of life was applied, were never heard of? Who has not been amazed at the way in which some, never associated in our minds with greatness, have shot up into well-merited prominence?"[18] He envisioned a roll call of his cadet company by a sorcerer with the gift of prescience, telling each man his fate. Gibbon, who graduated 20th in a Class of 38, began the Civil War as a captain and ended it as a brevet major general, being wounded several times and promoted for bravery at Antietam, Fredericksburg, Gettysburg, Spottsylvania and Petersburg. He was born in Pennsylvania but grew up in North Carolina and was appointed to West Point from there. His three brothers fought for the Confederacy and his family disowned him as a traitor. His entry to West Point was delayed a year because on his entrance exam he did not know the correct date for Independence Day. Of the Class of 1847 as a whole, sixteen would rise to general officer rank, but none of the generals came from the top five "star men" of the class. Four of the class would die in combat, including one of the generals, Ambrose Powell "A. P." Hill, who was killed at Petersburg in the last week before Appomattox.

Professor Mahan, unlike Gibbon, was a believer in the infallibility of the Thayer system. The continual process of testing and ranking the cadets—not just twice yearly but weekly—was to him an objective winnowing, and its product as accurate an indicator of future potential as could be devised. This, of course, was easy for a star man to believe. John C. Tidball of the Class of 1848, who rose to the rank of brevet major general in the Civil War and who was briefly Commandant of Cadets in 1864, wrote later that Mahan "regarded Grant, Sheridan and others who did not have high class standing as mere freaks of chance." The high-ranking graduates who held important leadership posts in the opening years of the war affirmed the judgment of the Academic Board; "but when success did not perch upon their banners hope fled, and when, finally, those of inferior standing rose to distinguished leadership the world was turned topsy-turvy. Then the days were indeed gloomy for the professor."[19]

One of the most noteworthy "freaks of chance" was indeed Ulysses H. (later S.) Grant, of the Class of 1843, whom Dabney Maury described as "a very good and kindly fellow whom everybody liked."[20] He is often thought to have been a Goat, but he was not, having graduated firmly in the middle of his class, 21st of 39. The idea that Grant performed poorly in school probably stems from a temptation to make him the anti-Lee. In many ways he was—Blue vs. Gray, westerner vs. easterner, son of the middle class vs. scion of the aristocracy, plainspoken vs. eloquent, rough-hewn vs. well groomed—it is too tempting to add to the list "Goat vs. Star."[21] But while not a Goat, Grant was hardly an ideal student. Looking back on his cadet years, he recalled that "military life had no charms for me, and I had not the faintest idea of staying in the Army even if I should be graduated, which I did not expect.... I did not take hold of my studies with avidity, in fact I rarely read over a lesson the second time during my entire cadetship." Grant said he spent most of his study time devouring novels, though "not those of a trashy sort."[22] When Congress debated a bill in December 1839 to close West Point, Grant favored the measure as "an honorable way to obtain a discharge."[23] Grant's lowest marks were in ethics and French, in which he was very poor, and in his final year his worst showing was in infantry tactics. But his other grades were decent and his disciplinary record was not extraordinarily bad; he did not get involved with hazing and he blew post to Benny's only once.

Grant's friend James Longstreet explained, "as I was of large and robust physique I was accomplished at most larks and games. But in these young Grant never joined because of his delicate frame."[24] Yet Grant was without equal in one area of study, horsemanship. He was a daring rider who took risks that others would not. The riding hall was a large space in the Academic building, which was not well adapted to the purpose, particularly because of the numerous iron support pillars around which cadets had to maneuver. They would guide their mounts about the hall, chopping at posts with straw-filled heads on top, poking their sabers through rings hanging above them, and leaping over wooden poles held by enlisted dragoons. Grant favored a foul-tempered sorrel called York that other cadets feared, and he would leap the animal over bars six feet high or higher. A hash was placed on the wall to mark Grant's highest leap, which was never beaten. Longstreet said that when Grant was in the saddle, "Rider and horse held together like the fabled centaur."[25] Once while Grant was riding a particularly spirited mount, the saddle girth broke, sending the rider tumbling. "Cadet Grant," the riding master said, "six demerits for dismounting without leave."[26]

Henry Heth was also credited as the best rider in his class, and was once given demerits for improvising a spur by placing a nail in his boot. Heth, like Grant, had no desire to compete for class ranking. "My four years career at West Point as a student was abominable," he wrote. "My thoughts ran in the channel of fun. How to get to Benny Havens' occupied more of my time than Legendre on Calculus. The time given to study was measured by the amount of time necessary to be given to prevent failure at the annual examinations."[27] Unlike Nathaniel Wyche Hunter, who constantly worried about being able to pass and feared the worst with every exam, Heth was fairly certain he could complete the curriculum, provided it did not interfere with his amusements, or vice versa. His previous schooling, especially at Peugnet's, may have helped inculcate this attitude. He found himself overprepared, or so he thought. "For the first six months [at West Point] I scarcely ever opened a book," he wrote. "I thought I knew it all, but often found, to my sorrow, that I was sadly mistaken when the X-rays of the professor were turned on my perfunctory knowledge of the subject."[28]

At the other end of the scale, the cadets in the first section had a "glamour of sanctity shimmering about [them] which causes its members to be regarded as a sort of intellectual aristocracy." This was Tidball's impression; he had worked his way up from the Immortals and was nervous about joining those whom he had made his peers:

> It was with palpitating forebodings I took my place among them; but I soon discovered I had little to fear on this score. I found, it is true, a very great difference between this section and those near the foot of the class, but I did not, on the other hand, find in it that transcendent brilliancy I had been led to believe existed there.[29]

Tidball discovered that those at the top were typically cadets who had excelled early in math and held on through hard study. He said there was an unwritten law that "none could be admitted to the first section in mechanics and engineering who had not been in the first section in mathematics. And this custom assisted in making the first section a close corporation, fostering the before-mentioned notion of intellectual aristocracy."

Those who aspired to join the top ranks would have to apply themselves diligently, and not everyone thought it was worth the effort. But perspectives on rank were relative, and proximity could breed contempt. Cadet George Derby, who had always done well in his studies and been consistently in the top ten, thought those above him were insufferable grinds who had an unseemly obsession with plaudits. (Those below, of course, might have thought the same of him.) He finished his third year ranked fifth in his class, a distinguished cadet aiming for a commission in the Engineers. He felt that he could have been first in the class had he tried, but he chose instead to do only enough to maintain the standing he needed. Anyway, the top of the class was not all it was made out to be; in Derby's opinion, the top men were insecure, egotistical and generally unlikable. "With moderate study I get calmly and comfortably along," he wrote in the fall of his final year, while

> the men above me are filled with envy, jealousy, and all sorts of bad passions, nothing is too small for one or two of them to do to get a better mark than those above them. They study nights, they draw on their problems at unauthorized hours, they neither think nor care for anything but their mark, and their continual bickerings, and jealousies, and boastings, and exultations are enough to make anyone sick of the sight of them. Now I dare say (and without much vanity either) that if I were to make such an ass of myself as all this I might stand above them all—but I should not gain much in self-respect, or in the opinion of any of my classmates or officers.[30]

Alas for Derby, he relaxed a bit too much in his final year and graduated seventh, missing both the designation of Distinguished Cadet and a commission in the Engineers. But he went on to become a hero in the Mexican War and to win more lasting celebrity as a humorist writing under the name John Phoenix.

One of those with whom Derby competed was the future Union army commander George B. McClellan, who had entered West Point at the age of sixteen and had also always ranked near the top. He was fourth in the class entering the final year, but as Derby dropped two slots, McClellan rose two, and he could have graduated first but for a disciplinary infraction. The top man, C. Seaforth Stewart, served honorably for forty years, but rose only to the rank of colonel.

The quest for rank and class standing became an unhealthy obsession for some. Plebe Benjamin Baden, for instance, passed away October 19, 1837, at the age of sixteen, because his classroom performance had been substandard. Cadet William Tecumseh Sherman, then seventeen, wrote to Ellen Ewing, then thirteen and a half (later his wife), that Baden was "proud and ambitious but unfortunately was not able to succeed in his studies which so mortified him that he was taken sick and five days afterwards was a corpse."[31]

The West Point entrance exam in those years required only an understanding of the four fundamental rules of arithmetic, the ability to read, good handwriting skills and passable spelling. Decades later William Gardner observed that "if the present high standard had then obtained, many men since distinguished in our national history would certainly have been rejected."[32] Among them in particular was his class-mate Thomas J. "Stonewall" Jackson, who arrived at West Point an unprepossessing figure wearing gray homespun and a wagon-master's hat, with a pair of worn saddlebags slung across his shoulders. Maury said that Jackson "was awkward and uncultured in manner and appearance, but their was an earnest purpose in his aspect which impressed all who saw him."[33]

Jackson had secured his position at West Point when another appointee decided not to attend at the last minute, and Jackson took his slot.[34] He failed his entrance examination, but was allowed to try again in September, and he passed. Jackson was something of a loner at West Point, a student who knew he had to study constantly if he wished to prevail. He spent most of his free time in his room, which he shared with George Stoneman, later a Union major general of cavalry and governor of California in the 1880s. Tidball said that "in consequence of a somewhat shambling, awkward gait, and the habit of carrying his head down in a thoughtful attitude, he seemed less of stature than he really was.... Being an intense student, his mind appeared to be constantly pre-occupied, and he seldom spoke to anyone unless spoken to, and then his face lighted up blushingly, as that of a bashful person when complimented.... When a jocular remark occurred in his hearing he smiled as though he understood and enjoyed it, but never ventured comment to promote further mirth."[35]

With rare exceptions, Jackson did not socialize with the other cadets or visit them in their rooms. Despite his eccentricities, he was not the victim of much hazing, except once in class when he was asked to go to the boards, and upon standing revealed that someone had chalked across his back, "General Jackson" in large letters.[36] Jackson's studies paid off. A year after he failed the entrance exam, he ranked 51st of 83 in his class, his worst showing (70th) being in French. A year later he had jumped up to 30th of 78, though he was in the Immortal section in drawing. He rose another ten spaces by the end of his third year, though he had not improved his skill at drawing, ranking third to last. This was balanced by his 11th place showing in philosophy. Jackson continued to improve his standing up to graduation, finishing 17th overall in the Class of 1846 and 5th in ethics, with his worst grades, like Grant's, coming in infantry tactics.

James Longstreet, an Immortal of the Class of 1842 who graduated third from the foot, and who would later serve with Jackson and A. P. Hill as one of Robert E. Lee's corps commanders, was another of those who used his intellectual gifts chiefly to make free time available for other pursuits. Longstreet was born in South Carolina. His mother moved to Alabama after his father died in a cholera epidemic, and he was appointed from that state by a relative, Congressman Reuben Chapman. "As cadet I had more interest in the school of the soldier, horsemanship, sword exercise, and the outside game of foot-ball than in the academic courses," he later recalled.[37] Longstreet managed to stay just above the line of deficiency until the January examination in his third year, when he failed mechanics for not being able to demonstrate pulleys. He had never really paid much attention to the lesson. "When I came to the problem of the pulleys, it seemed to my mind that a soldier could not find use for such appliances," he explained, "and the pulleys were passed by." He was given a few days to study before being reexamined, at which point he was quizzed over the entire mechanics curriculum and allowed to continue. But in the June exam he was again faced with the problem of the pulleys. "The professor thought that I had forgotten my old friend the enemy," Longstreet wrote, "but I smiled, for he had become dear to me—in waking hours and in dreams."[38] He passed that part of his exam with a perfect score, but it did not rescue his overall academic standing that year; and he ranked in the bottom ten of the entire Corps in conduct.

It was nearly impossible to escape demerits. "Few men have tried harder than myself to avoid demerit," Cadet Derby wrote, "yet some little act of carelessness would fix them upon me, in fact when the cadet officers seek a man doing his best or as it is called 'boning conduct' they instead of assisting him rather take pains to report him when possible, probably with the benevolent object of making him still more careful."[39] The cadet officers would "skin" their fellows just to show higher authorities that they were being attentive to their duties, and officers brought elastic interpretations to the regulations that made obeying the rules a largely subjective enterprise. Edmund Kirby Smith of the Class of 1845 (brother of Ephraim, the Goat of 1826), nicknamed "Seminole" since he came from Florida, complained in a letter to his mother, "If I obeyed the regulations to the letter, I should make a perfect anchorite of myself. The Professors—Superintendent, etc.—twist-turn & change them to suit their fancies & should not we poor devils evade them to meet our necessities?"[40] Edmund fared better than his older brother academically, graduating 25th of 41. He would go on to fame as commander of the Trans-Mississippi Department of the Confederacy, who did not lay down his arms until over a month after Lee's surrender at Appomattox.[41] He died in 1893, the last of the Confederate full generals.

Henry Heth's disciplinary record was impressively long, filling three and a half folio pages. He was mostly skinned for the kind of infractions one might expect from someone seeking to perfect the role of the Goat as bon vivant: lateness, inattention, wearing slippers at reveille, visiting, being caught out of barracks (a serious infraction, worth eight demerits), distracting sentinels at post and making boisterous noise, talking in ranks, and looking around, swinging arms or spitting on parade. Pickett's disciplinary history was of a similar sort, exhibiting the familiar social behavior, and was only a quarter page shorter than his cousin's. But Pickett was more daring in allowing points to accumulate, and in his final year he came within five demerits of expulsion.

Cadet Lewis Addison Armistead, a future brigade commander in Pickett's division and a relative of Heth's, was less careful. Armistead came to West Point the product of a distinguished military family. He was named after two uncles who had died in the War of 1812. His Uncle George had commanded Fort McHenry during that war and defended the original "Star-Spangled Banner" against the British. His father, Walker K. Armistead, was the third graduate of the Military Academy and a brevet brigadier general in 1833 when he secured his son a presidential appointment. Despite years of prep school, Armistead was not academically gifted. Sickness prevented his taking the January 1834 exam and he was forced to resign. He was reappointed later that year and in January 1835 barely scored high enough to remain. At the end of the year he ranked 52nd of 57 cadets and was turned back. He raised his grade significantly by January of 1836, coming in 31st of 59 cadets, but he ranked close to the bottom of his class in discipline. His best-known infraction came when he cracked a plate over Cadet Jubal Early's head in the mess hall in the winter of 1836. "Old Jube," a future division commander under Lee, was also a member of the Class of 1837, along with such Civil War notables as Joseph Hooker, John Sedgwick, John Pemberton, Braxton Bragg and William H. T. Walker, the Immortal who survived four musket balls at the Battle of Okeechobee.[42] On January 17, 1836, Armistead was placed under arrest for "disorderly conduct in the mess hall."[43] He was held for twelve days, after which he tendered his resignation from West Point rather than face trial and possible dismissal. But Armistead did not give up his dream of following in his father's footsteps. He was commissioned a lieutenant in 1839 and served the next three years in Florida, one year as his father's aide. In the Mexican War he won three brevets for bravery, and he served with distinction in the Army of Northern Virginia until falling mortally wounded at Gettysburg, leading his brigade in the Angle during Pickett's Charge.[44]

Some cadets prevailed against all odds to get through West Point. Randolph Ridgely, for example, a hero of the Mexican War, was a rare case of a cadet who went through three plebe years. He was a classmate of Armistead's, appointed from Maryland. Ridgely was first admitted in 1830 when he was just under sixteen years old, and had accumulated 198 demerits by 1831 when the 200 limit was instituted. The seven cadets below him were expelled. Though saved by a hair in discipline, Ridgely was found academically deficient. He was readmitted in 1832, grappled fitfully with his studies, and was turned back at the end of the academic year to start a third time. He worked doggedly for the next four years and finally graduated 42nd of 50 in the Class of 1837, seven years after he first came to West Point.

FLIRTATION WALK

THE ACADEMY THAT HENRY HETH arrived at in 1843 looked much like the school that Nathaniel Wyche Hunter had left ten years earlier, but day-to-day life had gradually improved for the Corps. North and South Barracks were still in use, and small groups of cadets still roomed with Mrs. Thompson, known as "Old Manny," in her cottage with her three now aging daughters. They were given permanent residence in recognition of the gallant sacrifice of her son at the Battle of Okeechobee. Beds appeared in all the rooms. Cadets had to pay a rental fee and buy the bedclothes, but it was better than sleeping on the floor. Yet the beds grew less comfortable once the mattresses began to wear out; Cadet William Dutton complained that he awoke each morning with traces of the iron bars on his body, since his mattress "has been lain on 8 years & is about 3 inches thick."[1] George Pickett sought to solve that problem and received three demerits for "having more bedding in use than is allowed by orders." All cadet furnishings and toiletries were standardized to the extent they could be, which made it harder for cadets to find items for barter, since things might turn up missing in any of the multiple daily inspections. Barter remained a necessity; cadets were paid $28 per month (until 1845, when their pay was reduced to $24), but were still not allowed to keep cash. All money was kept on account, and was not issued until graduation. Those who had to make purchases at the cadet store did so against their accounts, which were monitored by the Supe. Those who sought to make other purchases adapted as best they could.

Rooms were still crowded, with up to six per room for the larger spaces. They heated them by wood fire, though coal was now permitted, which was warmer and burned more evenly but did not give sufficient light to study. Whale-oil lamps were used for illumination, "the smell of which was, similar *if not worse than* that which Jonah must have experienced during his sojourn in the whale's belly."[2] There was still no running water, and cadets would line up at the old wooden pump every morning to carry buckets back to their rooms. The cadet latrine, "a place of barbaric filthiness, whose odors, but not those of Araby, pervaded the whole neighborhood around," was referred to as "Number Ten" due to its proximity to sentry post no. 10, and the term became slang for latrines throughout the Army.

The food that Wyche had complained about had improved slightly, but was still not praised by cadets. In one letter home, Cadet George Derby noted that "India rubber boiled in Aqua forte could give no idea of the toughness of our roast beef, and we are so accustomed to stale bread that the sight of a hot biscuit might occasion hysterics."[3] Bread was as a rule served cold, except, as the joke went, when a cat had slept on a loaf. Fruits and green vegetables were unknown in the mess hall.[4] Coffee and tea were in abundance, as were dairy products from local farms. Fish was served on Friday, frequently sturgeon caught in the Hudson and known as "Albany beef." But Tidball noted that there was at least a purpose to the culinary poverty. It was "still the epoch when soldiers—and with them were classed cadets—were fed with Spartan simplicity, so that their stomachs might be trained to meet every vicissitude of service, even to subsisting for a fortnight by chewing a greasy rag, or to enduring the fare of a rebel prison. All beyond the bare necessaries of life were deemed *effeminacies* unworthy of a solider."

Cadets continued to make hash in the winter, despite stern warnings from the authorities. In fact, the illegality of the act improved the taste of the fare. The hashes consisted of bread, meat and potatoes, "mashed and mixed together with plenty of butter and seasoned generously with pepper; the whole cooked in some kind of a vessel, generally a frying-pan." The tall, aptly named "forage hat" in use at the time provided a useful means of smuggling or "hooking" food from the mess hall, and "a steady marching cadet, one who could preserve a level head, could carry at one time enough of bread, potatoes, meat, and butter as was necessary for a very respectable hash for himself and a half dozen or so of his friends."[5] Frying pans were in short supply and were passed from cadet to cadet as the need arose. Most feasts were planned for Saturday night, when officers were more likely to be engaged in their own diversions and there were no lessons in the morning. Sentinels were bribed with portions of the hash. But the hash feast was not a bacchanal; cadets could not risk having the smell of the hash alert the authorities, so the meal was "scooped hot from the frying-pan and eaten on slices of bread or toast with a relish equaled only by the dispatch with which it had to be done; and then the guests flitted to their rooms with the innocence of uncaught thieves."[6]

Hazing had become more prevalent over the years, but had not reached the severity it would in later decades. It was an initiation ritual, "just sufficient to awaken alertness on the part of the new comers, but *seldom* anything malicious."[7] Before encampment, prospective plebes were called "things" and "beasts" (which is the origin of the contemporary term "beast barracks") and their ignorance of the rules made them prime targets for all kinds of mischief. Many incoming plebes wore their hair long, which was the fashion, and helpful cadets would direct them to a room in the old North Barracks where another cadet, posing as a barber, would proceed to give them a most uneven and unattractive cut.[8] Cadet Jesse Valentine from North Carolina was the victim of an elaborate haze authored by Henry Heth, who pretended to borrow Valentine's civilian clothes to facilitate a visit to Benny Havens'. The two were "discovered," placed under arrest, and taken to the hot, musty cockloft of the old North Barracks, a windowless gathering spot unknown to the Tacs, for immediate court martial. A cadet sat as president of the body at the head of a long table, with twelve others wearing blue furlough coats, sashes and plumed hats arrayed about him. A long list of invented charges was read, the prosecution and defense made speeches, and Cadet Valentine nervously pleaded his case. The prisoner was removed to the passage while the court deliberated; he was called back in and the sentence was read: "Plebe Valentine, the court, after mature deliberation, have pronounced in your case the following sentence: that you be taken tomorrow morning to the statue of the great and glorious Washington, and at sunrise precisely you be shot to death with musketry, and may God have mercy on your soul." The blood drained from Valentine's face; outside the room he collapsed to his knees, bemoaning his foul fate. Presently he was called back into the court and told that he had been given a reprieve. He was sentenced instead to stand all night with his head in a mortar. The next morning an officer came upon the curious site, and when he heard Valentine's story he told the plebe that he had been the victim of a prank.[9]

Not every plebe was as ingenuous as Cadet Valentine. In another case, some upperclassmen feigned offense at a plebe's behavior and arranged for a duel. They met just after reveille, and the plebe was given his choice of loaded muskets. The duelists marched fifteen paces, turned and fired. The upperclassman fell and lay still. The seconds and spectators stood by mournfully; but the plebe began to reload his musket.

"What are you doing plebe?" one of the upperclassmen said. "Don't you see you have killed your man?"

"Well," the plebe responded, "if he is dead, a little more killing won't do him any hurts." The "dead man" jumped up and the assembled apologized to the plebe.[10]

William Gardner explained, "With us [hazing] was rough horse play and fun, and the cadet who showed himself to be equipped with a powerful pair of fists and a strong disposition to use them on provocation was usually exempt from annoyance. Any such brutal violence as is not uncommon nowadays would in my time have been checked summarily by the student himself, with a bayonet thrust, knife stab or pistol shot." He was not engaging in hyperbole. In the summer of 1844, Heth and some companions were deviling a plebe on sentinel duty, who became so enraged he threw his musket, bayonet first, at his tormentors. The weapon struck Heth in the thigh, narrowly missing his femoral artery, the point emerging from the other side. "I fell as though I had been shot by a cannon ball," he wrote.[11] The wound put Heth in the hospital for weeks. The plebe in question was punished severely—not for wounding Cadet Heth, but for parting with his weapon.

There were occasional personal disputes, which could lead to violence. One such altercation involved Derby and Cadet William Logan Crittenden, a member of the famous Crittenden clan, who came to West Point from Kentucky in 1839. He was the son of Henry C. Crittenden, who had been murdered by a noted desperado of the time named John A. Waring. Henry's brother was John Jordan Crittenden, an 1812 war vet who served as governor, U.S. attorney general, congressman and senator. It was in the latter capacity that he formulated the "Crittenden Compromise," a failed last-minute attempt to stave off the Civil War. John's sons served on both sides in that conflict—George Bibb Crittenden (USMA 1832) was a Confederate general who resigned his commission in 1862 after his forces were badly mauled at the Battle of Mills Springs. His brother Thomas Leonidas Crittenden rose to the rank of major general in the Union army. Their cousin Alexander Parker Crittenden graduated from West Point in 1836; he soon resigned his commission and later became a politician and lawyer in San Francisco. He was gunned down by his mistress Laura Fair in 1870, and her highly publicized trial featured a pioneering defense linking the insanity plea to the menstrual cycle.[12]

William Logan Crittenden was a mediocre student—he entered with the Class of 1843 but was turned back twice, graduating as the Goat of 1845. His disciplinary record was not remarkably poor, but the incident with Derby almost led to his expulsion. One Sunday morning in 1844, Derby was returning to North Barracks after church when he passed Crittenden, who was a cadet lieutenant. The two were not on good terms, and they caught each other's glance.

"What do you mean, sir?" Crittenden demanded.

"Mean by what, sir?"

"By looking at me, sir."

"Do you consider yourself too good to be looked at, sir?" Derby said.

"Yes sir, I do," Crittenden said, "and if you give me any more of your words, God damn you, I'll run you through." Crittenden placed his hand meaningfully on the pommel of the sword on his belt. Derby, smaller, lighter, but with nerve, was not intimidated.

"You must be a miserable coward," he snapped, "to threaten an unarmed man with a sword." Crittenden did not hesitate. He drew his weapon and slashed three times at Derby, cutting his chin and throat, right arm and shoulder. Derby was put in the hospital for three weeks. Crittenden was placed under arrest, and Superintendent Delafield recommended dismissal to Secretary of War William Wilkins, but the request was not approved—political connections, Derby reasoned. Instead, the Superintendent restricted Crittenden to West Point, reduced him to the ranks, and relieved him of his sword and chevrons.[13] All things considered, he got off easy.

Crittenden later had a dispute with Cadet Winfield Scott Hancock, which they resolved to settle by fisticuffs. But Crittenden was so much larger than Hancock that the fight was deemed unfair, so by mutual agreement his place was taken by Cadet Alexander Hays. The resulting contest was said to have lasted three hours and been given to Hays on a decision. The authorities never found out about it and no one was punished.[14]

"Benny Havens', Oh!"

THE CADET'S LIFE WAS STILL regimented, moving cyclically day in and out to the beat of a drum. They marched to and from mess, had parade every afternoon, and manned regular tours of sentry duty. The only officially sanctioned variation in the schedule came when it rained and drill was canceled. Tidball called rain "a veritable Godsend—a positive intervention of Divine Providence in behalf of cadets." Free time was limited and closely proscribed, at least officially. Cards and other games were still prohibited.[15] The Dialectic Society debated, and hunting, fishing, hiking and swimming were permitted. Hiking was a popular escape; cadets were allowed to fish in the river or in the nearby mountaintop lakes, and a tradition grew of leaving a stone on the cairn at the top of the prominent peak north of the Academy called the Crow's Nest.

Smoking had been forbidden at the Academy since 1823, and the smell of tobacco in a room would quickly lead to demerits and extra guard tours on the weekend. But banning smoking only increased the desire of cadets to get away with it. Cadet Grant, later famous for his cigar habit, noted that "the fact that tobacco in every form was prohibited, and the mere possession of the weed punished, made the majority of the cadets . . . try to acquire the habit of using it."[16] Cadets would make bargains with tobacco traders in New York to buy cigars and pipe tobacco on credit and pay after graduation when they were given the balance of their accounts. "The very recklessness of it was captivating," Tidball wrote.[17] Some were more reckless than others—George Pickett received eight demerits one fall day for "highly unsoldierlike conduct walking around parade ground smoking tobacco improperly dressed."[18]

Alcohol and the means of obtaining it still commanded a great deal of cadet energies. DeRussy had loosened the drinking regulations, but Delafield cracked down on alcohol. He opened a "soda shop" at the Academy as a conciliatory gesture, meant to give cadets an alternative to the mess for some treats and hopefully forestall them looking elsewhere. For those who chose to "run it" in search of harder stuff, Bum Owens was still on hand to bedevil them.[19]

Benny Havens' remained very much part of the West Point experience, but by the 1840s Benny had some competition. A tavern had opened across the Hudson in the town of Cold Spring, behind Constitution Island and the site of the West Point foundry, famous for its ordnance production in the Civil War. The tavern was accessible by boat or over ice in the winter, though one was liable to be spotted crossing the barren ice, and furthermore, if the ice broke while a cadet was on the wrong side, he might find himself stranded. A man named Avery opened a tavern between West Point and Benny Havens', which was also convenient to the prep school established just south of the Academy by former Tac Zebina J. D. Kinsley (whom Edgar Allan Poe's roommate had pretended to decapitate). Another liquor merchant known as "the Pirate" would periodically appear on the river shore below the hospital (at a spot aptly known as "Pirate's Cove") to trade in whiskey, tobacco and other necessities. Tidball noted that "dealings with this individual were considered of a sneaking, low down order as compared with the *rollicksome recklessness* attending upon running it to Benny Havens."

Benny's remained the preferred cadet retreat, a tavern that was enshrined in myth and even in song. In the winter of 1839–40, an assistant surgeon named Lucius O'Brien visited some friends at West Point, who decided to show O'Brien where they used to while away the hours back in their cadet days.[20] O'Brien was so taken with Benny Havens' (or so under the influence) that he penned a drinking song to the tune of the Irish standard, "The Wearing o' the Green," which he called, "Benny Havens' Oh!"

> Come, fill your glasses, fellows, and stand up in a row,
> To sing sentimentally, we're going for to go;
> In the Army there's sobriety, promotion's very slow,
> So we'll sing our reminiscences of Benny Havens', oh!
> Oh! Benny Havens', oh! Oh! Benny Havens', oh!
> We'll sing our reminiscences of Benny Havens', oh!

O'Brien's song became an instant hit among the cadets, and his original few stanzas were supplemented in the scores by succeeding classes. Today the verses read as a compact history of West Point and the Army. One early and tragic addition commemorates O'Brien's own death in Florida during the Seminole War:

> From the courts of death and danger, from Tampa's deadly shore,
> There comes a wail of manly grief, "O'Brien is no more!"
> In the land of sun and flowers his head lies pillowed low,
> No more he'll sing "Petite Coquette" or "Benny Havens', oh!"

Benny remained popular with the cadets, a friendly purveyor of good cheer in many forms. Henry Heth was a regular, along with Pickett and another member of their clique, Heth's roommate, a tall, handsome cadet from Indiana named Ambrose Everett Burnside. Heth's first roommate was Augustus H. Seward, son of William H. Seward, recently governor of New York, later a senator and secretary of state under Presidents Lincoln and Johnson (in the latter capacity negotiating the purchase of Alaska from Russia, known then as "Seward's Folly"). Gus Seward, like Heth, began to accumulate demerits, and the Superintendent decided to separate them and place them with well-behaved cadets so they might learn from their example.[21] Heth was matched up with the respectable Burnside, but the Supe's plan backfired. Rather than Burnside reforming Heth, the fun-loving Virginian found "a very ready pupil" in the charismatic midwesterner.

"Burnside had but a few demerits when he came to live with me," Heth recalled, "in a few months he had over a hundred."[22] Burnside's total record of delinquencies covered two and a half pages. He stayed very close to the edge; he had 198 his first year and 190 his last. Most were for visiting after hours and being late.[23] In the fall of 1844, he was sentenced to seven days in prison for feuding, allegedly for assisting another cadet, Tom Lowe, in assaulting the unfortunate Derby (who at that point was only days away from his bloody encounter with Critten-den). The Superintendent hoped that the sentence "afforded a favorable time for Cadet Burnside to reflect in the solitude of his prison walls upon the errors and improprieties of his past conduct."[24]

Whether Burnside's imprisonment had any salutary effect is arguable, but it certainly did not end his forays to Benny Havens'. Heth said they would go on a spree at least twice a week. Burnside, with his rich, resonant singing voice, would entertain regularly at the tavern. Benny declared Burnside and Andrew Jackson to be "the two greatest men that ever trod God's foot-stool."[25] Burnside had a habit of socializing when returning to barracks under the influence, and Heth had to get him back to the room before he was discovered and expelled. "I would put him to bed and frequently stood at my door with my musket clubbed," Heth said, "threatening to knock him down if he attempted to leave the room."

During his final encampment, Heth found a means to augment his opportunities for revelry. He was sent to the hospital with swollen glands, and the doctor wanted him to be treated in a ward the entire summer. Heth asked that he at least be allowed to attend military drills, riding and artillery practice, and the doctor consented. "By this arrangement," Henry wrote, "if the doctor came to my ward and found me absent, I was supposed to be attending some of these duties and nothing was said. I was thus enabled to visit New York and Newburg, and go pretty much where fancy and inclination prompted; of course I was running a great risk, but I was so in the habit of taking risks, that I presume I became callous."[26] Heth was never caught. Burnside, on the other hand, got five demerits that summer for visiting Henry at the hospital without permission.[27] Burnside was not the only one to fall victim to Henry's frolicsome influences. During his hospital stay, Heth made friends with a Scottish steward named Stoddard who became his regular drinking buddy. Stoddard was fired for missing a morning appointment with the doctor after a night of adventures with Heth. But Henry would not expose his friends to risks he would not take himself. One late night during the 1846 encampment, returning from a round of drinking with Stoddard, Heth happened on a horse and decided to charge the encampment. He dashed through the tents on his mount, exited the Plain and concealed himself in Fort Clinton. Patrols were sent out, but Heth was not discovered. When the camp settled, he charged through again. The search process repeated, again with no result, and Henry made a third charge before he decided that he was tempting fate and headed back to the hospital.

The greatest change in cadet life in this period was in the social sphere. The Academy was no longer the martial monastery it used to be. West Point was well on its way to becoming one of America's leading resorts. This peculiar development was the product of various circumstances, one of them being the proximity to New York City, less than a day's trip by riverboat. With the advent of steamboats, the number of passenger vessels making the journey to Albany and back increased, and many made stops at West Point. This was also the heyday of the Hudson River school of painting, with its emphasis on nature and particularly the Hudson Valley, the Catskills and the Berkshires. Works of literature, such as *The Last of the Mohicans,* also raised awareness of the region.

Visitors were discovering what cadets had always known—that West Point is a place of great natural beauty. Nathaniel Wyche Hunter had described it as "the most beautiful place in the world" in one of the same letters in which he begged his father to be allowed to come home. Cadet Grant described the setting eloquently, saying it was "decidedly the most beautiful place I have ever seen ... it seems as though I could live here forever, if only my friends could come too."[28] Henry Heth wrote, "I have crossed and hunted in the Rocky Mountains, the mountains of Virginia, Tennessee and North Carolina but to me no view equals the view from the back porch of Roe's Hotel on a moonlit night."[29] The hotel was located at the north edge of the Plain, above the bend in the river, with sweeping views of the valley. It was built in 1829 using proceeds from wood cut on the public lands of the post. The "old north stoop" was also a favored place to escort young ladies, a fact that may have enhanced Heth's memory.

Traditionally, cadets had their greatest opportunities for social interactions during the furlough after their second year. Furlough was universally praised; as Grant said, "This I enjoyed beyond any other period of my life." Tidball described it as "that ticket-of-leave period of a cadet's life when, for the period of two months, he walks the earth a free man, astonishes every beholder with the glitter of his much bebuttoned furlough dress and smashes the hearts of ladies as a cider-mill crushes apples."

Cadets wore a special uniform on their furlough, which was intended to draw attention to them and represent the Academy with style. The coat was blue and cut in the manner of a dress jacket, with long swallowtails and ten buttons down the front. The dress shirts were also fancy, with gilt buttons. The cap was an Army regulation forage cap, with the addition of a black velvet band on which was pinned a gold wreath crest with silver letters "USMA" in Old English script. Wrote Tidball, "With our neat duck pants, this coat and this cap, we went forth armed like knights of old to down every competitor and win the plaudits of all ladies." Heth, echoing Grant, said, "these two months were among the most enjoyable of my life. The Duke of Wellington, after defeating his great enemy at Waterloo, could not have felt more exalted, or more pleased with himself, than the West Point cadet dressed in his furlough coat, with brass buttons, when strutting along the streets, or on entering the parlor of some young miss who had given a party in honor of his return to his native city or village."[30] During his cadet furlough, Heth met a young schoolgirl named Teny Selden. Twelve years later, they were married.

The custom of the time was for cadets to bestow "spoony" buttons from their coat and shirt to the girls they favored. The grand prize was the cap crest, which a cadet would not give up until the end of the trip. Being unique, the crest could be presented only once, and one can only imagine the competition or the means of obtaining it. Tidball later reminisced that his furlough days "passed away as a dream. They were full of those little incidents falling to the lot of all college students on vacation, but unworthy of record except in lovesick novels. I was greatly flattered by the attention I received on all sides; attention no doubt due more to the glamour of my furlough dress than to any merit of my own. But they were attentions all the same and I will not have the ungraciousness of now looking the gift horse in the mouth." There were, of course, the usual risks. In the fall of 1843, Derby noted that "several (3) cadets of the second class are in arrest and will probably be summarily dismissed for contracting a horrible disease while on furlough." He was not of the opinion they should be dismissed, since "their conduct was probably owing to thoughtlessness, rather than to want of principle and they are all very fine fellows, and stand pretty well."[31]

By 1840, cadets who spent the summer at the Academy also had their share of opportunities for feminine companionship. The Independence Day dinners had grown to be a major public affair; on July 4, 1845, there were two hundred visitors at the hotel, and crowds for special events could number over five hundred. "Three boats landed with excursion people on board, among them bands, glee clubs etc. without number," Derby wrote. "Of course the cadets enjoyed themselves highly and I think I never saw the Point present so gay an appearance as it did then—Last evening we danced until 12 o'clock."[32] Dances were common year round, and particularly in the summer. During the encampment of 1840 there were two dances per week in the mess hall, and cadets frequently held "stag dances" on the parade ground.[33] These were all-cadet affairs, in which lights were placed in rows on the Plain and the dancers took turns in the center showing off their steps. Some cadets would tie handkerchiefs around their necks and play the parts of girls. It was a characteristic form of entertainment in the western part of the country, and an opportunity to engage in hilarity to entertain the onlookers. Cadet William Sherman enjoyed the stag dances because a cadet "can shuffle and cut up as much as he pleases provided he goes through the figures."[34]

The summer's frolics were capped with a large formal ball, which became a signature event of the year for the fashionable young belles who were able to attend. Hundreds of invitations were sent out, and people came from across the country. Cadet Sherman described the scene:

> The Ball was a grand affair, in a fine large hall the walls decorated with wreaths of laurel and cedar—Crossed Swords, Sabers, and Bayonets—and the flags of nearly all nations of the world. From the ceiling hung a great number of elegant and tasty chandeliers, and when filled with ladies and officers both naval and military in their uniforms it presented the most dazzling and brilliant appearance I ever beheld.[35]

Food and drink were in abundance; as Lieutenant Jeremiah M. Scarritt, Class of 1838 and principal assistant professor of engineering, noted, there was "Champagne for the dull who would feign to be witty, sherry for those who were just forgetting their first flames, brandy for those who had no love in them."[36] Drinks were of course off limits to cadets, but those who could obtain clandestine supplies would indulge, preferably elsewhere and with their dates. The night before camp was broken, cadets held the "Illumination." Candles were lit in and around tents, casting a gentle glow about the entire Plain, best viewed from the upper floors of the hotel or surrounding buildings. The officers' tents had transparencies with the names of their companies. Rockets were fired, and an immense stag dance was held.[37] The Illumination remained a tradition until encampment on the Plain ended in 1943.

For the Corps, encampment had become a three-month celebration of idealized Army life, with martial drills during the day and festivities at night. For those who visited West Point in the summer, it seemed that this was all the cadets did, which raised some criticism, but not from the young female visitors. "To the young and gay of the female sex the hops are the chief feature of West Point," Tidball wrote. "In their estimation the Military Academy was established *solely* for such entertainments, and cadets maintained by a thoughtful government expressly to furnish them with young and nimble dancing partners." Young civilian men who might be on hand were unable to compete with the dash of the uniformed cadets, and they had to "stand in the corners and chew the bitter cud of jealousy, while their envied rivals are whirling off their fair charmers." For the women, West Point was a laboratory of flirtation. They could experiment as they wished in complete safety. It was an artificial environment, in which the men were tightly controlled and women could leave at will without the social repercussions that might attend them in their hometowns. In addition, for those so inclined, there was the thrill of corrupting the cadets, "the very essence of stolen fruit." It became something of a fad, as Tidball noted:

> Cadets were greatly sought after by the ladies, who seemed proud of being beaued by those stripling gallants.... [A]s the proportion of anxious ladies to cadets increased, a spirit of rivalry sprang up among the fair ones as to who should have the latter. Blushing young misses, flirtatious married women, and prancing widows, vied with each other in the contest. This strange infatuation developed at one time, into a species of feminine mania—a sort of contagious epidemic; it was in fact called and known as the "cadet fever," a malady every woman, whether young or old—not too old—coming to the Point was expected to catch, and until caught, the usual morning salutation was, "have you got it?"

The cadets of course were much pleased with the attention. Some took the dalliances more seriously than others, becoming infatuated, at their peril; others played their roles with no expectations other than enjoying themselves. Sometimes these relationships would result in engagement and even marriage, but more often they were summer flings, of varying intensity. A facilitating circumstance was the advent of fly trousers around 1845. Until then, cadets had worn a traditional front-flat pattern, and the more stylish design, then in use across the country, was resisted on grounds of decorum. Tidball noted that "The social element of the Point ... opposed it as being a shocking innovation." Shocking, perhaps, but very practical from the cadet point of view.

The traditional West Point trysting place was the Revolutionary War era Fort Clinton, in the northeast corner of the Plain, next to the river. The overgrown stone walls and battlements made the fort a labyrinth of grassy, bush-topped mounds, strategically located adjacent to both hotel and encampment. The fort was guarded nightly, and it was a strange and lonely place to stand watch, rendered eerie with its shadowy indistinct forms, the cries of night birds and the lowing from calf boats floating downriver at night, heading for the New York butchers. The spookiness of the place only added to its allure as a site for romance. There was an unwritten code that a sentry would turn a blind eye to another cadet making a rendezvous with a young lady at Fort Clinton, though the sounds of couples so engaged could be an uncomfortable experience.

A very important event in the history of social life at West Point occurred when the Superintendent extended the permitted area to include the old chain walk, the access path along the river shore that had been used during the Revolutionary period to maintain the massive chain across the Hudson that blocked passage by British warships.[38] This pathway was quickly exploited by the cadets and was soon known by the nickname "Flirtation Walk." The walk extended along the riverbank from the wharf below the hotel south to a spot known as Kosciuszko's Garden. Thaddeus Kosciuszko was a Polish officer who had designed West Point's fortifications during the Revolution. His garden was a ledge on the side of the river bluffs, which he had used as a private retreat. Maria Scott, wife of General Winfield Scott, would hold parties in the garden for several dozen cadets at a time. The Scotts and their daughters were fixtures at West Point in the summers, where the general would regale the cadets with tales of the War of 1812 and other adventures.[39] Kosciuszko's Garden was also used for dueling, usually with fists, though once with muskets, a prank played on a newcomer who did not know they were unloaded.

Flirtation Walk and Kosciuszko's Garden had what the Tacs might call a terrain advantage. The Plain is bordered on its north and eastern sides with a 150-foot escarpment, sheer in places, terraced in others. From most locations at USMA, anyone below the level of the Plain is out of sight. At one point, the path is overhung by a large boulder that came to be known as "Kissing Rock" for obvious reasons. In addition, the coastline is rugged, creating many shadowy nooks, and in the summer, the undergrowth along the slopes is dense. This afforded cadets a variety of options depending on how adventurous their guests were. "Flirty" became the scene of many contests and conquests, of one form or another. "Many youthful maidens," recalled R. W. Johnson (USMA 1849), "with their breasts heaving with emotions they could not suppress, and with their voices tremulous with excitement, have said 'yes' when 'no' would have been far better for their future comfort and happiness." Johnson noted that he did not speak to a woman during his entire cadetship—a record of sorts, he claimed—"hence no woman has any cause to regret a hasty and inconsiderate promise made to me in any of the love-making nooks in or about that historic place."[40]

Each class chose representatives as emissaries to the hotel to invite ladies to the dances and escort them there if they needed. It was choice duty, since it allowed the ambassadors to reconnoiter and have first preference, or at least first opportunity. The representatives for the Class of 1847 were, predictably, A. P. Hill, Ambrose Burnside and Henry Heth. The three were notorious rakes. Burnside had a steady girl at West Point named Nora, to whom he was engaged until one night when he was so drunk he fell out of his chair, and she ended it. Burnside sent Heth to plead his case, and Henry argued strongly for his friend, but came up short when Nora asked him point-blank if he would advise his own sister to marry Burnside. Heth had no good answer to that question, and the engagement was off permanently. Burnside quickly recovered, going on to be one of the great ladies' men of the pre–Civil War Army.

In the summer of 1846, Hill and Heth became particularly attached to two sisters who were accompanying their mother on an extended visit to West Point. Henry's sweetheart was named Josephine. One evening that August, Henry suggested a postprandial stroll on Flirtation Walk. Miss Jo agreed and met him in the hotel parlor with a package of gingerbread. After walking and talking, the pair found themselves on one of the many trailside benches. She produced the cake, ten inches square and an inch thick.

"Do you know the latest and most delightful way to eat cake?" she asked.

"I do not," he replied.

"I will show you," she said. She took his knife and cut an inch-wide strip of cake, placing one end in her mouth and the other in his. They slowly worked their way towards each other until their lips were brought together.

"The entire gingerbread was after awhile consumed," Henry wrote. "I found it the most delightful way to eat cake I ever tried, and I must say after the cake disappeared, our lips came together a good many times minus the gingerbread."[41] Eventually the pair wandered back up to the Plain, where there was a great commotion. A rumor had spread that Miss Jo had drowned in the river, and her mother was inconsolable.

Henry and Jo were spotted, and they dashed to the hotel, where Jo ducked into her room. Henry was quickly apprehended and confronted by her mother, who demanded to know where her daughter was. Henry said she was in bed asleep.

"Where have you been and what have you been doing?" she asked forcefully.

"Taking a walk and eating cake," he replied, innocently.

"Do you have any idea what time it is?" she said, pointing to the hotel clock. Henry thought it was about ten, but the clock said 2:15 in the morning. For this adventure he was confined to his tent for two weeks and had to perform eight extra guard tours. He was also banned from the grand ball at the end of the encampment. This was harsh punishment, and despite the intercession of Mrs. Scott and one of the tactical officers, the Supe did not budge. He called Henry "the worst boy in the Corps, [who] deserved no leniency, and none would be shown."[42] For her part, Miss Jo was shamed by her mother and sister, and was forced to end her relationship with the dashing Virginian. "All this trouble I attributed to ginger cake," he later wrote. "Should this ever be read by an aspirant for military glory at West Point, let him beware of a pretty miss, ginger cake, and Flirtation Walk."[43]

Home Sweet Home

GRADUATION WAS KNOWN AS "the kicking of the hats." At the final assembly for the graduating class, the Corps would be drawn up and called to attention, and the first class would march on to join them, carrying the Academy colors. The firsties would be marked by their moustaches, which they were allowed to grow for the several months leading up to graduation. They also bore their class rings, a tradition that had begun with the Class of 1835 and would spread to every college in the country. When they took their places, the band would play "Auld Lang Syne," and the weight of the moment would descend. "These men who had been here four years and who were to leave forever covered with honor the next day," Derby wrote, "as they thought of the trials and hardships they had overcome, of the intimacies they had formed, were much affected at this time, there was not a dry eye among them."[44] The first class was called to step forward, and the order was read relieving them of duty at the Academy. The band struck up "Home Sweet Home," and when the Corps was dismissed, the firsties flung off their caps, tossed them in the air, kicked them around on the ground, jabbed them with swords and bayonets, whooping and hollering and generally going wild.[45] Some would start singing, and Captain Frederick A. Smith's wife wrote a song for Heth's class that was to become an enduring graduation theme, with the refrain, "Change the Gray for the Blue":

> Hurrah! For the merry, bright month of June!
>   That opens a life so new;
> When we doff the cadet and don the brevet,
>   And change the gray for the blue.

The new officers would hurriedly switch to their Army uniforms, that very day if they had made arrangements with the tailors who had visited the Academy throughout the spring taking orders and preparing for the graduation. The graduates would not waste time in leaving West Point. Most would take steamers to New York the next day, to begin the brief furloughs before reporting to their new commands. Cadet Sherman wrote that members of his class were making plans months in advance.

> [F]rom morning to night we are laying schemes of what we intend to do when we graduate and if even half of these are realized a most happy set we'll be, but should some little Indian War break out, or the Canadian Patriots rise again or anything else interrupt with our furlough upon which all our expectations are centered we'd be in a pretty plight, instead of dancing hunting fishing and the like we might be sent to some remote corner of the Globe to drill drunken Irish recruits by way of saving our country.[46]

Graduation was a time of celebration, but for the Classes of 1836 to 1842, it meant the possibility of going to fight the Seminoles. Indeed, after the Dade Massacre, the entire Class of 1836 volunteered to leave early, and most of that class and those that followed did tours in Florida. For Goats like Pickett, Heth, Crittenden and others in the Classes of 1845 to 1847, graduation meant facing a very different enemy. Theirs were the first post-Thayer classes to be given an opportunity to put their education in conventional warfare to immediate use, in the conflict that was then raging in Mexico.

Henry Heth spent his final day at West Point in contemplation, looking for the last time at the familiar buildings and natural loveliness of the post, remembering his adventures, and thinking about the future. It had been a happy four years; but now he began his life as an officer. He knew he had to shed his adolescent ways and assume the responsibilities of adulthood. The next day, he headed south with Burnside. The two of them wound up in Richmond, where they stayed for a few weeks and "had a jolly good time."[47]

ZEB INGE

O
N MAY 9, 1846, Captain Ephraim Kirby Smith awoke on the field of Palo Alto, Texas, among the men of his company of the Fifth Infantry regiment. Kirby had returned to the Army several years after his court martial for flogging troops after the Fort Mackinac mutiny sixteen years earlier. He spent another decade and a half on the frontier, in Illinois, Wisconsin and Minnesota, still frustrated at the path his military career was taking. He was not called to fight in his family's home territory of Florida and did not volunteer to go either. Yet on this morning, in this dry, beaten field, two months shy of twenty years since he left West Point, Kirby had reason to be proud. The previous day, outnumbered American forces under the command of Brigadier General Zachary Taylor, moving to lift the siege of Fort Brown on the Rio Grande, fought Mexican troops under General Mariano Arista to a standstill, in the first major engagement in the as yet undeclared war with Mexico. It was Kirby's first taste of battle.[1]

Palo Alto was in the main an artillery duel. The infantry spent the day in line or square, watching the distant movements of the Mexicans in their resplendent uniforms, warding off cavalry attacks and protecting the artillerymen as they delivered their deadly fire. It was also an eventful day for Major Samuel Ringgold, fifth in Thayer's first class of 1818, a pioneer in the development of light artillery tactics.[2] The American guns were smaller, but more mobile and swiftly reloaded. Ringgold had developed methods of fire and maneuver that made his light cannon more lethal than the heavier, more ponderous Mexican pieces. Red-flannel-shirted gunners moved their guns, unlimbered, loaded, fired a few rounds, then limbered to move to new positions before the enemy batteries could bring them under counterfire. Before Palo Alto, this had been only a concept, but there it was tested in warfare and proved its worth under Ringgold's deft and daring leadership. He was assisted by his junior officer, Lieutenant Randolph Ridgely, the determined Immortal of the Class of 1837 who suffered through three plebe years. Throughout the battle, cannonballs fell amidst infantry drawn up in close order, ricocheting into packed bodies of men, or skipping harmlessly past them into the tall dry grass. "The enemy's shot were playing briskly through our ranks," Kirby wrote, "the wounded and dying at our feet producing no effect upon the admirable discipline of the men."[3]

After an hour of dueling, a smoldering wad from one of the American guns landed in some scrub and the wind-whipped prairie caught fire. The spreading flames and heavy smoke forced a pause in the fight, and each side sought to maneuver to advantage under cover. After the fire moved on, the battle reignited, raging through the afternoon and into evening. When a large force of Mexican cavalry threatened on the right flank, Taylor dispatched the Fifth Infantry to intercept them. Kirby's company rushed across a quarter mile of prairie to meet the advancing dragoons. "Here they come!" someone shouted, and the infantrymen formed a square, standing shoulder to shoulder in multiple lines, muskets poised, bayonets bristling. The mass of cavalry, eight hundred strong, rode towards them at a gallop, then at a charge. At one hundred feet out, the Mexicans fired their side arms, drew sabers and kept coming. Some Americans fell, but the rest stood coolly, and a moment later returned a devastating volley. Off to the right, twenty mounted Texas Rangers under Captain Samuel H. Walker picked off Mexican officers with deadly-accurate rifle fire. The horsemen veered left, and were met by raking canister fire from two of Ridgely's field pieces, sending the cavalry back to their lines in a rout. It was Kirby's baptism of fire. "The spectacle was magnificent," he wrote. "The prairie was burning brilliantly between the two armies and some twenty pieces of artillery thundering from right to left, while through the lurid scene was heard the tramping of horses and the wild cheering of the men."[4]

Combat ended when darkness fell. The Mexicans got the worst of it, but many Americans fell as casualties too, among them Ringgold himself—hit in the side of the leg by a Mexican cannonball that passed through his horse and blasted out through his other thigh. He was taken from the battlefield, surprisingly calm. Ringgold lived for sixty hours, cheerful to the end. Back on the field, soldiers worked by the orange light of the retreating prairie fire, treating wounded and burying the dead. The infantry made bivouac in their squares, sleeping on the ground, on their muskets, mindful of the enemy still on the field. It was a clear, cool night, the moon gently lighting the battlefield behind wisps of smoke. The air was tainted with the smell of burned grass and gunpowder. From both sides came the sounds of the wounded, the dying, or those suffering under the surgeon's saw.

When morning broke the next day, the Mexicans had departed, slipping from the field unnoticed and withdrawing down the road towards the Rio Grande and their headquarters at Matamoros. After a quick breakfast, Taylor called his senior commanders together for a council of war. Ringgold was not present—he was in the hospital tent at the moment, showing signs of improvement, attended by his friend Ridgely, who had assumed command of the battery. Ridgely said he hoped "old Zack will go ahead, and bring the matter to close quarters." But few other officers agreed. The Mexicans had removed to a stronger defensive position, closer to their base of supply and reinforcements, and to the besieged Fort Brown. The Americans were still outnumbered and would have to leave their pack train behind, along with a force to protect the supplies and the wounded. The odds did not look good. Nine of Taylor's commanders advised either entrenching to await additional troops, or withdrawing to the supply head at Port Isabel. Only four voted in favor of renewing the battle. Taylor listened pensively to the arguments and concluded the council by saying, "I will be at Ft. Brown before tonight, if I live."

Manifest Destiny

IN 1844, THE REPUBLIC OF TEXAS was a sovereign state, recognized by the United States, Britain and France, but not by the country from which it won independence, Mexico. The Tyler administration had sought to annex Texas and negotiated a treaty to that effect. To deter Mexico from seeking to reconquer its wayward northern province, Tyler sent a secret "Corps of Observation" to the border, commanded by brevet Brigadier General Zachary Taylor, hero of Okeechobee. But when the annexation treaty went before the Senate in June, Tyler suffered a setback. Sectional issues, particularly the understanding that Texas would be admitted as a slave state, coupled with divisions within the Whig party, led to a 35 to 16 defeat.

The slaveholding states, greatly outrepresented in the House, sought to maintain parity in the Senate in order to block any legislative efforts to end their "peculiar institution." Florida was on the verge of statehood, and the accession of Texas and lands to the west would supply territory out of which could be carved future slave states, to prevent a free state lock on government. The issue was thrown into the cauldron of the 1844 presidential race. James K. Polk, a protégé of Andrew Jackson's, known as "Young Hickory," ran on an annexationist platform, seeking to balance sectional feelings by also making an issue of the Oregon boundary dispute with Britain, coining the expression "54'40" or Fight!" Whig candidate Henry Clay, who opposed annexation, tried to straddle the issue, but wound up alienating his abolitionist base and lost the election.

Annexation was voted on again in a controversial joint resolution that President Tyler signed March 1, 1845, three days before leaving office. The offer was taken to Texas by the chargé d'affaires, Andrew Jackson Donelson, nephew of the former president and second-ranked graduate of the USMA Class of 1820, whom Thayer had attempted to expel.[5] A July 4 popular convention in Austin approved the offer, and Texas was formally admitted to statehood on December 22, 1845.

The resolution admitting Texas left an important omission: it did not define the southern border of the new state. Texas claimed all lands south to the Rio Grande, and Mexico claimed the area north to the Nueces, a matter of thousands of acres of sparsely inhabited, lawless territory, where the bleached skulls of victims of the incessant violence decorated the roadside bushes and mesquite trees. Polk sought to reach a diplomatic solution, as he would with Britain over the boundary in Oregon.[6] There was also interest in the Mexican lands of California, which some felt had too much potential to stay under weak Mexican stewardship. It was thought that if the United States did not annex the area, Britain might. The American negotiators offered fifty million dollars and a renunciation of Mexican debts to the United States for all the lands from Texas to the Pacific. But the deal was rejected. The loss of Texas had been a blow to Mexican honor, and the domestic political climate in that country had swung decidedly in favor of war.

In July 1845, Taylor moved his Corps of Observation south to Corpus Christi on the Nueces, renaming it the Army of Occupation. This same month, the eastern newspaper *Democratic Review* first used the term "Manifest Destiny" as a rationale for annexation of Texas. Corpus Christi was a wild frontier town, lawless, anarchic and rife with disease. But for the officers encamped there, it became a grand reunion. Taylor's force numbered over four thousand, around half the total Army strength. It grew to be the largest body of regulars assembled since the Revolution. It was a gathering of decades of West Point classmates and friends, in many cases together again for the first time since graduation. Kirby wrote "[I] was greeted frequently, as I passed the camp, by cordial welcomes from the well-known voices of old companions I had not met for years."[7] This brotherhood of arms, young men mostly in their twenties and thirties, included some fresh from West Point, others coming from service in Florida, and still others, like Kirby, from the frontier. The roster of the scores of officers at Corpus Christi stands as a roll call of future greats in a not too distant war that was then thought inconceivable—Grant, Meade, Pemberton, Bragg, Reynolds and Longstreet among them.

At the Academy, rumors of imminent war were rife, and it was said that the Class of 1846 would graduate early and be sent to Texas; but at Corpus Christi, the waiting continued. Second Lieutenant George Gordon Meade (USMA 1835), a topographical engineer sent to help determine the location of the true border, wrote his wife, "There are a thousand reports in the camp, making the period of our remaining almost any length from one month to a year; but I presume the truth is nothing is known about it, even at Washington."[8] The delicate negotiations were disrupted in December when the moderate Mexican president Joaquin Herrera was overthrown in a coup by Major General Mariano Paredes, who renewed Mexico's claim of Texas to the Louisiana border. There followed five months of increasing tensions, as politicians on both sides sought to use the issue to their advantage, and diplomatic initiatives floundered.

In March 1846, by order of the president, Taylor advanced the 150 miles to the Rio Grande, establishing a fort opposite the Mexican town of Matamoros, which had a large garrison. The river at that point was swift and deep, two hundred yards wide, with twenty-foot-high sheer banks. A standoff resulted, neither tense nor cordial. American soldiers took some interest in the young Mexican women who had a habit of swimming naked in the river in the afternoon, and Kirby watched some of the younger officers swim out to meet them. "The Mexican guards were not, however, disposed to let them come much nearer than the middle of the river," he wrote, "so they returned after kissing their hands to the tawny damsels which was laughingly returned."[9] In the evenings, the citizens of Matamoros would gather by the riverbank to listen to the serenades of the American regimental bands, and it was said that a number of enterprising Americans slipped the pickets to make rendezvous with the forbidden señoritas.

In April, the opposing forces came under the command of Major General Mariano Arista, a red-haired Mexican native who had spent years living in Cincinnati. Moving quickly to end the standoff, Arista reinforced his position at Matamoros and sent a column downstream with orders to cross the river, head north and cut Taylor's supply line to Port Isabel on the Gulf of Mexico. Taylor strengthened his defenses at the newly named Fort Texas, then withdrew most of his troops to the

Gulf, both to protect his lines of communication and to draw fresh supplies. But in separating his forces, Taylor gave the Mexicans an opportunity. Arista laid siege to Fort Texas and placed the bulk of his infantry
and cavalry on the road between Taylor and the fort. At Port Isabel,
Taylor's men heard the siege guns in the distance. Despite continuous
bombardment over several days, only two Americans died in the siege,
one of whom was the commander, Major Jacob Brown, a sergeant in
the War of 1812 commissioned for gallantry, after whom the post was
renamed.[10]

Taylor's column of 2,200 moved southwest on May 7 and met
Arista's 3,700 men at the road junction of Palo Alto. Shortly before leaving Point Isabel, Nathaniel Wyche Hunter, still with the Second Dragoons, wrote his fiancée, Sarah K. Golding, "I do not know how Arista
can avoid fighting—if he does fight we will have a tough thing of it."
Taylor was outnumbered, his force divided, bandits on his flanks, his
supplies uncertain, and he faced a well-trained enemy who knew the
terrain. But he had told his superiors, "If the enemy oppose my march,
in whatever force, I shall fight him."

The night before the Battle of Palo Alto was miserable; mosqui-
toes swarmed, and howling, famished wolves prowled the edges of the
American encampment. Among the troops was First Lieutenant Zebulon Montgomery Pike Inge, Second Dragoons, the Goat of the Class
of 1838. He had arrived at Port Isabel only days before with a group of
new recruits, just in time to march with Taylor. Zeb was from Tuscaloosa,
and was appointed to the Academy from Alabama. He was tall, well
mannered, decidedly handsome, and he attracted attention wherever
he went. Like many Goats, he was a good-natured and popular fellow.
His demerit record was low for an Immortal, and he was made a cadet
corporal in his yearling year. But in his two final years at USMA he
racked up back-to-back 160 demerit totals and lost his stripes.[11] Zeb
was known at West Point as an excellent rider, a reputation he took into
the service in the dragoons. He was also reputed to be the best swords-
man in the service. He served in Florida against the Seminoles, then
spent some time on recruiting duty on Long Island, where he met and
married Rosa Williams of Maryland. He left his young bride in Baltimore to join the Corps of Observation, taking along his favorite pointer,
since he had heard that the hunting in Texas was excellent.

Zeb dropped by the tent of his commander, Captain Charles
Augustus May, who was the son of a prominent Washington physician
and the grandson of John May, a wealthy Boston merchant and "Son of
Liberty" who had participated in the Boston Tea Party. His brother

Henry studied law and became a congressman from Maryland, but
Charley craved a life of adventure. He joined the Army in 1836 to fight
in the Seminole War, during which he captured a chieftain named King
Philip, Coacoochee's father. May was well known at the time as the
archetypal dragoon—tall, distinguished, flamboyant, with wildly long
hair and a woolly beard that went almost to his waist. He once rode his
horse into a fashionable Baltimore hotel lobby on a bet. Longstreet
described him as "amiable of disposition, lovable and genial in character."[12] He and Zeb were boon comrades.

That night, Zeb told Charley that Samuel Ringgold had invited
them both for drinks, to make the night pass more agreeably.

"I go to see Sam so often," May said, "I am afraid I'll drink up all
of his whiskey; but I'll tell you what I *will* do." May proposed a scheme
whereby they would join Ringgold, and when offered a drink, May
would decline but Zeb would accept. "When you two fill up," May said,
"I'll say, 'I hate to see you fellows drinking alone; I think I'll join you.'"
Zeb agreed, and the two went over to Ringgold's tent.

When Ringgold offered May a drink, he said no, as planned. "Well
Zeb, come along," Sam said, "if Charley won't take anything, you will,
won't you?"

"Thank you, Sam," Zeb replied innocently, "I believe not; I, also,
must swear off for the night; follow Charley's example, you know."[13]

"Remember Your Regiment and Follow Your Officers!"

NOW THE PALO ALTO BATTLE was over. The next morning, Kirby
moved forward with his company across the burned battlefield, through
the former Mexican positions, witnessing the carnage that the American guns had wrought the previous day.[14] Dozens of bodies lay there,
singly and in heaps. One observer described the scene:

> One [Mexican] had been nearly severed in two by cannon-ball; others
> had lost a part of the head, both legs, a shoulder, or the whole stom-
> ach.... One man, who had been shot between the hips with a large ball,
> lay doubled up as he fell, with his hands extended, and his face down-
> ward, between his knees. Another, whose shoulders and back were shot
> away, seemed to have died in the act of uttering a cry of horror. Dead
> horses were scattered about in every direction, and the buzzards and
> wild dogs were fattening upon their carcasses.[15]

The Fifth Infantry was in the advance of Taylor's column, led by
Lieutenant Colonel James Simmons McIntosh. A native of Georgia,

McIntosh was a tough old Army regular, a veteran of the War of 1812 who had been bayoneted in the neck and left for dead on the battlefield at Black Rock, New York, in 1814. He had seen service in Florida, at one time commanding Fort Brooks in Tampa, where he was a previous owner of Luis Pacheco, the guide who had led Dade's column to its unhappy destiny. McIntosh was one of the four officers in Taylor's war council who had voted to attack. The American troops moved forward steadily, all carrying twenty-six pounds of weapons and ammunition, their packs left behind with the baggage train and the wounded.

Arista had drawn up his forces at Resaca de la Palma, a marshy former riverbed eight miles from Palo Alto. The *resaca*, or ravine, was two hundred feet wide and ten feet deep, bisected by the main road to Matamoros, and on either side grew dense thorny brush called chaparral. The Mexicans had long used the spot as a camping and training ground—they knew every ditch. They had thrown up earthworks behind the ravine and established a mile-long triple line of defenses, with skirmishers positioned in ambush in the chaparral, men in the riverbed, and reinforcements behind the berm on the far side. Their flanks were anchored in stands of water and heavy brush. Artillery batteries were positioned at the right and left, and seven pieces were placed astride the road. The Mexican forces were veteran infantry regiments, and the Tampico Battalion, which was famed for bravery, supported the center. It was an imposing defensive position, and Arista was so confident it would hold that he left battlefield command to Brigadier General Rómulo Díaz de La Vega and retired to his tent in the rear.

Kirby heard the sound of musket fire as the American skirmishers made first contact. His men moved off the road as Ridgely rushed his light battery forward, then Kirby plunged into the thickets to the left side of the road, followed by his company. Second Lieutenant William Logan Crittenden, also of the Fifth Infantry, followed close behind. Other regiments moved into the brush on the right, and James Longstreet and Sam Grant led their small commands into the fray. The thick, thorny bushes made movement difficult, tearing clothes and scratching hands and faces. Men literally pushed each other through the bracken. Units became disorganized, breaking down into squad-sized groups, and Mexican ambush parties began engaging the men in desperate hand-to-hand combat. Kirby and his brother Edmund fought alongside each other "in the thickest of the fight—men falling around us on all sides." Reloading was difficult, and the struggle in the chaparral was reduced to bayonet, sword and knife. Kirby eventually tired of swinging his sword and resorted to his fists.

Colonel McIntosh boldly rode his horse into the brambles, exhorting his men to advance, but was waylaid by a squad of Mexican infantry.
They killed his horse, and he was thrown to the ground. A Mexican
rammed his bayonet down towards the colonel, shoving the spike into
his mouth, knocking out some teeth, the point emerging behind his ear,
pinning him to the ground. McIntosh grabbed the musket with his left
hand for leverage and hacked at his attacker with his sword. Two more
enemy set upon McIntosh, shoving bayonets through his arm and hip,
fastening him down like an insect. At that moment American soldiers
came upon the scene and drove off the attackers, rescuing McIntosh,
who was still alive but bleeding profusely and out of the fight. James
Duncan, who was pressing forward with his artillery battery and had
not seen McIntosh go down, called on him for assistance. The colonel
spat through his bloody mouth, "Show me my regiment, and I will give
you the support you need."[16]

As the infantry pressed forward towards the Mexican line, enemy
artillery fire intensified. "The enemy's grape and canister from ten pieces,
nines and sixes, were whipping the bushes about our ears," Kirby wrote,
"the small shot falling thickly among us."[17] From the start, Ridgely had
been raining fire down on the Mexican batteries from his position at
the center of the road, suffering few casualties from the counterfire
that went over his head. But the force of the Mexican barrage stalled
the advance. Taylor, watching from a position on the road behind
Ridgely's batteries, knew the Mexican guns had to be taken out of action.
He beckoned to May, who was sitting mounted with his men farther
back down the road. When May trotted up, Taylor said, "Charley, your
regiment has never done anything yet—you must take that battery."

May turned to his men. "We must take that battery," he said.
"Remember your regiment and follow your officers. Forward!" May
and Zeb Inge led the squadron of eighty dragoons towards the enemy
in a column of fours, sabers drawn. Ahead was Ridgely's battery; the
gunners were bare-chested, working their guns furiously a scant 150
yards from the enemy positions. Ridgely saw the horsemen approaching and understood what was about to happen. He bade the dragoons
stop.

"Hold on Charley, while I draw their fire!" he shouted. The American cannon boomed and were answered by the seven Mexican guns,
at which point May gave the order to charge. The dragoons gave a terrific yell, spurred their mounts and shot down the road. It was a spectacle that some on the field watched in disbelief. Cavalry charging
artillery was reckless; it verged on the suicidal. It was the kind of charge

that would take place eight years later on the field of Balaklava when the Light Brigade was cut to pieces in a tragedy immortalized in verse. It was a race against time, the speed of the horses and their riders against the skill of the Mexican gunners, furiously attempting to reload their weapons, as the dragoons crossed the shrinking space separating them. The infantry mêlée continued in the thickets to the right and left of the road as the cavalry thundered by, hair and beards flying in the wind, and the soldiers began cheering the riders on.

May and Inge raced side by side, jockeying for the lead position. May pulled slightly ahead at one point, and Zeb called out, "Hold back Charley, 'tisn't fair!" Zeb spurred his horse forward and overtook May, as moments later the two bore down on the Mexican tubes, nearly ready to fire, their gunners frantically shoving in powder and grape. Several cannon sounded on the flank; some dragoons went down. But the forward edge of the column was already among the main body of Mexican gunners, slashing at them with their sabers, leaping over the guns, scattering the crews, and crashing through the position to the Mexican works beyond. Some horses balked at the breastwork and threw their riders into the ravine. Corporal James McCauley, a former riding master at West Point, and a half dozen other men broke entirely through the Mexican lines and continued down the road to Matamoros, killing the officer of a platoon of lancers who tried to stop them and putting the rest to flight.[18]

Zeb surmounted the berm and reined his horse, turning back towards the battery. At that moment, a small group of Mexican infantrymen popped up from behind the earthworks, leveled their weapons and fired a volley. Zeb was blown from his saddle, landing in a shallow pool in the ravine, his body pierced by nine balls. He died instantly.[19]

May attempted to rally his scattered force and returned to the guns, where he found a Mexican officer swinging his sword, imploring his men to fight. May approached the officer with weapon drawn and ordered him to surrender.

"Are you an officer?" he asked.

"I am," said May.

The Mexican presented his sword. "You receive General La Vega a prisoner of war," he said.[20]

Longstreet, who was rushing to assist, said that May's "appearance as he sat on his black horse Tom, his heavy saber over General La Vega, was grand and picturesque."[21]

With the pressure of the guns removed, the American infantry surged forward, jumping into the ravine and overwhelming the center of the Mexican line. "The enemy here fought like devils," Kirby wrote. "Our men, however, knew that if conquered they would get no quarter and there was no possibility of a retreat, and though surrounded by vastly superior number fought with desperation."[22] American troops found a weak point on the right flank, and the Mexican position began to collapse. Kirby and Edmund rushed up the opposite slope of the ravine and in amongst the Mexican guns, Edmund leaping atop one of the pieces, slashing at the defending infantrymen, jumping down and dragging the piece back towards the American lines. Mexican lancers counterattacked but were driven off by concentrated musket fire. The Tampico Battalion valiantly tried to stem the tide, but the bulk of the Mexicans fled and the Tampico were annihilated, their tricolor standard captured.

The Mexicans fled down the road to Matamoros, pursued by dragoons. The flatboats at the riverbank filled quickly and hundreds of fleeing troops leapt into the river to swim across, coming under artillery fire from Fort Brown, whose cheering defenders watched in amazement as the Mexican army disintegrated before their eyes. Scores drowned in the retreat, including some officers and the army's priest. The Mexicans left behind their baggage train, supplies, Arista's personal papers, and a large feast that had been prepared to celebrate their expected victory.[23] They lost hundreds killed, wounded and taken prisoner. The Americans suffered 122 casualties, of them 39 killed. May's command had lost 8 men and 18 horses killed, 10 men and horses wounded. Zeb Inge was buried where he fell. His dog was cared for by his comrades.[24]

Four days after the battle, Kirby's brother Edmund wrote their mother, "You may banish all concern for our safety. The war is pretty much over."[25]

CHURUBUSCO

"TWO SUCH BATTLES UNDER ALL THE circumstances have never been fought in the United States," Wyche wrote from Fort Brown, two days after Resaca de la Palma and three after Palo Alto. "They are really glorious victories, and I have no doubt they will be appreciated as such by the country at large." He was right. The opening battles of the Mexican War were remarkable triumphs, psychologically as well as militarily. In the weeks leading up to the conflict, few foresaw a favorable outcome, and most commentators predicted disaster, a fact that magnified the impact of the Mexican rout. The battles were celebrated in song, and Zachary Taylor was courted by Whig politicians as a potential presidential candidate. May's charge had made him a national hero and he received two brevet promotions. His feat became the basis for the design on the shield of the Second Dragoons' coat of arms, and his order, "Remember your regiment and follow your officers," became their motto. The United States formally declared war within days, copying the text from the declaration of war against Britain in 1812.

Nevertheless, the war was not universally popular. Congressman Abraham Lincoln opposed it and later participated in a Whig effort to have it declared unnecessary and unconstitutionally begun. The *American Whig Review* called the war "as gross an outrage on our part as was ever committed by one civilized nation on another."[1] Henry David Thoreau went to jail rather than contribute taxes to support it, and he wrote the tract "Civil Disobedience" in which he characterized the Mexican War as "the work of comparatively a few individuals using the standing government as their tool; for, in the outset, the people would not have consented to this measure."[2] But the majority opinion was echoed by Walt Whitman, writing in the *Brooklyn Eagle:* "Let our arms now be carried with a spirit which shall teach the world that, while we are not forward for a quarrel, America knows how to crush, as well as how to expand."[3]

Mexican politics mirrored American volatility. There was substantial debate over whether outright war was necessary, and a response to the war declaration was not issued until July 1. A month later, General Paredes was deposed, and on August 16, General Antonio Lopez de Santa Anna reached Vera Cruz in the ship *Arab,* returning from exile in Cuba. He was given free passage through the American blockade, in the belief that he would be more amenable to a peaceful solution. Santa Anna marched on the capital to great acclaim, as Napoleon had in returning from Elba. By the end of the year he would be both president and commander in chief of the Mexican forces; but he would be no more disposed to peace than Paredes.[4]

The opening battles in Texas were a windfall to the Regular Army soldiers, and to the West Pointers in particular. The outnumbered Americans defeated the enemy with dash and bravery, helping to dispel the image of the West Pointer as a lazy intellectual who was either unwilling or afraid to get into a hard fight. Furthermore, the officers were finally able to put their training in conventional warfighting to use. As well, they did without the participation of the militia, so there would be no question as to who was responsible for victory, as there had been in previous wars. The regulars were conscious of this fact even before the battles began. Three days before Palo Alto, George Meade wrote,

> We are all anxious to give [the Mexicans] a sound thrashing before the volunteers arrive, for the reputation of the army; for should we be unable to meet them before they come, and then gain a victory, it will be said the volunteers had done it, and without them we were useless. For our own existence, therefore, we desire to encounter them.[5]

Ephraim Kirby Smith echoed this sentiment afterwards, saying, "It is a glorious fact for the Army that there were no volunteers with us."[6] The validation of West Point was the one aspect of the war that pleased the Whig critics. In the same piece that denounced the conflict in harsh terms, the *American Whig Review* stated: "West Point has nobly vindicated herself from the attacks of [its critics], and her brave sons that lie on those fierce fought battlefields shall forever silence their slanderous tongues."[7]

Congress voted to increase the size of the Army to prosecute the war effort, and veterans of the opening battles were dispatched on recruiting duty, heroes from the front who could inspire others and tell stories of the heroism they had witnessed and participated in firsthand. Nathaniel Wyche Hunter was sent out as a recruiter, wrapped in the glory of the Second Dragoons, and he took the opportunity to marry

Sarah Golding on August 18. William Logan Crittenden went to Philadelphia, and George Meade asked him to pay a visit to his family and give a detailed account of the two battles.[8] Volunteer regiments began forming across the country, many of them led by West Pointers. When the war commenced, 523 USMA graduates were on active duty and nearly equal that number returned to the colors, most of them with militia regiments from their home states. John Taylor Pratt, the first Goat, was a major general in the Kentucky militia and commander of the state's Third Division when the war broke out. He petitioned to lead forces in Mexico, but the governor would not grant him a command. "I was so unfortunate as to be a Democrat," he wrote, "[and] of course had no favor in a Whig governor's eyes." He resigned his commission "in disgust" and was reelected to the Kentucky House of Representatives.[9] Franklin Saunders, the Goat of 1837, who had served one year with the Second Dragoons in Florida before resigning, returned for a year as a captain in the First Kentucky Volunteers. George C. McClelland, the Goat of 1843, resigned from active duty while in Texas, a week before the opening battles. He returned as a private in the First Pennsylvania Volunteers, fighting in several battles, being recommissioned, and ultimately cashiered for "conduct unbecoming an officer and a gentleman" and "drunkenness on duty."[10]

Among the West Pointers who volunteered for service in Mexico, perhaps the most distinguished was Jefferson Davis. He had only recently reentered public life. In 1835, he had married Sarah Knox Taylor, daughter of Zachary Taylor, who at the time was his commanding officer. He resigned his commission to become a cotton planter in Mississippi. Sarah died three months later, and Davis went into seclusion for almost a decade. In 1844, he ran for Congress as a Democrat and won, serving from March 1845 to June 1846. Representative Davis then resigned his seat to command the First Regiment of Mississippi Riflemen. He joined Taylor's army as it moved deep into northern Mexico. There followed a series of battles, most significantly at Monterey in September 1846, and Buena Vista in February of 1847. At Buena Vista, Davis and his Mississippi Rifles plugged a hole in the American line at a critical moment, backed up by artillery under Captains Thomas W. Sherman and Braxton Bragg. Davis was wounded in the process, but became a national hero.[11]

Taylor believed he could continue his march through the whole of Mexico, but political pressures stayed his advance. The seat of war moved to the south and to a new commander. On March 9, 1847, U.S. forces under General Winfield Scott made what was then the largest amphibious landing in history south of the port city of Vera Cruz, near the spot where Cortes had landed in 1519. After a twenty-day siege the city fell, opening the way into Mexico. The Americans began to move inland, along the great national road leading to Mexico City. The line of march was ripe with defensive possibilities, but Santa Anna made only one serious stand, at the town of Cerro Gordo. Here the Americans won an unexpected victory. Most of the credit went to Brigadier General William J. Worth, of Seminole War fame, who was the operational commander; Lieutenant Colonel William S. Harney, another Florida hero, who headed the assault force; and topographical engineer Captain Robert E. Lee, whose personal reconnaissance deep into the enemy's positions made possible the bold flanking maneuver that carried the day. Captain George W. Patten of the Class of 1830, a poet, was severely wounded in the battle, and his friend Kirby paid a visit to "Poet Patten" afterward. "All his left hand but the forefinger and thumb having been carried off by a grape shot," Kirby noted. "He was doing well and is very cheerful. I consoled him with the fact that though he could no longer play the guitar he might write better poetry than before."[12]

The victory at Cerro Gordo created even greater political turmoil in Mexico and hampered efforts to mount an effective defense against the American column as it wended its way towards the capital. Two days after the battle, the Mexican government made proposing peace an act of treason, but the May 15 elections showed significant gains for the peace party headed by former president Joaquin Herrera, causing Santa Anna (called "the Great One-Legged" by the American troops) to threaten resignation. The internal dissension and continual political gamesmanship hampered Mexican ability to resist the small American force moving into the interior.

Vera Cruz was the supply head for the American Army, but communications were tenuous. The Mexican population was not cooperative, guerillas and banditti prowled along the road, and soldiers were murdered if caught alone in towns or the countryside. Stragglers were especially in danger, and those who fell sick and could not keep up with the column were in bad straits. Supply trains were raided and patrols ambushed. "The guerilla system is already in operation," Kirby wrote along the march. "It is dangerous to go about alone or unarmed, indeed the orders are that no one shall leave his quarters without arms."[13] Eventually General Scott decided that attempting to maintain supply from Vera Cruz was untenable, and he chose to live off the land, requisitioning supplies along the way. " 'Forward' is the word," Kirby wrote, "the 'Halls of the Montezumas' our destination."[14]

The march into the interior of Mexico went through some of the most picturesque terrain in the world. The main road ascended steadily, and the route was overlooked by high, snow-capped volcanic mountain peaks. At one point Kirby was so overcome by the view that he dropped to his knees "to breathe a prayer and a thanksgiving to a good God who made such a glorious world."[15] The column passed through areas showing evidence of the older Spanish civilization that had been flourishing in the Americas a century before the rudimentary settlements at Jamestown and Plymouth. Kirby made bivouac at an old palace, a marble-columned hacienda long abandoned, with trees growing in some of the rooms. "It was probably erected by some of the Spanish nobles who came to this country soon after the conquest by Cortes," he wrote. "Here knights have armed for the battle and celebrated their victories on their return. Here blushing beauty has listened to the amorous tale breathed in her ear by her warrior lover. Where are they all now? The beauties have mouldered in the tomb forgotten. The very memory of the knights is gone."[16]

Kirby's letters home show the familiar thoughts of the soldier between battles—of family, the local conditions, when the next battle would be, or perhaps when peace would break out. Like others, he discussed the brevet promotions being awarded for bravery, which were very controversial. In those days, there were no medals; they were considered a European custom unsuited to the American democratic culture. But brevetting created the same strains and jealousies. Whenever promotion lists came out, complaints were raised that not all who got them deserved them, and that many of those who deserved them were overlooked. "I have just seen the *villainous* order of promotions and brevets in which the Fifth is entirely neglected," Kirby wrote his wife at one point. "I am utterly disgusted with the service and were it not for you and the dear children would resign at once, but for your sakes I must continue to endure.... It is too frequently the sycophant who flatters the foibles of his commanding officer, he who has family political influence, of whom some accident makes conspicuous, who reaps all the benefits of the exposure and labor of others.... Success is a lottery and government rewards are by no means dependent on merit."[17]

Kirby wondered how the war would progress, and whether the United States should have been harsher in its prosecution. Perhaps, he mused, the Americans should not have been so accommodating, paying for supplies and protecting the inhabitants where they could, but should instead have laid waste to the land and "carried fire and sword to the heart of their country," treating them with contempt—perhaps then would the war have ended sooner and "peace on advantageous terms been offered?... *Now* we must fight it out with but little hope of a termination of the struggle in many years."[18] A year had passed since he was first under fire, and despite the string of victories the Americans had enjoyed, Kirby felt a creeping pessimism:

> Our prospects in the Army, I think, grow more gloomy every day. Not only does peace seem to be more distant, but when it does come we are in danger of being disbanded. I almost envy the old and disabled officers, and wish that a respectable wound would enable me to quit the field. I should like to spend the remnant of my days in the bosom of my beloved family, in the quiet of some neat country place raising my own cabbages à la Van Buren! ... I ought not, however, to complain. For twenty years I have worn the sword without facing an enemy. A few years of war will only fit me for a respectable old age, or put to rest my unquiet spirit forever.[19]

The column halted at the town of Puebla, where Scott reorganized his forces and awaited reinforcements. Diplomatic initiatives were under way, prompted by the arrival of Nicholas P. Trist, chief clerk of the State Department, bearing three million dollars to help smooth the negotiations. Trist was a native of Louisiana who had been a leading member of the USMA Class of 1822, but resigned in his final year to study law under the tutelage of Thomas Jefferson. Stories of imminent peace were rampant, but Kirby was not impressed. "I see no result but an armed occupation, colonization, and years of guerrilla warfare," he said.[20] "Madame Rumor" was rife; one story held that Santa Anna had been killed, another that Mexican troops had opened a civil war and the capital was undefended. But Kirby did not believe them. "The thousand lying rumors which are constantly circulated with regard to the enemy have ceased to excite the slightest attention," he said. "Lying is so universal here that I am almost afraid I shall fall into the habit myself."[21]

At Puebla the officers and men got a chance to interact with the locals, to sample Mexican cuisine and drinks such as mescal. The women, at least those of the established families, were generally not permitted to associate with the Americans. Assistant Surgeon Richard McSherry, USN, noted that "the most trivial acts of civility or courtesy are jealously watched by prying eyes; and the *poblana* who once nods her head to an American, is marked by a fierce and cowardly mob for future insult."[22] And the Americans were short on currency, which limited their carousing.

One day, Second Lieutenant William M. Gardner was hailed by his classmate George Pickett: "Gardner, would you like a julep?" It was a fine offer, since the junior officers were usually in want of money, and those who came into a sum were expected to share. The two went to a *fonda* that was full of young officers awaiting a similar invitation. Pickett and Gardner stood at the bar awkwardly for some time, not wanting to drink in front of their thirsty comrades, but lacking enough money to buy a round for the house. The other officers watched hopefully as Pickett reached into his pocket and withdrew a half dollar. He tossed it onto the bar and addressed the crowd.

"Fellows," he said, "I have asked Gardner to take a drink, and I am simply bound to have one myself. Now if anyone can squeeze any more liquor out of that coin, let him step up and imbibe." Juleps being twenty-five cents, that settled the matter.[23]

In August, with diplomatic measures stalled, Scott moved to bring the war to a conclusion. His enlarged force left Puebla, taking three days to clear the town. They advanced towards Mexico City, up winding ways through mountain vales and passes, finally peaking at 10,700 feet above sea level. The road then plunged down into the Valley of Mexico, "a most glorious spectacle," Kirby said, "which we beheld from the same point where Cortes first gazed upon it."[24] The soldiers moved down into the valley towards the Mexican defenses, in high morale, confident in their leaders and themselves. Kirby grimly appreciated the fact that they were heading for the climactic battle. "Welcome the danger, welcome the toil," he wrote, "welcome the fierce conflict and the bloody field, if it will but close the war."[25]

"The Day Will Be Ours!"

THE CITY OF MEXICO WAS well sited, being surrounded by lakes, marshes, and hardened lava flows known as *pedregal.* Santa Anna had incorporated the natural chokepoints into a system of interlocking defenses. General Scott had scouted the Mexican positions, much of the dangerous reconnaissance work done by Robert E. Lee and George McClellan. Scott attempted a flanking maneuver, around the western edges of Lakes Chalco and Xochimilco, towards the villages of Contreras, San Antonio and Churubusco. He opened his attack on August 20, carrying the first two objectives after a hard fight, and sending the Mexican forces into headlong retreat north towards the city. Santa Anna, hoping to stop the rout, sent reserve troops under Major General Manuel Rincón to hold the Franciscan convent of San Mateo and the nearby *tête-du-pont,* a fortified bridge over the Churubusco River along the line of retreat. The river, which at that point was walled like a canal, cut perpendicularly across the road, and a line of Mexican forces deployed along the stone banks between the two fortified positions. Scott ordered an immediate two-column assault against the convent and the bridge-head. The Americans were tired and in some disorder, but Scott pushed forward, hoping to outrace the retreating Mexicans. If he could cut the road at the bridge, he would have a substantial number of their troops in a bag.

The Mexican position at San Mateo was strong; the convent had high, thick adobe walls and was fronted with earthworks. Among its defenders was the San Patricio battalion of foreign mercenaries and American deserters, who fought furiously, knowing their fate should they lose. They beat back several waves of American attacks, inflicting heavy casualties. With the left flank stalled before the convent, it was up to Worth's division to storm the fortress bridge. The road to the *tête-du-pont* was soggy from a drenching rain the night before, and heavy traffic from the Mexican retreat had created viscous mud that was impassable to artillery. However, seeing the disorganized mass of enemy troops, Worth was confident he could take the objective. He sent the Sixth Infantry regiment straight up the road. But the position was stronger than Worth expected, and the unit was twice repulsed with bloody losses. Among them was First Lieutenant John Danforth Bacon, the Goat of 1840, who fell mortally wounded, leading his platoon. Worth then deployed the two other regiments of the Second Brigade, the Fifth and Eighth Infantry, into the cornfields to the right side of the road to attempt to outflank the Mexicans.

Kirby Smith had yet to get into the fight that day. Earlier, he and the Fifth had bypassed the Mexican positions at San Antonio, seeking to cut off the retreat towards the strongpoints at Churubusco. For two hours the Americans raced across the rough, difficult *pedregal,* the enemy in column to their right, moving rapidly up the road towards the bridge, parallel to their line of advance, just out of musket range. North of San Antonio, the Fifth emerged from the *pedregal,* made a right oblique, and slammed into the Mexican column, starting a vicious mêlée. "It will be entirely impossible for me to give any lucid description of this terrible battle," Kirby wrote to his wife. His company was a mile and a half behind the main action when he came to the road, "a broad stone causeway with corn fields and pastures on each side of it, divided by broad ditches filled with water from three to six feet deep, the corn very tall and thick."[26] Rain had left the irrigation ditches full and the fields ankle-deep with mud. Kirby moved a mile up the road, then was ordered to assault the eastern flank of the Churubusco defenses. His men deployed in line in a field behind a tall stand of corn, then moved forward.

The corn was higher than the soldiers' heads, and the men could see only a few files in front. Unseen officers shouted orders, sometimes contradictory, adding to the confusion. Soldiers lost sight of their regimental standards, and the units began to break up. Long-range Mexican cannonballs tore through the plants as they advanced, and there were sounds of a hot battle taking place in front of them. Kirby moved forward blindly, knowing only that he was headed for action. "Immediately in front of us, at perhaps five hundred yards, the roll of the Mexican fire exceeded anything I have ever heard," he wrote. "The din was most horrible, the roar of cannon and musketry, the screams of the wounded, the awful cry of terrified horses and mules, and the yells of the fierce combatants all combined in a sound as hellish as can be conceived."[27] The first waves of Americans had stumbled into the strongest Mexican defenses yet encountered in the war.

Kirby charged forward through the corn, emerging suddenly into the clear, and into a scene of horror. American dead and wounded lay across the field before the bridge, and those who were still able to fight were scattered, seeking cover in ditches or behind a nearby copse of trees. William M. Gardner had been in the first wave, and he lay seriously wounded at the edge of the corn stand. Many of his command had dropped in the first volley, and those who were not able to stumble back into cover were bayoneted by the Mexicans as they lay on the field. A storm of crossfire, both musket and grape, rained down on Kirby's men as they emerged, its sheer volume knocking the men back into the concealment of the corn.

The soldiers dropped to the ground, seeking shelter from the balls whipping through the leaves. Kirby stood, trying to rally them, finally forming his company. He could see no other officers, and the battalion was collapsing. Kirby gave command to his second, Lieutenant Farrelly, and ordered his men to charge. They set out against the stronghold while Kirby sought to assemble the remaining companies. He formed another group and was about to lead them against the fortress when he heard a desperate cry rising from the left.

"We are repulsed!" Terrified officers and men appeared, rushing back through the corn, bowling over Kirby's men, breaking his line. The American front was crumbling and panic had set in.

Kirby disentangled himself from the mass of retreating men. The battle hung on this moment. He drew to full height, placing himself in front of the panicking mass, and shouted:

"Men! We are *not* repulsed! Form up! Form up! Charge! The day will be ours!"

The rout slowed, then stopped. The men turned, encouraged each other, began to form. Colonel C. F. Smith appeared as the men rallied. Kirby shouted, "Forward! Forward!" The cry was echoed through the field and he and his men burst out through the corn, charging the Mexican defenses.

★ ★ ★

AROUND THIS TIME, ON THE EXTREME RIGHT flank of the American line, elements of the Eighth Infantry approached the *tête-du-pont*. The line moved over the fields to within 150 yards of the strongpoint, where concentrated fire stalled the advance, near one of the large irrigation channels. Some Americans struggled forward. The standard bearer of Company H came up to the ditch and fell, and the unit began to move back. Company commander Captain James V. Bomford (USMA 1832) picked up the colors and charged ahead with his junior officers, Lieutenant James Longstreet, and Second Lieutenants James Snelling (USMA 1845) and George Pickett.[28] The men of Company H, seeing their officers dashing towards the fortress, rallied, and the rest of the regiment began to follow.

Bomford reached the ditch, handed the colors to Longstreet and jumped in. He waded quickly across to the other side and clambered up the stone wall. Longstreet threw him the colors, and he, Pickett and Snelling navigated the passage under fire, with their men leaping in after them. Some were shot down by musket fire or grapeshot; some were wounded in midpassage and sank beneath the surface, drowning. But most made it across and followed the officers, who had raced up under the walls of the *tête-du-pont*. They probed for weakness in the fort as their men provided covering fire. Finally Bomford himself, standing on the shoulders of his men, forced an entry through one of the embrasures, with Longstreet and Pickett close behind, handing up the colors as they went. Other soldiers followed, and after a sharp hand-to-hand skirmish on the top of the fortress, the regimental banner was raised, to the cheers of the men below.

At this moment, Kirby and the Fifth regiment came charging onto the scene, emerging from the cornfield with a shout and running down the Mexican defenders outside the fort. The Mexicans inside panicked and tried to crowd out through the north entrance. Those who got out ran down the road towards Mexico City. Many were bayoneted or shot in the back as they fled. Pickett and Longstreet stood in the fort, watching the Mexican rout through the firing holes, hearing the cheers of their men, the regimental banner now joined by the Stars and Stripes. Outside, Kirby watched the same sight, as the banner of the Fifth Infantry was added to the display. San Mateo soon fell, netting General Rincón and most of the deserters. Rincón was one of eight generals captured that day, two of whom were also members of the Mexican Congress. In total, August 20 saw 4,000 Mexican casualties and 3,000 prisoners. The Americans lost 1,000 killed, wounded or missing.

The next day, Kirby was given command of the funeral parties, "a sad, a solemn service," he wrote. "In our haste we performed no burial rites—paid no honors—but laid our dead in the earth in the bloody garments in which they died, most of them on the spot where they fell. Indeed many were so torn and mangled by the shot it was entirely impossible to move them."[29] Many were trampled in the mud, some so completely that it was difficult to tell if they were American or Mexican. The field was strewn with the debris of battle, dead horses and mules, muskets, swords, boxes, pieces of uniforms, and packs. "Immense damage appears to have been done to their music bands," Henry Howe observed, "as prodigious quantities of musical instruments were scattered all over the field—drums, fifes, bugles, clarinets, trombones, ophicleides, etc."[30]

General Scott might have made for Mexico City on the 20th; some of William Harney's dragoons daringly rode up to the city gates before retiring under fire. But the troops were too tired and disorganized from the several victories they had already achieved that day. Instead, Scott agreed to an armistice, in hopes that a negotiated settlement could be attained without further loss of lives. The negotiators on the American side were Nicholas Trist and Major Abraham Van Buren, son of the former president and penultimate graduate of 1827, who had returned to service in 1846. Former president Joaquin Herrera led the Mexican negotiators. The Mexican delegation was instructed by its political leaders to "treat for peace as if we had triumphed!"

During the truce, neither side was supposed to reinforce or prepare for further conflict. The Americans were able to draw supplies from Mexico City, but were not allowed to enter the city in force. General Scott agreed to the armistice in good faith; whether Santa Anna planned it as a deception or was simply keeping his options open is debatable. Few held out hope for a diplomatic solution. Scott was not disposed to disrupt the negotiations, even as rumors reached him of Mexican violations, particularly of preparations for renewed battle. A resident of the city brought information of Mexican violations to Kirby, who forwarded them to Scott. The general dismissed the intelligence, calling the native source a liar. Nevertheless, by September 6 even Scott had to admit that the truce had been merely a ruse to allow the Mexicans to reestablish their defenses after the crushing defeats at Contreras and Churubusco. "Fatal credulity!" Kirby wrote his wife. "How awful are its consequences to us! By it, the fruits of our glorious victory are entirely thrown away."[31]

The Americans were encamped in the shadow of the castle of Chapultepec, which stood atop a 150-foot natural mound just west of the gates of the city. The area was one of the most beautiful spots in the valley, a favorite of Montezuma, called by the Aztecs "Grasshopper's Hill." The castle was built during the Spanish period as the home of the viceroy, El Conde de Galves (after whom Galveston was named). In 1847, it was the home of the enemy's military academy, the Mexican West Point. Most believed that Chapultepec would have to be taken before Mexico City could be conquered.

Yet before fighting that battle, Scott had prepared another mission. The general had received intelligence that the bells of the City of Mexico had been removed from the churches and were being made into cannon at the foundry at Molino del Rey (the King's Mill), a massive stone-walled collection of buildings and houses outside the city gates, two-thirds of a mile west of Chapultepec. The powder for the guns was being stored at Casa Mata, a fortified magazine five hundred yards west of the Molino. The area was lightly defended, and Scott sought to seize the buildings and the weapons, destroy the foundry, and capture or blow up the powder. He believed this could be done quickly, with minimal forces, and he projected the casualties at about twenty men.

General Worth, whose division was to be the assault force, thought the position was stronger than Scott assumed, and last-minute intelligence arrived that the foundry was in fact nonoperational. The machinery had been moved inside the city the day after Churubusco, and Santa Anna was reinforcing the area, inviting attack. Scott, for whatever reason, chose to ignore this information. He envisioned a three-pronged attack. On the extreme right, a brigade under Lieutenant Colonel John Garland would approach the south and east sides of the Molino. In the center, a forlorn hope of five hundred men led by Major George Wright

(USMA 1822) would pierce the Mexican defenses between the two strongpoints and wheel right into the Molino complex.[32] On the left flank, the nine-hundred-man Second Brigade under the command of Colonel McIntosh, recovered from his wounds at Resaca, would storm Casa Mata. Kirby was given command of the Light Infantry Battalion, which would act as a reserve, backing up the forlorn hope should it be necessary.

Scott briefed his commanders on the evening of September 7. That night, Kirby retired to his tent to write to his wife. "In my opinion a much bloodier battle is to be fought than any which have preceded it," he wrote. "This operation is to commence at three in the morning. Tomorrow will be a day of slaughter. I firmly trust and pray that victory may crown our efforts though the odds are immense. I am thankful you do not know the peril we are in. Good night."[33]

CHAPULTEPEC

A T SIX IN THE MORNING on September 8, as dawn broke over the valley of Mexico, the silence was cut by the sound of bugles blowing reveille at Chapultepec. Hours earlier, American troops had moved into their assault positions, and they listened to the cry of the horns as they waited for the battle to begin. As the bugle call echoed from the distant hills, the first rounds of American artillery were fired and the assault commenced. Captain William H. T. Walker, Immortal of 1837 and hero of Okeechobee, started across the 600-yard glacis towards the Mexican lines. It had taken two years for him to recover from the wounds he suffered in Florida. He had served gallantly with the Sixth Infantry at Churubusco on August 20 and had volunteered for the forlorn hope at Molino.

Walker led his men across the downward slope to the level plain two hundred yards from the walls, and soon they began to take scattered fire from Mexican artillery and light infantry. The order was given to march double-time, and the men moved ahead quickly. The weak fire did not slow them, and when they were within musket range, the Americans loosed a volley.

Captain James L. Mason (USMA 1836) dashed ahead and saw no serious opposition.[1] "Forward men!" he shouted, waving his hat. "There's no one here!"

"Charge bayonets!" was ordered, and the forlorn hope rushed the Mexican guns, scattering the gunners and throwing back the defenders.

★ ★ ★

ON THE LEFT FLANK, Colonel McIntosh began his advance with artillery support, seeking to hit the enemy lines just outside the small fortress magazine and cut it off from the rest of the defensive line. He rode into battle mounted, the only officer to do so. His men took some fire from the defenders in the ditch outside the fort, who then withdrew inside its walls as the Americans neared. Then the Mexican guns fell silent and McIntosh's unit advanced unopposed. At a hundred yards from Casa Mata, the Mexicans finally opened up. The Americans realized that the position was defended more strongly than they had anticipated. McIntosh's 900 men faced 1,500 Mexicans in prepared positions. The fire was intense; McIntosh urged his men forward, and the advance continued. They reached the embankment of the ditch twenty-five yards from the magazine and began to return fire. But the exposed Americans could not penetrate the enemy's outer works. Mexican fire intensified, and the battle became a slaughter.

The officers were cut down while imploring their men to fight. McIntosh, still leading from horseback, was shot from his mount. Major Martin Scott, his second in command, was killed, and Major Carlos A. Waite, the next commander, was wounded. Assistant Surgeon Roberts rallied a small group to charge, and was killed as he gave the command. Eventually an enlisted man gave the order to retire, and the brigade limped back towards the American lines.

THE FORLORN HOPE'S SUCCESS in the center had not lasted long. Captain Mason had not observed that most of the Mexicans were lying down behind the ditch. Seeing the relatively small size of the American force, the defenders leapt up and began a murderous fire, joined by others from inside and atop the buildings of the Molino. In minutes, eleven of the fourteen officers with the assault party went down, along with a large number of men. Walker was shot twice and collapsed.

The forlorn hope disintegrated and fell back. Mexican reinforcements came onto the scene and advanced beyond the walls, knifing and bayoneting American wounded as they came. They noticed Walker, but he was injured so severely they took him to be dead and moved on. After the Mexicans had returned to their positions, Walker chanced to move and a musket ball from the rooftop struck close by. He was well in view of the defenders, but was growing weak from the loss of blood. He reached for his canteen, bringing a volley of fire, which missed him. He knew his options were few at that point and sensed he would be dead one way or another, so he boldly grabbed his canteen, lifted it to his lips, and commenced to drink his fill, as Mexican soldiers raised a cloud of dust around him with repeated musket shots.[2]

★ ★ ★

GENERAL WORTH HAD WATCHED with growing concern as the assault ground down, and he ordered Kirby's reserve force into the fray. The Light Infantry, enraged by the enemy depredations on the wounded, swept down into the battlefield, through the remnants of the forlorn hope, and up to the enemy's guns, where they tore through the surprised Mexicans in a flurry of bayonet thrusts and sword strokes. Kirby led his men down the walls of the Molino, secured an archway to the rear of the structure, and barreled inside. Some Americans climbed sheds and surmounted the walls directly. The fighting at the complex was building to building, room to room, and across the rooftops. The Mexican troops abandoned the southwestern side of the compound and retreated to more distant buildings. American artillery, positioned to interdict possible reinforcements from Chapultepec, now redirected fire against the clustered Mexicans, causing some to panic.

Kirby returned to the outer works, rallied as many men as he could find, and charged towards the remaining Mexican batteries. Despite fire from the cannon and from infantry on the rooftops, Kirby's makeshift unit carried the enemy guns, which he quickly turned on the retreating Mexicans and the houses in which they sought cover. As Kirby was leading his men in this final victorious rush, a Mexican ball pierced his left eye, emerging from his ear. He fell on a pile of stones, smashing the right side of his face. The battle rolled over him, and he was carried from the field, barely conscious.

On the left flank, James Duncan's artillery had given cover to McIntosh's brigade as they retreated, and kept up a punishing fire on the magazine. Seeing the Molino defenses crumbling, the Mexican defenders abandoned their position and retreated north and east towards the city. Soon afterwards, Casa Mata caught fire and exploded, killing a few Americans.

The fight was over by midmorning. The Mexicans suffered 3,000 casualties, and another 2,000 soldiers deserted. The morale of the enemy was again shaken, and it seemed as though the Americans could carry any position, no matter how strongly defended. But Molino del Rey was proportionately the deadliest battle of the war for the Americans. They took 787 casualties, 58 of them officers. Half the number were in McIntosh's storming party. Colonel McIntosh was wounded twice in the battle, and both wounds healed. During his convalescence, however, the injury he had sustained in 1812 reopened and he bled to death. First Lieutenant Charles F. Morris, Eighth Infantry, the Goat of 1841, first injured at Resaca, was mortally wounded assaulting the enemy's works and died on September 17.[3] Captain Moses Emery Merrill of the Fifth Infantry, Kirby's friend, classmate and fellow Immortal of 1826, who had fought in every major battle of the war, was killed in action. His son, William Emery Merrill, would graduate first in the Class of 1859. Ephraim Kirby Smith was taken to the headquarters of his uncle, Major Edmund Kirby, who was serving as chief paymaster on General Scott's staff. He was attended to by the finest surgeons available and lingered semiconscious for two days. He sank into a coma on September 10 and died the next day.

When Molino del Rey was inspected, no operational gun works were found. There were some old gun molds, but no weapons or signs of recent activity. Cannon fire from Chapultepec made it impossible to hold the position at the mill, and it was burned and abandoned. By one o'clock in the afternoon, the Americans were again where they had started.

"God is a Yankee."

SANTA ANNA WAS NOW BACKED into his capital, holding only the castle of Chapultepec outside the city gates. The hill was unassailable on the north and the east, the natural rock being too steep. Ten-foot-high walls and deep ditches reinforced the other slopes, with eight gates, strongly defended. One thousand men commanded by General Nicolas Bravo manned the ramparts; among them were fifty teenage cadets who had refused orders to leave the Academy. Santa Anna could not send reinforcements, since most of his men were guarding the southern gates of the city against a possible attack by a division commanded by Brigadier General David E. Twiggs, whose troops Scott had sent as a show of force to keep Santa Anna guessing. On September 12, Scott subjected Chapultepec to a fourteen-hour bombardment, which did severe damage to the buildings and according to the general made a "good impression." That night the attacking parties made their way into the abandoned mill. The American bombardment recommenced on the 13th at six o'clock for two hours, after which the assault force moved in. Given the carnage five days prior, many officers on Scott's staff watched their progress nervously. Worth had uncharacteristically predicted defeat, and Scott himself had misgivings.

The storming parties were picked men, seasoned veterans carrying crowbars, pickaxes and ladders. The lead units moved in quickly on the western edge of Chapultepec, 260 enlisted men led by eighteen officers. Among them were Lewis Armistead, who had been wounded at Churubusco; James Longstreet, bearing the colors; and George Pickett. They ran forward through the grove of centuries-old cypress trees leading up to the western slope, carrying the outer defenses in a rush. They moved quickly towards the palace, across the rocky slope, taking fire from above. A large ditch ringed the hill at the base of the retaining wall beneath the buildings on the summit. The men with the scaling ladders had lagged behind, and Mexican troops and cadets fired from the windows and rooftops while Americans took cover and returned fire. Armistead raced up with a ladder and jumped into the ditch. He pushed the first ladder against the wall, and troops began to climb up. A Mexican ball caught Armistead and he went down. Some of the first men up the ladder were thrown back down into the ditch by the defenders, but presently lodgments were made and streams of soldiers and marines ascended. Longstreet and Pickett ran up. Longstreet paused to pick up a musket that had been discarded by one of the wounded. As he raised the weapon, he staggered—he had been hit by a Mexican ball and suffered a severe wound. He sank down, handing the colors to Pickett, who took the flag and ascended the wall, mounted the top and fought his way towards the palace.

Santa Anna viewed the action from an observation post in the city. Thousands of citizens clustered on rooftops and church towers watching the course of the battle. On the American side those troops who were not fighting sought vantage points on the tops of houses and in trees. Assistant Surgeon McSherry described the scene:

> The column, undaunted, moved steadily onward; sometimes there was a momentary suspense, but it was for physical obstacles; directly again, the onward, upward motion was resumed. You may imagine, but I cannot describe, what the feelings of the spectators were. I thought of all excitements I had ever known, or witnessed, and felt how far they fell short of this most engrossing spectacle.... Heads of regiments and companies were seen to sink in the ditch, then mount the walls. See them— they stop to wave the regimental flags, as they go over, then a period of the closest fighting, and shortly, the tricolour falls, and the American ensign waves over the proud Castle of Chapultepec.[4]

Legend has it that a seventeen-year-old Mexican cadet was on the palace roof as the Americans closed in. He had come to bring down the Mexican flag, to deny its capture to the enemy. As the Americans came up the stairwells, he lowered the flag, and clutching it he made for the back stairs. But as he ran across the parapet, he took an American bullet. The cadet stumbled and pitched off the high roof, falling to the rocks below. When his broken body was later found, he still held the flag. As the cadet plunged to earth, George Pickett dashed onto the roof, attached the American flag to the pole and hoisted it skyward.[5] Seeing the Stars and Stripes waving atop the palace, an officer standing next to Santa Anna shook his head and sighed, "God is a Yankee."[6]

★ ★ ★

THE CAPTURE OF MEXICO CITY ended major combat operations in the Mexican War, though small-scale fighting continued for some time afterwards. The American effort had astonished the world. A force of not over 11,000 men, having faced down an army three times their size, in the middle of a hostile country with uncertain supply lines, took possession of a city of 200,000. The Duke of Wellington said of General Scott, "His campaign was unsurpassed in military annals. He is the greatest living soldier."[7]

Scott gave a great deal of credit for the victory to West Point. "I give it as my fixed opinion," he said, "that but for our graduated cadets, the war between the United States and Mexico might, and probably would have lasted some four or five years, with, in its first half, more defeats than victories falling to our share; whereas, in less than two campaigns, we conquered a great country and a peace, without the loss of a single battle or skirmish." Philip Hone, who had strongly opposed the war, wrote of the Academy in his diary, "The utility of this establishment has been proved to the full extent of the favourable predictions of its friends, and the utter overthrow of the disparaging prognostications of its enemies. The students of West Point have been foremost in the career of glory in the Mexican war, in the front of the battle, reckless of danger, adding to the most chivalric bravery the benefit of military science acquired at this excellent national school."[8] As evidence of the bravery of the West Point graduates, the Academy published figures showing that the combat death rate of officers of the volunteer regiments was around 3 percent, while for West Pointers the rate was twice as much. For the West Point Goats, the rate was even higher. Fifteen Goats served in Mexico, of whom four—Zeb Inge, John D. Bacon, Charles F. Morris and Ephraim Kirby Smith— were either killed or mortally wounded in action, a death rate of 27 percent.

Disease killed far more Americans than battle, before, during and after the war. Dysentery, yellow fever, cholera, the grippe and other diseases, some with bizarre symptoms, unknown and never diagnosed, raged indiscriminately through the American forces. Second Lieutenant James Overing Handy of the Eighth Infantry, the Goat of 1842, died in Corpus Christi on September 26, 1845. First Lieutenant John Howard Hill of the Second Dragoons, the Goat of 1839, died of sickness at Puebla, July 29, 1847. Nathaniel Wyche Hunter returned to Mexico after recruiting service, but did not see further action. "Noble hearted Hunter" went home to Athens on sick leave of absence in 1848 and died in Charleston, South Carolina, April 25, 1849. He and Sarah had no children. Twelve days later, in San Antonio, brevet Major General William J. Worth, the "young Cortes," former Commandant of Cadets and hero of many campaigns, succumbed to Asiatic cholera.

After the battle of Molino del Rey, William H. T. Walker was taken to a small house used as an infirmary to die. His brother John lay nearby, shot through the legs. Walker lay quietly, staring at the ceiling, suffering greatly but not uttering a sound. Next to him lay a young lieutenant who had been hit by a piece of masonry dislodged by round shot, a painful but not serious wound. The lieutenant moaned and groaned, and was generally an annoyance to the rest of the men.

Finally Walker turned to him and said, "Lieutenant, are you suffering very much?"

"Not much," the young man said stoically.

"Then confound it shut up!" Walker said. "I am!"

Walker lingered on, to the amazement of the surgeons, the other patients, and especially himself. He suffered immensely, as much from not knowing his fate as from his wounds, but he refused to give up the fight. One day he told William Gardner, who was recovering from wounds suffered at Churubusco, "If I could only be certain that I had no chance to get well I'd send to the market for a turtle—the biggest to be found—dine on turtle soup, and die like a gentleman."[9]

Walker soon learned that his sacrifice had not gone unnoticed— he was brevetted major for gallantry on August 20, and lieutenant colonel for unexcelled bravery at Molino. He vowed that he would return to New York to see his wife and children. Walker was taken by stretcher to Vera Cruz, thence by steamer to New York. He spent nearly a year bedridden, but as with Okeechobee, he survived to return to active duty. General Scott said that Walker had endured through sheer willpower; any other man would have been dead.[10] In 1849 he was presented a sword of honor by the state of Georgia, on which was inscribed, "Okeechobee, Vera Cruz, Churubusco, Molino del Rey."

On March 13, 1849, Fort Inge was established in Texas, between San Antonio and El Paso, on the east banks of the Leona River, south of a small round mountain that was also named for Zeb Inge. Eight months after he was killed, Zeb's body was brought back to Alabama by his brother, Judge Robert Sturdivant Inge, along with his loyal hunting dog. A funeral was held in Mobile on January 28, 1847, and the lead casket containing the body was loaded onto the steamer *Tuscaloosa* for the journey home. Ten miles above Mobile, the vessel's boilers exploded; the ship burned and sank. The casket was never recovered. The pointer went down with the ship.

Randolph Ridgely, hero of the opening months of the war, declined a brevet promotion to captain for his actions at Palo Alto and Resaca de la Palma. He later served on Taylor's staff. Ridgely was thrown from his horse in the streets of Monterrey on September 24, 1846, and died three days later, leaving behind a wife and an infant child. Late in life, Longstreet wrote, "Many gallant, courageous deeds have since been witnessed, but none more interesting than Ridgely's call for the privilege to draw upon himself the fire that was waiting for May."

In May 1847, Jefferson Davis was appointed to the Senate seat of the recently deceased Mississippi senator Jesse Speight. Davis was subsequently elected to the office and served from August 1847 to September 1851, when he resigned to run for governor of Mississippi but was defeated.

Lewis Armistead recovered from his wound at Chapultepec, and was brevetted for gallant and meritorious conduct at the Battles of Churubusco and Molino del Rey. Richard B. Screven, Eighth Infantry, Goat of 1829, entered the war as a captain but left as a brevet lieutenant colonel, being recognized for bravery at Monterrey and Molino. The former Eggnog Mutineer served only three more years, succumbing to sickness and dying at New Orleans, May 15, 1851, at age forty-three. James Longstreet, seriously wounded carrying the colors at Chapultepec, received brevets for Churubusco and Molino. George Pickett was brevetted for gallantry at Churubusco and Chapultepec. Both were cited for "noble exertions and gallant conduct."

Ephraim Kirby Smith was buried in Mexico, but in 1848 the citizens of Syracuse, New York, had his body moved there, to be near his wife and three children. His uncle, Major Kirby, and General Twiggs saw to it that Ephraim received posthumous brevet promotion up two grades, to lieutenant colonel, for his gallantry at Churubusco and Molino. He thus finally received the recognition denied him in life.

THE MEMBERS OF THE CLASS of 1847 arrived in the theater too late for major combat, though A. P. Hill did participate in some small battles after the fall of Mexico City, as did Edward D. Blake, who had graduated just above Henry Heth. "It was something we could not comprehend," Heth wrote, "that General Scott could have captured the city of Mexico without the assistance of the Class of 1847."[11] It was the opinion of the class that Scott had somehow made a mistake. "How were any of us to gain the brevets for gallant conduct which we had assured our sweethearts we would do?" Heth wondered. He reached Mexico City in the fall of 1847 and was assigned to William H. T. Walker's old company as a second lieutenant. Walker's command had been given to Heth's kinsman Lewis Armistead. Heth, Armistead and Winfield Scott Hancock became messmates, "and never was a mess happier than ours."[12]

Heth looked up Ambrose Everett Burnside, who was stationed nearby at Tacubaya, and was regaled with tales of his friend's amorous adventures and cautioned against dallying with multiple Mexican women simultaneously. Burnside had already had several affairs, and at least one jealous paramour had attacked him with a knife. "One Mexican daisy is enough at a time," he counseled.[13] Burnside complained that his current live-in girlfriend Anita watched him like a hawk. "She is right," Heth said, "and you will bear watching, Burn."[14]

Heth made his own forays into the Mexican social scene, usually with Hancock, "a magnificent specimen of youthful beauty ... tall, graceful, a blonde, with light hair, the style of all others that once captivated the Mexican girls."[15] Hancock also took Heth around the battlefields, showing him where he had been wounded and where the Sixth and other regiments had made history. Heth's now-famous cousin Pickett took him to the roof of the citadel at Chapultepec and showed him the flagpole where he had raised Old Glory. These were pleasant days for all the old friends and classmates.

Before leaving West Point, the members of the Class of 1847 had agreed that when the City of Mexico was captured, they would have a cadet hash in the Halls of Montezuma. One afternoon they gathered for the "royal hash," which was prepared with local ingredients, and "in place of old Benny's whiskey there was *aquardiente* galore."[16] The festivities went on late into the evening, with much singing and telling of tales. Burnside got "gloriously tight," and at the end of the feast, Heth escorted him back to his room, just like old times. There he talked his way past Anita and rolled Burn unconscious into bed. Leaving his friend in Anita's care, he returned to his quarters. "I loved Burnside more than I ever loved a man," Heth later wrote, "and I know my love for him was reciprocated. I told his wife, after he was married, that she was the only person of whom I had ever been jealous."[17]

James McNeill Whistler

O N NEW YEAR'S MORNING 1849, the Corps of Cadets marched
to the wharf, accompanied by spirited tunes of the West Point
Band. They formed a square near the pier, the band within,
still playing. Forty picked cadets boarded a docked ship. Moments later
they returned in line, each bearing a banner captured in Mexico. The
cadets marched to the center of the square and cast the colors down
one at a time. "A great many of them were torn and covered with blood,"
plebe George L. Hartsuff observed. "They must have passed through
some hard fighting. Some of them were very neat and pretty. They were
probably worked by the fair Mexican maidens and presented to their
favorite youths no doubt with strict injunctions to preserve them or die
(a Yankee girl would say at least so) but Alas! for them they were met
by those who never were beaten (nor ever will be)."[1]

The captured Mexican banners were presented to the Academy
by General Scott and the secretary of war. The advance team had come
two weeks earlier, led by the chief clerk of the War Department, Archie
Campbell, who had graduated 24th in the Class of 1835. He served only
a year in uniform before becoming a civilian engineer. In 1845 he joined
the War Department, where he served in various high-ranking administrative capacities.

On Christmas Eve, Campbell joined a dozen other graduates for
a trip to Benny Havens' to relive old times. It was a bright, chilly, moonlit night. Two feet of snow lay on the ground. The officers walked briskly
down the road to Buttermilk Falls, in high spirits, chatting amiably.
They rounded a bend and found themselves face to face with a group
of first-classmen heading back from their own revelries.

The officers fell silent and stopped. The stunned cadets made a
quick calculation. They knew that they could not retreat or scatter into
the woods—if the officers returned to the post and called roll, they
would be found missing. The only option was to charge. They threw

their capes over their faces and rushed the officers, who started laughing. After all, most of them had done the same thing in their day, and
Christmas Eve was traditionally a time for bending the rules. But Captain George Cullum, instructor of practical engineering, third in the
Class of 1833 with no demerits and a well-known stick-in-the-mud, was
not amused. He angrily grabbed hold of one of the cadets as he passed.
The cadet got tangled up in his own cape and was nearly overpowered,
but knowing that capture would probably mean expulsion, he recovered, braced himself and swung Cullum bodily over the stone wall at
the edge of the road and down a steep snow-covered slope. Cullum slid
down the hill crying, "Help, Archie! Help!" as the cadet hightailed it
after his fellows. The group made it back safely to the barracks, and the
inevitable inspection later that night found all in place, studying or
asleep.

At the wharf, the banners were again taken up. The cadets took
their places in the ranks and tramped up the hill to the tune of "Santa
Anna's March." At the top, the Mexican flags were lowered and a salute
was fired, the American flag held high. The procession continued to
the front of the library, where the standard bearers moved forward.
They stood in ranks as the Corps and the faculty raised three cheers.
In his special order of the day, the Superintendent stated that the war
with Mexico "has removed the prejudices heretofore existing against
the West Point academy, and that the reproach can no longer be brought
against us of being Holiday Soldiers, fostered by an aristocratic and useless institution.... It is a source of no little gratification to us that the
President has been pleased to bestow this mark of his appreciation of
the services of the graduates of the Military academy, in selecting it as
the depository of these trophies, and it requires no assurance that it will
be equally our pride and pleasure to preserve these precious memorials of our country's glory."[2]

Among the cheering cadets was a firstie named James McQueen
McIntosh, the son of Colonel James Simmons McIntosh, who had died
heroically at Molino del Rey a year and a half earlier. He was born in
1828 at Fort Brooke, Tampa, where his father was then commanding.
Cadet McIntosh could trace his lineage to Brigadier William McIntosh,
a leader in the Jacobite uprising of 1715. In 1736, the brigadier's grandson John Mohr McIntosh brought most of the clan to America, settling
in Georgia and the Southeast. Cadet McIntosh's great-great-uncle General Lachlan McIntosh was commander of the Georgia militia during
the Revolution. He frequently came into conflict with Button Gwinnett, the chair of the state executive council (essentially the governor),

and a signer of the Declaration of Independence. Repeated provocations culminated in a duel on May 16, 1777. Both were wounded. McIntosh recovered, but Gwinnett did not; he succumbed three days later, the first signer to die. McIntosh was tried and acquitted, but could not comfortably stay in Georgia. He joined George Washington at Valley Forge, serving honorably through the difficult winter, and thereafter as a brigadier in the regular Army. Lachlan's nephew John, who was Cadet McIntosh's grandfather, also fought in the Revolution, as commander of Fort Morris in Sunbury, Georgia. In 1778, a British force of five hundred landed nearby and demanded the surrender of the fort and its two hundred defenders. McIntosh responded, "Come and take it!" He successfully beat back the attack, and was awarded a sword with his defiant statement engraved on it.

Although he came from a long line of fighting men, Cadet McIntosh was the first to receive formal military education. As it happened, he did not excel at his studies, but consistently ranked at or near the bottom in his courses. McIntosh was the inspiration for a very angry letter by Dennis Hart Mahan to the Superintendent, Captain Brewerton, dated September 28, 1848. Mahan was observing the Immortal section being taught physics by Lieutenant Hunt. McIntosh was at the boards and was asked what measured the moment of a force. After some time, he admitted that he did not even know what "the moment of a force" meant. Mahan then snapped at McIntosh, calling him a disgrace, having just passed the course in mechanics yet "evincing such ignorance of its simplest elements." He sent McIntosh back to his quarters to reeducate himself on the topic before being allowed to return. But what made Mahan most angry was the fact that many cadets, like McIntosh, maintained that "having passed on the subject referred to in the preceding classes, he considered any subsequent display of ignorance on them as beyond the reach of authority." In other words, once tested on a subject, the cadet felt he had fulfilled his part of the bargain and promptly forgot the subject matter, a practice still known in West Point slang as "spec and dump." "The entertainment of such a view of this subject by Cadets is, I apprehend, more general than a right thinking person would be willing to believe," Mahan wrote. He believed this evil was increasing year to year and a remedy needed to be found.[3] None ever was.

Like many Immortals, McIntosh was not well disciplined. He was tough and wiry, always ready for mischief. He racked up many demerits, usually for the kind of harmless antics one expects from the Immortal section, but occasionally he would get into more serious trouble. For

example, in June 1848, McIntosh got into a vicious fight with Walter
H. Stevens, a respected firstie who was about to graduate fourth in his
class. They were court-martialed and found guilty. Stevens was placed
under house arrest but allowed to graduate with his class. McIntosh
was given a week in light prison, three weeks' confinement to camp,
and fifteen extra guard tours.

McIntosh entered his final semester twenty-two demerits short
of dismissal. He tried his best to avoid crossing the line, but kept stumbling. On May 13, 1849, he was acting as officer of the cadet guard
when he received a report from Cadet Corporal John Edwards of several cadets committing an infraction. McIntosh took the report but did
not pass it up the chain to the Commandant. He was found guilty in a
court martial on May 28. This could have ended his career, but instead
he was given twenty days' confinement during recreation hours and
four extra tours. The Superintendent said he thought McIntosh had
displayed poor judgment rather than ill will. Nevertheless, when the
time came to graduate, McIntosh had racked up exactly twenty-two
demerits. Perhaps as an act of kindness, or maybe in recognition of his
father's heroism, the Superintendent reviewed his records and decided
to retroactively forgive one demerit—February 17, "Forage cap out of
order at class parade"—and McIntosh was allowed to march with his
class as the Goat of 1849.

The Mexican War brought more than captured banners to West
Point. In the years after the war, cadets found themselves being taught
by men whose exploits they had read about in books and newspapers.
Brevet Captain George McClellan came to West Point in 1849 as an
assistant instructor of practical engineering. And William H. T. Walker,
having recovered from the near-fatal wounds he suffered in Mexico,
was Commandant of Cadets from 1854 to 1856. He was as tough and
practical in this capacity as he had been in the field. For example, when
upperclassmen began deviling plebes on sentinel duty, Walker ordered
the youngsters to defend themselves with their bayonets. What had
befallen Henry Heth by accident, Walker made a policy. It worked.

But by far the most notable Mexican War hero to return to the
Academy was Superintendent Robert E. Lee, who had served together
with Walker at West Point for a year. They were a study in contrasts.
Lee had graduated second in his class, with no demerits, and was very
proper, always a gentleman. Walker had graduated near the bottom of
his class, earned many demerits, and projected the image of the hardened warrior he was. Both were bona fide heroes. Their experiences
gave them a good understanding of cadets and what they needed to

succeed as officers. They made a grand combination, and young men in search of personal inspiration could choose either model.[4]

Robert Weir painted a portrait of Lee while he was Superintendent, one of only two known portraits of him from before the Civil War. It shows a refined man, thoughtful and reserved. He was a model of decorum, and was held in some awe by the cadets, one of whom recalled, "Cadets living in the front rooms of barracks were apt to go to the windows to see him walk by on the opposite side of the street on his way to and from his office. . . . [T]here is nothing more attractive than a superb man in motion."[5] Lee seemed to have boundless energy, though he was sometimes seen napping through sermons on Sunday. He was very popular with ladies, especially the young ones. The first time she met Lee, Jefferson Davis's wife called him "the handsomest person I had ever seen."[6] His wife and children enjoyed living at West Point, and by coincidence Lee's tenure as Supe took place during the final years of his son George Washington Custis Lee's education. The young Lee surpassed his father, graduating first in the Class of 1854.

Lee was strict but fair in his dealings with cadets. He did not enjoy discharging his duty; he described relieving those "found" at examination "the most unpleasant office I am called on to perform."[7] Once when he was out riding in the afternoon with his youngest son, they came upon a group of cadets at the bend in the road to Buttermilk Falls. The cadets leapt over the low wall and disappeared down the ravine. A minute later, Lee said, "Did you know those young men? But no!—if you did, don't say so. I wish boys would do what is right, it would be so much easier for all of us."[8]

Lee's objectivity was tested in December 1853, when five cadets faced court martial for liquor violations, among them Fitzhugh Lee, his nephew. Fitz Lee was decidedly cut from the "Walker" model more than the "Lee"—he was an Immortal of the Class of 1856 who amassed 197 demerits in his yearling year, 196 the next. A contemporary described him as "a sturdy, muscular and lively little giant . . . with a frank, affectionate disposition—he had a prevailing habit of irrepressible good humor which made any occasion of seriousness in him seem like affectation."[9] The only subject he excelled in was cavalry tactics. He was a daring, even reckless rider. He once ran a horse into Execution Hollow, where they both tumbled down the slope; then he leapt up and said to the animal, "Now, damn you, I hope you've had enough!"[10] In the case of the liquor violations, Superintendent Lee treated Fitz as though he were any other cadet. Fitz was found guilty, received harsh punishment, lost his furlough, but was not expelled. One night during his lost summer, Fitz slipped post and was caught in the act. He was certain to be relieved, but the Class of 1856 "took the pledge" not to repeat the offense. Lee withheld clemency until every member of the class agreed.

Fitz Lee was spared with the concurrence of the secretary of war. The previous secretary, Charles Conrad, was in the habit of overturning Superintendent Lee's directives, which undercut his authority. This changed with the election of Franklin Pierce and the appointment of a new war secretary in March 1853—Lee's old friend Jefferson Davis.

Davis was an active, forward-thinking and reform-minded secretary of war. He raised four new regiments, encouraged the development of new mounted rifle tactics (drawing from his wartime experience), sponsored the adoption of a rifled musket, undertook mapping expeditions of the Trans-Mississippi, and experimented with a camel corps for operations in the desert Southwest. Lee and Davis worked well together. Davis for the most part supported Lee's decisions, knowing that a strong Superintendent was important for the discipline of the Corps. However, when Lee had Rinsler's Rock wired for demolition to remove the ancient gathering place for mischief, Davis countermanded the order, probably for sentimental reasons. The rock remained in place until the 1890s.

Davis brought several reforms to the Academy, some more consequential than others. One of his first acts as secretary was to deny firsties the prerogative of growing whiskers from May 1 to graduation. A group of cadets petitioned him to reconsider, since it was a longstanding tradition and it made them look less youthful, so visitors attending graduation might not think them incapable of commanding bearded men. The Superintendent, Commandant and chief of engineers all supported the cadets. But Davis declined, saying that whiskers disturbed the Corps's uniformity of appearance and noting the absence of beards on such notables as Washington, Jackson, Taylor and Scott. By this time, the "kicking of the hats" had also fallen into disfavor, and graduation day had little official ceremony to speak of.

The most important of Davis's academic reforms was the switch to a five-year curriculum in August 1854. The incoming class was divided in two, half of which were to graduate in 1859. Robert E. Lee was a strong supporter of the five-year curriculum, and it had been recommended by the Academic Board and several Board of Visitors reports. But Thayer opposed it and had a dim view of Davis generally. "Neither [Davis] nor my opinion of him has changed since I knew him as a cadet," he wrote. "If I am not deceived, he intends to leave his mark in the Army and also at West Point and a black mark it will be I fear. He is a recreant and unnatural son, would have pleasure in giving his Alma Mater a kick and would disown her if he could."[11]

Davis's poor academic record became a stick for his political opponents. An anonymous letter to the *New York Times* in 1855 reviewed his indifferent standing in great detail and concluded that "the above facts show conclusively that he has no particular aptitude for either literary or scientific pursuits. He is indebted, for his present position, to his towering pride, great firmness and power of will, and good luck in escaping, but slightly scathed, the dangers of the battlefield; as in no position in which he has ever been placed, has he ever given evidence that he possesses more than fair mental abilities." An anonymous answer was published two weeks later, noting that while the system of merit at West Point was perhaps "as perfect as can be devised," the Academy "seeks not to extend it beyond its own limits," nor asks that graduates be rated years later by a scale "only to be found by ransacking its daily records." "Least of all," the writer concluded, "does it desire that these records shall be held up to public notice for the purpose of disowning the well-earned reputations of those of its *élèves* who have proved their capacities by the only sure tests—trial in the actual realities of life and faithful and brilliant services."[12]

By this time, the Academy was beginning to see many legacy cadets, sons of graduates from previous decades following in their fathers' footsteps. George W. C. Lee was one conspicuous example. William Emery Merrill, whose father Moses was an Immortal and classmate of Ephraim Kirby Smith's, and who died with him at Molino del Rey, graduated first in the Class of 1859. Kirby had once written to his brother Edmund, "the Army in our country is certainly not a desirable profession for any young man who has ability and perseverance to succeed in any other.... I by no means desire that *my* sons should ever wear a sword. I would certainly prefer that they become honest, industrious mechanics."[13] But his eldest son, Joseph Lee Kirby Smith, thought differently. He had been raised on frontier posts, idolized his father and his famous uncle, and saw military service as an honorable profession.[14] He entered West Point in 1853. Young Kirby Smith's experience at the Academy was nothing like his father's—he was well liked and attentive to his studies, and graduated sixth in the Class of 1857.

"Silicon is a gas ..."

JAMES MCNEILL WHISTLER WAS ANOTHER West Point legacy.[15] His father was George Washington Whistler, who graduated tenth in the Class of 1819. Whistler's grandfather was a British soldier of Irish birth who served under Burgoyne at Saratoga, and after discharge returned to America and joined the U.S. Army. George Whistler was born in Fort Wayne, Indiana, where his father was post commander. He was appointed to USMA from Kentucky when he was fourteen. He married Mary Roberdeau Swift, the younger sister of his classmate Captain William H. Swift, the Goat of their class. He later partnered with his West Point friend William Gibbs McNeill, Class of 1817, and worked on some of the first major railroad projects, including establishing the route for the Baltimore and Ohio. (Most of the pre–Civil War rail and canal routes were laid out by West Point graduates.) In 1833, the older Whistler resigned from the Army to work at the Locks and Canals Company in Lowell, Massachusetts, where he built locomotives. He designed the first American locomotive equipped with a steam whistle, which, coupled with the coincidence of his last name, led to the belief that he had invented it. (Actually it was invented in Britain.) After his first wife died, Whistler married William McNeill's sister, Anna Matilda. In 1834, their first child was born, James Abbott McNeill Whistler.[16]

In 1842, George Whistler accepted Tsar Nicholas I's invitation to build a railroad between St. Petersburg and Moscow, and moved his family to Russia. The project presented an engineering challenge since the tsar had decreed that the railroad run in a perfectly straight line between the two cities. Legend has it that he placed a ruler on a map and drew the line himself. However, his thumb bumped the pencil, causing a slight jog in the line, which planners faithfully recreated rather than dare question the tsar's hand-drawn route. The work was difficult, mostly because of the intrigues and jealousies of the Russian court, which Whistler was ill disposed and ill equipped to handle. He died of cholera in St. Petersburg in 1849, before the project was finished.[17]

James Whistler, then fifteen, was offered a chance to enter the Russian Imperial School for Pages. His mother decided instead to return to her home in Connecticut and seek admission for James to West Point. In December 1850, Whistler's tutor, Roswell Park, top man in the Class of 1831 and former West Point chaplain who went on to become a noted clergyman, wrote an appeal to President Millard Fillmore seeking an at-large appointment for the boy, which was granted. "Little Jimmy"

Whistler entered West Point on July 1, 1851, ten days shy of his seventeenth birthday.

Whistler took a relaxed view of Academy life. His roommate, Henry M. Lazelle, called him "one of the most indolent of mortals. But his was a most charming laziness, always doing that which was most agreeable to others and himself." During the day he would rather make sketches than attend to his lessons. During evening study sessions Lazelle would look up from his book invariably to find Whistler sitting upright, asleep. Like Henry Heth, Whistler was intelligent but unmotivated. He had enough education to pass most subjects with little effort, albeit at very low rank. Lazelle's academic record was hardly better: he was a turnback, and an Immortal of the Class of 1855 who graduated fifth from the bottom. Like many Immortals, however, Lazelle went on to confound his doubters. He was severely wounded fighting Indians in 1859, brevetted for gallantry as a Union officer in the Civil War, and he returned to West Point as Commandant of Cadets, 1879–82, following in the tradition of William H. T. Walker.

Whistler was bold in his occasional ignorance. At a history exam when asked the date of the Battle of Buena Vista, he confessed that he did not know. "What!" the instructor said. "You do not know the date of the Battle of Buena Vista? Suppose you were to go out to dinner and the company began to talk of the Mexican War, and you, a West Point man, were asked the date of the battle. What would you do?"

"Do?" Whistler replied with hauteur. "Why, I should refuse to associate with people who could talk of such things at dinner!"

Whistler was not imposing physically. He was short, thin and nearsighted. This might have accounted in part for his remarkably poor horsemanship. One day when he went tumbling over his mount's head, the instructor, Major Sackett, observed, "Mr. Whistler, I am pleased to see you for once at the head of your class." ("But I did it gracefully," Whistler later recounted.) The horse in question was named Quaker— "No friend to me," Whistler observed, and in fact no friend to any cadet. The horse was so ill tempered it was periodically withdrawn from the training squadron. But Quaker, the same horse that Fitz Lee had tumbled down Execution Hollow, posed a challenge to the more adventurous cadets. Whistler remained skeptical of horses generally, and after falling from a mount three times, he said, "I don't see how people can ever ride for pleasure."[18]

Whistler was occasionally in poor health, and was so sick with rheumatism he was unable to take his second-year examinations with the rest of his class. The cadets called him "Curly" because of the thick, curly black hair that he insisted on wearing longer than regulations allowed. He tried to cajole Old Joe the barber into letting him keep some of his locks at the required monthly trimming, but Joe stuck to the regulations, causing Whistler some angst later in front of the mirror.

Whistler was one of the group of cadets privileged to mess with Mrs. Thompson, then quite advanced in age. He lost his rights when, as one story goes, Mrs. Thompson caught him flirting with the maid. He explained that he was just looking for his cat, an implausible tale since cadets were not allowed to keep pets. Another story has it that the precipitating event was a joke he arranged in which the cadets came to the dinner table claiming there was a cat on the roof, each new cadet adding a cat until Whistler arrived, claiming there were twelve cats. Mrs. Thompson failed to see the humor. Allegedly he got back in her good graces by looking admiringly at the portrait of the late Colonel Thompson that hung in the parlor, and saying aloud, as though to himself (but knowing she was within earshot), "To think that West Point should have produced such a man, and that we have his portrait here to remind us of what we ourselves may attain to!"

Whistler's forte at the Academy was drawing. Having begun sketching at the age of four, he quickly established himself as a talent, ranking at the head of his drawing class. He was fond of his own work and not given to having it altered. One day when he was sketching a peasant girl in art class, Professor Weir stopped to examine the composition. The professor then went to his desk and filled a brush with ink—Weir was an inveterate editor of his students' work—and moved back towards Whistler. The young artist saw him coming, raised his hands and said, "Oh, don't sir, don't! You'll spoil it!"

Like Poe, Whistler developed a reputation as a prankster, an afterhours cook, and a daring soul who was always willing to "run it" to Benny Havens'. As Poe with his satirical poems, Whistler became known for his comedic sketches. He would take the opportunity to make drawings wherever he went, on loose paper, in books, on tent flaps, desks or stools. In 1852 a Whistler drawing decorated the dance cards for the academy ball, and he sketched the cover for sheet music to "Song of a Graduate."[19] George Ruggles (USMA 1855), brevetted four times in the Civil War and present at Appomattox, recalled Whistler's "keen sense of the ridiculous. In the recitation room, at church and almost everywhere . . . he would sketch, in a second or two, cartoons full of character and displaying the utmost nicety of appreciation of its ludicrous points." In the summer of 1852 he produced a four-frame sequence entitled "On Post in Camp." In the first drawing, "First half hour," a cadet stands at attention with his musket shouldered. The second half hour shows him leaning against the tree, checking his watch. In the third half hour he sits at the base of the tree, and in the last half hour he is sound asleep. Whistler would depict cadets, members of the faculty and young women, but rarely landscapes—allegedly because of his nearsightedness he was not as enchanted with the Academy vistas. Some of his early studies of women involved Maria "Kitty" Bailey, daughter of Jacob Whitman Bailey, the professor of chemistry, with whom Whistler had made friends. He sketched Kitty at the Bailey house during free time on weekends. Tragically, Kitty and her mother both perished on the steamboat *Henry Clay* when it caught fire on the Hudson in July 1852. Professor Bailey and his son, William, survived.

It was inevitable that the artist and dandy would have romances at the Academy. He left a fragment extolling the virtues of "little 'Em' ": "a beauty by Jove! The belle of the Point!" who had "large, languishing deep black eyes" and "such beautiful, *really* beautiful rich red lips … delicious lips—not a bad resting place either—*parole d'honneur!* and when I last heard her 'Goodbye' I was 'right sorry' to leave them!"

Whistler showed the same talent for barrack-room barratry as Jefferson Davis. One cold morning he was on surveying duty with some other cadets and decided he'd rather be in the warm barracks. He made his way back unseen by way of a ditch. But an impromptu roll call found him missing, and he was written up. When shown the report, Whistler said, "Have I your permission to speak?"

"Speak on, Cadet Whistler," the officer said.

"You have reported me, sir," he began, "for being absent from parade without the knowledge or permission of my instructor. Well, now, if I was absent without your knowledge or permission, how did you know I was absent?" The officer was so amused by the defense that the report was dropped. But despite his wayward ways, Whistler was a man of honor. Once he and Lazelle had just finished playing cards after taps when Captain Edmund Kirby Smith, the inspecting officer, walked in. The cards were on the table and Kirby Smith saw them. He said that he would write the cadets up for "cards in possession" rather than the greater offense of "playing cards," since he had not actually seen them playing.

"No sir," Whistler said, "we had been playing." For his honesty, he and Lazelle lost their cadet furloughs.

Whistler was popular with cadets and faculty alike, and the son of a West Point legend. But no cadet can escape the consequences of low grades and high demerits. In his plebe year Whistler ranked in the bottom ten of his class overall, though was in the top ten in French. He had 190 demerits, which brought him close to expulsion. His offenses were for the most part not serious—inattentiveness, lateness, careless-ness, the kind of thing one would expect. In his yearling year, he was not examined in most subjects due to ill health, but ranked first in his class in drawing. He brought his demerits down to 168, hardly respectable but leaving a greater margin for error.

Fate struck in his third year. At the final chemistry examination, Whistler was asked to discuss silicon.

"I am required to discuss silicon," he began. "Silicon is a gas . . ."

"That will be all," the instructor said, and Whistler was marked deficient.[20] The Academic Board voted to expel him. It was rare for a cadet to be found in the third year, and Whistler was mortified. On July 1, 1854, he wrote a lengthy letter to Secretary of War Davis asking for a reexamination. He argued that his overall grade point average was higher than some cadets who had not been dismissed, and that while he "certainly did not do well" in chemistry, he had only failed one recita-tion, which could happen to anybody. It was also true that he had many demerits, but none were "vicious nor immoral." He said that after three years at the Academy, "all my hopes and aspirations are connected with that Institution and the Army, and that by not passing, all my future prospects are ruined for life."

Davis referred the letter to General Totten, the chief of engineers, who handed the matter to Superintendent Lee. On July 8, Lee wrote a detailed memo to Totten about Whistler's case. It was true that Whistler's grade point average was higher than some of those who were not dismissed, in part because he ranked first in drawing. But he had been declared deficient by a unanimous vote of the Academic Board. Further, Lee had shown Whistler every courtesy in trying to deal fairly with his delinquencies. In the last four months of 1853, Whistler had amassed 136 demerits, which was enough to expel him (at this time a cadet could not accumulate more than 100 per semester), but Lee reviewed the records with the reporting officers and was able to elim-inate 39 of the lesser demerits. Whistler's lax behavior in January 1854 showed that he had not appreciated Lee's efforts, and the Superinten-dent personally cautioned the young artist to mend his ways. In June, Whistler was again over the limit, and Lee reviewed the record. He found enough cause to remove 25 demerits, but Whistler was still 21 over the semester limit and had a year's total of 218. "I can therefore do nothing more in his behalf," Lee wrote, "nor do I know of anything entitling him to further indulgence. I can only regret that one so capable of doing well should so have neglected himself and must now suffer the penalty."[21] Davis concurred, and Whistler's expulsion stood. When Whistler departed West Point, Professor Weir observed that "with only the most ordinary industry [he] would make a name as an artist."[22]

Whistler always looked back fondly on his experience at West Point. He said he looked "dandy in gray," and he spoke highly of Academy discipline and the honor code. After he became famous, he presented a book to the West Point library inscribed, "From an Old Cadet, whose pride is to remember his West Point days." Later in life he reflected on the examination that had cost him his military career. "If silicon had been a gas," he said, "I would have been a Major General."

"I am the Bison"

JOHN C. TIDBALL, WRITING in the 1880s, noted the story of Cadet Thomas Freeman McKinney McLean, who by then had become "a sort of mythological character" at the Academy. He was better known as Bison McLean or simply as Old Bison. "So remarkable was Bison's career as a cadet," Tidball wrote, "that he has been handed down as one of the traditions of the Academy. Yet but few knew . . . his full history, and he is probably now regarded by many as a purely mythical being—a sort of Jack the Giant-Killer."[23]

Bison came to West Point from Smithland, Missouri. He was a nephew of John McLean, senator from Illinois, who no doubt was helpful in securing his appointment. The scruffy westerner got his nickname the day he arrived on post:

> When coming up river he lost his hat, blown from the steamer, arrived at West Point, carrying his all in a pair of leather saddle bags, slung over his shoulder, he struck straight across the plain towards the barrack. His frowzy, yellow hair gave his head a shaggy appearance, heightened by a scraggy beard on a pair of broad round jaws, as yet untouched by razor. A cadet seeing him from a window of barracks, at once spotted him as a new cadet, and calling to him, inquired from whence he came. Being answered, from Missouri, (then the land of the bison) the cadet replied "Oh yes, a bison!" and immediately yelled out "turn out to see the bison!" Whereupon every window was immediately filled with jeering faces.

Bison was six feet tall and heavy, not muscular-looking but very powerful. "He could ride like a Centaur and leap like a kangaroo,"

Tidball said. He had small, gray, deep-set eyes, pale skin, and scars on his face from fights in Texas when he was a youngster. Intelligent and studious, he stood in the first section in all his subjects and racked up few demerits his first two years.[24] Bison was something of a loner, though friendly and affable when the occasion called for it. He could be a good comrade, but when angered he could fly into a rage.

Shortly before his class was to leave on summer furlough, Bison was reported for "losing step marching to the mess hall" by Cadet Captain David R. Jones of Georgia. This was a minor offense, the type usually committed by plebes, somewhat embarrassing for a yearling. For some reason, Bison was outraged. The following afternoon he found Jones strolling with some friends on the Plain and proceeded to beat him thoroughly. "The friends of Jones sprang to his assistance," Tidball wrote, "but these Bison cast from him, throwing them against trees and fences, as a terrier handling rats in a pit." Bison lost his furlough because of the incident, and while his classmates were away he befriended William H. Morris of the Class of 1850, "a blasé youth from New York City who, although a scion of respectable lineage, was accomplished in all the wickedness of the town."

Bison and Morris began to get into various forms of trouble, chiefly "running it" to Buttermilk Falls, not so much to patronize Benny Havens' as to consort with townswomen. Bison became notorious locally, and the citizens formed a vigilance committee against him. "He became a terror to all the maids and matrons roundabout," Tidball wrote. "He grew in reputation until he became a sort of tantrabogus, or bug-a-boo, of this part of the Highlands, and mothers subdued their unruly urchins by threatening to give them to the Bison." Allegedly he "ruined a pretty girl," Effie Conklin, under false promise of marriage. Sergeant Owens couldn't catch him. Others tried and failed. The few times he slipped up, he invented plausible stories to evade severe punishment. Sometimes the excuses were exaggerations, other times flat-out lies. His reputation was well known on the post. In one of Reverend Sprole's sermons he called on Bison, with intended irony, to describe the conditions of a thoroughly depraved mind.

Despite these escapades, Bison maintained his grades, though not as high as they had been. He ranked 20th in his third year, down seven from the year before, doing best in philosophy (11th) and with only 80 demerits. He also did well in his final year, coming in 11th in engineering, the most challenging of the courses. Nevertheless, his conduct caught up with him. In mid-May 1848 he had 222 demerits. Then he racked up 36 more for being off post and for breach of arrest. Bison was brought before a general court martial in June, where he faced many charges, dating back months. They paint a picture of a cadet who for some reason had simply given up. Bison went to Buttermilk Falls without leave May 4, 5, 6, 7, 9 and 11. He was charged with being "in company with two girls of bad fame" on May 6 and "was seen in company with a girl of ill fame, in open day," on May 7 (found not guilty on both charges). After these events he was confined to his room, but breached arrest by visiting other cadets on May 17 and 18. He was also accused of having lied to get out of previous charges, and was found guilty of enough of these matters to be dismissed.[25] He was relieved from duty June 22, by which time he had already departed, and was officially dismissed August 7, 1848.[26]

Bison McLean left West Point in disgrace, but his myth was just beginning. He was soon reported brawling in Galveston, Texas, and on a California steamer heading for the gold fields. He was said to have been shown a secret gold mine in Arizona, the "Lost Yuma," by an Aravaipa Apache chief named Eskiminzin, which is still being sought today. But most colorful and enduring were the stories that placed Bison McLean living among and fighting alongside the Indians.

In 1850, Captain Nathaniel Lyon (USMA 1841) went on a punitive expedition to Clear Lake and Russian River in California. On September 26, 1849, Indians had killed Captain William H. Warner (USMA 1836) in the Sierra Nevada while he was searching for a suitable railroad route. He had been pierced with nine arrows. Captain Lyon fought two skirmishes with hostiles during his excursion, one of them on an island in the Colorado River. Some believed the Indians were commanded by Bison McLean, who was seeking vengeance against the Academy. In the summer of 1852, another West Pointer encountered Bison with the Gila Apache Indians, where he had been adopted and "had a wife or two." The account stated, "At this meeting he declared to me that he would never forget nor forgive the injustice and injuries he had received from his classmates and the academic authorities at West Point."[27]

Another alleged Bison sighting took place in 1858. Lieutenant Joseph C. Ives (USMA 1852, fifth in his class, later architect and engineer of the Washington Monument, Confederate colonel and President Davis's aide-de-camp, 1863–65), was exploring the Colorado River and the Grand Canyon. His expedition followed a previous one by George Derby.[28] One day some Mojave Indians came into his camp and they spoke awhile in Spanish. The chief then said in English, "How does it come, Ives, you're not wearing the uniform? You didn't fall down at the Point, did you?"

"Great Scott!" Ives cried. "What do you know about the Point?"

"Ives, do you know me?" the chief said. The Indian leader was half-naked, with feathers in his hair and rings in his nose and ears, but he spoke perfect English. Ives looked closely but did not recognize him. "I am the Bison," the chief said. "We were at West Point." He explained that his band had wanted to kill Ives and his men, but Bison convinced them that it would be best to let them finish the survey—it was more lucrative to rob the boats that would come later to trade.[29]

The myth of Bison McLean reached its pinnacle after the Custer massacre in 1876, when the story began to circulate—promoted by Cadmus Wilcox of the Class of 1846—that Sitting Bull was actually Bison. Not much was known about Sitting Bull at the time, and little still is certain about his early life. One proponent of the theory stated that "to the close observer, Sitting Bull has shown as much skill and judgment as an educated civilized soldier could have done. It would not be strange if Sitting Bull proves to have been educated at West Point, and it seems to us probable that this is the case."[30] Alas, the myth had finally outrun reality. According to a story in the *St. Louis Republican* written after Little Bighorn, Thomas F. M. McLean was killed by Indians near Tubac, Arizona, around 1870. This was confirmed by Lieutenant William Preble Hall (USMA 1868) of the Fifth Cavalry, who was with General Crook in Arizona at the time and knew Bison's relatives in Missouri. "Of Bison I suppose it may be said that his greatest fault was that of having an ungovernable temper," Hall said, "which he knew and which no doubt led him to pass his life beyond the confines of civilization. . . . As to who Sitting Bull is, the writer of this does not know. But certain it is that he is not Bison."[31]

William Logan Crittenden

WILLIAM LOGAN CRITTENDEN, THE GOAT of the Class of 1845, had fought well in Mexico, but had not received a brevet or attained the recognition he felt he deserved. One of his classmates and fellow officers said he was "a brave, fearless officer—I may say a somewhat reckless fellow."[1] Lucy Holcombe, a renowned Texas belle and Crittenden's fiancée, gave a more sympathetic description:

> [He] must have been in early youth very beautiful; for the free careless grace of childhood still lingered on the bold brow of the man, though passion had pressed its pallor on his cheek. The lines around the mouth denoted thought, even care; and the smile of the lip, though sweet, was uncertain. It was a frank and generous face ... [with] large fearless eyes, with their half tender, half defiant charm.[2]

Seeing no future as a career officer in peacetime, Crittenden resigned his commission in March 1849 to seek more profitable opportunities as a mercenary. He was certainly well qualified, being young, ambitious, West Point trained and experienced in war. The years after the Mexican War were a time of ferment in Latin America, hence a time of opportunity for men with military experience and a sense of adventure. To some young men the war was an inspiration: if a relatively small army of Americans could humble mighty Mexico, what might others do in the less powerful, less stable countries to the south? A journalist and adventurer named William Walker—no relation to William H. T. Walker—"conquered" Baja California, then landed in Nicaragua with a group of fifty-eight followers calling themselves "the Immortals" and established himself temporarily as Emperor. These and other mercenaries were called "filibusters," a term originally used to refer to Caribbean pirates.[3]

Crittenden joined a group seeking to liberate Cuba from Spanish

133

rule, led by a tall, white-haired, distinguished-looking Spaniard, General Narciso Lopez, who was born in 1799 to an aristocratic landowning family in Venezuela. They had been driven from the country by Bolivar's rebels around 1815 and emigrated to Cuba. Young Lopez pursued a career in the Spanish Army, rising to the rank of general, and commander in chief of the Spanish National Guards. He was a dashing officer, a natural leader with an aristocratic air: tall, dark-complexioned, with gleaming black eyes. "A face once seen, never forgotten," one observer noted.[4]

Lopez became involved in the Cuban independence movement and joined a plot to foment revolution. An abortive uprising in June 1848 sent him to the United States for sanctuary. His lands were confiscated, and in March 1849 a Spanish court condemned him to death *in absentia*. In exile, Lopez worked tirelessly for the revolution, supported by American backers with financial interests on the island. He met with politicians, opinion makers and others whose support might benefit Cuban liberation. Speaking through translators, he painted a picture of the island on the brink of rebellion, its people oppressed, one-third of the island enslaved.[5] He produced letters written by eminent Cubans pleading for assistance. If five hundred men would accompany him to Cuba, he said, they would be joined by ten times that many Cuban patriots. This would set off a general uprising in all parts of the country, and Captain General Concha and his Spanish government would be driven out.

Militarily the idea had some promise. The coastline was long and lightly garrisoned, and it would be difficult to defend the island against invasion by *filibustros*. Mountains in the interior could provide sanctuary, and poor internal communications would hamper the Spanish response. However, the situation in Cuba was more complex than Lopez let on. There were 1.3 million citizens, of whom 730,000 were free whites and persons of color, the other 570,000 slaves of African origin.[6] Opinion in Cuba was intricate and many-layered, with different groups holding varying opinions about Spain, slavery, independence, and the possibility of annexation by the United States. Cuba had seen 340 years of Spanish rule. It was one of the last outposts of a once great empire in the Western Hemisphere, which had stretched from the tip of South America to San Francisco, from Florida to California. But the Spanish Empire had been gutted by revolution and corruption, dwindling to a few possessions, the largest of which was this "coral bound jewel of the Antilles." Loyalist Cubans, mainly landed and wealthy, opposed independence. Others might have favored it but feared that without Spanish protection Cuba would be absorbed by the United States, or worse, by Britain, which would mean the immediate emancipation of their slaves. Only a small group of educated liberals, nationalists and American expatriates actively favored annexation, though to speak openly about it could court the charge of treason.

Americans had eyed Cuba with interest for decades. Thomas Jefferson and John Quincy Adams had seen Cuba as a potential strategic asset, bringing with it command of the Caribbean. In an 1823 letter to President James Monroe, Jefferson called Cuba "the most interesting addition which could ever be made to our system of states."[7] There was some fear that Cuba might fall to imperial Britain, as Gibraltar had. President James Polk counseled annexation, and Secretary of State James Buchanan sought unsuccessfully to purchase it. Some of those who supported Lopez were idealists, caught up in the spirit of liberal revolution then sweeping Europe. There was a popular mania for the Hungarians, who declared independence from Austria in 1848, and some called for U.S. intervention. (The mania was as short-lived as the Hungarian republic, which was quickly extinguished by Russian military intervention.) The slavery issue also hung over the debate. As with Texas, southern politicians supported annexing Cuba as a way of increasing the number of slave states and maintaining parity in the Senate. John Calhoun made this argument in 1848.[8] Time was of the essence because there were persistent rumors that Spain was on the verge of proclaiming emancipation, and it would be much easier, they thought, to assume control of an existing subject population than to have to reintroduce slavery.

Lopez appealed to all these interests, even when they were contradictory; but he knew that without military assistance the rebellion would not succeed. He first sought to recruit William Worth to lead the expedition. Worth was renowned for his exploits in Mexico and would lend prestige to the venture, as well as attract American volunteers. Worth expressed interest, and President Polk worked behind the scenes to supply materiel support. Unfortunately, Worth died in May of 1849. By then, Polk had been succeeded by Zachary Taylor, who opposed aggression against Cuba and a few weeks into his presidency issued a proclamation that called the planning of such measures "in the highest degree criminal, as tending to endanger the peace and compromise the honor of this nation."[9] He noted that the Neutrality Act of 1818 forbad private citizens from launching international military expeditions, and he pledged that his administration intended to enforce the law.

Lopez was undeterred. Around February 1850, seeking a replacement for Worth, he met with another hero of the late war with Mexico,

Senator Jefferson Davis. He offered Davis command of the expedition at a salary of $100,000, with another $100,000 or a coffee plantation after Cuba had been liberated. Davis declined the offer, but suggested that Lopez meet with another of the war's notables, his friend Colonel Robert E. Lee, then stationed in Baltimore. Lee gave the proposal serious consideration and discussed it at length with Davis. But he too turned it down, reasoning that he "had been educated in the service of the United States, and felt it wrong to accept place in the army of a foreign power while he held a commission."[10] The revolutionaries also approached Governor Quitman of Mississippi, a Mexican War hero, and General Edward G. W. Butler (USMA 1820), a ward of Andrew Jackson's who lived in Louisiana. While sympathetic to the cause, neither desired to take the command. Finally Lopez decided to lead the expedition himself, and he began seeking funds and volunteers.

Crittenden joined Lopez on his recruiting drive, using the experience he had gained while temporarily on recruiting duty during the Mexican War. He helped raise filibuster units across the country, particularly in Kentucky, Mississippi and Louisiana. Other volunteers signed up in Boston, Baltimore and New Orleans. Many of them were Mexican War veterans who wanted to see more action. Liberal Spanish-language newspapers fanned the enthusiasm, and pro-liberation and pro-annexation clubs (usually called *juntas*) were formed in the United States with Cuban and American members.[11]

Lopez launched his invasion in May 1850. Crittenden, still recruiting, was slated to join the expedition leading reinforcements. Lopez landed at Cárdenas with five hundred men, overwhelmed the Spanish garrison, and intended to march to Havana, rallying peasants from the countryside as he went. But the people, while hospitable, were not enthusiastic. After a futile twelve hours trying to stimulate rebellion, and facing increasing restiveness among his American troops, Lopez loaded his forces back aboard ship and withdrew. They raced Spanish ships all the way up to the entrance to the harbor at Key West. Most of Lopez's men abandoned the cause, but the public, especially in the South, hailed the general as a hero.[12] The Taylor administration, on the other hand, was embarrassed. Lopez was arrested and placed on trial in the federal district court in New Orleans.[13] Crittenden testified as a defense witness. He was then working at the Customs House in New Orleans, recruiting volunteers, collecting intelligence and easing the movement of people and supplies for the filibusters. Three juries failed to convict Lopez, and southern public opinion was in his favor. The charges were dropped and Lopez went free.

On April 25, 1851, President Millard Fillmore, who took office when Zachary Taylor died in July 1850, issued a strong statement against filibusters thinking about new expeditions. Lopez meanwhile carried on with preparations for a second invasion. He promised to pay each recruit $2,000 to $4,000. He raised money by issuing bonds against public lands in Cuba, under his authority as "Chief of the 'Patriotic Junta' for the promotion of the political interests of Cuba," "contemplated head of the Provisional Government," and "commander in chief of the revolutionary movement." By the summer he had assembled another force of around five hundred men. They came from every state, as well as from England, Ireland, Germany, Hungary, Poland, France and Canada. They had worked in many occupations: clerks, carpenters, drivers, farmers, merchants, boatmen and laborers. Lopez again commanded, with a staff featuring some noted Hungarian expatriates, such as his chief of staff General Pragay, a famous commander in his day, and other officers whom Pragay had fought with in Europe. The steamer *Pampero* was readied to take them to Cuba sometime in mid-August.

Through his post at the Customs House, Crittenden learned that the *Pampero* was to be seized by government agents on Monday, August 4, three days hence. Lopez pushed his timetable forward to be away the night before: He moved the ship to Lafayette, Louisiana, where it was loaded with supplies and the troops assembled. More men had volunteered than the ship could hold, so one company had to stay behind to serve as the second wave of the invasion. Lopez departed at four in the afternoon, to the cheers of hundreds of well-wishers who had gathered on the pier.

The *Pampero* carried slightly more than four hundred men, divided into three nominal regiments of three companies each. Crittenden commanded the First Regiment of Artillery, a notional designation since they had no cannon with them, although there were a few howitzers in Florida they hoped to bring later. Colonel Downman commanded the First Infantry Regiment, and Captain Oberto commanded the forty-nine-member First Regiment of Cuban Patriots, which was expected to swell with recruits once they arrived on the island. Conditions aboard the *Pampero* were disordered. The speedy departure accounted for it in part, but the inexperience of the soldiers also showed. They brought far more baggage than necessary—trunks, barrels and boxes crowded the deck. General Pragay, standing amidst the men, said he had been in forty-eight battles in Hungary and had never taken more with him than the clothes on his back, "two shirts, two pairs of drawers and stockings, two handkerchiefs, a cloak, a pair of pistols, this sword, which has faithfully defended me in all dangers, a spy-glass and a pocket compass." He said they would soon regret bringing so much.

Given the likelihood of being intercepted by Spanish patrols, the volunteers were drilled to take cover at the sound of the alarm, "Yankee Doodle." They also learned techniques to repel boarders. But several days passed without incident. The men cleaned and readied their muskets and complained about the rations. As the *Pampero* neared Key West on the ninth, it became clear from the amount of coal they had used that the ship was leaking steam. Lopez knew that even with more fuel he could not make it to his planned landing point on the south shore in the Central Department. After hastily coaling in Key West, Lopez altered his plan. He decided to make straight across to Bahia Honda, fifty miles west of Havana, where according to some Creoles he spoke to in port there were active pockets of rebellion. He knew the area, since his former plantation was not far inland. They made the passage in darkness, navigating by the stars. But they strayed off course and dawn found them heading directly into Havana Harbor. "Yankee Doodle" sounded and the soldiers took cover. The *Pampero* came around quickly and steamed away, Lopez expecting Spanish warships to appear at any minute in quick pursuit.

They made for Las Palmitas, sixty miles west of Havana. The site looked good: no patrol ships in sight. As they neared the disembarkation point, the men donned their new uniforms, blue shirts and gray trousers. The force landed at midnight, August 12. They were unobserved and unopposed—the only gunfire was a musket shot fired into the air from the first landing boat. It took four hours to complete the transfer of men and equipment. Lopez and his staff came on the last boat. The general was dressed in a trim white coat and trousers, a red sash around his waist. His face showed expectation and excitement. He hopped ashore, knelt down and kissed the ground. "*Querida Cuba*," he said, "Beloved Cuba."

The *Pampero* left immediately to return to New Orleans to pick up the second wave of troops, the howitzers and supplies. Lopez was confident he had achieved surprise and decided to make his way inland towards the hilltop hamlet of Las Pozas, twelve miles distant, where he believed the rebels would be waiting to join his force. He took 280 men, leaving 110 under the command of Crittenden in charge of the baggage train, with orders to follow in a few hours once wagons could be found.

Lopez reached Las Pozas at two in the afternoon and found it largely deserted. There were no rebels, and only a few curious townsmen who had stayed behind while the rest of the village fled. Lopez was disappointed, though he did not show it. He assured his men that the rebels were farther inland, and they would link up with them in the mountains. He was confident that he was not in immediate danger, either because he felt that he commanded the road over which he had moved or because Spanish troops would take a long time to reach them. He sent carts back to Crittenden and advised him to abandon the heaviest baggage and come up swiftly to unite the force for the move towards the mountains. Then they waited.

By the next morning, Crittenden had still not arrived. Lopez's men were taking breakfast when a volley was fired from a house on the edge of the village. The men scrambled for their weapons and hastily formed into their units. Lopez deployed his forces for battle, scarcely able to believe the Spaniards had already found him. But in fact Captain General Concha had received reports of the *Pampero*'s wayward voyage along the Cuban coast the previous day and had sent several columns to encircle the area he thought most likely to be Lopez's landing zone. He guessed well. Seven Spanish companies had arrived at Bahia Honda at two in the morning and marched through the night to reach Las Pozas, picking up the road Lopez had taken just north of the town. The Spanish forces were under the command of the dashing General Don Manuel Ena. His second in command, Colonel Nadal, had known Lopez in earlier years and considered him a friend, and hoped he could talk the old general out of this escapade.

Ena had achieved surprise, but quickly lost his advantage. Lopez's small force of Cuban volunteers charged the enemy soldiers in the house and drove them from their position. They spread out to other buildings on the edge of town and picked off soldiers in the main body of Spanish troops, who were advancing in the open. Ena sought to exploit his superior numbers and made two charges in column directly up the road into the town. Both were repulsed bloodily, under the cool and accurate fire of the American volunteers. The fighting went on for several hours. The Spaniards were well trained but tired from their forced march and thirty hours without sleep. The filibusters made up for their inexperience with enthusiasm, firepower and brave leadership. Lopez acquitted himself in his usual dashing manner—his cheers of *"Bravo Americano!"* and his limited English vocabulary of "Fire!" and "Go ahead, boys!" sounded over the battlefield.

General Ena withdrew his forces to the north, along the road where Lopez had advanced. Two filibuster companies followed them from a distance for several miles, eventually giving up the chase and returning to the village. The volunteers were flush with their victory over the Spaniards, but concerned that Crittenden had not joined them, and they still awaited the promised rebel army. Lopez sent five volunteers with messages for Crittenden warning him of the danger and urging him to try to reach Las Pozas before midnight. Then he readied to move south towards the mountains.

At eleven o'clock, Captain Kelly and his company from Crittenden's command arrived with chilling news. They had fought a battle, and Kelly and his men were the only ones in the column to escape destruction. Lopez decided to move without delay. He was forced to leave the wounded, including the officers, Pragay and Gotay, who were later killed by the Spanish. Lopez headed for the mountains; he told his men that there they would find patriots and they should not give up hope.

But there were no rebel bands; and within a few weeks, Spanish forces rounded up Lopez and his tattered army. The Americans were sent to Spain in chains to work at hard labor in the mines at Ceuta, an island off the coast of North Africa, but Lopez had been under a death sentence since 1849. He was taken to Havana, and on September 1, 1851, a large crowd assembled to watch the execution. Captain General Concha made a vitriolic speech, calling Lopez a traitor to Spain and to Cuba. Nevertheless, Lopez maintained his composure to the end, showing no fear and bearing himself on the platform with great dignity. He was executed by garrote. He was seated in a chair, the strangulation device fitted around his neck, the executioner behind him. At Concha's behest, the crowd watched in silence. Lopez's last words were, "My death will not change the destinies of Cuba."[14] The executioner turned the wheel, the crowd heard a loud crack, and Lopez's head fell forward to his chest.

"I will die like a man."

CRITTENDEN HAD BEGUN HIS MOVE inland the day Lopez fought the Spanish at Las Pozas. He had been delayed by the search for transport and was unaware of the Spanish threat. The oversize baggage train slowed his advance, as did the local oxen, which had been hard to find and were difficult to drive. "We traveled at the rate of about one mile an hour," one of Crittenden's men wrote, "every hundred yards the oxen refusing to draw, and the Americans expending a great many oaths and useless blows from the butts of their muskets upon the backs of the weary animals."[15] They lightened the load by tossing out the large carpetbags and trunks that should never have been brought in the first place, "belonging to those who expected to dress in patent leather boots and the latest French style of clothing" upon entering Havana.[16] As Pragay had predicted, they had come to regret it.

Halfway to Las Pozas, Crittenden halted the train, determined to find more oxen. Captain Kerr's company formed a foraging party and moved several hundred yards ahead, stopping at a tavern by the road. They decided to take a short break, and sought refreshments. While they were resting, musket fire erupted from the brush. They had made contact with the northern edge of Ena's column. The Americans quickly took defensive positions in the tavern, repulsing several Spanish attempts to rush them. The men down the road heard the rapid musket fire and grabbed their weapons, running towards the battle whooping and howling. They joined the force in the tavern and poured fire onto the enemy. Seeing they were outmatched, the Spanish retreated to join another unit on an overlooking hill and began firing down into the tavern yard.

Crittenden soon realized his position was untenable. He had no idea how far away Lopez was, whether he would hear the battle and march to their relief. He also did not know how many Spanish forces he was facing, whether enemy reinforcements were en route, or how secure his flanks were. If he stayed in the tavern yard, his men would be picked off one by one, and the column would probably wind up surrounded when more enemy troops arrived. The only certainty was that if he did nothing, he would be defeated. Therefore, he decided to attack. He formed two companies of about twenty-five men each, leaving Captain Kelly's command to hold the rear and secure the baggage train. He led the attack force out of the tavern yard and moved quickly into the brush by the road, attempting to flank the forces on the hill.

For an hour, Kelly's men suffered sniping from the Spanish. Crittenden was nowhere to be seen. They held a council and decided it would be best to abandon the tavern and the baggage train and make for a distant copse of trees to the east. Kelly agreed. The whole group hightailed out of the tavern, into the brush, and was gone.[17]

Meanwhile, Crittenden had undertaken a complex flanking maneuver that slowly brought him up unseen behind the Spanish on the hill. His men attacked with fury and drove the enemy south up the road to Las Pozas. Crittenden then returned to the tavern to find Kelly and his men gone, but where or how he did not know. He assessed his situation: half of his small command had vanished; he was in hostile territory, with unknown numbers of enemy on his flanks. Spaniards, commanding the road, stood between him and Lopez, who had not come to his assistance. Lopez's main body had disappeared into the interior, and for all he knew, it had been wiped out. The promised peasant uprising had not materialized; in fact, they had seen few Cubans at all, and none of them looked particularly interested in being liberated. The filibuster was finished. What mattered now was survival. Crittenden could not risk returning to port directly, since he suspected that Spanish cavalry patrols would soon be after them. He abandoned the baggage and took cover in the thick brush off the main road, which in time was swarming with Spaniards, as he expected. Crittenden and his men stayed hidden for a day and a half until the enemy troops moved on. Then, tired, hungry and despondent, they made their way furtively back to the shore. Crittenden commandeered four small fishing boats, and he and his men set sail for Florida.

The small flotilla was spotted in the late afternoon of August 15, near Levisa Key, by the Spanish warship *Habanero*. The weak, dehydrated men were apprehended without a fight, taken to Havana and transferred to the ship *Esperanza*. They sat on the deck, their hands bound tightly, while their fates were deliberated. The Spanish gave the fifty-one filibusters a perfunctory trial and condemned them to die at noon the next day.

On the morning of August 16, 1851, the American prisoners aboard the *Esperanza* were unbound and given pen, ink and paper. They were allowed the opportunity, if they wished, to write letters to their families, which would also serve as their confessions. Crittenden wrote to his friend Lucien Hensley, explaining, "I have not the heart to write to my family." He gave Hensley a detailed description of the tragic expedition, noting that in his "short sojourn in this island," he had not met a single Cuban patriot. "This is an incoherent letter," he noted, "but the circumstances must excuse it. My hands are swollen to double their thickness, resulting from having them too tightly corded for the last 18 hours." He asked Hensley to have a mutual friend write to his mother. "I am afraid that the news will break her heart," he said. "Farewell," he closed. "My love to all my family. I am sorry that I die owing a cent, but it is inevitable."

He found he had time to write a second letter, and addressed it to his uncle, the Hon. J. J. Crittenden, Attorney-General United States, Washington City:[18]

Ship of War Esperanza, Aug. 16, 1851

Dear Uncle: In a few moments some fifty of us will be shot. We came with Lopez. You will do me the justice to believe that my motive was a good one. I was deceived by Lopez—he, as well as the public press, assured me that the island was in a state of prosperous revolution.

I am commanded to finish writing at once.

Your nephew,   W. L. CRITTENDEN

I will die like a man

The men were bound and ferried to the wharf of Castle Atares in Havana Harbor. Two U.S. Navy vessels were in port, the Frigate *Saranac* and the gunboat *Albany,* whose crews stood on deck and watched the sad procession, unable to take any action to save their countrymen. A large crowd of Cubans had gathered ashore and cursed the Americans as they walked by. The doomed men were gathered in a cluster on the rocky ground at the base of the castle walls, and then were led out to the firing squad in groups of ten, Crittenden leading the second party. Spanish tradition was for the condemned to kneel with their backs to the executioners. When the order was given, none of the men moved. The commander of the firing squad demanded that Crittenden have his men turn their backs and kneel. Crittenden looked at him evenly. "A Kentuckian turns his back on no man," he said plainly, "and kneels only to God."

Some say the filibusters were shot down where they stood. One story has it that Spanish soldiers smashed Crittenden's lower legs with their rifle butts and forced him down, but he managed to whirl around before the shots were fired. He was struck in the forehead, an eyewitness said, his cranium literally blown off.[19] The rest of his men followed him.

Francis Day Newcomb stood nearby on the roof of his hotel, watching the tragic scene. Newcomb was a special correspondent for the New York *Journal of Commerce* who had lived in Cuba for six years. He was also a West Point graduate, an Immortal of the Class of 1824, graduating fifth from the foot in the class Dennis Hart Mahan had headed. After the firing party executed the last group of Americans, an officer made a speech congratulating them on their loyalty to Spain and her queen. Then Newcomb watched as the crowd rushed in and "that horrid, brutal and unnatural work of mutilation was done."[20] Some of the corpses were defiled, some torn to shreds. Body parts and bloody clothes were later displayed in the city. What was left of the executed men was piled into makeshift hearses and taken away for burial.

When news of the execution of Crittenden and his men filtered back to the United States, the public was horrified. The pathos of the final letters, which were widely reprinted, and tales of mutilation of the corpses sparked outrage. Emotions boiled over in New Orleans the evening of August 21. A crowd had gathered in front of a tobacco shop owned by Mr. Gonzales, a Cuban loyalist who began provoking the mob. They descended on the shop, led by some of the filibusters who had not made the passage to Cuba, forcing Gonzales to flee. "Cigars were cheap," one of the volunteers wrote, "everybody filled their hats and pockets, and some ran off with boxes."[21] The rioting spread to other Cuban tobacco shops and coffee houses, which were thoroughly looted. One coffee shop, the Jenny Lind, was razed to the ground. A French eyewitness saw "the lawyers of New Orleans, filling their hats and pockets at the sack of Romagosa's handsome cigar establishment."[22] The office of the Spanish consul was also attacked and the interior stripped. Police tried but failed to stem the violence, and while there was substantial material damage, no one was injured. A pro-Spanish commentator said that the people of New Orleans showed the world "that, of all the despicable barbarians in creation, they are the lowest on the scale of civilization."[23]

Congress authorized $25,000 in compensation for the New Orleans riot. The government also voted a small indemnity for the American prisoners being held by Spain. In 1852 the filibusters were released as a goodwill gesture, and President Fillmore ordered the Spanish flag to be saluted.

Lucy Holcombe, William Logan Crittenden's fiancée, wrote a lengthy romantic novel, *The Free Flag of Cuba*, dramatizing the story of the fateful expedition. In 1858 she married Congressman Francis W. Pickens of South Carolina, whom President Buchanan had appointed ambassador to the court of Tsar Alexander II. Pickens returned to the United States late in 1860 and was elected governor of South Carolina shortly before the state seceded. Lucy's beauty, social grace and generosity earned her the nickname "the Queen of the Confederacy." The Holcombe Legion from The Citadel was named in her honor, and she funded the unit by the sale of jewels given her by the Romanovs. She was the only woman to appear on Confederate currency, on several versions of the one-dollar and hundred-dollar bills, the latter of which were called "Lucys."

Crittenden and his men were buried in a mass grave on a hillside near Castle Atares. In 1859 some Americans surreptitiously placed a small pyramid of white marble on the spot, but it was quickly removed by Spanish authorities. The grave was rediscovered in 1898 after Cuba's liberation by American arms. The first enemy battle flag captured in the Spanish-American War was taken June 23, 1898, by the men of Company B, First U.S. Infantry regiment, commanded by William Logan Crittenden's distant cousin, Captain John J. Crittenden.

THE BATTLE OF BLUE WATERS

ON OCTOBER 1, 1855, THE *New York Times* reported the death of Captain Henry Heth at the Battle of Ash Hollow, better known as Blue Waters, on the Platte River in the Nebraska Territory. Scores of Indians were also killed, including, it was reported, Brulé Sioux chief Little Thunder. Henry Heth was last seen charging over a ridge pursuing fleeing Sioux warriors, pierced with six arrows.

All who knew Heth mourned the loss of the gallant, spirited young officer. The *Richmond Evening Post* said Heth was "beloved by his classmates and respected by his professors." Lieutenant Julian McAllister organized a fundraising effort for the Class of 1847, for a memorial to be erected in the West Point cemetery. On October 4, the *Times* ran a poem by an anonymous classmate, "Meditation: Lines to the departed Henry Heth, of the 10th Infantry":

> Called to the other world of happiness and purity, thou wilt find a place more suited to thy kindly nature;...
>
> A studious scholar at the noble *Point* thou didst give promise of a fair career; and surrounded by thy young companions, didst beguile their leisure hours by some pleasing narrative....
>
> At length, however, in a hostile struggle, the "pale-face officer" is killed.
>
> And like some beauteous, healthy plant, fresh in all the vigor of its youth, nipped in the bud by some unlooked for tempest.
> Thou didst yield thy youthful frame to God....
>
> Shall thy class-mates leave thy bones to prairie-soil, to waste away like those of some lost traveler?
> No! no! Let one and all join manfully to show their grief by a soldier's grave in some choice spot—

Where the monument of a departed friend may stand as
a warning to the wicked, that a soldier's life is short;
    And to the just, give pleasing hopes of meeting *Thee* in
Heaven!

As it turned out, reports of Heth's demise were greatly exaggerated.

Heth had left Mexico after the war in 1848 for Jefferson Barracks, Missouri. The next year he fell ill, and doctors diagnosed severe dysentery. He was given a furlough to return to Virginia, and was so weak that the doctors expected him to die there, if not en route. He headed east via the Erie Canal escorted by his friend Winfield Scott Hancock. While passing through New York City they chanced to stumble into a riot at the Astor Opera House over a performance by English actor William C. MacReady. The rioters were defending the honor of American actor Edwin Forrest, with whom MacReady was feuding, and who had recently been panned in London. Police attempting to quell the mob were pelted with cobblestones.[1] The New York militia was called out to put down the disturbance, and twenty-two people were gunned down. They were the first shots Heth heard fired in anger. "I did not enjoy the whistle of the bullet," he wrote, "and I must confess, though having heard many since, that I could never understand the pleasure the musical whistle of the bullet conveys to some I have met."[2] Later Heth and Hancock dined with General Winfield Scott, and afterwards the general forced them into a lengthy game of cards. It was not the night on the town they had expected. Heth said that Mrs. Scott defined *ennui* as "a tallow candle, a game of whist, and General Scott."[3]

When he reached Virginia, Heth's family doctor, Nathaniel Chapman, one of the leading physicians in America, took him off the medications he had been taking and gave him a more homespun prescription: rest, a diet of rare meat when he could eat it, hunting when strong enough, cutting back on juleps, and taking the water at White Sulphur Springs. Heth followed the instructions to the letter, and was soon in full health.

Heth returned to the West in 1850. He served for three years at newly erected Fort Atkinson on the Arkansas River, two miles west of present-day Dodge City, an isolated sod-walled outpost intended to help secure transit on the Santa Fe Trail.[4] It was a dreary place, known colloquially as "Fort Sod." Indian agent Thomas Fitzpatrick called the fort "beneath the dignity of the United States." It presently was overrun with field mice, which threatened the food stores. Heth requisitioned twelve cats from Fort Leavenworth, which was most likely the first time cats were inventoried as Army property.[5]

He frequently visited with his brother John, who was post sutler of Fort Kearny on the Oregon Trail after coming west in 1851 at Henry's urging, to recover from respiratory illness. While at Fort Atkinson, Henry became an accomplished bison hunter, claiming to have killed over one thousand animals. "I became a buffalo fiend," he said. "I never enjoyed any sport as much as I did killing them." Heth said that he had become expert at shooting from horseback because of his constant training for bison hunting. He could down a bison from a galloping horse with one pistol shot. He said he could hit running jackrabbits too, dropping his pistol and firing where he looked without aiming.[6] Each year he also killed more than five hundred wolves and coyotes, numerous antelope, ducks and other game. He once took a trip to the Black Hills to hunt bear, but wound up with his hunting partner high in a hackberry tree with a furious grizzly tearing the bark off below.[7] Heth supplied the fort with fresh meat year round. He also traded with Indians for buffalo tongues, at six tongues for a cup of sugar. He would pickle and smoke the tongues, then ship them to friends to sell back east. Bison tongue was a prized delicacy, selling for fifteen cents each. In one year he cured over 1,500 tongues.[8]

Heth befriended the Indians who came peaceably to the post. They sometimes camped in the thousands outside the sod walls, awaiting emoluments, and could easily have overrun Fort Atkinson had they so desired. It was once rumored that they stormed the fort, killing everyone within, causing a minor panic farther north. The story was without foundation, however, and despite a few small incidents, relations were good between the Army and the bulk of the Indians in this part of the plains, the spirit one of live and let live.

Over the years, Heth associated with many Indians of different tribes and grew to know and understand their culture. He observed that the greatest difference separating the Indian way of life from that of the whites was how the women were treated. To the Indians, women were no better than slaves. But because of all the manual labor they did, the women were stronger than the men, Heth noted, and he "enjoyed, on several occasions, seeing a young woman, a squaw, administer to her husband a sound thrashing, which I have no doubt he richly deserved."[9] Heth and his men spent one particularly severe winter living in teepees and found them very comfortable, more so than the fort.[10] Heth became friends with the Kiowa chief Tohausen, and informally adopted an adolescent half-Kiowa girl who lived in the fort. When she died suddenly of a seizure, Heth was heartbroken. His Indian name (probably Comanche) was Yo-ba-me-atz, "Sways When He Walks," or perhaps "One Who Swaggers."[11]

Cheyenne warriors who stayed at the fort gave Heth hunting tips, and he managed after many attempts to bring down a bison from horseback using a bow and arrow, "the most difficult job I had ever undertaken."[12] Accounts of this event were embellished by fellow officers and grew in the telling, so that in its mature form Heth was riding bareback, clad in a loincloth, the bridle in his teeth, taking down buffalo at will. Another time Heth was antelope hunting and told the sergeant who accompanied him that when the herd came within two hundred yards they would stop and look at the hunters for ten to fifteen seconds. He said he would shoot the lead buck in the right eye. When the antelope paused as expected, Heth took his shot, and in fact did hit the center of the buck's right eye. Heth admitted privately that it was just luck, but as the story grew, he heard he was able to shoot running bucks square in the eye every time. He became known as the finest rifle shot in the Army. "So reputations are sometimes made," he mused.[13]

Despite the good relations with most of the Indians, incidents sometimes occurred. Heth did not hesitate to secure the trail, which often involved pursuing bands of renegades that had robbed emigrants. He fought several skirmishes, usually very close-quarters fighting. But occasionally situations arose that demonstrated where the power on the plains really lay. Once while investigating the murder of a traveler, Captain Simon Bolivar Buckner (USMA 1844), commander of Fort Atkinson, ordered Heth to take thirty men and two cannon to the Kiowa village on the Arkansas River and bring back the killer.[14] Heth left on his mission, intending to avoid trouble. Once he reached his destination, however, the head of the village grew angry at the warlike appearance of Heth's party. Word spread and five hundred Kiowa appeared, ready for a fight. Heth stayed calm and asked to see the head chief Tohausen, who arrived a short time after. The old warrior took in the situation and spoke quietly to the angry village leaders. He then went to Heth and said, "Yo-ba-me-atz, you had better take your men back to the fort." Heth did so immediately, knowing that Tohausen had just saved his life. Buckner later approved Heth's course of action, and the matter was resolved through negotiation.

In the summer of 1852, Heth spent some weeks in St. Louis procuring supplies, and was able to spend more time with his friend Hancock and another officer he had befriended in Mexico, brevet Captain Ulysses S. Grant, who was in Missouri on leave from his post in Michigan. Grant's regiment was deploying to California, and his wife was planning to stay temporarily with her parents in St. Louis. One evening Grant gave Heth a buggy ride to the arsenal, showing off his pony, which he claimed was a fast pacer. Heth had his doubts, so Grant laid on the whip and the pony took off. "I had never been behind anything with so much speed," Heth wrote.[15] They rounded a sharp bend and ran straight into a cow. Heth was thrown to the sidewalk, landing between two baskets of cranberries. Grant landed on the curb and was knocked unconscious. He was taken to a nearby apothecary, where he soon came to and insisted they complete their journey to the arsenal. There they visited with General Clarke, the department commander, his adjutant Irvin McDowall, Captain Braxton Bragg and their old friend Hancock—and despite their shaken condition, as Grant later recalled, not one of them offered the two officers a drink.[16]

The Grattan Massacre

THE EVENTS LEADING UP TO the Battle of Blue Waters began the summer of 1854 when a lame cow owned by a Mormon emigrant wandered away from the wagon train and into an Indian camp in the Nebraska Territory. Fifteen hundred warriors were there, mostly Brulé Sioux led by Chief Conquering Bear, having raised six hundred lodges in an encampment that stretched for three miles. They were awaiting the arrival of the Indian agent, Major Whitfield, to distribute the "presents and annuities" they collected under terms of an 1851 treaty, in exchange for not molesting settlers on the Oregon Trail. Among the Indians was a youngster named Curly, thirteen years old, later called Crazy Horse. Prudently, the cow's owner did not enter the camp to retrieve it. A Miniconjou named High Forehead, who was staying with the Brulé, killed the cow, and he and others ate it.

Arriving at nearby Fort Laramie, however, the farmer reported the cow stolen. Second Lieutenant Hugh B. Fleming (USMA 1852), acting commander of the fort, offered to negotiate with Conquering Bear. He dispatched Second Lieutenant John Grattan of the Sixth Infantry with twenty-nine soldiers from G Company, two pieces of horse artillery and an interpreter, Lucien Auguste, to investigate and bring back whoever killed the cow. This was the same potentially dangerous scenario Henry Heth had faced with the Kiowa a few years earlier. But Grattan (USMA 1853) was new to the plains, and unlike Heth, he harbored a high degree of contempt for the Indians. He vowed to teach the savages a lesson.

Grattan and his men arrived in the camp on August 19 and demanded that the Indians turn over the man who killed the cow. Conquering Bear took him to High Forehead, who refused to go with

Grattan. He claimed that the cow was found, not stolen, and thus fairly killed. High Forehead promised to fight if Grattan tried to force him to go. The parlay lasted around thirty minutes and may have been made more contentious by interpreter Lucien Auguste, whom some say was intoxicated. The lieutenant returned to his men. He faced several chiefs other than Conquering Bear, such as Little Thunder, Big Partisan and Man Afraid of Horses. Vastly outnumbered, Grattan should have been diplomatic; but instead he rolled the cannon into the camp and stood next to one of the pieces in a threatening manner, believing he could intimidate the Indians.

Conquering Bear demonstrated his contempt for the young man by striding up to him, calling him a squaw and a coward, and counting coup by jabbing him with a spear. Grattan, surprised, drew his revolver and fired several rounds at the chief at close range, mortally wounding him. He elevated and fired the cannon, apparently to frighten more than to kill; or perhaps the Indians ducked. Either way, no one was injured, the shot hit the tops of the teepees, and a general mêlée ensued. Grattan ordered his men to fire their muskets and his first volley wounded many. But there was no chance to reload. Grattan was hit with several arrows, one going through his head, and he fell over the cannon. The soldiers broke and ran, pursued by a mass of Indians, who cut them down. Only one member of the party, Private John Cuddy, made it back to Fort Laramie, assisted by a local trader. He had been hit by seven arrows and died three days later.

The Sioux had their blood up. They looted some local homes and the nearby American Fur Company outpost, then surrounded the fort, which was defended by Fleming and ten men. They demonstrated wildly before they were prevailed upon to leave. Forty reinforcements showed up a short time later, but the Sioux could easily have taken Laramie if they had wanted. Several other depredations followed, including the massacre of a mail party as retribution for the death of Conquering Bear.

The remains of Grattan's party lay exposed for three days. Fleming would not risk sending out a burial detail, and ultimately local traders were hired to undertake the task. Grattan was found under his blood-stained gun, his body pierced with two dozen arrows and several bullets. The Indians had filled his cannon with manure, and Grattan's boots protruded from the muzzle. James Bordeau, whose home was looted after the massacre and who helped bury the bodies of the soldiers, later said that "placing the infantry on a prairie to fight with Indians is just the same as putting them up as targets to be shot at."[17] The shallow graves were insufficient to hold the corpses, and settlers passing the scene of the massacre months later were horrified to see the heads of the victims peering back at them from ground level.

Grattan got much of the blame from those familiar with the facts. But he had his defenders. One of his classmates, then in Salt Lake City with the Third Artillery, wrote a letter to the *New York Times* alleging that the traders were blaming Grattan in order to avoid an Indian war, which was very bad for their business. "I knew Grattan well as a man of undaunted courage," he wrote. "If he was rash, he paid the extreme penalty, and died at his post like the gallant gentleman and soldier that he was."[18]

By the following spring, a general war against the Plains Indians was being debated. One colonel stated that there was only an Indian uprising "in the imagination of our Administration." There had been some excesses, but they were transitory or, in the case of the Grattan Massacre, "the effect of great misconduct on the part of the Lieutenant." Another observer said that the Indians were "determined not to fight the whites" and were "awaiting to hear from their Great Father in Washington." The *Times* declaimed the costs of war in general, noting that Indian conflicts since 1833 had cost $30 million (mostly spent in the Seminole War). It was more important to do justice on the plains than to fight immoral wars—"we should never by any construction leave it possible that we are the aggressors." The editorial concluded sarcastically, "The Sioux must be taught that to shoot even the cow of a Mormon Emigrant Company may drag down upon them the Great Father's vengeance, and a visit from Secretary Davis' new and most brilliantly equipped companies."[19] The Indians, initially alarmed by the tough talk of those who wanted war, began to boast that the government was afraid to face them.[20] For President Franklin Pierce and especially Secretary of War Jefferson Davis, an opportunity had presented itself.

Pierce personally gave command of the Sioux expedition to General William S. Harney with instructions to "whip the Indians for us."[21] Harney could be counted on to make certain the operation was punitive. His heroism in Mexico had not eclipsed his earlier notoriety from the Seminole War. He would regale his men with tales of surviving the Caloosahatchee massacre and later paying back the Seminoles in kind. The *St. Louis Republican* noted that "if the Sioux Indians can be found they will be chastised into a proper respect for the people of the United States. Nothing short of this will do, and though the expedition is somewhat late in moving we have no doubt that Gen. Harney will strike terror into the enemy wherever he may meet them."[22]

Heth described Harney as "a singular man. If he liked you, all that you did pleased him; if not, the reverse."[23] He was also a great swearer, the greatest Heth had ever heard.[24] Harney favored Heth and asked him to join his staff for the expedition. Heth naturally accepted. When he arrived at Harney's headquarters at Fort Leavenworth, Heth was informed that he had been chosen to be a captain commanding Company E, Tenth Infantry, one of Secretary Davis's four new regiments. Heth at first thought it was a practical joke dreamed up by Hancock, but it was not. Heth, the Goat of his class, was the first to achieve the regular rank of captain.[25]

Heth was ordered east to hand-pick the members of his new company. In Washington he met with the adjutant general, Colonel Samuel Cooper (USMA 1815), a New Yorker who would later be one of the few Yankees to join the Confederate army. Heth knew Cooper, and inquired why he, a man with no political influence or significant Mexican War record, was chosen for the high-profile position.

"To whom do I owe the favor?" he asked.

"You owe your promotion to the Secretary of War," Cooper replied. "Do you know him?"

"I do not even know the name of the Secretary of War," Heth replied.

"Come with me," Cooper said, "and I will introduce you." Taken to meet Jefferson Davis, Heth thanked the secretary and again expressed his surprise at being chosen.

"I think, Captain, you have fairly earned your promotion," Davis said. "You have been in the Indian country four years; you have kept your routes open; you have had several Indian fights and have done well. And," he added, "I understand you are a wonderful buffalo hunter and a fine horseman, and that you have killed buffalo riding bareback with a bow and arrow."

Heth listened attentively. Who was he to contradict the secretary of war?

"It is a very pleasant thing to be killed."

THE EXPEDITION SET OUT from Fort Kearny on August 24, 1855. Harney assured Davis there was "no possibility of failure."[26] They were guided by maps made by a topographical party that had explored the area earlier that summer, led by Lieutenant Gouverneur K. Warren, second in the Class of 1850. Harney's force was over five hundred men strong, but a trader at Fort Laramie believed the War Department had sent insufficient forces for the pacification. "Our Great Father at Washington never will learn anything from experience or take the advice of those who know," he wrote. "I fear that this Sioux war will be intrusted to incompetent hands, and all sorts of plans will be adopted, until millions upon millions have been expended, and hundreds of lives sacrificed, and the end no nearer than the first. . . . The pitiful force of Gen. Harney entering the country at the tail of the season is worse than ridiculous, it only tends to encourage the Indians."[27]

Thomas S. Twiss, second in the Class of 1826, then serving as the Indian agent at Fort Laramie, issued a warning that "friendly and peaceable" tribes should congregate near the fort, south of the Platte River, and many did.[28] The show of force began to have an effect. In late August, word reached Harney that the Sioux were willing to give up the murderers of the mail party, but not those who killed Grattan and his men because it was a "fair fight."[29]

On September 1, Harney's force made camp on the banks of the North Platte, two miles from the Sioux encampment on the Blue Waters. In the evening, Heth and Harney were sitting near the commander's tent when cavalry commander Lieutenant Colonel Philip St. George Cooke (USMA 1827) reported for orders for the following day.[30]

"We will continue our march up the Platte," Harney said. Cooke saluted and left. Heth was incredulous. Harney turned to him. "I wonder what those damned Indians will say of my not attacking them."

"I know exactly," Heth said, goading him. "They will say they came where they are now and offered to give the big White Chief, the Hornet, as they call you, a fight, but that you tucked your tail between your legs and ran away."

The general jumped up. "God damn them, will they say that, Captain?" he roared.

"That is precisely what they will say," Heth replied.

Harney shouted after Cooke to return, and when he did, Harney issued a new set of orders:

"Colonel Cooke, I intend to attack those damned red skins this morning. Take your cavalry and make a circuit; get on the far side of the village; conceal your force among the hills; start at two o'clock tonight; I will move on their village so as to reach it by light, with the infantry and artillery; they will break and run towards you, don't let a damned one escape."

Cooke saluted and went back to his tent to plan the night flanking march. Later, Heth stopped by.

"What did you say to Harney that made him change his plans so suddenly?" Cooke asked. Heth told him. "He is not fit to command," Cooke said. "*Of course* he should attack; these are the very fellows we are looking for and another such opportunity will never occur again."[31]

In a few hours, Heth set out with Cooke on the long flanking maneuver, moving quietly to avoid detection. They completed the movement by 3 A.M. and discovered that there was not one Sioux village but many, stretching three miles up the river. Cooke took position across the river half a mile beyond the farthest Indian encampment, out of sight behind a ridge formed by a dry tributary to his left. Heth's men, serving as mounted infantry, dismounted and took positions along the ridgeline, their rifles trained on the probable Indian escape route. They lay for two hours awaiting the sound of battle being joined by the advancing infantry.

Harney moved up the Blue Waters at dawn. The Indians were caught by surprise, but once they sensed the advancing force they began breaking camp. Little Thunder hurried south to parlay with Harney on neutral ground. Harney set simple terms: hand over those responsible for the Grattan Massacre, the mail party ambush and the other depredations and you may go; otherwise, take the chances of battle. Little Thunder refused the demands; but Harney would present no other terms. The two parted. The Indians began to pull back, and the infantry deployed to attack.

Heth saw activity across the river. The Indians were packing their camp and the men assembling for battle, but he had not heard the sound of the infantry attack. Then two young braves rode towards his position, stopped, and began daring the men on the ridge to fight. The soldiers had been seen; surprise had been lost. But Cooke stuck to the plan and ordered his men to hold fire.

The Indians gathered near the bluff on the opposite bank, which was steep, rocky and virtually impassable from Cooke's direct line of approach. To the north, the slopes were gentler, and there was open country beyond. Cooke believed the enemy would break in that direction at first sound of gunfire. The moment volleys were heard from the infantry, Cooke and his cavalrymen leapt in their mounts and galloped down into the valley, across the river, and wheeled towards the lower banks on the opposite side. But as Cooke moved to the north, the Indians atop the heights saw that if they descended straight down the steep bank and headed northeast up the dry tributary, they could evade the cavalry arcing towards them, leaving Cooke stranded. Cooke noticed the same thing and called back for Heth to mount up and take his force down the slope to the left and block that escape route, with a mounted company commanded by A. P. Howe, an artillery officer, in support.

Harney's five companies of infantry to the south meanwhile had ascended the bluffs downriver and advanced on the village, firing with their long-range rifles. Some Indians took cover in caves along the river bluffs and fired back. The infantry concentrated their fire into the caves, killing women and children who had sought refuge along with braves.

The larger group of mounted warriors made for the escape route that Cooke had seen too late—they careened down the steep banks on their nimble ponies and headed directly for Heth's small blocking force. Howe's men, inexperienced with horses and having taken some casualties from Indian rifle fire, were stalled back near their starting point and had failed to back Heth up.

A chaotic fracas developed up the valley. Riflemen fired from the bluffs at the backs of the retreating Indians, but also towards Heth's company. Some of Cooke's men made it back down the way they came and were able to give chase. The Indians collided with Heth's force and broke through, the mounted infantry gamely pursuing as the Indians fired arrows back at them. There was a running fight for five or six miles, lasting several hours. Heth spurred his mount forward, using the riding skills he had displayed at West Point, firing his pistol as though hunting buffalo, riding far out in front of his men, eventually disappearing down the dusty valley.

When the dust cleared, eighty-six Indians lay dead, with many more wounded. Harney's force had suffered four dead, seven wounded and one missing. Overall, the battle had been successful. The Sioux had been dispersed, and from Harney's point of view, properly punished. The soldiers took some satisfaction in having avenged Grattan. Harney praised many of his officers in his after-action report, among them Warren for his reconnaissance. But Warren, seeing his first action, was appalled. He noted in his journal the scene of the field covered with the dead and wounded, "women and children, crying and moaning, horribly mangled by the bullets." He and others tended to the wounded as best they could. Soldiers scoured the battlefield, picking through the discarded belongings of the Sioux looking for evidence and souvenirs. The troops discovered pictorial representations of the Grattan Massacre, the murder of the postal party, and another raid on a wagon train; a letter from the captured mail; two white women's scalps; and some clothing from Grattan's party, which seemed to serve the cause of proving this was the same group of Indians.[32] Harney ordered the remaining clothes, weapons and other remnants burned in bonfires.[33]

Captain Howe was court-martialed for not going to Heth's aid. Howe was "not worth the powder and lead it would take to kill him," Harney stated. "He is as damned a coward as was his brother Marshal Saxe Howe, whom I have often court-martialed, and I shall put charges against this fellow."[34] Proceedings were ordered, but Howe got off on a technicality—Harney could not both convene the court and be the officer of record bringing charges. But Howe earned a reputation for cowardice and incompetence that he never shook.[35]

After the battle there were a few more Sioux raids. The Indians sent a message to Harney to "come on with his young men—that they were ready and wanted his horses."[36] But by October, Harney was making peace with the Indians. He held talks with the Oglala and Brulé chiefs shortly after the battle, and they agreed to give up the murderers of the mail party.[37] In January 1856, the Indians sent word to Harney that they would hold a general peace council. They said they had never wanted to fight and had not expected that their small raids would lead to a general war. One observer believed that the expedition had achieved its aims. Blue Waters "was proof positive that the Government was in earnest, and thus produced a most salutary effect." The upcoming pow-wow "may result in a strong and durable peace."[38] The Indians gave Harney a new and respectful nickname, "Mad Bear."

The speed and effectiveness of Harney's attack and the thoroughness of his victory were both admired and reviled. He had administered the bold stroke that Secretary Davis thought was necessary, and for this he won both fame and infamy. The *St. Louis Republican* called it "one of the most gallant and complete victories ever obtained over an Indian enemy."[39] The *New York Times* said that in his frank report of the battle, Harney wrote "without apology, without any attempt to conceal [the attack's] atrocious character, evidently considering it his business to kill Indians and not to justify himself for doing so. . . . Is there no way of adjusting and concluding this conflict of races except by the extirpation of the weaker?"[40] A letter published in the *Times* declaimed "the lamentable butcheries of Indians by Harney's command on the Plains," which had "excited the most painful feelings. The so-called battle was simply a massacre. . . . I trust the time has passed forever when Americans can look upon these holiday campaigns against Indians with exultation." The writer stated that were these matters left in the hands of the Interior Department instead of the War Department, this would never have happened.[41] Another letter claimed that the battle was only fought to justify the growth in the size of the Army that Secretary Davis had spearheaded. "It is not unlikely that some further outrages will be committed in order to convince Congress of the expediency of very large appropriations to meet the contingencies of Indian wars."[42]

Blue Waters was used by both sides in the debate over Indian policy, and its significance was muddied in the partisan exchanges. However, the early press reports of the battle were exaggerated in some respects. Chief Little Thunder was not killed. Neither, as it turned out, was Henry Heth. He had not been struck with six arrows, or even one, though he said "one would have been sufficient." Heth never learned the source of the report of his demise, though it was understandable in the chaos that he might be thought dead. If he was alive, it certainly was not for lack of effort on his part. He found the affair very amusing and looked forward to giving copies of his glowing obituaries to his grandchildren. "It is a very pleasant thing to be killed," Heth later wrote, "if you live to read the nice things your friends say about you."[43]

SOLOMON'S FORK

THE FOUR NEW REGIMENTS THAT Secretary of War Jefferson Davis created in March 1855 were the First and Second Cavalry and the Ninth and Tenth Infantry. They were experimental units, intended to fight in innovative ways with the latest equipment, part of an effort by Davis to transform the Army, to adapt to new technologies, missions and ways of fighting. Davis and Archie Campbell, who was again chief clerk of the War Department, pored over lists of officers, seeking the right kind of men to command their new units, men with initiative and dash. While looking at names of potential cavalry officers they came across Second Lieutenant James M. McIntosh, Goat of 1849, who had spent the years since he graduated from West Point as a scout in Texas. He had a commendable record but was low on the seniority list. Campbell recognized the name; he told Davis the story of the trip to Benny Havens' on Christmas Eve 1848 and how a charging cadet tossed George W. Cullum down an icy hill. After graduation, when it was safe to tell the tale, the culprit admitted what he did—bragged about it, in fact. Archie heard that the cadet who hurled Cullum was James M. McIntosh.

"I never liked Cullum much," Davis said, and he appointed McIntosh the senior first lieutenant of the First Cavalry.[1] Of the bottom ten graduates of the Class of 1849, eight were promoted to first lieutenant in March 1855; one more was promoted in December; and the remaining one had returned to civilian life. Secretary Davis, it seemed, had great faith in the Immortals.

The roster of McIntosh's new regiment had many names that would later be well known—Joseph E. Johnston, John Sedgwick, George McClellan, Alfred Iverson and James E. B. Stuart among them. McIntosh adapted well to his new position and made captain within two years. In 1857 he was commander of D Company, and his second in command was First Lieutenant David S. Stanley (USMA 1852), who graduated ninth in his class.

After Harney concluded his treaty with the Sioux, he recommended an expedition against the Cheyenne—he did not like their indifferent attitude and thought they needed a lesson. Several Cheyenne raids in the summer of 1856, mainly attacks on immigrants and travelers, seemed to vindicate his position. But at the time, the Army was busy with peacekeeping duties in Bloody Kansas and could not afford to mount another operation.

The Cheyenne attitude was understandable; in his survey of the plains, Warren noted, "We are in the habit of looking on the power of the United States as invincible, but it is far from being so regarded by the savages on our frontier. Many of them have neither seen or felt it." This feeling was reinforced when the Indians gathered and saw their combined size and strength. A large number of tribes assembled at a grand council on the north fork of the Cheyenne River in the summer of 1857, and a Dakota chief said that "their hearts felt strong at seeing how numerous they were; that if they went to war again they would not yield so easily as they did before. At that council they solemnly pledged to each other not to permit further encroachments from the whites, and he fully believed they were able to whip all the white people in the world."[2]

But continuing incidents and political pressures to secure the frontier were bringing matters to a head. Davis authorized the Cheyenne expedition in October 1856. It was planned that winter and officially ordered by the new war secretary, John B. Floyd, the following April.[3]

The plan was to send two columns marching west from Fort Leavenworth on May 18, skirting the Cheyenne territory, regrouping in the west and heading back east through the heart of their domain. The First Cavalry would supply the striking force, with troops attached from the Second Dragoons and the Sixth Infantry. The northern column was led by regimental commander Colonel Edwin V. Sumner, up the North Platte to Fort Laramie, along the Oregon Trail route. Major John Sedgwick led the southern column, following the Santa Fe Trail route to the Arkansas River and up to Fort Pueblo. They planned to converge at Fort St. Vrain on July 4. A flying column commanded by Lieutenant Colonel Joseph E. Johnston would provide flank security, patrolling the Kansas border to the south against possible Kiowa activity.

McIntosh rode in Sedgwick's column, one of his three squadron commanders. They made good time along the familiar trail, marching twenty or more miles per day. The weather was excellent for campaigning, and game was plentiful, for food and sport. The column had a beef herd but the men preferred to feed off the land. Beyond the tree line,

they made fires with buffalo chips, the *bois de vache,* "wood of the cow."
Delaware scouts preceded the column, keeping an eye out for trouble.
Over three weeks they encountered settlers, Kansas and Arapahoe Indians with whom they had no quarrel, and numerous Mormon emigrants
heading for Utah. The Cheyenne were not to be seen.

But the march was not without incident. One day as the column
was moving up the valley of the Arkansas River near Plum Buttes, they
spied bison grazing miles ahead. It was a massive herd, almost as wide
as the valley, a great brown blotch on the grassy plain. The soldiers
thought nothing of it; maybe some of them looked forward to a little
hunting. But when the column was about two miles from the herd,
something happened. A group of the animals started moving; first a few,
then many, and soon the entire mass began to swirl and flow, surging
towards the column. A huge rolling dark brown wave thundered down
the valley between the river and the bluff, funneled towards the soldiers who sat nervously on their mounts.

Sedgwick watched, fascinated, as the herd grew nearer. He was
uncertain what to do. He was a Seminole War vet and brevetted twice
in Mexico, but he had no real experience on the plains. The troops could
not retreat, and they were penned in on the left by the river and on the
right by the escarpment. Yet they had to do something, and fast. Sedgwick turned to Senior Captain Sam Sturgis, Class of 1846, who had
spent the last six years in Kansas and New Mexico fighting Indians.[4]
Sturgis took charge immediately, gathering in the column and deploying a firing party in a line on the edge towards the bison. When the animals were near enough, the men started firing. They shot as quickly as
they could, pumping round after round into the rushing dark mass of
hair and horns. Some bison stumbled and fell, but it was hard to kill
them firing at their thick skulls protected by dark matted hair. The bison
moved closer. Their grunts and brays were audible, punctuated by the
rounds from the firing party. Others joined in. More beasts went down.
The bison filled the horizon and their pounding hoofs shook the earth.
The fire intensified. Finally, a gap began to open, then widen. The leading edge of the herd was now hard on the firing line, and the men on
the wings fell back into a V formation. Bison ran by on left and right,
enveloping the soldiers in a cloud of dust. Some began shooting the
passing animals in the side, which brought many more down. The bodies of the fallen pushed the rest farther from the clustered soldiers.
They were now in the thick of the herd, with grunting, galloping bison
in every direction. They kept up the fire, and were soon surrounded by
a ring of dead and dying animals. After a half hour, the herd thinned,

then the trailing edge passed. The troopers were elated and exhausted. Sturgis had averted a catastrophe. While the column reorganized, foraging parties went out to collect the fresh meat.

The two columns reached the rendezvous on schedule and moved down the South Platte, erecting Fort Buchanan (after the president) on July 7, 1857. Sumner's plan was to head downriver for five days, then head southeast across the plains towards Beaver Creek, where Pawnee scouts said the Cheyenne were camped. They would then assess the situation and give battle if circumstances warranted. Sumner, known as "Old Bull," had the reputation of a martinet and was frequently impatient with his subordinates. But he was also known for his honesty and directness, and for his eagerness to get in the fight. "He was a man of great soldierly qualities," Stanley wrote, "but so brusque in his manner as to be rude at times, and there were many people who disliked him. Yet, he was a man truthful, honest and kindhearted."[5]

The column departed on July 13. After leaving the river, they found the terrain more difficult, traversing a treeless plain with sandy soil and sparse grass. Sand hills were interspersed with fields of scrub populated by prairie dogs. There was meager forage and little game. The midsummer sun was hot; the men, horses and cattle were thirsty; and water was in short supply. Periodically they crossed streams—tributaries of the South Platte, many of them dry. Ten days after leaving Fort Buchanan, the column crossed the bed of the Republican River, symbolic boundary of the heart of Cheyenne country. The next day, scouts reported that they were within a day of the village. So they were; but when the column arrived at the site, it had been abandoned. There was evidence of hundreds of teepees, a sobering indicator of the size of the Cheyenne band they were pursuing. The next day, moving across increasingly hilly and grassy terrain, the soldiers found another abandoned village site, and on the following day yet another.

Scouts continued to report that they were nearing the main body of Cheyenne, and Sumner increased security. March order was tightened, with cavalry leading and securing the flanks, infantry and the baggage train to the rear. Sumner banned bugle calls and the discharging of firearms, hoping to move as unobtrusively as possible.

However, Sumner's column had been under observation for weeks. The Cheyenne knew all about them—a force that large could not move through their lands without being seen. The Indians were ahead, preparing their weapons and discussing the best site for the inevitable battle, finding the ground on which they would make their stand. They chose a long narrow valley on the south fork of the Solomon River.

"Draw Sabers!"

ON JULY 29, OVER THREE HUNDRED Cheyenne left their village to do battle with the white soldiers, joined by some Sioux observers, including young Crazy Horse. They departed in high spirits, resplendent in their war paint and regalia. Two shaman, Ice and Gray Beard, told the Cheyenne warriors they had strong medicine. Bullets would not hurt them, and their own firearms would not miss. En route to the battlefield they held a ceremony at a small lake, dipping their hands in holy waters to make the medicine, to ensure that the enemy's rounds would fall harmlessly to the ground. They rode ten miles from the holy waters to the south fork valley, crossing the soft ground at the riverbank and gathering near the scattered cottonwood trees at the east end. The valley was two miles long and over half a mile wide, bisected by the twisting river. The Cheyenne rested in the shade while their horses grazed. At one in the afternoon, scouts reported that the enemy was drawing near. The Indians eagerly mounted their horses, formed a battle line, and waited.

James McIntosh rode steadily at the head of his company. Their mounts were worn from the steady pace of the pursuit—they had covered 140 miles in the last week and many miles already that day. But there was a sense of expectation. Scouts had told Sumner that Cheyenne braves had assembled a few miles ahead in the valley. Not a village this time, but a gathering of warriors. The cavalrymen were nearing the battle they had come to fight. The soldiers paused briefly to prepare, securing mounts, loading and checking weapons. As they drew near the enemy, Sumner was worried that the Indians might try to escape—he didn't know about the medicine, that his bullets could not harm the Cheyenne, that in fact this was their chosen ground, and their battle. He told his infantry and artillery commanders that he would take the cavalry ahead and they should not try to keep up. If he could pin down the enemy, they could join the battle later; if the Indians fled, only the cavalry would be able to give chase. Sumner gave the order to move out and his six cavalry companies of three hundred men headed down the north bank of the Solomon at a trot.

Ahead and to the left rose a sharp ridge called Sandy Point, which forced the river to hook south and then twist northeast. The column skirted the base of the ridge and emerged into the wide flat valley, following the river course. Sumner halted, looking ahead with field glasses. He saw the Cheyenne, lined up on horses, facing him, waiting. It was an odd sight, more akin to a conventional formation, not what Sumner was expecting. They must have seen him, but they showed no signs of flight.

Sumner called his companies "front into the line," and they spread out from the column, forming for battle. McIntosh was in the center, next to Sumner. The commander then ordered an advance at the trot. McIntosh relayed the order to his men and moved forward. The Cheyenne were also advancing, slowly at first, then with increasing speed. The painted, multihued Cheyenne, wearing war bonnets, waving bows, lances and rifles, chanting and singing war songs, stood in contrast to the blue-clad, yellow-trimmed, black-hatted, silent, expectant and orderly cavalrymen. It was a scene never before witnessed in the Indian wars: two lines of mounted warriors, roughly equal in number, closed on each other in a remote valley in Kansas, ready to give battle.

At rifle range, Sumner's scout Fall Leaf dashed ahead and fired at the advancing Cheyenne. The Indians howled derisively and fired a few shots in return. Sumner turned to Lieutenant Stanley and said, perhaps with irony, "Mr. Stanley, bear witness that an Indian fired the first shot." Sumner then ordered a gallop. The Indians were still advancing. McIntosh readied to draw his .58 caliber rifled carbine; he was also armed with a .36 caliber navy revolver, which he would use after the initial volley. They had trained for months at this maneuver, testing the new cavalry concepts, and were now ready to prove them on the field. The line of horsemen drew to well within range. Sumner raised himself on his stirrups and bellowed the command.

"Draw sabers!" Old Bull's voice echoed down the valley.

McIntosh paused, then gripped and drew his dragoon saber. The men were surprised, but followed the order mechanically. Three hundred blades flashed in the afternoon sun.

"Charge!" Sumner cried, and the cavalrymen let out a terrific yell and spurred their mounts forward towards the enemy.

The Cheyenne stopped, bewildered. They had not expected this. Their medicine was against bullets, not long knives. They wondered what had gone wrong, how the whites had known not to shoot at them. Their war chiefs urged them forward, but their morale was fast fracturing. When the cavalry closed to one hundred yards, the Indians fired a volley of arrows, then fled, breaking into small groups and scattering towards the hills.

Sumner's men gave pursuit to the bulk of the enemy, who had crossed the river and were riding south towards their village. The cavalrymen hit the soft ground near the river at the end of the valley and many became mired, giving the Indians a fair chance to escape. Company order broke down as the fastest horses charged out ahead. McIntosh was out near the lead, with Stanley, Lieutenant Lunsford Lomax (USMA 1856), also of D Company, Lieutenant James B. McIntyre (an Immortal of 1853, graduating fourth from the foot), and J. E. B. Stuart, whose horse Dan could outrun them all.

The battle became a series of small unit actions, or man-to-man fights with Cheyenne braves whose horses had gotten stuck or who were otherwise unlucky. It was a running battle that lasted almost two hours and stretched for miles. One trooper, Private Lynch, caught up to a large Indian band on his out-of-control horse; the Cheyenne split ranks and obligingly let the charging animal pass by, then killed Lynch from behind.

Eight miles from the battlefield, Lomax saw an Indian approaching one of his corporals. It was a chief named White Antelope. He stretched out his right hand to the corporal as if in friendship, but he was holding a revolver behind his back.

"Shoot him!" Lomax cried and rode towards them. By then the two had clasped hands, and White Antelope shot the corporal. Lomax was right on top of them, and the Indian turned and fired again, the ball passing just over Lomax's leg and under his bridle arm. "How he missed me at this short distance I cannot tell," Lomax wrote. Stuart then rode up swiftly and shot White Antelope, hitting him in the thigh. The chief fired back at Stuart but missed. Stanley and McIntyre also closed.

"Wait! I'll fetch him," Stanley said. He fired from his saddle but the barrel was near his horse's ear, and the discharge frightened the animal. Stanley leapt from the saddle and cocked his weapon, aiming at the chief. But the hammer stuck and the weapon would not fire. Seeing Stanley's predicament, White Antelope went after him, his own pistol poised. Stuart spurred forward and struck the chief in the head with his saber; but the Indian was able to bring his gun around and fire his last bullet within a foot of Stuart, hitting him in the chest. McIntyre and another man then finally killed the wounded White Antelope. "He threw everything he had at us," Lomax later said.[6]

J. E. B. Stuart dismounted slowly and lay on the ground. Lomax collected some sabers, jammed them in the ground and fashioned a tent with a blanket, to give Stuart some shade. Men gathered around him as the pursuit wound down, and Sumner rode up, gravely concerned. They carried the suffering Stuart back to the battlefield. The wound was painful, but it was not mortal, nor, as it turned out, even critical; the round had deflected to the left once it entered his body, lodging beneath the skin in his breast and not penetrating any organs.

Recall was sounded at 3:00 P.M. For all the action, the battle was not particularly bloody. The soldiers had lost only two men killed, with nine wounded, mostly from arrows. The Cheyenne had no more than nine killed, with many more wounded. Private James Murphy of E Company, a notorious Irish wit, when asked how many Indians he had killed, claimed, "I killed as many of them as they did of me."

One Cheyenne brave was taken prisoner. Some Pawnee scouts, who had generally not been as useful as the Delaware during the campaign but had been collecting trophies from the dead, asked to be allowed to torture the prisoner to death and take his scalp too. They even offered to pay for the privilege. Disgusted, Sumner refused.

The next day, the two dead troopers were buried with due ceremony. Cacti were piled in the graves just below the surface to deter wolves from digging up the bodies. Sumner let the men and horses rest, and the next day most of the command set off after the Cheyenne.

The wounded remained behind, protected by Company C of the Sixth Infantry, commanded by Captain Rennselear W. Foote and tended to by Dr. Edward Covey. The soldiers erected a sod earthworks, dubbed Fort Floyd in honor of the secretary of war. The fort was designed by Stuart's twenty-five-year-old classmate Second Lieutenant John McCleary. Hailing from Ohio, McCleary was from a poor family but through hard work had matriculated at St. John's College in Cincinnati. His name had been sent up for consideration for a cadetship along with that of a young man from a wealthy family who was a Yale alumnus. McCleary's congressman, Lewis D. Campbell, noted that in addition to his personal qualities, McCleary's family had already made sacrifices for the country. His brother fought with the Ohio militia in Mexico and died of yellow fever at Vera Cruz. McCleary also had recommendations from St. John's and his brother's former commander with the Fourth Ohio Volunteers. For these reasons, the congressman felt that McCleary should have precedence and that he would perform with credit at West Point.

Four years later, McCleary graduated the Goat of the Class of 1854. He was sent west after commissioning and soon saw action, commanding the lead infantry assault company at Blue Waters. He was with the infantry column at Solomon's Fork, where he did not get into the fight, but the small sod fort that he built for the bivouac was "quite respectable for the means at hand," according to Stuart.[7] Its worth was tested the night of August 4, when a party of twenty to thirty Cheyenne mounted a surprise attack. They were beaten back without casualties. The next day, five of Sumner's Pawnee scouts arrived on foot, having been attacked by the same Cheyenne war party, their ponies stolen. They brought orders for Captain Foote to return directly to Fort Kearny. The small group left Fort Floyd on August 8, making their way north across Cheyenne territory without a compass, guided by the Pawnee and the stars. Three wounded men were carried on litters lashed to horses Indian-style, with the poles bound together and dragging on the ground. Stuart was able to ride. They were low on rations, some of the men were barefoot, and their ammunition was only what they could carry.

The Pawnee assured them that it was only a few days' journey to Fort Kearny. They moved slowly, ten to fourteen miles per day, hoping they would not encounter one of the many bands of Cheyenne that were now wandering the area. On the 14th they awoke to a heavy fog, and after packing to depart they found that the Pawnee scouts had slipped away. They asked the Cheyenne prisoner if he could guide them, and though none had command of the language, he seemed to know what they wanted. They marched twenty miles farther and did not find the fort.

The next day, Stuart and McCleary volunteered to form a scouting party to find the fort, so as to save the strength of the company and particularly the wounded. Captain Foote sent along three other men, among them a Mexican guide, whom Stuart said was a coward and was "all the time creating discontent." They also led some mules packed with supplies. The fog was still thick, but the suffering of the wounded compelled the party to set out on horseback at noon. It was a tense journey—lack of visibility meant they would have no warning if they came across a band of Cheyenne. They headed roughly northeast, obscured from each other in the fog, staying in teams of two and trying to remain in sight and on course. That evening they camped along a grassy ravine, and just as they were bedding down, a storm "of great violence" whipped up. "There we sat," Stuart wrote, "every man squatted on his saddle, revealed in gloomy outlines only by the lightning's flash, a picture I can never forget." They had not realized that they were camped in the flood zone of an intermittent stream, but after they had been dozing in the downpour for some hours, a flash of lightning revealed that their picketed animals were standing in water halfway up their bodies and rising. They quickly saved their mounts and mules and moved to higher ground.

The next day, McCleary suggested building a fire to warm and dry themselves, but Stuart disagreed—they had to press on to Kearny, wherever it was. McCleary agreed. The day was overcast, but a brief sighting of sun in the morning showed they had been off course all along, heading due east. They turned north, but knew they had probably gone fifty miles in the wrong direction. Fortunately, there were still no signs of Indians. The group rode through the day across the plains, hitting an impassable stream in the later afternoon. They diverted course southeast to find a ford, and were amazed to stumble onto a wagon trail. Thinking it was the road to Fort Kearny, they set off at a trot. But three hours later they began to wonder if they were going in circles, "for a tree on our left was visible constantly, and apparently at the same distance." They encamped that night, running low on food, anxious for the men they had left behind and for themselves. But the sky finally cleared and they were able to get a reading from the stars, which indicated that the trail was leading towards Kearny.

On the 18th they continued on the trail, and soon encountered another seemingly impassable stream. Stuart suggested taking the chance crossing, McCleary wanted to find a ford, and the Mexican refused to do either, protesting, "Me no swim!" Stuart and another man decided to make the crossing regardless. The current was stronger than expected, and halfway across, Stuart's horse Dan fell over and he was thrown from the saddle. Stuart swam to the other side, fully clothed. Then the mules crossed, followed by McCleary and the other soldier. This left the Mexican, who kept protesting that he could not swim. "I could not be deaf to the voice of humanity," Stuart wrote, "and planned an arrangement to help him, when to our amazement, the rascal swam over better than anyone had done."

The group picked up the trail again and figured they had just crossed the Big Blue, fifty miles from Kearny. They dashed down the road, cold and wet but hoping to make the fort that day. At midday they encountered a mail carrier and got some food, "a piece of hard bread, the most delicious morsel I ever tasted," Stuart wrote. They arrived at the fort that afternoon, to the relief of the officers there, who had heard from some Indian scouts that they were in the area. They arranged for a relief party to retrieve Foote's company, which was safely back at the fort four days later.

The Light Mules

JAMES MCINTOSH RODE SOUTH from the battlefield with the main body of Sumner's column, over rolling, grassy brown hills, following the trail of the retreating Cheyenne. It was a clear morning two days after the battle. The men were rested and ready for more action. The Delaware scouts had reported a large Cheyenne village ahead. After a fourteen-mile ride the troopers topped the edge of the Saline River valley. Below, in a horseshoe bend, they saw the village, or what was left of it. They could see no Indians, no corralled horses, no fires; there were many lodges, but clearly there had been many more. The soldiers moved slowly down into the valley and towards the village. As they neared, they spotted three Cheyenne on horseback, watching them approach. Just as they were sighted, the Indians turned and moved quickly, but not too quickly, south, vanishing over the opposite rise.

The soldiers made camp upriver and then began exploring the village: 171 lodges were still standing, and an equal number lay disassembled and ready to move. Many more had been taken. In the center stood an eighteen-foot-high lodge hung with new buffalo hide, a grand gathering place, completely intact. Evidently the flight had been swift. Much had been abandoned. The soldiers found clothing, furnishings, skins of all types, cooking utensils, children's toys and various personal items—but no weapons to speak of. There were immense stores of dried buffalo meat, and the troops packed as much as they could carry. They took down the lodges and gathered them up in big piles. The greatest loss to the tribe was the many prime lodge poles, difficult to replace on the open plains. McIntosh watched as the remains of the village were put to the torch, the smoke rising in great columns in the clear sky. "The destruction of their entire camp equippage injured the Indians more than the killing of a few braves did," Stanley wrote. "We burned everything and it did touch my heart to see the implements of the kitchen and the half-dressed skins, upon which the poor squaw had almost broken her back in toil, and even the playthings of the little children, committed to the flames."[8]

Sumner's men searched for weeks for the scattered Cheyenne, but came up empty. Some Indians had gone east, separating into small family groups, melting into the plains. Others went south, taking refuge among the camps of the Kiowa and Comanche beyond the Arkansas River. One group went north to Sioux territory over the South Platte. After the main village was found and the foe dispersed, the campaign had not amounted to much. For soldiers looking back on events, the only noteworthy accomplishment was the battle in the valley, the deed itself. In the days before medals, and when brevets were rare (as they were in the Indian wars), often the deed was all one had.

Initial reports said that Sumner's men had slaughtered four to five hundred men, women and children.[9] Another, from the *St. Joseph's Journal,* depicted a battle fit for a parade ground, with Sumner's men seeming inexperienced and in poor morale, the Indians masters of the field: "the Indians wheeled into rank, and formed as well as any disciplined troops could have done. . . . The Indians received the fire of the Americans coolly, and returned it with effect."[10] Accurate details took some time to get out, since Sumner was still in the field. However, the Cheyenne, though scattered, could still strike back. On August 11, 1857, a band of Cheyenne and Comanche attacked a cattle drive twenty-seven miles from Fort Kearny, stampeding the cattle, killing one driver and wounding another.[11] There were similar events in the following days and weeks, raising questions why Sumner did not kill more of the Cheyenne when he had the chance.

Critics noted that Sumner had made a mistake drawing sabers; he should have used rifles, as was intended. Criticism grew to the point where General Persifor Smith made Sumner stand a court martial for the battle.[12] Though he faced a variety of charges, his crime, simply stated, was letting the Indians get away. He had "a favorable opportunity of destroying that bold, blood-thirsty tribe of Indians known as the Cheyennes, and that, through mismanagement and unsoldierly conduct, he allowed them to escape." He was faulted for not waiting for the infantry to catch up before attacking, and "because he only used the saber and not the revolver or rifle." Sumner's defenders said he acted in "the most prudent manner possible"—waiting for the infantry would have given the Indians a chance to escape, and since most of his men were new recruits, he did not trust that they could have used the rifles effectively.

The truth, that the battle occurred the way it did because the Cheyenne thought they had strong medicine and decided to make their stand, was not yet known.[13] The Battle of Solomon's Fork was a unique confrontation. Both sides ignored the principles of war. The cavalry could have held off at a distance, goaded the Indians to charge and shot them down with their new rifles. The Indians could have adopted defensive positions in the trees, on the slopes, or on the approaches to their village, loosing arrows or balls at the troops as they attempted to traverse the rough terrain, disrupting their movement and falling back— techniques used to good effect by the Apache. But the battle had become a conclave of warriors, the Cheyenne emboldened by the medicine to believe that they were invulnerable to fire, Sumner in the last moment choosing cold steel over hot lead, for reasons never satisfactorily explained.

The trial generated other controversies, and since the campaign was over, there was ample time to engage in personal and political squabbling. Harney was a member of the court martial, and Sumner objected because he felt that Harney was prejudiced against him (they had been feuding since the Mexican War). Harney did nothing to dispel this belief when he said that in fact he "never had any, or very little, respect for Colonel Sumner as a soldier."[14] After his court martial, Sumner wrote Harney asking to meet him "at any place he might designate" to settle their differences. Harney read this as a challenge to a duel and took the matter to the secretary of war as a violation of Article 25 of the Articles of War. Another court martial was ordered. After several days of hearings at Carlisle Barracks, the court returned a not guilty verdict in fifteen minutes. Secretary of War Floyd objected to the finding, but Sumner was not punished.

Harney damaged his reputation by seeking Sumner's court martial for challenging him to a duel. Harney had always said he would meet any man above the rank of lieutenant who called him out; but Sumner was known as a dead shot, and it was whispered that Harney was simply afraid.[15] It was also considered unseemly and beneath the dignity of gentlemen to settle their private affairs by exploiting official channels. "General Harney's conduct throughout the whole affair has been utterly unworthy of his position," the New York Times wrote, "and eminently unbecoming an officer and a gentleman."[16] Harney should have just declined the challenge; his actions had the appearance of a vendetta. Harney later said he had refused because of his superior rank. Sumner replied that "a man who could insult a brother officer, and then shield himself from the consequences on the plea of superior rank, was not worthy of the notice of any gentleman."[17] When the dust settled, the two were put in separate commands: Sumner was appointed commander of the Department of the West, and Harney became commander of the Department of Oregon.

★ ★ ★

IN SEPTEMBER 1857, HAVING COVERED hundreds of miles and not found any Cheyenne, James McIntosh's company made its way back to Fort Leavenworth. Four of the six companies of the First Cavalry regiment had been taken from the column to be rushed to Utah on a show of force to pacify the Mormons. The remaining two companies, which included Company D, gave their extra supplies and most of their horses to the units heading west. McIntosh had fewer than a dozen horses left, but more than adequate pack animals, so he rode his command to Fort Leavenworth using the means at his disposal, his unit now dubbed "the Light Mules."

THE PIG WAR

ON JUNE 15, 1859, Lyman A. Cutlar, a Kentuckian who had settled on San Juan Island in the Pacific Northwest, noticed a pig
in his garden. It had knocked over his fence and was rooting
about his vegetables. Cutlar knew the pig; it belonged to Charles Griffin, the Hudson's Bay Company agent on the island. Cutlar had previously complained to Griffin about the pig, demanding that he keep it
out of his potatoes. Griffin replied that it was up to Cutlar to keep his
potatoes out of the pig. Cutlar, feeling he had given fair warning, got
out his rifle and killed the interloper. Griffin was outraged. He sought
to have Cutlar tried in a British court. Cutlar declined to cooperate,
though he offered to pay for the pig. The animal was worth about ten
dollars, but Griffin stated that the pig, a Berkshire boar, was a champion breeder, and he demanded ten times that. The offer fell through
and James Douglas, governor of British Vancouver Island, whose nickname was "Old Square Toes," dispatched a sloop carrying his son-in-
law, Alexander Dallas, to arrest the trespassing American. Cutlar, rifle
in hand, told Dallas that his farm was on American territory, and if they
wanted to arrest him they would have to take him in by force. "Crack
the whip," he said defiantly.[1]

Around this time, Brigadier General Harney, in his capacity as
commander of the Department of Oregon, was on an inspection tour
of American forts in the Puget Sound area. He stopped off on San Juan
Island and was met by most of the eighteen American settlers, including Cutlar. They had just celebrated Independence Day and raised the
Stars and Stripes. When they told Harney the story of the pig shooting
and the British response, the general was outraged. He felt it was an
insult to the American flag and the rights of U.S. citizens. Harney conferred with Washington territorial delegate Isaac Stevens, who coincidentally had graduated at the top of the USMA Class of 1839, and
resolved a plan of action.[2]

On the night of July 26, 1859, under Harney's orders, sixty-eight soldiers of Company D, Ninth U.S. Infantry from nearby Fort Belling-ham steamed across the Rosario Strait on the *Massachusetts* and occu-pied San Juan. They established a fort on the Cattle Point peninsula at the southern end of the island, ran up the American flag and claimed San Juan as sovereign U.S. territory. They defied the British to take any steps to dislodge them and offered to do battle if that's what they wanted. The company commander set precisely the tone Harney had wanted. He had hand-picked the leader of the expedition; he wanted someone who was daring and brave, and whom he could count on in a fight. He sent Captain George E. Pickett.

Pickett had made a name for himself with his feat at Chapulte-pec and his bravery throughout the Mexican War. He left Mexico in 1848, serving the next seven years at various posts in Texas. Pickett said most of this time was spent in the field, "being under canvas nearly the whole time." He saw many of his West Point comrades over the years, notably serving with his friend Longstreet at Fort Bliss, 1854–55.

In March 1855, Secretary Davis promoted Pickett, as he had fel-low Goats Heth and McIntosh, and gave him command of Company D of the new Ninth Infantry. Pickett's second in command was Lieu-tenant James W. Forsyth, a turnback from the Class of 1856.[3] After a training period at Fort Monroe, the unit went to the Pacific Northwest. The area was rife with Indian raids on the settlers who were streaming into the Oregon Territory. Pickett was posted at Fort Steilacoom at the southern end of Puget Sound. In 1856 he established Fort Bellingham at the northern end, across the strait from San Juan. The Indians in Pickett's immediate area, mainly Nootka and Chinook, were for the most part peaceful towards the whites, and Pickett used his fort as neu-tral ground to encourage the Indians to allow him to arbitrate disputes between them. Pickett earned the respect of the locals, who called him *Nesika Tyee*—"our chief."

Like Heth, Pickett took an interest in Indian culture, setting up schools and translating the Lord's Prayer into the local tongue. He took a much more personal interest in one Indian in particular, Sâkis Tiigang, or "Morning Mist." She was a princess (as Pickett described her, more accurately the daughter of a chief) of the Kaigani Haida tribe whom he met on a survey expedition to Semiahmoo. They met again at Fort Bellingham, and Pickett soon proposed. This was Pickett's second betrothal; in 1851 he had wed Sallie Harrison Steward Minge of Rich-mond, who died the same year.

Pickett and his princess were married sometime in 1856 in a tribal ceremony, in which, it was said, they each wore a white glove and joined hands.[4] They later had a U.S. civil ceremony, which shows that Pickett's commitment exceeded that of most frontier soldiers, who would participate in tribal weddings with the intention of later deserting their wives, feeling no personal obligation or legal responsibility.[5] But Pickett doted on his bride. He built a house for her, the first permanent residence in Bellingham.[6] On December 31, 1857, she bore him a son, James Tilton Pickett, named for his friend Major James Tilton. However, there had been complications with the delivery and Sâkis Tiigang died within a few weeks. Pickett struggled to raise Jimmie as best he could, with the help of his wife's family, but his duties made it increasingly difficult for him to be a single father. In 1859, the young captain arranged for Catherine and William Collins to raise Jimmie. For ten years, through the Civil War and after, Pickett sent them what financial assistance he could.

Pickett ran a model frontier post, his men in good spirits. Pickett's friend Rufus Ingalls was quartermaster of the Department of Oregon at Fort Vancouver, 1859–60, and the two went hunting together when they could. (Pickett later named his hunting dog Rufus.) Pickett grew enough produce (potatoes, for example) to supplement the feed stores and sold what was left over at the local market. His main duties were preventing whiskey smuggling to the Indians; alcohol tended to cause fights and other incidents, both among Indians and between them and the growing immigrant population. The Fraser River gold rush in 1857–58 exacerbated these problems. It was important to keep the Indians from fighting with each other and the whites, as well as to prevent white reprisals when incidents took place. Pickett handled his territory well and impressed Harney as a competent officer who kept the peace.

The most significant problems were caused by Indians who raided from British Columbia. They were more warlike, and after their raids they fled north across the border and out of U.S. jurisdiction. There were too few troops in the area to prevent these incursions. One of the gathering points used by the raiders was San Juan Island, which is one of the larger islands in the straits between Washington Territory and Vancouver. There were frequent incidents between marauders and the few settlers who lived on the island, resulting occasionally in killing. When Harney visited the island in July 1859, the settlers petitioned him for protection. On inhabitant stated that "the butcheries around the islands . . . had driven away all hope of settling in safety."[7]

A jurisdictional issue complicated the problem. The 1846 treaty that set the boundary between U.S. and British territories in the Northwest was unintentionally vague—it specified that the line would be drawn in "the middle of the channel which separates the continent from Vancouver Island." Unfortunately, there were two channels, the Rosario Strait to the east of the island group and the Haro Strait to the west. The discrepancy was never clarified. In the 1850s, British and American settlers alike came to the sixteen-mile-long island. The Hudson's Bay Company, which called the island "Bellevue" and claimed sole administrative privileges, established a sheep herding concern. In 1855 an American sheriff impounded three dozen of the sheep for back taxes, but the State Department papered over the dispute. For the most part, regardless of local sentiments, London and Washington would rather ignore the issue than go to the trouble of resolving it. But it was hard to ignore George Pickett.

According to Harney's Special Order No. 72, July 18, 1859, Pickett's mission was to protect the inhabitants of the island from Indians operating from British or Russian territories, and to defend the rights of inhabitants from British intimidation or force.[8] Clearly the Indians would be deterred by the presence of soldiers on the island, so the issue would turn on the British response. It was quick in coming. A representative of Hudson's Bay Company arrived, told Pickett he was trespassing on Bellevue and asked him to leave. Pickett responded that he had been ordered to San Juan by lawful authority and would stay there until he received orders to the contrary.

By coincidence, the British were about to send a magistrate to govern the island, a tall, one-eyed Irishman, Major John de Courcy. Hearing of Pickett's preemptive occupation, the government dispatched three frigates, the *Tribune,* the *Satellite* and the *Plumper.* Pickett was enjoying an afternoon smoke near the shore with settler Paul Hubbs when HMS *Tribune* pulled up offshore. Hubbs observed that the situation had "turned a bit uncomfortable."

"Not in the least," Pickett replied.[9] He relocated his encampment to slightly more favorable ground, but they were still under the banks of naval guns. On August 3, Captain Geoffrey Phipps Hornby of the *Tribune* met with Pickett in his small camp. The post must not have appeared very impressive to the British officer: eighteen peaked canvas Sibly tents in a field near the shore, manned by a relatively small detachment. Hornby took a relaxed approach to the affair, suggesting a joint occupation until the diplomats worked out a solution. Pickett said he was not authorized to agree to such an arrangement; it would be in contravention of his orders. He did not think anything would happen if they maintained their current arrangement, with Americans on the land and the British at sea; but if Hornby sought to force the issue, the consequences would be on him. Hornby threatened a landing that day. Pickett declared that he would resist "as long as I have a man."

"Very well, I shall land at once!" Hornby declared. Pickett suggested a forty-eight-hour delay in order to communicate with Harney. "Not one minute," Hornby declared, and left.

Pickett quickly saw to his defenses. He drew his forces up in line of battle near the beach to repel the landings. Each man was armed with sixty rounds of ammunition and three days' rations in case they had to withdraw to the interior. The American settlers were there, rifles in hand, forming a sharpshooter militia. They took positions behind the regulars, seeking to pick off the British officers as they came ashore.

"Don't be afraid of their big guns," Pickett told his men. "We will make a Bunker Hill of it!" The troops stood to throughout the night, but no attack came.

The British could easily have taken the island at that point. Pickett was vastly outnumbered and outgunned. He wrote his commander at Fort Steilacoom, Lieutenant Colonel Silas Casey—an Immortal of the Class of 1826, who graduated two places above Ephraim Kirby Smith—that "it is not comfortable to be lying within range of a couple of war steamers. The *Tribune*, a thirty-gun frigate, is lying broadside to our camp, and from present indications everything leads me to suppose that they will attempt to prevent me carrying out my instructions." Pickett kept a brave front, hoping that his tenacity would deter the British, which it did. They made no move, but stayed at anchor with guns trained on his little outpost. Hornby met several more times with Pickett and came away impressed, writing to his wife, "He speaks more like a Devonshire man than a Yankee."

On August 3, Pickett wrote to headquarters, "they have a force so superior to mine that it will be merely a mouthful for them." He privately recommended suggesting a joint occupation, because if the British chose to land elsewhere, there was nothing Pickett could do to prevent it, so they might as well make a virtue of the inevitable. But Harney had no interest in joint occupation and told Pickett to stick to his position and await reinforcements. On August 9, American troops from the Ninth Infantry with artillery landed under the cover of heavy fog, passing directly under the *Tribune*'s guns. Colonel Casey took command.[10] More reinforcements arrived on the twelfth, and by mid-August the American force numbered five infantry and four artillery companies, about 450 men. They built heavy earthworks facing the Hudson's Bay Company compound and prepared for a siege. The British added two more warships, bringing the size of their force to 167 guns and over 2,000 men. Governor Douglas urged an attack, but Rear Admiral Robert L. Baynes, commander of British naval forces in the Pacific, refused to start a war over a "squabble about a pig."

President Buchanan, who as secretary of state had negotiated the 1846 treaty that had led to the problem, learned of the events on September 3. He took a characteristically noncommittal stance: If Harney's actions were preemptive against British aggression, they were commendable. If not, not. But until the facts were in, the president declined to "form any decided opinion" of the affair and counseled caution. American opinion was skeptical. "If an American Colonel in a petty post," the *New York Times* wrote, "and an English Colonel at the head of a petty colony, can drive England and America into a war, we shall shortly be cannonading our dearly beloved cousins across the sea."[11] The Crown protested that the action was unilateral, aggressive, and disruptive to the patient work of the boundary commission.[12] The British press charged the Americans with piracy and called for action. They would show "the licensed ruffians of the Federal Army that they must not appropriate British Territory as coolly as if they were cutting off another slice of Mexico." The Vancouver government debated whether the occupation already constituted open war, and some fiery speeches were made, but in the end the firebrands failed to muster the votes necessary to mobilize the militia. Despite the rhetoric on the mainland, the opposing forces on and around the island maintained cordial relations, visiting in Camp Pickett and aboard the British ships. American officers regularly attended the Sunday sermons by the British chaplain aboard the *Satellite*.[13]

Ultimately Buchanan delegated the problem to the Army chief of staff, General Winfield Scott, who had previously negotiated the Aroostook boundary dispute in 1839 (his pretext for leaving Florida after failing to pacify the Seminoles), which established the northern border of Maine. Buchanan gave Scott wide discretionary powers. He advised the general that a joint occupation was not objectionable, but should the British force a conflict, the United States would respond in kind. The *Times* surmised that in sending Scott, "It looks very much as if the Administration had already decided that *the island is to be surrendered*" [emphasis in original] and that the general was sent to lend a sufficiently martial air to what was actually a defeat.[14]

Scott met with Harney on October 21. They had a prior history, but not a good one. Harney had been Scott's cavalry commander during the Mexican War. Scott did not trust Harney's judgment and had relieved him of command after the landing at Vera Cruz. Harney appealed over Scott's head to President Polk and the secretary of war, William Marcy, and the order was overturned. Harney then went on to serve brilliantly during the war, which could not have improved Scott's opinion of him. Their meeting did not amount to much. Scott then conferred with Pickett on the disputed island.

When Scott met with Governor Douglas, he proposed a joint occupation with one hundred men each side. Douglas refused, saying he could not consent without instructions from London. After protracted negotiation they agreed *ad interim* to reduce the American presence to one company only ("any company except Pickett's," Douglas demanded). Scott made the agreement without further consulting Harney or the territorial governor, Richard D. Gholson. Scott believed that Harney and Pickett were "proud of their conquest of the island" and jealous of his "interference," so he felt no special need to include them in his deliberations. He saw Harney as impetuous and rash, the territorial government as irrelevant. On November 7, Scott ordered all U.S. troops off the island except a company from the Fourth Infantry commanded by Captain Lewis C. Hunt (USMA 1847), an Immortal of Heth's class. Pickett returned to Fort Bellingham, though the post he had established on the island continued to be called "Camp Pickett."

Scott departed without giving Harney a briefing on the discussed joint occupation, though he did give Harney the option to leave his command to go to St. Louis. Harney declined. For his part, Pickett was offended. He claimed that the president's instruction had been to leave his company on the island, and that Scott had acted at the behest of Douglas. "General Scott has however cast an implicit censure upon me for *Obeying Orders*," he wrote.[15] Local sentiment was decidedly in his favor. In December 1859, the Washington territorial legislature formally condemned Scott's actions as high-handed and insulting. It praised Harney for "the gallant manner in which he ... flew to the protection of our citizens against the insults and menaces of those who contemplated still further and more intolerable impositions." And to Pickett they gave "cordial thanks for his gallant bearing and prompt discharge of his duty in the face of overwhelming forces," assuring him that "although displaced of command at the demand of, and sacrificed to satiate British rapacity, he is not disgraced, but a ten fold degree elevated in the estimation of his countrymen." Pickett's "greatest crime was daring to do his duty in the face of British threats and British cannon." On January 11, 1860, the legislature unanimously voted to thank

Pickett formally "for the gallant and firm discharge of his duties under the most trying circumstances while in command on the Island of San Juan."

Meanwhile, visitors and settlers were flocking to San Juan, for the most part because of its celebrity. In the first few weeks of the stand-off, Pickett estimated he had five hundred callers. Increasing population brought familiar troubles and made Hunt's task more formidable than Pickett's. Some on the island were dissatisfied with Hunt, finding him too ready to interfere in their affairs (they were running rum, by Hunt's account). They petitioned Harney to have him removed. But others contended that the trade in illegal alcohol was widespread and very dangerous, which tended to support Hunt's position. Harney decided it would be a diplomatic move to place a new officer there, one with a reputation for fairness, so on April 1860, Pickett returned. Harney said, "without questioning the merits of Captain Hunt for firmness, discretion and courtesy, it is no disparagement of him to say he does not excel Pickett."

Harney had another, more pressing motive. On March 21, 1860, eighty-five Royal Marines landed at Garrison Bay on the western edge of the island under command of Captain George Bazalgette, who had recently arrived from China. Harney either was unaware of or chose to ignore Scott's joint occupation agreement. The Marines were ordered not to create an incident, but to defend the rights of Crown subjects in areas under their control, and not to interfere with the American citizens. "You will place yourself in frank and free communication with the commanding officer of the U.S. troops," Bazalgette's orders read, "bearing in mind how essential it is for the public service that the most perfect and cordial understanding should exist between you, which I have every reason to feel assured you will at all times find Captain Hunt ready and anxious to maintain."

However, Hunt was removed and Pickett put back, to the consternation of the British. One London newspaper stated that Harney had believed Hunt had "English proclivities" and described Pickett as "a commander of a very different character, the same gentleman whom he selected as his instrument when he first seized upon the island."[16] The locals, on the other hand, were delighted. Pickett was a man they could trust, both to stand up to the British and to bring order to the island. Meanwhile, Harney stoked the fires by issuing orders indicating that he did not recognize General Scott's joint occupation arrangement, since it had not been vetted by the territorial governor nor by the commanding general (himself). Some in Britain talked again of war, but most favored a diplomatic solution. "A fleet of near 200 guns and 2,000 men is a costly way of pleading the case for an island which nobody heard of till the other day," the *Times* of London noted.[17] What all agreed was that Harney was the source of the problem and had to be removed.

When Scott received the news of Hunt's replacement and Harney's statement, he went to the secretary of war and Harney was ordered to relinquish his command and return to Washington. He was later given command of the Department of the West in St. Louis.[18] The Department of Oregon was given to Colonel George Wright (USMA 1822), commander of the Ninth Infantry regiment, a veteran of many conflicts who was wounded leading the forlorn hope at Molino del Rey. Wright, who knew Pickett well, left him in place.

British fears of Pickett were unfounded. His reputation as a mischief maker was belied by his natural charm and easygoing temperament. He and Bazalgette got along well. They established a working relationship to deal with their common problems. By then, San Juan had become a law-free zone. Criminals went there because they claimed that civil authority did not and could not exist, so they could not be prosecuted. Indians went there to drink whiskey, resulting in fights and other troubles. Pickett, who believed his mandate was to enforce territorial law, did so without worrying about whether or not he had the power in theory. He appointed E. C. Gillette justice of the peace and U.S. commissioner for the island, promising to back up his authority with military support if needed. This calmed things down quickly. The British authorities handled matters similarly with their citizens, and each side handed over suspects to their proper national authorities. It was a practical solution to an impractical diplomatic situation.

Open conflict was averted. The only casualty in the Pig War was the pig.

Contemporary interpretations of the San Juan affair tied it to the exacerbated sectional dispute that would soon erupt into violence. Major Granville O. Haller, who commanded Fort Townsend, believed that Harney and Pickett were attempting to incite Britain to fight the United States, giving the South an opportunity to secede and make separate terms.[19] He noted that Harney was from Tennessee and had married into a slave-owning Missouri family. But in fact the general opposed secession, and he served with the Union in the Civil War. George B. McClellan, who at the time of the events was a railroad executive, had a more charitable though still speculative interpretation. He wrote in 1875 that the occupation of San Juan "had [its] origin in the patriotic attempt on the part of General Harney, Governor Stevens ... with the knowledge and zealous concurrence of Captain Pickett, to force a war with Great Britain in the hopes that by this means the then warring sections of our country would unite in a foreign war, and avert the civil strife they feared they saw approaching."[20]

Pickett was on San Juan Island on June 25, 1861, when he resigned his Federal commission and returned to the East to offer his services to Virginia. He left behind a decorated red camphorwood Chinese tea chest for his son Jimmie, containing his Army commissioning papers, a letter describing Jimmie's mother, Sâkis Tiigang, the two white gloves they had worn when they were married, and a Bible in which he inscribed, "May the memory of your mother always remain dear. Your father, George E. Pickett."

George Armstrong Custer

T HE RETURN FROM FURLOUGH was a bittersweet time for cadets. They left behind their families and friends, the comforts and adventures they enjoyed during the summer. Nevertheless, they returned to West Point with the first leg of their education behind them, and now stood a few short years from graduation. The "cows" congregated in New York to arrive en masse just before the end of encampment, in order to take advantage of the end of summer festivities. This was also their last chance to stock up on supplies for the coming year. The New York stopover was "a chance of a lifetime," according to George C. Strong of the Class of 1857, "and we made the most of it; for with a discretion and foresight that would have done credit to any quartermaster or commissary department in the world, we failed not to procure supplies for a long campaign."[1] They bought all the things denied them at West Point: tobacco, liquor, cooking utensils for hashes, decks of cards—anything they thought they could successfully sneak into the barracks. "All these things," Strong wrote, "the essentials of many a half hour's postprandial and social smoke, were ... contraband of war and had to be smuggled."[2] Tobacco and cigars were crammed into "every available inch of space" in their trunks. They bought pipes for their personal use or to give as gifts to those who had stayed behind. Cadets who were flush shared with those who came back from furlough broke (usually those who had had to travel a great distance). Since they were not allowed to have cash at the Academy, the cadets spent it all, less the $1.25 fare for steamboat passage upriver.

The returning cadets greeted the sight of West Point with mixed feelings; they cheered when the flag came into view, though Strong noted, "it must be confessed this enthusiasm at realizing the return of our subjugation to discipline, was rather external than otherwise."[3] They landed at the wharf and walked up to the South Gate, where their comrades who had spent the summer in the encampment met them with approbation. For their friends who had remained behind, the return of the furloughmen was a time of celebration, as captured in cadet verse:

> The "Furloughs" are coming and now must be near,
> There is dust, there is shouting, the "Furloughs" are here.
> They are here! What a cheer! As their comrades they hail;
> At the sight, what delight and affection prevail.[4]

The members of the Furlough Class of 1859 came through the gate August 28, their booty safely hidden, greeting their friends on the way to report for haircuts, shaves, and the mandatory in-briefing with the Commandant. Plebe John Montgomery Wright recalled that as the furloughmen were passing through the gate, the cry went up "from a hundred throats . . . 'Here comes Custer!' " Wright saw "an undeveloped looking youth, with a poor figure, slightly rounded shoulders, and an ungainly walk . . . an indifferent soldier, a poor student and a perfect incorrigible . . . a roystering, reckless cadet, always in trouble, always playing some mischievous pranks, and liked by everyone." The next time Wright saw him a few days later, Custer was in the process of "yanking" the plebe from his tent in the middle of the night, dragging him in his blanket across the Plain and sending him flying down the slope, laughing the whole time.[5]

Custer's return from furlough caused great commotion. He was well known to every class in the Corps. In his first two years, he had established himself as a cadet bon vivant, a ringleader of numerous escapades, charismatic, fun and loyal to a fault. Morris Schaff, who graduated ninth in the Class of 1862, wrote that "West Point has had many a character to deal with; but it may be a question whether it ever had a cadet so exuberant, one who cared so little for its serious attempts to elevate and burnish, or one on whom its tactical officers kept their eyes so constantly and unsympathetically searching as upon Custer. And yet how we all loved him; and to what a height he rose!"[6] Custer was a unique cadet in those days, or any day since. Schaff observed his inborn qualities: "His nature, so full of those streams that rise, so to speak, among the high hills of our being. I have in mind his joyousness, his attachment to the friends of his youth, and his never-ending delight in talking about his old home."[7]

George Armstrong Custer was born December 5, 1839, in the east Ohio town of New Rumley. His father, Emmanuel, was a blacksmith from western Maryland, son of a Hessian solider named Küster who had stayed in America after his unit surrendered during the Revolution. Part of a large and close-knit family, he was a charismatic youngster, with bright blue eyes and curly red-gold hair. Custer attended public school, where he got a decent education.[8] At school he was friendly, outgoing, athletic and mischievous, the latter a quality he got from his father, who said he was "always a boy with the boys."[9] His cousin Mary said he was "full of life and always ready to do anything which had a semblance of daring in it."[10] When he was four years old, "Autie," as he was called, started drilling with the local militia unit, the martially named New Rumley Invincibles, and became their mascot. The militiamen called Autie "a born soldier."

At the age of thirteen he moved to Monroe, Michigan, to live with the family of his older half-sister Lydia Reed. There he entered Alfred Stebbins' Young Men's Academy. He passed in most subjects, at least those he chose to favor with study, but like many future Goats, Custer was more interested in finding time to make mischief. It was an enduring impulse, one he was aware of and content with. One of his boyhood teachers relates the following conversation when Custer was caught in the act of some type of rascality:

"I know I was wrong," Custer said, "but I could not help it."
"Could not help it?" the teacher replied.
"No Sir. I wanted to do it."
"But could you not restrain your impulses?"
"Don't know Sir—never tried."
"But don't you think you ought to try?"
"What if I could; but I don't feel like trying."[11]

Custer was very personable and made friends easily, but he was known also for his temper. Once while Custer was in class during a recitation, another boy made a face at him through a window he was next to, and Custer put his fist through the glass and socked him.[12]

In Monroe, Custer did odd jobs for Judge Daniel S. Bacon, a local civic leader, which is when he first caught sight of Elizabeth, Judge Bacon's daughter. "Libbie" Bacon was attractive and lively, and Custer was naturally interested in getting to know her, but their social divisions kept the two apart, and they only passed a few words in the years he was there. Custer graduated from Stebbins' Academy at age sixteen and returned to Ohio, where he became a teacher in the one-room Beech Point schoolhouse in Hopedale, about ten miles from his parents' home. He was popular with the children, very animated in the classroom, and known to rough-house with the older boys who were not much younger than he. However, Custer had greater ambitions than to be a rural school-teacher. He wanted to be a famous solider or, failing that, a great educator at an eastern college. Custer saw attending West Point as a way to get a free education and to further his many ambitions. "I think [West Point] is the best place that I could go," he wrote his sister in 1856. Moreover, he noted that he would be paid $28 a month, and when he got out, he would be five years' pay ahead. His mother, Maria, opposed the idea; George had been named after a Methodist preacher, and she felt he should take the cloth. But Emmanuel approved. The trick then was getting an appointment.

Custer was a vocal Democrat from an openly Democratic family in a majority Whig/Republican area whose Republican congressman, John A. Bingham, was not likely to send a committed Democrat to fill his allotted slot at West Point.[13] But a local farmer named Alexander Holland, who was influential in Republican circles and with whom Custer was boarding, made an appeal on the young man's behalf. Holland may have been impressed with Custer, or perhaps he wanted to break up a budding romance between Autie and Holland's daughter Mary. Whatever the case, Congressman Bingham interviewed Custer and was impressed enough to grant him an appointment. It arrived in early 1857, signed by Secretary of War Jefferson Davis.

CUSTER REACHED WEST POINT in June 1857 and called it "the most romantic spot I ever saw."[14] He was soon making friends in the Corps, and like most cadets he picked up a nickname, "Fanny," for his beautiful long, curly locks and his peaches-and-cream complexion. It was an unbecoming moniker for a warrior, but cadets could be harsh with those who too obviously paid attention to their grooming. One cadet was hazed in camp after taking too long before a mirror; his fellows drew up a charge of "effeminate conduct, unbecoming an officer and a gentleman, and to the prejudice of good order and military discipline," specifying that the cadet in question did "look, in a shameless and effeminate manner, and for five consecutive minutes or thereabouts, into a mirror; and that with unmistakable signs of self-approval."[15] Custer tried to escape his feminine nickname by shaving his head. While previously he had been written up for having his hair too long, now he faced reports for having his hair too short; so he took to wearing a wig to stay within regulations until his hair grew out.[16] Later he was called "Cinnamon" for the cinnamon hair oil he used, and was also known by Whistler's nickname and—ironically, given what was to come—Crazy Horse's boyhood name, "Curly."

Custer was passionate about the things that interested him. Studying, for most of the year, was not one of them. He was consistently at or near the bottom of his class academically. He was not a great reader—after his first year at West Point, he never checked a book out of the library. Like many other Goats, Custer could have done better at his coursework if he had wanted to. But he consciously balanced academics against amusement and allowed the latter to dominate. He did not have to work hard to pass. Simply getting to graduation was good enough for him, whatever his class rank. He was not courting failure; he was unquestionably determined to earn his commission. After his first year at West Point he wrote his sister, "I would not leave this place for any amount of money because I would rather have a good education and no money than have a fortune and be ignorant."[17]

Custer's letters show that he at least claimed to study (or "bone," in cadet argot) a great deal around exam time. Perhaps he and other Immortals who could have been star men might not have wanted to graduate near the top and become engineers and artillerymen. A place near the bottom guaranteed entry into the Infantry, Dragoons, Mounted Rifles or Cavalry, and for those who wanted adventure, these postings were preferable. They were much more likely to be sent into action on the frontier, and Custer noted also that "the cavalry offered the most promising field for early promotion."[18] His qualifications were mixed; like many Immortals, Custer earned a reputation as an expert rider, yet his worst grades in his final year were in cavalry tactics.

Tully McCrea, a fellow Ohioan of the Class of 1862, who roomed with Custer his first year at West Point, observed that "the great difficulty is that he is too clever for his own good. He is always connected with all the mischief that is going on and never studies any more than he can possibly help." Yet Tully "admired and partly envied Custer's free and careless way, and the perfect indifference he had for everything. It was all right with him whether he knew his lesson or not; he did not allow it to trouble him."[19]

Graduating from West Point had gotten easier over the years, or so statistics indicated. In the period 1812 to 1821, when Thayer's reforms first took effect, only 29 percent of cadets admitted to the Academy actually graduated. In the ten years before the Civil War, the number had risen to 52 percent.[20] Custer's class began with 108 candidates, of whom 68 passed the January exam; 12 were later dismissed and 22 resigned to join the Confederacy. The classes of the late 1850s were on the five-year program that Jefferson Davis had instituted while secretary of war. On

October 11, 1858, Davis's successor John B. Floyd reverted back to the four-year curriculum, and the top two classes were combined. The cadets were extremely pleased, especially those in their fourth year who looked forward to being released early. They told their families and friends, made travel plans, and bought their lieutenant's uniforms. But on April 5, 1859, with graduation so close the cadets could taste it, the secretary changed back to the five-year plan.[21] The top two classes were again divided, and the cadets who thought they were going to graduate had to store their blue uniforms for another year. One cadet wrote home that the change was "probably accomplished by one of the most disgraceful intrigues ever known in the City of Washington."[22] In the fall of 1860, a commission visited West Point with a view to recommending improvements. Senator Jefferson Davis was one of the commissioners.[23] They submitted a 350-page report on December 13, 1860, recommending a radical overhaul of the entire Academy, but leaving the five-year course in place. The cadets in private cursed the committee for not finding against the five-year curriculum—an unlikely outcome, since it had been Davis's own reform. A Georgia cadet wished that Davis would go to hell—but then quickly said, "No, I take that all back; for I believe the day is coming when the South will have need of Mr. Davis' abilities."[24] A week later, South Carolina seceded, and events overtook the reforms.

"Custer's Luck"

IN HIS FIRST SUMMER at the Academy, Custer noted that he had "escaped with but few demerit marks" and observed that "a person has to be very careful in his conduct."[25] Four years later, he had racked up one of the highest demerit totals in West Point history. "Custer was constantly in trouble with the school authorities," according to Peter Michie, second in the Class of 1863 and a leading professor at West Point for thirty years. ". . . He had more fun, gave his friends more anxiety, walked more tours of extra guard, and came nearer being dismissed more often than any other cadet I have ever known."[26]

Custer is widely thought to hold the record for demerits, with 726 in four years. This is an impressive achievement, but whether or not it constitutes a record is open to interpretation. A number of graduating cadets had higher totals. For example, George W. "Poet" Patten had 1,077 demerits over four years, and Charles H. Larnard, Class of 1831, previously mentioned as the one-year record holder, had a career total of 1,658 demerits. However, these two cadets gained most of their demerits before the 200-point annual limit was imposed. There was also the matter of the demerit multipliers in the 1830s and 1840s. The rules had been relaxed by Custer's time. For example, when Custer was a plebe, he enjoyed a one-third demerit reduction at the end of each half year, in recognition of being "less experienced, and more likely to err."[27] In his plebe year, he earned 226 demerits, which dropped to 151 after one-third were forgiven. The demerit multipliers of earlier years were also done away with, so for example a firstie would no longer suffer the additional half-point penalty. Thus, Custer had it easier than cadets who preceded him, in that he could afford to court higher demerit totals with a reasonable expectation of graduating. He kept as close to the line as he could, right up to the end of his West Point career. He had 97 demerits in the six months up to June 6, 1861, when the term ended. In the next three weeks, knowing his class would probably graduate early, he racked up 52 more, 8 of them the day before graduation.

But Custer still had a strong contemporary challenger for the crown of "worst disciplinary record." It was Marcus A. Reno, with whom Custer's fate was intertwined. Reno was admitted as a member of the Class of 1855. He was always near the bottom in merit, and in the first half of his final year at West Point, Reno amassed a stunning 225 demerits. He was recommended for discharge. The secretary of war commuted this to suspension, and Reno returned to repeat his firstie year. However, in 1856 he was again dismissed, this time for being caught off post drinking, and again he was reinstated. Reno finally graduated in the middle of the Class of 1857, with 1,031 skins over his six-year career at West Point. While Reno beat Custer in absolute terms, his annual average was lower (171.8 demerits per year, versus Custer's 181.5). And in any case, Custer clearly had more fun.

Custer said his "offenses against law and order were not great in enormity, but what they lacked in magnitude they made up in number."[28] The record bears this out. Of his five and three-quarters folio pages of demerits, most were relatively small, one- to two-point violations, some in the three-to-four range, and a few fives. He was marked down for being late, talking, napping, being absent, skipping class, neglect of studies, collar turned up on coat, long hair, room in disorder, idling, visiting, laughing, throwing bread at dinner, trifling, loitering, unshaven at inspection, hair brush out of place (one of the pickier violations), throwing snowballs, throwing stones, rusty musket, playing cards, riding despite being on sick report, and the counterpart, absent from hospital when sick (copying Henry Heth's ploy).

Custer spent a good deal of time "walking extras," doing additional guard duty on weekends to reduce his demerit count. A tour lasted four hours, walking a thirty-yard interval, in full uniform with musket. Each tour would eliminate one demerit. Custer estimated he spent sixty-six Saturdays so employed—it was the only way he kept within the 100-point semester limit. For example in the spring of 1860 he accumulated 129 demerits (he had earned 53 in February alone), and walked off 30 of them to stay within the limit. Tully McCrea said that "extra guard duty is severe punishment, as I know from experience." He preferred confinement to quarters.[29] But in a letter home, Custer noted that "everything is fine" after describing walking punishment tours. To him they were a safety valve, a way of redeeming himself after going over the line, and showing the authorities that despite his obstreperous ways, he was committed to the institution and its ultimate authority. He never complained about punishment but accepted it as the price he had to pay for living the life he had chosen. If the pressure was too great, he could go weeks at a time without demerits; the spring of 1860 was noteworthy in that he received no demerits at all.[30]

Custer was hardly the only cadet who courted trouble. As in years past, the cadets continued to relish the cat-and-mouse game with the Tacs. They had devised a "telegraph system" to alert each other during surprise inspections. The new barracks, built in 1851, had a central heating system, with furnaces in the basement that forced hot air through shafts, and gas lighting fed through pipes. When an inspection commenced unexpectedly, cadets on the lower floors would tap the pipes to warn the rest of the Corps. Cadets like Custer who lived on upper floors could quickly order their rooms before the officers arrived.[31] But the Tacs played the game as well, some in the same spirit of sportsmanship. Cadmus Wilcox, Class of 1846 and instructor of infantry tactics, 1853–57, would sneak about the barracks in rubbers to muffle his footsteps, springing in on the unsuspecting cadets in their rooms. He was so effective he inspired an ode to the tune of "They Stole My Child Away"[32]

When evening's shadows gently closed around us,
We used to take out the "papers" to play;
Till "Cadmus" came one fatal night and "hived" us,
He "skinned" us all, and took our cards away.

I hear the old rascal upon the stairs;
In spite of his rubbers, I hear him there.
He stole! He stole!
He stole my pipe away!

The factor working against cadets the most was institutional memory. Most of the officers had previously attended the Academy themselves, and some had impressive demerit totals. Wilcox, for example,
was an Immortal of his class, graduating five spots above Pickett, with
160 demerits his final year. He knew the tricks, and most of the other
Tacs did too. So the old standby of concealing cooking utensils in the
chimney would no longer work, as Custer learned when an officer
inspected his fireplace and "hived" his hidden hash kitchen.

★ ★ ★

IN AUGUST OF HIS FIRST YEAR at West Point, Custer noticed that some
of the cadets would don civilian dress and "have the boldness to cross
the sentinels posts at night and go to a small village two or three miles
down the river for the purpose of getting things which are not allowed,
such as ice cream, candies, fruit and (I am sorry to say) some even go
for wines and other liquors."[33] Custer soon joined this bold crowd, and
later in life he reflected that "the forbidden locality of Benny Havens'
possessed stronger attractions than the study and demonstration of a
problem in Euclid, or the prosy discussion of some abstract proposition of moral science."[34]

Benny Havens' remained a center of cadet life and imagination,
though by the late 1850s "the barriers between it and the barrack-prison
have been made too strong, by more modern discipline, to be passed
by any save the most daring."[35] While the proportion of cadets at Benny's
declined, they were offset by the returning officers, "the bravest and
wisest, gray-haired veterans making a last pilgrimage to Benny's sylvan
shrine."[36] Benny himself was also white-haired by this time, nearing
seventy years old, but still spry. One former cadet of that era described
him as "of uncertain age, over fifty and under eighty, with a ruddy clean-
shaven face which displayed soft little wrinkles about his eyes and
mouth." Benny was "full of wise saws and quaint stories" about former
cadets who had gone on to fame as Army officers, "which he would
relate with a merry twinkle of his eyes and a genial quaver of voice that
made them fascinating to youngsters." He was assisted by his three
grown daughters, also objects of cadet fascination. It was said that the
two dominant cadet traits at Benny's were "chivalry and hunger." Being
recognized or inquired after by Benny or his daughters "was an honor
to which no cadet was indifferent."[37]

Custer used a common stratagem to foil late-night inspections.
One occasion was Thanksgiving of 1859. Custer and some of his friends

were invited to a ball in Buttermilk Falls. Of course, they were not permitted more than half a mile from the barracks and they had to pass a bed check at 10:00 P.M., but, Custer reasoned, "because we are in bed at ten o'clock is no reason why we should remain there until reveille." After the bed check, the cadets donned civilian mufti and placed items under their covers approximating the size and shape of a person in case there was an unannounced check. They slipped off the post and went to the ball, where they "passed a very pleasant night," returning a few minutes before reveille. They changed into their uniforms, but Custer noted that he "was in poor humor for hard study during the next day" and he was "almost (*but not quite*) sorry" he had gone to the ball. "Instead of a 'Thanksgiving dinner,'" he wrote, "I had a 'Thanksgiving' dance."[38]

Custer drank, but did not smoke; yet he was skinned more than once for tobacco smoke in room. Whenever smoke was detected, the cadet who was in charge of the room that day got the demerits. Custer sought a letter of permission to smoke from his father, but he explained that all he really wanted to do was be able to obtain tobacco for his roommate, who might then obtain other things for him. "Nothing could induce me to use tobacco either by smoking or chewing as I consider it a filthy, if not unhealthy, practice.... I can say what very few of my age can, and that is I never 'chewed' of tobacco in my life and what is more I do not think I ever will."[39]

Custer delighted in hazing "beasts" and plebes and others who did not know better. Some Custer pranks we can only guess at by the reports they engendered. The night of July 9, 1860, during encampment he was cited for being out of his tent without hat, coat *or pants* after 10:00 P.M. (one demerit) and interfering with a new cadet on guard (five demerits). Custer once stole a rooster belonging to Lieutenant Henry Douglass (USMA 1852), because it bothered him with its incessant crowing. He got rid of the evidence by eating the bird. Another cadet volunteered to throw away the feathers, but was careless enough to leave a trail of evidence leading back to him. Custer was never punished.

He was a class cut-up who once asked the Spanish instructor how to say "Class dismissed" in Spanish, and when the instructor answered, Custer led the class out of the room. In French he was bidden to translate *Léopold, duc d'Autriche, se mittit sur les plaines*, and began, "Leopard, duck and ostrich ..."[40] Wright noted that Custer's bravery in battle did not surprise anyone who had seen him "walking up with calm deliberation to the head of the section-room to face the instructors with the confession that he knew nothing of his lesson."[41]

Most of Custer's escapades at West Point were harmless; and when he was caught, he submitted to punishment with equanimity. But he did have some nerve-racking moments, one of which came in his final semester. The January 1861 examination was one of the most difficult in West Point history. Thirty-three cadets were found deficient, among them President Buchanan's nephew Edward Y. "Buck" Buchanan. It was expected that the president would intervene on behalf of his nephew and for the sake of appearances, at least, spare some other cadets as well. But Buchanan, then a lame duck watching the Union disintegrate and claiming he was powerless to stop it, saved only his nephew. McCrea called this "the most flagrant piece of injustice that this corrupt administration has been guilty of yet."[42]

One unsaved victim of the January 1861 examination was Charles Nelson Warner of Custer's class, a diminutive, brown-haired, freckled lad from Montrose, Pennsylvania. He thought he had done well on the exam, but he soon learned that he had been found "not proficient" both in ethics and in infantry tactics. The examiners noted that Warner was "rather studious" but showed very little aptitude for these two subjects. His disciplinary records show a very social cadet, receiving skins for visiting, loitering or being out late, and the previous term he had come within five points of expulsion. But Warner never seemed to be overly worried—about demerits or anything else. His letters from West Point are full of idealism and gratitude for the opportunity to serve his country and improve his station. "I am very well and never enjoyed myself so much in my life," he wrote his mother in May 1860. "West Point will be a familiar word with me as long as I live. I think it has done more for me than any other place would, and I hope when I leave here I shall be prepared for a happy and useful life." Being "found" so close to graduation was a crushing blow to Warner, who returned to Pennsylvania dejected and ashamed.

The reason for the severity of the exam can be traced to Custer. He had been more concerned than usual that he might not pass the January exams, so he sought a means of improving his odds. It was customary for professors to prepare lists of questions for each cadet to be asked by the examining board. The lists were closely held; if a cadet managed to get his hands on the list, he could study only those topics he knew he would be questioned on, and thus secure a much higher grade than he deserved. Custer knew that one of his instructors roomed at the hotel on post, and, waiting until he knew the room was empty, sneaked in unobserved. After a quick search he found the notebook in which all of the questions were recorded and began copying the list of queries he would face. At some point in the middle of the process he heard someone approaching. Custer panicked; without thinking through the consequences, he tore the page he was copying from the notebook and fled. The instructor naturally noticed a page missing, and he had a good idea who might have taken it.

Custer was not the only cadet who tried to cut corners. Several cadets successfully obtained copies of the French exam and passed it without being detected. Another cadet trying to copy the rhetoric exam had to hide in a trunk when the instructor returned to his room unexpectedly; a sympathetic female servant helped distract the officer later, allowing the cadet to duck out the back way. But when Custer's theft was detected, all the questions for everyone were changed, and Custer and some others were arrested.[43]

It did not look good for Custer. McCrae said he would be sorry to see him go. But three weeks later, Custer was let off, while others involved in the cheating scandal were not. "Custer with his usual good luck was also reinstated, and he was the only one in his class, while the rest were sent off," McCrea wrote. "He does not know why it is he was more fortunate than the rest, but I am quite sure that he will be more careful in the future and study his lessons more."[44] It was another example of what would come to be known throughout the Army as "Custer's Luck."

ABSENT FRIENDS

THE CADETS AT THE ACADEMY in these days studied, played pranks and ran it to Benny's not knowing that soon they would be playing important roles in a war that would pit them against each other and divide the West Point fraternity. While sectional passions had excited the country repeatedly in the decades leading up to the war, the Academy had been for the most part free of political passions. George C. Strong from Massachusetts, writing under the pseudonym R. Rankanfile, related an experience in which some instructors questioned him about his politics:

"You are appointed from the Acorn State, are you not, Sir?" an officer asked.

"Yes Sir."

"What are your politics, Mr. Rankanfile?"

"I'm an Administration man, Sir," he replied, thinking it was a safe bet to back the commander in chief.

"Just as I expected, Sir," the officer said. "It is evident you have mistaken your calling. You should have known, ere this, that an officer of the Army has nothing to do with politics."[1]

Politics aside, there were some cultural manifestations of sectional feelings. Nathaniel Wyche Hunter thought the Yankee faculty was out to get him, for example, but sometimes the northerners felt the same way about southern instructors. A British observer who stopped at West Point during the Thayer era commented, "There is a remarkable difference between the cadets of the Northern and Southern States: the former are generally studious and industrious; the latter, brought up among slaves, are idle and inattentive, so that they are almost all dismissed; consequently, the Academy is not 'in good odor' with the planters; for they imagine that favoritism prevails, and that the dismissals are not impartial."[2] The question was debated outside of West Point as well. Southerners were regarded as less prepared and were seen as underachievers.[3] In 1849, Cadet George Hartsuff, born in New York and appointed from Michigan, observed that "the Southern boys with some few exceptions have not the energy and perseverance of the Northern and consequently do not as a general thing stand so high in their class. But they are generous high-spirited fellows and among them I can name many of my best friends."[4]

An 1855 article noted that of the thirty-four cadets graduating that year, only five hailed from the South, and at that rate the Army would eventually be led by northern officers. The article asserted this was due to poor grades and high demerits by the southern cadets.[5] Another article stated that "the difference in favor of the North cannot be the result of accident."[6] A rejoinder noted that at the time, 40 percent of Army officers were southern, so the results of 1855 were clearly an aberration.[7] But the popular notion of the underachieving southern cadet was reversed during the war in the face of Confederate prowess on the battlefield. One observer noted in 1863 that one thing "which has given the rebels a great advantage in this contest . . . is the large number of military colleges in the south."[8] There were several important southern military schools, such as the Virginia Military Institute, founded by Francis H. Smith (USMA 1833), the South Carolina Military Academy (a.k.a. The Citadel), and the Louisiana Seminary of Learning and Military Academy, headed by Superintendent Colonel William T. Sherman. In October 1853, Secretary of War Davis refused to recommend creating a southern military institute on the West Point pattern, saying it would "create and increase sectional jealousies."[9] In 1855, the State of Kentucky proposed that USMA be moved to Andrew Jackson's former home, the Hermitage (with the endorsement of Tennessee). These were among the many periodic proposals to either do away with USMA, move it somewhere else, or create more schools just like it.

One of the rare intrusions of sectional politics in West Point life was on March 15, 1841, when the Dialectic Society debated the question, "Has a state a right to secede from the Union?" The issue came down to a tie vote, which was broken when Sam Jones of Virginia, Class of 1841 and president of the society, voted yes. Jones, who graduated nineteenth in the class, went on to become a Confederate major general.

Custer later said that the sectional divisions between the cadets were "at first barely distinguishable" but grew more sharply defined over the years. The watershed event was the John Brown raid and subsequent trial, which took place between October and December 1859. The raid on Harper's Ferry affected the Corps personally; one of the hostages Brown held was Colonel Lewis Washington, the father of plebe

James B. Washington of Virginia, and great-grand-nephew of George Washington. The Marine unit that ended the siege and captured Brown was commanded by the former Superintendent, Robert E. Lee, and his aide-de-camp, J. E. B. Stuart. After the raid, trial and execution, sectional feelings at West Point became more acute and more overtly political. On December 2, 1859, the day John Brown was executed in Charleston, Virginia, he was hanged in effigy at West Point, dangling from a tree in front of the barracks until removed by members of the garrison.

The John Brown trial was the subject of intense cadet debate, and it contributed to the first shedding of blood between West Pointers on the question of slavery.[10] Emory Upton of the Class of 1861 was appointed to the Academy from New York. For the previous two years he had been a student at Oberlin College in Ohio, which in 1835 was the first college to admit African American students and in 1837 became the first coeducational college. It was a noted center of antislavery studies, and its first president, Asa Mahan (no apparent relation to Dennis Hart Mahan), was an active abolitionist. When Upton came to West Point he declared himself firmly in the abolitionist camp, the first cadet to do so openly. Custer remarked that "the cadet who had the courage to avow himself an abolitionist must be prepared to face the social frowns of the great majority of his comrades and at times to defend his opinions by his physical strength and metal."[11] Schaff stated more bluntly, "this made [Upton] a marked man."[12]

Wade Hampton Gibbes, Class of 1860, was from Columbia, South Carolina, the son of a slave owner who had grown up on a plantation. Gibbes embodied all of the firebrand tendencies one might expect from a young man of his background, and he disliked Upton intensely. One day Gibbes and other southern cadets were having a bull session, and Gibbes strongly implied that Upton, among other things, had been sexually involved with black women while at Oberlin. Upton got wind of the comment and confronted Gibbes, who would not back down from the charge. They agreed to settle the matter as gentlemen, and word spread that a fight was on, to be held in the barracks near the sally port, on the first floor.

A mob of cadets crowded around for a view of the brutal contest, while the nearest sentinel called vainly for the corporal of the guard. The battle went on for many minutes, until Upton emerged, his face bloodied. The southern cadets shouted threats as Upton made his way towards the stairs, when Upton's roommate, a big Pennsylvanian named John I. Rodgers, appeared at the top of the steps and said to the jeering southerners, his eyes "glaring like a panther's" according to Schaff, "If there are any more of you down there who want anything, come right up!"[13] None did.

The fight between Gibbes and Upton, wrote Schaff, "was the most thrilling event in my life as a cadet; and, in my judgment, it was the most significant in that of West Point itself." Schaff saw it as prophetic of the war to come, reflecting both "the courage and the bitterness with which it was fought out to the bitter end."[14] He believed that the northern temperament, which stood insults, tended to encourage the southerners, who misconstrued taciturnity for lack of courage. "It took Gettysburg and the Wilderness and Chickamauga to prove them their fatal error," Schaff later wrote.[15]

In October 1860, some southern cadets held a straw poll for preference in the upcoming presidential election. John Lane of Oregon, an Immortal of Custer's class and one of his roommates, had a particular interest since his father, Senator Joseph Lane, was the vice presidential nominee of the Southern Democrat faction headed by Breckenridge.[16] Lincoln received 64 votes out of 278, or 23 percent of the cadets, and the incensed southerners began to hunt out the "Black Republican Abolitionists in the Corps."[17] Only 30 cadets would admit they backed Lincoln, and all of them were from west of the Hudson. Schaff, a Lincoln backer, called the unwillingness of the New England Republicans to stand by their votes "the most equivocal if not pusillanimous conduct I ever saw at West Point."[18] Shortly before the actual election, Lincoln was hanged in effigy, like Brown, in front of the barracks.

Lincoln's victory on November 6, 1860, was the final impetus putting events in motion that would sunder the brotherhood of West Point. McCrea, another of the Ohio Lincoln supporters, celebrated the Republican victory. "As we rejoiced the other parties mourned," he wrote, "the southerners [fumed] and (as is customary with a great many of them), they threatened to do all kinds of terrible things, and blustered around at a great rate." McCrea noted that they had threatened to resign if Lincoln was elected, and he thought this "would be a blessed good thing" because "it would clear the institution of some of the worst characters."[19] On November 9, the *Guardian* of Columbia, South Carolina, published a letter from the West Point cadets of the Palmetto State pledging to stand by their homeland if it left the Union. "All we desire is a field for making ourselves useful," they said.[20] Ten days later, Henry S. Farley of South Carolina became the first West Point cadet to resign for the South. James "Little Jim" Hamilton, also of South Carolina, followed him four days later. South Carolina finally seceded on December 20, 1860, and on the same day Major William H. T. Walker, Immortal of 1837, hero of the Seminole and Mexican wars, and former Commandant of Cadets, became the first Regular Army officer to resign his commission and join the rebellion. The indestructible Walker, survivor of grievous wounding at the Battles of Okeechobee and Molino del Rey, was finally felled in the Battle of Atlanta on July 22, 1864.

Of the 278 cadets at the Academy at that time, 86 (31 percent) were from the South. Among these, 65 ultimately left or were discharged for reasons connected to the war; 6 left for other reasons; and 15 (17 percent of the southern cadets) sided with the Union.[21] The southern cadets did not leave en masse, but departed in small numbers as the Union slowly disintegrated through the winter and spring of 1860–61.

"No one speaks of anything but war and everyone in this part of the country firmly believe that we will hear in a few days that hostilities have commenced," Custer wrote on April 10. "I feel confident that we will have war in less than a week, and if we do I never expect to graduate here … as we would be ordered to join regiments at once." Custer's words were prophetic. Two days later, Confederate forces attacked Fort Sumter in Charleston Harbor. P. G. T. Beauregard of Louisiana, second in the Class of 1838 and USMA Superintendent for five days in January 1861 until his state seceded, commanded the Carolinian forces and gave the order to fire on the fort. The signal shot of the siege was fired from Fort Johnson by Company C, First South Carolina Artillery, with Upton's tormentor Lieutenant Wade Hampton Gibbes at the lanyard.[22] A moment later, Lieutenant Henry S. Farley, the first cadet to resign, fired the first mortar round into the fort.

Events at Sumter had an electric effect on the North, according to Custer. "Opponents in politics became friends in patriotism," he wrote, "all differences of opinion vanished or were laid aside."[23] Custer doubted the nation would ever see that type of unity again. The cadets assessed the attack according to their predispositions and state loyalties. There were West Pointers on both sides of the bombardment, and the cadets soon met one of them. On April 27, Captain Truman Seymour, nineteenth in the Class of 1846 and one of the Fort Sumter defenders, came to West Point to visit his father-in-law, Professor Weir.[24] He gave the cadets his account of the battle, hardening the resolve of the Unionists. Custer observed that the men leaving for the South were "impatient, enthusiastic and hopeful," while their northern counterparts were "reserved almost to sullenness; were grave almost to stoicism."[25] Custer had always gotten along with the southern cadets, in part because he was a strong Democrat and an anti-abolitionist who openly denounced the "Black Republicans." He felt that the Republicans were most responsible for the pressures that were tearing the Union apart. Also, he knew the southerners better; he was a member of D Company, composed chiefly of Immortals, most of whom were from the South or the West.

One Saturday, Custer was walking an extra, as usual, when across the Plain he saw a group of cadets carrying two others towards the wharf on their shoulders. Custer recognized them as his classmates Charles P. Ball of Alabama, a popular, academically gifted cadet first sergeant, and John Herbert Kelly of California, an Immortal of his company. As the men were borne away, they saw their friend Custer and raised their hats to him across the Plain in farewell. It was too far for Custer to shout back, so, after looking to see if he was being watched, he saluted them by bringing his musket to "present." Ball commanded the Eighth Alabama Cavalry regiment during the war, and afterwards became an inventor. Kelly, in November 1863 at age twenty-four, became the youngest general in the Confederacy, a counterpart to his friend Custer, who achieved the same distinction in the Union army six months earlier. Kelly was killed in 1864 during a raid near Franklin, Tennessee.

Thirty-three cadets resigned on April 22, 1861, the largest one-day group. Among them was another of Custer's friends, Thomas Lafayette Rosser of Texas, an Immortal of the Class of May 1861. Two months earlier, Custer and Rosser had engaged in their own form of sectional conflict. On February 22, at 11:30 A.M., the Corps of Cadets marched to the chapel to the tunes of the West Point Band. President Lincoln had ordered that in honor of Washington's birthday they "listen to the friendly counsels, and almost prophetic warnings," in his Farewell Address.[26] Commandant John F. Reynolds (USMA 1841) led the group into the chapel.[27] The cadets took their seats and listened as Washington's words were read, entreating them to "properly estimate the immense value of your national union" and to frown on "every attempt to alienate any portion of our country from the rest, or to enfeeble the sacred ties which now link together the various parts."[28] Then the cadets were released for the customary holiday. It was a cloudy day, and most spent it indoors, discussing the political crisis or studying. The cadet barracks was on the south side of the Plain. The North and South Barracks had been demolished and the new building completed in 1851. It was a marked improvement. The facade resembled a stylized castle, with towers, crenellations and other such design elements. The building had two major wings, east and west, with a small wing extending south from the west wing used for officers' quarters. There were 136 cadet rooms, fourteen by twenty-two feet, with 40 rooms for officers.[29] Between the two large wings on the ground floor was a sally port. Over the years, the cadets had perhaps unconsciously, certainly without plan, segregated themselves, northerners on the east side of the port, southerners on the west.

At 9:30 P.M., the hour of evening tattoo, the band formed near the morning gun on the north side of the Plain and marched towards the barracks playing "Washington's March." Cadets gathered at the windows to watch and listen. The band marched directly into and through the sally port, striking up "The Star-Spangled Banner." When it emerged on the south side of the barracks, the music burst out, and Custer, whose window faced that side, began a cheer, which was soon taken up by all of the northern cadets. The cheering was against regulations, but it persisted. The southern cadets, led by Rosser, responded with massed cheers for "Dixie." The northerners "flung back a ringing cheer for the Stars and Stripes; and so cheer followed cheer," Schaff wrote. "Ah, it was a great night! Rosser at one window, Custer at another."[30] It is a poignant scene, these boys in their cheering sections in a contest animated as much by mirth as by anger, who would meet again as men on the battlefield.

One of the last and most difficult partings was that of Lieutenant Fitzhugh Lee, nephew of Robert E. Lee, who as a cadet was saved from expulsion when the Class of 1856 took the pledge. He had returned to West Point as a tactical officer, the commander of Company A and assistant instructor in cavalry tactics. He had spent the previous two years as a cavalry scout, being involved in several actions against the Comanche, almost dying after taking an arrow in the lung at Crooked Creek, Kansas, May 12, 1859, and fighting a fierce hand-to-hand struggle near Camp Colorado on June 16, 1860. Schaff said he was "the most popular officer that I have ever seen at West Point."[31] His father, Captain Sidney Smith Lee, USN, patriarch of the Lee family, was the first of the five Lees in uniform to resign. Sidney's brother Robert E. Lee soon followed. Fitz Lee struggled with the decision, but in the end sided with Virginia. He resigned May 21, 1861, a month after his Uncle Robert. The day before he left, he went to his cadets and shook their hands, one by one. As one of them later remembered, "with tears in his eyes and a voice tremulous with emotion, he bade us farewell, left an impression that will not be effaced so long as memory lasts."[32] That evening the officers serenaded him, and the next morning after breakfast he boarded a carriage and headed for the South Gate. The cadets had gathered in front of the barracks, and when Lee passed, they silently waved their caps goodbye.

★ ★ ★

WITH HOSTILITIES UNDER WAY, the Class of 1861 petitioned to graduate early. They did not hear back on their request, but as the Corps
was forming to march to supper on May 6, the first class was diverted
to the library. There, without ceremony, they were informed that they
were to graduate. Each cadet was called forward, recited the oath of
allegiance, and was handed a diploma.[33] They were instructed to report
to Washington without delay. After they had graduated, the classmates
went to the mess hall "and were received by the other cadets with such
rounds of applause as was never heard before."[34] The newly commissioned officers left quickly for New York, where they spent their accumulated pay equipping themselves with side arms and other
accouterments of war. They proceeded to Philadelphia on ship, landing at ten in the evening only to be promptly disarmed and placed under
arrest by a posse at the Walnut Street wharf. News had reached police
chief Ruggles that a large band of secessionists had left West Point heading south and had bought weapons in New York. The former cadets
broke into laughter when they realized the mistake, and after explaining the mix-up were allowed to continue to Washington.[35]

Custer's class also petitioned to leave early and to miss their final
year. Custer predicted that his class would be gone by June 25, "if not
sooner." They were being rushed through a compressed version of the
fifth-year curriculum—a "course of sprouts," said one cadet.[36] Custer
said the pace was so physically punishing that they were all becoming
thin and pale. "There was never an instance of so severe studying being
done as is now done by my class," he wrote. He stayed up boning until
one in the morning, catching a few hours' sleep before rising again at
five. Nevertheless, he tested poorly in the 1861 exams, coming in at the
foot of the class. He later claimed that some of the southern cadets,
had they remained, "would probably have contested with me the debatable honor of bringing up the rear of the class."[37] This is certainly possible. Custer had been last in his class in the third year as well, but the
five cadets above him all fought for the Confederacy, and they could
have been contenders for the last man.[38] The sixth was Charles Nelson
Warner from Pennsylvania, found deficient and sent home. James P.
Parker of Missouri, one of Custer's roommates, who later joined the
Confederacy, is sometimes identified as ranking below Custer because
his name appears after Custer's in the June 1861 Register of Officers
and Cadets.[39] But Parker was listed last in the register only because he

was deficient in conduct, and after his resignation he was struck from the list of graduates.[40]

Custer's prediction was nearly on the mark. On June 30, 1861, his class was relieved of duty and ordered to "report to Washington City without delay." Officers were needed to lead the volunteer units that were then being hastily organized. This effectively ended the five-year curriculum. Of the eighty-nine graduates of the two classes of 1861, forty-three were at the Battle of Bull Run on July 21. Adelbert Ames, number five in the May class, was wounded and received the Medal of Honor. Emory Upton, number eight, was also wounded, his horse shot from under him. Sheldon Sturgeon, the Goat of May 1861, arrived in time to be captured. (He was later exchanged and became a Union mustering officer.)

The graduates of June 30, 1861 were listed in order of merit, ending with Frank A. Reynolds. Custer was not on the list. Fate had a final trick to play on Cadet Custer. On the evening of June 29, 1861, while serving as officer of the guard in encampment, he heard a disturbance some distance from the main camp and rushed over to find a crowd of cadets ringed around two of their fellows, who were spitting invective. Just as Custer arrived, the two came to blows. Seeing Custer and fearing he would put the pugilists on report, some of their friends rushed in to separate them. Custer should have arrested the two; but as he later wrote, "The instincts of the boy prevailed over the obligation of the officer of the guard."[41] He waded into the mob of cadets, pushing back those who were interfering with the mêlée, and called out, "Stand back, boys; let's have a fair fight!"[42] The crowd pulled back; in fact, it immediately evaporated, and Custer too late noticed the cause. Lieutenants William E. Merrill and William B. Hazen, the officer in charge, were approaching.[43]

"Why did you not suppress the riot which occurred here a few minutes ago?" Hazen demanded. In Custer's opinion, a fight between two boys could not properly be described as a riot. This was not a satisfactory answer, and the next morning Custer was interviewed by Commandant Reynolds and placed under arrest. Hours later, the order arrived for his class to depart for Washington, without him.

Custer sat at West Point for two weeks before his case was taken up by a general court martial, presided over by Lieutenant Stephen Vincent Benét.[44] "I was arraigned with all the solemnity and gravity which might be looked for in a trial for high treason," Custer recalled.[45] Cadet "George W. [sic] Custer" was charged with "neglect of duty" (for not breaking up the brawl) and "conduct to the prejudice of good order and military discipline" (for calling for a fair fight). He pleaded guilty on both counts, then awaited the results as his classmates pulled whatever strings they could in Washington to secure the release of their class Goat. "Fortunately some of them had influential friends there," Custer observed.[46] On July 17 a telegram arrived instructing that Custer be released to report to the adjutant general in Washington in person. Custer was sentenced only to be reprimanded in orders. The court noted that it was being lenient "owing to the peculiar situation of Cadet Custer represented in his own defense, and in consideration of his general good conduct, as testified to by Lieutenant Hazen, his immediate commander."[47]

By the time the verdict was finalized, however, Custer had departed, and he never learned the decision of the court. Within days, he was in action at Bull Run. Weeks earlier he had written, "It is useless to hope or to suppose that the coming struggle will be a bloodless one or one of short duration. It is certain that much blood will be spilled and that thousands of lives lost, perhaps I might say hundreds of thousands. In entering the contest everyone must take his chance and no one can say that he will live through it, but this is a necessary consequence and cannot be avoided. If it is to be my lot to fall in the service of my country and in defense of my country's rights I have or will have no regrets."[48]

JAMES McQUEEN McINTOSH

WHEN THE CIVIL WAR BEGAN, few institutions in the country were as well positioned for tragedy as West Point. Its fraternity represented every state, and classmates who had hitherto lived and fought together under the same flag faced the possibility that they might meet in battle. Only the graduates of the Naval Academy and the members of the United States Congress were in similar straits, and rarely with the same consequences. Of the 821 serving Army officers who were West Point graduates, 184 declared for the Confederacy. They were joined by 99 graduates who returned from civilian life to fight for the Rebel cause. Likewise, 115 civilian graduates rejoined the ranks for the Union.[1] In the course of the war, 45 West Pointers were killed or died of wounds fighting for the South; the North lost 60.[2] The first to die was E. B. Holloway of the Class of 1843, accidentally killed by his own men on May 16, 1861, at Independence, Missouri, two days after he resigned to join the Confederate army.

Joseph Lee Kirby Smith (USMA 1857), son of Ephraim Kirby Smith, served as a topographical engineer in the years before the war. As the southern states began to secede and officers with southern sympathies began to resign their commissions, he wrote to his Uncle Edmund seeking advice. Joseph's grandmother in Florida was eager for him to join the Confederate cause, and Edmund said that in his own case he would answer the call of his state. Joseph agreed; but he had been born in New York of a northern mother, and so he went with the Union.

During the war, Joseph served as colonel in command of the 43rd Ohio Volunteers in the Army of the Mississippi. He received brevet promotions for gallantry at the capture of Island Number Ten in the Mississippi River, and at the siege of Corinth in May 1862, where he led the repulse of a Rebel sortie. He returned to Corinth that fall as part of a new Union offensive. Kirby's division commander was Brigadier General David Stanley, who had fought beside James M. McIntosh against the Cheyenne at Solomon's Fork. Kirby told Stanley, "I want to go into one fight where there is a storm of bullets, just to see how I can behave."[3] He soon got his wish.

Kirby's regiment moved into position along the crest of a ridge overlooking the town on the night of October 3, defending a section of line between two batteries. Early the next morning, the regiment came under Confederate artillery fire, followed by sniper attacks lasting several hours. The main push came at noon. Three columns composed of Texas and Arkansas regiments emerged from the woods north of Corinth and bore down on the Union lines. One column advanced on Kirby's right flank. They gained the parapet and focused intense fire on the unit. Nine of the thirteen officers of the regiment were killed or wounded. Leading the counterattack, Kirby was shot in the face, like his father. General Stanley rushed in to take command, completing the complex maneuver and driving the enemy off the parapet with the help of other units that had come to their aid. Colonel John W. Fuller, Kirby's brigade commander, wrote later that Smith "enjoyed not only the confidence and esteem of every officer of this command, but was respected and beloved by the whole army." Stanley noted in his report, "I have not the words to describe the qualities of this model soldier or to express the loss we have sustained in his death. The best testimony I can give to his memory is the spectacle I witnessed myself, in the very moment of battle, of stern, brave men weeping as children as the word passed, 'Kirby Smith is dead.' "[4]

Not every southern graduate went with the Confederacy; in fact, only about half did. Of the 330 serving graduates appointed from the southern states, only 168 joined the Rebel ranks, while 162 defended Old Glory. Those southerners who chose to remain loyal to the Union frequently met with harsh recriminations from friends and family back home. Lieutenant William Terrill of Bath County, Virginia, Class of 1853, received the following letter from his father:

> I am *overwhelmed* by the position you have taken. It is the bitterest cup that has ever been commended to my lips. You are surely *demented*. Your talk about loyalty to your oath is all *stuff*. Oh! How it makes my heart bleed to think that while Virginia's sons are rallying to the defense of her firesides and her homes, that my son is found playing the part of Benedict Arnold. You will never be permitted to revisit your native state but to die.[5]

His father threatened that he would be ostracized from the family, but Terrill kept to his word and soon saw battle. His artillery battery won fame at Shiloh, and he was made a brigadier in September 1862. The next month, Terrill was mortally wounded at Perryville, Kentucky. His brother James Barbour Terrill was an 1858 VMI graduate who remained loyal to Virginia. He was made a brigadier general on May 31, 1864, and killed in action that same day near Bethesda Church, Virginia. Their grieving father was said to have erected a monument to his two sons inscribed, "God alone knows which was right."[6]

There were twenty-four living "Last Men" from the classes of 1818 through June 1861. Of them, sixteen were serving, and they split evenly: eight for the Union, eight for the Confederacy. Only two of the civilians returned to the colors, one for each side. Albert Gallatin Edwards, Goat of 1832, had served three years in the Mounted Rangers and Dragoons when he retired from active duty. He was a St. Louis merchant and a Missouri bank commissioner when he was appointed a brigadier general of the Missouri Volunteers. He did not see action during the war. Hugh McLeod of Georgia, the Goat of 1835, had resigned his commission long before the Civil War—he was en route to his first posting at Fort Jesup, Louisiana, when he left the Army to head west to fight for Texas independence. He served on the frontier battling Indians, and as a brigadier general he commanded the 1841 Santa Fe expedition, which failed, owing in part to his ill health. McLeod was taken captive by the Mexicans and was released in 1842. He later served as inspector general of Texas and as a member of the Texas House of Representatives. When the Civil War broke out he became lieutenant colonel and then colonel of the First Texas Infantry regiment, and marched to Virginia to fight the Yankees. But the scrappy Texan never saw action; he died of pneumonia at Occoquan, Virginia, on January 2, 1862.[7]

John T. Pratt, the Academy's first Goat, who had been denied a commission during the Mexican War because of partisan politics, was willing to do his part. He was a merchant in Georgetown, Kentucky, and still vigorous in his old age. "I am now nearly sixty-three years old in good health and quite a boy in activity and should occasion require could do better service than I did in Johnson's Regiment on the Thames [in] 1813," he wrote, referring to his service in the War of 1812. "I have plenty of this world's goods to support life to the end without asking or even wanting a pension from my government."[8] Pratt was not given the opportunity to prove his mettle again.

Harold Borland of Arkansas, of the Class of 1860, signed on quickly to the Confederate cause. Harold was a turnback from the Class of 1859, tagged "Ginger" because his hair was the color of ground ginger. During a recitation in ordnance he was asked how many pieces a twelve-pound shell will burst into, on average. Borland pondered the answer and finally said, "Not less than two." He narrowly graduated Goat of the class, in a tight race with George W. Vanderbilt of New York, probably due to his last-place standing in ethics. Schaff said that after Borland received his diploma, he "came down the nave with an inane smile, and was greeted with the heartiest applause."[9] He was assigned to the Mounted Rifles but resigned to join the Confederate cause on March 31, 1861, a month before his state left the Union.[10] He went directly to Montgomery, Alabama, to tender his services to Jefferson Davis. He was commissioned a major in the Confederate service, and served in Florida as an engineer and quartermaster. He became the assistant adjutant general on the staff of General Slaughter, and was sent in this capacity to accompany the steamer *Alice Vivian* in an attempt to run the blockade from Mobile to Havana, carrying 550 bales of cotton. The ship was intercepted by the USS *De Soto* on August 16, 1863, and Borland was captured. He was sent to Fort Warren, in Boston Harbor, where he was exchanged October 1, 1864, for a Major Forbes of Boston.[11]

Harold's father, Solon Borland, was an Arkansas medical doctor, former senator and U.S. minister to Nicaragua. When the war broke out, he raised a Confederate cavalry brigade, and in March 1861 he led a force of one thousand up the Arkansas River to Fort Smith, to capture the post and its garrison, which was commanded by Captain Samuel Sturgis (USMA 1846) and his adjutant, Captain James McQueen McIntosh, Goat of 1849. A member of Borland's expedition wrote that "to the young men and boys . . . it was a picnic excursion, heartily enjoyed all the way up. They were welcomed at every town, landing and wood yard by the new-born secessionists." As they neared Fort Smith, a small boat hailed them. It was Captain McIntosh. He had resigned his commission from the Federal army and was en route to volunteer his services to the Confederacy. He told Borland's party that news of their advance had reached the fort, where "hurried preparations were making in the fort for either a fight or a flight. He bade us God-speed and went on down the river."[12]

McIntosh made his way quickly from Fort Smith to the Confederate capital, then at Montgomery, Alabama. Convinced that the Confederacy needed a frontier force, he volunteered to take a leading role in organizing it. General Albert J. Pike, who was President Jefferson Davis's representative to the Indian Territory, asked for McIntosh by name. "We must also have several regular officers to command the bodies of Indians enlisted," he wrote to the secretary of war. "Among these I hope Captain McIntosh . . . will be included. He desires to go into the service in the Indian country, and I should, if I were to command here, much desire to have him." McIntosh was immediately given a commission, but to his disappointment he did not get a major frontier command. He became colonel of the Second Arkansas Mounted Rifles.[13]

David S. Stanley, previously McIntosh's second in command, said that his former commander had joined the southern cause less because of sectional ties than from ambition; he "coolly calculated his chances of promotion, [and] thought them better in the Confederacy."[14] It is true that the war meant quick promotion, on both sides. At the start of the conflict, no West Point graduate was a general officer. Of the 800 who served, 297 attained the rank of general, 152 Confederate and 147 Union (including Stanley). Yet these were no desk jobs; 27 Confederate and 21 Union West Point graduates died in battle as generals. And Stanley's charge of opportunism was based on his belief that McIntosh was from New Jersey, when in fact he was a native Floridian who had married a Virginian and had historic family roots in Georgia. So McIntosh had ample Confederate bona fides, and he followed his head and heart. However, his brother, John Baillie McIntosh, did live in New Jersey. He was one year James' junior, also born on the Florida frontier. He had served as a midshipman in the Navy during the Mexican War, then went into private business in the Garden State. When his brother James joined the Confederate cause, John cast his lot with the Union and was commissioned a second lieutenant in the Second U.S. Cavalry.[15]

James McIntosh was soon back west of the Mississippi, and he brought his usual enthusiasm to his new command. He first won acclaim by bloodlessly capturing over 130 Union troops of the Third Missouri and their supplies at Neosho, Missouri, on July 5, 1861. The Federal troops were commanded by Captain Joseph Conrad, who surrendered unconditionally. It was hailed as the first Confederate victory on Union soil. In the early summer of 1861, Confederates under Major General Sterling Price were driven out of the state by Union forces under Brigadier General Nathaniel Lyon, eleventh in the Class of 1841, noted earlier as having reputedly fought Indians led by Bison McLean. Lyon was short, red-haired, intellectually gifted and dynamic, well respected by friend and foe alike. All believed he had a brilliant career ahead of him. A combined force consisting of Price's men and others commanded by Brigadier General Benjamin McCulloch of Texas, a former Texas Ranger and commander of the Indian Territory, moved north again in August and met Lyon's forces at Wilson's Creek on August 10, 1861.[16]

Lyon achieved tactical surprise against the Rebel forces, opening the battle with a blow to their rear. But the southerners fought back doggedly, and eventually carried the day. McIntosh directed the fight on the Confederate right flank, through an area known as "Ray's corn-field." His Second Arkansas, and Colonel Louis Hébert's Third Louisiana Volunteers, faced "galling fire" from U.S. regulars as they advanced, and slowed when they came to the fence on the edge of the field. McIntosh rallied the regiments by leaping over the obstacle, followed by Hébert, and then their combined forces piled over the obstruction and advanced in a rush. They drove back the enemy and secured the flank. McIntosh was slightly wounded by Federal grapeshot during the charge. Colonel Hébert said McIntosh deserved "unlimited praise" for his actions in the cornfield. Brigadier General N. B. Pearce, commander of the First Division, Army of Arkansas, wrote, "I deem it lost time for me to attempt to sound the praises of the brave and chivalrous McIntosh. Always in the midst of the fight cheering and leading his men forward to victory, his name and conduct were a host in our behalf." After the battle, General McCulloch wrote, "To Colonel McIntosh, at one time at the head of his regiment and at other times in his capacity of adjutant-general, I cannot bestow too much praise. Wherever the balls flew thickest he was gallantly leading different regiments into action, and his presence gave confidence everywhere."

Wilson's Creek was a bloody fracas. S. B. Barron, Third Texas Cavalry, on viewing the scene after what was his first battle, wrote, "We continued our ride until satisfied for that time, and for all time, so far as I was concerned, with viewing a battlefield just after the battle, unless duty demands it."[17] While walking the field, McIntosh found the body of General Lyon, the first Union general officer to die in combat in the war. Lyon was wearing a plain captain's coat; McIntosh recognized him when he stopped to take some papers from his pocket. With the Union forces in retreat and their leader killed, the Confederates had a fleeting opportunity to press the matter deeper into Missouri. Sterling Price, a Missourian who held his commission as a member of the state militia, wanted to exploit the victory and move north towards Springfield. He thought if they moved rapidly enough they could push the Union retreat all the way to St. Louis.

But while Price counseled swift exploitation, Ben McCulloch hesitated. He and Price had never gotten along. Dabney Maury observed that "in person, in manner and in character, McCulloch presented a strong contrast with Price."[18] McCulloch was eccentric, imperious, and not held in high regard by those who did not serve under him. He was known for his outlandish uniforms and monumental ego. William Baxter, clergyman, poet, and president of Arkansas College, commented that McCulloch "was extremely unpopular through all that region where he had so long held the chief command; his appearance was neither that of a great man nor a good soldier; his manners were coarse; his conversation thickly interlarded with oaths."[19] But his men loved him for his drive—he led from the front.[20]

Sterling Price, known as "Pap," was temperate, moderate and friendly, well loved by the people of the region. "The ladies called to see him," the Confederate Military History stated, "and the most enthusiastic kissed him, as he sat to give them a reception. The little girls he took upon his knee."[21] Though he outranked McCulloch on paper, the fact that he held a commission from a state that was not yet part of the Confederacy gave McCulloch enough of an excuse to disregard Price's orders. They had moved on Lyon at Wilson's Creek only because Price gave command to McCulloch; and afterwards, when McCulloch refused to move north into Missouri, Price went anyway. His advance soon stalled as Union forces reorganized. A. W. Sparks, who served in McCulloch's command as part of the Ninth Texas Cavalry, and who respected him greatly, said that the failure to back up Price was "the most egregious folly capable of being committed by a man having the least pretension to reason and common sense."[22]

Winter hit the plains hard. December 1861 was bitterly cold, with heavy snow and frozen roads, widespread illness and low morale on both sides. McIntosh, temporarily in command of McCulloch's division in their winter encampment at Van Buren, Arkansas, pondered the course of his career. He had created hard feelings the previous September by claiming that his commission in the Confederate army antedated all others, making him the senior colonel in the theater. The claim may not have been literally true, but McCulloch backed him up.[23] However, McIntosh had seen no major action since August, and despite his previous opportunities for heroism, spending another quiet winter on the frontier was not the war he had signed on to fight.

On December 15, a despondent McIntosh sent a message to General Samuel Cooper (USMA 1815), who was now the Confederate adjutant general in Richmond, requesting a transfer.[24] "I have the honor to apply to be removed from this section of the country after the return of General McCulloch," he wrote. "I do not think any battle of importance will be fought during the next year west of the Mississippi River. Probably none other than a guerrilla war will be kept up. I therefore desire and respectfully apply for service where the tug of war will be, and where I can be of more service than here." He also hoped to be closer to the center of political power in order to make his views known more effectively and to "have the same chances that many of the regular officers of the Army, younger in rank than myself, have had, and rise at least to their level."[25] Clearly McIntosh felt that the East was where careers could be made; and he may also have been annoyed by the fact that his former adjutant Stanley had been made a Union brigadier the previous September.

The next day, McIntosh was at a barn dance when word arrived of a mutiny among the Confederacy's Cherokee allies in the Indian Territory. They had rallied to the cause of Creek chief Opothleyahola and his pro-Union "Pin" Indian faction. McIntosh saw an opportunity for action and he took it. He quickly sent a dispatch to Adjutant Cooper:

> GENERAL: Since my communication of day before yesterday I have heard more of the disaffection of the Cherokees and of the rapidly increasing force of Opothleyahola, the Creek chief. I have deemed the troubles there of sufficient importance to send additional force, and will myself take command and march against Opothleyahola. I start to-morrow, and will march with upwards of 2,000 men. . . . I hope soon to settle matters in the nation.

McIntosh was about to involve himself in a very old feud between two Creek Indian factions, which had started in 1825 when Opothleyahola and his followers murdered a rival chief named William McIntosh. Chief William's son Chilly McIntosh now led the tribe, and whether James McIntosh knew it or not, there was more to the situation than a coincidence of names. The Creek chiefs were in fact his distant kin.[26] Chilly McIntosh and the Lower Creeks signed a treaty of alliance with the Confederacy after meeting with General Pike; the Cherokee, Chickasaw and Choctaw had already sided with the Confederates, and within a few months there were four Confederate Indian regiments, two Cherokee, one Creek and one Choctaw-Chickasaw.[27] Colonel Daniel N. McIntosh, Chief Chilly's son, led the Creek regiment. He was more than happy to have the support of the other tribes, not to mention the Confederacy, in settling his family's business with the hated Opothleyahola.

Opothleyahola was moving north towards Kansas with a mixed band of 4,000, mostly Creek and some Cherokee, Choctaw, Kickapoo, Shawnee, Yuchi, Delaware and Comanche, as well as numerous fugitive slaves. The group was pursued by a 2,000-man Confederate force, composed of the Indian regiments and the Fourth Texas Cavalry regiment, and led by Colonel Douglas Hancock Cooper, a close associate of Jefferson Davis's who served with him in Mexico, later a well-regarded Indian agent who was an honorary member of the Chickasaw tribe. In early December, Opothleyahola had encamped at Chusto-Talasah, or

Caving Banks, on Bird Creek. He offered to negotiate with the Confederates, and Cooper sent one of his aides, Major Pegg, accompanied by three companies of Cherokee. The Cherokee were loath to fight the Creeks, and at the negotiations Opothleyahola virtually ignored Pegg, summoning his powers of oratory to appeal directly to the warriors. He urged them to abandon Cooper's force and not raise their hands against his people, who had been their friends on their ancient lands. Swayed by the old chief's words, the Cherokee deserted Pegg, who dashed back to Cooper with only a small band of followers. The next day, December 9, Cooper attacked. Opothleyahola's forces were strongly emplaced in a horseshoe bend in the creek, surrounded on three sides with thirty-foot banks, the line of approach fortified with natural brush and log breastworks. They fought a pitched battle, sometimes hand to hand, for four hours. Eventually Opothleyahola judged that his group's women and children in their wagon trains had reached relative safety and he ended the struggle. His forces melted away at sundown; and the next day, the Confederates found the camp empty.

Cooper, shaken by the desertion of the Cherokee and fearing further rebellions, sent a message to Colonel James McIntosh asking him to join his force. This was the opportunity McIntosh had been waiting for. After he sent notification of his plans to Richmond, he made a forced march from Van Buren to Fort Gibson with elements of five Texas and Arkansas cavalry regiments totaling 1,400 men. At Fort Gibson his men drew some supplies and McIntosh conferred with Cooper. They planned a two-column envelopment, McIntosh and his forces in the front, with Cooper in the rear to engage the pursuit. McIntosh moved out on December 22, and three days later sighted smoke from enemy campfires rising from the hills ahead. He wanted to attack as soon as possible; morale was high with the enemy so close, and the men were ready for a fight. Cooper's column, however, was delayed and would not be in position. McIntosh, outnumbered, went ahead with the attack anyway.

Opothleyahola had dug in at a position in present-day Osage County, Oklahoma, a place called Chustenahlah, "shoal in the creek," so named because of the creek that ran at its base. His band needed rest, and he had received word that reinforcements were on the way. But when McIntosh arrived, Opothleyahola readied for battle. He had reason to be confident: his 1,700 infantry stood in sheltered positions on a steep, rocky hill covered with oak trees, his mounted troops behind it as a reserve. The lower reaches of the hill were manned by Seminoles led by Halleck Tustenuggee, the last of the major Seminole leaders to surrender in the Seminole War twenty years before, and leader of the Martin's Point massacre that had killed the wife of Lieutenant Alexander Montgomery, the Goat of 1834. Among his company commanders were veterans Billy Bowlegs, Alligator and Gopher John. Opothleyahola rode amongst his men, offering encouragement, and the vividly war-painted Indians howled at the Confederates as they began to advance. McIntosh deployed three Texas regiments in a line, with his Arkansas troops as the reserve. As they approached the creek at the base of the hill, the lead elements began taking heavy fire. "Each tree on the hill-side screened a stalwart warrior," McIntosh wrote. He threw out flanking forces, with orders to dismount when they were in position. His next move, with enemy fire still raking his forces, was related by A. W. Sparks: "The impetuous McIntosh, who cannot brook a tardy skirmish salutation, orders the charge."[28]

"It seemed a desperate undertaking to charge a position which appeared almost inaccessible," McIntosh wrote later, "but the order to charge to the top of the hill met a responsive feeling from each gallant heart in the line, and at noon the charge was sounded, one wild yell from a thousand throats burst upon the air, and the living mass hurled itself upon the foe." McIntosh led the assault as the hillside erupted with defensive fire. The engagement quickly turned into a series of small, hand-to-hand skirmishes. The Confederates pushed back the enemy before them, muscling their way upward towards the summit, dispatching warriors as they went with shot, sword and bayonet. One old Seminole, said to be Alligator, who had given the order to fire on Dade's column in Florida in 1835, bravely fought the onrushing Confederates:

> An old warrior fired upon a party of eight or ten from behind a tree. The men did not wish to kill him, and even used entreaties to induce him to surrender; but, with death imminent, he continued to load his old rifle with a sublime indifference never attained by the Cynic philosophers of Greece, and having loaded he coolly proceeded with the priming, when his admiring foes were compelled to dash out his old brave life.[29]

Some scaled sheer rock while engaged in dangerous fighting with Indians above. Several officers and men went down, but the speed and daring of the attack overcame the will of the defenders, who scattered for the gullies and gorges north of the hill. McIntosh's men pursued and some were met with effective resistance in the rocky terrain. But for the most part, the Indians had no alternative except flight. A small group that rallied to defend Opothleyahola's main camp three miles into the hills was overwhelmed, and the mounted Creek forces were routed.

The battle was over by four o'clock in the afternoon. McIntosh lost nine killed and forty wounded. He had crushed the enemy and captured most of their baggage train. Chief Stand Watie's three hundred Second Cherokee Mounted Rifles joined McIntosh as the battle concluded, and took over the pursuit. Opothleyahola's band fled north as evening fell, into the face of a blizzard that had begun in the afternoon. The group struggled along, their winter clothing still in the baggage train, some of them barefoot, as Stand Watie's men hunted them, shooting them down in the snow. Nearly a hundred were killed over the next several days before they reached relative safety in Kansas.[30]

In his report to Richmond, Cooper complained that had McIntosh waited for his forces to arrive before attacking, they could have bagged all of the Indians. McIntosh's report was more sanguine. The enemy had been defeated and the rebel Cherokee were returning to the fold. "I think the march of our force into the nation has had a most happy effect," he concluded.[31] To the higher headquarters it appeared that McIntosh's dash had achieved what Cooper's caution could not. A few weeks later, McIntosh received his commission as a brigadier general.

Between Death and Glory

BY THE SPRING OF 1862, McIntosh's reputation was well established. A. W. Sparks wrote that "the impetuous McIntosh . . . was at home only amidst the raging of wild elements, and . . . courted the missions of danger with a fondness not surpassed by the affection of a lover for his mistress." He was "the soul of honor and chivalry; the *beau sabreur* of the Western army."[32] B. W. Stone, one of his regimental commanders, wrote that McIntosh was an officer "in whose courage the troops had the most implicit confidence."[33] Lieutenant George Griscom of the Ninth Texas Cavalry called him "gallant but rash."[34] Yet his rashness (or gallantry) had served him well. McIntosh had achieved the general officer rank he sought and had been given command of the First Brigade in McCulloch's division. He led five regiments of Arkansas and Texas cavalry, a total of over 4,400 men. He no longer sought transfer, and events were conspiring to bring more action to the Trans-Mississippi theater, along with more opportunities for glory.

The McCulloch/Price feud had stalled any effective military action in Missouri, and in order to break the deadlock, Jefferson Davis appointed a commander over both their forces. His first choice was Henry Heth, but he later settled on a fellow Mississippian, Earl Van Dorn, an Immortal of the Class of 1842, who graduated fourth from the foot, two steps above his classmate Longstreet. Van Dorn had seen action in most of the major battles in Mexico, being brevetted for his deeds at Cerro Gordo and Churubusco. He helped storm Chapultepec and was wounded occupying the City of Mexico. Later he served on the frontier with the Second Cavalry, chiefly in the Southwest, where he was wounded in several Indian fights—four times in one battle. When he was given command of the Trans-Mississippi, Van Dorn set his sights on St. Louis. "I must first have St. Louis," he wrote his wife, "then, Huzza!"[35] Van Dorn planned to concentrate his scattered forces, bypass the Union forces garrisoned along the main approach to the city, move as swiftly as possible to seize it, and rally support from the countryside while awaiting Confederate reinforcements.

After Lyon was killed at Wilson's Creek, command of Union forces in southwest Missouri fell to Brigadier General Samuel R. Curtis from Ohio, an Immortal of the Class of 1831 who had graduated sixth from the bottom. Curtis had resigned after a year of active duty to become an engineer and lawyer. He fought in Mexico as a colonel of volunteers, and then returned again to private life. In 1857 he was elected to the House of Representatives from Iowa; he left Congress in 1861 to help defend the Union. Curtis unknowingly disrupted Van Dorn's campaign plan by starting his own advance south in January 1862, slowly pushing Sterling Price's forces back into Arkansas. Martial law had been declared in Missouri in December, and Curtis's men, particularly his German troops, burned towns and villages along their route. After fighting some skirmishes with Price, and wary of his lengthening supply lines, Curtis dug in about eight miles over the Arkansas border on a bluff overlooking Sugar Creek. He had a strong position—the bluffs ran east-west, a bow-shaped plateau with natural flank support, straddling the road. It was a formidable natural defensive position, which he augmented with trenches and log breastworks.

Van Dorn took command of the Trans-Mississippi on February 28, and seeing an opportunity in Curtis's forward position, immediately ordered Price, McCulloch and Albert Pike (who commanded the Confederate Indian regiments) to mass their divisions north of Fayetteville. They began their combined advance towards Missouri on March 2. Four days later, several inches of snow lay on the ground, and though the sun was bright, the cold was numbing. Curtis's forces were foraging, and he had no knowledge of the Confederate advance or reason to believe he was going to be attacked. However, his southernmost foragers at Bentonville observed a large enemy force approaching them rapidly. McIntosh's men were in the van of the Confederate column, and they moved to flank the city and cut off the Union troops. But the Federals anticipated the movement and set up an ambush at the point where McIntosh's force rejoined the road. Once the trap was sprung, McIntosh, in his usual fashion, drew his saber and charged into the teeth of the enemy guns. As the momentum of the charge ebbed, he grabbed the flag and waved it over his head, imploring his men to make a second effort as Union musket balls whipped by him. A running battle ensued, and most of the Federal forces made it back to Curtis's bastion along Sugar Creek by nightfall.

That evening, the Confederates went into bivouac on a hillside near the Union lines along Sugar Creek. They were worn from several days of forced marching across fifty-five miles. Most lacked tents, and there was little food. "It was impossible to sleep," one Confederate sergeant wrote, "for the night was bitter cold; no one will ever know how much we suffered from cold and hunger; no tongue or pen can paint it."[36] Curtis spent the night preparing his defenses for battle. The fires of the Rebel camp were visible a few miles to the southwest, scattered across the snow-covered hills in the nearly moonless night. Curtis suspected he was outnumbered, but to what degree was open to question. The wildest reports had 50,000 Rebels ready to descend on him. In fact, Curtis faced 16,000 of Van Dorn's men, of which 1,000 were Albert Pike's group of Choctaw, Creek, Chickasaw and Cherokee. Curtis could field 10,500 effective troops.

Van Dorn held a council of war to consider his options. The main line of attack was up the Telegraph Road, which ran in front of Curtis's line parallel to Sugar Creek before turning north through his position, going northeast past the two-story Elkhorn Tavern, and thence towards Springfield. It was not a promising avenue of advance, and Curtis had spent weeks readying his defenses for just such a battle. But McCulloch and McIntosh knew a different route, a less-traveled road eight miles long, leading northeast from Telegraph Road below Curtis's position behind an outcropping called Pea Ridge and rejoining Telegraph Road north of Elkhorn Tavern. By taking this route, Van Dorn could bypass Curtis's forward defenses, flank him on the detour in a long loop, and swoop down in his rear in a two-pronged attack around both ends of Pea Ridge. Secrecy was critical to maintain the element of surprise, so Van Dorn undertook a night march. They began to move at 8 P.M., first Price's force accompanied by Van Dorn, then McCulloch's, then Pike's. Fires were left burning in the bivouac to give the impression the Confederates were still in front of Curtis's position. The movement was complicated. Curtis's men had felled trees along the detour, which were difficult to remove in the darkness. As well, the men were still very tired, having not been given adequate rest, and some of them misunderstood their orders and had to countermarch several additional miles. The attack was not ready until 10 A.M., but despite the hardships, Van Dorn's flanking action was successful.

Morning dawned with a thin fog over the Sugar Creek valley, and Curtis readied for the expected attack. As the mist began to clear, however, he observed that the valley was empty. Reports then came in that supply wagons had been seized in the rear. Curtis quickly realized what had happened and just before Van Dorn's attack began he ordered an about-turn to meet the threat. He supposed the attack would come from the northwest, through the settlement of Leetown, and sent his left flank forward under the command of Colonel Peter Osterhaus. They advanced right into Pike's Indians, who, seeing the enemy, charged ahead whooping. The sight of the painted Indians shook Osterhaus's mainly German immigrant force, and Pike's men routed the Union troops, captured their battery and broke the advance. But the Indians failed to exploit their victory; they gathered around the captured battery, "a mass of Indians and others in the utmost confusion, all talking, riding this way and that, and listening to no orders from any one."[37] When another Union battery opened up on them, the Indians, who traditionally feared artillery, scattered to the woods from which they had charged and would not advance again.

Van Dorn and Price attacked at 10:30. Curtis, exploiting his interior lines, had managed to throw in place a hasty defense that withstood the Rebel attack remarkably well under the circumstances. Price's first two assaults failed to dislodge the Federal line, but he rallied his men and on the third advance they pushed the enemy back south of Elkhorn Tavern. The tavern owner J. C. Cox and his family took refuge in the cellar during the battle, while the space above the tavern was used as a hospital. As the battle progressed and the wounded were brought in, the family listened to the sounds of fighting, the groans of the soldiers and the surgeons at work. When blood began to seep down through the floorboards and drip on them, they finally fled into the open for fresh air and to escape the horror.[38] As the Confederate left advanced beyond Elkhorn, it became clear that the Union forces were on the verge of a major defeat. Van Dorn sent a dispatch to McCulloch urging him to press the right flank and close the trap.

McCulloch, five miles away at the southern end of Pea Ridge, had started his attack at the first sound of Price's guns. His men advanced in a long line, heading roughly southeast, feeling for the enemy. His cavalry regiments were drawn up on the right, led by McIntosh, advancing in five columns of four abreast. The infantry were on the left under the command of Hébert. The terrain was mixed: cleared fence-lined fields separated by strips of oak woodland, in which Union troops were hastily establishing gun emplacements and ambushes. As the infantry advanced, a Union battery situated behind a rail fence next to a log cabin opened up from three hundred yards, pouring destructive fire into the Confederate infantry. McIntosh instantly ordered his cavalry brigade to charge. The bugles sounded, the men whooped, and thousands of horses thundered across the field. Colonel B. W. Stone of the Sixth Texas Cavalry wrote that "the heavens resounded with the tramp of warriors' steeds as they swept the field and rushed impetuously on the enemy's battery."[39] McIntosh was out front, as usual, waving his saber and shouting. The Union support troops fired a volley and then ran as the Confederate horsemen descended on them. The Rebels captured the three guns as the gunners fled. Momentum carried many of the horsemen through the enemy lines, and a running gun battle erupted with the Third Iowa Cavalry. The Union front was stabilized with the arrival of a division under the command of the ironically named Jefferson C. Davis.

McCulloch meanwhile organized an infantry advance, which steadily pushed back the Union forces. During a pause in the action he rode forward to reconnoiter. He was unmistakable in his white hat, black velvet uniform, pantaloons cut to the knee and boot-length stockings. He was on the edge of a tree line, looking through his field glasses, when Union sharpshooters from the 36th Illinois regiment fired a volley. A soldier named Peter Pelican was credited with firing the shot that dropped the general. Pelican and others then allegedly ran forward and stole McCulloch's gold watch. Not far to the east, McIntosh and Lieutenant Samuel M. Hyams Jr. of the Third Louisiana regiment were watching as McCulloch fell. They immediately spurred their horses and rode down the line.

"I fear the General is killed," McIntosh shouted to Lieutenant Frank Crawford Armstrong, the assistant adjutant general.[40] "A whole company of skirmishers fired upon him; he clasped the pommel of his saddle and fell forward." McIntosh then saw the Federals moving up towards the general's body. He called out to the men from his old command the Second Arkansas, and ordered a charge. Private Rose of the Ninth Texas Cavalry wrote that McIntosh, "with that conspicuous gallantry which was part of his nature, led the foremost, sword in hand."[41] As McIntosh neared the edge of the tree line, the Union sharpshooters got him in their sights and felled him.[42]

With McCulloch and McIntosh down, the attack on the Confederate right flank dissipated. Colonel Hébert, the remaining brigade commander, rode to a group of soldiers to try to rally them, learning too late that they were Federals, who captured him. Through the afternoon the battle drifted, and towards evening Albert Pike led the remnants of the right wing of the attacking force back to the road. Overnight they made their way northeast to join Price's forces. The next day, the Confederates regrouped at Elkhorn Tavern, at least those who still wanted to fight. They discovered that their supply train had been sent to Bentonville, leaving them with little food or ammunition. Curtis went on the offensive, redeploying his forces to face the remaining Rebels, and opened the battle at seven in the morning, pushing the enemy back steadily. Three hours later, Van Dorn decided to abandon the field; he retreated ten miles to Huntsville, Arkansas. Curtis, his men tired and lacking significant cavalry, was in no position to exploit the turn of fortune.

William Baxter was in his home in Fayetteville the night of the second day of the Battle of Pea Ridge when he heard the sound of a wagon coming from the direction of the battlefield. The wagon contained a body, escorted by officers of the elite Third Louisiana. The body was taken to the house of a friend of Baxter's, and he went in. He recognized it as James M. McIntosh. Baxter described the lonely scene: "there he lay, cold and stark, just as he was taken from the spot where he fell; a military overcoat covering his person, and the dead forest leaves still clinging to it. His wound had not been examined; I aided in opening his vest and undergarments, and soon found that the ball had passed through his body, near, if not through, the heart."[43] McIntosh was buried at Fort Smith, his last post as a Federal officer, where his grave remains today. A. W. Sparks predicted that the Goat of 1849, "had he lived, would have written his name high upon the memorial roll of Fame. With McIntosh, there was no intermediate rest between death and glory."[44]

CHARLES NELSON WARNER

C ADET CHARLES NELSON WARNER returned to Pennsylvania
in the spring of 1861, despondent over being "found" so late in
his West Point career. It was particularly nettlesome that he
had been sent away the day before the declaration of the Confederate
States. While many of his classmates were leaving West Point to join
the Rebel cause, he was not allowed to remain to defend his beloved
Union. He may have been deemed "not proficient" in ethics, but he
certainly had no problems with loyalty. And while his classmates graduated and rushed to the battlefront, Warner helped drill local militia
units in Montrose and pondered his options. But that fall the young
cadet was granted a reprieve. The need for West Point officers was so
great that Warner, who had completed the majority of the curriculum,
was too valuable an asset to waste. He was reinstated in September
1861 as a firstie, slated to graduate in the spring of 1862, as he had originally expected.

When Warner was tested the following June, he passed both ethics
and infantry tactics, albeit at the bottom of the class. He had also not
improved his conduct, amassing ninety-six demerits his final semester,
second worst in his class. Nevertheless he graduated, as the Goat of
1862. He wrote his sister Emma, "I can't help feeling proud of graduating at this place, although I may not have a very high standing in my
class. I appreciate the privileges which I have enjoyed and am now
enjoying, more than I have always done. I am perfectly satisfied with
my position and would not exchange it for any that I know."[1] He realized that his time at West Point had not been perfect, but he was looking towards the future and getting into the war. "Thank fortune it is not
too late," he wrote Emma,

> ... I am infinitely better fitted for my profession than I would have been
> if I had graduated last year. Taking everything into consideration I do

not believe I shall ever be sorry for coming home last year. Temporarily it seemed a great misfortune, but in the end I think it may be a permanent advantage. I am older now than a great many who graduate here, but I feel I am none too old. Plenty young enough for the experience I may have. If I had gone into the Army last year I should have had a much higher rank, but now I have a very much better education. No one ever could have better advantages than I have had. I only hope that they have not been thrown away, which I am going to try to demonstrate.[2]

Warner had pondered his branch assignment, saying his choice was between infantry, cavalry and artillery. "I don't know if I can get into artillery," he wrote Emma. "If I can I intend to take it."[3] He liked infantry for the drill and rapid promotion prospects; cavalry was a harder life, but he enjoyed riding and the pay was better. "But I prefer artillery," he wrote, "because there are fewer non-graduates in it, because ... it is more scientific, because the service is easy, because it is more stationary, that is, you remain longer in one place, but principally because I would stand a better chance of being posted East, where I would not be entirely separated from my friends."[4] He said he thought he could get an artillery commission, "because a great many citizens have been appointed into it, and also men who have been found deficient here. If I am not able to get into it, it will certainly not be because I am incompetent, when you consider what kind of men are now in the Corps."[5]

It was a rare Goat who branched artillery. Under normal circumstances it would have been impossible, since artillery commissions were reserved for higher-ranking graduates. But with a war on there was a need for trained artillery officers, and a West Pointer, even one like Warner who scored last in his class in artillery tactics, was looked on with more favor than a volunteer. Warner got his wish, and on June 17 was made a brevet second lieutenant of the Second Artillery regiment. He was assigned to Battery D, which at the time was commanded by Emory Upton.

By July 30, Warner was with McClellan's Army of the Potomac in camp at Harrison's Landing, Virginia, during the latter days of the Peninsular Campaign. The major battles around Richmond had been fought and lost weeks before, and the large Union force had withdrawn to a defensive posture, still capable of action, but doing little beyond reconnaissance. "Here we are, lying day after day, doing nothing, and costing the government an immense amount," Warner wrote. "It seems a great pity that we couldn't go on and do something, and then return to our homes. Waiting seems to be characteristic of McClellan." Warner continued to believe that the war could be brought to a close swiftly, with the proper exertions: "I don't expect to have always as pleasant and comfortable a time as I am having now. War brings trouble and misery upon us all.... It is perfectly practicable to end it in a few months, if the country would show that it was in earnest about the matter.... I think the time has gone by when we should count the cost or any other sacrifice which is necessary to be endured to bring this war to a close. We have a great deal to do and a great deal to risk, but I hope we may all do our duty, live through the war, and enjoy for a long time the blessings of peace, which I trust we may be able to appreciate."

He finally got his chance to see action in September. Following up his success at Second Manassas in late August 1862, Robert E. Lee invaded Maryland. By a quirk of fate, his operations plan fell into Union hands, wrapped around some cigars, on September 13. Lee's invasion force was divided at the time, and quick action could have allowed Federal forces to engage it piecemeal. But McClellan was hesitant, as Warner had noted, and the Rebels regrouped and almost escaped back over the Potomac. Not wanting to risk a river crossing with McClellan nearby, Lee drew his forces up in a defensive position on a ridge above Antietam Creek, outside the town of Sharpsburg, Maryland.

September 17, 1862, became the bloodiest single day of the war. Warner wrote Emma, "I have taken part in the most destructive battle of the war and we are victorious." Then part of the First Division, Warner was miles away at Crampton's Pass when battle was joined. His unit moved quickly towards the sound of the guns. They arrived on the field at noon, taking a position in the center of the Union line, near Dunkard Church on the Hagerstown and Sharpsburg Turnpike, relieving part of the right flank of Sumner's II Corps.[6] There Battery D engaged in an artillery duel until sundown.

"We were under a very warm fire for several hours from the enemy's artillery and sharpshooters, and were very fortunate that we had so few casualties," Warner wrote. Two men were wounded by sniper fire and two horses killed. "You cannot imagine what horrid noises fall on the ear on the battlefield. I do not speak of the groans of the wounded, I heard much of that, but that being caused by the air being filled with the different kinds of missiles of destruction. The whistle of bullets, explosion of shells, roar of artillery, crackling of musketry almost like a pack of fire-crackers, all going off at once, when two hostile lines come together, is indescribable." The next day was mostly quiet, and Warner saw only some skirmishing. Soon a truce was declared and both sides tended to the wounded and buried the dead. On September 19, Warner's unit had reveille at three in the morning and then readied to renew the contest. They moved into position before daylight; but Union pickets reported that the enemy had left. Later, Warner moved across the field, noticing bodies "corded up like wood" for burial. "It was so dark I could see very little," he wrote, "but the stench arising from the dead bodies was intolerable."[7]

Warner's unit soon moved south in pursuit of the Rebels, but on September 28 he returned to the battlefield, looking for his brother Fletch, who was in Ambrose Burnside's command. Ten days earlier, Burnside's men had attempted to storm a stone bridge on the southern end of the field and were cut down by a small force of well-emplaced Rebel sharpshooters on the heights above. The Union forces eventually overwhelmed the Confederates, but not before making "Burnside's Bridge" a watchword in military history for the hopeless attack. Fletch was not in camp; Warner was told he had been gravely wounded. That evening he and a friend set out to find his brother. "Started at dusk with Charley Frink for his hospital, or rather, barn," he wrote. "When we arrived we found the surgeon engaged in the horrid operation of cutting off a man's arm. . . . [I]t seemed to me like a land of blood, and made me realize more forcibly than ever before, the dreadful horrors of war—whence the hasty disappearance of a vast amount of military ardor."[8] They found Fletch, still bedridden ten days after the battle, but no longer in grave danger. They stayed with him the rest of the night, and the next day set him up in nearby Rohrersville with their family friend Allie Rohrer.

By December, Charles' other brother, Ed, was also wounded and sent home. "I feel glorious to have Ed and Fletch at home and I the only one away," he wrote Emma. "I have no one to trouble myself about but myself. I am going to do my duty and trust to luck, and Divine providence especially. I am going to try to rough it through this war and I hope to gracious it will be over pretty soon. I have seen enough of it."[9] Nevertheless, Charlie was an optimist. His letters constantly made reference to the better times ahead. "Oh! There is a good time coming Emma, when the war is over," he wrote in December 1862, "and war is exhilarating, but I think peace is near. It is winter now and next year will end the business. A few more battles, and I hope for a little more glory, and a better appreciation of peace when it comes. I don't care much for the glory, though. I am not very ambitious. I want to do my duty and be respectable. That is about all I care for in way of reputation."[10] And despite the hardships he was facing, he noted that "this way of living is a thousand times better than being at West Point."[11]

At eight in the morning on December 12, 1862, soon after Warner predicted the coming end of the war, his battery crossed the

Rappahannock River and took up a position south of Fredericksburg near a creek called Deep Run. His battery advanced cautiously towards the front line and established themselves just behind the pickets. It was a quiet day, and the men settled in. Mail arrived and Warner was about to read a letter from home when guns from A. P. Hill's division opened up on the battery, blasting them out of position. "Were cleaned out by a battery of the enemy and took refuge in a gully," Warner wrote in his war diary. "Several narrow escapes in the battery. One of my men wounded and another scared out of his wits—both missing for some time. There was one close shot on myself.... That one shot made me temporarily sick of war. At dusk moved out of the gully and encamped on a large pile of straw." The next day they moved back into line of battle but did not engage, though they were under fire all day. To the north there was "such a roar of musketry near us for two or three hours as I never heard before." It was the sound of the luckless Burnside's catastrophic attack on Marye's Heights west of the city. A few days later, Warner's unit was withdrawn.

In April 1863, Warner's battery was among those troops reviewed by President and Mrs. Lincoln. General Joseph Hooker (USMA 1837) had taken over as commander of the Army of the Potomac. Warner observed, "I think Hooker will put us through pretty hard. If he has any fault, in my opinion, it is not over cautiousness, which some people ascribe to McClellan."[12] Warner was at Camp Amparo, across the Rappahannock from Fredericksburg, where he had been since the battle. "I must say I rather like the idea of participating in active operations again once more," he wrote. "There is pleasure in excitement, in change or novelty, in risk. Of course at home you will be afraid that I shall get hurt. War troubles everybody but those who are engaged in it. Soldiers get fond of the business after awhile, and the more they see of destruction and suffering the less they think of it." He pledged to take no unnecessary risks. "I don't pretend to be courageous either. I don't like to hear the little balls whistle, or big balls roar, or great shells burst. I would not like to be hit by any of them.... The idea is, I am tired of camp life ... and would enjoy moving and seeing new things, perhaps meeting with some little adventures. All people like excitement of one kind or another."[13]

On April 26, around midnight, Warner received word to move his battery quietly to the banks of the Rappahannock, half a mile south of Fredericksburg. Along the road they passed lines of infantry carrying pontoons. The night was cloudy and dark, and visibility was low. The assault boats launched just before dawn, and several hundred men rowed stealthily across the river. At midstream a volley of fire erupted from the other side. A dozen men fell, but the river assault went forward. The Union troops landed, took the Rebel defensive works, and seized many prisoners. Warner's division was quickly thrown across to defend the bridgehead while the bridges were constructed for the rest of I and VI Corps to cross. Warner's battery was placed on the eastern shore, behind an old Confederate rifle pit. "We considered it quite an honor that our Battery should be chosen to defend the crossing," he wrote, "as it was a very responsible and dangerous duty."[14] They stayed there as the bridge was built and the Union forces crossed. "I hope we will not be obliged to cross the river again," he wrote from his position. "I have seen enough of the other side."

This movement was the opening of the Battle of Chancellorsville. The landing to the south of the city was a small part of an ambitious plan. Over the next few days, Hooker executed a bold flanking maneuver, crossing fords miles upriver from the city and depositing his main force in Lee's rear. He hoped to present Lee with a quandary: if he moved from Fredericksburg to face Hooker, I and VI Corps would move on the town and take it. If Lee stayed where he was, V, XI and XII Corps would bottle him up in the city from the rear. The only other option was retreat south. On April 30, after completing this movement, Hooker announced to his army, "It is with heartfelt satisfaction the commanding general announces to the army that the operations of the last three days have determined that our enemy must either ingloriously fly, or come out from behind his defenses and give us battle on our own ground, where certain destruction awaits him."[15] Hooker believed that the most significant part of the battle had already been completed and that victory was assured. But the subsequent contest raged for three days, encompassing both Stonewall Jackson's famous flanking movement and his death by friendly fire. And while this contest was played out on the Union right flank, on the left Warner watched as the planned assault on Fredericksburg took shape.

On the evening of May 1, the Union forces formed on the north edge of the plain on the opposite bank of the river, a line a mile and a half long, clearly visible under a full moon. "We had a splendid view of it," Warner wrote. "It was the most beautiful line I have ever seen." The band assembled just in front of Warner's battery and began playing as the troops formed. They played "Yankee Doodle," "Hail Columbia," "Dixie" and other songs. "I thought the rebs would fire on them from their batteries and put a sudden stop to the music, but they did not choose to. After the band had stopped, the Rebels yelled like infuriated demons. They yelled so long and it seemed so loud and near that I thought they were charging on us for certain. Then our men returned it, and such defiant hideous noises on both sides you never heard."[16] That night there was a hot skirmish between the pickets. Warner stayed in his position, suffering some Confederate shelling the next morning and returning in kind. "The rebels have honored us with a few shots this morning which made a great deal of noise and came so close that I could see them bounding along on the ground. Their shells caused considerable commotion."[17] He noted the sound of the battle west of the city. "It is said there has been a very hard infantry fight," he wrote. "I hope we shall whip them. The prospect seems favorable."

On the night of May 2, the rest of VI Corps was ordered over the bridge to assemble for the attack. "I never saw so fine a sight as the crossing of these troops," Warner wrote a few hours later. "They are all drawn up in battle array, twenty-seven thousand strong beneath the heights of Fredericksburg. We shall make an attack at daylight tomorrow, and then we shall have a desperate fight. Sunday is the day for battles, you know. The rebels are making huge fires as if to say, Come on, we are ready for you, what do we care for you? I think we shall whip them. I want to be a member of our victorious army in Richmond in a few days. . . . I hear we are going to attack at daylight and the batteries are to be shoved ahead. I think I shall pass through this rumpus all right. Good bye."[18]

Warner got only an hour's sleep. Reveille was at 1 A.M., and at daylight the battery moved out. Almost immediately the Union forces came under fire from Rebel artillery positioned on the heights. The fire was punishing. The Federals were under some cover, but the shells began to land among them "with enough force to go through half a dozen men."[19] A piece of shell from an exploding round came right at Warner and he dodged it. Another shell wounded a soldier nearby and within minutes he was dead. A twenty-pound solid shot landed square on the head of another man standing right in front of Warner "with an awful thud," killing him instantly. "He never moved," Warner wrote. "No-one appeared to think much of it. His comrades were thick all around him." They threw a cloth over him during a pause in the battle, and later the soldier's friends carried the body away. The shelling continued for hours until the infantry charged up the heights and took the positions. Said Warner, "It was a beautiful sight."

Warner marched through Fredericksburg and west up the heights, under close fire from fresh Rebel batteries. "It seemed very much like a triumph when we went through the detested place," he noted. The column passed many dead by the side of the road, both blue and gray. They advanced two miles down the plank road towards Chancellorsville. The retreating enemy had established a line of defenses in a belt of dense woods near a brick building called Salem Church. At five in the evening, Warner watched as Union troops moved across the open plain towards the woods. They "advanced in splendid style," he wrote, "and then the slaughter commenced."

The Union forces were attacking a brigade commanded by Cadmus Wilcox, which was soon reinforced by three more brigades of Lafayette McLaws' division. McLaws had graduated in the bottom ten of Longstreet's Class of 1842. He had fought in Mexico, where his career was almost cut short when he was accidentally shot by William Logan Crittenden. "When the front line of the [Federal troops] reached this wood," McLaws wrote, "they made a slight halt; then, giving three cheers, they came with a rush, driving our skirmishers rapidly before them. Our men held their fire till their men came within less than 80 yards, and then delivered a close and terrible fire upon them, killing and wounding many and causing many of them to waver and give way."

Warner watched the Union regiments disappear into the woods, "line after line, with banners streaming," followed by the roar of muskets for fifteen minutes. Then the Union troops began to reappear. "Some fell back slowly and in good order, disputing the ground inch by inch," he noted, "while others fled ingloriously, perfectly terror stricken." The Rebels emerged from the woods, and the retreat threatened to become a rout. The air was alive with musket balls, and the stragglers were running back towards the town as other units bravely attempted to stem the tide. Colonel Charles H. Tompkins, the chief of artillery, ordered Warner's battery to the front at a gallop, to prevent the entire line from collapsing. The battery raced ahead to the forward edge of the battle and set up straddling the road. Battery commander Lieutenant Edward B. Williston began firing spherical case rounds with a fuse delay of one and three-quarters seconds into the mass of advancing Rebel troops. "The effect of this fire proved so disastrous to the rebels that they retreated in great confusion," Williston wrote, "and crossed the road to the left-hand side." This placed them directly in front of Warner's guns. Warner and Williston pumped a dozen round shot down the road like bowling balls, bouncing and ricocheting into the massed Confederates. The Rebel forces were severely disrupted and the fighting paused for ten minutes as they reorganized. Then they advanced again, attempting to charge the battery, and were again met with a storm of canister and shot. General Sedgwick was nearby, urging the artillerymen on. The fight was intense. "We fired about an hour with effect I believe, under a warm musketry fire," Warner wrote. "I was so tired I could hardly stand up."[20] Eventually the fighting ceased and Warner's battery was relieved. They moved back a mile from the front, dirty, sweaty and exhausted.

"That night, I must say, I was horrified," Warner recalled. "In that repulse we lost a great many men, quite a number that I knew very well. Between us and the woods, about eight hundred yards, I could see black spots all over the ground. They were dead bodies. A great many of our dead and wounded fell in the edge of the woods. The woods were afterwards set on fire by the rebs, and a great many must have burned." The battery had stopped near a house that was being used as a staging area for the wounded, and Warner was treated to more horrifying sights. "They were all alone and uncared for, and one who was gasping very nearly his last rolled his eyes around at me. I do not forget how he looked. I suppose I am not very much of a soldier or I would not mind such things, but I never was so much impressed with the horrors of war as I was that night."[21] Warner soon learned that his close friend Lieutenant Justin E. Dimick, an Immortal of his original Class of June 1861, had been mortally wounded. Another friend, Lieutenant Edmund Kirby, a cousin of the Kirby-Smiths and tenth in the Class of May 1861, had lost his leg; he died of his wounds three weeks later. For the moment, however, Warner could not comfort them. When his unit reached their bivouac, he took his blankets from the wagon, dropped them directly on the ground, fell to earth and was asleep. May 3, 1863, he later recalled, "was the longest day I ever knew."

The next day, Warner's battery was on the field but not engaged. By then, General Hooker had lost confidence in his plan (or, as he admitted, in himself) and ordered a withdrawal. Warner recrossed the Rapahannock around 1 A.M. on May 5. He and his men slept on the opposite shore, within range of the Rebel shells that occasionally fell nearby. "I did not know but I should wake up in the morning and find myself dead," he noted. After a brief rest they were ordered to go nine miles to Richard's Ford to block a possible crossing by Fitz Lee's cavalry, which was trying to flank the retreating Union army. They established a defensive position, but the attack never came. They waited for two days in the rain, and then withdrew and headed north.

Afterwards, Warner noted that Lieutenant Williston, the battery commander, was "in very high feather" because of the reputation the battery had established with their stand at Salem Church. Warner related the battle to Emma with characteristic modesty. "We were in action perhaps half an hour and it is said did very good service. I believe we did. Some say we would have been driven into the river if it had not been for our battery. I think we killed a few and scared a great many more."[22] A few days later he wrote, "It is pleasant after a fight to be able to say that you were in it, and if you should not happen to last as long as the fight does, that is what you might call hard luck."[23] But he passed through the rumpus all right.

GETTYSBURG

"THE 'BATTLE OF GETTYSBURG' was the result purely of *an accident*," Henry Heth wrote, "for which I am probably, more than anyone else, accountable."[1] Two days before the most famous battle of the Civil War, Major General Heth was encamped at the small hamlet of Cashtown, Pennsylvania, leading the main body of Robert E. Lee's invasion of the North. The march from Virginia had been fatiguing. Heth's men needed supplies, particularly shoes, and the general wanted a new hat. He asked his quartermaster what was available, and the latter produced a box of about a dozen, all of which were too large. Heth was frustrated, but his clerk said, "General, I think I can fix one to fit you." He folded up a dozen large sheets of paper and placed them behind the hat band, thereby saving his commander's life.[2]

Henry Heth was a captain on leave in Virginia when the war broke out. There was no question that he would support his native state's cause. He resigned from the Army when Virginia left the Union, and on the same day wrote to Jefferson Davis offering his services to the Confederacy. Someone on Davis's staff wrote on Heth's letter, "Special attention, this is a first rate soldier and of the cast of man most needed."[3] Within months Heth was promoted to full colonel and served as inspector general of Virginia. He witnessed some early but futile fighting in western Virginia, serving under former secretary of war John B. Floyd, whom Heth considered incompetent. He appealed to Davis to send him to another command where he might do some good, and Davis called Heth in for an interview.

"Young man, how much rank can you stand?" Davis asked.

"Mr. President, you must be the judge of that," Heth replied.

"Well, I will make you a Major General and send you to the Trans-Mississippi; Price and McCulloch are fighting each other there harder than they are fighting the enemy."[4]

It was a prestigious post, and Heth could not refuse it although he would rather have stayed in the East defending Virginia. Then, Heth said, "a kind of providence, in this event, came to my assistance."[5] His promotion became a matter of contention between Davis and the Confederate Congress.[6] Missouri had recently been admitted to the Confederacy (having seceded October 31, 1861), and its congressional delegation wanted native son Price to command. Davis saw this as a challenge to his power, and a political dispute ensued. Price's partisans charged that Heth was too young and inexperienced, and said disparagingly that he was a "West Point Cadet." President Davis strongly objected to this slighting of his candidate and the Academy (and by extension, himself):

> If it is designed, by calling Heth a West Point Cadet, merely to object to his education in the science of war, it may pass for what it is worth; but if it be intended to assert that he is without experience, his years of active and distinguished service on the frontier of Missouri and the territory west of it will, to those who examine before they censure, be a sufficient answer.[7]

But Heth chose not to try to convince his critics that he was suited for the job, and eventually Earl Van Dorn received the appointment. Heth was consoled with promotion to brigadier general on January 9, 1862.[8]

In May of that same year, Heth drove back a Union advance at Giles Court House, Virginia, commanded by future president Colonel Rutherford B. Hayes of the 23rd Ohio, but a few weeks later he was defeated by Union forces in Lewisburg.[9] He then transferred west to serve as a division commander under Edmund Kirby Smith in Tennessee. Here he participated in the daring 1862 invasion of Kentucky. The Confederates defeated a superior Union force at Richmond, then advanced to Lexington, where they paused to regroup. Heth argued forcefully that they strike while the enemy was disorganized, and move on Louisville or Cincinnati. Kirby Smith permitted Heth to move towards Cincinnati, which he did swiftly with six thousand men. The city was undefended and thrown into panic at Heth's approach. His men faced no resistance until he reached the outskirts of the riverfront town of Covington, Kentucky. There he routed local militia and prepared to move on the town proper. Yet before he could depart, a courier arrived with orders from Kirby Smith not to attack; a decisive battle was expected between Braxton Bragg (a star man of the Class of 1837), commander of the Army of Tennessee, and Don Carlos Buell (USMA 1841) of the Army of Ohio, after which, according to Kirby Smith, "Cincinnati and

Louisville will fall like ripe apples into our hands."[10] But Bragg's contest with Buell at Perryville on October 8 was inconclusive, and his unexpected withdrawal from Kentucky three days later aborted the entire invasion. Heth was forced to pull back, and he and Kirby Smith concluded that "General Bragg had lost his mind."[11]

In the fall of 1862, the Confederate Senate denied Heth promotion to major general, and he requested to be transferred to Lee's command: "General Lee has always been my personal friend, and I should much like to join him for many reasons." Among them was his desire to help defend Virginia and to clear his name from the defeat at Lewisburg. Lee enthusiastically endorsed Heth's proposal (he had already asked for Heth by name in February), and Heth was sent east on January 17, 1863. Lee sent a strong recommendation to Stonewall Jackson: "I think the interest of the service, as well as justice to individuals, requires the selection of the best men to fill vacant positions."[12] Jackson replied, "From what you have said respecting General Heth, I have been desirous that he should report for duty."[13] Jackson made Heth a brigade commander in his classmate A. P. Hill's division.

Heth reported for duty too late to face his old friend Ambrose Burnside at Fredericksburg, but he did take part in Jackson's famous flanking maneuver at Chancellorsville. Hill's division was the third line of Jackson's attack, and when Hill was wounded by friendly fire (of the sort that killed Jackson), Heth took over command for the third day of the battle. His troops saw heavy fighting and led the attack on the Union entrenchments. He was wounded but refused to leave the field, and acting corps commander J. E. B. Stuart especially noted Heth's heroic conduct.

When Lee reorganized his army after Chancellorsville, he sought to advance Heth's career. He wrote to President Davis that he wanted Heth to take over A. P. Hill's division if and when Hill was made a corps commander.[14] But Hill wanted Dorsey Pender (USMA 1854) to succeed him. Since Heth had previously been turned down for promotion, Lee was hesitant to foment a squabble, so he formed a new division, thus arranging for two vacancies. On May 30, Hill was made a corps commander, and his division was placed under command of "Maj. Gen. Harry Heth."

One month later, Heth's was the lead division of III Corps, encamped at Cashtown, nine miles west of Gettysburg, through which elements of II Corps had passed en route to York three days earlier. Thinking the town secure, and believing that shoes might be available

there, Heth dispatched General James J. Pettigrew's brigade to the city
to retrieve them and other supplies, and to return that day. Pettigrew
came back sooner than expected, reporting that he had seen a Union
cavalry force while en route to the town and he suspected there might
also be infantry nearby. A. P. Hill stated that he did not believe there
was a significant force in Gettysburg; George Gordon Meade's army
had not had time to move so far north, he reasoned, and these were
probably local home guard units. Heth concurred.

"If there is no objection," Heth said, "I will march my division
tomorrow, go to Gettysburg and secure those shoes."

"None in the world," Hill replied.[15]

General Lee was looking for a fight, but not this one. Late on June
28, Lee had received reports of Federal troops moving to intercept him
and was seeking to unify his scattered forces. His objective was to assume
an advantageous defensive position and let Meade attack him. The invasion of Pennsylvania was based on the Napoleonic principle of strategic offense/tactical defense: seize ground the enemy cannot afford to
lose, and then exploit the tactical benefits of being on the defensive. It
was the same principle Hooker had tried to employ two months earlier
at Chancellorsville. Gettysburg was a natural rallying point, the inter-
section of eleven roads. Whether Gettysburg was planned to be the site
of the decisive battle or whether Lee would have moved elsewhere is
unknown. But given his supply trail through the Cashtown Gap, Gettysburg could not have been left undefended. The II Corps, commanded
by General Richard S. Ewell (twelfth in the Class of 1840) was thirty
miles away, nearing Harrisburg. Lee could plan on their return by July
1. But he had no idea where his cavalry was.

"Every officer who conversed with General Lee for several days
previous to the battle of Gettysburg," Heth wrote, "well remembers
having heard such expressions as these: 'Can you tell me where General Stuart is?' 'Where on earth is my cavalry?' 'Have you any news of
the enemy's movements?' 'What is the enemy going to do?' 'If the enemy
does not find us, we must try and find him, in the absence of our cavalry, as best we can!' "[16] Lacking his principal reconnaissance arm, Lee
was unable to assess Meade's strength, position or movements, which
meant he was unable to plan his next moves. His subcommanders did
not know what Lee intended. He had told some of his generals, among
them A. P. Hill, that he did not wish to become decisively engaged. But
Hill was sick the morning of July 1 and did not convey this essential
command guidance to Heth. In any case, both Hill and Heth believed
that they faced only local militia, not regulars, and that no serious fight

was in the offing. Furthermore, given the Army of Northern Virginia's recent record of battlefield success, the Rebel troops were confident of victory no matter what they encountered. "There was not an officer or soldier in the Army of Northern Virginia, from General Lee to the drummer boy," Heth wrote, "who did not believe, when we invaded Pennsylvania in 1863, that it was able to drive the Federal army into the Atlantic Ocean."[17]

Heth set off at five o'clock the next morning, moving southeast down the Chambersburg Pike towards Gettysburg.[18] Around 7:30, Heth's skirmishers came into contact with Union screening forces on Whistler's Ridge, west of town. Tradition has it that battle was opened with a carbine shot from Lieutenant Marcellus Jones, Company E, Eighth Illinois Cavalry. Jones served under Brigadier General John Buford (sixteenth in the Class of 1848), who had been with Heth on the Sioux expedition in 1855. Like Heth, Buford was a division commander, in charge of the 3,000-man First Cavalry, screening the left flank of Meade's forward movement. Buford had encountered Pettigrew's men the day before and knew the Confederates would return in force. He was prepared to fight a delaying action until reinforcements could be brought up.

Under pressure from Heth's men, the Union pickets slowly withdrew to Buford's main position on McPherson's Ridge, less than two miles from the center of the town. Along the western edge of the ridge was Tidball's Battery A of the Second Artillery, attached to Buford's division and commanded by Lieutenant John Haskell Calef. An Immortal of the Class of 1862, coming in fifth from the bottom in artillery tactics, Calef was already a veteran of many battles only a year after graduating. His six guns were spread out along the ridge to give an illusion of strength. At Buford's command, his battery fired the opening Union artillery salvo of the battle.[19]

Heth set his troops into battle line, deploying two brigades along Herr Ridge on either side of the Cashtown Road: Brigadier General James J. Archer to the right and Brigadier General Joseph R. Davis, nephew of President Davis, to the left. He positioned two batteries on the ridge for support. At eight o'clock, after some probing attacks, Heth ordered the brigades forward on what he thought was a reconnaissance in force, seeking to brush aside the lightly armed cavalry forces.

"It may not be improper to remark that at this time," Heth wrote, "I was ignorant what force was at or near Gettysburg, and supposed it consisted of cavalry, most probably supported by a brigade or two of infantry."[20] For the moment, Heth was by and large right; Buford's men were outnumbered and outmatched. Nevertheless, through rapid carbine fire and Calef's deft use of artillery (his men "fought on this occasion as is seldom witnessed," Buford wrote), they managed to put up a spirited defense. Buford knew he could not hold the ridge by himself; his purpose was to delay Heth long enough to allow units from the Union I Corps to arrive.

The I Corps was commanded by former USMA Commandant Major General John F. "Old Pop" Reynolds. He left West Point in June 1861 and was soon made a brigadier. Reynolds fought in the Peninsular Campaign in the summer of 1862, where he was briefly a prisoner of war. He took command of I Corps after he was exchanged that fall. Reynolds was seven miles south of Gettysburg the morning of July 1, and when he received orders to head north at four in the morning, he moved slowly, the urgency still developing. But as he neared the town, he could hear the sounds of battle, and he hurried ahead across the farms south of town towards Seminary Ridge. His lead brigades came onto the field around ten o'clock, just as Heth's men were making their way up. Reynolds' Second Brigade, under Brigadier General Lysander Cutler, arrived first, occupying the ground to the right of Chambersburg Road, opposite Davis's brigade. Reynolds' First Brigade, the so-called "Iron Brigade" commanded by Brigadier General Solomon Meredith, arrived just as Archer's men were entering McPherson's Woods. The Iron Brigade was recognizable by their distinctive black hats, and the Confederate force realized that there was a considerable fight ahead of them.

Reynolds was in the thick of it, urging his men from his mount as they engaged the advancing enemy. "Forward men!" his voice rang out. "Forward for God's sake and drive those fellows out of the woods!" As Reynolds looked back, a bullet struck him at the base of the skull, and he fell from his saddle, dying almost immediately.

Command of I Corps fell to Major General Abner Doubleday (USMA 1842) of baseball fame. After a sharp fight, Archer's brigade was driven back and the general was captured. As he was being led to the rear, he encountered Doubleday, whom he had known in the Army.

"Good morning, Archer!" Doubleday said jovially. "How are you? I am glad to see you!"

"Well I am not glad to see you by a damned sight!" Archer spat back.

Meanwhile Davis's brigade had been severely mauled after becoming trapped in a railroad cut on the Union right flank. Every field officer but two became casualties, and the unit fell back. This ended the morning fighting for Heth's division, which reformed on Herr Ridge and awaited further orders. A. P. Hill arrived and began to deploy the rest of his corps.

About this time, Ewell's corps came onto the field at the far north end of the ridgeline and readied for battle. Robert E. Rodes' division of eight thousand began their assault at 1 P.M., moving south against a hastily organized Union defense. As the attack developed, Heth sought out A. P. Hill and found him with Lee, who had arrived on the field not long before. Lee was perturbed by the morning's developments. This was not the battle he had come to fight. Heth argued strongly that regardless of what Lee had planned, this was the fight they had, and he wanted to move quickly to support the flanking action.

"Rodes is very heavily engaged," Heth said. "Had I not better attack?"

"I do not wish to bring on a general engagement today," Lee replied. "Longstreet is not up." But Lee had to acknowledge that events had overtaken his plan, and around 2:30 he allowed Heth to move forward. He sent in all four of his brigades.

Heth's line moved from Herr Ridge facing light opposition from Union artillery. At the base of the ridge was a creek called Willoughby's Run, and as his men began to cross it they came under hot musket fire. But they pushed ahead, dressing their formations as they advanced. The afternoon fighting on McPherson's Ridge was some of the fiercest of the battle, indeed some of the bloodiest of the war. Heth's men outnumbered the Union defenders, and his line extended well beyond the Union left flank. But the Iron Brigade, reinforced by some Pennsylvania regiments from Chapman Biddle's brigade, hung on stubbornly and the carnage was terrible.

"I lost 2,300 men in 30 minutes," Heth later said.[21] The 26th North Carolina, in Pettigrew's brigade, had the worst of it. They were in the center of the line and moved directly against the Iron Brigade in the woods. The resulting firefight was devastating. "In one instance," Heth wrote, "when the Twenty-Sixth North Carolina Regiment encountered the second line of the enemy, [its] dead marked his line of battle with the accuracy of a line at a dress parade."[22] Overall the regiment took over 85 percent casualties, and John Lane, its commander, claimed that this unit lost more men than any other unit on either side in any battle in the entire war. Company F of the 26th North Carolina, with 3 officers and 88 men, had the distinction of suffering 100 percent casualties.

Heth's men continued to push back the Union troops, breaking through their first line of defenses, then their second. The Federals withdrew slowly in front of the determined assault. Heth, leading the attack in McPherson's Woods, watched with satisfaction as the enemy finally broke before his advancing troops. It was the last of the engagement he saw. A musket ball struck Heth in the forehead. He fell to the ground, unconscious, bleeding, his skull cracked, but alive. The force of the round had been deflected just enough to save his life by the rolled-up paper in his overlarge hat.

PICKETT'S CHARGE

HENRY HETH'S DIVISION WAS NEAR the spearhead of Lee's invasion of Pennsylvania; his cousin George Pickett's was the rear guard. When Lee's army moved north in June 1863, Pickett was left at Hanover Junction, Virginia, with orders to keep the Union forces guessing as to the Confederate movement. When he was finally allowed to head north, he was ordered, to his consternation, to leave behind two of his five brigades to guard against possible Union moves on Lee's line of communications. Though reduced in strength, Pickett's men were in high spirits. On June 27, Pickett wrote from the march, "the officers and men are all in excellent condition, bright and cheerful, singing songs and telling stories, full of hope and courage, inspired with absolute faith and confidence in our success."[1] Captain H. T. Owen of the Eighteenth Virginia regiment observed that the youthful enthusiasm of the Rebel forces had given way to the purposeful confidence of seasoned troops. "The bright uniforms and braided caps of earlier days were gone and had given place to the slouched hat, the faded threadbare jacket and patched pantaloons," he wrote. "The veterans' faces were tanned by summers' heat and winters' storm and covered with unkempt beards. Boys who enlisted in their teens appeared with long tangled locks, changed and weather-beaten, now, apparently, into men of middle life."[2]

The march north wore on the troops. More than once, Pickett's men had to reverse course and spend hours readied for battle, on rumor that enemy troops were heading in their direction. His troops made bivouac near Chambersburg in the days leading up to the battle, and on July 1 again stood ready all day to repulse an expected attack that never came. From the northeast came the faint sound of cannon as Heth's men joined battle with Buford on McPherson's Ridge. In the early morning hours of July 2, Pickett was resting under a tree when he received orders to move to Gettysburg. The division set out an hour later, and by early afternoon had covered twenty-seven miles to Marsh Creek, near Cashtown, around three miles west of the battle front. Pickett left his men to rest and pressed forward with his aide S. P. Baird, arriving on the field sometime after three in the afternoon. Longstreet's attack on the Union left flank was about to commence, and Pickett had sent word to Lee that he was ready to join the fray if he was needed. For his part, Longstreet wanted Pickett in the attack. "I never like going into battle with one boot off," he told General John Bell Hood (USMA 1853).[3] Pickett rode to Longstreet's headquarters and paid his compliments. Old Peter (as Longstreet was called) "was mighty glad to see me," he wrote.[4] But as the two discussed the battle plan, word arrived from Lee that Pickett's division was not needed right away. "I will have work for them tomorrow," Lee said. Pickett returned to his bivouac, where he and his men listened to the distant sounds of battle throughout the afternoon.

George Pickett had been skeptical about secession. He was loyal to Virginia, but did not think it would be in his native state's best interest to leave the Union. He did not oppose secession on legal grounds; he believed it was every state's right. But he objected for reasons of expediency. Pickett argued that the war was being pushed on Virginia by radicals in the Deep South. On February 13, 1861, while on duty in the Northwest, he wrote to Benjamin Alvord, "I do not like to be bullied nor dragged out of the Union by the precipatory and indecent haste of South Carolina."[5] Nevertheless, when Virginia finally left the Union on April 17, Pickett rallied to the Confederate cause. Union loyalists in the Northwest knew well his sympathies, and he left the Washington Territory a hunted man, almost being detained at Fort Vancouver, then traveling under an alias from San Francisco to New York. Since it was dangerous to move south directly (as demonstrated by the mass arrest of the Class of May 1861), Pickett made his way to Virginia via Canada.

Like many West Pointers on both sides, Pickett rose swiftly in rank. By February 1862 he had gone from captain to brigadier general, serving in Major General Longstreet's division. He led 2,500 men, almost thirty times as many as his command during the San Juan affair. Pickett's first big battle was at Williamsburg, Virginia, in May 1862, a delaying action during the early part of the Peninsular Campaign. Pickett was in the thick of the fight, and afterwards Longstreet reported that he "used his forces with great effect, ability, and his usual gallantry." At the Battle of Seven Pines on June 1, Pickett distinguished himself for tenacity in the attack when his brigade successfully opposed a Union division commanded by Silas Casey, Pickett's commander during the

San Juan affair. Pickett's unit was dubbed "the Gamecock Brigade." Three weeks later, he was shot in the shoulder at Gaines Mill, which took him out of action until the fall. "As poor a marksman as the Yankee was who shot me," he noted, "I wish he had been poorer still."[6]

In September 1862, Longstreet was promoted to lieutenant general and became a corps commander. Two months later, Pickett was made a major general and took over Longstreet's division. According to Major G. Moxley Sorrel, Longstreet's assistant adjutant general, Longstreet was "exceedingly fond" of his old messmate Pickett and looked out for him. Longstreet made certain his staff gave Pickett extra attention, either to ensure that he was clear on the commander's intent, or more likely to restrain his well-known aggressive tendencies. Longstreet even looked the other way when Pickett was spending too much time courting the young belle LaSalle "Sallie" Corbell in Richmond. Lee, however, was not as accommodating. In the spring of 1863 he banned Pickett and his staff from using rail transport in an effort to stop his frequent liaisons and keep him at the front; Pickett responded with an appeal to the secretary of war, noting the ban's "great detriment to the facilities of expediting military movements of importance."[7]

Pickett saw little action during his first six months as a division commander. He was present at Fredericksburg but did not see heavy fighting. "I can't help feeling sorry for Old Burnside, proud, plucky, hard-headed old dog," he later wrote of his friend's luckless assault.[8] Pickett was absent from Chancellorsville, being farther south with the bulk of Longstreet's corps. Like his cousin Henry Heth, he would face his first serious battle as a division commander at Gettysburg.

"A singular figure indeed!" was how Sorrel described Pickett. "A medium-sized, well-built man, straight, erect, and in well-fitting uniform, an elegant riding whip in his hand, his appearance was distinguished and striking." Most impressive was Pickett's hair: "Long ringlets flowed loosely over his shoulders, trimmed and highly perfumed; his beard likewise was curling and gave out the scents of Araby."[9] During the march into Pennsylvania, women would ask the handsome Lee for a lock of his hair, and he would refer them to Pickett, who, he said, had plenty to spare. Pickett was called a dandy, a fop, a cavalier, a romantic. Sir Arthur J. Lyon Fremantle of the Coldstream Guards, a British observer who by luck had accompanied Lee on the invasion, thought Pickett "altogether a desperate looking character."[10] And while some were skeptical of Pickett's effectiveness as a commander, none would question his physical bravery; it was said that "if necessary he would charge the gates of Hell itself."[11]

The early morning of July 3 was overcast, threatening rain. Pickett sat with his brigade commanders, Armistead, Kemper and Garnett, in what he called "a heart to heart powwow."[12] They knew they were going to lead the Confederate assault that day. The plan was not yet set, orders had not been given, but they were certain that their time had arrived. Armistead was particularly emotional, and offered Pickett a ring to give to Sallie with his compliments. A message arrived from Longstreet as they were talking, summoning Pickett to the front. Pickett and his commanders shook hands.

"Good luck, old man," they said. The brigadiers left to ready their men for the march while Pickett mounted his horse and headed east. Bernhard Domschke, a Union prisoner held behind the Confederate lines, saw Pickett as he rode away from camp. "The archetype of a Virginia slave baron strutted briskly, proud in bearing, head lifted in arrogance," Domschke wrote. "On horseback he looked like the ruler of a continent.... He galloped proudly that morning from his tent to the front."[13] A few miles down the road, Pickett happened to pass Fitz Lee, who had arrived the previous day with Stuart's cavalry.

"Come on Fitz, and go with us," Pickett said as he trotted past. "We shall have lots of fun there presently."[14]

Pickett found General Lee and Longstreet in a serious discussion. When Lee had arrived in Longstreet's sector in the early morning, he was surprised to see that no preparations were being made to attack. Lee had wanted the blow to coincide with an assault on Culp's Hill, on the Union extreme right flank, which was already in progress. These orders, however, were not conveyed to Pickett (there is some doubt whether the plan was formulated at all), and he did not move from camp until daylight, when Lee had wanted the battle to be under way. Lee and Longstreet conferred on how to modify the original plan, but could not come to an agreement. Lee suggested that Hood's and McLaws' divisions continue their attacks from the previous day, with Pickett's division in support. Longstreet objected; those divisions had seen very hard fighting and needed to rest. Furthermore, if they pressed forward it would create gaps in the line, opening them to Union flank attacks.

Longstreet then returned to the argument he had originally made late on July 1, and again on July 2, that Lee should attempt to swing wide around the Union left flank and establish a position between George Meade's force and Washington. The idea was to use the maneuver to place Meade in an untenable situation so he would have to withdraw, a plan that was more in the spirit of the original concept of operations. Longstreet had sent a reconnaissance force out late on July

2 to study the flank movement, and they reported back favorably. Nevertheless, Lee again rejected the suggestion.

"The enemy is there," Lee said, pointing to the Union line, "and I am going to strike him." The two commanders rode north along the line, moving forward towards the Rebel pickets and coming under sporadic Union skirmisher fire. They were joined for a time by A. P. Hill and Henry Heth, who had partially recovered from his head wound, but was still not ready to resume command from Pettigrew. While the commanders debated the attack plan, Pickett's men began to appear on the field. They took a position behind Seminary Ridge, moving quietly, lying down to conceal themselves from Union lookouts. As Lee, Longstreet, Pickett and the others rode by surveying the battlefield, Pickett's men, mindful of orders not to reveal their presence, rose and stood silently, holding their hats above their heads in salute.

Lee eventually focused on the northern portion of Seminary Ridge. The previous day, 1,400 Georgians of Brigadier General Ambrose R. Wright's brigade charged across the fields and achieved the ridgeline, somewhere south of a copse of trees on the forward edge of the Union position. It was over three-quarters of a mile between the lines, a twenty-minute march.[15] Wright later said, "It is not so hard to *go there* as it looks.... The trouble is to stay there."[16] But Lee believed that this was the decisive point of the Union line, and a major blow would break it. He improvised the final plan on the spot—a direct infantry assault prefaced by a massed artillery barrage, hitting the line near the copse of trees. The artillery was to push forward during the attack in support, especially to protect the flanks. Fifteen thousand troops would take part: Pickett's division from Longstreet's corps; Heth's division, commanded by Pettigrew, from A. P. Hill's corps; and reinforcing brigades from Pender's and Anderson's divisions. Lee made Pickett the battlefield commander. After Lee finished explaining his attack plan, Longstreet voiced his final objection: "I can safely say there never was a body of fifteen thousand men who could make that attack successfully."[17] Lee ended the discussion. The attack would go forward.

The plan was set by around eight in the morning. Longstreet explained the concept of operations to Pickett with a heavy heart; but Pickett was in high spirits. He was confident of success, and in fact the possibility of failure never occurred to him. The Army of Northern Virginia had faced great challenges in the past two years and had consistently emerged triumphant. Like many, Pickett had unwavering faith in the generalship of Robert E. Lee. Moreover, Pickett had been in similar situations before. In Mexico the Americans had marched hundreds of miles into enemy territory and prevailed against superior numbers of enemy soldiers in entrenched positions—it was all a matter of the will to see it through, to overawe the adversary, to advance fearlessly and fight bravely. Above all, Pickett was delighted that Lee had placed such confidence in him, that he had given him the honor of leading the decisive assault. Previously Pickett had not been in a position to fight, to earn glory, to prove himself yet again. Now the entire battle hinged on him.

Pickett and his staff set about developing the operational details. His division would be on the right, with Heth's division, commanded by Pettigrew, on the left. The two wings of the advancing line would converge on an area around one-fifth the length of the formation, to concentrate their mass and punch through the Union line.

Five brigades of Anderson's division were placed under Longstreet's control for the battle, including Wilcox's brigade, supporting the right flank. Major General Isaac Trimble commanded two brigades of Major General Dorsey Pender's division, supporting the left. Trimble was sixty-one years old, a graduate of the Class of 1822 and classmate of the Creek Indian David Moniac. He was one of the oldest graduates to join the Confederacy. Trimble was known for his aggressiveness in battle, and two days earlier had begged the hesitant General Ewell to allow him to attack Culp's Hill. Ewell refused, and the hill became the anchor of the Union right flank, ably defended by sixty-two-year-old Brigadier General George S. Greene of Rhode Island, who graduated second in the Class of 1823.

As Pickett was working with his staff, Colonel Birkett D. Fry rode up. He had been on point in Heth's advance on the first day of battle, and was now acting commander of Archer's brigade. His unit was in the center of the attack formation and Pettigrew had sent him to discuss how the lines would be dressed. Pickett greeted his old classmate warmly, and Fry noted his enthusiasm and optimism. Pickett observed that they had "been together in work of that kind at Chapultepec," and they would see this one through as well.[18] Pickett also met with Lieutenant Colonel George T. Gordon of the 34th North Carolina regiment, Scales' brigade, Pender's division. Pickett introduced Gordon to staff officer Captain Robert A. Bright: "This is Colonel Gordon, once opposed to me in the San Juan affair, but now on our side." "English Gordon" was skeptical of the attempt, and told Pickett so.

"Pickett, my men are not going up today," he said.

"But Gordon," Pickett said, "they must go up; you must make them go up."

"You know, Pickett, I will go as far with you as any other man, if only for old acquaintance sake," Gordon said. "but for the last day or two [my men] have lost heavily under infantry fire and are very sore, and they will not go up today."[19]

Gordon spoke for many on the left flank; Heth's division had already seen hard fighting. Pickett's men were arriving unbloodied and with something to prove. Longstreet observed that Pickett's boys showed a "zest for fighting," since they were "coming up fresh and feeling disparaged that the army had won new laurels in their absence."[20] Yet he was still troubled. He knew the risks of the attack, and he felt so little confidence it would succeed that he did not want to give the order that started the advance. Around noon, he sent a message to his artillery commander, Colonel Edward Porter Alexander:

> Colonel: If the artillery fire does not have the effect to drive off the enemy or greatly demoralize him so as to make our efforts pretty certain, I would prefer that you should not advise General Pickett to make the charge. I shall rely a great deal on your good judgment to determine the matter, and shall expect you to let General Pickett know when the moment offers.

Alexander had graduated third in the Class of 1857 and spent most of his career as an assistant instructor of military engineering. He had been given tactical control of I Corps's batteries by Longstreet on July 2. Though Alexander was only twenty-eight years old, Longstreet had great faith in him. Alexander had performed heroic duty at Fredericksburg and Chancellorsville, and Lee's artillery chief Brigadier General William N. Pendleton, who had graduated fifth in the Class of 1830, said, "we have no more accomplished officer." But Alexander was also skeptical of the plan. He said the spot selected for the attack was "almost as badly chosen as it was possible to be."[21] He thought Cemetery Hill a preferable point of attack, where all the Confederate artillery could be brought to bear. Alexander wrote back to Longstreet:

> General: I will only be able to judge of the effect of our fire on the enemy by his return fire, for his infantry is but little exposed to view and the smoke will obscure the whole field. If, as I infer from your note, there is any alternative to this attack, it should be carefully considered before opening our fire, for it will take all the artillery ammunition we have left to test this one thoroughly, and, if the result is unfavorable, we will have none left for another effort. And even if this is entirely successful it can only be so at a very bloody cost.

But Longstreet was adamant; if the order was to be given, he wanted Alexander to do it. He replied:

Colonel: The intention is to advance the infantry if the artillery has the desired effect of driving the enemy's off, or having other effect such as to warrant us in making the attack. When that moment arrives advise General P[ickett], and of course advance such artillery as you can use in aiding the attack.[22]

Still hesitant to bear the burden, Alexander went to Pickett to gauge his mood. He found Pickett "very sanguine, and thought himself in luck to have the chance" to lead the attack.[23] Time was passing, and Alexander knew that further delay would reduce the chance for success. He wrote Longstreet, "General: When our artillery fire is at its best, I shall order Pickett to charge."

"Let the batteries open," Longstreet ordered, and then lay down in the shade to think. The cannonade began at 1:00 P.M. with two signal shots. Lee had dedicated 164 of the 248 cannon he had on the field to the attack. It was probably the largest sustained artillery barrage in history to that point, and surely the largest in support of an infantry assault. John Gibbon, commanding the U.S. Second Division, called it "the most infernal pandemonium it has ever been my fortune to look upon. Very few troops were in sight and those that were, were hugging the ground closely, some behind the stone wall, some not, but the artillerymen were all busily at work at their guns, thundering out defiance to the enemy whose shells were bursting in and around them at a fearful rate, striking now a horse, now a limber and now a man."[24] But the Rebel fire was not as devastating as Lee had hoped. Faulty fused rounds failed to detonate on target, or at all; and because the Confederate fire was directed at a ridge, shells frequently passed over the front to wreak havoc in the reserve and headquarters areas behind the lines.

Soon the Rebel guns were answered by eighty or so Union artillery pieces. J. H. Moore of the Seventh Tennessee Infantry wrote that "no imagination can adequately conceive of the magnitude of this artillery duel. It surpassed the ordinary battery fire as the earthquake or some convulsion of nature surpasses the muttering of an ordinary thunderstorm."[25] John T. James of the Eleventh Virginia regiment observed, "I have heard and witnessed heavy cannonading, but never in my life had I seen or heard anything equal to this. Some enthusiasts back in the Commissary Department may speak of it as grand and sublime, but unless grandeur and sublimity consist in whatever is terrible and horrible, it was wanting in both of these qualities."[26] Another soldier recalled, "turn where you would, there was to be seen at almost every moment of time guns, swords, haversacks, human flesh and bones flying and dangling in the air or bouncing above the earth, which now trembled beneath us as shaken by an earthquake."[27] But Captain John Holmes Smith of the Eleventh Virginia saw Longstreet ride by during the bombardment, "quiet as an old farmer riding over his plantation on a Sunday morning."[28] Kemper, who saw Longstreet ride the line, said that "his bearing was to me the grandest moral spectacle of the war."[29] Pickett too trotted down the rear of his division, entreating the men to make ready for the advance and to "Remember Old Virginia!"[30]

Around 1:30 P.M., Pickett was with his staff when a note arrived from Alexander. "If you are coming at all you must come at once, or I cannot give you proper support; but the enemy's fire has not slackened at all; at least eighteen guns are still firing from the cemetery itself."[31] Alexander's lack of ammunition was acute, and unexpected. When the Union counterfire began, General Pendleton had ordered the ordnance train out of range of Federal shells, slowing the resupply effort. "Granny" Pendleton, a former Episcopal clergyman in Alexandria, Virginia, was not held in high regard as a warfighter, being considered too cautious. This limited Alexander's options: if he paused for resupply, the enemy could reconstitute; if he kept up his rate of fire, the attack would have to launch immediately.

Pickett looked at his men. "Boys, let us give them a trial," he said, and ordered his brigade commanders to form their regiments.[32] Then he rode off in search of Longstreet, whom he found sitting on a fence, watching the effects of the bombardment. He was "like a great lion at bay," Pickett later wrote. "I have never seen him so grave and troubled."[33] As Pickett approached, he was handed another terse message from Alexander:

> The 18 guns have been driven off. For God's sake come on quick or we cannot support you, ammunition nearly out.

Pickett read the note, then handed the paper to his friend.

"Sir, shall I advance?" he asked.

Longstreet looked silently at Pickett. It was bad luck that Pickett had sought him out, and that the second note arrived when it did. He had hoped Pickett would step off on Alexander's order. Now Pickett had inadvertently placed Longstreet in the very position he sought to avoid. Longstreet had to give the order. He tried to say it, but he could not. Instead, he held out his hand. The two men shook, and Longstreet nodded wearily.

"Then, General," Pickett said, "I shall lead my division on." He turned his mount and rode quickly away. It was, Longstreet wrote, "one of the saddest days of my life."[34]

Pickett rode south down the line to his division. His brigades had loosely formed and the soldiers were waiting for the order to advance. He rode out before them, proud, buoyant, eager to begin the advance that he felt certain would determine the course of the battle and the fate of the Confederacy.

"Up men, to your posts!" Pickett said. "Don't forget that you are from old Virginia!" Orders were relayed. "Forward! Guide center! March!"[35] Drums sounded. A band struck up a tune. Pickett turned his horse and began to advance. All around, his men called out to him, "We'll follow you, Marse George! We'll follow you!" as they set off towards the Union lines. Across the field, General Alexander Hays (USMA 1844), commander of the U.S. Third Division, called to his men, "Now boys, look out; you will see some fun!"[36]

Meanwhile Longstreet had ridden out to Alexander's forward position. Alexander told him that the guns were nearly out of ammunition and that, while he was hopeful, he might not be able to give the attack all the support he would like.

"Stop Pickett immediately and replenish your ammunition!" Longstreet barked. But Alexander said he could not. The supply wagons were too distant, and if the tempo of battle slowed, Meade would be able to reconstitute his position.

Longstreet saw the inevitable, and his tone became fatalistic. "I don't want to make this attack," he said. Alexander stood silently, letting Longstreet, in his words, fight his battle out alone. "I would stop it now," he continued, "but that General Lee ordered it and expects it to go on. I don't see how it can succeed."[37]

As Longstreet spoke these words, the Confederate line emerged from concealment. "Pickett's Division swept out of the wood and showed the full length of its gray ranks and shining bayonets," Alexander recalled, "as grand a sight as a man ever looked on."[38] Around fourteen thousand men materialized from the woods in a line a mile and a half long. There were regiments from Virginia, North Carolina, Alabama, Mississippi, Georgia, Tennessee and Florida. The extreme right stretched down to the Peach Orchard, and Pickett was somewhere around Spangler Farm on the southern half of the line. Longstreet watched as his old friend set off down the slope of Seminary Ridge and into the fields.

"As he passed me he rode gracefully," Longstreet recalled, "with his jaunty cap raked well over his right ear and his long auburn locks, nicely dressed, hanging almost to his shoulders. He seemed rather a holiday soldier than a general at the head of a column which was about to make one of the grandest, most desperate assaults recorded in the annals of wars."[39]

Captain Scott of the 126th New York Infantry watched the advance from the Union lines. "The guns and bayonets in the sunlight shone like silver," he wrote. "The whole line of battle looked like a stream or river of silver moving towards us.... The movement of such a force over such a field, in such perfect order, to such a destiny, was grand beyond expression."[40] Many on both sides also noted the fantastic sight of the assault force moving en masse across the rolling farmland. At Longstreet's order, Alexander's artillery opened up with a few final supporting rounds after the lines passed, attempting to suppress what remained of the Union artillery. But it was a vain effort. Soon the perfect lines of infantry were rent by gunfire from all along the Union line. Enfilading fire from Little Round Top was particularly effective. But the guns did not slow the assault. The Rebel lines closed up smoothly as men were struck down, and the advance continued.

Pickett rode between the first and second lines, encouraging his men and keeping an eye on the disposition of the brigades as they advanced.[41] About halfway across the field they executed a left oblique, a 45-degree left turn to take advantage of protection afforded by the rolling terrain, to keep the enemy guessing at where they intended to hit the line, and most importantly to consolidate the mass of the assault on the objective at the copse of trees. Shortly thereafter, about 750 yards into the charge, Pickett noticed that his left flank was wavering. Brockenbrough's and Davis's brigades of Heth's division had run into trouble.[42] They had suffered greatly on the first day of the battle and were not in high spirits. As they advanced over a fold in the ground, troops from the Eighth Ohio regiment who had been on picket duty sprang up and surprised the Confederates with a close-range volley, which shook their confidence and caused panic. Many began to flee the field. Pickett sent his brother, Major Charles Pickett, to rally the column. "Unless they support us on the left," Pickett said, "my division will be cut to pieces."[43]

The advance continued, Pickett's right flank angling to meet the center near the copse of trees. Pickett paused maybe four hundred yards from the objective, in low ground, sheltered from the worst of the enemy fire, to dress his lines and consolidate for the final push, trying to maintain the cohesion of the attack. His four staff officers relayed instructions to the brigade commanders as they advanced, and Pickett watched his flanks warily, hoping the expected reinforcements would arrive soon. He crossed the Emmitsburg Road south of the Codori Farm, about three hundred yards from the Angle. Kemper's and Garnett's brigades had swept ahead on either side of the farm buildings and were about to hit the Union line.[44]

As his main force readied to cross the Emmitsburg Road, Pickett sent his aide Captain Bright to Longstreet asking him to commit the reserves, else the position could not be held. Longstreet had already ordered three support brigades to shore up the left flank when he saw Brockenbrough's men retreating. He halted them before they moved beyond the artillery line, sensing that the battle was already decided. Bright found Longstreet sitting on a fence alone. He relayed Pickett's message, and Longstreet asked where the flank support was. "Look over your shoulder and you will see them," Bright replied, referring to the small groups of stragglers already making their way back.

At that moment Colonel Fremantle, the British observer, rode up, saying he wanted to witness the "magnificent" charge. "I would not have missed it for the world," he gushed.

"The devil you wouldn't!" Longstreet retorted. "I would like to have missed it very much; we've attacked and been repulsed." Fremantle looked out on the field and saw the soldiers "slowly and sulkily returning" in "small and broken parties" towards the start line. "Captain Bright," Longstreet said, "ride to General Pickett and tell him what you have heard me say to Colonel Fremantle."[45] As the astonished Bright rode off, Longstreet called after him that they could use Wilcox's brigade if they needed to.

From Longstreet's point of view, the battle may have been decided, but for the men at the forward edge of the attack it had hardly been joined. The center of the assault force had reached the double line of fences running across their advance at the Emmitsburg Road. Many were cut down trying to cross this unexpectedly difficult barrier. J. H. Moore wrote that "the time it took to climb to the top of the fence seemed to me an age of suspense. It was not a leaping over; it was rather an insensible tumbling to the ground in the nervous hope of escaping the thickening missiles that buried themselves in falling victims, in the ground and in the fence, against which they rattled with the distinctness of large rain drops pattering on a roof."[46] One section of fence, sixteen feet long and fourteen inches wide, took 836 hits.[47]

Brevet Lieutenant Tully McCrea, Light Company I, First U.S. Artillery, had been viewing the advance from his battery in Ziegler's Grove, on the northern edge of the attack. He watched the advancing lines of Pettigrew's men as they came to the road. "Could a finer target for artillery practice be imagined? Three lines of infantry, two deep, advancing over such ground in the very face of our artillery." The guns had not been driven off, as Alexander had believed. They had fallen silent to conserve ammunition. When the Confederate lines neared,

the Union cannon commenced a murderous fire. "When we opened
on them one could see great gaps swept down," McCrea wrote, "it was
impossible to miss."[48] The survivors reformed and crossed the clover-
covered slope leading up to the Union emplacements. Colonel Joseph
C. Mayo of the Third Virginia regiment noted Captain Thomas J. Lewis
of Company C forming up his command, "looking as lazy and lackadaisi-
cal, and, if possible, more tired and bored than usual."

"Pretty hot, Captain," Mayo said as he passed.

"It's redicklous, Colonel," Lewis replied, "perfectly redicklous."[49]

Sensing an opportunity, Colonel George Stannard's Thirteenth
and Sixteenth Vermont regiments moved out into the field to harass
Pickett's right flank. Around the same time, a similar maneuver was
made on the left against Pettigrew by the 108th and 126th New York
regiments and the First Massachusetts Sharpshooters, moving south
from Ziegler's Grove. Pickett sent Bright to ask for artillery support
from Dearing's battery directly to his rear, but he was told they had only
three round shot left. Pickett sent his brother Charles to entreat
Longstreet for more help, but Charles could not find him.

The fight was thick now as the Confederates neared the objective. Pettigrew's men surged towards the Angle but were stopped at the
wall. Trimble's two brigades advanced through the remnants of Pettigrew's division, reached the wall on the left flank near Bryan Farm, and
were forced back. Trimble, who had advanced on his horse Jinny, took
a round to the ankle and turned command over to John Lane before
leaving the field.[50] Garnett, riding just to the rear of his men and coolly
managing his part of the assault, was shot in the head and fell from his
mount less than twenty-five yards from the stone wall. He died on the
spot. But the Union line was buckling, and his men reached the wall
and planted their flags. Armistead, moving quickly to assist Garnett, led
his men forward with his hat on his sword. As they crossed the stone
wall he entreated his men to "Give them the cold steel, boys!" About
two to three hundred of his troops made it over the wall at the Angle.
The fighting was brutal, point-blank musket fire and vicious hand-to-
hand struggle. As Armistead attempted to turn the Union cannon, a
round hit him and he sank down next to a gun carriage, mortally
wounded. As Heth wrote, "Armistead was killed by Hancock's troops,
and Hancock was wounded by one of Armistead's command. What a
commentary on the Civil War!"[51] About an equal number of Kemper's
men had penetrated to Armistead's right. They drove off the first line
of defenders, and Kemper, raising himself in his stirrups, cried out,
"There are the guns boy, go for them!" At that moment, Kemper was

knocked from his horse by a round that penetrated his thigh and lodged at the base of his spine. Moments later his troops were devastated by a double-canister volley from Battery B, First New York Artillery, at a few yards' range.

Around this time, Wilcox's and Perry's brigades (the latter under the command of Colonel David Lang) finally moved forward to support Pickett's right. They knew that the attack had failed and that they were moving too late to be effective. Moreover, they could not see the troops they were sent to support, and the brigades advanced on a line that took them south of the main body. They moved through the field under hot artillery fire, crossed Emmitsburg Road and advanced into the depression at the head of Plum Run, where they took more punishment from cannon and musket. The Sixteenth Vermont, still extended on Pickett's right and between the reinforcements and the main body, turned about and delivered withering fire into their flanks. The two brigades soon abandoned their hopeless mission, Wilcox having taken 204 casualties and Lang around 150.

Henry Heth, who had watched the attack from the start line, remarked, "as was said of the famous charge of the six hundred at Balaklava, *c'est grande, mais c'est ne pas la guerre* [*sic*]."[52] Alexander said, "no-one could have looked at that advance without feeling proud of it."[53] Colonel Emory Upton, commanding the 121st New York Infantry, who had viewed the charge from Little Round Top, called the attack "imposing and sublime."[54] But the fight had been grim and unforgiving; and as the assault collapsed, the retreat became something less than sublime. J. H. Moore, who had reached the wall, said that "it was death or surrender to remain. It seemed almost death to retreat."[55] Men feared that if they withdrew slowly, they would be shot in the back, so some began running to get out of range as fast as they could. But many were left on the field. "There were literally acres of dead lying in front of our line," Captain Scott recalled. "The dead in every direction lay upon the field piled in heaps and scattered as far as the eye could reach."[56] Pickett watched as his command crumbled, and then rode out along the disintegrating line, imploring his men to reform; but it was a hopeless task. As one observer remarked, "They were panic stricken, and no effort could induce them to form anew while under that terrific storm of fire."[57] Pickett finally withdrew, muttering, "My brave men! My brave men!"

Back along the artillery line, a group from the 24th Virginia had rallied around their standard, one of two regimental colors that had not been lost. As Pickett rode up, the standard bearer, Charles Belcher, shouted, "General, let us go at them again!" (A year later, Belcher would desert the South and join the Union cause.) Such enthusiasm was cut short when litter bearers brought up the desperately wounded Kemper.[58] Just then General Lee approached and the soldiers clustered around him. Lee went to Pickett and clasped his hand. Pickett began to weep.

"General Pickett," Lee said, "place your division in rear of this hill, and be ready to repel the advance of the enemy should they follow up their advantage."

"General Lee," Pickett said, his head hanging, "I have no division now."

"Come, General Pickett," Lee said, "this has been my fight and upon my shoulders rests the blame. The men and officers of your command have written the name of Virginia as high today as it has ever been written before."[59] Lee then went to console Kemper, and Pickett galloped off in search of Longstreet. William Youngblood, Longstreet's courier, saw Pickett approaching, "his long black hair waving in the wind."[60]

"Where is General Longstreet?" Pickett yelled. Youngblood took Pickett to Longstreet, and he approached his old friend in obvious torment.

"General, I am ruined," he cried. "My division is gone—it is destroyed." Longstreet attempted to console Pickett, noting that his division was just scattered, and that his men would probably begin to regroup in a few hours. He sent Pickett off to begin gathering them up. Meanwhile the stragglers were pushing back beyond Seminary Ridge, tossing aside their muskets and equipment and making for their encampment. Some attempted to rally at a chokepoint along a road leading away from the battlefield, but they were confronted by a teary-eyed Pickett, who told them, "Don't stop any of my men. Tell them to come to the camp we occupied last night." He then left the battlefield, heading west.[61]

"The moans of my wounded boys," Pickett wrote a few days later, "the sight of the dead, upturned faces, flood my soul with grief—and here I am, whom they trusted, whom they followed, leaving them on that field of carnage."[62]

Gettysburg was the greatest disaster of Pickett's life. His division lost 499 killed or mortally wounded, 1,473 wounded, 681 missing or captured—a total of 42 percent casualties.[63] Garnett was dead, Armistead mortally wounded, Kemper believed to be dying.[64] Of his 32 field officers, 12 were killed, 19 wounded, and only one, a major, not wounded significantly. Heth's division, already battered from the first day's fighting, was devastated. Only about 1,800 men mustered when they crossed the Potomac back into Virginia.

Pickett would never recover emotionally. The irresistible confidence he had felt that morning was replaced with anguish, a sense of betrayal, and guilt. Pickett was convinced that his men took the ridgeline, but had lost it because he was not reinforced. Had he had the use of his two brigades that had been left in Virginia, he reasoned, he would have broken the Union center. Pickett wrote a bitter after-action account of the battle, which was so critical that Lee asked him to destroy it. "You and your men have crowned yourselves with glory," Lee wrote Pickett, "but we have the enemy to fight, and must carefully, at this critical moment, guard against dissensions which the reflections in your report would create. I will, therefore, suggest that you destroy both copy and original, substituting one confined to casualties merely. I hope all will yet be well." A few days later, Lee wrote the still-anguished Pickett, "No one grieves more than I do at the loss suffered by your noble division in the recent conflict, or honors it more for its bravery and gallantry."[65]

Henry Heth, writing decades after the battle he began by accident, sided with Longstreet and believed that in retrospect Lee did as well. "I think the fight of the 3d of July was a mistake," he wrote, "that General Lee should have so manoeuvred as to have drawn Meade from his stronghold; and such I believe to have been General Lee's views after the fight, as he remarked to me, at Orange Courthouse, during the winter of 1863–64, when, animadverting upon the criticisms made upon the Gettysburg fight, especially referring to the fight of July 3, 'after it is all over, as stupid a fellow as I am can see the mistakes that were made.'" But, Lee told Heth, "I notice, however, my mistakes are never told me until it is too late, and you, and all my officers, know that I am always ready and anxious to have their suggestions."[66]

LAURENCE SIMMONS BAKER

W RITING LONG AFTER THE EVENTS at Gettysburg, Henry Heth echoed what was by then a common critique of the battle: "The failure to crush the Federal army in Pennsylvania in 1863, in the opinion of almost all the officers of the Army of Northern Virginia, can be expressed in five words—*the absence of our cavalry.*"[1] When General Lee moved north, he had given J. E. B. Stuart some discretion on his route, ordering him only to stay in contact with the right flank of the Army of Northern Virginia. Stuart took a liberal view of his mission. On June 25, as the rest of the army marched north up the valley behind the mountains, he headed east into Maryland, swinging around the Union right flank, seeking to raid supplies and create confusion. But with the Union forces between himself and the Confederate main body, he could no longer communicate with Lee, thus leaving the Army of Northern Virginia blind to the movements of the forces massing to intercept them.

Colonel Laurence Simmons Baker was one of Stuart's officers, commander of the First North Carolina Cavalry. Baker hailed from a notable North Carolina family. His grandfather and namesake commanded a regiment in the Revolution and was a Federalist delegate to the North Carolina convention to debate the Constitution. Baker attended Norfolk Academy in his native state and was appointed to West Point in 1847. He was not a distinguished student, coming in consistently at the lower end of his class and ultimately graduating as the Goat of 1851. He was commissioned in the Mounted Rifles and served on the frontier, first in Kansas and the Dakota Territory, later in Texas and New Mexico. During the latter tour he fought a skirmish with the Kiowa at Ojo del Muerto (Dead Man's Springs) on March 12, 1857.

Baker joined the Confederacy in May 1861, and within a year he commanded the First North Carolina. Like many cavalry officers, Baker was known for his dash. In June 1862, during the Seven Days Battles outside Richmond, Baker made a forced march from North Carolina and was thrown into the line, commanding all cavalry not then with J. E. B. Stuart. Lee ordered Baker to make a night scout on June 29 to ascertain the location of Union forces retreating after the Battle of Savage's Station. Baker led five companies of his regiment towards the town of Willis Church, where there was rumored to be an enemy camp. As Baker moved down the Quaker Road, he encountered a small group of Union cavalry and charged them with sabers, believing them to be a minor covering force. The Federal horsemen broke, and Baker rushed his command forward towards the campfires just ahead, bursting through the perimeter and into the center of the encampment. There he made an important discovery. "I was compelled afterward to retreat from their camp," he noted laconically in his report, "which I found to be their main army." His men came under heavy fire from the massed Union troops, but in the darkness and general confusion caused by his unexpected arrival they were able to escape with few casualties. If nothing else, Baker was able to report to Lee that he had accurately ascertained the Union position.

By July 28, 1862, Baker's regiment was part of General Wade Hampton's brigade. Hampton was very wealthy, reputed to be the largest slave owner in South Carolina. He was physically imposing and a dead shot with a pistol. Under Hampton, Baker fought in most of the significant cavalry engagements in the East and built a reputation for coolness under fire and willingness to take the battle to the enemy. After the 1862 invasion of Maryland, J. E. B. Stuart wrote that Baker had conducted himself "with the utmost gallantry, and sustained a hot fire of artillery and musketry without flinching or confusion in the ranks." At the Battle of Brandy Station on June 9, 1863, Baker conducted a series of charges that Stuart called "most successful and brilliant."[2]

Baker arrived in Gettysburg with Stuart's forces late on July 2. Stuart commanded six thousand men in four brigades, and also had in tow 125 captured wagonloads of supplies, which had slowed his advance and delayed his rejoining the main force. Stuart went in search of Lee's headquarters, where he was given a chilly reception by his commander. Meanwhile Baker, with the rest of Hampton's brigade, was stationed at Hunterstown, five miles east of Gettysburg. Hampton had received word that a Union cavalry force was moving in his direction, apparently attempting to get to Lee's rear. He was ordered to stop them. Battle was joined on a road near the town, and after skirmishing briefly, the Union cavalrymen attempted a charge.

"The charge was most gallantly made," Hampton wrote, "and the enemy were driven back in confusion to the support of his sharpshooters and artillery, both of which opened on me heavily." The Union attack was made by Company A, Sixth Michigan Cavalry, commanded by Captain Henry E. Thompson. He was accompanied by another officer clad in a black uniform and black hat, with long golden hair. His horse took a bullet in the head and fell, throwing the rider from his mount. Thompson also went down, severely wounded, as did his aide, Lieutenant S. H. Ballard.[3] The Rebels surged forward as the black-clad officer staggered to his feet. A Rebel moved to cut him down, but a private named Norval Churchill rode up, shot down the Confederate cavalryman, hoisted the officer onto his horse and hightailed it back up the road. It was another narrow escape for George A. Custer.[4]

War was the ideal arena in which to give free reign to Custer's talents and instincts. He had always sought to create his own world, bending and breaking rules as he thought necessary, and he found in armed conflict the opportunity to realize his ambitions. The cavalry was the perfect medium for Custer; it played to his strengths, giving him a greater measure of freedom of action, the ability to move on the enemy rear and flanks, sowing chaos, exploiting opportunities, imposing his will on the foe. Speed, dash and surprise—these were the primary elements of Custer's way of war.

Captain James H. Kidd of the Sixth Michigan Cavalry, who would lead the Michigan Brigade in 1864 after Custer was promoted to division commander, described him as "tall, lithe, active, muscular, straight as an Indian and as quick in his movements."[5] Joseph Fought, a boy bugler who met Custer in the opening days of the Civil War, said, "He was a conspicuous figure from the first, attracting attention wherever he went."[6] Custer's hair curled about his neck and shoulders; during the Peninsular Campaign he vowed not to cut it until he entered Richmond, a vow he kept, although it took three years. Like Ben McCulloch, he wore a distinctive uniform as brigade commander: "a velveteen jacket with five gold loops on each sleeve, and a sailor shirt with a very large collar that he got from a gunboat on the James," as Fought described it. "The shirt was dark blue, and with it he wore a conspicuous red tie—top boots, a soft hat, Confederate, that he picked up on the field."[7] Lieutenant Colonel Theodore Lyman, one of Meade's aides, said, "He looks like a circus rider gone mad!"[8] But Custer explained, "I want my men to recognize me on any part of the field."[9]

Kidd said that Custer was "brave, but not reckless; self-confident, yet modest; ambitious, but regulating his conduct at all times by a high sense of honor and duty; eager for laurels, but scorning to wear them unworthily; ready and willing to act, but regardful of human life; quick in emergencies, cool and self-possessed, his courage was of the highest moral type: his perceptions were intuitions."[10] He was the kind of man who inspired fanatic loyalty and bitter jealousy. Joe Fought remarked that "all the other officers were exceeding jealous of [Custer]."[11] They secretly, and not so secretly, wished for him to stumble.

Custer cheated death repeatedly. He was never wounded severely, but he had seven horses shot from under him on the Gettysburg campaign alone. During a bridging operation over the Chickahominy River, a shot from one of Fitz Lee's batteries hit a log that Custer was sitting on, knocking it out from under him but not harming him.[12] At Front Royal in August 1864, a bullet sheared off a lock of hair from the side of his head. Another time near Monticello, three Confederate sharpshooters had a bead on him in easy range and all three missed. Once before a battle his horse stepped in a post hole, flipped over and landed with Custer beneath. Men rushed forward to help, thinking he was critically wounded or worse; the horse rolled off and revealed that Custer was dusty but relatively unharmed. After a few minutes he was again seeing to the disposition of his troops.[13]

Custer was also conspicuous in physical bravery. He made his first charge in his first battle, at Bull Run. At the Battle of Williamsburg, May 5, 1862, serving as a volunteer aide to Brigadier General Winfield Scott Hancock, he rushed a Confederate position along with attacking Union infantry, taking six enemy prisoners and capturing a battle flag. Three weeks later, he led a reconnaissance in force across the Chickahominy, again exposing himself to grave danger. A report of the action singled him out as "the first to cross the stream, the first to open fire upon the enemy, and one of the last to leave the field." His boldness earned him promotion to captain of volunteers and assignment as aide-de-camp to General McClellan. One story has it that he had come to McClellan's direct attention when his column stopped near the Chickahominy. McClellan was discussing with his staff how deep the river was and where it might be forded. Custer, farther back in the column, rode out into the four-foot-deep water and up to the general. "That's how deep it is, sir," he said.

McClellan's first impression of Custer was "a slim, long-haired boy, carelessly dressed." While on his staff, McClellan came to know

Custer as reckless and gallant, "undeterred by fatigue, unconscious of fear; but his head was always clear in danger, and he always brought me clear and intelligible reports of what he saw when under the heaviest fire. I became much attached to him."[14]

Custer was a great admirer of McClellan during the war and afterwards. In many ways McClellan was the opposite of Custer, particularly in academics (George McClellan graduated second in the Class of 1846) and also in his cautious nature. But both were strong-willed men, and Custer admired McClellan's systematic and businesslike approach to command. He considered McClellan the ablest of the Union generals, a master strategist who was defeated not by Lee but by the Washington politicians who conspired against him. "Few persons can realize or believe at this late day the extent of the opposition which McClellan encountered from those from whom his strongest support and encouragement should have come," Custer wrote long after the war. "This opposition was well known at the time; in fact there was little if any effort to conceal it."[15] McClellan likewise appreciated his young protégé's energy and enthusiasm, and sought to promote his career.

During the early years of the war, Custer achieved the distinction of becoming one of the first Army aviators. Observation balloons had come into use during the Peninsular Campaign, but most soldiers were dubious about their value because the contractors who owned the balloons also conducted the reconnaissance. Custer saw the problem with this monopoly: "They could report whatever their imagination prompted them to, with no fear of contradiction." In order to combat this tendency, the Army decided to send officers aloft, and Custer was among those chosen. He whimsically said that this was "an order which was received with no little trepidation; for although I had chosen the mounted service from preference alone, yet I had a choice as to the character of the mount, and the proposed ride was far more elevated than I had ever desired or contemplated." Custer's first ascent was made without incident, though he remained seated in the basket until he could get up the nerve to stand. The young officer marveled at the view and the history encompassed in the countryside, from Jamestown to Yorktown, the legend of Pocahontas to the victory over the British in the Revolution. After completing his reconnaissance he descended, with much less trepidation about the experience. For several weeks he made almost daily ascents.[16]

Custer frequently encountered friends from his West Point days, and sometimes they wore an enemy uniform. In May 1862 during the

Peninsular Campaign, Custer's former roommate, Confederate lieutenant James B. Washington, serving on Joseph E. Johnston's staff, was captured. Custer had their picture taken together, and the photo of the reunited West Point chums was republished throughout the country. As a result of this publicity "James B. Washington" dog tags were minted and distributed as collectables in the North.[17]

Confederate captain John W. "Gimlet" Lea, I Company, Fifth North Carolina regiment, was wounded in May 1862 at the Battle of Williamsburg and also taken prisoner. Lieutenant Alexander C. M. Pennington, who graduated eighteenth in the Class of 1860 and knew Lea, found him lying in a barn stall, his wounds untended. Pennington brought him to Custer, who saw to it that Lea was well taken care of, despite his protestations. Custer later described the reunion:

> When we first saw each other he shed tears and threw his arms about my neck, and we talked of old times and asked each other hundreds of questions about classmates on opposing sides. I carried his meals to him, gave him stockings of which he stood in need, and some money. This he did not want to take, but I forced it on him. He burst into tears and said it was more than he could stand. He insisted on writing in my notebook that if ever I should be taken prisoner he wanted me treated as he had been. His last words to me were, "God bless you, old boy!" The bystanders looked with surprise when we were talking, and afterwards asked if the prisoner were my brother.[18]

Gimlet Lea was taken in by Williamsburg resident Margaret Durfey, wife of the Confederate colonel Goodrich Durfey, and during his convalescence he became engaged to their daughter, also named Margaret. As the Union army prepared to withdraw, Custer secured permission to visit Lea. The wedding had been set for the following week, but Lea was determined to have Custer as his best man and moved the nuptials up to the next evening. The ceremony was held at the Durfey house, called Basset Hall. The groom wore a fresh, gray Confederate officer's uniform with gold trim; the best man was resplendent in his blue full Federal dress. The bride, Margaret, and her cousin Maggie, the bridesmaid, both wore white. "I never saw two prettier girls," Custer later wrote.

After the ceremony cousin Maggie began crying, and Gimlet, supposing she was weeping because she was not married, said, "Well, here is the Minister and here is Captain Custer, who I know would be glad to carry off such a pretty bride from the Confederacy."

"Captain Lea," she replied, "you are just as mean as you can be!"

As they retired to the reception, Custer asked Maggie how she could take the arm of a Union officer, being so committed to the southern cause.

"You ought to be in our army," she replied.

Custer stayed at Basset Hall for two weeks, entertained by Maggie at the piano (she played pro-southern tunes in a vain attempt to get Custer's goat; he simply laughed), and playing cards with Gimlet Lea, the stakes being the Confederacy. "He won, every time," Custer wrote.[19] Custer left when the last of the Union forces withdrew. By September, Lea had been exchanged and was again with the Confederates, "fighting," Custer said, "for what he *supposes* to be right!"[20] The man Lea was exchanged for was assistant quartermaster Captain Alexander Montgomery, the Goat of 1834, whose wife had been killed in Florida by Halleck Tustenuggee in 1840.

D. H. Strother, who knew Custer around this time, called him "one of the most agreeable acquaintances I have made among the juniors of the Staff." He described him as "rather a handsome youth, with light, curling hair and lithe figure," whose "friends, it seems are pushing him for a Brigadier's commission to serve in the cavalry, and his comrades frequently joke him on the subject. Custer takes their chaffing pleasantly, and replies, with a shake of his curly head, 'Gentlemen, I don't know whether or not I am worthy of such promotion; but if they give it to me, I promise that you shall hear of me.' "[21]

But Custer's career was at a crossroads. His patron McClellan was disgraced after the Peninsular Campaign, and after Antietam he lost his position as head of the Army of the Potomac. When Custer left McClellan's staff, his rank dropped back to lieutenant, and his immediate prospects did not look good. He knew that as a Democrat he could not get a colonel's commission in an Ohio volunteer regiment, given the strong Republican sentiments there. He sought out a Michigan commission, but the state's governor, Austin Blair, was also a Republican (in fact, a founding member of the party) and would not help him.

Custer's luck changed dramatically when he came to the attention of Brigadier General Alfred Pleasonton, a District of Columbia native who graduated seventh in the Class of 1844. Pleasonton was a brevetted Mexican War veteran who had participated in May's Charge at Resaca de la Palma and spent the years leading up to the Civil War on the frontier. During the war he had engaged in several important battles, being brevetted lieutenant colonel for bravery at Antietam. In

June 1863, he was promoted to major general of volunteers and placed in command of the newly organized Union Cavalry Corps. Pleasonton was tasked with finding bold brigade commanders, the kind of men who could stand up to J. E. B. Stuart's famed horsemen. He had recently observed Custer at the Battle of Aldie in June 1863 and praised him as "conspicuous for gallantry throughout the fight." Pleasonton nominated Custer to command the Second Cavalry Brigade, made up of four Michigan regiments and known as the Michigan Brigade.[22] Lieutenant Custer received his commission as a brigadier general of volunteers on June 29. It came as a total surprise.

"I owe it all to Gen'l Pleasonton," Custer wrote his fiancée Libbie. "He has been more like a father to me than a Gen'l."[23] Custer was twenty-three, the youngest American general officer in history at the time. But his promotion was not unparalleled; there were generals in their twenties on both sides. The youngest was the Union brigadier Galusha Pennypacker, promoted in April 1865 at age twenty. On the Confederate side, Brigadier William Paul Roberts of North Carolina was twenty-three when he was promoted in the waning months of the war. Custer's West Point friend P. M. B. Young was a month shy of twenty-seven when he was made a brigadier. Brigadier General Hugh Judson Kilpatrick, Class of May 1861, was twenty-seven and Custer's division commander. The two were healthy rivals, both on and off the field—they may have competed for the affections of a young nurse from Cambridge named Anna Elinor "Emma" Jones, who was, in her own words, "a companion to the various commanding officers ... a private friend or companion." Wesley Merritt (USMA 1860) was made a brigadier at age twenty-nine. These promotions were a function both of the rapid expansion of the armies and of the desire to have as many West Pointers as possible in higher command positions. Some might see it as an expression of the West Point bias, but Custer had earned his position through his daring, his judgment, and his willingness to take calculated risks.

A few days later at Gettysburg, Custer's unit was detached to assist Brigadier General David McMurtrie Gregg against a possible move by J. E. B. Stuart against the Union right flank, along with Battery M, commanded by Custer's friend and now brevet Captain Alexander Pennington. Gregg was a staid and unfussy commander whose nickname was "Old Steady." He graduated eighth in the Class of 1855 and saw combat in the Northwest frontier before the war. Gregg fought in the major cavalry engagements against Stuart in the East, and a few months earlier had participated in "Stoneman's Raid" towards Richmond. In some respects, Gregg was very much the anti-Custer. He cared little for his image, sported a long unkempt beard and wore a scruffy uniform. Gregg did not seek public acclaim, and he barred journalists from his command, saying, "I do not propose to have a picture reputation."[24]

Pleasonton had ordered Gregg to support the Union positions at Culp's Hill to the rear, and sent Kilpatrick's men even farther south to the Union left. Gregg, however, knew that he had to hold the area to his front, and he subtly found ways to delay executing the pullback order. He withdrew his forces slowly and tried to locate reinforcements from any of Kilpatrick's men still lingering in his sector. He found Custer at the stopover of Two Taverns on the Baltimore Pike where he had gone for the night, and requisitioned him to remain behind.

The Confederate cavalry was moving south steadily, nearing Gregg's position. Stuart's plan was to swing around the Union right and descend in their rear between the Hanover Road and the Baltimore Pike, to disrupt and divert attention, support Pickett's attack and reduce Meade's freedom of action. Even should Longstreet's assault fail, penetrating the Union line would have serious consequences.

Stuart paused on Cress Ridge near the Rummel and Trostle farms, overlooking the Union lines. The Low Dutch Road–Hanover Road area, near Rummel Farm, was not ideal cavalry terrain: broad, rocky fields were traversed by stone and wood fences, and copses of trees stood on the fringes. Stuart opened the engagement by firing a volley from the Louisiana Guard Artillery; he had the battery fire a round in each direction of the compass, for reasons never explained. He may have been seeking to flush the enemy cavalry reported to be nearby.

Custer had come on the scene and was assembling his troops when the four shells fired. They were answered by Pennington, commanding Custer's horse artillery. Stuart knew the battle was on and sent forward dismounted skirmishers from Ferguson's and Chambliss's brigades. Custer responded by deploying dismounted elements of the Fifth and Sixth Michigan, who moved forward in skirmish line, formidably armed with Spencer repeating rifles.

It was midday, and the threat to Culp's Hill was abating. Pleasonton saw the wisdom in Gregg's position and decided he should stay put. However, he ordered Gregg to send Custer back to Kilpatrick to participate in a planned move around the Confederate right flank. Custer's position was to be taken over by a brigade commanded by Colonel John Baillie McIntosh, brother of the Confederate general James McQueen

McIntosh. But seeing how the situation was developing ahead of him, and with reports from XI Corps of a large Rebel cavalry force moving on his position, Gregg decided that Custer would have to stay. He used the pretext that Custer's orders to redeploy were verbal, not written, and until he had written authority stating otherwise, Custer would remain with him. He noted that Custer, "fully satisfied of the intended attack, was well pleased to remain with his brigade." It was well for Custer that he stayed put. Later in the day, Kilpatrick's attack on Confederate positions near Big Round Top resulted in the loss of 65 men, of whom 13 were killed, 25 wounded and 27 captured. Brigadier General Elon John Farnsworth, who led the attack, was among the dead, struck down by five bullets. The futile assault had no effect on the outcome of the battle.[25]

McIntosh moved forward to feel the enemy with dismounted troops of the First New Jersey and the Third Pennsylvania, relieving members of Custer's Fifth and Sixth Michigan. As they were exchanging positions, they heard the opening of the great barrage in support of Pickett's Charge. James H. Kidd wrote, "The tremendous volume of sound volleyed and rolled across the intervening hills like reverberating thunder in a storm."[26] Shortly thereafter, Stuart began his attack, intending to clear the way to Hanover Road and southward. Artillery from Cress Ridge played among Custer's men while the Rebel skirmishers moved up. Custer pulled his men back in good order, covered by deadly fire from Pennington's battery that silenced the Confederate guns. Gregg later praised Pennington, saying, "The fire of the artillery during this engagement was the most accurate that I have ever seen."

Custer observed Confederates moving on McIntosh's flanks as his units advanced, and sent Major Noah Ferry of the Fifth Michigan with some men to bolster McIntosh's position. They moved forward quickly and ran into an ambush laid by the 34th Virginia Battalion, which cut down many while others broke and ran. Major Ferry was trying to rally his men when he was shot in the head. The battle now began to mount by degrees. McIntosh threw in what was left of his unit, and Stuart committed the rest of Ferguson's brigade, and some of Chambliss's and Hampton's. The Confederates bore down on the small group of Union defenders. A fierce fight developed at Rummel Farm, and it appeared the Federals had the worst of it. However, a counterattack by artillery directed by Gregg thwarted the Confederate move, and the Rebels fell back. Before the Union soldiers could reform and consolidate their defenses, Stuart's famed First Virginia Cavalry regiment of Fitz Lee's brigade charged without warning towards the Union right-center. Stuart wrote, "The impetuosity of those gallant fellows, after two weeks of hard marching and hard fighting on short rations, was not only extraordinary, but irresistible. The enemy's masses vanished before them like grain before the scythe, and that regiment elicited the admiration of every beholder, and eclipsed the many laurels already won by its gallant veterans." McIntosh had no more reserves to commit and the charge scattered his men to the protection of nearby woods.

Quick action by Stuart in support of the First Virginia might have given his forces the field, but he failed to follow up his advantage; and behind the Union lines, Custer's Seventh Michigan Cavalry was moving forward. The Seventh was a small, inexperienced but eager regiment. Gregg noted the fresh troops coming on line and ordered a counterattack. This was Custer's moment. He rode to the front of the Seventh, drew his saber and gave the order to charge.

"Come on, you Wolverines!" he shouted, spurring his horse ahead. Custer rode bareheaded into battle, his golden locks streaming in the wind as the Michiganders charged after him across the field. The Ninth and Thirteenth Virginia regiments, dismounted, opened up on them as they passed. A volley from the Thirteenth sent half of the riders headlong into a fence, where they were stalled in a mass. Some troops from the First Virginia dismounted on the other side and a point-blank mêlée ensued. It was a brutal and chaotic fight, a tangle of seven hundred men and their mounts, fighting with pistol, saber and carbine. Captain William E. Miller of the nearby Third Pennsylvania Cavalry said that "the meeting was as the crash of ocean waves breaking on a rock bound coast, and men and horses rolled and tossed like foam upon the crest."[27] Some of Custer's officers dismounted and broke down the fence, allowing their men to set upon the Virginians, who scattered with the Seventh in pursuit. Meanwhile, Custer and the rest of the Seventh swept on towards Rummel Farm, but lost contact with the enemy and, their momentum spent, turned to go back.

Wade Hampton had been watching the action with some concern. "I sent to Colonel Baker," he wrote, "ordering him to send two regiments to protect Chambliss, who had made a charge (I know not by whose orders), and who was falling back before a large force of the enemy." Laurence Baker ordered his First North Carolina regiment and the Jeff Davis Legion under Waring to prepare to move in support of the First Virginia. They were in the process of forming when they saw the Seventh Michigan turning. Sensing an opportunity, Baker ordered a charge. His horsemen flew across the field and slammed into Custer's rear. The Union cavalry, startled, began to stampede back. They retreated along the same route as McIntosh, again running the gauntlet of dismounted Virginians, who joined the two mounted regiments in the pursuit. McIntosh rode out among the fleeing horsemen and tried to rally them. "For God's sake men," he implored, "if you are ever going to stand, stand now, for you are on your free soil!"[28]

Remnants of the Fifth Michigan and some of McIntosh's men hit at the Rebel flanks, and a general mêlée of pistol and saber developed. Hampton saw that Baker had followed the enemy too far, and in his desire to bring them back he impetuously rode out into the field alone, heading towards the mass of troops. His adjutant, Captain T. G. Barker, mistakenly believed that Hampton wanted a general assault and committed almost all of the rest of the brigade. Then Fitz Lee, seeing Hampton's brigade move, followed suit. The two brigades emerged from behind Cress Ridge in good form, sabers drawn, first at a walk, then a trot, then a gallop. "In superb form, with sabers glistening, they advanced," wrote James Kidd. "... It was an inspiring and imposing spectacle that brought a thrill to the hearts of the spectators on the opposite slope."[29] Captain Miller said, "a grander spectacle than their advance has rarely been beheld. They marched with well-aligned fronts and steady reins. Their polished saber-blades dazzled in the sun."[30] Hampton, still riding ahead, noticed with surprise what was happening behind him, but since there was nothing he could do to stop the developing charge, he rode on. The Rebel cavalry thundered across the field behind him, drawing deadly Union artillery fire.

There was no organized Union resistance ready to receive the blow. Gregg looked for reinforcements and saw the First Michigan coming onto the field. They were vastly outnumbered, a single regiment facing elements of two brigades, but Gregg ordered them to meet the charge. Custer rode over to the commander of the regiment, Colonel Charles Town, to relay the order. "Colonel Town, I shall have to ask you to charge," he said, "and I want to go on in with you."[31] Custer once again led the advance, repeating his rallying cry, "Come on, you Wolverines!" as they rushed forward, sabers held high.[32]

"In addition to this numerical superiority," Custer wrote, "the enemy had the advantage of position and were exultant over the repulse of the Seventh Michigan Cavalry. All these facts considered, would seem to render success on the part of the First impossible. Not so, however." Custer's horse Roanoke fell, but he leapt onto another mount and rode into the saber clash. The forces collided headlong and a terrible fight commenced. "Then it was steel to steel," Kidd wrote. Captain Miller said the sound of the collision of the two forces was like "the roaring crash when woodsmen fell a great tree.... The clashing of sabers, the firing of pistols, the demands for surrender and cries of the combatants now filled the air."[33] Miller's men had been holding a flank position, and he ordered them to join in against the Confederate left, violating direct orders to hold his position. Miller was wounded in the arm, but his move contributed materially to the repulse of the Confederates. In 1897, he was awarded a Medal of Honor for leading the attack, despite disobeying orders.

Hampton and Baker were in the midst of the struggle, fighting hand to hand with sabers. Hampton shot three federal troopers from their horses and ran a fourth through with his sword. Wiley C. Howard of Cobb's Legion saw Hampton in grave danger. "Being hard pressed and partially disabled," he later wrote, "while protecting himself with saber from a furious onslaught of three of the enemy and cornered against a fence, another came up in his rear and shot him in the back. An eyewitness who with others was flying to his relief, said that while he parried manfully the blows being rained on his devoted head by his antagonists in front, he turned his head with those snapping eyes flashing upon the man who shot him and said, 'You dastardly coward—shoot a man from the rear!' and continued to fight the foes in front until rescued from his perilous position."[34] Hampton transferred battlefield command to Baker and was taken from the field. But by then, the impetus of the assault was spent.

"For minutes," Kidd recalled, "and for minutes that seemed like years—the gray column stood and staggered before the blow; then yielded, and fled."[35] Custer recalled, "For a moment, but only a moment, that long, heavy column stood its ground; then, unable to withstand the impetuosity of our attack, it gave way into a disorderly rout, leaving vast numbers of their dead and wounded in our possession, while the 1st, being masters of the field, had the proud satisfaction of seeing the much-vaunted 'chivalry', led by their favorite commander, seek safety in headlong flight." The momentum of the Confederate charge was broken. The outnumbered and disorganized Union troops had mounted a fierce enough resistance to halt Stuart. Laurence Baker led the Confederate cavalry back to Cress Ridge. They were not pursued, nor did they reappear that day. The Baltimore Pike and the Union right were saved. Custer returned to Gregg, his face spattered with blood. His unit had taken the worst of it—of the 254 Union losses in the fight near Rummel Farm, 219 were from Custer's brigade. But they had secured their place in history and that of their commander. Custer later rather immodestly wrote in his report, "I challenge the annals of warfare to produce a more brilliant or successful charge of cavalry."[36]

FIVE FORKS

CHARLES N. WARNER STOOD ON THE Gettysburg battlefield on July 4, in heavy rain. His battery had moved seventy-two miles in the last four days, rushing towards the battle from the south. They had marched through the night on July 1 and all day July 2, arriving in the Union rear late on the 2nd. On the 3rd, they were held in reserve and not engaged. He wrote that evening, "The battle has been very severe nearly all day and is still going on, and favorably I believe."[1] His cousin Edward R. Warner joined him in camp that night. He had graduated 21st in the Class of 1857, and was currently lieutenant colonel of the First New York Light Artillery and on the staff of Brigadier General Henry Hunt, Meade's chief of artillery.[2] It had been his task during the battle to coordinate the movement of Union artillery in and out of the line during the barrage and subsequent defense.

Charles walked up to the front lines and saw the results of the previous days' fighting. The battlefield showed dreadful signs of the recent carnage. Confederate trooper Robert Stiles wrote of July 4, "The sights and smells that assailed us were simply indescribable—corpses swollen to twice their original size, some of them actually burst asunder with the pressure of foul gases and vapors. I recall one feature never before noted, the shocking distension and protrusion of the eyeballs of dead men and dead horses. Several human or unhuman corpses sat upright against a fence, with arms extended in the air and faces hideous with something very like a fixed leer, as if taking a fiendish pleasure in showing us what we essentially were and might at any moment become."[3] Warner wrote, "Our loss has been very severe and a great many have been killed that I am well acquainted with. The artillery has lost a great many.... A large proportion of artillery officers are killed, West Pointers that I have long been intimate with."[4] Lieutenant George A. "Little Dad" Woodruff, First Artillery Battery I, sixteenth of Warner's original Class of June 1861, was mortally wounded in Ziegler's Grove. His command was taken over by Warner's friend and classmate Tully McCrea. Alonzo H. Cushing, Fourth Artillery Battery A, twelfth in the same class, was severely wounded in the legs during the fight in the Angle, but refused to leave the field. He stayed with his gun until he was killed.[5] Colonel Patrick O'Rourke, first in their class, had died July 2 in a heroic counterattack on Little Round Top. No class suffered as greatly at Gettysburg as the Class of June 1861. For Warner's part, he said he was "sorry we could not have been called into action, but somebody had to be kept in reserve."

Warner walked along the stone wall in the Angle and back amongst the field hospitals behind the line. "This is a glorious but a sad 4th," he wrote. "We have gained a great victory but I do not feel like rejoicing." He saw wounded with the cap emblem of the 151st Pennsylvania—A and C Companies of which came from his home of Susquehanna County. They were known as the Schoolteacher's Regiment because of their nine-month enlistment. The regiment was part of Doubleday's division in I Corps, and on the first day fought hard on Seminary Ridge. The 151st was fronted against the 26th North Carolina in Heth's division, firing at each other in lines twenty paces apart. The North Carolinians suffered over 85 percent casualties, the worst of any Confederate unit on the field. The Pennsylvanians took 69 percent casualties, the second worst of any Union unit.[6] On July 3, the 151st faced the right flank of Pickett's Charge while the 26th advanced on the left.

"I see no signs of moving and we may remain here all day," Warner commented. "Everybody is mad because we are not pursuing them." Indeed, in some quarters it was not evident who had won the battle. The Union general Daniel Sickles, who had lost a leg on the second day, said that the delay was due to a difference of opinion over the outcome. "It was by no means clear," he told the Committee on the Conduct of the War, "in the judgment of the Corps commanders, or of the general in command, whether they had won or not."[7] Brigadier General John D. Imboden, one of Lee's cavalry commanders, said that the third day at Gettysburg was generally understood to be a defeat, "but it was surmised in camp that with tomorrow's dawn would come a renewal of the struggle." Lee had already made his decision, however. When Imboden met with him after midnight on the 4th, the Confederate commander was exhausted, and Imboden observed "an expression of sadness that I had never seen before upon his face." Lee and Imboden exchanged a few words, and then Lee lapsed into reverie. Finally, he said, "'I never saw troops behave more magnificently than Pickett's division of Virginians did to-day in that grand charge upon the enemy. And if they had been supported as they were to have been,—but, for some reason not yet fully explained to me, were not,—we would have held the position and the day would have been ours.' After a moment's pause he added in a loud voice, in a tone almost of agony, 'Too bad! Too bad! OH! Too BAD!' "[8] Lee told Imboden that there would be no fighting in the morning. The army was returning to Virginia.

Lee's army began its withdrawal in heavy rain at 4 P.M. on July 4, and the tail of the seventeen-mile-long column finally cleared Gettysburg at dawn the next day. The Confederates reached the Potomac on July 7, but the crossing took a week because of flood conditions on the river. Meade was not able to exploit this good fortune, and most of Lee's army escaped. But there was a notable coda to the Battle of Gettysburg. Ten days after the withdrawal, Henry Heth was with James J. Pettigrew on the north side of the river at Falling Waters, their forces serving as Lee's rear guard covering the crossing. A squadron of forty of Custer's cavalrymen inexplicably waylaid them. It was a foolish move. The Federals were greatly overmatched and quickly wiped out, but not before one of them mortally wounded Pettigrew, who died three days later.

Heth continued to see action in the next year as the battlefront returned to Virginia. In October 1863, at the Battle of Bristoe Station, Heth's men fought bravely but A. P. Hill's inconsistent leadership contributed to their defeat. Heth saw heavy action in the Wilderness battles in late spring 1864, as Grant began his move south towards Richmond. On May 7, Heth went head to head with his beloved friend Ambrose Burnside at Spottsylvania, where his entrenched troops repulsed three Union assaults with no losses, inflicting hundreds of casualties. Heth also fought an important action against his old messmate Winfield Scott Hancock. In late August 1864, Hancock's II Corps attempted to cut the Weldon Railroad five miles south of Petersburg at Reams' Station. Wilcox mounted a counterattack but was repulsed. Heth then led three brigades of Hill's corps in an attack against the Union entrenchments. As the battle was about to commence, Heth walked out to the skirmish line ahead of his column and bade the commander, Lieutenant D. C. Waddle, find a standard bearer and bring him there. Waddle returned with Thomas Minton, the color bearer of the 26th North Carolina regiment, which had suffered so terribly at Gettysburg. Minton had been one of the wounded. Heth asked for the flag.

"General, tell me where you want the flag to go and I will take it," Minton said. "I won't surrender my colors." Heth repeated his request, and the soldier again refused.

"Come on, then," Heth said, taking Minton by the arm, "we will carry the colors together." They waved the flag and two Confederate brigades broke from their positions and rushed yelling towards the Union lines. Heth and Minton dashed ahead of the infantry through the wire-laced abatis in front of the Union position and planted the flag on the enemy's works. The bold move demoralized the Union defenders, who managed only one volley before either fleeing or surrendering. Heth's men took two thousand prisoners. Heth later said, "If Hancock's heart could have been examined there would have been written on it REAMS as plainly as the deep scars received at Gettysburg and other fields were visible."[9]

Heth occupied the extreme right of the Confederate lines around Petersburg during the siege of Richmond, with orders to attack Grant every time the Federals made a flanking move to cut the rail lines to the capital. Heth estimated that between September 1864 and April 1865 his division was in combat every ten days on average. General John Brown Gordon recalled one planning session at which the commanders in the sector gathered to discuss a possible Union attack. After talking about the disposition of troops, the officers retired to a nearby hut to pray to God for guidance. "As we assembled," Gordon recalled, "one of our generals was riding within hailing distance, and General Harry Heth of Hill's corps stepped to the door of the log cabin and called to him to come in and unite with us in prayer." The officer, who was Heth's brother, did not understand the nature of the invitation, and replied, "No, thank you, brother Henry, no more at present; I've just had some."[10]

Heth made his headquarters at the Pickeral House, four miles from Petersburg, where his wife, Harriet, and their children joined him. Lee was a frequent visitor, given both their close friendship and the importance of Heth's position on the line. Lee was a welcome guest, conversing with Mrs. Heth and playing with Heth's daughter, once giving her a lock of his hair and a button from his coat. As the Confederate position grew more tenuous, however, Lee became troubled.

"I don't think it is safe for you to be here," he said to Harriet. "General Grant may break through these lines some day and capture you and your little children, and it would grieve me to hear that General Grant had taken you for his cook."[11] Three days after Heth's family returned home, Lee's fears were realized, and the Confederate line around Petersburg collapsed.

Grant's breakthrough came after a series of events in which George Pickett played a prominent role. In late March 1865, Grant ordered

General Philip Sheridan to outflank Lee on the right, to cut the South-side railroad and thus compromise Richmond. Lee sent three brigades under Pickett to block Sheridan, and if possible, push him back. Pickett commanded a 10,000-man force of five brigades, six guns, and the cavalry of Thomas Rosser, W. H. F. "Rooney" Lee and Fitz Lee. Their objective was a critical crossroads aptly named Five Forks. Pickett planned to drive off the Union forces holding the strategic position and then move on Sheridan's headquarters at Dinwiddie Courthouse to the south.[12]

Pickett attacked on March 31 and won a signal victory. His forces rolled up the Union flank in a dramatic sweeping maneuver, and by evening the Federal troops were retiring towards Dinwiddie Court House, where Sheridan's cavalry was massed. Pickett's advance was checked half a mile from the town by Union troops who had rallied under the leadership of George Custer.

General Lee had expected Pickett to pursue the enemy south-ward and perhaps take Dinwiddie Court House. Pickett might have been able to do so; but it would have left him isolated, out of contact with the right flank of the Confederate line, and subject to envelop-ment by Sheridan's mobile forces. He also knew that Major General Gouverneur K. Warren's V Corps was moving in from the east. To con-solidate his position Pickett withdrew five miles and established a defen-sive line around Five Forks, blocking the roads and protecting the route towards the railroad. Lee sent a terse missive, "Hold Five Forks at all hazards. Protect road to Ford's Depot and prevent Union forces from striking the south-side railroad. Regret exceedingly your forced with-drawal, and your inability to hold the advantage you had gained." Pick-ett then awaited the reinforcements he thought were coming.

The morning of April 1 was cold and quiet. Frost covered the ground. Pickett's five brigades began to dig in and make ready to accept the expected Union counterattack. "I immediately formed line of bat-tle upon the White Oak Road and set my men to throwing up tempo-rary breastworks," Pickett wrote. "Pine trees were felled, a ditch dug and the earth thrown up behind the logs. The men, God bless them, though weary and hungry, sang as they felled and dug. Three times in the three hours their labors were suspended because of attack from the front; but they as cheerily returned to their digging and to their 'Annie Laurie' and 'Dixie' as if they were banking roses for a festival."[13] There were reports of Union movements to Pickett's front and some skirmish-ing, but by noon no serious action had materialized. Pickett assumed that the window for an attack had passed and that none was coming.

His men were occupying well-prepared defensive positions along a three-mile front, which he felt would be able to hold off a Union probing action until he could make further dispositions. His position secured to his satisfaction, Pickett went with Fitz Lee to Rosser's headquarters on the north bank of Hatcher's Run some two miles behind the lines, where a fish fry was in progress.

The Weight of Renown

GETTYSBURG HAD BEEN PICKETT'S third brush with national fame. The doomed attack on the third day soon became known as "Pickett's Charge" largely through the influence of the media. The Richmond papers had highlighted the exploits of Pickett's Virginia division, which was the only unit of that size composed of soldiers from a single state. Northern writers later relied mainly on Richmond papers for southern accounts, perpetuating the belief, widely held by then, that the assault was mainly if not exclusively a Virginia affair. This caused great and understandable consternation among veterans from other states who had participated in the charge, particularly North Carolinians who went to great lengths to demonstrate that there were more of them present, they went farther and took more casualties than the Virginians.[14] Some responded by spreading stories that diminished Pickett's contribution to the battle, even claiming he did not advance with his troops. However, the term "Pickett's Charge" is not a misnomer; Pickett was the operational commander of the assault. He gave the order to advance; he managed the battlespace; and he bore the burden of the repulse. The attack remains one of the most famous exploits of a "last man," truly one of the best-known actions of any graduate of the Academy.

On September 15, 1863, George Pickett married fifteen-year-old Sallie Corbell. Sallie idealized George, seeing in him the spirit of the young officer who stormed the walls of Chapultepec. But things had not gone well for Pickett since Gettysburg. The war had aged him. Though only in his late thirties, photos from later in the war show his weariness, the lines under his eyes, wrinkles, and added weight. He drank too much, and his old jauntiness and confidence had faded, replaced by a growing sense of bitterness and pessimism.

In the fall of 1863, Pickett became a department commander in southeast Virginia and northeast North Carolina. He was tasked with countering Union raids on the countryside from their havens on the coast. It was hard, irregular fighting, almost a guerilla war, where the rules of conduct observed in other theaters had broken down. Pickett

Definition of "Goat" from the 1909 *Howitzer,* which also contains the original term "Immortals." The Goat Coat of Arms is from the 1912 *Howitzer;* Bijay (B.J.) is short for "Bold Before June." [USMA Special Collections]

Femme, n. A girl.

Fess, v. To fail entirely.

Fess, n. A complete failure in any recitation or undertaking.

File, n. One of the masculine gender. To bone files, v. To seek higher academic standing.

Find, v. Pechol's delight; to find deficient, hence, to discharge.

Flirtation, n. Chain Battery Walk; the favorite resort of spoonoids.

Formation, n. Any gathering. 2. A misunderstanding between two or more persons.

Found, adj. Discharged.

Fried-egg, n. Dress-hat ornament.

Goat, n. A man who would have stood first if he had boned.

Grind, n. A joke, genuine or attempted.

Gross, adj. Stupid; lacking in intelligence.

Growley, n. Heinz Ketchup, served in the messhall to disinfect slum.

Growley, v. To blush.

Gum up, v. To make a botch of anything.

Gum Stick, n. Essential equipment of a gross file.

Hell Cats, n. The heralds of the dawn; privates of the fife and drum corps.

Hive, v. To comprehend intelligently. 2. To catch one in the act of wrong-doing, a Tac's ambition.

Hundredth Night, n. A play given by the Corps of Cadets on the hundredth night before June 1st.

Immortals, n. The Goats.

Juliet, n. A cadet who enters after the time designated for the entrance of his class.

L. P., n. Lemon Pie; a femme whose beauty and age are good subjects for debate.

L. P., v. To sting.

Limits, n. Sacred precincts to which cadets are supposed to confine their wanderings.

Make, n. One of the Com's elect; a cadet officer.

Makings, n. The ingredients for twirling a dream; tobacco and papers.

Mathy, adj. Skilled in Mathematics.

Mar, n. The maximum mark.

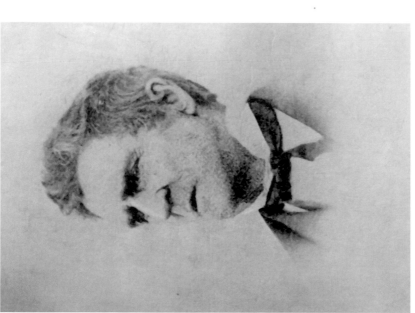

Tavern keeper Benny Havens offered succor to generations of West Point Cadets, and became an American legend celebrated in song for over a century. [USMA Special Collections]

Above, The Goats' nemeses: Sylvanus Thayer, Father of the Military Academy; *left,* Engineering Professor Denis Hart Mahan, as uncompromising as he was brilliant; and *right,* Superintendent Robert E. Lee, who graduated second in the Class of 1829 with no demerits over four years. [USMA Special Collections]

Above left: Cadets could strike demerits from their record by walking weekend punishment tours, at a rate one demerit every four hours. Cadet George A. Custer estimated he spent sixty-six Saturdays so engaged. [USMA Special Collections] *Left:* The West Point grounds at the time of the Civil War, showing the characteristic gray stone fortress architecture. [National Archives] *Above:* Smoking, drinking and playing cards were all infractions for which cadets could be "skinned." [USMA Special Collections]

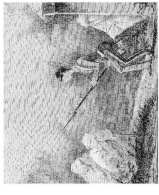

Top left: Bed Check: Cadets used mannequins to fool inspectors when they "blew post"—unless they were caught in the act. [USMA Special Collections] *Bottom left:* "Devilling" plebes on guard duty during summer encampment was a favorite pastime of more experienced Cadets. [USMA Special Collections] *Right:* Flirtation Walk, along the Hudson River shoreline, was the scene of many engagements, numerous conquests, and countless retreats. [USMA Special Collections]

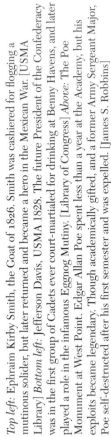

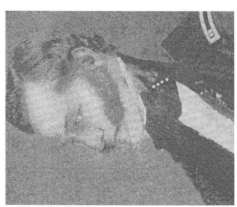

Top left: Ephraim Kirby Smith, the Goat of 1826. Smith was cashiered for flogging a mutinous soldier, but later returned and became a hero in the Mexican War. [USMA Library] *Bottom left*: Jefferson Davis, USMA 1828. The future President of the Confederacy was in the first group of Cadets ever court-martialed for drinking at Benny Havens, and later played a role in the infamous Eggnog Mutiny. [Library of Congress] *Above: The Poe Monument at West Point. Edgar Allan Poe spent less than a year at the Academy; but his exploits became legendary. Though academically gifted, and a former Army Sergeant Major, Poe self-destructed after his first semester and was expelled. [James S. Robbins]

Last Half Hour.

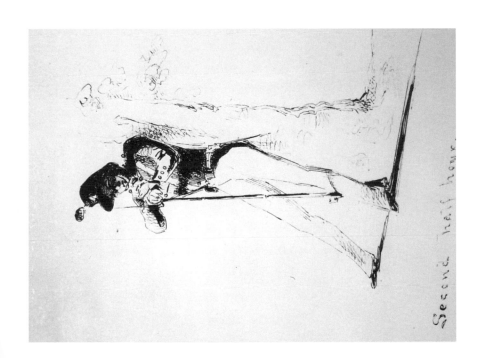

Second half hour.

Cadet James M. Whistler's view of guard duty from his series "On Post in Camp." Whistler failed chemistry in his third year and appealed to Superintendent Robert E. Lee for clemency, but had too many delinquencies to remain at the Academy. [USMA Special Collections]

Left and middle: Confederate General George E. Pickett, the Goat of 1846, and his wife LaSalle "Sallie May" Pickett. [Library of Congress] *Right:* Confederate General Henry "Harry" Heth, the Goat of 1847. Heth, along with his cousin George Pickett, future Union General Ambrose Burnside and future Confederate General A. P. Hill, formed the core of a Cadet clique dedicated to pursuing good times on every possible occasion. [Library of Congress]

Top: The heroic charge of the Second Dragoons at Resaca de la Palma during the opening days of the Mexican War. Z. M. P. Inge, the Goat of 1838, was killed in action at the head of the column. [Tomes, *Battles of America*] *Bottom:* The 8th US Infantry storming the *tête-du-pont* at the Battle of Churubusco, led by Lt. George Pickett and his friend Lt. James "Pete" Longstreet, who graduated third from the bottom in the Class of 1842. [Library of Congress]

The Light Infantry charging at the Battle of Molino del Rey. The charge was led by Captain Ephraim Kirby Smith, the Goat of 1826. He received two brevet promotions for valor, but was severely wounded and died several days later. [Coffin, *Building the Nation*]

American Soldiers and Marines storm the Mexican stronghold of Chapultepec in the last major engagement of the war. Lt. George E. Pickett received the flag from the severely wounded Longstreet and raised it atop the captured fortress. [USMA Library]

BATTLE OF PEA RIDGE, ARK.

Top: The execution of Colonel William Logan Crittenden, the Goat of 1845, at the Castle Atares in Havana Harbor, Cuba. Crittenden had joined the ill-fated 1851 Lopez expedition to liberate the island from Spanish rule, but the expected uprising did not materialize and fifty Americans faced a Spanish firing squad. [USMA Library] *Bottom:* General James M. McIntosh, the Goat of 1849, leading the Confederate cavalry charge at the Battle of Pea Ridge, Arkansas, March 7, 1862. Fearless in battle, McIntosh was felled later that day by Union sharpshooters. [Library of Congress]

Above left: Cadet George Armstrong Custer, the Goat of June, 1861. Custer said that while at the Academy his "offenses against law and order were not great in enormity, but what they lacked in magnitude they made up in number." *Left:* Cadet Charles N. Warner, the Goat of 1862. Originally in Custer's class, Warner was sent home after failing an examination, but was readmitted when the Civil War broke out. Within a year of graduation, he had fought at Antietam, Fredericksburg, and made a heroic stand with his battery at Chancellorsville. [USMA Special Collections] *Below left:* Confederate General Laurence S. Baker, the Goat of 1851. When he received word of the surrender of Confederate forces at Appomattox, he told his men that they were going to keep on fighting. [Library of Congress] *Above:* Pickett receives the order to charge the Union line at Gettysburg from General James Longstreet, July 3, 1863. Longstreet later wrote, "It was one of the saddest days of my life." [Library of Congress]

Left: Custer pictured in 1862 with a prisoner of war, his former roommate Confederate Lieutenant James B. Washington, great grandnephew of George Washington. The picture of the West Point chums reunited on the battlefield was circulated widely in the North. [Library of Congress] *Right:* Custer reinvented his image after the Civil War. The "Boy General" of the Union cavalry became a buckskin-clad Indian fighter. He is shown here in a photo studio with visiting Russian Grand Duke Alexis. [Denver Public Library]

dead for the want of propper Care and nourishment

28th this morning we went to burry the and Now Comes the most hertrendering tale of all as I have said before General Custer with five Companies went below the village to Cut them off as he supposed but instead he was surrounded and all of them Killed to a Mon 14 officers and 250 men Their the Bravest General of Moddern times met his death with his two Brothers Brother in law and Nephew not 8 yards apart surrounded by 42 men of E Company. Oh what a slaughter how Mainney homes are made desolate by the sad debaster every one of them were scalp and otherwise Mutelated but the General he lay with a smile on his face The indians

Top: A page from the diary of trooper Pat Coleman, 7th Cavalry, a few days after the Battle at Little Big Horn. He notes that in death Custer "lay with a smile on his face." [USMA Special Collections]
Bottom: The grave of Lt. John J. Crittenden, a washout of the Class of 1875 who was determined to live a soldier's life, and died alongside Custer. He was buried where he fell at the request of his father, General Thomas L. Crittenden, who said, "There can be no fitter resting place for the true soldier than that spot which his blood has hallowed." [Denver Public Library]

The statue of Custer erected at the Academy in 1879. Custer's widow Libby so disliked the monument she waged a relentless and ultimately successful campaign for its removal. Its current location is one of the enduring mysteries of West Point. [USMA Special Collections]

was sent word of alleged Union atrocities that winter. One communiqué from Colonel Joel R. Griffin of his command read, "Enemy have escaped me by river bridge, Pasquotank River. . . . They hung Private Daniel Bright, of Company L, of my Sixty-second Georgia Regiment; hung him to a beam in a house; body remained suspended forty hours. Lieutenant Mundin's wife, with other ladies, were arrested, tied, and placed in jail at Elizabeth City, and carried in irons to Norfolk; even their feet tied. Negroes killed a child in Camden County, committing all other kinds of excesses."[15] Events such as these would form the backdrop for another controversial episode in Pickett's life.

On January 20, 1864, Lee ordered Pickett to retake the city of New Bern, North Carolina, which Burnside had seized in February 1862 by amphibious assault. Pickett planned a complex joint operation of thirteen thousand men and fourteen cutters operating on the Neuse River, and launched his attack on February 1. But the Confederate force met stronger than expected resistance, and after two days Pickett withdrew, to the disappointment of Lee and President Davis. During the battle, Pickett's troops captured fifty-four North Carolina soldiers who had left their regiments and joined the Union forces. Pickett treated the men not as prisoners of war but as deserters. In Pickett's mind they were no better than the Americans captured with Mexican forces at Churubusco who were ceremonially hanged when Pickett raised the flag atop Chapultepec. Twenty-two of the North Carolinians were "duly executed according to law and the customs of war" in the town of Kinston. The scene was heartrending—the wives and families of the men, who lived in the area, pleaded for their lives, to no avail. The bodies were stripped before they were returned, and for good measure Pickett threatened to kill ten Union POWs for every Rebel executed in retaliation. Pickett may have been acting with his accustomed zeal, but his superiors thought the executions unnecessarily harsh, both in concept and in implementation. A controversy arose and Pickett was removed to the district command of Petersburg.

In early May, Longstreet appealed to Lee to return Pickett to his division, and Lee assented. Pickett was ordered north to assist in opposing Grant's drive towards Richmond. However, on May 5, before Pickett resumed his old command, Union troops under General Benjamin Butler launched a surprise amphibious assault on Petersburg. Pickett's 600 troops, about a third of whom were "second class militia" (boys under seventeen and men over fifty), faced off against 36,000 Union soldiers. The defense of Petersburg may have been Pickett's finest hour; relying on scarce resources and his own talents, he rose to the occasion and saved the city. Pickett was a whirlwind in the battle, using his small, inadequately supplied force in inspired ways—but after he had won the battle, he had a minor breakdown from the strain. A week later, he had recovered enough to return to his old division.

Pickett's defense of Petersburg had impressed Lee and helped erase the stigma of the incident at Kinston. On June 17, 1864, Pickett again distinguished himself at the Battle of Bermuda Hundred, east of Richmond. Union forces had seized a portion of the Rebel lines and Lee ordered Pickett to counterattack. Lee then thought better and cancelled the order, but word had not reached Pickett. His men charged the Federal lines and retook the works in a "dramatic rush." Lee wrote to Lieutenant General R. H. Anderson, acting commander of Longstreet's corps (while Longstreet was recovering from wounds): "I take great pleasure in presenting to you my congratulations upon the conduct of the men of your corps. I believe they will carry anything they are put against. We tried very hard to stop Pickett's men from capturing the breastworks of the enemy, but could not do it."

During the long siege of Richmond, Pickett's division manned seven miles of line north of Petersburg between his headquarters at the Howlett House and Swift Creek, an area called the Howlett Line. It was a key defensive point, the spot opposite the Bermuda Hundred where the James and Appomattox rivers narrowed.

Like the Heth family, Pickett's wife joined him at the front during the summer. In July she returned to Richmond to give birth to their first child, George Edward Pickett Jr., and Pickett asked Lee's permission to leave the lines to go into the city to see his new son.

> But when I applied to the great *Tyee* for a pass to Richmond, saying, "My son was born this morning," he replied, "Your country was born almost a hundred years ago." It was the first word of reproach Marse Robert ever spoke to me; but he was right and I was reckless to ask.[16]

Lee soon relented and gave Pickett a pass and a congratulatory note— which George placed in his infant son's hand. Back at the front, Pickett's men had lit bonfires all along their positions, and observing this from his own lines, Grant asked the cause of the celebration. His scouts soon learned the reason, and Grant said, "Haven't we some kindling on this side of the line? Why don't we strike a light for young Pickett?" Days later, Federal troops arrived under flag of truce to deliver a baby's silver service, engraved, "To George Pickett, Jr. From his father's friends, U.S. Grant, Rufus Ingalls, George Suckley."[17]

Despite such lighthearted moments, conditions in the Rebel siege lines were difficult. Boredom and desertion were constant challenges, and the situation grew much worse as winter approached. Dr. Henry Alexander White witnessed the trying scene:

> Winter poured down its snows and its sleets upon Lee's shelterless men in the trenches. Some of them burrowed into the earth. Most of them shivered over the feeble fires, kept burning along the lines. Scanty and thin were the garments of these heroes. Most of them were clad in mere rags. Gaunt famine oppressed them every hour. . . . With dauntless hearts these gaunt-faced men endured the almost ceaseless fire of Grant's mortar-batteries. The frozen fingers of Lee's army of sharpshooters clutched the musket barrel with an aim so steady that Grant's men scarcely ever lifted their heads from their bomb-proofs.[18]

Pickett had a difficult time keeping order among his men, and in January 1865 Lee chastised Longstreet to "correct the evils in Pickett's division." Their morale had been crushed by the failure of the Hampton Roads Peace Conference held on the Union transport *River Queen* on February 3, 1865. Pickett wrote:

> The anxious, despairing faces I see everywhere bespeak heavy hearts. Our commissioners knew that we were gasping our last gasp and that the Peace Conference was a forlorn hope. Because of the informality of the conference and my knowledge of Mr. Lincoln, his humanity, his broad nature, his warm heart, I did believe he would take advantage of this very informality and spring some wise, superhuman surprise which would, somehow, restore peace and in time insure unity. Now, heaven help us, it will be war to the knife, with a knife no longer keen, the thrust of an arm no longer strong, the certainty that when peace comes it will follow the tread of the conqueror.[19]

The Waterloo of the Confederacy

WHILE PICKETT, FITZ LEE AND ROSSER enjoyed their repast at Hatcher's Run near Five Forks, couriers arrived periodically with reports of fresh Union movements. The commanders were at first unconcerned. Later, when informed about possible Federal moves on their left flank, Pickett ordered Fitz Lee to extend his cavalry to the east. As the afternoon wore on, more reports arrived. Fitz left to check on his command. Pickett began to suspect that an attack was developing. He wrote messages to his brigade commanders and gave them to couriers to take back to the front. Pickett watched the messengers ride south down the road.

They neared the stream, then stopped. Men in blue uniforms emerged from the edge of the woods. Pickett looked on in disbelief as his couriers were taken captive by Union skirmishers. He leapt on his mount and thundered down the road, running the gauntlet past the Federals, who fired wildly at him.

When Pickett had ordered Fitz Lee to extend his line, he had no idea the size of the force he was facing. Sheridan had sent Warren and V Corps against Pickett's left. Units under Major General Samuel W. Crawford made a sweeping move through the woods up to Ford's Road, the main north-south route, near where Pickett was having lunch. The cavalry could not have stopped them. After dislodging the Confederate left, Sheridan feinted to the west with Custer, then smashed into Pickett's front with a division.

The center of Pickett's line was held by a brigade under Brigadier General George Hume Steuart of Maryland. He was an Immortal of the Class of 1848 who graduated next to last. Before the war, he had served with the Mounted Rifles, chiefly in the Southwest, fighting the Mogollon and Navajo Indians. He served as a member of the honor guard for Abraham Lincoln's 1861 inauguration, and joined the Confederacy six weeks later. He was a strict but fun-loving commander; he had a habit of deviling his sentries by sneaking up on them at night and taking them by surprise, a favorite West Point prank.[20] His nickname was "Maryland Steuart" to distinguish him from J. E. B. Stuart, and during the invasion of Pennsylvania when his unit crossed the Potomac he knelt down to kiss the soil of his native state. He fought bravely on Culp's Hill at Gettysburg, where his brigade suffered more casualties than any other in General Edward A. Johnson's (USMA 1838) division. Steuart and Johnson were both captured on May 12, 1864, during the Battle of Spottsylvania Court House by Sergeant George W. Van Vlack of the 64th New York. They were taken back to Winfield Scott Hancock, who greeted Steuart warmly.

"Why Bob Steuart," he said, extending his hand, "how do you do?"

"I am Brigadier General George H. Steuart of the Confederate Army," Steuart said, straightening, "and under the present circumstances I decline to take your hand."

"Under any other circumstances I would not offer you my hand," Hancock replied. He turned to Johnson and the two old comrades shook hands cordially.

"General Hancock, this is worse than death to me," Johnson said.

Hancock commiserated briefly with Johnson, and then clapped Van Vlack on the shoulder. "My God, Orderly, you made a splendid haul," he said. "Steuart is a spicy fellow, look out for their safe keeping." Steuart was exchanged that August and given a brigade in Pickett's division.[21]

When the attack developed at Five Forks with Pickett absent, Steuart quickly took control of the situation. He refused his left in good order to face V Corps's flanking maneuver, mounting a spirited but ultimately doomed defense. Fighting all along the line was desperate. Private Theodore Gerrish from Maine wrote, "It was hot work, and in many places it was a hand to hand fight. Men deliberately pointed their rifles in each other's faces and fired. Clubbed muskets came crushing down in deadly force upon human skulls. Men were bayoneted in cold blood. Feats of individual bravery were performed on that afternoon which, if recorded, would fill a volume."[22]

Pickett arrived on the scene to see his front beginning to collapse. He tried to organize the units that were falling back, and gave some orders to his artillery commander, Colonel William J. Pegram, who had commanded the battery under Heth that fired the first Confederate shots at Gettysburg, and who was directing his guns effectively against the Union onslaught. They parted with the Northwest Indian salutation, *"Kla-how-ya, Tik-egh."*[23] A few seconds later, Pegram was struck in the left side and fell, mortally wounded. Pickett then gathered some men and manned an artillery piece himself, getting off eight rounds before the axle broke. The situation had grown dire.

"Charge after charge was made and repulsed," Pickett wrote, "and division after division of the enemy advanced upon us. Our left was turned; we were completely entrapped. Their cavalry, charging at a signal of musketry from the infantry, enveloped us front and right and, sweeping down upon our rear, held us as in a vise." One of Pickett's men handed him a bloodstained battle flag and Pickett began waving it, trying to rally his men to meet the next Union charge. Some of his men began singing "Rally 'round the flag" and Pickett joined in. Enough of the troops stood to face the final assault, and in Pickett's words, "overpowered, defeated, cut to pieces, starving, captured, as we were, those that were left of us formed front and north and south and met with sullen desperation their double onset. With the members of my own staff and the general officers and their staff officers we compelled a rally and stand of Corse's Brigade and W. H. F. Lee's Cavalry, who made one of the most brilliant cavalry fights of the war, enabling many of us to escape capture."[24] But where Pickett and many of his men escaped, thousands of others had not. Sheridan's attack isolated Pickett's army, cut the Southside railroad, disrupted the main supply lines to

Petersburg, and compromised Richmond's right flank. The defense of the Confederate capital became untenable, and the next day President Davis departed for Danville. The Richmond defenses collapsed as Lee withdrew his army and headed west.

The Battle of Five Forks has been called the Waterloo of the Confederacy, and was one of the most significant battles of the war. The collapse of Pickett's front was the catalyst that spelled the end of the Confederate States. One ignominious footnote to the battle took place when Sheridan relieved Warren of command of V Corps. Warren had performed heroically, at one point grasping the V Corps standard and leading a charge himself. Private Gerrish called it "the most gallant deed of the whole day's battle." But he had been slow to advance to Sheridan's aid on the previous day and Grant had already authorized his dismissal. It was an embarrassing event, with the war nearly over, and given Warren's foresight in saving Little Round Top. Warren would be exonerated by a postwar court of inquiry, which published its findings in November 1882, three months after he died. His last words were "The flag, the flag, oh the flag!"[25]

There followed a week of chaos as the Confederate forces fled to the west, some in good order, some completely disorganized, seeking sanctuary in Roanoke or Danville. Robert Stiles wrote of the retreat from Petersburg:

> No Confederate soldier who was on and of that fearful retreat can fail to recall it as one of the most trying experiences of his life. Trying enough, in the mere fact that the Army of Northern Virginia was flying before its foes, but further trying, incomparably trying, in lack of food and rest and sleep, and because of the audacious pressure of the enemy's cavalry.... The somewhat disorganized condition of the troops and the crowded condition of the roads necessitated frequent halts, and whenever these occurred—especially after nightfall—the men would drop in the road, or on the side of it, and sleep until they were roused, and it was manifestly impossible to rouse them all.[26]

The retreating units were short of food and ammunition, cold, tired and harassed by the relentless Union cavalry. General John B. Gordon, who commanded at the leading edge of the Confederate flight, wrote:

> Fighting all day, marching all night, with exhaustion and hunger claiming their victims at every mile of the march, with charges of infantry in rear and of cavalry on the flanks, it seemed the war god had turned loose all his furies to revel in havoc.... [T]hus came short but sharp little battles which made up the side shows of

the main performance, while the different divisions of Lee's lionhearted army were being broken and scattered or captured. Out of one of these whirlwinds there came running at the top of his speed a boy soldier whose wit flashed out even in that dire extremity. When asked why he was running, he shouted back: "Golly, captain, I'm running cause I can't fly!"[27]

"The horrors of the march from Five Forks to Amelia Court House and thence to Sailor's Creek beggars all description," Pickett wrote. "For forty-eight hours the man or officer who had a handful of parched corn in his pocket was most fortunate. We reached Sailor's Creek on the morning of the sixth, weary, starving, despairing."[28] According to an officer who saw Pickett during the flight west, he was "hopeless, demoralized and prostrated. He did not look like Pickett but like an old and broken man."[29]

APPOMATTOX

O
N APRIL 6, LEE TRIED TO MAKE the turn south to Danville
and was engaged by Union forces at Sailor's Creek. The resulting battle was devastating, as Robert Stiles recalled: "By the
time we had well settled into our old position we were attacked simultaneously, front and rear, by overwhelming numbers, and quicker than
I can tell it the battle degenerated into a butchery and a confused mêlée
of brutal personal conflicts. I saw numbers of men kill each other with
bayonets and the butts of muskets, and even bite each other's throats
and ears and noses, rolling the ground like wild beasts."[1] What remained
of Pickett's division was effectively destroyed. Those who escaped death
or capture were "broken down, nearly famished, and mostly without
arms."[2] Seven thousand Confederates were captured, including Generals Richard S. Ewell, Custis Lee and Joseph B. Kershaw. The senior
Rebel officers were brought before the commander of the Union division that had captured them. Kershaw saw "a spare, lithe, sinewy figure, bright, dark, quick-moving blue eyes; florid complexion, light, wavy
curls, high cheek bones, firm set teeth—a jaunty close-fitting cavalry
jacket, large top-boots, Spanish spurs, golden aiguillettes, a serviceable
saber . . . a quick nervous movement, an air telling of the habit of command—announced the redoubtable Custer whose name was as familiar to his foes as to his friends."[3]

Custer had been a ubiquitous presence during the retreat, continuously at the front, pressing the Confederate forces, raiding their
baggage, netting prisoners among stragglers, fighting skirmishes, and
doing what he could to get ahead of the Rebels. Custer's brother Tom
had joined his staff and emulated his gallantry. He had been wounded
at Sailor's Creek, leading an assault on Confederate works. George
described his brother's action in a letter home:

Tom led the assault on the enemy's breastworks, mounted, was first to leap his horse over the works on top of the enemy while they were pouring a volley of musketry into our ranks. Tom seized the rebel colors and demanded their surrender. The color bearer shot him through the face and neck, intending to shoot him through the head. So close the muzzle Tom's face was spotted with burnt powder. He retained the colors with one hand, while with the other he drew his revolver and shot the rebel dead.[4]

"Armstrong," Tom said to his brother as he came up, "the damned rebels have shot me, but I've got my flag."[5] It was the second flag Tom had captured that week, and for his gallantry he was awarded two Medals of Honor, the only soldier in the war to receive the medal twice for separate actions.[6]

The spurs that Kershaw noted Custer wearing were a recent acquisition, a loan from Confederate artilleryman Colonel Frank Huger, an Immortal of the Class of 1860 whom Custer had captured that day. He was the son of General Benjamin Huger, who had graduated eighth in the Class of 1825. Both had resigned their commissions to join the Confederacy. The elder Huger had been Winfield Scott's chief of ordnance and artillery in Mexico, and Scott had presented him with an unusual gift, a set of large and intricately carved spurs. They had belonged to Santa Anna and been presented to Scott by the Mexican leader as a gesture of respect after Scott returned his sword. General Huger in turn had given the spurs to his son Frank when he graduated from West Point. Young Huger wore the spurs through the war, right up to the engagement at Sailor's Creek, where he was captured by his friend Custer. For the rest of the day, Custer kept Huger with him, as he said, "to let you see how I am going to take you fellows in."[7] Huger then loaned his spurs to Custer, and he wore them for the rest of the war.

"Little Phil"

CUSTER HAD ENJOYED A BRILLIANT career since Gettysburg. The Union leadership had come to realize the importance of an independent cavalry arm and began to exploit the opportunities presented by mobile forces. Custer fought in many battles, and as a result of his bravery and imagination had been promoted to major general and given a division command. He owed much of his professional success to his new patron, General Philip H. Sheridan.

Sheridan bore little resemblance to Custer's original supporter George McClellan. Though both stood about five and a half feet tall,

"Little Mac" by his bearing, his intellect and his sense of self projected an air of significance that few could ignore. Not so "Little Phil." James H. Kidd observed that there was nothing marked about Sheridan, nothing in particular that distinguished him from other officers, no single factor on which one could pin his eventual success. He had to be taken as a whole. "There is no solider of the Civil War with whom he can be fairly compared with justice to either," Kidd wrote. "If he had not the spark of genius he came very near to having it." Sheridan was calm, unhurried, thoughtful, confident. "In his bearing was the assurance that he was going to accomplish what he had pledged himself to do. . . . The outcome to him was a foregone conclusion."[8] David S. Stanley, who rode in a coach with Sheridan while on their way east to enter the Academy, called him "the most insignificant looking little fellow I ever saw."[9] Wharton J. Green, who was acquainted with Sheridan at the Academy, recalled, "If, at that time, I had been called upon to designate the man on that historic spot who would later on reach the high rank Sheridan attained, he would probably have been one of the very last to have come under consideration, and such, methinks, would have been the almost unanimous forecast of all who knew him. Proof that is, that the boy is not always father of the man, gauged by the world's criterion—success."[10]

Sheridan, like Custer, was an Ohioan, of Irish ancestry, born in 1831. As a teenager he thrilled to stories of the Mexican War. "The stirring events of the times so much impressed and absorbed me," Sheridan wrote, "that my sole wish was to become a soldier, and my highest aspiration to go to West Point."[11] His slot at the Academy opened when the original claimant failed the math portion of the entrance exam. Sheridan was not gifted at mathematics either, but had the benefit of a helpful roommate, Henry W. Slocum.[12] Sheridan recalled:

> After taps—that is, when by the regulations of the Academy all the lights were supposed to be extinguished, and everybody in bed—Slocum and I would hang a blanket over the one window of our room and continue our studies—he guiding me around scores of stumbling-blocks in Algebra and elucidating many knotty points in other branches of the course with which I was unfamiliar.

With Slocum's tutoring, Sheridan was able to pass the January boards. In the years that followed he was consistently in the lower half of his class, though not in the bottom section in most subjects. (His French, however, was abominable.) Neither did he earn large numbers of demerits. But in his third year he got into an altercation with Cadet Sergeant William Terrill of Virginia, the same who would bring such shame to his family by dying in defense of the Union. He did not like the tone of an order Terrill had given him and broke from the ranks, threatening, "God damn you sir, I'll run you through!" Sheridan recalled:

> While my company was forming for parade, having, given me an order, in what I considered an improper tone, to "dress" in a certain direction, when I believed I was accurately dressed, I fancied I had a grievance, and made toward him with a lowered bayonet, but my better judgment recalled me before actual contact could take place. Of course Terrill reported me for this, and my ire was so inflamed by his action that when we next met I attacked him, and a fisticuff engagement in front of barracks followed, which was stopped by an officer appearing on the scene. Each of us handed in an explanation, but mine was unsatisfactory to the authorities, for I had to admit that I was the assaulting party.[13]

Sheridan was suspended from the Academy for a year. He returned to graduate 34th of 52 in 1853, with his worst showing (47th) in infantry tactics; he also had amassed an uncharacteristic 189 demerits, 11 shy of expulsion. After graduation he went off to serve on the frontier in Texas. He was a captain when the war broke out, and then became chief quartermaster of the Army of Southwest Missouri. Captain Sheridan developed an uneasy relationship with his commander, General Curtis, and after the Pea Ridge campaign Curtis accused Sheridan of stealing horses from private citizens. With a court martial looming, Sheridan was saved by Major General Henry W. "Old Brains" Halleck, third in the Class of 1839, and soon to be chief of staff. Halleck made Sheridan a member of his staff, and shortly thereafter Sheridan was given a volunteer colonelcy and command of the Second Michigan Cavalry.

Sheridan began to distinguish himself in battle. He was a division commander at Perryville, and before the battle he was able to make peace with Terrill. "In 1862, when General Buell's army was assembling at Louisville, Terrill was with it as a brigadier-general," Sheridan wrote, "and I then took the initiative toward a renewal of our acquaintance. Our renewed friendship was not destined to be of long duration, I am sorry to say, for a few days later, in the battle of Perryville, while gallantly fighting for his country, poor Terrill was killed." By May 1863, Sheridan was a major general, promoted for gallantry at Murfreesboro. He came to the attention of General Grant during the Battle of Chattanooga, where his troops took Missionary Ridge in a nearly suicidal assault. The charge was led by the 24th Wisconsin, the colors borne by eighteen-year-old Lieutenant Arthur MacArthur, who though wounded led his men up the ridge and took the enemy positions. Sheridan embraced the lad and said, "Take care of him. He has just won the Medal of Honor."[14] When Grant headed east, he took Sheridan with him, and in March 1864 made him cavalry commander of the Army of the Potomac, replacing Pleasonton, who was sent to the Department of Missouri.

Custer came to Sheridan's attention at the Battle of Yellow Tavern, May 11, 1864. It was Sheridan's first face-to-face battle with Stuart, and the Union horsemen were being pummeled by Confederate batteries strongly emplaced on a hilltop. Custer's men had been taking hot fire from the guns and from Rebel sharpshooters in nearby woods, and he rode about his command saying, "Lie down, men—lie down. We'll fix them!" He rode to General Wesley Merritt and told him he was going to silence the Rebel battery. Merritt said he would support the move in any way he could. As Custer went about readying his troops for the dangerous exploit, Sheridan arrived at the headquarters, and Merritt told him of Custer's plan.

"Bully for Custer!" Sheridan said. "I'll wait and see it." Custer had his regimental band blow a salutation and then play "Yankee Doodle" as his regiments trotted towards the battery. His men descended into a depression, crossed a ditch over three small bridges, and then broke into a charge up the rising ground to the cheers of the men in the line behind them. The Rebel cannon could not be depressed enough to come into effective play, and Custer's men routed the artillerymen and their support troops. It was a replay of May's Charge at Resaca de la Palma, but on a much grander scale. J. E. B. Stuart, trying to rally his men and stem the tide, fell mortally wounded, depriving the Confederacy of its *beau idéal*.[15]

Custer soon became Sheridan's primary offensive instrument in his many campaigns. "Where work was to be done that had to be done, and done quickly and surely," Kidd wrote, "Custer was apt to be called upon."[16] Custer was the manifest expression of the type of intrepid warrior that President Lincoln had been seeking to vigorously prosecute and win the war. He was the point man for the will of the commander in chief, as expressed by the chain of command: Lincoln had Grant, Grant had Sheridan, and Sheridan had Custer. Kidd observed that "Custer was a fighting man, through and through, but wary and wily as brave. There was in him an indescribable something—call it caution, call it sagacity, call it the real military instinct—it may have been genius—by whatever name entitled, it nearly always impelled him to do intuitively the right thing." Custer was a true professional who "went about the work of fighting battles and winning victories as a railroad superintendent goes about the business of running trains." In battle he was all business; "in camp he was genial and companionable, blithe as a boy."[17]

Custer never asked his men to do something he himself would not do. In camp he was extravagant, but on campaign he was a ruthless hunter—ruthless with himself most of all. While many men died for him, he took the same or greater risks, so they respected and loved him. He reciprocated their respect. "Always when we met Custer on a march," James Avery recalled, "he would lift his hat to each company, and was greeted with hearty cheers by the passing soldiers. All loved him, yes, they idolized the curly headed General, who led them in many a hard fought battle."[18] Kidd observed:

> The popular idea of Custer is a misconception. He was not a reckless commander. He was not regardless of human life. No man could have been more careful of the comfort and lives of his men. His heart was tender as that of a woman. He was kind to his subordinates, tolerant of their weaknesses, always ready to help and encourage them. He was brave as a lion, fought as few men fought, but it was from no love of it. Fighting was his business; and he knew that by that means alone could peace be conquered. He was brave, alert, untiring, a hero in battle, relentless in the pursuit of a beaten enemy, stubborn and full of resources on the retreat.[19]

Someone as energetic, intractable and talented as Custer would inevitably conjure jealousy, and Custer's natural competitiveness did not help matters. He would, explicitly or by implication, criticize other officers, particularly those whom he had little contact with or use for. Custer was particularly critical of other cavalry officers, and his feud with Hugh Kilpatrick was well known. Their differences may have influenced Sheridan's decision to move Kilpatrick west to Sherman's command in the summer of 1864. Custer's competitive spirit was something of a surprise to those who had known him at West Point, where he considered vying for class rank a meaningless preoccupation. This race was keener, and it struck to the heart of what Custer thought an officer should be. Custer was a warfighter; his function was to drive the enemy from the field. It was a responsibility he took literally. Even as a division commander he led from the front. And when battle had subsided, he wanted others to know what he did. Custer adopted a practiced modesty when placed in the spotlight, giving all credit to his men—yet he always managed to arrange where the spotlight would fall. His fame was well earned, but also well cultivated.

Custer's rise to stardom began shortly after Gettysburg. A few weeks after the battle, Kidd was riding a train to Washington and observed that "the name of Custer, the 'boy General,' was seemingly on every tongue and there was no disposition on our part to conceal the fact that we had been with him."[20] Several factors conspired to give Custer center stage. His winning personality, affableness and eccentricity contributed. So did the fact that he was fighting in the East, close to the centers of power and the press. The *New York Times* reporter E. A. Paul attached himself to Custer's staff and began writing a series of glowing articles, transmitted by telegraph and quickly in print.

Custer also had a secret weapon in his wife, Elizabeth "Libbie" Bacon, whom he had married in Monroe, Michigan, in February 1864. Her father, Judge Daniel Bacon, had never approved of their relationship, believing Custer was below the Bacons' social station. But after Custer became a general officer, Judge Bacon relented. The newlyweds stopped at West Point for a day on their honeymoon and Custer grew jealous when some cadets showed Libbie Flirtation Walk. They set up a home in Washington, and while George was at the front fighting, Libbie was meeting the right people, making connections, and managing perceptions of her husband. She passed on to George all the adulation she heard, fanned no doubt by her own flirtatiousness with the glib politicians who began to protect and promote Custer, to feed off his fame and bask in his reflected glory. Custer was received by Congress and the president in March 1864. The Custers were hugely popular on the Washington social circuit. George was his usual charming and witty self, Libbie attractive and intelligent—the perfect couple, a prize for Washington hostesses. They were the ideal combination of charisma and authenticity—Custer had "been there," and when he arrived in uniform he was instantly the center of attention. The fame spiral became self-reinforcing; Custer believed his own press, even as he created it. Notoriety flowed from him naturally, an expression of his romantic self-image. And it was hard to argue with the results; Custer usually won his battles, and his superiors loved him. When Grant took command of the Army of the Potomac, George and Libbie accompanied him to the front.

In October 1864, after the Battle of Cedar Creek, Custer escorted a delegation of soldiers to Washington to present ten captured Confederate banners to Secretary of War Edwin Stanton. Custer recounted tales of his men's heroism, saying that their victory was "the most complete and decisive which has been achieved in the Shenandoah."

Secretary Stanton announced that the soldier who had captured the flags would be awarded medals. "And," he continued, "to show you how good Generals and good men work together, I have already appointed your commanding General a Major General." He shook Custer's hand. "General Custer, a gallant officer always makes gallant soldiers."[21]

The timing of these events was critical. The 1864 presidential election was nearing, and Custer's former patron McClellan was the Democratic nominee against Lincoln. Custer had worked hard to overcome his reputation as a Democrat and a McClellan protégé. Regardless of his recent achievements on the battlefield, certain memories could be long in Washington. In the winter of 1863–64, Custer received a letter from a senator who was to vote on his much-delayed confirmation as a brigadier general. "Before I can vote for your confirmation," the senator wrote, "I desire to be informed whether you are what is termed, 'a McClellan man.'"[22] Custer took umbrage at the implications of the note—did his personal views matter? did they interfere with his performance in the field? had he ever shown disloyalty to the commander in chief?—but he understood their import, and he understood, too, that he needed to remove any doubt that he was solidly behind Lincoln. He took the opportunity of his pre-election visit to Washington to make his opinions known on the Democratic Peace Platform and proposals for an armistice: "I am a peace man, in favor of an 'armistice' and of sending 'Peace Commissioners,'" he told the press. "The Peace Commissioners I am in favor of are those sent from the cannon's mouth. The only armistice I would yield to would be that forced by the points of our bayonets." He felt that proposing an armistice was "madness" given the successes of the armies in the field, and that if a general were to call for a halt to fighting when the enemy was crumbling on the battlefield, he would be "cashiered for cowardice and treachery." Rather than talking peace, he counseled that the armies at the front should be reinforced and the matter pressed vigorously. In addition—alluding to the election, but not being able as a professional officer to make a political statement—he said, "let the people, at the proper time, speak in such tones as will guarantee to the soldiers in the field a full and hearty support."[23]

Custer's father disapproved of his son's newfound views, but Custer was steadfast. He wrote a lengthy defense of his opinion, noting that he had risked his life on scores of battlefields and that the time for conciliation had long passed. "Since the South has chosen to submit our troubles to the arbitrament of the sword," he stated flatly, "let the sword decide the contest."[24]

"Have all the bloodshed you want!"

AFTER THE ROUT OF THE Confederates at Sailor's Creek, Sheridan wired to Grant, "If the thing is pressed I think Lee will surrender." Word came back shortly from President Lincoln: "Let the thing be pressed."

Sheridan sent his troops west, harrying the Confederate southern flanks and attempting to cut off their retreat. He had already chosen Appomattox as the point where he would swing in front of Lee and try to block him in. Custer was in the van, on the leading edge of the pursuit, taking prisoners and raiding supplies as he went. He surrounded himself with a personal guard of men who had shown particular valor, bearing the dozens of Confederate battle standards he had captured, each banner signifying the destruction of a regiment. After Sailor's Creek, Custer's honor guard carried thirty-one Rebel flags. By Appomattox they would have forty. Ahead of them flew the red-and-blue silk banner with crossed sabers, Custer's personal standard, which Libbie had sewn for him. For the next several days, Custer was a blur of activity, always at the front, engaging the enemy in wild, disorganized charges. Colonel Newhall of Sheridan's staff described Custer's approach to warfare during the pursuit as "Custer against the world."[25]

On April 8, Custer's men cut the Lynchburg Pike and Appomattox Road, Lee's last escape routes. Sheridan recalled the mood that evening: "To-morrow was to end our troubles in all reasonable probability, but it was thought necessary that the infantry should arrive, in order to doubly insure the result.... Happiness was in every heart. Our long and weary labors were about to close; our dangers soon to end. There was no sleep; there had been but little for the previous eight or nine days."[26]

Morale was not as high among the Confederates. Brigadier General Edward Porter Alexander wrote that "day by day, death, wounds and capture were robbing us heavily of comrades with whom we had been through many campaigns, and now our army was reduced to little more than a collection of fragments, out of food and nearly out of ammunition."[27] But those who remained were still willing to do their duty and to follow Robert E. Lee as long as he would lead them.

On the evening of April 8, Lee called his corps commanders, Longstreet, Gordon and Fitz Lee, to a final council of war. Earlier that morning, General Pendleton had suggested that the time had come to think of surrender, but Lee had been unequivocal. "Oh, no, I trust that it has not come to that," he said. "General, we have yet too many bold men to think of laying down our arms." But the events of the afternoon had raised the question again. The four men spoke long about their options, few as they were—the possibility of breaking through Sheridan's force to the west, to head for Lynchburg, or perhaps Roanoke, maybe to link up with General Johnston's army to the south. It seemed a hopeless task; but they were unanimous in deciding to give it a try. Longstreet was particularly adamant that they fight to the last. Fitz Lee and Gordon would strike Sheridan with Longstreet guarding the rear, then the entire army would push through west. When General Gordon asked where he should stop to make camp, Lee replied, "the Tennessee line."[28]

The Confederate attack launched at daybreak. Gordon's infantry advanced and pushed back the Union forces, briefly clearing the road to Lynchburg. Some of Fitz Lee's cavalry had in fact broken through. But soon Union reinforcements reached the field and vigorously pressed the counterattack. Among the Union defenders was Second Lieutenant Samuel Hall Kinney, Second Artillery, the second West Pointer appointed from Utah and the Goat of the Class of 1864. He had fought in the siege of Petersburg since graduation. Kinney pulled back with the rest of the Union center, but his fighting withdrawal helped stabilize the line. Major General George Crook, fifth from the bottom in the Class of 1852, singled Kinney out for gallantry, and he received two brevet promotions for his heroic actions that day.

Lee sent word to Gordon asking his prognosis. Gordon replied, "Tell General Lee I have fought my corps to a frazzle, and I fear I can do nothing unless I am heavily supported by Longstreet's corps." Lee realized that continued resistance was futile. He turned to his staff officer Lieutenant Colonel Charles S. Venable and said, "There is nothing left me but to go and see General Grant, and I had rather die a thousand deaths." Meanwhile, George Pickett, who was with Longstreet's reserve forces, penned a note to his wife, Sallie:

> Lee's surrender is imminent. It is finished. Through the suggestion of their commanding officers as many of the men as desire are permitted to cut through and join Johnston's army. . . . It is finished! Ah, my beloved division! Thousands of them have gone to their eternal home, having given up their lives for the cause they knew to be just. The others, alas, heartbroken, crushed in spirit, are left to mourn its loss. Well, it is practically all over now. We have poured out our blood and suffered untold hardships and privations all in vain. And now, well, *I* must not forget, either, that God reigns. Life is given us for the performance of duty, and

duty performed is happiness. It is finished—the suffering, the horrors, the anguish of these last hours of struggle.[29]

Lee summoned Longstreet and met him wearing a new uniform, sword, sash and golden spurs. Lee told him that the situation was hopeless and he was going to see Grant. Longstreet concurred grudgingly, but added that if Grant would not give them adequate terms, Lee should come back and fight it out.

Longstreet returned to his command. Fighting raged all along the front, and shortly after he left Lee, Longstreet saw Gordon's corps weakening. He began to form a last defense, the final battle line of the Army of Northern Virginia. Alexander deployed his remaining batteries. Pickett brought forward the scraps of his division and whatever stragglers had joined him during the retreat. Henry Heth took the left flank, assembling the remnants of A. P. Hill's corps. Hill had been killed at Petersburg, April 2, 1865—the last Confederate officer who had graduated from West Point to die in the war. Men dutifully fell into their places in the ranks, but this was not the army it once was. "Their faces were haggard, their step slow and unsteady," a member of McGowan's South Carolina brigade wrote. "Bare skeletons of the old organizations remained, and those tottered along at wide intervals."[30]

Lee belatedly requested that word be sent to call a truce, and Captain Robert Sims rode forward to the Union lines with an improvised white flag. The firing slowed, then ceased. Presently Longstreet saw a delegation approaching, composed of Major R. W. Hunter of General Gordon's staff, Major Wade Hampton Gibbes, who had fired the signal shot at Fort Sumter, and a Union officer with "flaxen locks flowing over his shoulders." The latter came up to Longstreet and declared brusquely, "In the name of General Sheridan I demand the unconditional surrender of this army!"

Longstreet looked evenly at young Custer, who was breathless, flushed, wearing his odd uniform, and showing precious little respect. Longstreet had not fought and sacrificed for the Confederacy for four years to see it all end like this. He drew himself up and spoke sternly.

"I am not the commander of the army," Longstreet said, "and do not have the authority to give its surrender. Nor do you have the right to request it. And you are within the lines of the enemy without authority, addressing a superior officer, and in disrespect to General Grant as well as myself; and even if I was the commander of the army I would not receive the message of General Sheridan."

Custer grew indignant. "If you do not surrender you will be responsible for the bloodshed to follow," he barked.

"Go ahead and have all the bloodshed you want!" Longstreet snapped back, and began to give orders to his staff to bring up divisions that he knew, but maybe Custer did not, existed on paper only. Custer grew more conciliatory and suggested that further fighting was not necessary, that it would be a pity to continue.

"As you are now more reasonable," Longstreet replied, "I will say that General Lee has gone to meet General Grant, and it is for them to determine the future of the armies."

Custer, chastened yet satisfied, left.[31] He was escorted back to his lines, where he sought out Alexander Pennington, by then one of his brigade commanders."Let's go and see if we can find Cowan," Custer said.

Colonel Robert V. Cowan of North Carolina, formerly of the Class of 1863, was the tallest man in the Corps in Custer's day. He had been found deficient in English and mathematics in his plebe year and sent home. During the war, Cowan was the commander of the 33rd North Carolina in Wilcox's division. His regiment had been in all the major battles in the East since Antietam. He was wounded at Chancellorsville and participated in Pickett's Charge under Trimble. Custer and Pennington went to the truce line on a stream bank and asked one of the Confederate pickets to ask for Colonel Cowan. Presently a rider approached; it was Cowan, who, seeing his friends, jumped his mount across the ditch.

"Hello, you damned red-headed rebel!" Custer said, and the three began laughing. Their reunion was shortly interrupted by their fellow Academy graduate Lieutenant Colonel Orville E. Babcock, third in the Class of May 1861, and then on Grant's staff. Babcock was a member of the party escorting Lee to the McLean House. Lee had seen the small get-together as he crossed a bridge 150 yards away, and sent Babcock to tell them he did not want fraternization. The classmates separated, and Babcock rode back to Lee, who was soon out of sight, on his way to meet with General Grant.[32] Then the group reconvened.

Custer had made a habit of seeking out his Rebel West Point comrades during the war. One of his roommates and a close friend was Pierce Manning Butler Young, from Cartersville, Georgia.[33] Morris Schaff called him "a very good fighter, and a very good hearted fellow."[34] He was also an unreconstructed southern partisan. During the John Brown trial in 1859, Young said he wished that he had a sword as long as from West Point to Newburgh, so he could cut off every Yankee head in a row. One day in the winter of 1860–61, while the cadets discussed current events, he made a prediction:

> Custer, my boy, we're going to have a war. It's no use talking; I see it coming.... Now let me prophesy what will happen to you and me. You will go home, and your abolition governor will probably make you colonel of a cavalry regiment. I will go down to Georgia and ask Governor Brown to give me a cavalry regiment. And who knows but we may move against each other during the war. You will probably get the advantage of us in the first few engagements as your side will be rich and powerful, while we will be poor and weak. Your regiment will be armed with the best of weapons, the sharpest of sabres; mine will have only shotguns and scythe blades; but for all that we'll get the best of the fight in the end, because we will fight for a principle, a cause, while you will fight only to perpetuate the abuse of power.[35]

Young resigned in March 1861, and as predicted he went to Georgia and became a well-regarded lieutenant colonel in the Cobb Legion Cavalry in Stuart's corps.[36] He never literally crossed swords with Custer, though they saw each other through binoculars across the battlefield, and their men sometimes came to blows. However, they once shared some meals in Virginia. On October 19, 1863, Young was having breakfast at Hunton House in Buckland Mills, attended by the two daughters of the house. J. E. B. Stuart had just left, advising Young not to be long because the enemy were in pursuit. Shortly thereafter a shell exploded nearby, and an aide called out, "They are coming, sir, we must hurry or be cut off from the bridge." Young and his men evacuated, and shortly Custer rode up. He politely asked the young women if they would make him breakfast. They said that breakfast was already on the table, that General Young had just left it.

"Very well, ladies," Custer said, "Young and I are friends. I will take his breakfast." After entertaining the sisters with tales of his and Young's exploits at West Point, Custer requested that in the evening they make some dinner for him and his staff, since they would most likely be in the vicinity all day. They did so, but as often happened in cavalry engagements, the fortunes of war shifted and Custer was forced to pull back. He paused at the gate during his retreat and said, "Ladies, give Young my compliments and tell him I took his breakfast. He can take my dinner."[37] Young became the youngest Confederate major general and ended the war serving in North Carolina against Sherman.

Fellow cavalryman Thomas Rosser had encountered Custer more frequently. He had been at Aldie in 1863 and noted Custer's bravery. Rosser had faced off with him at Gettysburg, after which he was promoted to brigadier general. The two fought each other periodically afterwards, and Kidd wrote that "Custer and Rosser, in war and peace, were animated by the same knightly spirit."[38] As with Young, they left each other messages in places they knew they would occupy in turn.

In September 1864, Rosser and James Dearing were instrumental in executing the great "Beef Raid" outside Petersburg, in which 2,500 head of Union cattle were boldly rustled from Grant's rear and herded back to Confederate lines. It was a huge embarrassment to the Union commander and gave the Rebels some much-needed provender. Sheridan was peeved at Rosser's successes, which had earned him the nickname "Savior of the Valley." Sheridan ordered the cavalry commander General Alfred Torbert to "either give Rosser a drubbing . . . or get whipped himself."[39]

Custer had his chance on October 9 at Tom's Brook. Jubal Early's supply train was strung out along a road and guarded by Rosser's cavalry. Rosser had drawn his men up in a defensive line, and Custer assembled his men for the attack. When his forces were in place, Custer rode slowly out in front of his command, towards Rosser's troops. He stopped several yards away from his men, doffed his wide-brimmed hat and saluted Rosser with a flourish. He then returned to his troops and immediately ordered the charge. His men swept forward against the Confederate line, which was quickly broken by the bold maneuver. Custer routed Rosser's men and captured his headquarters and baggage, many pieces of artillery and scores of wagons. Rebel cavalry were pushed back twenty-six miles to Woodstock, Virginia, and the battle soon became known as "the Woodstock Races." Jubal Early, commenting on the performance of Rosser's "Laurel Brigade," said tartly, "The laurel is a running vine."

The next day Custer delighted his staff by appearing before them in Rosser's captured uniform.[40] Rosser paid Custer back December 22 near Harrisonburg, Virginia. Custer was moving south and had vowed to spend his Christmas at Lynchburg. Rosser made a predawn attack on his division as it advanced, driving it back and taking forty prisoners.

Stephen Dodson Ramseur of North Carolina, who had graduated sixteenth in 1860, joined the Confederacy and became Lee's youngest brigadier. Schaff described him as "dark eyed, stern [and] dignified," and he was known as an uncompromising fighter.[41] He saw most of the

battles in the East and performed bravely at Gettysburg.[42] He was a
division commander under Jubal Early at Cedar Creek, where he fell
severely wounded. Custer was in the pursuit after the battle and overtook a Confederate ambulance. Private James Sweeney of the First Vermont Cavalry asked who was in the back, and a voice said, "Do not tell
him."

"Is that you, Ramseur?" Custer said. He had Ramseur sent to
Sheridan's headquarters to be tended to, and there he saw his fellow
West Pointers Wesley Merritt, Henry DuPont and Alexander Penning-
ton. The group had last gathered in 1860 just before graduation when
Custer and Rosser arranged a going-away party at Benny's for Ramseur,
Merritt, Pennington and Wade Hampton Gibbes. Ramseur died the
next morning.[43]

Souvenirs

GRANT AND LEE HAD CONVENED in Wilmer McLean's parlor to discuss terms. When the meeting concluded Babcock opened the door,
glanced out at the assembled, placed his forage cap on one finger and
twirled it around, "and nodded ... as if to say, 'It's all settled.' "[44] Lee
emerged, and the Union officers sprang to attention and saluted. Lee
mounted his horse and with great dignity rode back up the road to his
lines. The men around the McLean House soon heard the cheering of
the Confederate soldiers as Lee returned to his army.

Custer, Pennington and Cowan had been reminiscing for some
time when they heard the cheers erupt from the Confederate lines.
Robert E. Lee had returned. They watched as he rode back down the
road.

"As he proceeded into his lines there was a grand rush toward him
of his men and officers," Pennington wrote, "cheering, I suppose, to
give him heart, for he seemed very much depressed as he rode by us."[45]
Custer and Pennington bade Cowan goodbye and left, heading back
towards the town.

The hunt for memorabilia of the event had begun immediately.
The apple tree under which Lee waited before being escorted to Grant
was "literally dug up by the roots," according to Alexander, "and not a
chip of it was left" after twenty-four hours. Years later Alexander regretted not getting a piece for himself, since he said he could not find a
shard as big as a toothpick. One enterprising Texan made a walking
stick for the trek back home.[46] Reporter E. A. Paul, present at the

surrender, noted, "before twenty-four hours I doubt if there is much of the [McLean] house left—such a penchant have Americans for trophies."[47]

Wilmer McLean had moved to Appomattox from Manassas to escape the war, and now not only had the war found him but Union officers were crowding his house, some offering him money for his household furnishings, others simply pocketing souvenirs. General Edward O. C. Ord (USMA 1839) paid forty dollars for the marble-topped table at which Lee sat. He later offered it to Grant's wife, who declined the honor, saying it should go to Ord's wife. Custer's chief of staff, Lieutenant Colonel Edward Whitaker, bought the chair Lee sat in, and Colonel Henry Capehart bought the one used by Grant. The story was that McLean had refused to sell the chairs, throwing to the floor the money that was pressed into his hands. The colonels forced their way out with the chairs anyway, and later a cavalryman appeared, handed McLean a ten-dollar bill, and rode off.[48] Horace Porter on Grant's staff had loaned his pencil to Lee, and retrieved it afterwards. Sheridan obtained the inkstand, and paid twenty dollars for the small wooden table on which Grant wrote the terms of the surrender. When Custer soon arrived at McLean House, Sheridan presented him the table to give to Libbie, along with a note saying,

> My Dear Madam: I respectfully present to you the small writing-table on which the conditions for the surrender of the Confederate Army of Northern Virginia was written by Lt.-General Grant, and permit me to say, madam, that there is scarcely an individual who has contributed more to bring about this desirable result than your very gallant husband.

Sheridan also gave Custer the white linen dishtowel that Sims had carried to the Union lines as a flag of truce.[49] Custer left McLean House holding the table slung over his back; Horace Porter said he looked like Atlas carrying the world. Custer gaily rode off balancing the table on his head. It had been a magnificent day. That night Colonel Whitaker found Custer sitting alone on a log before a campfire, upright, a cup of coffee in his hand, sound asleep.

The Reunion

O N THE MORNING OF APRIL 10 in occupied Richmond, John Beauchamp Jones, late clerk of the Confederate War Department, noted in his diary, "Raining. I was startled in bed by the sound of cannon from the new southside fort again. I suppose another hundred guns were fired; and I learn this morning that the Federals declare, and most people believe, that Lee really has surrendered his army—if not indeed all the armies." Later that day he wrote, "It is true!... This army was the pride, the hope, the prop of the Confederate cause.... All is lost!"[1]

News of Lee's surrender had traveled quickly back to Washington. The War Department issued an official bulletin at 9:00 P.M. on April 9, and celebration broke out immediately. "The tidings were spread over the country during the night, and the nation seems delirious with joy," Navy Secretary Gideon Welles wrote in his diary. "Guns are firing, bells ringing, flags flying, men laughing, children cheering; all, all are jubilant."[2] Charles Mason, the federal commissioner of patents—who had graduated first in the Class of 1829, just ahead of Lee, but left the service after two years—noted, "At dawn of day cannon were booming to celebrate the surrender of Lee and his army which has doubtless taken place. I am not taken by surprise. I hope this will end the war. It can be made to do so if we are reasonable."[3] Crowds serenaded President Lincoln throughout the day, and at one point he asked a band to play "Dixie," calling it "one of the best tunes I ever heard" and adding that he considered it a lawful prize of war.[4] The *New York Times* ran the Grant/Lee correspondence on the front page under the headline, "Hang Out Your Banners: UNION: Victory! Peace!"

The news reached the Military Academy midmorning on April 10. "It was a glorious day for us all," plebe Paul Dahlgren wrote. "Routine as usual throughout the day—studies—descriptive geometry, but no French on account of the good news.... The whole Union is perfectly wild with excitement."[5] The second class marched to Battery Knox on the riverbank, where they fired a 200-gun salute, answered by another 200 guns fired by the first class at Fort Putnam. That evening after taps, Dahlgren and five friends had a "candy hash" until midnight. Then, seeking further merriment, he and his classmate William T. Ditch went to the gym and removed all the wooden horses and iron men (the targets used for cavalry drills) and set them up in formation on the Area. The officer of the day, brevet Lieutenant Colonel Francis U. Farquhar, second in Custer's class and a veteran of many battles, came upon them in the act, and they immediately fled, with Farquhar in pursuit. "So close did he press on me," Dahlgren wrote, "that I lost both shoes." He and Ditch were not caught, but they did not get back to barracks until two in the morning.

April 10 dawned drizzly at Appomattox, a slow, cold morning, with the two armies in contact but no longer anticipating bloodshed. It was a relief from the confusion of the last week, particularly among Lee's men, who could relax for the first time since leaving the lines around Richmond and Petersburg. Confederate artillery commander Edward Porter Alexander said that April 10 "seemed to usher in a new life in a new world. We had lived through the war. There was nobody trying to shoot us, and nobody for us to shoot at. Our guns were gone, our country was gone, our very entity seemed to be destroyed. We were no longer soldiers, and had no orders to obey, nothing to do, and nowhere to go."[6] Custer's redheaded Rebel friend Robert V. Cowan could not bear it. An order had come down from General James H. Lane that Cowan make the formal surrender of the regiment. Cowan and Major J. A. Weston read the order sitting under a large oak tree. After reading it, Cowan jumped to his feet, his eyes flashing.

"I won't surrender," he declared, and turned to Weston. "Major Weston, take charge of the regiment." Then he mounted his horse and rode off. Weston never saw Cowan again.[7]

For most others, April 10 was an opportunity to meet the men they had been fighting, and in some cases renew old friendships. "Morning dawned," wrote brevet Major General Joshua Chamberlain, the Union hero of Little Round Top at Gettysburg, "and then, in spite of all attempts to restrain it, came the visiting and sightseeing. Our camp was full of callers before we were up." They came to "see what we were really made of, and what we had left for trade." The visiting and bartering grew to the point that "it looked like a county fair, including the cattle show."[8] William Swinton of the *New York Times* wrote, "Hostile devisement gave place to mutual helpfulness, and the victors shared their rations with the famished vanquished. In that supreme moment these men knew and respected each other."[9]

Lee was in his tent that morning, editing General Order No. 9, his farewell to the men who had fought under his leadership these last four years. He assured them that he agreed to the terms of surrender not out of lack of confidence in them, but "feeling that valor and devotion could accomplish nothing that could compensate for the loss that would have attended the continuance of the contest, I determined to avoid the useless sacrifice of those whose past services have endeared them to their countrymen."[10] At nine o'clock he was informed that General Grant had ridden to see him, but had been stopped by Confederate pickets. Lee quickly rode out to meet him. The two raised their hats and shook hands. Grant was accompanied by several of his senior officers, and his adjutant general, Seth Williams (USMA 1842), a brevetted Mexican War veteran who had returned to West Point to serve as adjutant when Lee was Superintendent. John Gibbon, who saw the two meet, said "there was nothing in Gen. Lee's face, as he gravely and courteously received [Williams], to indicate that he had ever seen him before."[11] The two commanders discussed the details of the surrender, the times and places the Confederate forces would lay down their arms. They agreed to a six-man commission to set the details. Grant also asked Lee to prevail upon President Davis to end the war, but Lee declined.

After the half-hour meeting concluded and Grant headed back, some of the officers in Grant's party requested permission of General Lee to visit friends in the Army of Northern Virginia. Lee granted the request, and Sheridan, Wesley Merritt, John Gibbon and Rufus Ingalls rode back into the Confederate encampment. Most of the Confederate generals had gathered at the Clover Hill Tavern, and the group soon returned with Pickett, Heth and Cadmus Wilcox, who had been best man at Grant's wedding. He was mounted on a half-starved gray horse, wearing a long thick overcoat. Gibbon asked him if he felt cold.

"It's all I have," Wilcox replied, opening the coat to show he was wearing only a shirt beneath. "That's all the baggage I have left," he said, pointing to his saddle bags. He turned to Sheridan, who had been a member of his company when he was a cadet captain. "You have captured all the balance, and you can't have that until you capture me!"[12] Heth, on the other hand, was resplendent in his finest uniform; he explained that when he realized all the baggage trains were being captured, he changed into his best clothes rather than let them fall into enemy hands.

The Confederate generals Gordon and Pendleton, who were members of the peace commission, joined in. They passed Longstreet and Lee on the way back and Longstreet went with the throng. They rode back to the McLean House, where the commissioners were set to meet. Grant recalled,

> Here the officers of both armies came in great numbers, and seemed to enjoy the meeting as much as though they had been friends separated for a long time while fighting battles under the same flag. For the time being it looked very much as if all thought of the war had escaped their minds.

Gibbon was talking to Colonel Theodore Lyman of Meade's staff when someone said, "How are you, Ted?" It was W. H. F. "Rooney" Lee, General Lee's second son, who had been a classmate of Lyman's at Harvard.[13] Meade, meanwhile, had ridden back to see his old friend Robert E. Lee, who seemed at first not to recognize him.

"What are you doing with all that gray in your beard?" Lee said.

"As to that," Meade replied, "you have a great deal to do with it."[14]

The six-man commission met in the same room where Grant and Lee had discussed the surrender, though it had been denuded of furniture by memorabilia seekers. Gibbon devised a practical solution to the lack of a writing surface. "Mindful of the prize I had seen Custer carrying off and having no surplus $20 gold pieces to pay out," he wrote, "it occurred to me to secure a cheaper table." The final agreement was signed on the pine camp table he had used through the war.[15] He later had a clerk sand down the top and inscribe the date and the use to which it had been put.

Longstreet went inside the house and was heading for the meeting when he heard someone call out his nickname, "Pete!" Grant stood and came forward, extending his hand. Longstreet had not seen Grant since a few years before the war. One day in St. Louis he ran into Captain Edmunds B. Holloway (USMA 1843), who had fought beside him in Mexico in the Eighth Infantry, along with some other friends, and they had repaired to the Planters House hotel to reminisce and play some hands of brag.[16] They were a hand short for the game, and presently noticed a shabbily dressed civilian come into the hotel, whom they recognized as Ulysses Grant. His forays into the business world had not gone well and he was in financial difficulties. The classmates coaxed him into playing a few hands and reliving old times. The next day Longstreet again ran into Grant, who had been waiting for him near

Planters House. Grant placed a five-dollar gold piece into his hand, repayment for a debt dating back to the war with Mexico. Longstreet tried to give the coin back, arguing that since he was still in uniform he did not need the extra money, and Grant could probably put it to better use. "You must take it," Grant said. "I cannot live with anything in my possession that is not mine." Longstreet, seeing Grant's determination, and not wishing to embarrass his friend, who was in obvious need, took the coin, shook his hand, and they parted.

Now, at McLean House, Grant took his friend's hand again. "Pete," he said, "let us have another game of brag, to recall the days that were so pleasant." They spoke awhile, and Grant gave Longstreet a much-appreciated cigar. Longstreet had to leave for the meeting, and they parted. Longstreet later recalled, "Great God! I thought to myself, how my heart swells out to such magnanimous touch of humanity. Why do men fight who were born to be brothers?"[17]

Henry Heth then stopped by, and Grant shook his hand and invited him to sit.

"Heth, do you remember when we were last together?"

"In St. Louis, I believe in 1852."

"Yes, and do you remember how near I came to breaking my neck and yours?" Grant was referring to the time he ran his buggy into a cow, throwing them both onto the street.

"Yes," Heth replied. "It would have made little difference, as far as history is concerned, if you had broken my neck, and now, as our troubles are at an end, I am glad that you got through safely [too]; but, Grant, during the past three years I have wished a thousand times you had broken your neck when you ran into that cow." Grant laughed, and reminded Heth that afterwards when they went to Jefferson Barracks not one of the officers present offered them a drink. The chatted for half an hour "about old times, kissing the beautiful girls in the army, about Mexico," but not about their recent war. When they concluded, Heth remarked that Grant had not offered him a drink either. Grant laughed again, and when Heth returned to his headquarters he found that two gallons of good whiskey had been delivered with Grant's compliments.[18]

George Pickett was outside with Ingalls and others, talking about their days in the Old Army. "Rufe" Ingalls was a member of the Class of 1843 and had been Grant's roommate their plebe year. In 1859 he was quartermaster general for Oregon, Pickett's hunting partner who supplied his men during the Pig War. In July 1862 he was appointed chief quartermaster, Army of the Potomac, and remained in that post throughout the rest of the war, rising to the rank of brevet major general. He had been present in the room with Grant and Lee the day before. Gibbon relates a story in which three major generals, one Union and two Confederate, were discussing what might become of them. The Union officer suggested that Lincoln "was known to be an exceedingly kind hearted man" and would probably not "feel disposed to pursue any very extreme course."

One of the Confederates turned to the other. "George," he said, "do you know what I would do were I in Uncle Abe's place, and had in my power fellows who have been doing what you and I have for four years?"

"No," replied George. "What would you do?"

He pointed to the nearby oak trees. "From every limb of these trees I should hang a rebel," he said. "I hope he won't do it though!"[19]

Custer started the day early. Like Lee, he issued a General Order to the Soldiers of the Third Cavalry Division: "With profound gratitude towards the God of Battles, by whose blessings our enemies have been humbled, and our arms rendered triumphant," he began, and went on to praise their courage, noting they had "never lost a gun, never lost a color, . . . never been defeated, . . . [and] captured every piece of artillery which the enemy has dared open up on you." He hoped that these actions had finally brought the war to a close. "Speaking for my self alone," he concluded, "when the war is ended and the task of the historian begins, when those deeds of daring which have rendered the name and fame of the Third Cavalry Division imperishable are inscribed upon the bright pages of our country's history, I only ask that my name be written as that of the Commander of the Third Cavalry Division."

Custer's tone was characteristically bombastic, but he bore the Rebel armies no ill will, and was eager to see more of his Confederate friends. He learned that Gimlet Lea was nearby; Lea had been in the center of the Rebel line, commanding Robert D. Johnston's brigade. Custer sent him a hamper full of food, providing lunch for his staff. Later the two had dinner together.

When Fitzhugh Lee ran into Custer, the two laughed, grabbed each other, wrestled themselves to the ground and rolled about like boys. Fitz had been with the group that had broken through, but instead of making good his escape he had come loping into the town. Gibbon first saw him on horseback near McLean House, looking uneasy. "Hello Fitz!" he said. "Get off and come in!" Lee did so, looking relieved. That evening Gibbon sent a note to his wife:

> I am seated at the table writing to you whilst before me lying on the floor is General Fitzhugh Lee who came in tonight and gave himself up as a

prisoner, and has just been paroled. He is cheerful as ever, sends his kindest regards to you, and his name on what he calls "the best kind of green back."

Fitz had taken out a five-dollar Confederate note and written on it, "For Mrs. Gibbon, with the compliments of Fitz Lee." He said to Gibbon, "Send that to your wife and tell her it's the last cent I have in the world. Tell her I am the last of the Mohicans."[20]

Thomas Rosser was in Fitz Lee's command, but was not present at Appomattox. He had fought bravely to the end. Rosser won the battle of High Bridge for the Confederate forces on April 7, the last battle they would ever win. In the process, he captured General David M. Gregg. The Confederate brigadier general James Dearing of Virginia was mortally wounded at that battle; he was a former member of the Class of 1862 who had resigned before graduating, the last person who had attended West Point to die in the war. The morning of April 9, Rosser had led a successful charge through Union lines to the Lynchburg Road, and escaped the Federal noose. There was some debate over whether his forces were included in Lee's capitulation, and ultimately it was decided that only those in the immediate vicinity could be considered surrendered. Rosser stayed briefly in the field, then retired to his wife's house near Hanover Court House in central Virginia. A few weeks later in May, while en route from Richmond to Washington, Custer made a detour to pay Rosser a visit. He pulled up his command and sent a note to the door:

> Dear Friend,
> The house is surrounded. You can't get away. Come on out and surrender yourself.
>   Regards,
>   G. A. C.

Rosser's war was over, but his friendship with Custer had survived.

Custer had arrived in Richmond on April 12. He had received word that Libbie was there, and he rode through the night to see her. She came to Richmond on the president's gunboat the *Baltimore* on April 10, having left Washington that morning. She spent the next two nights at the former Confederate White House, in Jeff Davis's bed. Custer walked into the room unexpectedly the morning of the 12th and said, "So, after all these years of fighting, you beat me into Richmond."[21] Custer was soon given honorary promotions to brevet brigadier general and brevet major general of the Regular Army. Everyone hailed him as a hero; as he rode through the Virginia countryside even southerners flocked to the roadside to see him, waving handkerchiefs and clapping.[22] His life was one of unbounded joy. George Custer was twenty-five years old.

Years after Appomattox, Morris Schaff wrote, "My heart leaps with pride, for on that day two West Point men met, with more at stake than has ever fallen to the lot of two Americans to decide.... These two West Point men knew the ideals of their old Alma Mater, they knew each other as only graduates of that institution know each other, and they met on the plane of that common knowledge.... The greatest hour that has ever come in the march of our country's years was on that April day, when Grant and Lee shaped the terms at Appomattox."[23] And the next day as well, when the healing began, when the United States was reborn; when classmates and brothers came together reunited in purpose and friendship, and gave new meaning to a verse of the traditional West Point graduation song:

> Though broken the tie that here bound us awhile,
> > Fate ne'er shall dissever the few
> Of a true-hearted band who, linked hand in hand,
> > Changed together the gray for the blue.

Laurence S. Baker's Final Ride

FOR LAURENCE S. BAKER, the Goat of the Class of 1851, the war was still on. He had not heard the news from Appomattox; when he finally did, it did not matter.[24]

Like Custer, Baker was building a stellar career after Gettysburg. Three weeks after the battle, when Robert E. Lee reorganized his cavalry into seven brigades in two divisions, Baker was promoted to brigadier general and took command of the First through Fifth North Carolina Cavalry regiments. Wade Hampton became Baker's division commander. Fitz Lee led the other division, with J. E. B. Stuart as the cavalry corps commander. Baker saw a great deal of action in the weeks after the battle as the respective cavalry forces sparred in the upper Shenandoah. At the Battle of Brandy Station on July 31, 1863, Baker helped drive back the Union forces, and was praised in the after-action report by General Lee. Unfortunately, Baker was wounded in the right arm and permanently disabled. Judged unfit for field duty, he was sent back to North Carolina, where, like Pickett, he was given a command in the rear areas, organizing the defense of the state from raids by Union forces established on the coast. He personally saw combat at least once, in

March 1865 when he led a regiment of green reservists under command of General D. H. Hill against a Union force at Kinston. They
were given their baptism of fire and hurt severely, but Hill noted that
Baker "did all that could be done to inspire his troops."

In the spring of 1865, Baker commanded the Second Military
District of North Carolina. His headquarters was at Weldon, an important railroad junction on the south bank of the Roanoke River, near the
border with Virginia. On paper, Baker was the head of four districts,
each commanded by a colonel with a regiment and an artillery battery.
But in fact he had fewer than three hundred infantry, an artillery battery with 125 men, twenty horsemen, and around seventy-five others—
stragglers, furloughed prisoners and convalescents. Baker's command
was between two arms of a strategic pincer movement. Grant sat outside Richmond to the north. Sherman's army was moving up from South
Carolina, pushing General Joseph E. Johnston (USMA 1829) in front
of him. In February, Johnston took over command of the remaining
Confederate forces in the area with hopes of buying time for the Confederacy, and perhaps uniting with Lee's forces at Danville, should a
retreat from Richmond become necessary. There was even talk of Lee
abandoning the capital temporarily to join Johnston in crushing Sherman, then swinging back to face Grant. But the grand strategic movement was never a serious possibility, and while Lee suffered Grant's
siege, Johnston fought a series of delaying actions against Sherman. On
the night of March 21, Johnston pulled back from Bentonville after a
two-day fight with Sherman's forces, withdrawing towards Raleigh. Sherman had linked up with Union forces advancing west from New Bern,
placing most of eastern North Carolina in Union hands. Rather than
pursue Johnston west, Sherman decided to link up with Grant's forces
by moving due north. His first objective was Weldon.

Baker was ordered to hold the city, to keep railroad contact open
between the Army of Northern Virginia and the Carolinas, and to collect and ship supplies to units that needed them, or at least to any unit
they could reach. The area was a central supply point for armies to the
north and south, and Baker had to hold it as long as he could, while
repelling raids from the ubiquitous Union cavalry. It was a tall order.
Baker had few men and much ground to cover. He spent his days riding circuit through his command, checking on conditions, gathering
intelligence, and executing his duty as best he could. For weeks the
command was "in a state of constant activity and excitement," wrote
Private James M. Mullen, Company A, 13th North Carolina Artillery.
Baker's movements were hampered by Union raiders who tore up the

train tracks, and his twenty-man cavalry force did not have a decent well-fed horse between them. The situation was summed up in a communiqué he sent to his commander, Braxton Bragg, on March 31, 1865: "Enemy at Spring Green, four miles from Fort Branch, 500 infantry, five pieces artillery, and some cavalry. Sixteen boats reported landing troops at Williamston. I have nothing to meet them."

On April 6, Baker was informed of the evacuation of Richmond. He was told to send all supplies and rolling stock down the rail lines west, and to "hold yourself promptly prepared to withdraw and save your forces as soon as you shall find them placed in jeopardy by the approach of the enemy from any direction." The next day, Johnston ordered Baker to remove all trains, artillery, supplies and anything of military value to the south side of the Roanoke, and for the bridge over the river to be burned. "Give your officer instructions to destroy any rolling-stock which would otherwise fall into enemy's hands," Johnston wrote, "railroad people cannot be trusted for this." These orders were echoes of the rolling tragedy that was befalling Lee's army in Virginia, though Baker did not know the full extent of the catastrophe. He began to ready his force for the expected redeployment and the hard fight ahead. He did not burn the bridge immediately but kept it open to allow his men to forage on both sides of the river. Old, broken-down horses were given away and fresh horses and mules impressed from the countryside. Small boats along the river were collected and destroyed to hamper Union crossings. Seeing these preparations, the townspeople began to panic. "The scenes in and around Weldon these few days were heart-rending," Private Mullen wrote. "The citizens in the country around, especially on the north side of the river, became panic-stricken, and came crowding into the town, imagining the direst calamities would befall them upon withdrawal of the troops."[25] On April 12, three days after Lee's surrender, orders arrived to abandon Weldon and to link up with Johnston near Raleigh. Baker's men departed, but the general stayed behind, burning the bridge as his last act.

The 13th opened with a hard rain, and the small force struggled forward over muddy, rutted, flooding roads. After a few hours they began to encounter small groups of stragglers heading east. One of them, a "weary-looking, foot-sore and jaded young fellow in the dirty and tattered uniform of a Lieutenant of Infantry," told them that he was heading home, that Lee had surrendered, and that the entire Army of Northern Virginia was paroled. Baker's men were incredulous. The last they had heard, Lee was still entrenched around Petersburg; they knew nothing of what had happened since the line broke April 2. The battery commander, Captain Lewis H. Webb, in temporary command while General Baker was coming up from Weldon, placed the officer and a few others under arrest until they could verify this fantastic story. It did not take long. Soon the roads were filled with parolees from the Army of Northern Virginia, North Carolinians returning to their homes. "I shall never forget the feeling that came over me when fully impressed with the fact that Lee had surrendered," Mullen wrote. "Until then I had never permitted myself to doubt the ultimate success of the Confederacy; and, as to the Army of Northern Virginia, I believed that under 'Marse Robert' it was simply invincible."[26] As the truth sank in and the hopes of the men in the small command buckled, further dismal news reached them. Sherman had taken Raleigh, and Johnston was retreating further inland towards Greensboro. That evening they made camp near Warrenton Junction, tired, hungry and dispirited.

The following morning, General Matthew W. Ransom rode up. He had been at Appomattox and confirmed the reported surrender beyond doubt. Webb was uncertain what course of action to pursue, and General Ransom, as a parolee, was loath to give advice. But he invited Webb to join him at the house of his brother, Major General Robert Ransom (USMA 1850), who lived nearby and was on sick leave, and thus still an active combatant. They went there and held a conference. Robert Ransom did not see the point in continuing. He believed the best course would be to send a flag of truce to Sherman and ask for terms. Hearing this, Matthew sprang to his feet, arm raised and eyes flashing, and said, "Never, under no consideration surrender until there is a force in your front sufficient to compel it!" He then caught himself. "But what am I doing," he continued. "I am a paroled prisoner and have no right to speak in this manner." He left the room.

Webb returned to find Baker's command in a state of near-mutiny, breaking into food stores and other supplies. Webb put a stop to the disorder, assembled the men, and told them what he had learned. He entreated them to hold together until they could ascertain whether in fact Sherman was in Raleigh. They advanced to the nearby railhead at Ridgeway, commandeered a steam engine and sent a small party south down the tracks towards Raleigh armed with Enfield rifles. They were under the command of Lieutenant John M. Blount of the Tenth North Carolina Artillery. Webb decided that if the reconnaissance team returned before General Baker, he would be forced to make a decision one way or another.

A few hours later, Baker finally caught up with his column. He also had heard the news of Lee's surrender and the rumors of Sherman in Raleigh. Lieutenant Blount returned at eight in the evening and confirmed the latter; he had gone to within twelve miles of the city and collected enough information to be certain. Sherman had changed his plans when he heard Lee had abandoned Richmond. He made directly for Raleigh and Johnston, seeking to keep him from moving north to link up with Lee. He marched from Goldsboro on April 10 and entered Raleigh on April 13, finding Johnston gone. Lieutenant Blount had seen nothing of Johnston's troops, but it was said they were still in the field and ready to fight.

That night Baker convened a council with his officers to discuss what they should do. Only a few wanted to keep fighting. Most wanted to send a flag of truce to Sherman and request the same terms that were granted Lee's army. Baker took a vote and the truce party won. On the morning of April 15, Baker assembled his command and made an announcement. They were to abandon the artillery and all unnecessary supplies, strip themselves down to as light a force as possible, use the artillery and transportation animals for mounts, and move around Sherman's rear to join Johnston's command. The officers were dumbstruck. Baker had completely disregarded their counsel. He wanted to keep on fighting. It was of course his prerogative as the commanding general, but this seemed an impossible mission. Nothing was done that day, and on the 16th, some of Baker's officers went to him urging that they send the flag of truce, arguing that the men would not follow his scheme. Baker listened politely, then said he would take it under advisement and announce his final plan at the evening assembly.

At sundown, Baker convened his command. He announced that he intended to head south and try to fight his way to Johnston. He would take with him any who chose to follow him; the rest could leave for home if they so desired. But he would not surrender. He asked the volunteers to come forward. About fifty men did so. They were given the best mounts and Enfield rifles. After midnight, Baker led his small force south by the light of a three-quarter moon.

Baker's band spent the next several days winding through the countryside of Franklin, Johnston and Wake counties, sticking to the forests and trails, evading Union patrols and seeking Johnston's army. They passed through the town of Louisburg, and the townspeople turned out enthusiastically, cheering on the one-armed general and his tattered crew of horsemen, pressing flowers and food into their hands. Private Mullen, who went with the general, said that the morale of the little band was not high; they believed they were on a "wild goose chase," but their sense of duty overcame any objections to the practicality of the venture. "Nothing but a sense of duty, and a reluctance to turn back as long as we were called upon to go forward, carried us on."[27]

On April 18 they halted at Earpsboro, due east of Raleigh and well behind Sherman's lines, where Baker was told that Johnston had surrendered. Baker was crestfallen. Their last chance to continue fighting had faded. He felt at that point that they had done all they could do and that further resistance would be futile. The next day Baker sent a flag of truce to Raleigh to tender his surrender—and later heard a rumor that Lincoln had been assassinated. Sherman replied that Johnston had not capitulated but that an armistice was declared, and they had agreed on general terms that "will, in my judgment, terminate the war and provide for all the armies of the Confederacy." Sherman offered Baker the same provisions as Grant had offered Lee. "If you wish to disperse your men let them deposit their arms and let a field officer sign a parole for them and send me the list. Any officer may safely come in, as hostilities are suspended."[28]

Later that day, Baker issued General Order No. 25 of the Second Military District of North Carolina, announcing that it had become necessary to disband his command. He thanked the men who had "remained with him to the last," and who would "carry with them the proud consciousness of having done their whole duty to their country, and of having laid down their arms only when they could be of no further service to the cause to which their lives were so freely devoted." He sent individual notes to each officer with personal thanks to each man under his command who "courageously remained at the post until the last moment, and who have not feared to trust their safety to him in the hour of adversity." Baker said that he had done all he could for these brave men, "and only surrenders them when it would be folly and madness to continue longer in arms." The officers and men were "allowed to return to their homes, where they will remain peaceably and quietly, until called forth again by the proper authorities." Following the terms originally set by Grant, the men were allowed to take their horses with them as private property to assist in reestablishing their farms. Mullen said, "the horse was the best pay I ever received from the Confederacy."[29] Thus ended the military career of the Goat of 1851. Laurence S. Baker rode home, his head unbowed, his honor intact.

CHARLES DEMPSEY

O N THE MORNING OF APRIL 15, 1865, five days after the cele-bration of Lee's surrender at Appomattox, the cadets were heading for mathematics recitation when academic duties were suspended. Someone handed Cadet Charles King a copy of the *New York Herald,* and he mounted a sundial pedestal on the edge of the Plain. The Corps gathered round, and despite orders to disperse, lis-tened as King read the account of President Lincoln's assassination. "When I finished," King recalled, "I had one glance at that little sea of upturned faces, white, awe stricken, and most of them quivering."[1]

Lincoln had been a popular wartime leader among the cadets and faculty. He had made a brief, unannounced visit to the Academy to see General Scott in 1862, the first presidential visit since before Thayer's tenure as Superintendent. Lincoln had enjoyed substantial support for reelection in 1864 among the students and faculty, even over West Point graduate George McClellan. Dennis Hart Mahan said that with the exception of Fremont, "the country has never had a name before it less qualified for the Presidential office than General McClellan."[2] Cadet Robert Fletcher, probably speaking for many of his peers, especially the younger ones, wrote in his diary, "If McClellan is elected the gov-ernment goes to ruin, and will surrender to armed traitors who are now almost crushed. If the Republican Party triumphs all is well."[3] After Lincoln won, he noted, "Now may loyal hearts rejoice and traitors tremble."[4]

But after guiding the country through four years of civil strife, Lincoln had been struck down in the very hour of victory. "With hearts overwhelmed at the sudden and awful calamity we retired to our quar-ters," Cadet Fletcher noted in his diary later that afternoon. "It seems hard to realize that it can be true, and yet the fearful fact is only too certain.... A Nation has lost its great head, now in its day of rejoicing, and joy is turned to sorrow profound."[5] A 13-gun salute was fired on the morning of Lincoln's funeral and a 36-gun salute in the evening, with a gun fired every half hour between. On the evening of April 25 the Corps ferried across the river to Garrison, formed along the railroad track and presented arms to honor the president as his funeral train wended its way west.

Six weeks later the mood of optimism was restored. Thousands traveled to West Point in anticipation of the graduation ceremony for the Class of 1865. Cozzen's and Roe's hotels were filled. Family, friends and spectators swarmed the Academy. Young women collected spoony buttons, and according to one observer "nearly every cadet has lost a majority of his coat buttons, and the ladies are heavy with the stolen metal."[6] But the Corps of Cadets was only one of the attractions this year. People had also come to see the returning graduates who had delivered the Union, and in particular the guest of honor, Ulysses S. Grant. "Gen. Grant is a short man," Cadet Fletcher recorded in his diary, "rather well built, small eyes; light eyebrows, dark brown hair, and light brown beard, well trimmed. He is dressed very plainly, having on a double-breasted regulation coat, and a plain black hat (slouched)."[7] Scores of people orbited Grant, seeking to shake his hand. After observing the parade and meeting with dignitaries, Grant rode by the barracks in a carriage and the cadets flooded outside to cheer him.

Grant came to West Point frequently in the years after the war, and any visit from him was the cause of much fussing by the officers of the Academy and the many visitors to the Point. "All those who had not seen him flocked to Roe's to catch a glimpse of the great chieftain who had led our armies to frequent and certain victory," read one report. "And those who had seen him only watched him the more, because he was there to be gazed at."[8] During his 1868 visit he looked fatigued, with the presidential campaign looming. He did not "present that hearty, florid appearance which distinguished him in the field while in front of Petersburg."[9] The reserved Grant accepted the ceremonies, engagements and reverence with aplomb, but one observer remarked, "we can see that the General would be very much obliged to the officers and Professors if they would let him kill time as he pleases."[10]

William T. Sherman also visited West Point in June 1865, and like Grant would be a regular visitor in years to come. Sherman became commanding general of the U.S. Army after Grant's inauguration in 1869, and when he handed out diplomas that summer, the finely groomed and polished cadets offered a contrast to the general in his plain black pants, unadorned and unbuttoned service coat, and old felt hat. A reporter described Sherman's arrival in 1873:

> The General came unaccompanied and in the plainest of civilian attire, his wide-brimmed straw hat and smooth-shaven face giving him more the appearance of a peaceful farmer than a stern soldier. To one who last saw the General in the dark days of the great rebellion it was curious to see how entirely has passed away that grim expression in his eyes and inflexible and severe bearing that were so well known then; and it was a very pleasant-mannered and jovial-looking gentleman who shook hands with and greeted his friends on the piazza at the hotel, where the President [Grant] and the Secretary of War sat.[11]

A grand hop was held the night before the 1865 graduation, and a "jollier crowd I never saw," one observer wrote. "The Cadets are simply ecstatic in their bliss. Released from [Superintendent George W.] Cullum, freed from professors, unbothered by regulations, unawed by demerits, caring nothing more for lessons . . . they one and all seem forgetful of the past, regardless of the future, but bent and determined on enjoying the present to the very full." Those at the head and middle of the class were "exhilarated by the prospect of a good standing, while those further down were consoled by the reflection that somebody must eat the burnt gingerbread." But even the bottom 50 percent "are sent to the Army with culture far superior to that afforded ninety-nine men out of every hundred in civil life."[12]

One of those in the bottom half was Cadet Charles A. Dempsey of Alexandria, Virginia, where his father was consul for the Danish and Norwegian governments. Dempsey had come to West Point in September 1861, only months after Virginia seceded, and he chose to remain loyal to the Union. Upon entering, he was sent to report to yearling Cadet William Ennis, then in camp. "I got in the guard house in less than fifteen minutes after I reported to him," he recalled. As with the rest of his class, Dempsey's tenure at West Point bridged the war. Most arrived in the summer of 1861, before the Battle of Bull Run, and they watched the entire course of the conflict from the Academy. Like Charles N. Warner, the cadets at first expected the war to be over quickly, but each year the classes preceding them graduated and went off to the front. They followed the events, studied the battles, and prepared to play their parts, nourished on tales of valor in letters from older grads who went to the fight, from faculty who had seen action and from incoming students who were themselves veterans. By late 1864, the war was still grinding on and the Class of 1865 thought they might play a part. However, the conflict ended a few weeks before they got their chance, and the Class of 1865 began their professional careers in a very different world.

Charles Dempsey was a case in point. He graduated as the Goat of 1865, was commissioned into the Seventeenth Infantry and sent to Texas. Frontier life was still difficult; Dempsey found himself in command of his company at one point when the captain and first lieutenant both died of yellow fever. But over the years he saw little action. He participated in the Nez Perce War in 1877 and the Red Cloud uprising in 1890–91, operations that were a far cry from the massive campaigns of the Civil War. Moreover, absent large-scale warfare there were no more meteoric career rises. Dempsey made captain twenty-three years after leaving West Point, and major ten years after that. He was notified of the latter promotion the day his forces landed at Siboney, Cuba, in 1898. He was awarded the Silver Star for his actions in the San Juan campaign. The Spanish-American War had its tonic effect on promotions and Dempsey was raised to lieutenant colonel a year later. Then he served a year in the Philippines operating against nationalist insurgents. He retired from active service in 1901, but periodically was active with the National Guard, and was brought back to active duty during the First World War, finally retiring as a brigadier general.

William Ennis, who had put Dempsey in the guardhouse his first day at West Point, died in 1938 as the oldest surviving West Point graduate, and passed the mantle on to Dempsey, who died in Richmond on June 4, 1941, on the eve of America's entry into the Second World War. He was ninety-six years old, the last of the Civil War–era graduates. Dempsey had lived through an age in which the United States and the world had seen dramatic changes. In his adult lifetime, America was transformed from a young nation riven by bloody internal strife to a country standing on the edge of a titanic global conflict that would lead to its establishment as the preeminent world power.[13] The era of the musket and the cavalry saber had given way to the machine gun, the tank, the aircraft carrier and the strategic bomber. Dempsey had witnessed a revolutionary series of military transformations. He could not have imagined what the future held when he walked into the cadet encampment of 1861.

The Civil War became West Point's central defining event. In its scope, its drama, and the sacrifice of the fraternity of the graduates, it was without parallel. Its battles have been studied at the Academy ever since, with a durability far greater than the engagements in Mexico or many of the wars that followed. The wartime cadets and those who came to the Academy in the years after the conflict benefited from an influx of faculty tempered by fire. During the war, paroled officers awaiting exchange of another of equal rank taught there, as did wounded officers convalescing. After the war, the faculty were predominately veterans, graduates who had tested the worth of their education on the proving grounds of war. When they lectured on tactics, they did so with the authenticity of men who had led in battle. But they taught all manner of courses as well. Tully McCrea, who had stood in Ziegler's Grove against Pickett's Charge, returned as an assistant professor of geography, history and ethics, and later mathematics. He taught with fellow artilleryman Edward R. Warner, Charles Warner's cousin. Joseph P. Farley, who as a cadet had shaken hands with the teary-eyed Fitz Lee as he left West Point for the Confederacy, served in the war as an ordnance officer and came back as a professor of drawing.

But most prominent among the returnees was Emory Upton. Ten years after his bloody fight with fellow cadet Wade Hampton Gibbes, Upton returned as the Commandant of Cadets. He had graduated eighth in the Class of May 1861, and served heroically in the war, rising to the rank of brevet major general. Around 1867 the manual of infantry tactics he had developed based on his combat experiences was accepted as Army doctrine.[14] Upton was thirty-one years old when he became Commandant, and was expected to be a leading light in the military intelligentsia. Cadet Ernest Albert Garlington of the Class of 1876 described him as "not handsome of feature, had a good presence, soldierly bearing, a very strong face expressing character and will power."[15] He served under Superintendent Thomas H. Ruger, third in the Class of 1854, veteran of many battles including Gettysburg, and recently military governor of Georgia. Garlington said Ruger had all the characteristics of a red-hot poker except the warmth.

Cadets also came to West Point fresh from the war. President Lincoln had a habit of recommending soldiers for appointment. Veterans were eligible for admission up to age twenty-four rather than the standard twenty-two. Over seventy-five veterans matriculated at the Academy between 1862 and 1868, and of them forty-five graduated. One of the graduates was John H. Gifford, who fought for a year as a private in the Sixteenth Indiana Volunteers before entering USMA on July 1, 1863. He graduated as the Goat of 1867 and served in the Second Artillery for thirty-one years. But the Academy was open only to Union veterans. On June 8, 1866, by General Order No. 56, men who had served in the Confederate army were banned from admission.

Cadets from the South returned slowly to West Point. Some records indicate a few dozen appointments from southern states in the latter years of the war, but these were unused southern slots given to the abovementioned Union veterans or to children of Federal soldiers fighting at the front. It was not until several years into Reconstruction that native-born southerners were first welcomed back, and the rebuilding process was uneven. In February 1870, a scandal broke when Benjamin Franklin Whittemore, a member of Congress from South Carolina, was censured for selling cadetships.[16] Whittemore was a carpetbagger from New England who had been a chaplain with the 53rd Massachusetts Infantry during the war. He admitted that he took the money—in the range of $300 to $500—ostensibly for the relief of the needy in his district, or to defray campaign expenses. It was rumored that other politicians in southern states were doing the same, and that it was a common practice. Whittemore resigned from Congress in February only hours before his certain expulsion. He was reelected in a special election in June, but Congress refused to seat him. Illinois congressman and former general John A. "Black Jack" Logan Sr., who had not attended the Academy, led the charge. Whittemore finally relented, and his seat was taken on December 12, 1870, by former slave Joseph H. Rainey, the first African American to serve in Congress.

Georgian Ernest Garlington was one of the first genuine postwar southern cadets. In the spring of 1872 he boarded a train for the ride north, passing through the war-damaged countryside. "Signs of the Civil War were in evidence throughout Virginia," he recalled. "Lines of entrenchments paralleled and crossed the railroad as we approached Petersburg, Richmond and Fredericksburg; redoubts crowned the hills; young pine trees were growing in and marking the lines." Garlington was not certain how he would be received at the Academy, but when he arrived, New Hampshire–born Professor Henry L. Kendrick (USMA 1835) put an arm around his shoulders and said, "I am delighted to see you young gentlemen of the South coming back here."[17]

But while southern cadets were again welcome at West Point, prior graduates who had fought for the Confederacy were not. The spirit of magnanimity that had animated Grant and other Union officers at Appomattox was not at first in evidence at the Academy. Superintendent George W. Cullum (1864–66) set the tone. He harbored a smoldering animosity towards the Confederate officers, and when he compiled his invaluable masterwork, the *Biographical Register of the Officers and Graduates of the United States Military Academy,* he refused to include the wartime records of those who had served the

South. Initially he even refused to note the fact of their resignation; and so serious was his objection to their actions that he left instructions in his will that future versions of his work never be altered, in order to forestall what in his view would be honoring treason if the Rebels were included. In November 1865, Cullum's old classmate Francis Henney Smith, the founder and superintendent of the Virginia Military Institute, wrote to him requesting permission to visit the post on business:

> War sometimes separates those who were once friends. Civil War always does. But peace has its healing and restoring qualities. I am now here on business connected with the Institution to which 26 years of my life have been devoted, and my purpose is, in this connection, to visit West Point. I have deemed it proper to advise you of this intention. . . . I remain, General, very truly, F. H. S.[18]

Cullum replied immediately:

> We were once attached friends, and now I have no unkind feeling towards you; but as the Superintendent of the U.S. Military Academy, I cannot at present, with a proper sense of the responsibilities of my position, receive one who is at the head of an institution which has done so much for the injury of my country.[19]

Smith responded in turn:

> I regret that your view of your public duty closes the door of the Academy to me. I shall return to Virginia, with no unkind feeling towards you, but pained that I have to add your letter to the record of losses, which war has brought upon our common country.[20]

Four years later, Cullum helped organize the USMA Association of Graduates. Not every graduate thought such an organization was necessary; George Custer wrote a detailed seven-page letter opposing the AOG, thinking it demeaning to the institution—why have an association to promote fraternity among a group of individuals who already cherished their alma mater? But most graduates approved the idea, and the first annual meeting of the AOG was held in New York City in 1870. It soon became traditional to meet at the Academy around graduation time. Initially the southern graduates were in an ambiguous position, either not feeling welcome or refusing to join while Reconstruction was ongoing and their citizenship status was in question. But at the 1874 meeting, at the initiative of the chairman, Professor Charles Davies (USMA 1815), one of the oldest living graduates, the members voted to invite members of all classes and all sections of the country to come to West Point the following year to commemorate the centenary of the Battle of Bunker Hill, in order to forge anew their brotherhood and abiding love of country. Davies, an old and beloved figure, invoked his own passing to bring people together, saying that amongst his last thoughts he would like to have the "consciousness, that union, fraternity, peace and mutual regard, had reached the heart and would regulate the life of every graduate of this institution."[21]

Francis H. Smith received a letter from his old friend Professor Davies inviting him to the reunion and saying he wanted a "strong delegation of Southern graduates." In Smith's account: "I told him, in reply, that I could not go. I was an 'unpardoned rebel,' with the 'rope' around my neck, and unless I could sit down with my old comrades as an equal, I had better not go at all." Davies assured Smith that he would be welcome and invited him to his house in Fishkill before the reunion so he could go as his guest.

Over one hundred alumni showed up for the 1875 reunion, which was held in the Little Chapel. Among them were seven of the dozen former Confederates then members of the AOG. Joseph Hooker was the highest ranking among the Union officers, and the Confederate contingent was led by James Longstreet. The Corps of Cadets lined up on the Plain in front of the Superintendent's house, and the graduates marched out led by Superintendent Ruger and Commandant Upton as the band played "When Johnny Comes Marching Home." Colonel Ruger welcomed the alumni and suggested they greet each other as a gesture of friendship and reconciliation. James Longstreet immediately turned to Horace Porter (USMA 1860), who had been awarded the Medal of Honor for his role fighting Longstreet at Chickamauga in 1863. He had last seen Porter at Appomattox. The two shook hands, prompting others to do the same.

At the formal meeting of the association, Charles Davies gave the address, welcoming all who came, and stating, "from this auspicious day all the graduates from this institution will recognize each other as friends. Henceforth and forever we have one flag, one country, one destiny."[22] He hearkened back to the unity of the time of the Revolution. Looking back over his own sixty-year association with West Point, he saw "a silver cord of tender recollections—of personal ties, and of dear friendships, which even the rude shock of civil war has not broken." After the speech, the graduates had dinner in the cadet mess, where according to an observer "there was a large attendance and it was a merry affair." Smith and Cullum, who had been avoiding each other, met on the stoop and were prevailed upon to shake hands, symbolizing that "the widest part of the breach" had finally been bridged.[23]

Despite his frail health, Professor Davies accompanied Francis H. Smith back to Virginia and spent two weeks with him at VMI, attending the annual examination of the cadets and renewing old ties. When he left, he said it was the happiest two weeks of his life. He passed away at his home in Fishkill the following year, on September 17, 1876.

The Passing of the Greats

DAVIES WAS ONE OF SEVERAL WHO had helped establish the enduring character of the Academy who passed into history in the decade and a half after the Civil War. General Joseph G. Swift, the first West Point graduate, died on July 23, 1865, at age eighty-two. He was honored at the Academy with an eleven-gun salute while the flags flew at half-staff. His grandson, Joseph Gardner Swift, was then a cadet in the Class of 1866.[24] Lieutenant General Winfield Scott, who had dominated the American military imagination for most of the nineteenth century, died quietly on May 29, 1866, a few weeks short of his eightieth birthday. Cadet Fletcher noted in his diary that he had recently seen Scott on post, "and although very old and decrepid [sic], yet he walked around easily by means of a staff."[25] The next day, the very religious cadet related a story of Scott's dying request: "Just before [Scott] died a servant came in and he asked him about his horse and told him to take good care of him. It was but a few moments after that he expired. It is dreadful to think of an immortal soul thus passing into eternity."[26]

The general's funeral was held a few days later. Fifteen thousand people turned out to honor him, among them Vice President Foster, Speaker of the House Schuyler Colfax, numerous senators and congressmen, Mayor Hoffman of New York, Generals Grant, Meade, Butterfield, Howard, Meigs and Ingalls, Admiral Farragut, Colonel Van Buren and "Poet" Patten. Representatives of the government of Mexico also attended. There was an open casket observation in the chapel, where Scott lay beneath pillars wrapped with the banners his army had captured in Mexico. He was dressed in a plain black suit, shrouded in an American flag. The observers went by slowly, silently, some simply curious, others holding back tears. Some had served with Scott as far back as the War of 1812. At 11:30 the Corps of Cadets filed through, passing on both sides of the bier. After the formal services, the coffin was sealed and the procession moved slowly and circuitously to the cemetery, led by General Meade. The coffin was lowered into the earth to the reverberations of signal guns echoing off the steep hillsides. The cadets fired a salute, and the crowds slowly dispersed to attend the many receptions being held in Scott's honor. While not a graduate of the Academy, Scott had been among its most influential supporters, and his "fixed opinion" of the value of West Point in securing victory over Mexico became part of the "poop" memorized by all incoming cadets.[27]

Sylvanus Thayer, the father of the Academy, died September 7, 1872, at the age of eighty-seven. At the time of his death, he was the oldest living graduate of West Point, and one of only a few remaining who had graduated from the "Old Academy" before his tenure as Superintendent. The Thayer system had survived in part through the efforts of his handpicked intellectual successor, Dennis Hart Mahan. But sadly, Thayer survived his heir. On September 17, 1871, plebe Hugh Lenox Scott, Class of 1876, wrote to his mother, "[Saturday] afternoon there was a report that Old Prof Mahan had committed suicide. He was coming up from New York on the *Mary Powell* and was sitting on a deck talking to a lady and got up, walked across the boat and off into the water where the paddle wheel struck his head and that was the last seen or heard of him."[28] Rumor had it that Mahan was "insane on account of another book he had been writing."

Mahan had been professor of engineering for forty years, a noted author and world authority on military and civil engineering. The several generations of officers who fought the Civil War passed through his classroom. He had faithfully maintained the Thayer system, and its durability probably owes as much to his doggedness as to Thayer's innovation. In the years before his death, Mahan had been a reliable roadblock to reform—of the curriculum, of the Academy's focus, of anything that would reduce the importance of engineering—all of which the Board of Visitors resented. In June 1871, the board recommended his retirement. The decision haunted him for weeks, and he had been depressed for most of the summer. He resolved to go to New York to consult with a physician and friend, and a servant girl was sent along to watch him. At one point he removed his jacket and put it on the back of a chair and said, "There, if you want something to watch, watch that." He then took off his shoes, placed them near the chair, turned and walked right off the ship. Small boats were lowered to save him, but he had vanished into the river.

The young girl got off in Yonkers and reported the terrible news. Mahan's body later washed ashore near Haverstraw. A few days afterward, Cadet Scott attended Mahan's funeral, which he described as "the most splendid thing I ever saw." The battalion marched to the chapel, and Mahan's rose-covered coffin was brought in, carried by soldiers, followed by his sons, Lieutenant Frederick A. Mahan, who like his father taught on the engineering faculty, and Commander Alfred Thayer Mahan, later the president of the Naval War College and pre-eminent American theorist of naval power. After the chapel ceremony, the battalion formed and marched "reverse arms" in a procession, the flag-draped casket on a caisson pulled by four large black horses, followed by the officers, faculty, friends and other mourners. "The band was playing the most splendid music I ever heard," Scott wrote, "so solemn it almost made me cry."

Tavern owner Benjamin Havens outlived them all. By the 1870s he had become an American legend. West Pointers had taken their distinctive drinking song with them to war, and around campfires both north and south Benny's name echoed in the night sky. The Civil War transformed "Benny Havens' Oh!" from a seditious West Point hymn to a camp song enjoyed by the whole Army. It was sung by officers and men who had never met Benny or been anywhere near his establishment. It was published as sheet music, and sung in parlors and taverns across the country. New verses were invented, numbering over a hundred, many never written down and soon forgotten. After the war, mustered-out soldiers being shipped up the Hudson back to their homes in New York, New England and the West serenaded old Benny as they passed by his house in Highland Falls. Lucius O'Brien's song remained an emblematic tune for over a century.

Benny Havens passed away on May 29, 1877, at the age of ninety-one. He was buried in the Highland Union Cemetery near the Academy whose cadets he had served, literally and figuratively, for over sixty years. At the graduation ceremony of 1890, in his final address to the Corps of Cadets on the fiftieth anniversary of his graduation, General Sherman, then retired, disparaged both the song and the man; he said that Benny Havens was "a rascal," and not worthy of remembrance. "Take a higher type than Benny Havens to think of and to sing of," he counseled.[29] Nevertheless, during his career Old Ben had helped shape the image of West Point and touched the lives of those cadets who found succor at his hospitable establishment. A death notice in the *Brooklyn Eagle* stated, "He knew all the 'boys' who had been at the Academy . . . and he was a great favorite with them, none of whom forget him, or ever will."[30] The Class of 1877, soon to graduate, added the following verses to the song that bore his name:

Now the soften'd summer winds
   Come whisp'ring to us low,
That he of whom we oft have sung,
   Death's hand lies on his brow.

For ninety years his eyes shone out,
   And friendly smiles met friend and foe.
But now the spark of life's gone out;
   No more we'll greet our "Havens, Oh."

These granite hills surrounding us,
   By sun all set aglow,
May they be guardian angels
   To our Benny Havens, Oh![31]

John Jordan Crittenden

I N MOST RESPECTS LIFE AT WEST POINT after the war was much like it had always been. The "rocks and hills and waters remain, and the new faces who come up seem like a mere repetition of those who went before them," an observer wrote. "You may take a photograph of that cadet on guard, and he is an exact copy of the one who stood there forty years before."[1] The rhythm of life had not changed. Exams arrived as always in January and June. In between came classes, study, drill and the boards. In the summer, there was the monotony of encampment and the thrill of furlough. There were the constant inspections, the threat of demerits and walking post, cadet hash and blowing post. They celebrated the same holidays, with the addition of Thanksgiving as decreed by President Lincoln. In the years after the war, the tradition of the Hundredth Night began, and the graduation ceremony took on its recognizable features. There were dances, grand balls, and encounters on Flirtation Walk. The young women who visited the Academy were still rapacious: one cadet on guard duty during encampment at the end of the summer season found himself face to face with a mob clamoring to visit the cadets in their tents. He wrote his mother, "If you had ever seen your son in front of a bloodthirsty crowd of women with an innocent musket in his hand and endeavoring to keep them at bay you would have trembled for his safety. The men I could keep off with my bayonet but the women I either had to let them pass or [be] smothered."[2]

There were of course some changes. The weapons the cadets trained with were updated. The trees planted in decades past had grown to maturity. There were several new buildings and improvements to some of the older ones—for example, in 1867 the barracks got steam heat. Many enhancements to cadet life came from an unexpected quarter. George W. Cullum became the Superintendent in 1864, bringing with him his well-earned reputation for stuffiness. But to the surprise and delight of the Corps, he began to ease some of the Academy's regulations governing cadet behavior. Under Cullum the library was opened on weekdays, allowing cadets a chance to read the daily papers and follow the course of the war. Food could be sent from home and cadets were allowed to receive and spend money. They were permitted off post during free time on weekends, which removed the subversiveness and mystery of "running it," taking away also much of the fun. Cullum tolerated smoking, and pipes and tobacco were issued to cadets. "Tobacco was created for some good and it is in such cases as this, when exhausted nature requires help, that it may be used as the very best of medicines and friends," plebe Charles W. Larned wrote his disapproving mother. He noted, however, that the tobacco issued to the cadets was very weak.[3]

Superintendent Cullum also opened a bowling alley in the fall of 1864, which soon became decidedly popular. (The idea had been suggested by Secretary of War Jefferson Davis in 1856.) But cadet creativity did Cullum one better. In the winter of 1865–66, some members of the second class decided to start a billiard club. They ordered a table from Griffiths in New York, paying $150 and having the table delivered to Garrison. After it arrived, the cadets borrowed a sled and smuggled the five-by-eight-foot table across the frozen river in the dead of night and secured it in the barracks. They had previously bribed one of the men who tended to the furnace to procure the use of one of the coal bins. They boarded up the windows, thoroughly cleaned the bin, and outfitted it with "a card-table, some half a dozen chairs, four kerosene-oil lamps with reflectors, a supply of pictures on the walls, pipes and tobacco, a keg of cider, a barrel of crackers, and a whole cheese—all the surroundings of a 'first-class' billiard-room, excepting spirituous liquors."[4] They mounted the table on two sawhorses and commenced to play.

The billiard club soon grew to about thirty members, each paying ten dollars in dues. The authorities soon learned of its existence when the check used to pay Griffiths somehow came into the possession of the Academy treasurer. The Tacs began periodic searches to uncover the mystery but never thought to look in a coal bin. Their failure to discover the whereabouts of the billiard table became a source of embarrassment to the Tacs, and of silent delight to the Corps. The cadets enjoyed their secret for almost a year until several club members were spotted entering the bin after hours, to the sound of clacking billiard balls. The Tacs set up for a major raid the following evening, but they themselves had been seen the night before. To deny the officers some of the satisfaction of their victory, the cadets tidied the room and left a note on the table addressed to the "Tactical Officers on Duty at the Academy":

> We, the members of the Billiard Club of the First Class of the Corps of Cadets, desire to present this billiard-table, with all its appurtenances, to the officers on duty at West Point, as a slight token of our gratitude to them, for the generous courtesy displayed by them towards us, in allowing us for so long a time to enjoy the privilege of the Club. The table was manufactured in New York nearly a year ago, and the room furnished at our own expense. From that time to the present we have freely indulged in this amusement, and we cannot but feel most grateful to you for your generous forbearance.

Cadet Oliver E. Wood commented, "One can imagine their mortification at being so completely outwitted by the cadets." No one was ever disciplined for the billiard club escapade. The table was later presented to the Superintendent's wife.[5]

Despite the noteworthy performance of West Point graduates in the Civil War, reformers still found reasons to criticize the manner in which the Academy pursued its educational mission. In 1867 the traditional entrance exam, which had focused on reading, writing and arithmetic, was expanded to include grammar, geography and history. In 1872 the Board of Visitors again criticized the education level of new cadets, concluding that the entrance exam was insufficiently rigorous. This led to even harder exams at the Academy, and competitive examinations in congressional districts for the chance at nomination, a practice that had some drawbacks. John C. Tidball, who served briefly as Commandant of Cadets during the war, noted that this method went "far towards insuring the appointment of those best prepared for the entrance examination, but not necessarily of those making the best officers. In such examinations youthful phenomena and hot-house plants are apt to carry off the prizes, while those of slower but of more sturdy development are left behind." As the education reformers saw it, there was no place for a Stonewall Jackson, a Philip Sheridan or a George Custer—even though recent history had demonstrated convincingly that there was no necessary correlation between classroom achievement and success on the battlefield. They sought instead to homogenize the Corps, to produce a single idealized type of officer, if possible starting from the day of arrival. This postwar emphasis on uniformity had a predictable effect. An observer of the graduation of the Class of 1871 noted that "while the class of graduates this season may be fairly esteemed as excellent and well-educated gentlemen, there are few of the old-time characters bristling with genius and *esprit du corps*."[6]

Ernest A. Garlington of the Class of 1876 was an example of a cadet whose academic record did not augur greatness. He had gotten in trouble a few times—"quite a long line of tragedies," he called it, even though his demerits were only in double digits—but he was in enough difficulty in the fall of his plebe year to lower his class standing significantly. "The result was inevitable," he wrote. "I hit a toboggan slide, as it were, and wound up in the 'Immortals' in both philosophy and chemistry, and began to pile up demerits."[7] He felt that he was being excessively punished, began to neglect his studies, and considered resignation. Lieutenant William P. Duvall, one of his math instructors, noted Garlington's sagging morale and walked with him one evening, giving him a pep talk in a very kindly way and assuring him that matters were not as dire as they seemed. "I surely appreciated this disinterested act of Lieutenant Duvall," Garlington recalled, "and will always remember it as a red letter day of my cadet life."[8]

By June 1875, all but four Immortals of Garlington's class were "found," but he was not among them. He improved his class standing somewhat, but still found ways to get into trouble. He estimated that he walked an "extra" every Saturday of his firstie year, and probably left still owing some time. He graduated 30th of 48, below what he knew he was capable of. He noted, however, that had he graduated higher in his class, he would probably not have been assigned to the Seventh Cavalry (since the regiment had not been his first choice), "would not have received my promotion as First Lieutenant within ten days after graduation; would not have had the fortunate opportunity for service with that gallant regiment and make the record I did make."[9] Garlington was awarded the Medal of Honor in 1893 for distinguished gallantry at the Battle of Wounded Knee in 1890, where he was severely injured.[10] Eventually he rose to the rank of brigadier general and was inspector general of the Army. Several of his classmates who graduated behind him also had distinguished careers. James Parker, who was just after Garlington, received the Medal of Honor for repulsing a night attack by insurgents in the Philippines in 1899. J. C. Gresham, 34th in the class, was another Medal of Honor recipient, also at Wounded Knee, fighting alongside Garlington. George Andrews, who graduated 35th, became adjutant general of the U.S. Army. Hugh Lenox Scott, the cadet who nearly cried at Professor Mahan's funeral, had originally been a member of the Class of 1875 but was suspended for a year after his yearling year; he graduated 36th, and returned as Superintendent of the Military Academy, 1906–10, and Army chief of staff, 1914–17.

Cadet discipline and hazing had grown worse during the war. Cadet Robert Fletcher arrived from his home in New York City during encampment in August 1864 and "[g]ot a reception which very much astonished me. Was surrounded by a crowd, hooted at, yelled at, questioned, and quizzed in every possible manner."[11] Three days later he wrote home, "If I had known, before I came here, what I should have to undergoe [sic], I do not think that I should have desired to come but now that I have been here, experienced the hardships and begun to get used to them, I should not like to leave."[12] The newcomers—called plebes, animals, conditional beasts—were treated to questions such as, "What's the cosine of Noah's Ark?" "How long is a piece of string?" "What is the height of impossibility?" Even enforcing the basics, such as coming to attention, was an opportunity for degradation. Garlington wrote, "I don't think it possible to devise a bodily attitude calculated to lower one more in one's own esteem than the position a 'Plebe' ... was made to assume in my time: head thrown back as far as possible; chin drawn in to the neck; chest thrown out; back curved; belly drawn up under the ribs; arms extended down the sides; little fingers along the trouser seam and palms of hands turned square to the front." He said that having to march in this position only increased the "mortification and humiliation."[13]

On January 15, 1864, at the suggestion of General Joseph G. Totten, the secretary of war ordered that before they would be eligible for furlough, cadets must sign a certificate stating that they have not in any way "interfered with, or molested, harassed or injured new cadets."[14] There was understandable resistance to this order, which cadets felt trespassed on a traditional privilege. In the summer encampment of 1865, the yearling class passed around a paper on which they pledged, on their honor, to yank plebes. All but three members of the class signed it. The general belief was that such a show of solidarity would force the leadership not to enforce the new furlough policy. Cadet Fletcher regretted signing the paper, which he said he did "hastily, and without reflection." Still, he noted, "the plebes are, without doubt, getting very fast, being impertinent, and not ready to work well in the opinion of our class generally."[15] Unfortunately for the yearlings, the plan did not work. That December, Fletcher noted ruefully, "the indications are that no member of the third class except Savage [who had not signed the pledge] can get a [Christmas] leave on account of the 'yanking' business last summer."[16] They were, however, allowed a month's furlough the following summer.

Hazing became a major issue after the war in part because of West Point's increased public profile. Events that in the past would have been of no interest to anyone not on the post became national news. Case in point: an 1871 letter from a plebe published in Chicago and reprinted nationwide, which began, "The romance of West Point has already worn off with me, and nothing but stern reality remains, and stern enough it is I assure you."[17] His complaints included having to do calisthenics, having to sleep on a blanket, rising at 5 A.M., drill before breakfast, and various types of harmless hazing (e.g. yanking and standing on his toes for an extended period). It was the kind of gripe letter that had been written by plebes for fifty years. These complaints were tame compared to everyday life in the Academy's early days, when living conditions were much more harsh, and when plebes standing watch were authorized—even encouraged—to bayonet devilers. "Anyone coming here expecting to have a nice time will find he was woefully mistaken before he has been here a week," the plebe continued. "I will have to get even on someone for the rough treatment I am receiving now. . . . Just as long as this Academy exists, so long will the cadets cut up, devil the 'Plebes' &c. You may put them on their honor not to devil new-comers, but they will get round their oaths—not breaking them strictly speaking—by many warps and prevarications."[18]

Yanking continued to be a popular prank; Fletcher had heard of a cadet being yanked forty or fifty times in one night. He noted that the cadet officers were largely indifferent to the pranks, having gone through the ritual themselves in their time. Fletcher himself avoided a great deal of hazing by arriving only days before the move into the barracks. There were the usual indignities, such as being constantly called to attention, being criticized roundly for small mistakes, having to repeat simple tasks over and over. In one case, plebes were forced to dance and sing, "Oh I just feel as happy as a big sun flower." In another, new-comers were made to stand on a fireplace mantle wearing their hats backward and whistling, with bayonets held like flutes, while other plebes danced a jig on the floor below. Older cadets also sought to place newcomers in situations in which there was no answer they could give that would not mean trouble. In one scenario, a cadet would approach a "beast" in a very determined and serious manner, snap him to attention and ask, gravely, "Are you a fighting man, sir?" If the nervous new-comer answers no, the cadet responds, "Then what do you mean, sir, by coming here? We want fighting men. Sir, go home and hoe corn." If the victim answers yes, the upperclassman replies, "Very well sir, you shall have enough to do. Come out and begin on me."[19] Garlington noted that "as a rule [deviling] was a harmless and more or less pointless exercise of their ingenuity in devising schemes to produce a reaction from the New Cadet; if he kept his temper, remained patient, and subordinate there was no fun for the other party; but if he lost his temper and showed it, the situation became unpleasant for the New Cadet."[20]

A tradition began to grow of establishing the kind of servile relationships common in English boarding schools, in which upperclassmen virtually adopted plebes as private servants. The authorities tried various methods to end this practice. One was a new furlough pledge, which "involved the preposterous idea that we had treated plebes as equals," Cadet Fletcher noted. "This failed. Men going on leave could not and would not and say they never will sign any such document. Plebes never can be considered equals."[21] The plebes also refused to promise not to do work for older cadets—probably for fear of having to break their word. "Maj. Egan in our company threatened with arrest any cadet making a plebe do work," Fletcher noted. "This had no effect but to unite the men in having work for them done by the plebes, so strong is the determination to maintain the custom."[22] The authorities tried a compromise in which an older cadet might ask a plebe to do nonmenial labor (menial tasks being making beds, sweeping tent floors and carrying water). This had mixed results. Officers finally ordered the plebes not to visit the quarters of older cadets, and thus avoid the predicament. "But we can't help it, we must go, and so we are between two fires," Cadet Larned wrote his mother. "If it wasn't for you I would not stay here five minutes longer, especially as the worst is yet to come."[23] When Larned was confined to his quarters for a minor offense a few days later it was a relief, because otherwise he would "in all probability have had to spend it in some other cadet's room, cleaning guns, etc."[24] After a few weeks at the Academy, he said that it would take a book to recount all the deviling he went through. But by the end of June, the hazing had mostly ceased, and he wrote, "I am getting more and more contented every day I stay here and really begin to feel a sort of liking for the place."[25]

Legacies were given an additional share of hazing. Being the son of a graduate, particularly a famous graduate, or anyone else of note brought down extra fire. Sheridan's son was forced to "re-create" his father's famous ride from Winchester to the Battle of Cedar Creek by mounting a broomstick. Admiral Farragut's son received extra penance, especially for being the son of an admiral. Most conspicuous among the children of fame was Frederick Dent Grant, Class of 1871. Not only was he the son of General Ulysses S. Grant, savior of the Union, but two years after he arrived at West Point his father was elected president.[26] But like his father, Fred Grant kept a low profile. "His personal appearance and manner is very quiet and unassuming," a reporter wrote, "and there is not a more popular young man in the institution. He seems to avoid all affectation, and acts utterly unconscious of being the President's son."[27] Fred Grant was universally liked among the Corps and faculty, but his performance at West Point was worse than his father's. He entered in July 1866, and in October he was granted a six-month leave, ostensibly for his health. "He seems to be in a pretty healthy condition," Cadet Fletcher noted archly.[28] He repeated his plebe year, with middling grades that declined in each successive year. By the end of his cow year of 1870 he was a confirmed Immortal, fourth from the bottom of his class, with 192 demerits.

At the start of his final semester at West Point, Cadet Grant was implicated in an event that gained national attention. On January 3, 1871, three plebes were placed under arrest by the Commandant. Cadet William Baird, son of Major General Absalom Baird (USMA 1849—ninth in his class and a Medal of Honor awardee in the Civil War), had been absent from the barracks the previous night; his roommate Enoch Horace Flickinger had reported him present knowing he wasn't; and McDowall Edgar Barnes made a false statement to a sentry while en route to visit Flickinger. Grant and other members of the first class met and decided to take matters into their own hands. One wrote, "If we failed to notice [lying] there could be no telling where this habit, so suddenly and auspiciously commenced, was about to carry us." They went to the plebes in the middle of the night, had them dress in civilian clothes, took them to Highland Falls, and told them that they were never to return to the Academy. Their trunks would be shipped after them. This kind of self-policing was not unusual at West Point. Lying was an honor code violation and the cadets did not countenance it within their ranks, either between each other or to the authorities. When detected, they would settle matters themselves, as they always had. The firsties did not enjoy what they were doing, but saw this as a humane alternative—had the cadets been tried for lying, they would forever carry the stigma. This way they could get on with their lives without a stain on their records.

That of course assumed that the plebes would leave quietly and the matter would never become public. But the three young men made their way back to the Academy, where they faced a court martial. Baird and Flickinger were suspended, but allowed to return to repeat plebe year. Barnes was expelled. But their preemptory ejection had come to the attention of the papers (probably in part due to young Grant's involvement) and a scandal ensued. "This was no boyish freak," the *New York Times* opined, "no manifestation on our part of youthful childish feeling. It was, on the contrary, from its very conception, a most serious affair."[29] The entire first class lost its privileges and was placed under arrest. The House of Representatives held hearings and nearly unanimously recommended their reinstatement, but called for an investigation to find ringleaders. (In a similar event in 1865 the organizers were sentenced to be dismissed, though the penalty was remitted.) The sanctions lasted through the spring, right up to graduation, and it seemed that the class would not be permitted to attend their own graduation ball. However, on June 5, 1871, Secretary of War William Worth Belknap relieved them from arrest, thinking they had learned their lesson. Grant graduated 37th of 41 in his class, coming in last in cavalry tactics and below last in discipline (lower than a cadet who was suspended). He had 194 demerits his final year. In the general role of merit he came in last in his class in French, Spanish, cavalry tactics and discipline, and next to last in infantry tactics. His father, the president, handed him his diploma to wild cheers. Years later when his own son, U. S. Grant III, was attending West Point he inquired to an old Academy friend how he was doing; Charles W. Larned, then professor of drawing, wired back, "Don't worry, Fred, your son is doing better in everything than you did in anything."[30]

The Wheels of Fate

JOHN JORDAN CRITTENDEN WAS A member of the same clan that had produced William Logan Crittenden, the Goat of 1845, who was executed with the filibusters in Cuba. His father was Thomas Leonidas Crittenden, a lawyer by trade who had volunteered to fight with a Kentucky regiment in the Mexican War. He served on General Taylor's staff at Buena Vista and after the war was appointed U.S. consul at Liverpool, England. President Lincoln commissioned Crittenden a volunteer brigadier general in September 1861, and in July 1862 he was promoted to major general for his gallantry at Shiloh. Crittenden served as a corps commander in Tennessee and Virginia until he unexpectedly resigned in December 1864. But when the Army expanded in 1866 he returned to the colors as a regular colonel of the Seventeenth Infantry, attaining brevet brigadiership the following year. Thomas's brother George Bibb Crittenden (USMA 1832) had been a Confederate major general during the war.

John J. Crittenden the younger was born June 7, 1854, in Frankfort, Kentucky, and was given an at-large appointment to the Academy in July 1871.[31] Crittenden's grades placed him in the Immortal section from his plebe year. He was not a disciplinary problem; he scored only in the mid double digits in demerits. In his academic records Crittenden comes across as a well-meaning young man trying his best to uphold a family tradition. However, in his third year he fell afoul of Lieutenant David A. "Dave" Lyle, twelfth in the Class of 1869, who taught the second and last sections of philosophy in the years 1872–75. He took a perverse pleasure in wielding his power over the cadets, and James Parker of the Class of 1876 called him "a satrap in his way." Lyle's practice was to mark down grades a week in advance, based on his expectations of cadets' abilities and without relation to how they actually performed in recitation. When Cadet Henry D. Borup observed Lyle making the anticipatory marks, he explained to the class, "I want you gentlemen to understand that my marks are of no consequence—in your final standing I will bring each of you out where you belong." Cadet Charles Wilson Williams was later up on questions, and answered all of them correctly but one. He was given only one-tenth out of a possible three points. When he protested that he had missed only one answer, Lyle replied, "Mr. Williams, that was a two and nine-tenths question." Williams graduated as the Goat of 1875.[32] Lyle ended John J. Crittenden's West Point career altogether by finding him deficient in philosophy in his third year. Whether Crittenden failed on merit or simply failed to impress Lyle is unknown; but by July 1874, he had left the Academy.[33]

The next year, Crittenden sought and received a direct commission from President Grant. On October 15, 1875, he was appointed a second lieutenant in the 20th Infantry, based at Fort Abercrombie in the Dakota Territory, commanded by Colonel and brevet Major General George Sykes of the Class of 1842. Crittenden was sworn in on October 23. Two days later, while on a hunting trip, he was injured in the left eye when a shotgun shell blew up in his face. He was declared unfit for duty and had to return east. A month later in Cincinnati, a surgeon removed Crittenden's damaged eye. At this point Crittenden might honorably have left the service and pursued a civilian occupation, but his drive to follow in his father's footsteps was strong. The subsequent spring he returned to the frontier.

Meanwhile a remote chain of events conspired to have a decisive impact on Crittenden's life. On December 9, 1875, Second Lieutenant Charles Braden (USMA 1869) was promoted to first lieutenant. Two years earlier, on the morning of August 11, 1873, Braden had been attacked in camp on the Yellowstone River. Braden's men were charged by several hundred Indians, who approached to within thirty yards of their position. Braden fought back coolly and held off the attackers, though he was gravely wounded. His commander wrote that Braden and his men "delivered such a well-directed fire that the Indians were driven rapidly from that part of the field, after having suffered considerable loss. Unfortunately, Lieut. Braden received a rifle-ball through the upper part of the thigh, passing directly through the bone, but he maintained his position with great gallantry and coolness until he had repulsed the enemy."[34] Braden went on leave of absence March 13, 1874, still recovering from his wounds, and though promoted he remained on sick leave until he retired for disability on June 28, 1878.[35]

Braden's slot was to be given to Edwin Philip Eckerson, who had been granted a presidential appointment May 2, 1876, specifically to fill the vacancy. His father was Theodore J. Eckerson, who had joined the Army as an enlisted man in 1840. He fought in the Seminole and Mexican wars under the command of Ulysses S. Grant. He was later given a commission and served as a quartermaster at Fort Vancouver. In February 1865, General Grant recommended him personally for promotion to major. During his career, Eckerson also published two poetry anthologies, his most famous work being "To My Old Knapsack." Edwin's brother Theodore was appointed to West Point by Grant and graduated an Immortal, third from the bottom in the Class of 1874. He served honorably as a cavalry scout. Edwin Eckerson had originally been commissioned in December 1872, but was court-martialed three years later for "absence without leave, conduct to the prejudice of good order and military discipline, and related charges," and dismissed. It was only through the longstanding friendship between his father and the president, and perhaps also his brother's record of service, that Edwin was given a second chance. He accepted the commission and was ordered to report for duty June 19. True to form, he showed up two weeks late.[36]

Meanwhile, General Alfred Howe Terry, commander of the Dakota Territory, was assembling a force for a punitive action against the Sioux, and John Jordan Crittenden begged his father to intervene on his behalf to be allowed to go on the campaign, to prove that he could still serve usefully as a soldier, even blinded in one eye. Terry was reluctant, but

Eckerson's tardiness left him with an opening, so at the last minute he granted Crittenden's request. It was this series of events that brought John Jordan Crittenden to join Company L, Seventh Cavalry, just in time for Custer's expedition to the Little Bighorn.

HURRAH FOR CUSTER

I N THE SPRING OF 1876, George Custer was in Washington, the star witness before the House Committee on Expenditures in the War Department, which was holding a series of public hearings investigating government corruption. Committee chairman Heister Clymer, a Democrat from Pennsylvania, had set his sights on his former Princeton roommate William Worth Belknap, the secretary of war. Belknap maintained a lavish lifestyle in Washington, too lavish for a public servant with a salary of $8,000 per year. Solid evidence existed that Belknap and his wife had accepted tens of thousands of dollars in bribes and kickbacks in return for rights to Army post traderships in the Indian Territory.

Custer testified twice against Belknap, stating that it was a common belief in the Army that the secretary was in league with the corrupt traders at Army posts and Indian reservations. Custer also knew that the traders were putting advanced weapons in the hands of the Indians for profit. He concluded his opening day's testimony with an impassioned statement of his confidence in the honesty of the Army and his dismay at the corruption of the civilians who ran the War Department. Belknap was incensed by Custer's statements, which were very dramatic but on closer examination lacking in substance. Custer came across as earnest and passionate, sometimes too much so; according to one report, "Custer testified like one spurred by a grievance."[1] The committee report against Belknap was read on the afternoon of March 2, 1876. Belknap had resigned that morning in an attempt to limit the damage to the administration, but the issue was too politically charged to be discarded; after another round of hearings, the House voted unanimously to impeach him.[2]

Custer was clearly out to settle some old scores, and he implicated others with whom he had grievances.[3] But he soon faced a controversy of his own over a shipment of corn. Custer had stated that while at Fort

Abraham Lincoln in September 1875 he refused to receive a delivery of eight thousand bushels because he believed it had been stolen from the Indian Bureau. He reported this through channels to the War Department, but word came back signed by the secretary of war that he was to accept the corn.[4] Custer then related the pitiable tale of a winter when the food supplies at the Standing Rock Agency were exhausted and the Indians were forced to eat their ponies. His implication was that it was another example of Belknap's perfidy—forcing stolen corn on his command while Indians starved and grew resentful. But when committee chairman Clymer asked the interim war secretary, Alonzo Taft (father of future president William Howard Taft), for a copy of Custer's original report, Taft could not locate it. "No report of that character can be found," the War Department reported, "nor is there any record of the receipt of such report, or of any directions to General Custer from the War Department or any of its bureaus respecting this subject."[5]

The story was front-page news. Had Custer lied? Was the War Department hiding something? Close review of Custer's prior testimony revealed that there was less to it than initially met the eye. None of his charges were verifiable; most were hearsay, rumor, personal belief or, some said, slander. "There is not a statement of fact in [Custer's testimony] tending to prove any fraudulent manner whatever that is stated on his own authority and personal knowledge," one observer noted.[6] "General Custer is losing something of his prestige before the investigating committee," the *New York Times* reported. "He is full of information as an egg is of meat, but somehow it is only hearsay and gossip, and no witnesses appear to corroborate it."[7] The administration was incensed and the House committee embarrassed. Some said this would cost Custer his next promotion; others believed he would lose his command. He was being vilified in the Republican press, and his old friends were deserting him. All over some sacks of corn. Could this absurdity possibly mean the end of his amazing career?

Custer had come a long way from his visit to Washington eleven years earlier, on May 23, 1865, when President Johnson had authorized a two-day tribute to the Union army, including a grand review of the Army of the Potomac and the Army of the West. The parade route went from the Capitol down Pennsylvania Avenue to the White House. President Johnson, Generals Grant and Sherman, many other officers and cabinet members watched from the reviewing stand outside the north porch, which was wrapped in star-spangled bunting. Grant later sketched the scene:

> The National flag was flying from almost every house and store; the windows were filled with spectators; the door-steps and side-walks were crowded with colored people and poor whites who did not succeed in securing better quarters from which to get a view of the grand armies. The city was about as full of strangers who had come to see the sights as it usually is on inauguration day when a new President takes his seat.

Spectators were hanging from windows and sitting on rooftops along the parade route, everyone cheering and throwing flowers. Many carried umbrellas to escape the hot sun and the morning rain, which helped keep the dust down. Bands played martial tunes, horses clattered on cobblestones, officers barked commands. It was a festive atmosphere, though tempered by awareness of the sacrifices that had recently been made. A sign on the Capitol proclaimed in large letters, "The only national debt we never can pay is the debt we owe to the victorious Union soldiers."[8] The building was still draped with black crepe from the Lincoln lying-in-state, and the flag flew at half staff in his honor. The portico of the Treasury Department building was draped with the flag of the Treasury Guard regiment that had hung below the presidential box at Ford's Theater the night Lincoln was shot. The end of the flag showed a large tear where John Wilkes Booth's spur had caught as he jumped from the balcony, sending him off-balance onto the stage and breaking his leg.

The Cavalry Corps led the review, fronted by Wesley Merritt and his staff, General Sheridan having been called to New Orleans to organize occupation forces. Custer's Third Division followed in a column eight horsemen across, and behind them the rest of the corps, eight thousand horses strong. Walt Whitman, who marched with his brother George and the 51st New York Volunteers (Whitman having served as a nurse in Washington), described the cavalry as he had seen them two days earlier during a review for the departing Sheridan:

> a strong, attractive sight; the men were mostly young, (a few middle-aged,) superb-looking fellows, brown, spare, keen, with well-worn clothing, many with pieces of water-proof cloth around their shoulders, hanging down. They dash'd along pretty fast, in wide close ranks, all spatter'd with mud; no holiday soldiers; brigade after brigade. I could have watch'd for a week.[9]

Custer rode at the head of his division, leading the review of what was the most powerful land army in the history of the world. He was at the high point of his fame as he passed up Pennsylvania Avenue to the cheers of the crowd: "Custer! Custer! Hurrah for Custer!" The column turned up Fifteenth Street, passed the Treasury Building and headed for the reviewing stand. Custer doffed his hat as he passed a chorus of three hundred young ladies in white, who threw flowers as they sang. One offered a wreath, which he caught on his arm. This spooked Custer's spirited mount Don Juan, which reared and galloped down the road, to the surprise and dismay of the spectators. Custer attempted to salute as he rocketed by the reviewing stand, dropping his hat and saber in the process. He stayed calm and steady in the saddle as the horse bolted down the avenue. When its fear subsided, Custer turned and trotted back to his men while the frenzied crowd cheered in relief and delight.[10] As usual, he had stolen the show.

"It was a pretty picture," a reporter wrote, "the horse, wreathed with flowers, running full speed; Custer sitting like a monument, and his long yellow hair, his hat having blown off, streaming in the wind."[11] Another noted that "In the sunshine his locks unskeined, stream a foot behind him. . . . It is like the charge of a Sioux chieftain."[12]

Hurrah for Peace

FOR HIS ENTIRE PROFESSIONAL CAREER, George Custer had known only war. He had gone literally from the Academy to the battlefield. It was an environment in which he thrived, the ideal setting to harness his abilities and proclivities in the interests of the Army and his country. But with the war over, Custer faced having to adjust to life in a peacetime force very different from the one he had fought with, and much changed from the antebellum Army. A new military had emerged, with new missions, and one in which West Point was no longer the dominant influence.

The Army, while significantly smaller than at the height of the war, was larger than it was in 1860. Congress in 1866 mandated a force three times the prewar force, to undertake the military occupation of the former Confederate States, meet frontier security needs, man the coastal defense force (which for decades was America's traditional form of homeland security) and deter a perceived threat from French-controlled Mexico. In 1869, Congress cut back the expansion to 35,000 officers and men, which was still about double the prewar level. Another round of downsizing in 1871 left the Army at 30,000. Officer slots peaked at 2,853, then settled at just over 2,100.[13]

The expansion of the officer corps did not translate into a career bonus for West Point graduates. The percentage of West Pointers on active duty declined markedly. In 1860, 68 percent of the 1,108 active duty officers were USMA graduates. By 1867, this had fallen to 23 percent of the 2,853 officers, and climbed back only to 35 percent of 2,178 officers in 1877. This was largely due to the number of qualified volunteer officers who had seen action in the Civil War. Congress gave strong preference to volunteer veterans in filling open slots in the expanded Regular Army. The commendable record of volunteer officers during the war was seen by some, especially in Congress, as proof that experience in actual warfighting was more important than education in producing leaders. It was an echo of the rivalry between the citizen-soldier and the professional that had framed the American military debate since the Revolution.

Officers who had enjoyed high temporary "brevet" ranks while leading volunteer units of state militiamen reverted to their original, lower Regular Army ranks when the volunteer units disbanded. For Custer this meant losing his general's stars, and two days after Lee's surrender he wrote to Libbie, with a hint of irony, "Hurrah for Peace and my little Durl. Can you consent to come down and be a Captain's wife?"[14] Sheridan lobbied for Custer's brevet major general's rank to be made permanent, but politics intervened. When his volunteer commission lapsed on January 31, 1866, Custer was reduced back to captain of the Fifth Cavalry, his rank in June 1863 before Gettysburg. His salary dropped from $8,000 to $2,000. The same thing happened to officers throughout the Army. Though they lost their ranks, the brevet officers were given the courtesy of their former titles, so Captain Custer was still referred to informally as "General."

The new officer corps was younger, and more experienced in war, but could look forward to neither rapid promotion nor major military action. There were too many other young men, which meant fewer retirements, thus a shortage of open slots and little upward mobility. Brevet promotion was out of the question—until 1890, brevets were not awarded for Indian warfare. By the time the regulations were changed, most of the frontier conflicts were over. Postwar graduates from West Point could face virtual career stagnation. Mason M. Maxon, the Goat of the Class of 1869, was a case in point. Maxon was commissioned a second lieutenant in the Tenth Cavalry, and was not made a first lieutenant until six years later. It was another fourteen years before he was promoted to captain. He retired at that rank in 1891, after twenty-two years of active duty. Maxon's career path was typical in the late nineteenth century, and Libbie Custer noted that when an officer died of accident or disease, or was killed in battle, the question of who would be promoted to replace him became a matter of great excitement and concern.[15] Given the limited opportunities for advancement, patronage became critical.

In many respects Army life returned to what it was in the 1850s or even the 1830s. Conventional war between mass armies gave way to unconventional warfare against the Plains Indians. Military men were again virtually segregated from the society they defended. A civil-military gap developed, which was ironic since the United States had more veterans than at any time in its history to that point. But the men still in uniform felt socially as well as physically separated from the society they protected. People again questioned why an Army was needed at all.

There were over 250 Army posts throughout the United States after the war, and few were worthy of the name. Sherman compared some of the forts to prairie dog towns. The frontier had moved west in the decades since Ephraim Kirby Smith guarded Michigan from the British and the Indians, stationed in primitive camps in the Great Lakes region. But frontier life, whether in Arizona or the Dakota Territory, was still difficult.[16] It was hard for the officers and harder for the men. There were few amenities and the food was substandard. At one point in 1867, Custer's regiment was issued bread baked in 1861—"probably in honor of the year I graduated," he quipped.[17]

The Army tended to attract immigrants (32 percent of the Seventh Cavalry were Irish), criminals, and people who wanted free passage west. There was 25–40 percent turnover per year due to death, desertion and end of enlistment.[18] Desertion rates fluctuated around 33 percent, as men left for more lucrative work in mines or on railroads. Flogging for desertion had been banned in 1861, but there were a variety of other punishments, including tattooing and being literally branded a deserter.[19] The Army was experiencing what later would be called a readiness crisis: training was poor, few men reenlisted, and postwar units were often severely under strength.

Pay was erratic in the more remote areas, as was the mail. There were few amusements. Gambling and whiskey remained the leading diversions. Organized sports had become more common, especially the new craze, baseball. There was also the traditional hunting, fishing and gardening to supplement rations. Disease, especially venereal disease, was rampant. Winters were still harsh, particularly on the plains. The official history of the Seventh Cavalry summed up the troopers' existence in these trying years:

> The summer's sun found it plodding over the arid, dusty plains as escort to commissioners, surveyors and what not, or dashing along in eager pur-

suit on a fresh Indian trail, and dealing vigorous strokes upon this savage enemy; the winter's snow served as a winding sheet to many of its gallant dead. The theatre of its operations was the scene of many well contested conflicts with its treacherous foe. Two seasons it fought the unseen but virulent enemy—Asiatic cholera. It subsisted for months on food unfit for human consumption, and as a consequence scurvy frequently prevailed among the men, weakening them to such a degree as to invite the more deadly disease—cholera. This varied and trying service developed officers of determination and endurance, of daring and skill; and at the same time eliminated the "deadwood" which it discovered.[20]

One Long, Perfect Day

POSTWAR SERVICE WAS LESS EXCITING for George Custer, and less forgiving. He found that he could no longer rely on a buoyant national mood, or exhibitions of personal bravery, to extricate him from his troubles. Custer had made glory a staple of his career, but it was much harder to come by when the great battles faded into the past. John Gibbon noted dryly that glory was "a term which, upon the frontier, has long since been defined to signify being 'shot by an Indian from behind a rock, and having your name wrongly spelled in the newspapers.' "[21] Furthermore, actions undertaken as a matter of course in wartime became more controversial in peacetime, as Custer soon found out.[22]

Custer went with Sheridan to patrol the Rio Grande in May 1865, chiefly to deter French forces then occupying Mexico from making any hostile moves. Custer commanded a new cavalry division in Texas, made up of western regiments. He found his new troops harder to manage, for several reasons. The western forces had always been less disciplined and informal than their eastern counterparts. Also, the men were less motivated than they had been during hostilities; many of them just wanted to go home. Finally, serving on occupation duty brought the temptation to take advantage of the situation through looting and other forms of misbehavior. Custer had been strict with his men in the East, and though they eventually came to admire and respect their young leader, at first they resented him. In Texas the men never got past the resentment. Custer's troops were always on the verge of mutiny, or so it seemed to him, and he responded with harshness. Some were flogged, "twenty-five lashes on his back, well laid on," although flogging had been abolished by the statute of August 5, 1861, and Custer's men instantly despised him.[23] According to a history of the First Iowa Volunteer Cavalry,

> The principal event which has taken place in the regiment since its service in Texas was the flogging of one of its members by order of General Custer, who in thus violating law and humanity, and from the hero of many a mad charge sinking into the hero of the lash, justly received the indignant condemnation of the people of Iowa, and of all who know that it takes something besides mere audacity to maintain the reputation of a soldier, not here to mention that of a gentleman also.

Governor Stone of Iowa protested the "barbarous code adopted by the long-haired young general," and requested that his unit be mustered out. Major General Fitz Henry Warren, an Iowan who as the editor of the *New York Tribune* had coined the expression "On to Richmond!" in 1861, took the matter to Secretary of War Edwin Stanton personally, and the unit was allowed to disband.[24]

Custer himself mustered out of volunteer service February 1, 1866. He flirted with the idea of seeking civilian employment or a government post. He could easily have left the service and capitalized on his fame, but Army life appealed to him. Around that time, he was offered a major general's commission in Benito Juarez's rebel Mexican army, an opportunity that promised high pay and high adventure. Grant and Sherman approved of the move, but Secretary of State William H. Seward did not, and he prevailed upon President Johnson to block it.

On July 28, 1866, Custer was commissioned a lieutenant colonel of the newly formed Seventh Cavalry stationed in Fort Riley, Texas. Custer had wanted the colonelcy and protested being made second in command, but to no avail. Command of the Seventh was given to brevet Major General Andrew Jackson Smith, son of a Revolutionary War veteran who later fought under Andrew Jackson at the Battle of New Orleans. A. J. Smith was born three months later and named after his father's commander. Smith was appointed to West Point from Pennsylvania, in 1834, and was in the Immortal section, graduating 36th of 45 in his class. Smith was assigned to the First Dragoons and spent his prewar career on the frontier. He fought in the western theater in the Civil War, and Grant singled him out for heroism in the fighting during the approach to Vicksburg. Custer's disappointment at not being given the command was mitigated by the fact that Smith also acted as commander of the District of the Upper Arkansas, leaving Custer as the regiment's de facto chief.

The Seventh Cavalry was soon given an opportunity to take to the field. On December 21, 1866, a column of eighty soldiers of the Eighteenth Infantry from Fort Phil Kearny were ambushed and wiped out by Oglala Sioux led by Chief Red Cloud. The soldiers were under the command of Captain William Fetterman, who gave his name to the massacre. There was a public outcry and Sherman, commander of the Military Division of the Missouri, who had clashed with Red Cloud at a peace conference the previous June, wanted to settle the score. He ordered Winfield Scott Hancock, commander of the Department of the Missouri, to mount an expedition in the spring. "Hancock the Superb," as he was known by then, raised a force of 1,400 men, including the Seventh Cavalry, to participate in the operation. "Wild Bill" Hickock was one of his chief scouts. It was a show of force, or at least became one when the Indians refused to fight. Hancock's men marched across the central plains with no specific objective from April to July 1867. There was a great deal of patrolling and pursuit, but for Custer, at least, no major battle. The only action of note was burning an Indian village at Pawnee Fork, though this predictably had the effect of stirring things up. And in any case, the Indians that Hancock was moving against had nothing to do with Fetterman's killing.

Persistent Indian depredations in the wake of Hancock's expedition led to another, smaller operation commanded by Custer. He was personally encouraged by Sherman to be ruthless, but he had a problem bringing the Indians to decisive engagement. The Indians gave battle on their own terms, usually against small, isolated groups of soldiers, preferably in ambush. In most other circumstances they would flee. It was the classic contest of superior mobility against superior firepower, the same calculus that faced the Army in the Seminole Wars, and later in the Philippines, Vietnam and Iraq.

During the summer, Custer faced a particularly acute desertion problem. It was an issue that affected every command, but in 1867 the rate in the Seventh Cavalry was double that of the Army at large. Thirty-five men deserted at the start of the summer expedition, and later a group of thirteen rode off boldly in broad daylight. Custer turned to his brother Tom, Lieutenant William W. Cooke and Major Joel Elliott, and said, "I want you to get on your horses and go after those deserters and shoot them down" if any resistance was offered.[25] The officers set out in pursuit. Seven of the deserters eluded capture, and of the other six, three either were shot while resisting apprehension, or were summarily executed, depending on whose version of events was to be believed. Hanging was common for desertion in the Civil War; Custer himself had carried out executions for desertion then. However, execution for desertion in peacetime had been outlawed in 1830; and though what Custer ordered was not technically capital punishment (he claimed it was self-defense), it did not sit well with many people. The wounded deserters who were brought back were denied medical care at first, though later Custer relented. But he had made his point, and desertion temporarily ended in the Seventh Cavalry.

On July 13, 1867, Custer's column arrived at Fort Wallace for rest and resupply. Custer had hoped to meet his wife there, but she had not made the journey, nor had word been sent why she was not there. Custer heard that a flash flood had hit Fort Hays, where Libbie was staying, and the news was too much for him. On July 15 he headed east for Fort Harker, where the civilians from Fort Hays had been evacuated, accompanied by four officers and seventy-two men. Custer drove his command mercilessly; they pushed 150 miles in 55 hours. Custer lost many horses in his haste, and several stragglers fell prey to Cheyenne attacks. When Custer refused to send a relief party to retrieve the wounded or the bodies of the dead, it caused a shock through his command. Twenty men deserted. But Custer continued doggedly towards his wife. He arrived at Fort Harker in the early morning of July 19 to find that Libbie had been sent safely to Fort Riley. He reported to Colonel Smith and asked permission to continue to Fort Riley without explaining why he was going there, or why he had come to Fort Harker in the first place. Smith, half-asleep and not knowing if Custer was operating on direct orders from Sherman, allowed him to take the first morning train. Libbie described his arrival several hours later:

> After days of such gloom, my leaden heart one morning quickened its beats at an unusual sound—the clank of a saber on our gallery and with it the quick, springing steps of feet, unlike the quiet infantry around us. The door, behind which I paced uneasily, opened, and with a flood of sunshine that poured in, came a vision far brighter than even the brilliant Kansas sun. There, before me, blithe and buoyant, stood my husband! In an instant, every moment of the preceding months was obliterated. What had I to ask more?... There was in that summer of 1867 one long, perfect day.[26]

Shades of Custer's stealthy trip to Richmond after Appomattox. But he was alone then, and no one had died. At the end of the "long, perfect day," Custer received word that he would be arrested.

Colonel Smith had brought charges against Custer for leaving his command in the field, and Captain Robert M. West raised the matter of shooting deserters without a trial under the rubric of "conduct prejudicial to good order and military discipline." Hancock concurred with the charges. Custer believed that Smith had acted on Hancock's order, and never forgave either of them. He went to Fort Leavenworth, where the court took up his case in September 1867. Custer mounted a thorough defense, giving his version of events while also objecting to the composition of the court, noting that four members were inferior to him in rank and another was a commissary officer he had censured for corruption.[27] To demonstrate his objectivity, Custer pointed out that one of the officers he objected to, brevet Major Stephen C. Lyford, was one of his classmates and a close friend. Nevertheless, the proceedings continued and the court rendered its verdict on October 11, 1867. Custer was found guilty on almost all counts. He was suspended a year without pay, which most observers considered a lenient sentence.

Captain West then attempted to bring civil charges of murder against Custer—a trooper in his command, Charles Johnson, was among the wounded who had been denied medical care and later died. But a judge ruled that there was insufficient evidence to pursue the matter. Custer retaliated by having West brought up on charges of drunkenness, garnering him a two-month suspension.

It was a low point for Custer. But if it affected him in any way, he did not show it. He had sat stiffly on his horse on parade as the orders of the court were read, his features betraying no noticeable reaction. George and Libbie spent the winter at Leavenworth, taken care of by Sheridan, who had replaced Hancock as commander of the Department of the Missouri. It hardly seemed like punishment; according to the diary of Libbie's cousin Rebecca Richmond, who visited the couple during this period, their time was taken up with singing, games, hunting, theater, hops and parties.[28] Custer never felt he had done anything wrong, and was not made to feel guilty. Reports of the time had him privately furious about the entire proceeding, the charges, the composition of the court, and the sentence. But his autobiography only alludes tangentially to the court martial, and treats the interlude of his suspension as though it were an extended vacation, while Libbie's book *Tenting on the Plains*, covering the same period, ends with George arriving for their long, perfect day. That spring they went back to Michigan to relax until the fall.

WASHITA

AFTER HANCOCK'S FAILED EXPEDITION, a peace commission was sent out to convince the Plains Indians to vacate the area between the Platte and Arkansas rivers, the main route for railroads and settlers heading west. Members of the commission included General Sherman, Brigadier General Alfred Terry, and old Indian fighter William S. Harney, Heth's commander at Blue Waters and Pickett's at San Juan, now retired. Harney would participate in several such peace delegations and become a strong advocate for fair play with the Native Americas. After his death in 1889, the Sioux bestowed on him the name, "Man-Who-Always-Kept-His-Word."

In October 1867, the delegates concluded a series of agreements with the Kiowa, Comanche, Cheyenne and Arapahoe, known as the Medicine Lodge Treaties. The tribal leaders agreed to move south of the Arkansas River and to end raids into Kansas and other settled areas. Many of the bands complied and this seemed to promise peace. However, such agreements often foundered on the cultural divide. Treaties were considered literal, legal and binding by the whites, but more as temporary guidelines by the Indians. Many bands could rightly claim not to be party to them. By spring and summer of 1868, disagreements, misunderstandings and the passions of unrestrained warlike youths led to a series of raids and skirmishes. Given Hancock's failure to bring battle the previous summer, Sheridan suggested mounting an offensive in the winter, when the Indians were at their least mobile and most vulnerable. Some thought this too risky and tried to dissuade him, but he "reasoned that as the soldier was much better fed and clothed than the Indian, I had one great advantage."[1] Sherman approved the concept, stating that "these Indians doubtless expect to relax their war efforts about December, when the grass will fail them, but that is the very time we propose to begin in earnest, and I hope that by the time the new grass comes a very small reservation will suffice for what is left."[2]

Sheridan sought to wage general war on the Indians, to unleash the kind of campaign he had done in the Shenandoah Valley in 1864. Moreover, he wanted his right-hand man back to lead the campaign. Custer was again to be his instrument. Sheridan and Sherman engineered an early release from his suspension; and when word reached him that he was returning to the Seventh Cavalry, a joyous Custer departed immediately for the West. He was given free rein by Sheridan—his orders were to follow his instincts. "I rely in every thing upon you," Sheridan wrote, "and shall send you on this expedition without giving you any orders leaving you to act entirely upon your judgment."[3]

On November 23, 1868, Custer and his regiment moved south from a staging post unimaginatively called Camp Supply on the North Canadian River in the Indian Territory, what today would be western Oklahoma. The weather was cold, and as the column began its march a fresh snowstorm blew in, adding to the deep snow blanket that covered the countryside. But Custer's force of eight hundred men was well trained and motivated. They moved slowly towards the Indian winter villages along the Washita River, led by Osage scouts. On November 26 they picked up an Indian trail that seemed to lead north to Kansas, and assuming it was evidence of a raiding party, they tracked it back to its source. Custer reconnoitered the Indian encampment personally, creeping through the snow along a ridgeline to look down on the valley by the light of the half-moon.

Fifty-one lodges stretched out along the dark ribbon of the river. It was one of history's ironies that Cheyenne chief Black Kettle led the band Custer had found. For years he had been among the more conciliatory Cheyenne leaders, seeking peace when it was possible, signing agreements when they were offered. Four years earlier Black Kettle's band had encamped in what they thought was safety at the Sand Creek Reservation in Colorado, flying an American flag to show their loyalty to the Union. But they were attacked by elements of the Colorado militia under Colonel John Chivington, and over two hundred men, women and children were killed. The Sand Creek Massacre became an enduring symbol of white inhumanity on the frontier. Chivington was investigated for possible criminal action, though because of conflicting jurisdictions he was never brought up on charges. An Army judge called Sand Creek "a cowardly and cold-blooded slaughter, sufficient to cover its perpetrators with indelible infamy, and the face of every American with shame and indignation."

Despite the tragedy, Black Kettle remained a "peace chief," and in November 1868 the sixty-seven-year-old leader was involved in ongoing negotiations with Colonel William B. Hazen over the release of a captured settler, Clara Blinn, and her two-year-old son, Willie, being held by the Kiowa. The deal stood at five ponies for the pair. Hazen, one of the officers who had placed Cadet Custer under arrest in June 1861 for the fistfight incident, was at Fort Cobb, a hundred miles downstream from Black Kettle's camp. His assignment was to determine which bands were keeping their agreements under the peace treaty. A week earlier, Black Kettle had admitted to Hazen that he could not prevent his young warriors from raiding settlements, though he was trying his best to keep the peace. The trail that Custer had followed could have been made by some of these raiders, or perhaps a hunting party. It made little difference either way.

Custer devised his attack plan on the spot. He left eighty men with the baggage train, and divided the remaining 720 into four columns, which would attack the village from separate directions. His men dispersed into position under clear, brilliantly starlit skies, moving cautiously through the deep snow. At dawn, Custer's hand-picked sixteen-man brass band signaled the opening of the battle by striking up the regiment's signature tune, "Garry Owen." Captain Francis M. Gibson recalled,

> [W]e listened intently for the signal notes of "Garry Owen" our charging call, and the death march as well of many a comrade and friend. At last the inspiring strains of the rollicking tune broke forth, filling the early morning air with joyous music. The profound silence that had reigned through the night was suddenly changed to a pandemonium of tumult and excitement; the wild notes of "Garry Owen" which had resounded from hill to hill, were answered by wilder shouts of exultation from the charging columns.

Afterward, Custer wrote to Sheridan, "With cheers that strongly reminded me of scenes during the war, every trooper, led by his officer, rushed toward the village."[4] Custer led from the front, as usual. He was the first in the village and fought through to the south side, where he directed the battle from atop a low hill.

The Indians were "caught napping," in Custer's memorable phrase. Many were cut down as soon as they emerged from their teepees. Some stood and fought; many more tried to escape. "In the excitement of the fight, as well as in self defense," Custer noted, "it so happened that some of the squaws and a few children were killed and wounded." In fact, around ninety-two women, children and old men were killed, along with ten warriors. Black Kettle and his wife were found together in the river, shot down as they tried to flee. Little Rock, the second senior chief, briefly took command of the defense until he was killed by Major Elliott.[5] The main struggle in the village was soon over, though sporadic fighting continued against pockets of resistance in the surrounding countryside. Elliott and nineteen troopers pursued a group of fleeing Indians downstream. "Here goes for a brevet or a coffin!" Elliott shouted as he rode away.[6]

Custer secured the village and took stock of his accomplishments. He had wiped out what he believed to be a hostile band and demonstrated that offensive operations in the winter were possible. His losses had been slight—only a few killed that he knew of, among them Captain Louis McLane Hamilton, grandson of Alexander Hamilton, handsome and ambitious, who had died in the initial charge, shot down at Custer's side. They had taken fifty-three women and children captive. Custer's men inspected the lodges and discovered evidence suggesting that some in the group had been raiding. Most of the rest of the captured material was burned, and the herd of eight hundred ponies and mules methodically shot down (a common practice, since the Indians relied heavily on the animals and leaving them behind would place them in the hands of other bands). Custer sent some memorabilia of the battle to the Detroit Audubon Club, including a buffalo hide shield, a bow and arrows, a beaded buckskin dress, and a ten-inch knotted scalp, said to be that of Little Rock.[7]

While Custer's men were mopping up and shooting the ponies, Indians from villages downstream began to appear along the ridgeline and take shots from a distance. Custer was in an exposed position, with his pack trains some distance to the rear and with evening approaching. He knew he could not stay at the village site for long. Custer organized his troops and the prisoners in column and began to move downstream, threatening the other villages. When the warriors withdrew to spread the alarm and prepare their defenses, Custer swung the column around and moved quickly back towards Camp Supply. He reached the post to great fanfare on December 2.

Major Elliott had not returned. Unbeknownst to Custer, Elliott's group had been ambushed and wiped out some miles downstream, probably by Cheyenne and Arapahoe warriors from other villages. Custer had left the scene without determining Elliott's fate, an error in command judgment that became a sore point for several of Custer's officers and many of the men. This event, combined with the circumstances of the forced march to Fort Harken in the summer of 1867, solidified Custer's reputation as a commander who would leave the wounded and dead in the hands of the Indians, violating one of the most sacred unwritten rules of the frontier force.

The bodies of Mrs. Blinn and her child turned up five to ten miles from the encampment. Where she had been and by whom she was killed were unknown. Colonel Hazen was outraged by the entire affair, which he believed was misdirected and unnecessary. Several years later, after Custer published an account of the battle in *My Life on the Plains,* Hazen countered with a pamphlet, *Some Corrections of My Life on the Plains,* in which he questioned key details of Custer's glowing account of Washita.

Custer called Washita a "complete and gratifying success" and "a regular Indian 'Sailor's Creek.' " Sheridan also approved. He wrote that Black Kettle's group was "one of the most villainous of the hostile bands," and if the chief himself did not participate in the depredations of the braves it was age alone that kept him back; he "freely encouraged them by 'making medicine,' and by other devilish incantations that are gone through with at war and scalp dances."[8] Custer had validated Sheridan's concept of winter operations, and rehabilitated himself from his court martial. Once again he had redeemed himself through battle.

The *New York Times* also praised the outcome of Washita: "Gen. Custer, in defeating and killing Black Kettle, has put an end to one of the most troublesome and dangerous characters on the Plains. . . . A permanent peace can now be obtained through energetic and successful war. . . . 'stout hearts' will do much; and one or two repetitions of Custer's victory will give us peace on the Plains."[9] Others were horrified at the killing of so many noncombatants, though the "exterminationist" fringe approved. Custer denied having specifically targeted women and children, and demonstrated through his actions later in the campaign that he was not an indiscriminate butcher, choosing negotiations over fighting when he could. But the bloody reputation he gained at Washita stuck in some quarters. Colonel Ned Wynkoop, the Indian agent for the Cheyenne who already had a low opinion of Custer, accused him of perpetrating a senseless massacre and resigned his position, stating, "I most certainly refuse to again be the instrument of the murder of innocent women and children."[10]

Sheridan's campaign continued through March, but without any further major battles. For Custer it marked his return to public notoriety. Some saw him as a hero, others as a man capable of atrocity. Either way he was being talked about. He took the opportunity to reinvent himself. Instead of the Union cavalryman and boy general, he was now the frontiersman, hunter and Indian fighter. The new image was much like the old — dashing, warlike, romantic. He adopted stylized buckskin garb, more a costume than a uniform, and was widely photographed. He promoted his image through his writings and in his social circles, carefully tending the Custer legend.

"The Most Complete Example of a Petty Tyrant That I Have Ever Seen"

HIS REDEMPTION AT LEAST PARTIALLY secured, Custer settled down to garrison life. He began to study the plains and the people who lived there. He grew comfortable dealing with Indians. His books and articles were filled with his observations of Indian life and culture. He learned sign language and gave respect to those he dealt with, particularly the Osage, Crow and Arikara scouts who worked with the Army against their traditional tribal enemies. The Indians returned his respect, and a scout named Red Star said that Custer "had a heart like an Indian."[11] Their nicknames for him included Long Hair, Creeping Panther and Son of Morning Star.

Nevertheless, there were limits to Custer's admiration of the Native Americans. He was critical of the literary notion of the "noble savage": "Stripped of the beautiful romance with which we have been so long willing to envelop him," he wrote, "transferred from the inviting pages of the novelist to the localities where we are compelled to meet with him, in his native village, on the war path, and when raiding upon our frontier settlements and lines of travel, the Indian forfeits his claim to the appellation of the 'noble red man.' We see him as he is, and, so far as all knowledge goes, as he ever has been, a savage in every sense of the word; not worse, perhaps, than his white brother would be similarly born and bred, but one whose cruel and ferocious nature far exceeds that of any wild beast of the desert."

On the other hand, he found that "Indian life, with its attendant ceremonies, mysteries, and forms, is a book of unceasing interest. Grant that some of its pages are frightful, and, if possible, to be avoided, yet the attraction is none the weaker. Study him, fight him, civilize him if you can, he remains still the object of your curiosity, a type of man peculiar and undefined, subjecting himself to no known law of civilization, contending determinedly against all efforts to win him from his chosen mode of life."[12] Custer saw something of himself in the Native Americans, though not those who consented to the civilizing effects of the reservation. "If I were an Indian," he wrote, "I often think that I would greatly prefer to cast my lot among those of my people who adhered to the free open plains, rather than submit to the confined limits of a reservation, there to be the recipient of the blessed benefits of civilization, with its vices thrown in without stint or measure."[13]

Like Henry Heth, Custer enjoyed the boundless opportunities for hunting that the plains provided. He was particularly eager to hunt buffalo, though in his first encounter with a bison he managed to shoot the horse he was riding, Libbie's favorite, called Custis Lee. On military expeditions he doubled as commander and chief huntsman, helping keep his regiment well stocked with fresh meat. He could frequently be seen galloping across the plains pursued by his pack of loyal hounds. Over the years, Custer became something of a naturalist, collecting live animal specimens that he sent to zoos in the East, as well as fossils he forwarded to scientists. He also learned taxidermy, a useful art to while away the winter months.

Libbie was a constant source of companionship. George had written to her daily during the Civil War. She followed him west to Texas in 1865, stayed with him in garrison and accompanied him on the march except on active operations. The two enjoyed each other's company on long rides and quiet evenings, as well as the many social events they attended. Libbie adapted well to camp life; she was gracious in her important though informal role as the commander's spouse, and patient with the hardships they faced. She was emotionally strong and had a very good attitude, especially as a daughter of privilege taken from the comforts of Monroe, Michigan. George doted on his bride, sometimes to the consternation of other officers and the enlisted men. They both attracted rumors of infidelity, spread chiefly by George's adversaries, but the scant evidence of philandering must be weighed against the copious epistolary record chronicling their close and loving relationship.

Custer populated the Seventh Cavalry with friends and family members to the extent possible. Tom Custer was of course assigned to the regiment. Later their civilian brother Boston accompanied the unit on several expeditions. Lieutenant James Calhoun was married to George's sister Margaret, and Captain Myles Moylan married Calhoun's sister Charlotte. Fred Calhoun, James' brother, married George's niece Emma Reed, and Custer asked that he be transferred to the unit. This was refused—the Army had reached the limit of the personal coterie they would allow Custer to assemble. This might seem unprofessional by contemporary standards, but it made sense in the days when there was virtually no lateral mobility in the Army. Soldiers stayed with the same regiment their entire career. Thus from Custer's point of view it made sense to introduce members of his actual family into his surrogate family, rather than all of them serving in separate units with little chance of ever seeing each other.

As the frontier became safer and more accessible, railroads brought both settlers and tourists. The Custers took every opportunity to entertain visitors, to help maintain their links to the East and reinforce George's celebrity status. George and Libbie played host to politicians and other prominent guests. They gave their company what they wanted: a taste of the vanishing frontier, including hunting buffalo, seeing and meeting actual Indians, and witnessing the pageantry of the cavalry drill. Custer's natural sense of showmanship guaranteed a memorable vacation. In January 1872, Grand Duke Alexis of Russia visited the West, and Sheridan imported Custer from a temporary post in Kentucky to lead the buffalo hunt.[14] Sheridan accompanied them, as did famed scout William F. "Buffalo Bill" Cody and several other officers, in addition to the imperial party.[15] The trip went well, with Alexis taking down several buffalo. Chief Spotted Tail and his Brulé warriors came along, displaying their hunting techniques, and in the evening putting on a war dance before a large campfire. Alexis was dazzled by the spectacle, and very taken by Custer's wit and charm and the tales of his escapades. Alexis was so impressed he asked that Custer be allowed to accompany him on the rest of his tour, west to Denver, then back east via Kansas, finally ending in Pensacola in February. This was the Custer that people loved—the winning personality, charisma unbound. Charles Godfrey Leland, a folklorist, scholar and journalist who had fought for the Union at Gettysburg, visited with him at Fort Riley and wrote, "There was a bright and joyous chivalry in that man, and a noble refinement mingled with constant gaiety in the wife, such as I fear is passing from the earth."[16]

Unfortunately, Custer was not enjoying financial or career success. He used his connections to pursue several money-making schemes, perhaps with a view towards leaving the Army, but none of them turned a profit. Sheridan worked assiduously for Custer's advancement, but could not find a way to move him up in rank. Custer believed he had a chance to assume the colonelcy of the Seventh Cavalry when A. J. Smith retired on May 6, 1869, but to his disappointment the command was given to Pickett's classmate Colonel Samuel Sturgis.[17]

Custer and Sturgis had a grudge dating back to shortly after the Civil War ended, and this did not improve things between them. To escape serving under Sturgis, Custer requested appointment as Commandant of Cadets at West Point. It would have been a dream assignment both for Custer and for the cadets, giving them a role model of the Immortal made good in the tradition of William H. T. Walker, who served in that post opposite Superintendent Robert E. Lee. But the assignment went to the more intellectual Emory Upton. However, like Colonel Smith, Sturgis was frequently detached on details, so Custer still commanded the regiment on a daily basis.

Custer in camp in these years was not the carefree spirit of old. His experience in Texas had not tempered him. He ran his regiment like a division, always seeking ways to keep people busy. Lieutenant Charles W. Larned, Fred Grant's friend from West Point, served in Custer's command. While at Camp Sturgis in Yankton, Dakota, in April 1873, he wrote, "Custer is not making himself at all agreeable to the officers of his command. He keeps himself aloof and spends his time in excogitating annoying, vexatious and useless orders which visit us like the swarm of evils from Pandora's box, small, numberless and disagreeable."[18] Larned remarked that Custer "wears the men out by ceaseless and unnecessary labor. . . . We all fear that such ill advised and useless impositions will result in large desertions when the command is paid off, as it will be tomorrow morning. Custer is not belying his reputation—which is that of a man selfishly indifferent to others, and ruthlessly determined to make himself conspicuous at all hazards."[19]

Captain Albert Barnitz, who served in the Seventh for four years and was seriously wounded at Washita, wrote his wife that Custer "spares no effort to render himself generally obnoxious."[20] Barnitz called Custer "the most complete example of a petty tyrant that I have ever seen. You would be filled with utter amazement, if I were to give you a few instances of his cruelty to the men, and discourtesy to the officers."[21] The arrival of Colonel Sturgis was met with joy, according to Larned; "for how long no-one knows . . . perhaps only for a few days—any time would be a relief." For his part, Sturgis said that "Custer was not a popular man among his troops, by any means. He was tyrannical, and had no regard for the soldiers under him."[22] Again, things had changed a great deal since the war.

Libbie Custer called the officers of the Seventh Cavalry "a medley of incongruous elements."[23] Custer had his favorites, chiefly his brother Tom, Myles Moylan, George W. Yates (who was from Monroe), Thomas B. Weir and Algernon E. Smith. Larned referred to them as his "royal family." But Custer also had his detractors. Abandoning Elliott at Washita had created enduring fissures in the Seventh, and Custer's later actions did not help. Through his behavior, he encouraged a command climate of favoritism. He fed off adulation, while he frowned on critical or independent thinking. Those who either disliked Custer or simply did not want to be among his throng grew alienated.

Most prominent among the Custer critics was Captain Frederick William Benteen, a Virginian by birth who had sided with the Union. His distraught father had stated that he wished his son would die with the war's first bullet, and that ideally it would be fired by a family member. The two were later reunited when Benteen's regiment captured a southern riverboat, and he found his father on board serving as chief engineer. All the crew but Benteen's father were paroled; Frederick had him jailed, more out of concern for his safety than out of spite. Benteen fought at Pea Ridge with Bowen's Battalion of Missouri Cavalry, on the Union right around Elkhorn Tavern. He fought at Vicksburg and other battles in the West, distinguishing himself for bravery. He ended the war as commander of the 138th Colored U.S. Volunteers. After the war he was given a Regular Army captain's commission and sent to the Seventh Cavalry.

Benteen was a self-styled contrarian, frequently at odds with authority. "I've been a loser in a way, all my life," he wrote, "by rubbing a bit against the angles—or hair—of folks, instead of going with their whims; but I couldn't go otherwise—'twould be against the grain of myself."[24] He was much like Custer in a way, and they were certain to either bond or clash. As it happened, Benteen took a dislike to Custer immediately, finding him vain and self-serving, and a braggart. Since Benteen was unable to provide Custer with the veneration he craved from subordinates, their relationship never improved. Benteen never forgave Custer for the death of Elliott, and he and Custer almost came to blows over private criticism Benteen had made of his conduct at Washita, which unfortunately made it into the St. Louis press. In 1873, Custer disallowed a request for emergency leave so Benteen could visit his desperately ill daughter, who later died. Given Custer's own behavior dashing off to Libbie in the summer of 1867, this must have seemed the height of hypocrisy.

★ ★ ★

IN THE SUMMER OF 1873, the Seventh Cavalry was assigned to guard an engineering and surveying party that was exploring a route for the Northern Pacific Railroad between Bismarck and Bozeman, up the Missouri and Yellowstone rivers. The commander of the expedition was General David S. Stanley, the same Stanley who was saved by J. E. B.

Stuart at Solomon's Fork, who commanded Joseph Lee Kirby Smith at Corinth, and who was awarded the Medal of Honor for gallant leadership at the Battle of Franklin in 1864. In 1873 he was commander of the 22nd Infantry regiment. Larned wrote that Stanley "seems to be very much liked and impressed me favorably when I met him. Large, handsome and dignified."[25] But Stanley and Custer did not get along. Stanley described Custer to his wife as a "cold blooded, untruthful and unprincipled man. He is universally despised by all the officers of his regiment excepting his relatives and one or two sycophants.... I will try, but am not sure I can avoid trouble with him."[26]

The chief engineer of the survey party was Custer's old classmate, friend and adversary Thomas L. Rosser. One afternoon Custer was resting when he heard someone asking which was General Custer's tent. "Halloo, old fellow!" Custer said. "I haven't heard that voice in thirteen years, but I know it. Come in and welcome!" The two men renewed their old friendship and spent many hours together reliving old memories. In a letter to Libbie, George related one of the talks they had while lying under the fly of Custer's tent on a buffalo robe: "We talk over our West Point times and discuss the battles of the war.... It seemed like the times when we were cadets together, huddled on one blanket and discussing dreams of the future."[27]

Custer was ordered to stay back with Rosser and his engineers advancing slowly while Stanley pushed forward to the Yellowstone. The rear was an unaccustomed position for Custer, and he soon decided to move out on his own. "Custer having been given a little tether must needs throw off Stanley's shackles altogether and start off with heels-in-the-air on his own hook," Larned recorded in his diary.[28] One day, rather than assisting the baggage train over the Muddy River, he pressed out into the van, sending a note to Stanley to send him rations and forage. Stanley instead dispatched an angry note ordering Custer to stop where he was and see to his own supplies, and never to act without direct orders again. "After a march of eleven miles with considerable delay on account of the heavy condition of the prairie from hard rains," Larned noted, "an orderly courier from Stanley overtook our 'flaxen haired' chieftain presenting him with a *billet doux* to the effect he should halt on the spot."[29] Custer "was just gradually assuming command," Stanley wrote, "and now he knows he has a commanding officer who will not tolerate his arrogance."[30]

By August, relations between Stanley and his unmanageable subordinate had settled down. Stanley had demonstrated his authority, but also began to allow Custer to forge out ahead of the column. Custer

always volunteered to do scouting. Stanley wrote that in the days following the incident, Custer "has behaved very well, since he agreed to
do so, went ahead every day to look up road and select the best camps."[31]
But finding the campsites was only Custer's pretext. If there was action
to be had, he would find that too.

In several skirmishes with bands of Indians numbering from under
a hundred to five hundred or more, Custer performed admirably, demonstrating his knowledge of Indian fighting methods. He was usually on
the defensive, and as often outnumbered. The largest of these engagements took place on August 11, 1873. Custer, encamped in a valley near
the Yellowstone, found himself attacked from two sides. The battle
opened with exchanges of sharpshooting and insults, and the cavalrymen were alerted to the main force attack when their Indian scouts
"came tumbling down the bluffs head over heels, screeching, 'Heap
Indian come.'" This was the battle in which Lieutenant Braden, the
man whose slot John J. Crittenden eventually got, was severely wounded.
Custer divided his command and charged in both directions, driving
the enemy eight to ten miles. "The Indians were made up of different
bands of Sioux, principally Uncpapas," Custer wrote in his after-action
report, "the whole under command of 'Sitting Bull,' who participated
in the second day's fight, and who for once has been taught a lesson he
will not soon forget."[32]

But the Indians of the 1870s had learned much since the early
days fighting the whites on the plains. They were much better equipped,
often with Henry repeating rifles that were superior to those carried
by the troopers. In one of the skirmishes, the antagonists fought for
three hours, "the Indians maintaining a perfect skirmish line throughout, and evincing for them a very extraordinary control and discipline."[33]
The Indians had adapted to modern fighting methods and were not as
easy to defeat as they used to be. Yet the lesson Custer took away from
the engagement was that disciplined and well-organized cavalrymen
employing coordinated firepower could hold their own against superior numbers of Indians.[34]

The Yellowstone expedition garnered Custer more press cover-
age and more fame. But as it turned out, the effort was for naught. On
October 1, 1873, the investment banking concern Jay Cooke and Company, financiers of the Northern Pacific Railroad, went bankrupt, precipitating the Panic of 1873. The railroad's finances collapsed and the
planned rail project was set aside for another seven years.

THE BOY PRESIDENT

IN HIS AUTOBIOGRAPHY, CUSTER noted that "the ways of Congress are sometimes peculiar—not to employ a more expressive term."[1] Custer had more than once seen his career threatened by politics, but in 1876 he chose to step into the middle of a political controversy that nearly cost him his command and saved his life.

If Custer had wanted a political career it would have been his for the taking. He turned down a chance to run for Congress in Michigan in 1866—a race he certainly would have won. In the immediate post-war years he was courted by both political parties. He hobnobbed with people at the highest level of politics and business, at dinners, parties, dances, receptions and other functions. He and Libbie were always in demand. He had achieved celebrity and promotion through the patronage of the Radical Republicans, particularly Secretary of War Edwin Stanton, but his natural inclination was towards the Democrats, and when Andrew Johnson succeeded Lincoln, the McClellan Democrats reached out to Custer.

Custer supported the short-lived National Union Party movement, which after Lincoln's death became a mainly Democratic group, promoting reunification of the two Democratic factions. Custer had briefly taken a hard line against the South, stating in May 1865 that "extermination is the only true policy we can adopt toward the political leaders of the rebellion, and at the same time do justice to ourselves and to our posterity."[2] But this was uttered in the angry days immediately after the Lincoln assassination. Custer was chosen to stand beside General Grant, Admiral Farragut and other luminaries during President Johnson's unity tour of the Midwest in the fall of 1866. Some crowds met Johnson with open disdain and a riot broke out in Indianapolis. Custer got into sparring matches with the rowdies, shaming them for treating the commander in chief with such disrespect.[3] To the Republicans, this defense of Johnson was Custer showing his true colors. They had always suspected he was a "McClellan man" and they were right—he praised McClellan as the finest general he had ever known and had a picture of Little Mac on prominent display in his quarters (beside his own portrait).

The Civil War was a boon for the young Republican Party. Founded in 1854, it had made a strong showing in congressional elections that same year, and won the White House with Lincoln six years later. During the war, the plum volunteer regimental commands usually went to Republicans, and the fraternity and network thus established contributed to fifty years of seldom-broken Republican political supremacy, with the Ohio faction dominating the party. But in the 1874 midterm elections, the Democrats took control of the House of Representatives, which gave them an opening. With their newly won subpoena power, the House Democrats began to take aim at members of the Grant administration, striking at its chief vulnerability, corruption.

The problems were particularly acute on the frontier. Frederick Benteen believed that fraud in the Indian Bureau was the root of all the conflicts with the Indians in America. There were no comparable wars in Canada, he observed, where the bureaucracy was more professionalized and more honest. Though the president himself was never implicated in the scandals, those close to him frequently were. In 1874, a controversy broke over a group that came to be known as the Whiskey Ring. Officials in Washington and St. Louis representing the Internal Revenue Service and other agencies defrauded the government of nearly three million dollars over the years 1871–74 by skimming from the whiskey tax on spirits shipped from St. Louis. Attention soon focused on Orville E. Babcock, Grant's private secretary who had been with him through the war and was present at Appomattox. Grant voiced strong support for Babcock, showing his characteristic loyalty. Babcock was tried and found innocent, to Grant's relief, but negative public opinion forced him to resign.[4]

The House Democrats were perennial foes of the Army. This was in part due to the fact that during Reconstruction it was sometimes used for political purposes that benefited the Republicans (primarily securing polling sites to allow freedmen to vote). The southern Democrat representatives who began to appear in Congress, many of whom were former Confederate soldiers, had no love for the Union army, and certainly no affinity for President Grant. The House Committee on Military Affairs, chaired by Democrat Henry B. Banning of Ohio, began a series of investigations in February 1876, followed by the hearings of Hieister Clymer's House Committee on Expenditures in the War

Department. Of course there were limits to what the House Democrats could achieve. The Senate was still in Republican hands, and Senator John A. Logan, chairman of the Committee on Military Affairs, blocked many of the congressional legislative excesses. "Black Jack" Logan was a former Union general and Medal of Honor recipient who had served under Grant in the West and was a strong supporter of the Army.

Custer was initially reticent when he was summoned to Washington in March 1876. Planning for the campaign against the Sioux was under way and he suggested testifying by telegraph; but he later withdrew the request and made the trip. He testified before Clymer's committee on March 29 and April 4. By then, William Worth Belknap had already resigned as secretary of war, and was about to be impeached nonetheless. Custer also testified before Banning's committee, and was granted the privilege of the floor during his visit. Custer used his time in Washington to good effect; he met with important people in office calls, at official functions, and at dinners and receptions. This was his state in life, a young man with direct access to the centers of power, someone trusted, respected, famous and influential. Congressmen sought his advice on legislation. Senator Thomas F. Bayard, a Democrat from Delaware, threw him a dinner attended by senators, congressmen and former Confederate generals. Custer spoke boldly of his plans to whip the Sioux whenever he was allowed to rejoin his troops.

Custer antagonized the president by openly socializing with Clymer and other Democrats, under the circumstances highly incautious for a serving military officer. He compounded his problems by giving testimony that painted vivid portraits of corrupt Army traders and Indian agents, and brought particular attention to Orvil Grant, the president's brother. He accused Orvil of taking a $1,000 bribe to award a trade post at an Indian reservation. President Grant was not close to his brother; he disapproved of what Orvil did, and had no contact with it. Yet this was a public embarrassment, and Custer drew unwanted attention to it. Some credited Custer with scrupulous honesty; others said he was simply naïve and ingenuous, or that he was compelled by the committee to testify. But Custer was habitually sensitive to the political winds and wise in the ways of power. He could have testified in a variety of ways that would have been less damaging to Grant.

Custer's motives are not clear. He had a good relationship with Grant during the war and afterwards. He was also very solicitous to Fred Grant, who went on the 1873 Yellowstone expedition as an observer. When Fred was called back east for his grandfather's funeral, George advised Libbie (then in Monroe) to hang the president's portrait in the parlor if Fred stopped by to visit her en route. The Custers attended Fred Grant's wedding to Ida Marie Honore in Chicago in October 1874. The president was there, as were Babcock, Secretary Belknap and General Sheridan. Charles Larned served as a groomsman.[5] But Custer may have been jealous of Fred, who had jumped to the rank of lieutenant colonel within a few years while serving on Sheridan's staff. Custer had been stalled at that rank for ten years, even with his wartime record. Fred was too young to have seen action, though at age twelve he had been wounded while with his father at the siege of Vicksburg. President Grant had never helped Custer achieve the rank and station he felt he deserved, and as commanding general did not intervene to stop the 1867 court martial. For his part, Custer had criticized Grant's Indian policy in *My Life on the Plains,* and worked behind the scenes to defame the administration through his close contacts in the Democratic media.

Custer may have hoped that his political machinations would lead to a brigadier's star; he had jumped up rank quickly before. The prospect of Custer becoming a brigadier under Democratic patronage was discussed openly in the press. He might also have wanted to be appointed secretary of war, which was plausible if a Democrat took the White House. The fact that he helped expose Belknap's corruption would have made him an attractive candidate, in addition to his record of service and national fame.

There is a persistent belief that Custer may have been seeking the Democratic presidential nomination himself. Thirty years later one of his Arikara scouts, Red Star, stated that Custer had told them that "he had been to Washington and that he had been informed that this would be his last campaign in the West among the Indians. He said that no matter how small a victory he could win, even though it were only against five tents of Dakotas, it would make him President, Great Father, and he must turn back as soon as he was victorious."[6] It is possible that Custer said this, though he may have been referring to a position other than president. In *My Life on the Plains,* Custer notes that the term "Great Father" in Indian parlance referred to the government generally, not necessarily to the president.[7]

Could Custer have been "informed" that he would get the nomination? He probably had some discussions with Democratic leaders— nothing official, of course, just the usual banter that proliferates around Washington in election season. The Democrats would not have seen Custer as a leading candidate, but as an option, either in 1876 or in the future. Had he achieved a great victory in the West (as he was promising to do) and had momentum suddenly built behind obtaining a slot for him, either at the top or as vice president, he would not have said no to the Democrats, as Sherman did to the Republicans. Custer may have had visions of the contentious 1868 convention, in which Horatio Seymour, who initially was not even a contender, emerged as a dark-horse candidate after twenty-two ballots.[8]

But even if Custer had thought seriously about running in 1876, securing the nomination would have been difficult. One factor working against him was timing. The Democratic Convention was set for June 27, and even if the Sioux expedition had gone out in the spring as planned and Custer had achieved a major victory, it would still have been difficult to translate his success into a nomination in a few weeks or months. Custer would have had to overcome the political machines of his opponents with no machine of his own. In particular, he would have had to outmaneuver Governor Samuel J. Tilden of New York. Tilden was the favorite to win the nomination, though some early reports implied that he was a lost cause, and there was a flurry of speculation over who might get the nod instead.[9] Custer's name, if it was mentioned, was not prominent, and most discussion focused on Governor Thomas A. Hendricks of Indiana, who had almost captured the nomination in 1868. But rumors of Tilden's political weakness were unfounded. Six names were put forward in nomination on June 28, 1876; Tilden gained a majority on the first ballot, and the required two-thirds on the second.

Tilden's issue was reform of corruption, an area in which the Republicans were vulnerable. However, the Republicans had their own readymade issue, the Civil War. It became traditional in postwar elections for the Republicans to "wave the bloody shirt," to invoke the conflict that they blamed on the southern Democrats. The GOP (which at the time stood for Gallant Old Party) won seven of the nine presidential elections from 1868 to 1900 with Civil War veterans. The Democrats won two nonconsecutive victories with nonveteran Grover Cleveland, who had to fend off charges of draft dodging. Running a military man would have made sense for the Democrats, and if they had wanted to nominate a Union general and war hero they did not necessarily need Custer. Winfield Scott Hancock, savior of Gettysburg, friend of Heth and Armistead, was ready to bear the standard. Soon after the war, he had become active in Democratic politics, though he remained a serving officer (like McClellan) and in 1876 was commander of the Division of the Atlantic. Hancock first stood for presidential nomination in 1868, and was briefly a contender in that fractious convention. He stood again in 1876, and eventually secured candidacy in

1880.[10] Even southern Democratic delegates, many of them former Confederate officers such as Fitzhugh Lee, rallied behind Hancock.[11]

Custer would have been a strong candidate in the general election. He was young, dashing, articulate, a northerner and a war hero. He had taken a stand on the corruption issue; the Democrats quoted Custer's testimony extensively in their 1876 national campaign briefing book.[12] Custer would have been a contender against Ohio governor Rutherford B. Hayes, a middling candidate who eventually defeated Tilden only after a disputed electoral vote count. Had Custer won all the states that Tilden won plus his native Michigan, the Boy General would have become, at age thirty-seven, the youngest man elected to the nation's highest office, the Boy President.

But rather than taking the oath of office on the East Portico of the Capitol, Custer sat in a hearing room in Washington, having his credibility challenged and being forced to answer questions about whether he lied when he made charges concerning misappropriation of funds related to some bags of corn. He had alienated the president, and the Republican press was attacking him as vigorously as the Democratic press was praising him. His old networks of influence and patronage were breaking down. The Sioux campaign awaited.

Custer left Washington on April 20, heading for New York, stopping off at the Centennial Exposition in Philadelphia. Four days later, the Senate managers of the Belknap impeachment called him back. Custer was very uncomfortable, sensing that he had overplayed his hand, and he wanted to get back to the frontier as quickly as possible. He argued that he should be released from Washington because all his evidence was hearsay, which ironically most of his detractors had already pointed out. He wrote to Libbie that he was being "called on to do more than I desire. . . . I do not care to abuse what influence I have."[13] But it was too late for such second thoughts.

Sherman then stepped in to help. He had pinned on his fourth star when Grant became president in March 1869, and proved to be an intelligent, uncompromising and independent-minded commanding general. He eschewed politics and resisted Republican efforts to elevate him to the presidency after Grant's second term. But political infighter Belknap systematically undermined Sherman's power over the Army, leaving him a figurehead. The general moved his headquarters to St. Louis just to get away from Washington and the politics of the War Department. He applauded Belknap's downfall and had no problem with Custer's role in it. Sherman had been cordial to Custer on his first visit, and now he asked Secretary of War Alonzo Taft to write a letter authorizing Custer to go back to Dakota. But Grant forbad it; he saw no reason to reward Custer for his behavior. The president ordered that another officer be chosen to lead the Seventh Cavalry in the Sioux expedition.[14] Sheridan reluctantly asked Brigadier General Terry to take charge.

Custer was frantic. The Belknap impeachment managers released him on Saturday April 29, and Sherman advised Custer not to leave Washington until he could get an audience with the president the following Monday. Custer had tried to see Grant two times before and been snubbed. He sought a third audience with Grant on May 1 to plead his case, waiting five hours at the White House. Rufus Ingalls, then the deputy quartermaster general of the Army, happened by, heard Custer's story and conferred with Grant. Ingalls told Custer that Grant would not see him and he might as well leave. Custer then checked out at the War Department and hopped a train west.

Custer was in Chicago on May 4 in a rail car readying to leave for St. Paul when he was placed under arrest. General Sherman had sent a telegram to Sheridan, stating: "I am at this moment advised that General Custer started last night for St. Paul and Fort Abraham Lincoln. He was not justified in leaving without seeing the President and myself. Please intercept him and await further orders; meantime let the expedition proceed without him."[15] Custer was charged with having left Washington without reporting to Grant (whom he tried vainly to see) or Sherman (who was in New York City). That same day, the *New York World* published a lengthy editorial entitled "Grant's Revenge," castigating the president for an act of "miserable vengeance" against Custer. The article contained details that could only have come from Custer himself.

Custer reported to Sheridan, who dressed down the young man in no uncertain terms—probably for his foolishness in getting involved with politics. Custer sent three telegrams to Sherman seeking clemency, but none was answered. On May 5, Grant ordered that command of the Seventh Cavalry during the expedition be given to Major Marcus Reno. For good measure, he denied Custer any role in the upcoming campaign against the Sioux; he was not even permitted to accompany his regiment. Custer was likely facing the end of his career. His friends could not help him and his foes were not disposed to. When the pro-Custer press made Grant's action a public issue, even Sherman was dismissive. "The Army," he stated, "possesses hundreds of officers who are as competent for the command of any expedition as General Custer."[16]

Custer went to see General Terry in St. Paul for one final try. Colonel Robert Hughes, Terry's brother-in-law, witnessed a tearful Custer on his knees begging Terry to help. Though they had had their differences, Terry needed Custer for his knowledge of the region, his understanding of the enemy, and his warlike spirit, his fearless force. Terry, a former lawyer, helped Custer draft a plea to Grant. "I appeal to you as a soldier to spare me the humiliation of seeing my regiment march to meet the enemy and I not share its dangers," he wrote.[17] Sheridan also supported executive clemency, alluding to how he had appealed for Custer's early return from suspension in 1868 with good result. And Terry finally cleared up the matter of the corn shipment, saying that he had never passed Custer's complaint along to the War Department and had authorized delivery himself. On May 8, Grant relented. Custer could go on the campaign at the head of the Seventh Cavalry, but Terry remained in command of the mission. The Democratic press hailed the outcome as the defeat of one general at the hands of another, younger and more able.

When word reached Custer, he was elated. He had once again been given a chance to salvage his career and reputation. Redemption on the battlefield had been his way, at Bull Run, on the Rappahannock, at Aldie, Gettysburg, Appomattox and Washita. There was a purity in the armed contest that was not possible in politics. From his point of view, battle was something objective, a matter of life or death with no middle ground. The prospect energized him; he was going to be given the opportunity to lay his life on the line again. But he needed to do something dramatic, and unambiguously his, with his men alone. A short while after Custer learned of Grant's decision, he chanced upon Captain William Ludlow, one of the two cadets he had urged to have a "fair fight" in the summer of 1861, and told him excitedly that once the campaign was under way he would "cut loose" at the first opportunity.[18]

THE SIOUX CAMPAIGN

THE PEACE COMMISSION OF 1867 that had concluded the Medicine Lodge Treaties and negotiated the Fort Laramie Treaty a year later established the Great Sioux Reservation in present-day South Dakota west of the Missouri River.[1] The purpose of the reservation was to convert the Indian nomads into farmers. The treaty "set apart for the absolute and undisturbed use and occupation of the Indians herein named." The United States agreed that no one except officers of the government on official business "shall ever be permitted to pass over, settle upon, or reside in the territory described in this article." In essence the treaty banned all whites from these Indian lands, from settling or even passing through.

The Fort Laramie Treaty allowed for certain unceded lands west of the reservation for the purpose of hunting game, which became a haven for dissenters who practiced the traditional ways of life. About three thousand Sioux and four hundred Cheyenne settled in the area north of the Platte River and east of the Bighorn Mountains, led by Hunkpapa chief Sitting Bull. This was the area that the surveying parties for the Northern Pacific Railroad penetrated in 1872–73, and these were the Indians that Custer fought then.

It wasn't long before a controversy developed over an unexplored area inside the reservation known as the Black Hills. These hills were considered sacred by the Sioux, though this was not an ancient claim, since they had only come to the area a little more than a hundred years earlier, displacing the indigenous Kiowa. More practically, the Black Hills was a good wintering spot, with ample game and winter firewood. There was an Indian legend of a mountain of gold, relayed by Father Pierre Jean De Smet, the first Catholic missionary to visit the area, who had been at the 1868 peace conference. The "mountain of gold" was in fact a formation of yellow mica, but even the hint of mineral wealth in the West conjured visions of El Dorado. The fact that the territory was off limits to whites excited speculation and jealousy, the lure of the unknown coupled with resentment of "savages" who didn't know what to do with the fortune they were sitting on. Rumor became the justification of desire, and denials only led to more speculation. Stories filtered out of prospectors being scalped, which fueled the indignation and the belief that the Sioux had something to hide.

In 1873, General Sheridan recommended establishing an Army post near the foot of the Black Hills in order "to secure a strong foothold in the heart of the Sioux country, and thereby exercise a controlling influence over these warlike people." In July and August 1874, Custer led a thousand-man expedition to the Black Hills, a reconnaissance mission seeking a site on which to build the post. William Ludlow was on the expedition as chief engineer of the Department of Dakota. Fred Grant also went along as an observer on Sheridan's staff. Geologists and prospectors accompanied the mission. Ore samples were brought back, with most serious geologists expressing skepticism that they portended gold in any meaningful quantities. Custer sent a dispatch from the field noting the discovery but adding the caveat that further study was needed.

The press was not so restrained. Sensational stories were written to confirm what most people already believed. Custer added to the rising mania by making less temperate remarks about the finds when he returned. Gold fever broke out and both prospectors and opportunists began moving towards the Dakota Territory. The expedition's chief geologist, Newton H. Winchell, doubted that gold had been discovered at all and raised the possibility that the samples offered as evidence had been planted. Fred Grant concurred. But Custer rebutted them in print, and also got into an exchange of articles with William B. Hazen over the value of land in the Dakotas. Custer represented the area in glowing terms, which pleased his friends at the Northern Pacific Railroad, who were attempting to leverage the value of their land rights to resuscitate their bankrupt firm. In return they gave Custer mostly free passage on the railroad.

Sheridan feared that gold fever in the Black Hills would lead inevitably to conflict as trespassers encountered young warriors seeking to protect their lands. "Many of the persons now crazy to go to the Black Hills never think of how they are to exist after they get there, or how they could return in case of failure," Sheridan wrote Sherman.[2] He deployed troops at key transit points to try to interdict prospectors. Yet the expected gold rush could not be stemmed. Miners and speculators flooded in, and outfitters founded a town they named after Custer. The government decided that another, more thorough survey was necessary to settle the gold question. Custer assumed he would lead it, but his boosterism made him unsuitable for the mission and it was given to Brigadier General George Crook instead. Crook explored the area in the summer of 1875, and his expedition revealed something less than an El Dorado. But enough evidence of gold was found to keep the fever alive.

By early 1876, twelve hundred miners were reported to be digging in the area.[3] Having failed to keep the trespassers out, the government opened negotiations to purchase the land from the Sioux. A Sioux delegation had visited Washington in May 1875 to get the government to address their concerns, such as the invasion of lands guaranteed them by treaty, the desecration of holy places in the Black Hills, and corruption in the Indian agencies. Chief Red Cloud responded to the idea of selling the Black Hills by saying, "Look at me! I am no Dog. I am a man. This is my ground, and I am sitting on it." Many discouraged Sioux began to leave the reservation to join the dissenters with Sitting Bull to the west. This precipitated an order from Secretary of the Interior Zachariah Chandler, in December 1875, decreeing that all Sioux must return to the reservation by the end of January or be sent back by force.

Sheridan wanted to move against the Indians in the winter, when advantages were with the soldiers—they were more mobile and better supplied; their horses would have comparatively more feed. It had worked well at Washita and Sherman was certain it would work again. But there was an appearance problem: the Indians hadn't done anything that would merit a full-scale campaign. Chandler's ultimatum was a means of establishing a pretext. On February 1, 1876, Chandler sent word to Secretary of War Belknap that since Sitting Bull's followers had not come to the reservation, they were considered to be hostiles and "turned over to the War Department for such action on the part of the Army as you may deem proper under the circumstances."[4] He absolved himself of whatever happened next. Frederick Benteen concluded that "this wasn't a fight instituted by the Army for glory going purposes, or anything of that kind; but rather, 'twas a little gentle disciplining which the Department of the Interior ... had promised would be given the Indians if they, the nomads of the tribe, declined to come in to agencies in the Spring."[5]

A column of eight hundred men was sent out in March 1876, led by Brigadier General Crook, an Ohioan and an Immortal of the Class of 1852, graduating sixth from the foot. He and Sheridan had been roommates at the Academy, and Crook later served under him in the Civil War. He ended the war at the rank of brevet major general. He had established a good reputation on the frontier and was declared the ablest of all men in dealing with the Indians, who referred to him as Gray Fox. They knew and respected Crook, and sometimes feared him. His column moved north through bitter cold, eventually locating an Indian village near the Powder River. It was thought to be Crazy Horse's, but was not. Crook's men burned the village, and some of the teepees, packed with ammunition, exploded. Then they withdrew.[6]

A major campaign was ordered for later in the spring or early summer. But by then, the number of Indians had swelled, mobility was restored, and the January deadline, then months past, had lost its authority. Meanwhile the rationale for the campaign was fading; the prospectors who had flocked to the Black Hills were discovering that the rumors of gold were much exaggerated, and some began to believe that the entire enterprise had been a fraud.[7] Land values in Custer City collapsed; lots that had sold for $500.00 dropped to $2.00. But the wheels of bureaucracy were moving and the expedition went forward.

A three-pronged campaign was planned:

• Brigadier General George Crook moving north with his command from Fort Fetterman, with over 1,300 officers and men.

• Colonel John Gibbon with 500 men of the Second Cavalry and the Seventh Infantry moving east down the Yellowstone River from Fort Ellis, Montana.

• Brigadier General Alfred Terry with over 900 men, predominately the Seventh Cavalry and including a small unit with three Gatling guns, moving west from Fort Lincoln, Dakota.

The three columns were to converge on the Indians, who were encamped somewhere east of the Bighorn Mountains, near the upper Little Bighorn River. Converging columns was a technique Sheridan had used before, in 1868 and in the 1874–75 Red River War. But the commanders had no idea how many Indians they faced or exactly where they were. Coordination of the separate elements of the campaign would be difficult; the columns would have to feel the enemy and attempt to herd them into a position where further resistance would be untenable. It was a delicate war of maneuver that did not have to end in major combat to be effective.

When Grant allowed Custer to go on the expedition, Sherman sent word to Terry, "Advise Custer to be prudent and not to take along any newspapermen who always work mischief."[8] Sherman was well known for his hostility to war journalists. During the Civil War he had banned the "dirty newspaper scribblers who have the impudence of Satan" from his command, and had Thomas Knox, a reporter for the

New York Herald, arrested for reporting the Union defeat at Chicka-saw Bluffs.[9] Custer had already arranged to send back anonymous reports of the campaign to the *Herald,* but General Terry disobeyed Sherman's guidance and granted permission for a reporter from the *Bismarck Tribune* to come along. Editor Clement Lounsberry, a former colonel of the First Michigan Sharpshooters, had hoped to go but could not, so he sent reporter Mark Kellogg in his place. Kellogg was a stringer for the Associated Press wire service with a nose for news, and he kept close to Custer, sending reports back for his own paper that were also carried in the *Herald.*

As the column prepared to march from Fort Lincoln, Custer was his usual flamboyant self, clad in buckskin, his hair cropped short. Kellogg reported:

> Gen. George A. Custer, dressed in a dashing suit of buckskin, is promi-nent everywhere. Here, there, flitting to and fro. in his quick eager way, taking in everything connected with his command, as well as generally, with the keen, incisive manner for which he is so well known. The Gen-eral is full of perfect readiness for a fray with the hostile red devils, and woe to the body of scalp-lifters that comes within reach of himself and brave companions in arms.

Libbie accompanied the column for a day before riding back to the fort, and the couple had an emotional leave-taking. This was later taken as premonition, but it was not unusual for them. The campaign was still a family affair; along for the adventure was Custer's eighteen-year-old nephew Armstrong "Autie" Reed, listed officially as a herder but really just out for the summer with his uncle. Boston Custer was there too, as a "guide."

Terry's column moved west in search of the foe, said to be nearby and in large numbers. Custer scouted, and found nothing. "All stories about large bodies of Indians being here are the merest bosh," he wrote.[10] But Indians were out there and did not wait for the campaign plan to unfold. A war party led by Crazy Horse struck first. Exploiting the advan-tage of interior lines, they moved south against Crook's column, hitting them near upper Rosebud Creek on June 17. The fight raged across the valley for six hours, and in the end Crook held the field but was out of ammunition. He pulled back to Goose Creek, near present-day Sheri-dan, Wyoming, to regroup and resupply. This effectively put his col-umn out of the campaign.

Meanwhile, unaware of Crook's engagement, Gibbon's and Terry's columns had united and were at the confluence of the Yellowstone and

Rosebud Creek. They still had not encountered the Sioux. A scouting mission was sent out under Major Marcus Reno, who, as noted earlier, had vied with Custer for the record number of demerits while at the Academy. Reno was a great friend of Cadet Whistler's, and later in life told the painter that had he made a career of the Army, no one would ever have heard of his mother. But this was an uncharacteristic moment of levity. Reno was generally taciturn and reserved. The Arikara scouts called him "Man with Dark Face." He had served in the Civil War as the commander of the Twelfth Pennsylvania Cavalry, part of the Army of the Potomac. He rose to the rank of brevet brigadier general, and after the war he was one of three majors in the Seventh Cavalry and the only one present on the Sioux campaign. Reno looked forward to his first Indian battle. He had not served directly under Custer before; this was the first time all the companies of the regiment had been assembled. When it appeared that Custer would not be allowed to go on the campaign, Reno had lobbied to be named commander in his stead—a fact that did not endear him to Custer. Reno went on his scout and reported possible signs of hostiles in the Little Bighorn Valley. He had exceeded orders on his scout and Terry chastised him, but the information he had gained was very valuable.

Given this fresh intelligence, Terry revised his operations concept. Custer would take the Seventh south up Rosebud Creek, turn west to the upper reaches of the Little Bighorn Valley and head north downstream as Crook's column was originally envisioned to do. Gibbon and Terry would meanwhile head south up the Bighorn to the Little Bighorn. If the timing was correct, they would catch the Indians in a pincer movement. One problem was not knowing exactly where the Indians were. It would be difficult to coordinate the two elements of the operation, and maneuvering on exterior lines would hamper communications. They would essentially be two independent forces attempting to wind up at the same place at the same time, not knowing exactly where that place was.

Compounding the situation was the fact that Custer could not be counted on to proceed cautiously, or to take steps that might have mitigated the communications difficulties. The only communiqué his superiors could expect was the after-action report recounting his brilliant victory. Terry amplified the problem by writing an order that gave Custer maximum latitude.[11] He ordered Custer to march up the Rosebud until he found evidence of the Indian trail discovered by Reno. He then had the option to engage the enemy if he thought it was necessary. "It is of course impossible to give you definite instructions as to your movements," Terry continued. "Even were it otherwise, the Officer in Command has too much confidence in your zeal, energy and skill to give you directions which might hamper your freedom of action when you have got into touch with the enemy." Terry then spelled out a detailed concept of operations in which Custer would coordinate with the second column and catch the Indians in the middle.

But Custer ignored most of the order. Read literally, it meant he did not have to follow the plan. He had every intention of using the latitude Terry had given him, whatever the situation. Kellogg's wire dispatch before the column moved out made this clear:

> [T]omorrow, June 22, General Custer with twelve Cavalry companies will scout from its mouth up the valley of the Rosebud until he reaches the fresh trail discovered by Major Reno, and move on that trail with all the rapidity possible in order to overhaul the Indians whom it has been ascertained are hunting buffalo and making daily leisurely short marches. Gibbon's part of the command will march up the Big Horn Valley in order to intercept the Indians if they should attempt to escape from General Custer down that avenue.

Custer had no intention of waiting to attack, and he saw the rest of the troops in the field as a backup force. His evening letter to Libbie highlighted the freedom of action he believed Terry had given him.[12] So far as Custer was concerned, it was akin to Sheridan's orders before Washita. He could use his own discretion. Later that night he mentioned to Second Lieutenant Winfield Scott Edgerly, an Immortal from the Class of 1870, "We are going to have a hard ride, for I intend to catch those Indians even if we have to follow them to their agencies."[13] He wanted to do it all himself and believed he could. Furthermore, he had a vital personal need to bring home a victory.

The next morning as the Seventh Cavalry departed, Gibbon said, "Now Custer, don't be greedy! Wait for us!"

"No, I won't," Custer replied.[14]

LITTLE BIGHORN

C USTER'S FORCE INCLUDED 31 OFFICERS, 566 men, 35 scouts and a dozen others. He left the Gatling guns behind, in the interests of mobility, and for the same reason took no artillery. He refused the services of four companies of Montana Volunteer Cavalry, who in any case did not want to serve under Custer's command. Terry also made him leave behind his brass band.

As Custer's regiment marched up the Rosebud (so called because wild roses grew on the banks), they came across some Sioux burial platforms, which the Crow scouts threw down, spilling the corpses wrapped in buffalo skins. On June 24 they discovered the site of a major village. At the center was an arbor two hundred feet in circumference around a thirty-five-foot pole made from a felled tree, around which were piled buffalo heads, evidence of a sun dance. In a sweat lodge the soldiers found pictures traced in sand that looked like a battle. It was the location where Sitting Bull, in an induced trance, saw soldiers falling upside down into the Sioux camp, later regarded as a premonition of the approaching encounter and the disaster to befall Custer.

Custer was not his usual self on the march. He held a planning meeting with his officers, and his customary tone, which was clipped, confident and businesslike, had become "conciliatory and subdued" according to Lieutenant Edward S. Godfrey. "There was an indefinable something that was *not* Custer."[1] They picked up the fresh Indian trail on June 24 and followed it until late in the afternoon, when it began to turn west. Custer went into camp and sent his scouts out to follow the trail. White Man Runs Him, Goes Ahead and Hairy Moccasin reported back that the trail led to the Little Bighorn Valley and a village was probably there, though they had not seen it. They could confirm in the morning from a promontory on the ridge between the valleys known as the Crow's Nest. At this point, Custer could have continued south to the upper Rosebud, near Crook's battlefield, then turned west and headed down the Little Bighorn towards the village. The timing would have been perfect to coordinate with Terry and Gibbon. He might have joined up with Crook, had Crook not withdrawn, a fact he was unaware of. This movement would have been more in line with the concept of operations that Terry had spelled out in his orders. But Custer had no intention of sharing the battle with anyone. After a brief rest, he ordered a night march west.

At midnight the regiment began the ascent up Davis Creek and the ridge between the two rivers. They marched six miles and made camp at two in the morning. Sunrise was before five, and at eight o'clock on the 25th, Custer's scouts returned and reported that they had spotted the village, fifteen miles away. "The scouts came in and reported a large village in our front—the General was highly pleased to hear it," trooper Pat Coleman noted in his diary. Coleman said this was the critical period; the old Custer had reemerged. "From the hour we left the Rosebud . . . his old-time restless energy had returned, and he seemed to think of nothing but to reach and strike the Indians." The pursuit was on in earnest. Custer's blood was up. "Every man feeling that the next twenty four hours would deside the fate of a good manney man," Coleman wrote, "and sure enough it did."[2]

At nine that morning, Custer went to the Crow's Nest to see for himself. He could not make out the village at first, but the scouts told him what to look for. The Indians believed it was a very large village based on the size of the pony herd (looking like "worms crawling in the grass" from that distance), with more braves than they could handle in two or three days. Custer made light of their estimate—one day, perhaps, he replied. Half-Yellow-Face, one of his Crow scouts, saw no reason for levity. He signed to Custer, "You and I are both going home today by a road we do not know."

The village stretched three miles along the river. "It is a lovely place," Pat Coleman wrote. "The valley is 1½ miles broad and four miles long, the river winding like a snake and dotted with Islands thickly studded with timber, the water clear as christal as it comes rushing from the Mountains." The river was "beautifully blue," according to Frederick Benteen.[3] Cottonwood trees and underbrush hugged the banks, and the surrounding hills were covered with long grass. The six tribal circles included numerous bands of Teton Sioux: Hunkpapa, Sans Arcs, Miniconjou, Oglala, Blackfoot, Two Kettle and Brulé. Other Sioux included the Yankton and Santee, and there were also 120 Cheyenne lodges. The Hunkpapa circle was at the southern end of the village, the Cheyenne to the north. Estimates vary on how many were there—at most 12,000 Indians total, of them 3,000 to 5,000 warriors and young men. Custer believed there were fewer, between 500 and 1,500.

Washita had taught Custer that Indians could be defeated if they were surprised in place. Indian warfare was based on mobile guerilla tactics, hit and run, each equally important. Faced with superior force and given the chance, they fled to fight another day. The key, at Washita as at Blue Waters, was to pin them down in their villages. This required speed and surprise. The traditional early-morning attack was not feasible on June 25. Custer had planned to do a careful reconnaissance, rest his troops and deploy them that night for a crushing dawn attack on the 26th; but he grew impatient as the morning went on. He questioned his scouts' assertions concerning the size of the village, which was much larger than expected. His own observations from the Crow's Nest led him to believe that the village was smaller. He grew more agitated when several incidents led him to believe that he and his men had been spotted, thus losing them the element of surprise. So he called his officers and said they would attack that day. According to Lieutenant Godfrey, Custer chose to attack because "our discovery made it imperative to act at once, as delay would allow the village to scatter and escape."[4]

Custer led the way towards the river, wearing a dark blue shirt, buckskin trousers, and a large white hat. He rode into battle flying his personal standard; the regimental banner was left furled in the pack train. His attack plan was reminiscent of Harney's at the Battle of Blue Waters twenty years earlier. Custer divided his regiment into three battalions, led by himself, Marcus Reno and Frederick Benteen.[5] Custer and Reno advanced in tandem down Reno Creek. Benteen was to scout south towards the south fork of Reno Creek looking for more Indians. Reno and his three troops of 112 men were to cross the river and engage the Indian village from the south while Custer and five troops rode ahead along the ridgeline to the right to hit the Indians in the flank, or pursue them as they broke and ran. Benteen was to take his three troops a short distance to the south to make certain the rear was secure before moving north quickly either to reinforce Reno or Custer, or to join the general rout of the Indians. According to Lieutenant Edgerly, in Benteen's command, this movement was not simply a reconnaissance mission; Custer may not have known exactly where the southern terminus of the village was, and Benteen's men were ordered "to go over to the left and charge the Indians as soon as we saw them."[6]

Around 2 P.M., Custer's group paused at a lone teepee about five miles from the village, within which was the body of a warrior killed in the engagement with Crook. Lieutenant Luther R. Hare (USMA 1874), Reno's chief of scouts, and Custer's lead scout Fred Gerard saw what they believed to be the Indians fleeing from the village, and reported this back to Custer. "Here are your Indians, General, running like devils!" Gerard shouted. Private Thomas O'Neill, looking at the village, recalled, "We could see the Indians, they looked very much like an ants nest that was disturbed running this way and that, and about a thousand of them in sight."[7] A half hour later, as the cavalry rode up over the ridge above the village, approximately three miles distant, Custer sent Reno across the river to move forward rapidly and commence the attack, adding "You will be supported by the whole outfit." The bulk of the Indian scouts were to secure the pony herd while Reno swept into the village.

Reno's troops galloped into the valley in columns of twos around 3 P.M. Lieutenant Charles A. Varnum (USMA 1872) rode ahead shouting, "Thirty days' furlough to the man who gets the first scalp!"[8] Reno crossed the river and set up a skirmish line with the right flank anchored on a wooded section of dry riverbed. Custer was wrong in one respect—they had achieved surprise. The Sioux who had seen Custer's force that morning were not from this village and the Indians in the valley were unprepared for an afternoon attack. When morning had passed without sign of soldiers, they drew in their scouts and believed they would pass the day in peace. The Indians at first were stunned, but quickly recovered and began to organize a defense. Women and children ran west for the hills as warriors headed towards Reno to meet the threat, and towards the pony herd to secure their mounts. Reno poured in rounds from 700–900 yards. Hundreds of Indians led by Crazy Horse swarmed out of the village, on foot and horseback, returning fire.

It became clear that Custer had underestimated both the size of the village and the will of the Indians to bring battle. It was not like Blue Waters, where the demoralized Indians chose not to fight. Two Moon, a Cheyenne participant, recalled the chaos of the mêlée. "I saw the white soldiers fighting in a line. Indians covered the flat. They began to drive the soldiers all mixed up—Sioux, then soldiers, then more Sioux, and all shooting. The air was full of smoke and dust."[9]

Indians got on Reno's left and began to turn his flank. Some infiltrated his line and engaged his men hand to hand. Reno saw he was about to be overrun, pulled back and pivoted counterclockwise 90 degrees, into a wooded bend in the river with his back to the water, a marginally more secure position but leaving him unable to execute the tactical plan. Fighting continued with Indians using the underbrush to creep slowly into his position. After about half an hour, Reno saw that the situation was hopeless and ordered a fighting withdrawal across the river back up the heights on the eastern bank. As he was doing so, Bloody Knife, Custer's favorite scout, who was next to Reno, was hit in the head with a bullet. His head exploded, showering Reno with blood and brains. Reno, shaken, bolted out of the timber and rode hard a mile upriver to the crossing. Some followed, at least those who had noticed what was going on. Others were left behind. Few units were able to mount a coherent defense as they pulled back, and the disorganized withdrawal meant death for many. The Indians, first believing that Reno was counterattacking, then saw he was withdrawing, and they surged forward and began pulling down riders or knocking them from their mounts with rifles and clubs. The river crossing was difficult, down a five- to ten-foot bank, across the four-foot-deep river and up a steep slope. The riders had no time to find a fording place, and they barreled over the river bank and into the water "like buffalo fleeing," according to Two Moon.

"What is this—a *retreat*?" said Lieutenant Benjamin "Benny" Hodgson as men bolted by him. Hodgson was an 1870 graduate who was left back his plebe year. He was an unruly student who racked up 747 demerits in his five years, beating Custer's total of 726 but taking an extra year to do it.

"It looks most damnably like a *rout*," another lieutenant replied. Hodgson made for the river but was shot from his mount as he went down the bank. He beckoned to a passing sergeant, "For God's sake, take me to the river!" The sergeant helped him across, having him hold the stirrup, dragging him through the water. But as Hodgson staggered up the steep bank on the other side, he was shot again, and that finished him.[10] Lieutenant Donald "Tosh" McIntosh, a half-Indian Canadian who was no clear relation to the McIntoshes of Georgia, lost his horse and a trooper insisted he take his mount. The lieutenant refused, but the soldier jumped off anyway, and McIntosh leapt on the horse and rode off. Minutes later he was dragged off and killed.

Meanwhile Custer had moved north and was unaware of what was transpiring in his rear. His exact route is speculative. When he finally saw the extent of the village, he was not afraid. "We've caught them napping," he said to John Martin, his orderly and trumpeter. Turning to his officers, he shouted, "We've got them!"

Sergeant Daniel Kanipe of Tom Custer's Company C recalled, "At the sight of the camp the boys began to cheer. Some horses became so excited that some riders were unable to hold them in ranks, and the last words I heard Custer say were, 'Hold your horses in boys, there are plenty of them down there for all of us.' "[11] Kanipe was sent back to urge Captain Thomas M. McDougall to bring up the pack train. Custer also sent trumpeter Martin bearing written instructions for Benteen. Martin, whose birth name was Giovanni Martini, was an Italian immigrant who had been a drummer boy for Garibaldi. He set off south and soon passed Boston Custer coming up from the pack train.

"Where's the General?" Boston said.

"Right behind that next ridge you'll find him." Boston rode off, the sound of gunfire already audible to the north.[12] Lieutenant Edgerly, with Benteen's troop, had seen Boston pass a few minutes earlier. "He gave me a cheery salutation as he passed and then with a smile on his face, rode to his death."[13]

Custer and his men rode down a ravine called Cedar Coulee, which joined Medicine Tail Coulee, ending at the river. At some point in this movement he released his Crow scouts White Man Runs Him, Goes Ahead, Hairy Moccasin and Curley. Three left, but Curley remained. He and famed scout Mitch Boyer witnessed Reno's retreat and sought out Custer at upper Medicine Tail Coulee, giving him the news. Custer sent two companies under George W. Yates down to the river while the rest withdrew to the heights. Indians were already moving up the ravine and Yates repelled them with fire before heading back to join the rest of the command.

Custer may have believed that Reno would try to consolidate the regiment, and he had already ordered Benteen forward. If he sent a similar order to Reno, it never got there. Custer may have been taking high ground to await their arrival, establish a defensive cordon and fight his way out. He had done it before—in June 1864 at Trevillian Station, Virginia, where he mounted a surprise assault on the Confederate rear but an expected attack on the front was delayed and the Michigan Brigade was nearly surrounded. Outnumbered five to one, Custer battled for three hours, at one point saving his brigade standard by wrapping it around his own body. He withdrew slowly, maneuvered through a miraculous river crossing and saved his command. When he returned to headquarters he found that he had been reported killed.

When Reno achieved the bluffs he was joined by Benteen. It was just after 4 P.M. Benteen had received the now famous message from Custer, borne by John Martin: "Benteen. Come on. Big village. Be quick. Bring packs. P[S] Bring pacs." Benteen had a low opinion of Martin, "a thick headed, dull witted Italian, just about as much cut out for a cavalryman as he was for a King."[14] Benteen had not found any

Indians, and Martin informed him that those in the village were "skedad-
dling." But there was the sound of heavy gunfire and Captain Thomas
B. Weir, one of Custer's coterie, counseled that they ride to the sound
of the guns. Benteen hesitated; Weir and Company D rode off alone.
Benteen followed, not waiting for the pack train. He arrived to see Reno
struggling up the hill under fire. His men helped drive off the Indians
who, at the sight of reinforcements, broke off the attack and swung
north to join the battle raging downstream.

"Where is Custer?" Benteen asked. Reno said he did not know.
Custer and his men were out of sight down the valley, obscured by the
rolling terrain and the dust cloud being raised by the hundreds if not
thousands of Indians now moving on his command from every side.

Reno began to prepare a defensive position, but sounds of battle
continued to the north, including several volleys that some of the men
interpreted as a distress signal. Reno showed no signs of taking action,
other than burying the dead. Some say Reno had gone insane, but loss
of nerve and judgment is closer to the mark. Again, Captain Weir took
the initiative. He moved his company north down the ridge heading for
Custer's position. One story has it that he and Reno had exchanged
harsh words beforehand. Weir mounted the heights above the southern edge of Medicine Tail Coulee about four miles from Custer's position. Through the swirling dust he saw horsemen riding, and the
distinctive swallowtail stars and stripes guidons of the Seventh Cavalry.

"That is Custer over there!" he shouted, and ordered the company to make ready to ride into the battle. A sergeant, standing next to
Weir, stayed him.

"Here Captain," he said, "you had better take a look through the
glasses." He handed Weir the binoculars, adding, "I think those are
Indians." Weir raised the glasses and studied the scene. He then lowered them, and had his men stand down. On the distant ridge, groups
of mounted Indians rode in circles, waving the guidons, shooting down
at the ground, dispatching the wounded. Others on foot, men and
women, had begun the grisly task of looting and desecrating the corpses.
Bodies of cavalrymen and their mounts lay scattered about the hill.

It is difficult to know what happened in Custer's final moments.[15]
There were hundreds of Indian survivors from Custer's sector, scores
of eyewitnesses to tell how the battle ended. Unfortunately, their versions vary widely.[16] Even Sitting Bull gave conflicting, sometimes highly
embellished accounts.[17] They generally credit Custer with having
achieved surprise, which caused some disarray among the Indians at
first, but from which they soon recovered. They mostly agree that Custer

and his men fought bravely, and Reno and his troops did not. "I never before nor since saw men so brave and fearless as those white warriors," Oglala chief Low Dog later recalled.[18] But much beyond this is speculative. That part of the battle has been reconstructed various ways, using participant accounts, archaeology, and especially the location of the bodies. As for details such as when and how Custer died, we will probably never know.

Yates' two companies went down to the ford following Medicine Tail Coulee. It would have been characteristic of Custer to be leading them. They were driven back, retreating up Deep Coulee to the north. Miles Keogh, posted on the heights, moved north to consolidate the forces. They linked up on Calhoun Hill, the southernmost prominence on Battle Ridge. Custer established his left flank a half mile north. The soldiers faced a three-pronged assault. Crazy Horse had crossed downriver and come up a ravine, striking from the northwest, primarily against F and I Companies (Yates and Keogh). Gall came up from the south and southeast, hitting C and L Companies (Harrington and Calhoun). E Company (Smith) faced a direct attack up from the river led by Cheyenne leader Lame White Man, who had rallied his warriors after being attacked by Harrington's men, and was later killed by friendly fire.

"This is a good day to die, follow me!" Low Dog said, as his braves galloped towards Custer's men.[19] "Then the shooting was quick, quick," Two Moon recalled. "Pop—pop—pop very fast. Some of the soldiers were down on their knees, some standing. Officers all in front. The smoke was like a great cloud, and everywhere the Sioux went the dust rose like smoke. We circled all around them—swirling like water round a stone. We shoot, we ride fast, we shoot again. Soldiers drop, and horses fall on them."[20] The cavalrymen were overwhelmed. There may have been little organized resistance. There was clearly some panic, which is understandable as the defensive crescent began to collapse. Battlefield archaeology indicates that the soldiers on Calhoun Hill mounted the more coherent defense, though a hundred years of souvenir hunting around Custer Hill may have removed most of the cartridge evidence on that flank.[21] Some accounts have Custer's position breaking first; others, for example from Gall, have the southern flank collapsing. Either way, Custer had done what he could with what he had. Edward J. McClernand (USMA 1870), who was with Gibbon's command, later wrote that "the position [Custer took] was the best obtainable; the line he established on the ridge, running from this position towards the river, showed more care taken in deploying and placing the men than, in my opinion, was shown on any other part of the field."[22]

Benteen had set off after Weir, but soon saw him and his men returning, "hordes of Indians hurrying them somewhat." The troopers consolidated their position and established a defensive ring on one of the hilltops, digging in with their hunting knives. They fought off Indian attacks for the rest of the day, through the night, and into the next day. Reno was in titular command of the defense but Benteen was the true leader, walking among the men, exhorting them to fight, and leading sallies outside the perimeter against Indian snipers. The battle finally ended late on the 26th. Sitting Bull explained, "I did not want to kill any more men. I did not like that kind of work. I only defended my camp. When we had killed enough, that was all that was necessary."[23] It was a magnificent stand, akin to the Battle of Roarke's Drift in the Zulu War, which would take place three years later. And as at Roarke's Drift, the defenders were recognized for their heroism. Twenty-four Medals of Honor were awarded for the stand on Reno Hill, one-twentieth of all the medals awarded in the Indian Wars. Most of the awards went to men who made the hazardous trip to fetch water from the river.

The Indians decamped south ahead of the relief column on June 27, moving towards the safety of the Bighorn Mountains. Gibbon's column arrived at ten that morning. They passed through the abandoned village site and then moved towards Reno's position. The Indians left behind a great deal of debris and several lodges hung with blankets containing dead warriors in funeral garb. Three burned human heads hung by a wire on one pole; on another was a man's heart. Charles F. Roe saw dark objects scattered on the hillside across the river from the village site and concluded they were dead buffalo. A few of Reno's men who had been left behind on the other side of the river emerged. They had hidden in the woods and been overlooked in the chaos of the battle. One was the trooper who had given his horse to Lieutenant McIntosh. Some of the men on Reno Hill thought the relief column was led by Custer, who had abandoned them as he had Elliott at Washita and was now returning. The men in Gibbon's command were aware that a battle had been fought but disbelieved that a tragedy of this scale could have taken place. It was inconceivable—not to Custer, who exuded a sense of immortality.

But Custer's luck had finally run out. Five of the twelve troops of his regiment were wiped out; 197 men died with Custer, 47 were killed with Reno and Benteen, and 52 others were wounded. For the Custers it was a family tragedy: brothers George, Tom and Boston were dead, along with Autie Reed and brother-in-law James Calhoun. Custer's Scottish wolfhound Tuck died alongside his master.

First on the scene on Battle Ridge was Lieutenant James H. Bradley, Seventh Infantry, who himself would be killed just over a year later fighting the Nez Perce at the Battle of Big Hole. The carnage was horrific. Roe noted in his diary, "June 27th—Arrived at Little Big Horn Valley—found Reno and remnant of 7th on hill fortified—Custer, 15 officers, over three hundred men killed, 50 wounded—dead horses and soldiers scattered all over valley for miles. The most terrible sight ever witnessed—I cannot write my thoughts." Roe later managed to compose himself and three days later wrote his wife: "The battle field Kate was awful, awful—dead men & horses in all directions. Everyone of the bodies stripped, scalped and mutilated." Roe said their column had seen the Indians retreating and had they attacked them immediately they would have routed them, but "the powers would not order it, so the very best opportunity we will ever have has been thrown away. . . . Such is fate, blunders are constantly made which can never be retrieved."

Pat Coleman and some others went across the river to search for a member of their company and "could not recognize him. All of them were scalped and otherwise horably mutilated. Some had their heads cut off, others arms, one legs. [The Indians'] hatred extended even to the poor horses they cut and slashed them before they were dead. . . . Oh, what a slaughter. How manney homes are made desolate by the sad disaster." Coleman found Lieutenant Benny Hodgson, "shot twise with Ball and once with arrow. Several other bodies lay close by. I Burried the Lieut on a nice Knowl overlooking the river with a cedar tree at his head. He was a Brave officer and a true gentleman." Besides Custer and Hodgson, three other West Point graduates died on the field: Lieutenant James E. Porter (USMA 1869), with Keogh's Company I; Second Lieutenant Henry M. Harrington (USMA 1872), commanding Company C; and Lieutenant James Garland Sturgis (USMA 1875), the son of Colonel Samuel Sturgis, who had joined the unit the previous September fresh from the Academy and was on his first campaign.

"Tosh" McIntosh was unrecognizable. He was identified by his brother-in-law, Lieutenant Francis Marion Gibson, who noticed some sleeve buttons his sister had given her husband before leaving Fort Lincoln. Journalist Mark Kellogg died with C and E troops. He was the first Associated Press reporter to die in battle. His last dispatch to Lounsberry read, "By the time this reaches you we would have met and fought the red devils, with what result remains to be seen. I go with Custer and will be at the death." His sun-bloated body was found scalped and was identified by his shoe.

John J. Crittenden, who had been so determined to live the life of a soldier, died with Calhoun. Edgerly noted, "The first dead soldiers we came to were Lieuts. Calhoun, Crittenden and the enlisted men of L troop. The bodies of these men were lying a short distance in rear of their men, in the very place where they belonged, and the bodies of their men forming a very regular skirmish line. Crittenden's body was shot full of arrows."[24]

Tom Custer was found severely mutilated. He could be positively identified only by a tattoo, spotted by Lieutenant Edward S. Godfrey, who had served with Tom in the 21st Ohio in 1861. Hunkpapa chief Rain in the Face was said to have torn out Tom's heart and paraded it through the Indian village on a pole, an act of personal vengeance. In December 1874, Tom Custer and a small party had arrested Rain in the Face for killing three men in Custer's command on the Yellowstone expedition. He was taken to Fort Lincoln but later escaped, vowing revenge, so it was said. Henry Wadsworth Longfellow wrote a famous poem about the event, averring that it was George Custer's heart that the chief "uplifted high in the air as a ghastly trophy, bore."[25] Rain in the Face later described in detail how and why he tore out Tom Custer's heart, but on his deathbed he recanted the story. He said he had simply taken credit for what was being rumored.[26] In fact it is highly doubtful that Tom Custer's heart was cut out at all. Rain in the Face also claimed to have killed George Custer. "I killed him. I made many holes in him. He once took my liberty; I took his life. I am glad I did."[27] He recanted this story too.

George Custer was found naked and unmutilated, with two wounds, in his left breast and left temple. He was propped in an angle formed by two of his men lying across each other, his arm across the top of them, the small of his back touching the ground, his head lying in his right hand as if in thought, smiling. Pat Coleman wrote of Custer's group, "Every one of them were scalped and otherwise mutilated but the General he lay with a smile on his face. The Indians eaven respected the great Chief." Low Dog explained that "the wise men and chiefs of our nation gave out to our people not to mutilate the dead white chief, for he was a brave warrior and died a brave man, and his remains should be respected."[28] It was not clear that the Indians knew it was Custer, just that he had led and fought bravely (implying he survived well into the attack). Hunkpapa chief Crow King stated, "No warrior knew Custer in the fight. We did not know him, dead or alive. When the fight was over the chiefs gave orders to look for the long-haired chief among the dead, but no chief with long hair could be found."[29] Low Dog concurred:

"I did not see General Custer. I do not know who killed him. We did not know till the fight was over that he was the white chief."[30] Sergeant Kanipe said that only the wounded were mutilated, that the squaws would not mutilate a corpse. It was a form of torture that was wasted on the dead.

One thesis has it that Custer committed suicide; another that they all did.[31] Robert Utley convincingly argues that tales of mass suicide originated with Indians who had come in to the agencies shortly after the battle who did not want to be blamed for killing any troopers. According to Sitting Bull, Custer fought bravely to the end. He gave his admittedly secondhand account in an 1877 interview:

> *Sitting Bull:* Well, I have understood that there were a great many brave men in that fight, and that from time to time, while it was going on, they were shot down like pigs. They could not help themselves. One by one the officers fell.... Any way it was said that up there where the last fight took place, where the last stand was made, the Long Hair stood like a sheaf of corn with all the ears fallen around him.
>
> *Interviewer:* How many stood by him?
>
> *Sitting Bull:* A few.
>
> *Interviewer:* When did he fall?
>
> *Sitting Bull:* He killed a man when he fell. He laughed.
>
> *Interviewer:* You mean he cried out.
>
> *Sitting Bull:* No, he laughed; he had fired his last shot.

An old trapper who had known Custer and lived among the Indians talked to the Sioux after the battle, and stated that while he thought Custer went down fighting like a "little devil," he was only speculating, and everyone else was too. "I do not believe there is a man living, red or white," he wrote, "who knows how Custer died."[32] Frederick Benteen, standing over Custer's body, made the definitive statement. "There he is, God damn him, he will never fight any more."[33]

My Every Thought Was Ambition

I T TOOK SEVERAL DAYS FOR THE first reports of the Little Bighorn tragedy to make it into the papers, and they competed for headlines with reportage from the Centennial celebration in Philadelphia. Generals Sherman and Sheridan were both there and dismissed the initial stories as rumor. Such tales had attached themselves to Custer many times before. A week later, detailed accounts sent by telegraph began to appear in the press. They had outstripped the official Army reports, which were sent overland by messenger. Official word did not reach Washington until 3 P.M. on July 6, more than ten days since the battle. General Sherman received confirmation while in the middle of an interview with the *New York Herald* in which he was denouncing it all as speculation.

Custer's death was an unimaginable story that grew in the telling. Given the emotional content, the lack of white eyewitnesses to the final moments, the geographical distance, the limitations of the communications media and competition among the press, many dubious tales got into print. In all cases, it was seen as an unparalleled military disaster. "The massacre of Major Dade and his command in the Florida war is alone comparable with it in American history," the *New York Times* opined.[1] There was of course the Fetterman Massacre in December 1866; also the murder of Brigadier General Edward Richard Sprigg Canby April 11, 1873, by Modoc Indian chief Captain Jack, during peace negotiations.[2] There was as well the slaughter that began in Minnesota on August 17, 1862, in which Santee Sioux under Little Crow killed 644 whites, and later 38 Santee were executed, the largest mass execution in American history. As for the number of soldiers killed at Little Bighorn, compared with many Civil War battles it was a minor affair. But numbers were not the determining factor in making Little Bighorn one of the defining battles in American history. Rather, it was the context. The Civil War had been over for a decade. People were not used to this kind of killing on the frontier. The Indians were not supposed to win. And they killed the immortal Custer.

Analysis of the event began immediately, and every pundit had his say. One commentator, wise to the ways of Washington, noted that "the affair will be made use of as an argument by those who insist upon transferring the Indian Bureau to the War Department, and also by those who oppose such legislation. It will be made an excuse for increasing the Army, and held up as a reason for cutting it down."[3] These were sagacious words; it did not take long for these and many other issues to be examined through the lens of the Custer tragedy, a process that continues well over a century later.

With 1876 being an election year, the event was quickly exploited for political gain. On July 16, a *New York Herald* editorial entitled "Who Slew Custer?" laid the blame on President Grant, both for pursuing a peace policy and for the corruption in the Indian agencies that had helped inflame Sioux passions. It became expedient for the Democrats to beat the war drums, making the president look weak and his war planning inadequate. The *New York World*—which supported Samuel Tilden for the presidency—suggested that Custer died because he was not in overall command of the expedition, the result of Grant's pettiness after Custer's testimony against Belknap. This charge is only partly true; Custer might have commanded Terry's column, but not the entire expedition, and what difference that would have made to the outcome is speculative. Probably none, since Custer was following his own counsel. "No military man ever charged Custer with conservatism, hesitation, excessive deference to the opinion of others, or unwillingness to 'go in and win,'" the pro-Republican *New York Times* countered.[4] Republicans noted that the Army had asked to establish military posts on the upper Yellowstone that could have served as better supply points, allowing more troops to have been deployed and thus staving off disaster—had the Democrat-controlled Appropriations Committee not refused to fund the measure. Others blamed the white invasion of the Black Hills for bringing about the situation in the first place. The Sioux expedition was conjured by mythical gold, but it cost the nation genuine blood and treasure. The irony of course was that Custer had encouraged the Black Hills gold rush.

The *New York Sun* sought to explain it through Custer's personality. Custer meant "to fight alone, and alone win a great battle and harvest the glory of a victory which should put an end to Sioux warfare. It was a great stake, gallantly but madly played for, and ruinously lost. The dashing cavalryman, charming gentleman, and accomplished scholar paid his life and the lives of his male relatives, and the lives of over three hundred of the best soldiers in the army, as the penalty for his rash ambition."[5] General McClellan's assessment was that "those who accused him of reckless rashness would, perhaps, have been the first to accuse him of timidity if he had not attacked, and thus allowed the enemy to escape unhurt. He died as he had lived, a gallant soldier; and his whole career was such as to force me to believe that he had good reasons for acting as he did."[6] Lieutenant Godfrey, in a letter to Charles Roe in 1918, noted that had Custer succeeded, "he would have been hailed as a genius and hero, and nothing ever would have been said about disobedience, rashness and blunders and court martial."[7] For his part, Colonel Gibbon chose not to speculate. "General Custer is dead and cannot tell his side of the story or of the motives which influenced his action," he wrote, "which I think ought to prevent us from severely criticizing his course."[8]

President Grant had no difficulty blaming Custer. "I regard Custer's Massacre as a sacrifice of troops, brought on by Custer himself, that was wholly unnecessary—wholly unnecessary."[9] Sherman and Sheridan also declared the attack rash and ill considered, though Sherman later told an anguished General Thomas L. Crittenden, whose son had perished in the battle, "when Custer found himself in the presence of the Indians, he could do nothing but attack."[10] General Samuel D. Sturgis, who also lost his son at Little Bighorn, was very vocal in his condemnation. He felt that Custer had been motivated by his need for notoriety after the clash with Grant, and this had clouded his judgment. "What I especially deprecate is the manner in which some papers have sought to make a demigod out of Custer, and to erect a monument to Custer, and none to his soldiers," he said in an interview a few weeks after the massacre. "Custer was a brave man, but he was also a very selfish man. He was insanely ambitious for glory, and the phrase 'Custer's luck' affords a good clue to his ruling passion." Sturgis denied that he was primarily motivated by anger at the loss of his son, but he still blamed Custer for it. "When I knew that my boy had gone out," he continued, "and that General Terry was in command I felt that we were tolerably fortunate. Terry has a matured judgment, and I looked for the campaign to be conducted on good military principles, instead of which Custer made his attack recklessly, earlier by thirty-six to forty-eight hours than he should have done, and with men tired out by forced marches."[11]

Terry's dispatch to Washington after the battle indicated that he had expected Custer to follow his detailed orders. Precise measurements had been made calculating distance covered and probable rates of march over several days. Had Custer gone to the headwaters of the Rosebud before turning west to the Little Bighorn, the two columns would have come on the scene simultaneously.[12] "The plan adopted was the only one that promised to bring the Infantry into action and I desired to make sure of things by getting up every available man," he wrote. "The movements proposed for General Gibbon's column were carried out to the letter and had the attack been deferred until it was up I cannot doubt that we should have been successful."

Others received equal or greater shares of blame. A portion landed on Benteen, but over time most fell on Marcus Reno. Author Frederick Whittaker, whose biography of Custer, rushed out in December 1876, was pure hero-worship, pushed for a Court of Inquiry on Reno's behavior in the battle. In Whittaker's opinion, Reno disobeyed orders and left Custer to die, perhaps intentionally. Thomas Rosser, then living in St. Paul and with no more information than anyone else who had not been on the scene, wrote a widely reprinted letter to the *St. Paul Pioneer Press and Tribune* blaming Reno for deserting Custer. The Army was loath to bring proceedings, but Whittaker made such an issue of it that Reno himself demanded the chance to clear his name. Reno was eventually found not culpable for Custer's death, but the decision was worded in such a way that neither side was satisfied. In the years following the battle, Reno was court-martialed twice for "conduct unbecoming an officer and a gentleman": once for attempting to take advantage of another officer's wife (1877), and the second time for drunkenness and lewd behavior directed at Colonel Sturgis's daughter (1879). He was found guilty both times, given clemency for the first offense, but dishonorably discharged for the second. Reno died penniless in 1889.[13]

Word of Custer's death reached the Corps of Cadets while they were encamped at the Centennial celebration in Philadelphia. Soon, two new verses were added to "Benny Havens', Oh!"

> In silence lift your glasses; a meteor flashes out.
> So swift to death brave Custer, amid the battle's shout
> Death called—and crowned, he went to join the friends of long ago
> To the land of Peace, where now he dwells with Benny Havens, Oh!
>
> We drop a tear for Harrington, and his comrades, Custer's braves,
> Who fell with none to see the deeds that glorified their graves.
> May their memories live forever, with their glory's present glow;
> They've nobly earned the right to dwell with Benny Havens, Oh!

In May 1877, General Sheridan proposed retrieving the bodies of the officers from the battlefield and giving them a proper military burial. His brother Colonel M. V. Sheridan was sent to oversee the exhumation and movement of the remains. General Sheridan himself visited the battlefield on the one-year anniversary of the battle.[14] Frank Palmer of Company C, Seventh Cavalry, who helped bury the bodies, said there was no chance of confusion regarding their identities. The bodies of the officers had been carefully buried and marked with slips of paper embedded in wooden disks or in spent cartridges, sealed with wax and driven into the ground at the head of the grave. But the graves of the enlisted men were not marked at all.[15]

Captains Yates and Tom Custer, Lieutenants Smith, McIntosh and Calhoun were buried at Leavenworth, August 3, 1877. It was a low-key ceremony, sparsely attended. The planned "imposing military display" was called off because most of the soldiers had been sent to St. Louis to help suppress the Great Railroad Strike of 1877, which had spread to other industries and shut the city down.[16] Lieutenant McIntosh was later transferred to Arlington National Cemetery. Boston Custer and Autie Reed were buried in the family plot in the Woodland Cemetery in Monroe, Michigan. The Custer Battlefield National Cemetery was established August 1, 1879, though the enlisted and unidentified dead were left in shallow graves until 1881, when many were reburied in a mass grave on Custer Hill. Charles F. Roe supervised the placing of the eighteen-ton granite monument marking the spot. The white stone markers showing where the men fell were installed in 1890.

Lieutenant John J. Crittenden had not been exhumed. His father, who after the massacre had transferred from the frontier to Governor's Island, New York, opposed reburial as a matter of principle. "There can be no fitter resting place for the true soldier than that spot which his blood has hallowed," General Crittenden wrote. "It would be vandalism to dig up and scatter widely the bones of those men who have been buried, as they died, shoulder to shoulder. They all perished together, fighting without hope, and the comradeship thus cemented should never be sundered."[17] Crittenden's remains were left buried where he fell until 1931 when they were relocated to the National Cemetery.[18]

Custer's body was taken to a vault at the Poughkeepsie Cemetery for storage until October, so that officers and cadets then on furlough could be present for the funeral, and also to allow others who might want to attend to make travel plans. The remains were in a wooden box, sealed in Fort Lincoln and bearing a certificate signed by post surgeon R. G. Read. A rumor spread a year later that the remains were not of

Custer but of a teamster.[19] However, with the body came a unique carved cavalry spur, one of two that Custer had worn for the past eleven years. It was one of the spurs he had borrowed from Frank Huger, originally belonging to Antonio Lopez de Santa Anna. Custer had never given them back after the war. Libbie eventually returned the spur to Huger.[20] Santa Anna had died in Mexico City four days before Custer, at age eighty-two, impoverished and forgotten.

Custer's body was taken through Poughkeepsie on October 10, 1877, with a military escort, the flag-draped coffin in a hearse followed by a riderless horse. The flag was the same one that adorned the coffin of Louis McLane Hamilton, killed at Washita, who was buried in Poughkeepsie. Ten thousand spectators thronged the streets. Custer was taken from Poughkeepsie down the Hudson on the *Mary Powell*—the same riverboat from which Dennis Hart Mahan jumped to his death. At West Point, Custer's coffin was carried from the south dock to the chapel to lie in state. Fresh flowers surrounded the dais, and atop was a two-foot-high column of dried flowers known as immortelles, near which were arranged Custer's sword and hat. At the foot was a wreath encircling the words "Seventh Cavalry," and above the head of the coffin at the back wall a festooned American flag and a blue silk banner with gold letters, "God and Our Native Land."

Thousands turned out for the procession to the cemetery. Elizabeth, weeping freely, walked close behind the caisson, supported by Superintendent Schofield. A riderless horse followed, with the regalia of a major general. At the cemetery, the service was brief. The remains were lowered into the grave; some dirt was sprinkled on top. The chaplain made a brief address and the Corps of Cadets fired three volleys in salute. George Custer had returned to West Point for the last time.

Custer once wrote, "In years long numbered with the past when I was merging upon manhood my every thought was ambition; not to be wealthy, not to be learned but to be great. I desired to link my name with acts and men and in such manner as to be a mark of honor not only to the present but to future generations." This was how Custer had lived his life, and was the way he met his death.

THE IMMORTALS

JOHN TAYLOR PRATT, WEST POINT'S first Goat in 1818, always wanted to return to the colors, but was never given the chance. He lived out his later years as a merchant and farmer. Before his death at age eighty-seven in Georgetown, Kentucky, on November 29, 1883, he was the oldest living graduate of the Academy.

William Walton Morris, Goat of the Class of 1820, remained in uniform his entire adult life. He had fought on the frontier in the 1820s, was with David Moniac at the Battle of Wahoo Swamp against the Seminoles, and was on Taylor's staff at Palo Alto and Resaca de la Palma. He served on the plains in the 1850s, and wore Union blue in the Civil War, commanding the Harbor Defenses of Baltimore during the conflict. When President Lincoln suspended rights of habeas corpus during the war, Morris became his chief enforcer in the border state of Maryland, imprisoning rebel sympathizers without trial. His actions led to several seminal Supreme Court cases; ironically, in 1787 his great-uncle Gouverneur Morris had proposed the language that enshrined the right to trial in the U.S. Constitution. Morris was promoted to brevet major general, U.S. Army, on December 10, 1865, for "faithful and meritorious services during the Rebellion." He died the next day at Fort McHenry, Maryland, age sixty-four.

Albert Gallatin Edwards, the Goat of 1832, was a brigadier general of the Missouri Militia during the Civil War, and from 1865 to 1886 served as assistant treasurer of the United States at St. Louis. In 1871 he made an unprecedented leap for a Last Man: he returned to West Point as a member of the Board of Visitors. In 1887, Edwards retired from federal service and founded the investment firm of A. G. Edwards & Son with his son Benjamin Franklin Edwards. He died in 1892 at age eighty.

"Ill-fated and mysterious man!" Edgar Allan Poe wrote in 1834, a few years after leaving West Point in disgrace, "bewildered in the brilliancy of thine own imagination and fallen in the flames of thine own youth!"[1] Poe became one of the geniuses of American letters, though his life remained tortured and tumultuous. He was found barely coherent on a Baltimore street on October 3, 1849, and died four days later of unknown causes.

James McNeill Whistler remained a friend of the Academy throughout his life, speaking favorably of the education he received there and the friendships he made. He left for Europe in 1855 and became one of the most controversial artists of the later nineteenth century, as much for his flamboyant lifestyle as for his artwork. Whistler recorded his thoughts on art and life in his appropriately entitled, *The Gentle Art of Making Enemies.* He died in London, July 17, 1903.

John McCleary, the Goat of 1854, fought at Antietam, Fredericksburg and Chancellorsville. He was brevetted major for gallantry at Gettysburg, fighting in the Wheat Field, and spent the rest of the war on garrison and recruiting duty. After the war he went to Charleston, South Carolina, as commander of the Union garrison. On February 25, 1868, at The Citadel, he suffered a stroke and died, age thirty-six. He was buried in Hamilton, Ohio.

Samuel Hall Kinney, Goat of the Class of 1864, who received double brevets for valor resisting the final Confederate assault at Appomattox, represented Battery A, Second Artillery at the laying of the cornerstone of the Soldiers' Monument at Gettysburg National Cemetery on July 4, 1865. He was later stationed in San Francisco, and in 1867 was sent to the newly acquired Alaska Territory. Kinney fell ill and died in the southern Alaska town of Sitka on December 3, 1868, at age twenty-five.

Charles N. Warner spent the rest of the Civil War in the West, fought in the Battle of Nashville, and was brevetted captain on April 2, 1865, for gallant and meritorious service in the capture of Selma, Alabama. After the war he took part in Winfield Scott Hancock's plains expedition and became a good friend of his fellow Pennsylvanian and Academy grad. A lifelong Republican, Warner considered voting for Hancock for president in 1880, but could not overcome his partisan predilections; hearing that the Democrats were going to deliver a "Solid South" for Hancock, he felt there should be a "Solid North" for Garfield on the other side.[2]

Warner married Eliza Brown Houston of Columbia, Pennsylvania, in 1867. He mustered out of the Army in 1871 and returned to Pennsylvania to study and practice law. He became a very successful lawyer, who for five years served as the town justice of the peace. Charles and Eliza raised six children, and for fifty years they lived together happily in Montrose, where they were pillars of the community. Warner was involved in the Four Brothers' Post of the Grand Army of the Republic, and in the Sons and Daughters of Veterans organization. In 1913 he visited the Antietam battlefield with his brother Fletch, who had survived his wounding at Burnside's Bridge. An active member of the Association of Graduates, Warner attended several West Point reunions, bringing his family along in 1882 and 1918. He died September 5, 1920, at Montrose, Pennsylvania, at age eighty-one. An obituary in his hometown paper spoke of him in words that could well apply in any era: he "passed on as others of his generation are fast doing, leaving to the patriotism and character of Young America the unfinished task of applying American ideals to the solution of the intricate problems which in peace and war every generation must face and care for that our nation may ever go forward in its God-appointed destiny."[3]

William H. T. Walker's fortitude and will to survive were an enduring memory among those who knew him. On July 10, 1885, former Confederate lieutenant general Simon Bolivar Buckner (USMA 1844) visited the ailing Ulysses S. Grant. The two had last seen each other when Grant accepted Buckner's surrender at Fort Donelson, February 1862.[4] Grant was dying of throat cancer and unable to speak, but communicated by writing notes on a pad of paper. Buckner, trying to raise Grant's spirits, recalled their days together in Mexico and Walker's dogged recovery after Molino. In response, Grant wrote, "I remember Walker's condition very well. He was, as I remember, many months unable to help himself. In my case I have not been confined to bed a single day; but there cannot be a cure in my case." Grant passed away two weeks later. In June 1893, Julia Dent Grant toured West Point, where she met Jefferson Davis's wife, Varina, and the two started up a friendship that lasted for the rest of their lives.

Long after the Civil War, Morris Schaff wrote that he could not think of the fates of many of his southern classmates "without seeing West Point suddenly take on the mysterious background and fated silence of the scenes of the Greek tragedies."[5] There was notably little spirit of retribution after the Civil War, even with Lincoln's assassination.[6] The Lincoln conspirators were hanged, as was Henry Wirz, the notorious commanding officer of Andersonville prison. The Radical Republicans wanted further prosecutions, but President Johnson began pardoning thousands of former Confederates, including Davis's vice president, Alexander Stephens, who later served in the U.S. Congress. Some radicals pursued former Confederates using military tribunals convened under emergency power provisions, prompting Johnson to declare the war officially over in April 1866, thus negating the rationale. Jefferson Davis had been held in chains without specific charges at Fort Monroe under military authority, and was transferred to civilian custody in May 1867. Bail for his release was set at $100,000.[7] The sum was immediately paid by a consortium of Richmond businessmen and northern abolitionists, including arch-Yankee Horace Greeley. There were several attempts to convene a treason trial, but disagreements arose over exactly how to do it, what law had been broken, and whether the Fourteenth Amendment superseded any such law. Davis was eager to have a trial in order to make his case that secession had been legal and his actions had not been treasonous, but in 1869, the government entered a *nolle prosequi* and gave up attempts to try Davis and thirty-seven other leading Confederates.

Davis lived relatively quietly after the war. He refused opportunities to reenter politics, for example turning down his old Senate seat from Mississippi in 1875. In 1876, he and his wife took up residence in Beauvoir, the home of a widow named Sarah Dorsey, near Biloxi, Mississippi, on the Gulf of Mexico. There he worked on his memoir, *The Rise and Fall of the Confederate Government.* Davis looked back wistfully on his West Point days and corresponded with some of his surviving classmates. On July 4, 1883, he wrote to Major Edward Watts of Hagerstown, Maryland, a washout of the Class of 1828, "It is sweet to renew the memories of schoolboy days, and though the body has grown old the heart may still preserve the freshness of the happy days when all was colored by hope, and, like butterflies, we looked for flowers without the knowledge of thorns."[8] He was far from his days of mirth at Benny Havens', or his twenty-second birthday at Fort Winnebago, where he rued the fact that the renown he had expected in life had not yet visited him.

Davis died December 5, 1889, and was buried in New Orleans. Many felt that Richmond would be a more appropriate location for his final resting place, and in 1893 the remains were removed and placed on a special train for Virginia. Wending its way through the former Confederate States, the train was shown the same reverence as the one bearing President Lincoln to Illinois twenty-eight years earlier. Veterans from South and North turned out to honor him, along with thousands of others who lined the tracks in every town. The train arrived in Richmond on Memorial Day. Davis lay in state in the capitol in Richmond, and there was an unbroken line of people paying their respects the entire day. The procession to Hollywood Cemetery went along streets decorated in black bunting along with American and Virginian but mostly Confederate flags. Henry Heth commanded the visiting troops and also acted as one of the honorary pallbearers, as did Laurence Simmons Baker. Dabney Maury was there, and George H. Steuart, Fitz Lee, Thomas Rosser and L. L. Lomax, among many other officers. Scores of Confederate veterans' organizations were represented, with delegations attending from every Confederate state. Uniforms, battle flags, drums and bands, men in columns horsed and on foot—it was the most diverse gathering of Confederate arms in Richmond since the war, and one of the greatest such gatherings of veterans ever.[9]

Laurence S. Baker, the Goat of 1851 who refused to surrender with Lee's army, was forced like many former Confederate officers to adjust to civilian life. He tried his hand at farming, trucking and selling insurance before becoming the station agent for the Seaboard Air Line Railroad in Suffolk, Virginia, in 1877.[10] He and his wife, Elizabeth, lived in Suffolk and raised two sons and a daughter. Baker preserved the pride of his service to the Confederate States and was an active member of the Tom Smith Camp of United Confederate Veterans. He passed away on April 10, 1907, at age seventy-seven. Harold Borland, the Goat of 1860 who was captured running the Union blockade, served in the West for the remainder of the conflict. He fought at Palmetto Ranch, Texas, the last battle in the war. He went briefly to Mexico with Kirby Smith but soon returned to the United States and lived the rest of his life quietly in Arkansas, as a teacher and an employee of the Revenue Service. He was married twice, and twice a widower. His two sons served in the First World War, one in the Navy, one in the Army. In his declining years he lived in the Confederate Veteran's Home in Sweet Home, Arkansas. He died in Little Rock on July 20, 1921, at age eighty-five.

Fitz Lee had always said he graduated fifth in his class, "if you counted from the bottom." Yet he had an extraordinary career in the Rebel Army and afterwards. He wrote several books, including an important biography of his Uncle Robert E. Lee. Active in politics, he served as governor of Virginia, 1885–89, and tried but failed to secure the Democratic nomination for the Senate. President Cleveland appointed him consul general to the U.S. Mission in Havana, which as it turned out was a fateful appointment. Cuban nationalists were fighting a liberation struggle against the Spanish rulers, the uprising that Narciso Lopez had predicted and William Logan Crittenden had expected almost fifty years earlier. Lee favored U.S. intervention to help the rebels, and advised that a warship be made ready to protect American lives and property. However, when the battleship USS *Maine* arrived in Havana

Harbor on January 25, 1898, Lee thought the timing of the provocative act was ill advised, and telegraphed his misgivings to Washington. On February 15, an explosion sent the *Maine* to the bottom of the harbor, and the United States and Spain spiraled towards war. Lee returned to the States on April 11. This was the first major conflict the United States had fought since the Civil War, and in order to promote sectional unity, President McKinley commissioned Lee as major general of volunteers with command of VII Army Corps. Another commission went to Joseph "Fighting Joe" Wheeler, an Immortal of the Class of 1859 who had been a Confederate lieutenant general. Wheeler saw some heavy fighting, but Lee's unit was scheduled to participate in a second wave that never materialized. Instead, his corps arrived as an occupation force and Lee served as the military governor of Cuba from 1899 to his retirement in 1901. He died four years later and was buried at Hollywood Cemetery in his U.S. Army uniform. This was a matter of some controversy, and to make a point, his family had the body wrapped in the Confederate flag that had draped Jefferson Davis's coffin during his funeral procession in 1893. Still, the blue uniform was said to prompt one Confederate veteran to wonder, "What'll Stonewall think when Fitz turns up wearing that!"

James Longstreet caused a furor in 1868 when he joined the Republican Party and recommended that other southerners do the same. He was influenced in part by the success of his friend Grant, who appointed him surveyor of customs for the Port of New Orleans. Longstreet later served in several other government posts, including ambassador to Turkey and U.S. marshal for Georgia. Jefferson Davis, with whom he had had a falling-out over a misunderstanding during the war, said that "by comparison, Judas Iscariot was a well meaning and much misunderstood lover of humanity."

On May 1, 1886, Davis was the featured speaker at the dedication of a statue to U.S. and Confederate senator Benjamin H. Hill in downtown Atlanta. It was part of his first series of public appearances in many years. Davis had begun his speech when shouting was heard in the back, then whooping that grew into a roar and a full-throated Rebel yell. It was Longstreet's men. Old Pete had appeared in his uniform, riding right up to the rear of the throng without announcement. Indeed, no one knew he was coming.

"By damn!" a veteran of the Fourth Texas Infantry, Hood's division, exclaimed, "if thar ain't Old Pete, sure as hell! Look at him boys!" The clamor swelled and the veterans demanded that Longstreet take the stage so they could all see him. He dismounted and went up the steps to the stage. He walked towards Davis, who met him halfway and without hesitation threw his arm around Longstreet's neck. "Forgive me," he said, and the two shook hands and bowed. The crowd went wild.[11]

Longstreet remained an active member of the Association of Graduates after attending the reconciliation meeting in 1875. His last visit to the Academy was for the Centennial celebration in June 1902. Longstreet was a major attraction at the festivities. His former artillery chief Edward Porter Alexander gave a speech on "The Confederate Veteran," and when he casually mentioned Longstreet's name, the cheers from the crowd were so loud and sustained that Alexander had to suspend his speech for a while. Longstreet died of pneumonia January 2, 1904, at his daughter's home in Gainesville, Georgia, six days before his eighty-third birthday. He is buried at the Alta Vista Cemetery in Gainesville.[12] Few of the Confederate veterans' organizations mourned Longstreet, however. His memoir, published in 1896, was not sufficiently reverential to Lee and did nothing to rehabilitate him in the eyes of many of his former comrades. As well, Longstreet consistently defended his lifelong friend George Pickett.

After the war, Pickett discovered that he was being investigated by the same prosecutor who had convicted Henry Wirz on war crimes charges in the Kinston hangings. He and his wife fled to Montreal, where they lived in exile as "Mr. and Mrs. Edwards," and Sallie tutored in Latin to help support them. The war crimes investigation returned its findings in December 1865, recommending arrest. Pickett chose to return to the United States to face the charges and plead his case, but Grant intervened, recommending to President Johnson that he pardon Pickett. Johnson demurred; he did not want to further alienate the Radical Republicans by issuing another high-profile pardon, yet neither did he make prosecuting Pickett a priority. The matter simmered through 1866, then faded away unresolved. In 1874, the Congress finally voted a bill to "remove the political disabilities of George E. Pickett, of Virginia."

George Pickett had to face life out of uniform, something for which he was ill prepared. His fame brought him offers of various kinds, especially in Virginia politics. He could easily have become a representative, senator or governor; but he had no desire to be a public figure and he turned all the offers down. He tried his hand at farming and business, failing at both. Eventually he became an agent in the Norfolk office of the New York–based Washington Life Insurance Company, but he did not like the work, which he found unseemly. "You don't know how abhorrent it is to me," he wrote Sallie. The company's literature listed him prominently as "Gen'l Geo. E. Pickett." People were more than willing to do business with the famous Pickett, feeling they could trust him based on his reputation, and in any case they could say they had a relationship with him. Perhaps others felt sorry for him and wanted to do him a good turn. Or maybe it was for old times' sake. Once, he insured two former members of his division. "One of them said they had to run me down and almost tie me to make me insure their lives," he wrote. "You know, dear, I can't do it. I'd sooner face a cannon than ask a man to take out a policy with me. Your soldier is *nothing but a soldier;* the war is over and he is no more account."[13]

The war was over, but the debate over what it had all meant was just beginning. Pickett played no role in the squabbles that erupted over various wartime controversies, whether real or manufactured. The Confederate backbiting accelerated with Robert E. Lee's death on October 12, 1870, as self-appointed defenders of the revered leader ground their axes in speeches and in print. Pickett's fame naturally attracted barbs from those who felt that his reputation was unearned or that it unfairly overshadowed the accomplishments of others. Some North Carolinians were particularly upset that Pickett's Charge came to be viewed as a primarily if not exclusively Virginia affair. They spread stories that Pickett had been drunk on the field, or absent altogether, both of which were false. Much was made of supposed bad blood between Pickett and Lee, for which there is scant evidence, and none of it firsthand.

Famed Confederate guerilla leader Colonel John S. Mosby, who barely knew Pickett, was the source for two of the most noted stories about him. In 1911 he told of a chance meeting between Pickett and Lee in March 1870, which he characterized as "cold and formal." As they parted, Pickett grumbled, "that old man ... had my division massacred at Gettysburg."

"Well, it made you immortal," Mosby replied.

Mosby further contended that after the disaster at Five Forks, Lee had ordered Pickett placed under arrest, and seeing him later during the retreat, Lee had said to his aide Charles S. Venable, "Is that man still with this army?"

But an eyewitness to the March 1870 meeting, who knew Lee much better than Mosby did, said he comported himself in his usual "cordial, dignified manner," which Mosby may have mistaken for stiffness. Pickett's personal physician, M. G. Elzey, who was with him through the latter part of the war and afterwards, said he "spoke of General Lee always in terms of the highest veneration and respect." He said Pickett was never under arrest. Pickett was on the final battle line of the Army of Northern Virginia, and he signed the parole documents for his division as general commanding. Elzey bemoaned the tendency of former Confederates to wage war on each other in the press. "The youngest hero of our lost cause is an old man now," he wrote. "It is sad to see old men, companions in a lost cause, who stand tottering on the verge of eternity, casting slurs upon each other, and even upon the reputations of the dead, their former companions in arms. . . . Comrades, in the name of God, in the name of the dead, who sleep, let us at last have peace among surviving heroes of our lost cause."[14]

Pickett attended few official functions related to the war, and none that are known of related to West Point. In 1869 he served as the chief marshal of a ceremony in Richmond to dedicate a ninety-foot granite pyramid that honored the eighteen thousand Confederate dead buried nearby. There he met again with many from his old division. Twelve thousand people walked in the procession to Hollywood Cemetery, amid "a stillness, an awesomeness, save for those necessary sounds— the clanking of swords, the tramp of horses, and the martial tread of men keeping time with funeral marches—the solemn requiem. No cheers, no applause; only loving greetings from tear-stained faces, heads bent in reverence, clasped hands held out to us as we passed along. . . . From their eternal silence, those who marched heroically to death looked down upon us yesterday. My darling, you cannot know," Pickett wrote to Sallie, "no, you cannot know!" In his speech he relived the awful splendor of Gettysburg, his men marching "in line of battle as on dress parade down that slope and across the stone wall one mile into the jaws of death, under fire from two hundred pieces of ordnance, and upon the center of the foe (who had been three days preparing) without support and *without faltering* oh grand but fatal day." This appearance at Richmond was the exception; for the most part Pickett kept a low profile. Captain George D. Wise said that he "moved so noiselessly along that some of us had forgotten we had a hero among us."[15]

Pickett's home life was also difficult. Sallie, who continued to idolize George, was recurrently ill, and their second son, Corbell, died of measles in 1874. Jimmie Pickett, George's first son with Indian princess Sâkis Tiigang, never met his father though he had followed his career closely. He corresponded with Sallie, and once met his half-brother George, though the meeting was awkward. Jimmie was a talented artist and a gifted student, but his life was cut short by tuberculosis, and he died in Portland, Oregon in 1889. George E. Pickett Jr. went to the

Virginia Military Institute and became an Army officer. The Pickett family returned to USMA with George Pickett IV (USMA 1944), great-grandson of the Goat of 1846.

In 1874, James Tilton, with whom Pickett had served in the North-west and after whom Jimmie Pickett was named, wrote his friend George suggesting he go to Egypt, where he could make a fresh start. Khedive Ismail Pasha was enlisting American officers to modernize his army. Tilton argued that Pickett was "one of the best infantry officers of our time," and that the Khedive "appreciates Americans." The Khedive wanted Pickett to be his commander in chief, and when Pickett was reluctant, a telegram arrived from Cairo instructing, "Forward Pickett at any cost." But Sallie opposed the idea and argued against it in a note she had him take to a dinner meeting to discuss the plan. "We've had glory enough, and war enough, with its hardships and separations and dangers," she wrote, "and now we just want each other forever and forevermore." Pickett refused the offer, and his friends said he was "signing the death-warrant to ambition and success."

In the summer of 1875, George and Sallie had planned to go on a family vacation to White Sulphur Springs, but business diverted George temporarily to Norfolk. Sallie went along with him despite his assur-ances that it would be a brief diversion and they could take up their plans shortly. On July 28 he fell ill, and died in a hospital two days later, his wife at his side. He was fifty years old. George Pickett's remains were placed in a vault in Cedar Grove Cemetery in Norfolk while arrangements were made for his reburial in Richmond. His funeral took place October 25, 1875, and was one of the largest seen in that city. One of the presiding officers was Pickett's surviving brigade commander James L. Kemper, who had been severely wounded at Gettysburg and was then governor of Virginia. There were 1,500 people in the official party, 40,000 spectators, and a procession a mile long, including the First Virginia regiment, cadets from VMI, the Monticello Guard, the Attucks Guard (a black unit), the Association of Veterans of the Army of Northern Virginia, the Richmond and Petersburg Commanderies of Knights Templar, and many others. Pickett's casket was carried on the caisson that later bore Jefferson Davis. He was laid to rest at Hollywood Cemetery near many of the men who had fought and died alongside him. He was at peace, resting with his boys.

George Pickett never wrote a memoir, and in later years the task of preserving his memory fell to Sallie. His unexpected demise was a terrible blow to her. The world she had known as a young plantation belle was destroyed; her hero husband whom she revered was dead.

"The light of my life is gone out," she said, and her autobiography ends at that moment even though she lived for many years afterwards.

Sallie worked in Washington as a pension clerk, uncertain what direction her life would take. But she was always her old soldier's wife, and in 1887 she attended a Gettysburg reunion where she was greeted with great acclaim and affection. Her first book about her husband, *Pickett and His Men*, with an introduction by James Longstreet, was published in 1899 and sold very well. Sallie published several more books and many articles, mostly based on letters George had written her, though her tendency to edit and embellish them has led historians to treat them with suspicion. In her writings, Sallie tapped into a sentimental nostalgia for times gone by. The war had been over for forty years, and many looked back to the innocent and uncomplicated antebellum golden age of their youth—time having obscured the passions and controversies that had made war inevitable. Sallie idealized her childhood on the plantation, the traditional southern way of life, and her hero husband, the pure-hearted soldier of the South, handpicked by fate to play a central role in the tragedy of the lost cause. Sallie died in 1931.[16]

Soon after the end of the war, Ambrose Burnside asked Henry Heth to visit him in New York. It was an emotional reunion; the two friends could not speak for fifteen minutes. Burnside had been elected governor of Rhode Island, and was also busy in railroads. He wondered what his friend Henry was going to do.

"I do not know," Heth replied. "I intend to pitch into the first thing that offers, whereby I can make an honest living." Burnside suggested that Heth reopen the coal mines his father had worked near Richmond, and advanced him $50,000. Heth agreed and worked the mines for three years before a combination of low prices for coal and water in the mines ended the enterprise. In the years that followed, he lived in Richmond and tried his hand at various pursuits, such as selling insurance and being director of a railroad project, none with much success. President Grant offered Heth the Indian Bureau in recognition of his wisdom in dealing with the Indians on the frontier, but he declined. He did serve as an informal advisor to the president and helped Grant rid his administration of corrupt officeholders.

Henry and his wife spent many years in Washington, where Harriet was active as president of the Southern Relief Association. They loved each other dearly, and he was pained that his journey in life had taken her from wealth to relative penury. Though the couple was not well off, they enjoyed an active social life among their many successful friends, particularly former Union officers who made names in politics, Grant, Hancock, Burnside and many others from West Point, the Old Army and the Confederacy. Heth remained a witty and sought-after dinner guest and companion.

At one dinner party thrown by then Senator Burnside in 1877, Heth had a discussion with Sherman about the war. At one point, Sherman made reference to "you damned rebels."

"Stop, Sherman," Heth said, "and think, if there are two men in the world that should go on their knees and thank the Almighty for raising up the rebels, those two men are Grant and yourself; but for the rebels you would now be teaching school in the swamps of Louisiana and Grant would be tanning bad leather at Galena."

Sherman placed his hand on Heth's shoulder. "That is so, old fellow," he said.[17]

Heth was active in preserving the history of the war in which he had played such an important role. In 1891 he served as Confederate representative for the official marking at the Antietam battlefield, and worked for several years at the War Department helping assemble Confederate documents for the Official Records of the War of the Rebellion.

From 1880 to 1884, Heth was a civil engineer in Georgetown, South Carolina. In 1885, during the Cleveland administration, Custis Lee helped him secure a job as special Indian commissioner, and for four years he toured the agencies, visiting the scene of his youth on the plains and renewing old friendships. Once, he visited the Cheyenne and Arapahoe Agency, asking for friends from his days on the Arkansas River in the 1850s. He learned that all the men he had known were dead, some of natural causes, others of combat with Indian enemies or the whites. But Eoneva, daughter of Cheyenne chief Feathered Bear, whom Heth had known, still lived there. She and her husband came to see him, and they spoke long in sign language about earlier, happier times, until Eoneva began to weep. Her husband, Young Whirlwind, son of Heth's friend Old Whirlwind, approached him with a pelt and said, "Yo-ba-me-atz, Eoneva and I give you this lion skin; keep it, and the road you travel our children shall follow. In forty years you have never told an Indian a lie."

In December 1898, Heth was diagnosed with the grippe and fell into paralysis. The following February he was found to have Bright's disease, now called nephritis, a serious kidney ailment. He battled mightily during the summer months, and was reported at death's door several times, but rallied back. Yet eventually the disease overcame his spirit, and Henry Heth died at his home on G Street, in the District of

Columbia, September 27, 1899, with his wife at his side. He was seventy-eight years old. At Henry Heth's funeral in Washington, the casket was covered with roses and orchids, at its head a Confederate flag made of immortelles. He was taken to Richmond, escorted by friends from both sides of the late conflict, and lay in state September 29. His casket attracted great crowds, especially aging veterans who had known and served with him. A large procession accompanied Heth that afternoon to Hollywood Cemetery, where he was interred. At his gravesite stands a granite cross inscribed, "In Action Faithful and in Honor Clear."

In the years following the Little Bighorn battle, the event became lodged in the popular consciousness and took on a mantle equaled by few other battles, growing well out of proportion to its military significance. Like the Gettysburg and Waterloo, it became a vehicle for art, literature, history, strong emotion and endless debate.[18]

In death, Custer was bestowed with even more glory than in life. *Galaxy* magazine, which had been serializing Custer's memoirs when he died, editorialized:

> Never was there a life more rounded, complete and symmetrical than that of George A. Custer, the favorite of fortune, the last cavalier. The manner of his death has cast a halo of glory round his name such as no man ever attained in contest with the savages. . . . To Custer alone was it given to join a romantic line of perfect success to a death of perfect heroism; to unite the splendors of Austerlitz and Thermopylæ; to charge like Murat; to die like Leonidas.[19]

One of the first and most influential biographies was *The Complete Life of General George A. Custer* by novelist Frederick Whittaker, who based his accounts of the battle on sensational news reports, letting his imagination fill in where facts were lacking. The book was published in December 1876 and drew immediate fire from military professionals, especially those who were directly or indirectly criticized. Serious critics panned it as drivel. But the public loved it, and it influenced popular perceptions and other writers for decades.

Painters, poets and serious writers also weighed in. When Walt Whitman viewed John Mulvaney's 1881 twelve-foot-high wall-sized mural *Custer's Last Rally* he "sat for over an hour before the picture, completely absorb'd in the first view." He cast the scene in terms of his thesis of the native superiority of the American over the European, even in tragedy:

> . . . it is all at first painfully real, overwhelming, needs good nerves to look at it. . . . swarms upon swarms of savage Sioux, in their war-bonnets,

frantic, mostly on ponies, driving through the background, through the smoke, like a hurricane of demons. . . . Altogether a western, autochthonic phase of America, the frontiers, culminating, typical, deadly, heroic to the uttermost—nothing in the books like it, nothing in Homer, nothing in Shakspere; more grim and sublime than either, all native, all our own, and all a fact. A great lot of muscular, tan-faced men, brought to bay under terrible circumstances—death ahold of them, yet every man undaunted, not one losing his head, wringing out every cent of the pay before they sell their lives. Custer (his hair cut short) stands in the middle, with dilated eye and extended arm, aiming a huge cavalry pistol . . . indeed the whole scene, dreadful, yet with an attraction and beauty that will remain in my memory.[20]

Elizabeth Custer, like Sallie Pickett, found herself alone and with no means of support. For all the memories, fame and glory, there was no Custer estate. She was left with a government pension of $30 per month, and the support of family and friends. She had no desire to remarry. She went to work for the Society of Decorative Arts in New York, but in time found her voice and began to write. She recorded her observations on many topics: art, culture, life, public affairs. Though her entrée to publishing was as "Custer's widow," she became a well-known commentator in her own right and spent summers with other women writers at Onteora Park in the Catskills. She traveled the United States and the world, and became independently wealthy.

But Libbie Custer never abandoned her role as the chief custodian for the preservation and promotion of the Custer myth. The task fell naturally to her; Libbie had helped create George's reputation starting during the Civil War, so it made sense that she would continue. She defended him against all comers. Between 1885 and 1890 she published three books of her observations while with George in the West: *Boots and Saddles*, *Tenting on the Plains* and *Follow the Guidon*. Like Sallie Pickett, she presented an idealized, unblemished vision of her husband, loving, grave, and with a hint of tragedy. This was the George Custer she wanted the world to remember.

Yet Custer had become a national treasure, and others sought to honor him in their own way. On August 30, 1879, four thousand spectators and many dignitaries gathered at West Point for the unveiling of a statue of the Goat of June 1861. It was located at the edge of the Plain, at the angle formed by the mess hall and the officers' headquarters. It stood on a granite pedestal faced with gold-bronze panels of western scenes in bas relief. The statue was draped with a large flag, and the sculptor, James Wilson McDonald, pulled the chord to the tune of "Garry Owen" and a thirteen-gun salute.[21]

It was a scene of Custer at bay, left foot forward, bent left arm gripping a pistol, right arm extended downward with sword at ready. But the position of the weapons was not natural. Custer's hair was neck-length and unattractively swept back. His forehead was wide and bulbous. He wore no hat, and had a long dress coat buttoned to the neck. The coattails were swept back, revealing high-topped boots that made his legs look spindly. The overall proportions were odd. The statue did not evoke action, bravery or tragedy. It was cartoonish. McDonald had based his sculpture on a drawing of the Last Stand by *Harper's Weekly* illustrator William Cary. One critic said "it is a representation of a harum scarum sort of fellow."[22]

The next day near Poughkeepsie, three thousand people attended the closing session of the Duchess County Peace Society. Among the resolutions being discussed were: that USMA be converted into a school for teaching international law; that the War Department be transformed into a Peace Department; and "that the honors paid yesterday, at West Point, to the memory of George A. Custer, the treacherous and unprovoked murderer of [Black Kettle] and the friendly Cheyenne Indians, are a national disgrace, as they proclaim to the world that the Government of the United States approves deceit, and indorses causeless slaughter."[23]

If Custer's critics disliked the statue, Elizabeth Custer loathed it. She had not been consulted on the design nor involved in the process. She boycotted the unveiling, and in fact was not even invited until the last minute. In April 1880, a bill was introduced in Congress for McDonald to erect a much larger monument to Custer and his officers in Washington, D.C., including a reproduction of the West Point statue. But Mrs. Custer objected strongly to McDonald's being the principal sculptor. "The statue could not be worse than it is," she wrote to Congress. "The face is of a man of 60, and the dress so unmilitary that his brother officers shudder in looking at it. . . . The whole costume is incongruous and incorrect." (An ironic complaint given Custer's taste for unorthodox and piecemeal uniforms.) "He is armed like a desperado, in both hands. . . . The statue is a failure as a likeness, as the representation of a soldier and as a work of art." She concluded, "I could not endure the thought of this wretched statue being repeated."[24]

McDonald's sculpture does not compare favorably with the statues on the Plain today. Each conveys a sense of the man, his time, his character or his memory. Washington, majestic. Thayer, mythic, cloaked, ancient. Sedgwick, firm, straightforward and realistic. MacArthur, imperious, uncompromising. Eisenhower, steady, quietly confident. Patton, in his leather winter jacket, helmeted, pistols on his hips, hands on lowered binoculars, looking at the horizon (or the library), a warfighter at war, immediately evoking the Battle of the Bulge and the relief of Bastogne, one of his greatest achievements. The statue of Custer that Libbie most liked has a similar feel. It stands in Monroe, Michigan. It was designed by sculptor Edward Potter and dedicated by President William Howard Taft in 1910. It is called *Sighting the Enemy*. Libbie kept a photograph of it in her foyer. It portrays Custer at Gettysburg, on horseback, looking into the distance. The name of the work tells the moment, of planning, intense thought, rush of adrenaline, of anticipation, the known and unknown in urgent collision. The moment of decision. It must have been Custer's best feeling.

Libbie's lobbying efforts blocked the proposal to have a copy made of the West Point statue, though the original still stood. In January 1882 she wrote to General Sherman, "I have been very much troubled for the past three years to think that I was obliged to submit to the statue of General Custer at West Point."[25] Her lengthy critique repeated earlier complaints about the statue, "so utterly bad" in her opinion, and castigated McDonald, "so wholly unable to carry out what surely requires genius." She continued, "I can no longer endure the idea that our whole country, all our foreign tourists, who invariably visit West Point, besides generations of cadets, will receive their impressions of General Custer from this frightful libel on his character."

Libbie's persistence prompted the Board of Visitors to debate the issue. Custer's former roommate Morris Schaff, then a board member, said that the statue "exaggerated Custer's worst characteristics," and he favored its removal. But others thought it was an accurate rendering of Custer's fiery spirit. The board's debate was inconclusive and the statue remained. In 1884, after Sherman's recommendation, the approval of a majority of the original donors, and on order of Secretary of War Robert Todd Lincoln (Abraham Lincoln's eldest son), the Custer statue was finally taken down. McDonald objected, but was overruled. The pedestal was moved to the Custer gravesite, and the offending statue was stored indefinitely. In 1905 an obelisk was placed atop the pedestal, inscribed "George Armstrong Custer, Major General, U.S. Volunteers."

But McDonald's statue staged a comeback. In December 1898, post quartermaster Major William F. Spurgin, a washout of the Class of 1862 who had fought with an Indiana regiment in the Civil War and would later rise to the rank of brigadier general, sent a note to the USMA adjutant saying that the Custer statue was stored in the quartermaster's stable. Spurgin must have known Custer, and he remarked that the head was a striking likeness. Since the statue had been rejected because of the pose, he suggested that the arms be removed and the statue cut off at the waist, leaving a very serviceable bust that "when mounted properly on a pedestal would secure to the Academy a most excellent work of Art." The scrap could be sold to finance the project.[26]

Libbie Custer liked the idea—perhaps because it would prevent the whole statue from ever being seen again, and involved destroying most of it. Two years later opportunity presented itself in the person of famed architect and designer Stanford White, the son of a noted Shakespeare scholar, who became one of the foremost architects in the country. He had apprenticed under Henry Hobson Richardson, a very influential architect who had failed to gain admission to West Point because of a speech impediment. White was later a partner in the firm of McKim, Mead and White, which in the late nineteenth and early twentieth centuries was the leading architectural firm in the world. White designed famous public structures, such as Madison Square Garden and the Washington Square Arch, many private homes, and memorials. White was also a notorious bon vivant, known for his lavish parties and a string of glamorous affairs.

White served as architect of the Battle Monument at Trophy Point, dedicated in 1897, honoring the 2,240 Regular Army soldiers killed in the Civil War. He also designed the Officers' Mess and the West Point memorial to his friend James M. Whistler. White had even grander plans for the Academy. In 1902 his firm was invited to compete for a commission to totally redesign the campus. White detested the characteristic Gothic style for which West Point was famous, and wanted to tear all the older buildings down and replace them with neoclassical structures. When his proposal was turned down, he said it was "a public calamity, a body blow to all those who are striving to raise architecture out of the heterogeneous mush."[27]

White was at West Point in 1900 for the dedication of Cullum Hall, which he had designed, and which was funded from a bequest from the estate of General George Cullum, who had passed away in 1892. White was approached about the statue project and agreed to undertake the modifications. The statue was shipped quietly to New York. By 1905 it had been dismembered. But the project was never finished. On June 25, 1906, while dining in the rooftop supper club at Madison Square Garden, White was gunned down by railroad heir

Harry Thaw, husband of White's former mistress Evelyn Nesbit. It was thirty years to the day from the Battle of the Little Bighorn.

Elizabeth Custer never visited the Little Bighorn battlefield, which over the years became a tourist attraction. In 1926 she listened on radio to the fifty-year anniversary ceremonies as part of her annual June ritual of press interviews. Late in life she lived on Park Avenue in New York and was regularly seen walking around the neighborhood or frequenting the Cosmopolitan Club. Many of those who might have been more critical of George Custer gave deference to Libbie, and she managed to outlive all of them. She died April 6, 1933, two days short of her ninety-first birthday. She was buried at West Point alongside George, the West Point Band playing "Garry Owen" as she was laid to rest.

WHITHER THE GOAT?

T HE SPIRIT OF THE GOAT DID NOT DIE with George Armstrong
Custer. It lived on in Powhatan Henry Clarke, the Goat of 1884,
like Custer a cavalryman, and the only Last Man to receive the
Medal of Honor. The son of a Confederate officer, Clarke was assigned
to the predominately African American Tenth Cavalry, known as the
Buffalo Soldiers. During the Geronimo campaign his unit was pinned
down in an ambush, and one of his men, Corporal Scott, fell wounded
in the crossfire. Clarke coolly ran out under heavy fire, picked Scott up
and pulled him to safety. "Well, what else could I do?" he later said. "I
was scared to death, but the man called to me and you know I couldn't
leave him to be shot to death." Clarke was a close friend of the illustrator Frederick Remington, who had campaigned with him in Arizona
and witnessed the rescue. Remington called the tall, charismatic Virginian the perfect model of a cavalry officer and based many of his drawings and sculptures on him. Clarke drowned in the Little Bighorn River
in July 1893, while stationed at Camp Custer.[1]

George Patrick Ahern, Goat of 1882, served as secretary to the
imprisoned Sitting Bull, and was granted the honorary title Chief Two
Crows. He explored the unmapped sections of Montana in the 1880s,
including Glacier National Park, where Ahern Glacier is named after
him. Ahern also showed his nerve under fire in Cuba, being awarded
a Silver Star in the Spanish-American War. Clarence Ransom Edwards,
the Goat of 1883, received three Silver Stars in the Philippine Insur-
rection, commanded the 26th "Yankee" Division in the First World War
and retired a major general in 1922. Charles Young, the Goat of 1889,
was the third African American to graduate from West Point, and the
last for almost fifty years until Benjamin O. Davis Jr. in 1936. Young
served in the war with Spain, and during the Punitive Expedition in
Mexico in 1916 he led a successful cavalry charge against forces under
the command of Pancho Villa to rescue pinned-down U.S. forces. At

the onset of the First World War, Colonel Young commanded the Tenth Cavalry regiment and was the highest-ranking African American in the U.S. Army, as well as the first to achieve the rank of colonel.

James Alfred Moss, the Goat of 1894, was a pioneer military cyclist who received the Silver Star for bravery in Cuba. He commanded the 367th Infantry regiment in France in the First World War. Afterward he founded the U.S. Flag Association and was the motive force behind the establishment of Flag Day. Daniel Duncan, Goat of 1895, was best known for his "remarkable run" in the 1893 football game against Princeton, in which he returned a goal-line fumble the length of the field for a touchdown, "the most remarkable play . . . ever witnessed in West Point." It was one of the first, if not the first, full-field defensive runs ever.[2] Duncan drowned in Lake Michigan two years after graduating.

These men and others established the tradition of the Goat, which endured through most of the twentieth century. After 1968, a "Goat fund" of a dollar per cadet was collected to give to the Last Man. It could be a considerable sum; for example in 1976 there were 855 graduates. But cultural changes and shifts in political fashion can bring a swift end to honored conventions, and so it was with the Goat. In 1978, West Point discontinued the General Order of Merit, and the Academy announced "The Last of the Last Man (or The Demise of the 'Goat')." The official rationale for the change was "the Military Academy's intensification of the pursuit of excellence in academics . . . to stress competition against a high standard of learning rather than to have the students compete against one another for class standing."[3] The report of the study group stated that academic ranking, which was supposed to encourage achievement, in fact discouraged most cadets. The study group isolated what they called the "goat syndrome," which was "a synthesis of all the negative attitudes on academic excellence." The study reasoned that "if cadets were not continuously and publicly given their relative standings, there could be no particular reason to adopt the goat attitude."[4] The study group objected especially to the "Goat fund," calling it the "quintessential manifestation of the 'goat' cult," and noting that the cadet in question "crosses the stage amid popping flashbulbs to receive a dollar from each of his classmates and greater acclaim than the top ten graduates."[5] The reformers maintained that only those who received top honors should be identified by rank, a system that would have "the added advantage of not attaching notoriety to those who barely escape failure."[6] One suspects that the study group was swayed by contemporary educational theories about promoting self-esteem by minimizing the public consequences of competition.

Today's West Point graduates are listed in the register in alphabetical order, except for the honor graduates. But the Goats have turned out to be tougher than expected. Unpublished class rankings exist, and there is still a "Last Man" in every class. Despite the best efforts to stamp out the custom, every cadet at the commencement ceremonies knows who the Goat is, and when his or her name is read in the alphabetical list, the crowd bursts into sustained cheers.

The reformers of the 1970s showed little understanding of the "Spirit of the Goat." It is not the product of defeatism but one of esprit. Graduating as the Goat was an object of rivalry among those on the bottom rungs of the class, and unlike competition for the top or "star" slots, going for Goat carried a degree of risk. A cadet had to do poorly enough to be last, but not underperform to the degree that he would be dismissed. Chuck Rittenburg (USMA 1973), said that the Goat would wind up studying more than others because he had to know exactly how many questions he could miss on a given test in order to maintain his razor-edge standing on the brink of failure—with margins that slim, the safest course was to know all the answers and be in a position to miss them selectively. Thus, competing for the coveted hindmost spot required a certain audacity and courage, traits with which Custer, Pickett and the rest would be on familiar terms.

When West Point gave up the Goats, it surrendered a part of its soul and turned its back on its history. The drive to standardize, to seek an ideal form of predefined excellence, unvarying across large and diverse groups of people, is both harmful and wasteful. The Army (indeed any organization) benefits from soldiers of spirit and a certain degree of nonconformity. Academic achievement does not necessarily presage a successful military career. Likewise, a poor academic record does not reflect a lack of honor, sense of duty, or physical courage. It does not mean one cannot be a good or inspirational leader. And it surely does not mean one cannot make sacrifices or act courageously.

Nothing in one's academic record can predict heroism; few who became heroes knew it was their destiny. The cadets of the 1820s and 1830s did not know they would have their baptism of fire in Mexico. The cadets of the 1850s foresaw service on the frontier fighting Indians, not waging war on each other in the greatest conflagration of the nineteenth century, led by the veterans of the Mexican War. Some West Pointers of the quiet 1920s found themselves on the Bataan Death March. Others who trained to lead soldiers against Soviet tank armies in West Germany in the 1980s wound up hunting terrorists in Afghanistan and Iraq. They did not know they would be given the opportunity to perform great deeds, some of which are well known, or to achieve the kind of intimate greatness attained in small engagements through actions known only to the men with whom they served.

The stories of the Goats are not tales of failure but of redemption. These were men who were last in their class academically but who persevered to live extraordinary lives of service and sacrifice. As many service members have done and do today, they forwent a stable family life, financial gain and personal freedom, until the time they were called upon to risk their lives to ensure the safety of our families, the protection of our freedoms, and the lives of their comrades. There are some today who stand guard at home or abroad in mean circumstances—questioning commitment, aware that the people they defend may not recognize the sacrifices they are making—who will one day move unexpectedly onto the stage of history to play a role that will be remembered and honored for all time.

No one knows his fate. None of these men did. They did not experience their lives as the prologue of greatness to come; they lived every moment uncertain of the future. Some risked all and lost. Others prevailed, some to lose later on. But all were united by a common bond of selfless service to America. To tell their story is to honor and preserve their memory, as they have honored us by building and defending our nation and our freedoms. In so doing, we learn that some virtues are not learned in classrooms.

A NOTE ON SOURCES

Most of the primary sources used in this book are in the United States Military Academy Special Collections. They include, *inter alia*, documents in the files compiled by George W. Cullum for his *Biographical Register of the Officers and Graduates of the U.S. Military Academy*, 3 vols. (3rd ed., 1891), also known as the "Cullum files"; the "x-files" of cadets who did not graduate; the Annual Reports of the USMA Association of Graduates; the 1952 Register of Graduates and Former Cadets; the Thayer Papers; the Register of Delinquencies, Staff Records, Post Orders, Special Orders, and other sundry records. Other biographical details are from Francis Bernard Heitman, *Historical Register and Dictionary of the United States Army, from Its Organization, September 29, 1789, to March 2, 1903* (Washington, D.C.: Government Printing Office, 1903). Civil War–era after-action reports, correspondence and other such records are from *The War of the Rebellion: A Compilation of the Official Records of the Union and Confederate Armies* (Washington, D.C.: Government Printing Office, 1902). Other sources are as cited throughout. Much gratitude and credit goes to the USMA Special Collections staff for their innumerable acts of kindness and expert assistance during the research for this volume.

NOTES

Introduction: The Spirit of the Goat

[1] *The Letters of Major General James E. B. Stuart,* ed. Adele H. Mitchell (Stuart-Mosby Historical Society, 1990), p. 43.

[2] 1910 *Howitzer,* p. 50. Beach graduated next to last in the Class of 1910 and later fought in the Verdun sector in the First World War. He retired as a colonel in 1945.

[3] The 1900 *Howitzer* defines a Goat as "a Cadet in the lowest section," and at an 1898 furlough dinner for the Class of 1900, the second toast, offered by Cadet George B. Comly, was "The Goats!" "West Point Cadets Dine," *New York Times,* June 10, 1898, p. 7. Comly graduated 51st of 54, and the Goat of his class, Richard Morgan Thomas, was awarded the Silver Star fighting Muslim insurgents in the Philippines.

[4] The fact that a goat is the mascot of the Naval Academy probably helped solidify the expression, but did not originate it. The first Navy goat, El Cid (the Chief), the mascot of the USS *New York,* was on hand for the 1893 Army/Navy football game. The Midshipmen defeated West Point 6–3, and lucky El Cid was offered shore duty at Annapolis, where he became the Navy's mascot. The last graduate in each class at Annapolis is called the more descriptive "Anchorman." The Air Force Academy has no such term, though "Tailgunner" comes to mind.

[5] "West Point Cadets Cheer War Veterans," *New York Times,* June 13, 1912.

Nathaniel Wyche Hunter

[1] Francis Henney Smith, "West Point Fifty Years Ago," an address delivered before the Association of Graduates of the U.S. Military Academy, West Point, June 12, 1879. Nathaniel Wyche Hunter letters and

diaries from the Hitchcock-Coit Papers at the F. W. Olin Library, Mills College, Oakland, California, and the Hargrett Rare Book and Manuscript Library, University of Georgia, Athens, Georgia. For general information on West Point in this era see *Cadet Life Before the Mexican War*, ed. Sidney Forman (West Point, N.Y.: USMA Printing Office, 1945).

[2] Cf., T. J. Cram (USMA 1826), "Recollections As a Cadet and As an Officer," typescript excerpts, USMA Archives; and Elizabeth Dey Jenkinson Waugh, *West Point* (New York: Macmillan Press, 1944).

[3] Waugh, *West Point,* p. 41.

[4] U.S. State Papers, 16th Congress, 1st Session, no. 176.

[5] U.S. State Papers, 16th Congress, 1st Session, no. 194.

[6] *North American Review,* January 1832, pp. 246–62.

[7] Smith, "West Point Fifty Years Ago."

[8] Simon Magruder Levy is often mistakenly called the first Goat because he is listed second of two graduates in 1802. But prior to 1818, Academy graduates were listed in the order they completed their coursework and were commissioned, not by the General Order of Merit (GOM), a rank-order based on academic achievement and to a lesser extent on disciplinary records. Since the curriculum was not standardized before 1818, cadets might take months to finish, or years. So Levy cannot claim the title of the first Goat, though cadets at the West Point Jewish Chapel are fond of noting that the first USMA graduating class was "50 percent Jewish." Only after 1818 did the expression "first (or last) in his class" have any particular meaning. There were also the "turnbacks," who had to repeat a year; and the "washouts," those who failed completely and were expelled. A "stay-back" is a newly commissioned officer who does not leave after graduation but stays awhile to help the new cadets.

[9] USMA, Record of Delinquencies, vol. 1822–1828, p. 416.

[10] Mason served two years and left the service. He was later a lawyer, newspaper editor, politician, and chief justice of the state of Iowa.

[11] Larnard was in the Fourth Infantry regiment and brevetted at Resaca de la Palma, and at Fort Steilacoom, Washington, 1853–54, and fought against the Sno-ho-mish Indians in Washington, 1854. He drowned March 27, 1854, in Puget Sound on his return from the expedition when the small boat he was in capsized in a storm. He was forty-five.

[12] Letter of October 17, 1829.

[13] Letters to his sister, April 5, 1832, and February 20, 1833.

[14] Albert E. Church, *Personal Reminiscences of the Military Academy from 1824 to 1831,* a paper read to the U.S. Military Service Insti-

tute, West Point, March 28, 1878 (West Point, N.Y.: Military Academy Press, 1879), pp. 31–32.

[15] Ibid., p. 16.

[16] Ibid., p. 12.

[17] Ibid., p. 13.

Benny Havens'

[1] Sources for information on Benny Havens include among others: *The West Point Sketch Book* by Major Ernie Webb, Captain John D. Hart and First Lieutenant James E. Foley; Lewis Beach, *Cornwall* (Newburgh, N.Y.: E. M. Ruttenber & Son, 1873), pp. 72–73; Benson J. Lossing, "West Point," *Scribner's Monthly,* July 1872, pp. 257–85; and other sources as cited.

[2] Albert E. Church, *Personal Reminiscences of the Military Academy from 1824 to 1831,* a paper read to the U.S. Military Service Institute, West Point, March 28, 1878 (West Point, N.Y.: Military Academy Press, 1879), p. 18.

[3] Nathaniel Wyche Hunter letter, February 20, 1833. Wyche shared recipes with Mrs. Havens for making cornbread and butter cakes, of which she knew nothing before. "I have often been down there for the pleasure of making and eating an ash cake."

[4] "Useful Sergeant Owens," *New York Times,* November 25, 1894. Clay graduated second in the Class of 1831. He resigned immediately. He was killed at Buena Vista, February 23, 1847, a lieutenant colonel in the Kentucky militia.

[5] Cf. generally, *The Papers of Jefferson Davis,* vol. 1 (1808–1840), ed. Haskell M. Monroe Jr. and James T. McIntosh (Baton Rouge: Louisiana State University Press, 1971); USMA Post Orders, vol. 4; Virginia Howell Davis, *Jefferson Davis: A Memoir* (New York: Belford Co. Publishers, 1890); Walter L. Fleming, "Some Documents Relating to Jefferson Davis at West Point," *Mississippi Valley Historical Review,* September, 1920, pp. 146–52.

[6] This is the name as given by Davis's wife, but there are no cadets by this name or any similar name in the years Davis was there.

[7] R. H. Stoddard, "Edgar Allan Poe," *Harper's New Monthly Magazine,* September 1872, pp. 561; G. E. Woodbury, "Poe's Legendary Years," *Atlantic Monthly,* December 1884, pp. 814–29; J. H. Ingram, "Unpublished Correspondence by Edgar Allan Poe," *Appleton's Journal,* May 1878, pp. 421–30; letters from the Poe Manuscript Collection, Valentine Museum, Richmond, Virginia; J. Thomas Russell, *Edgar Allan Poe: The Army Years* (West Point, N.Y.: USMA Press,

1972); Thomas W. Gibson, "Edgar Allan Poe at West Point," *Harper's New Monthly Magazine,* November 1867, pp. 754–56. Gibson ranked 45th of 55 cadets in his surviving year group, and the ten below him were turned back. In discipline he was second to last of the entire Corps for 1831 with an impressive 337 demerits. He did not make it past his yearling year.

8 In 1966, a copy of this edition was up for auction and USMA authorized a bid of $5,000. The Academy was outbid, but a benefactor put up the additional money to obtain the volume. It is now in a room near the Poe Memorial Arch. Russell, *Edgar Allan Poe,* pp. 25ff.

9 December 20, 1831.

10 Hunter letter, December 1832. He also wrote: "Though opposed to Jackson as president, I still like him as a man. He has been very partial to the Cadets in his official capacity." (Wyche opposed Jackson's position in the Nullification crisis.) October 20, 1832.

11 Anderson was mortally wounded at the Battle of Churubusco.

12 Francis Henney Smith, "West Point Fifty Years Ago," an address delivered before the Association of Graduates of the U.S. Military Academy, West Point, June 12, 1879.

13 Hunter letter, April 30, 1832.

14 Hunter letter, August 7, 1829.

15 Smith, "West Point Fifty Years Ago."

16 Hunter letter, February 20, 1833.

17 Thayer continued in service to the country until 1863, when he retired from active duty. He died September 7, 1872, having never returned to the school that has ever afterwards borne his imprint. Five years later his body was reinterred in the West Point cemetery. On June 11, 1883, Wyche's classmate and former Superintendent, Major General George W. Cullum, unveiled a granite statue of Thayer, which currently stands in the northwest corner of the Plain, in front of the superintendent's house. The inscription reads, "Colonel Thayer, Father of the United States Military Academy."

Ephraim Kirby Smith

1 Dwight H. Kelton, *Annals of Fort Mackinac* (Mackinac Island, Mich.: Mackinac State Historical Parks, 1992).

2 Some background information on Smith's family can be found in Joseph Howard Parks, *General Edmund Kirby Smith* (Baton Rouge: Louisiana State University Press, 1954). *The Diaries of Samuel Peter Heintzelman, USMA 1826,* vol. 3 (1830) at the USMA Archives is an invaluable source for frontier life in Michigan.

[3] The Battle of Lundy's Lane was fought between British and American forces on July 25, 1814, near Niagara Falls, Canada. U.S. forces were defeated after a pitched battle and retreated to Fort Erie.

[4] House Document 193, April 11, 1820.

[5] Ephraim Kirby Smith, "To the officers of the Army, the following is submitted, the defense of Lieutenant E. K. Smith, delivered in court on the occasion of his late prosecution," December 1826.

[6] Heintzelman diaries, p. 56.

[7] Reprinted in Lynda J. Lasswell, "Jefferson Davis Ponders His Future, 1829," *Journal of Southern History,* November 1975, pp. 519–20.

[8] Heintzelman diaries, pp. 101–2.

[9] Ibid., p. 85.

[10] Lasswell, "Jefferson Davis Ponders His Future, 1829."

[11] "Report on the Subject of Desertions," Adjutant General's Office, January 25, 1830.

[12] Mark A. Vargas, "The Military Justice System and the Use of Illegal Punishments as Cause of Desertion in the U.S. Army, 1821–1835," *Journal of Military History,* January 1991, p. 11.

[13] Heintzelman diaries, p. 45.

[14] Quoted in Francis Paul Prucha, "The United States Army as Viewed by British Travelers, 1825–1860," *Military Affairs,* Autumn 1953, p. 116. Another traveler, Captain Basil Hall of the Royal Navy, believed the problem in the U.S. military was *not enough* flogging. Ibid., p. 118.

[15] Quoted in Vargas, "The Military Justice System," p. 3.

[16] Ironically, Congress legalized flogging as punishment for desertion on March 2, 1833.

The Seminole War

[1] *American State Papers: Military Affairs,* vol. 7, 1837–38 (Washington: Gales & Seaton, 1861), pp. 425–26.

[2] See for example, the lengthy "Dade's Massacre," which appeared in the *Southern Literary Messenger,* July 1837, pp. 437–38. The tone of the poem is reflected in this stanza:

> Now furious grew the desp'rate fight
> And well each soldier made his stand—
> Oh! 'twas a great and glorious sight,
> The prowess of that little band.

The event would inspire poems long afterwards. See "On the Massacre of Dade's Detachment," *Southern Literary Messenger,* October 1859, p. 276.

[3] Philip Hone, *The Diary of Philip Hone, 1828–1851*, vol. 1 (New York: Dodd, Mead, 1889), p. 196. Entry date January 27, 1836, shortly after the first reports of the month-old Dade Massacre reached New York. General reference works for this section include: John T. Sprague, *The Origins, Progress and Conclusion of the Florida War* (New York: D. Appleton, 1848); John K. Mahon, *History of the Second Seminole War, 1835–1842* (Gainesville: University of Florida Press, 1967); George Rainsford Fairbanks, *History of Florida* (Philadelphia: J. B. Lippincott & Co., 1871).

[4] See Alligator's testimony in Frank Laumer, *Dade's Last Command* (Gainesville: University Press of Florida, 1995), pp. 239–41.

[5] There is a notable parallel between the killing of Charley Emathla and the assassination of Ahmed Shah Massoud by al-Qaeda on September 8, 2001.

[6] The officers were: Major F. L. Dade, Fourth Infantry; Captain S. Gardiner, Second Lieutenant W. E. Basinger, USMA 1830; Second Lieutenant R. Henderson, USMA 1835; all of the Second Artillery; Captain U. S. Frazer; Second Lieutenant R. R. Mudge, USMA 1833 and a Tac, October 1834 to September 1835; Second Lieutenant J. L. Reais; all of the Third Artillery; and Assistant Surgeon J. S. Gatlin.

[7] Luis Pacheco's role is disputed, and he later denied complicity in the massacre. He was sent west on a transport by General Jesup, where he became free. Luis was later the subject of the "Pacheco Claim," an attempt by his owner's heirs to secure government compensation for what they saw as misappropriated property. The bill was introduced several times and because of its implications for the slavery issue was hotly debated. See for example HR 197, February 9, 1848, which placed compensation at the sum of $1,000. In January 1849 it came down to a narrow 91 to 89 passage. However, a recount found that the vote was actually 90 against, 89 for, with the Speaker abstaining. The bill was revisited ten days later and passed 101 to 95. Abraham Lincoln voted in the negative. The Senate passed the bill without debate. Luis Pacheco lived into the 1890s, protesting his innocence in the Dade Massacre until the end.

[8] Quoted in Laumer, *Dade's Last Command*, p. 240.

[9] *North American Review*, January 1842, p. 8.

[10] The total number of Indians in Florida, men, women and children, was probably 5,000, with 1,400 Africans, either slaves of the Seminoles or runaways. Fairbanks, *History of Florida*, pp. 276, 282. If even 20 percent of these could take to the field, their numbers were well beyond official estimates.

[11] Report of Lt. J. T. Sprague, April 1, 1837, National Archives, M234, roll 238, frames 738–56; letter S.249.

[12] Lane was a classmate of Jefferson Davis's, ranked 10th in the Class of 1828, and had served on the West Point faculty for a year afterwards. He had gained notice of the president while stationed in Washington, where he assaulted Representative John Ewing of Indiana, a critic of Jackson's. Some said this contributed to his getting the assignment. Lane was a gifted engineer as well, and he invented the pontoon bridge, which was used throughout the war.

[13] For general information on David Moniac, see Benjamin Griffith, "Lt. David Moniac, Creek Indian: First Minority Graduate of West Point," *Alabama Historical Quarterly,* Summer 1981, pp. 99–110; Carolyn Thomas Foreman, "The Brave Major Moniac and the Creek Volunteers," *Chronicles of Oklahoma,* vol. 23 (1945), pp. 96–106; and Captain Kenneth L. Benton, "Warrior from West Point," *Soldiers,* February 1974.

[14] Washington gave Sam a medal, which he always wore and eventually was buried with.

[15] *American State Papers, Military Affairs* (Washington: Gales & Seaton, 1861), vol. 2, p. 7.

[16] The event took place August 14, 1821. The USMA Archives has an original copy of Adams' four-page speech.

[17] Pvt. Alexander Moniac and Pvt. Samuel Moniac also served in the unit.

[18] The reason was a matter of some dispute. One newspaper report stated, "So much has been expected of [Lane] that it is not to be wondered that the total failure of his high ambition should have produced despondency." See clipping in Lane Cullum file. Those closer to Lane totally rejected the suicide thesis. Lane's mother immortalized her son's demise in verse, wondering where he was buried and if the spot was marked. "Oh! Is there no rude stone, / To designate the spot, / And is our country just, / To let him be forgot?" See Papers of Charles Davies, USMA Archives.

[19] Quoted in Benton, "Warrior from West Point."

[20] Brown later served in Mexico and was twice brevetted. In the Civil War, he commanded the troops that put down the New York City draft riots. He served until 1867.

[21] Quoted in Sprague, *The Origins, Progress and Conclusion of the Florida War,* p. 166.

[22] Letter from the Adjutant General's Office, January 27, 1838.

[23] The detailed estimate is in the notebook of John C. Casey, USMA 1829, Cullum #551. Casey was a staff officer for Zachary Taylor at the time.

[24] See Patricia R. Wickman, *Osceola's Legacy* (Tuscaloosa: University of Alabama Press, 1991).

[25] See Sidney Herbert, "Kill and Burn Orders," *New York Times,* June 1, 1902, p. 31.

[26] See "General Jesup on the Capture of the Seminole Chief Osceola," *New York Times,* October 25, 1858, p. 2. Jesup said that if he found himself in the same situation, he would do it again.

[27] Allegedly, Colonel Gentry had suggested this maneuver before the battle but did not survive to give his account.

[28] Walker, Cullum file #936.

[29] John C. Casey notebook, December 25, 1837. Casey was not at all easy on the Missourians, writing privately, "The volunteers behaved as is usual with citizen soldiers, i.e., they disgraced themselves."

[30] Fairbanks, *History of Florida,* p. 317.

[31] Harry A. Kersey Jr. and Michael Peterson, " 'Was I a member of Congress . . .' : Zachary Taylor's Letter to John J. Crittenden, January 12, 1838, Concerning the Second Seminole War," *Florida Historical Quarterly,* 1997, pp. 447–61.

[32] Nathaniel Wyche Hunter diary, February 27, 1840. (See n. 1 for ch. 1 above.)

[33] Ibid., March 15, 1840.

[34] Ibid., March 20, 1840.

[35] Ibid., March 21, 1840.

[36] Ibid., March 24, 1840.

[37] Jackson had made retiring the Revolutionary War–era public debt a priority, and he achieved it. For two years, 1835 and 1836, the United States was debt-free. It was the first and last time to date.

[38] Hunter diary, April 2, 1840

[39] *Congressional Globe,* March 9, 1840, p. 252.

[40] Quoted in Mahon, *History of the Second Seminole War,* p. 270.

[41] Ibid.

[42] Henry B. Dawson, *Battles of the United States* (New York: Johnson, Fry & Co., 1858), p. 442.

[43] Hunter diary, April 14, 1840.

[44] Ibid., April 15, 1840.

[45] General James Taylor, a relative of Zachary Taylor, was founder of the town of Newport, and one of the largest landowners in the West.

LAST IN THEIR CLASS

[46] The story is told by George Washington "Poet" Patten, USMA 1830, 36th of 42, in his *Voices of the Border* (1867). He had written a poem on the occasion of the departure of a column of troops to hunt down the Indians who committed the crime, entitled "Pale Eve on Wing of Starlight Rays." Patten was stationed in Florida at the time. There are other versions of the story that vary in some details.

[47] Note that the Marines had been active in the war from early on. In 1836, Colonel Archibald Henderson, the commandant of the Marine Corps, put a "Gone to Florida" sign on his Washington office, raised a Marine battalion and headed south. This war was the going concern and the Marines were going to be in it. Henderson personally led his troops in battle in January 1837, alongside W. W. Morris, who was then commander of the Creek Volunteers.

[48] For the full details, see Robin O. Warren, "Hamlet Rides Among the Seminoles," *Southern Cultures*, vol. 7, no. 4 (2001), pp. 32–63.

[49] At the time, the expression was spelled "hough."

[50] Theophilus F. Rodenbough, *From Everglade to Cañon with the Second Dragoons* (New York: Van Nostrand, 1875), p. 57.

[51] Fairbanks, *History of Florida*, p. 345.

[52] Mahon, *History of the Second Seminole War*, p. 315.

[53] Cf. *North American Review*, January 1842, p. 24.

[54] Ibid., pp. 1–2.

Henry Heth

[1] Dabney Maury, *Recollections of a Virginian in the Mexican, Indian and Civil Wars* (New York: Charles Scribner's Sons, 1894), p. 22.

[2] James L. Morrison Jr., *The Memoirs of Henry Heth: The Young Cavalier*, Master's Thesis, The University of Virginia, 1960. Includes the full text of Henry Heth's autobiography.

[3] Heth, July 25, 1843.

[4] Other attendees included P. G. T. Beauregard and W. H. F. Lee, son of Robert E. Lee.

[5] *Memoirs of Brigadier General William Montgomery Gardner*, edited and compiled by Elizabeth McKinne Gardner, Special Collections, USMA Archives, p. 8. Tidball said that the Immortals included "the wild and reckless as well as the idle and stupid." See John C. Tidball, *Getting through West Point by One Who Did and for Those Who Want to Know*, unpublished ms., USMA Archives.

[6] See for example, Samuel T. Williamson, "The Drama Behind the Gettysburg Epic," *New York Times*, July 3, 1938, pp. 16–17; "Lincoln

Started Gen. Pickett's Career," *New York Times,* December 5, 1927, p. 20.

7 "Reminiscences of Washington," *Atlantic Monthly,* December 1880, p. 805.

8 *Collected Works of Abraham Lincoln,* ed. Roy P. Basler (New Brunswick, N.J.: Rutgers University Press, 1953), vol. 1, p. 377.

9 Pickett and Garber both served in Texas 1853–54, though in different units and places; and both served in the Northwest in the late 1850s, though again not obviously crossing paths. Garber died of sickness in Oregon in 1859.

10 He is sometimes said to be a Goat because his name appears last on the 1812 list, but this was prior to the use of class ranking, and his position indicates only that he was chronologically last to leave West Point that year.

11 Quoted in George S. Pappas, *To the Point* (Westport, Conn.: Greenwood Publishing Group, 1992), p. 224.

12 George H. Derby letter, December 25, 1843. Ironically, in 1838 Cadet Sherman had written, "On Christmas and New Year's we have always had good dinners (things always welcome in this quarter of the globe) I am confident that Maj. Delafield is too much of a gentleman to interfere with them." Sherman letter to Ellen B. Ewing, December 10, 1838.

13 Tidball, *Getting through West Point.*

14 Derby letter, November 1, 1845.

15 The younger Mahan grew up at West Point but chose to go to Annapolis, and afterwards served in the Union Navy during the Civil War. His later fame in the academic world eclipsed that of his father; he was a noted author, president of the Naval War College and the preeminent theorist of naval strategy in the late nineteenth and early twentieth centuries, whose works are still studied in military schools worldwide. See Captain W. D. Puleston, *Mahan: The Life and Works of Captain Alfred Thayer Mahan, USN* (New Haven: Yale University Press, 1939).

16 Tidball, *Getting through West Point.*

17 Mahan had been only a second lieutenant when he wed, albeit a very old one.

18 Remarks of Brigadier General John Gibbon, June 12, 1886, West Point, New York.

19 Tidball, *Getting through West Point.*

20 Maury, *Recollections of a Virginian,* pp. 23–24.

21 Few ever think of Grant's close partner and fellow "westerner" Sherman as a Goat, and for very good reason—Sherman had an exemplary academic record, and graduated sixth in the Class of 1840.

[22] *Personal Memoirs of U.S. Grant* (New York: Charles L. Webster & Co., 1885).

[23] Such bills were suggested periodically; during one attempt in 1843, Francis Henney Smith wrote a lengthy defense of the Academy. See the *Southern Literary Messenger,* November 1843, pp. 665–70.

[24] Longstreet quoted in *New York Times,* July 24, 1885.

[25] Ibid.

[26] Jacob Dolson Cox, *Military Reminiscences of the Civil War* (New York: Charles Scribner's Sons, 1900), vol. 2, ch. 32.

[27] *Memoirs of Henry Heth,* pp. 16–17.

[28] Ibid., p. 14.

[29] Tidball, *Getting through West Point.*

[30] Derby letter, November 19, 1845.

[31] Sherman letter, October 22, 1837.

[32] *Memoirs of Brigadier General William Montgomery Gardner,* p. 5.

[33] Maury, *Recollections of a Virginian,* p. 22.

[34] Cf. John C. Waugh, *The Class of 1846* (New York: Ballantine Books, 1994), Part 1.

[35] Tidball, *Getting through West Point.*

[36] *Memoirs of Brigadier General William Montgomery Gardner,* p. 9.

[37] Longstreet's memoir, *From Manassas to Appomattox* (Philadelphia: J. B. Lippincott & Co., 1896).

[38] Ibid.

[39] Derby letter, October 3, 1842.

[40] Quoted in Joseph Howard Parks, *General Edmund Kirby Smith* (Baton Rouge: Louisiana State University Press, 1954).

[41] Kirby Smith surrendered on May 26, 1865.

[42] The disciplinary records for this period were destroyed in the fire of 1837. Walter H. Harrison, the inspector general of George Pickett's division in the Civil War, wrote that Armistead had resigned from West Point following a "youthful escapade," which he had been told was "the partial cracking of Jubal A. Early's head with a mess hall plate." Neither Armistead nor Early wrote of the incident; Early stated that "there was nothing worthy of particular note in my career at West Point. I was never a very good student, and was sometimes quite remiss, but I managed to attain a respectable stand in all my studies." He graduated 18th in a class of 50, although he was nearly expelled in 1836 when he ran up 196 demerits.

[43] Battalion Order No. 6, January 17, 1836.

[44] Sources on Armistead: Armistead Cullum file, particularly "List of Orders Relating to Cadet Lewis Addison Armistead"; Wayne E. Motts,

"Trust in God and Fear Nothing": General Lewis A. Armistead, CSA (Gettysburg, Pa.: Farnsworth House Military Impressions, 1994); Lieutenant General Jubal Anderson Early, CSA, *Autobiographical Sketch and Narrative of the War Between the States* (Philadelphia & London: J. B. Lippincott & Co., 1912).

Flirtation Walk

[1] William Dutton to his cousin Lucy J. Matthews, February 18, 1843.

[2] John C. Tidball, *Getting through West Point by One Who Did and for Those Who Want to Know*, unpublished ms., USMA Archives. Kerosene had not yet been invented.

[3] George H. Derby letter, February 26, 1845.

[4] Tidball said that "Even the common tomato was unknown to our tables, and I yearned for it as did the Israelites for the flesh-pots of Egypt." *Getting through West Point.*

[5] Ibid.

[6] Ibid. Many cadets recorded the wonders of the hash, "a species of conviviality, hospitality, and good-fellowship that cemented friendships among cadets like drinking out of the same canteen among old campaigners."

[7] Ibid.

[8] The actual post barber was a shoe-black named Joe Simpson, who could quickly and efficiently give a cadet a clean and even cut.

[9] James L. Morrison Jr., *The Memoirs of Henry Heth: The Young Cavalier*, Master's Thesis, The University of Virginia, 1960, pp. 34–38. Valentine attracted a great deal of unwanted attention from cadets and officers alike. Tidball attributed it to the fact that he was old for a plebe and looked older still; plus he was awkwardly built, large with a bullet-shaped head and arms disproportionately short. All the attention being paid to Valentine took the pressure off the rest. Jesse, though a schoolteacher before he came to West Point, dropped out after his second year.

[10] In Wharton J. Green, *Recollections and Reflections* (Raleigh, N.C.: Edwards & Broughton Printing Co., 1906), p. 286.

[11] *Memoirs of Henry Heth*, p. 17.

[12] Holly Streeter, *The Sordid Trial of Laura D. Fair: Victorian Family Values*, Gender and Legal History in America Papers (Washington, D.C.: Georgetown Law School, 1995).

[13] USMA Post Orders, November 22, 1844; and Derby, November 21, 1844. In Tidball's account, both men are armed and it is Crittenden who is wounded. *Getting through West Point.*

[14] Hays was a close friend of Grant's and the two fought together in Mexico. In the Civil War, Hays rose to the rank of brigadier general. He was killed leading his troops in battle in the Wilderness in 1864.

[15] Tidball: "to play at cards, which last was deemed the vilest of all depravity. As well might a person be caught with a kit of burglar's tools as for a cadet to be detected with a pack of cards, or even one card. It was proof positive of guilt in the first degree." In *Getting through West Point.*

[16] Quoted in Joseph B. James, "Life at West Point One Hundred Years Ago," *Mississippi Valley Historical Review,* June 1944, p. 36. Grant died of throat cancer, believed to have been brought on by his lifetime of smoking.

[17] Tidball, *Getting through West Point.*

[18] Register of Delinquencies, October 25, 1843.

[19] In April of 1846, the Corps pledged en masse to abstain from the use of liquor, in order to save a fellow cadet who was about to be expelled for drinking. The pledge worked, but the cadet never graduated.

[20] Another account places the event in June 1838, with O'Brien accompanying recently graduated Ripley A. Arnold, who had allegedly fought a duel at Benny's while a cadet.

[21] Seward graduated 34th of 38 in 1847.

[22] *Memoirs of Henry Heth,* p. 25.

[23] Burnside got eight demerits August 29, 1846, for being off limits near the wharf, but only five demerits for being AWOL September 21–22.

[24] USMA Post Orders, October 28, 1844.

[25] Tidball, *Getting through West Point.*

[26] *Memoirs of Henry Heth,* pp. 20–21. The post surgeon was named Dr. Wheaton, and those who evaded duty by pretending to be sick were said to be "Wheatoning it," a term that came into general use in the Army.

[27] Register of Delinquencies, June 22, 1846.

[28] Grant quoted in "While at West Point," *Cincinnati Times-Star,* July 29, 1885.

[29] *Memoirs of Henry Heth,* p. 49.

[30] Ibid., p. 18. Note that Grant says he spent most of his furlough with his friends, and does not go into detail about what other activities may have made it so memorable a time.

[31] Derby, September 6, 1843.

[32] Derby, July 5, 1845.

[33] Derby says there were three stag dances a week.

34 William Sherman to Ellen B. Ewing, August 21, 1839, and August 30, 1837. See also Derby, July 2, 1842.

35 Sherman to Ellen B. Ewing, August 21, 1839.

36 In a letter dated November 20, 1839, Scarritt describes a ball given by Mrs. Totten in November for her two nieces who were visiting. "Imagine two large rooms thrown into one as the scene of the action—the walls hung with choice engravings—paintings and portraits of which latter the most conspicuous was one which informed how our hostess looked twenty years since—native plants and exotics arranged in the deep windows so that those in rear should overlook those in front—just as though the room had been a theater—we the actors and those plants the audience seated in parquet, boxes and gallery. . . . The ladies were all muslin and smiles, the officers all lace and formality."

37 Derby, September 6, 1843. The Illumination was a tradition until encampment on the Plain ended in 1943.

38 The chain was the reason West Point existed. The fortifications such as Fort Clinton and Fort Putnam had been built to defend the chain, and thus prevent the British from using the Hudson as a communications link to Canada, which would have effectively split New England from the other states.

39 Maria was a family friend of the Heths' and had treats sent to Henry daily when he was laid up after his accidental bayoneting.

40 R. W. Johnson, *A Soldier's Reminiscences in Peace and War* (Philadelphia: J. B. Lippincott & Co., 1886), pp. 25–27. Johnson graduated 30th of 43 in his class, and was a brevet major general in the Civil War.

41 *Memoirs of Henry Heth*, p. 39.

42 Ibid., p. 41.

43 Ibid., p. 41.

44 Derby, July 2, 1842.

45 Tidball observed decades later: "Recently it has become customary to deliver the diplomas with considerable ceremony; and orations, music and mirth contribute interest to the occasion. All of which is but slow, common-place, and country-like compared with hat-kicking." *Getting through West Point.*

46 Sherman to Ellen B. Ewing, November 1, 1839.

47 *Memoirs of Henry Heth*, p. 50.

Zeb Inge

1 General sources used for the Mexican War chapters include: John S. Jenkins, *History of the War Between the United States and Mexico,*

from the Commencement of Hostilities to the Ratification of the Treaty of Peace (Auburn, N.Y.: Derby, Miller & Co., 1850); Richard McSherry, *El Puchero; or, A Mixed Dish from Mexico, Embracing General Scott's Campaign, with Sketches of Military Life, in Field and Camp, of the Character of the Country, Manners and Ways of the People, etc.* (Philadelphia: Lippincott, Grambo, 1850); John Frost, *Pictorial History of America, from the Earliest Times to the Close of the Mexican War* (Philadelphia: J. B. Smith & Co., 1857); Henry Howe, *Adventures and Achievements of Americans: A Series of Narratives Illustrating Their Heroism, Self-Reliance, Genius and Enterprise* (New York: G. F. Tuttle, 1859); K. Jack Bauer, *The Mexican War 1846–1848* (New York: Macmillan, 1974); John Edward Weems, *To Conquer a Peace: The War Between the United States and Mexico* (Garden City, New York: Doubleday & Co., 1974); *Appleton's Cyclopedia of American Biography,* ed. James Grant Wilson and John Fiske, 6 vols. (New York: D. Appleton & Co., 1887–1889). Ephraim Kirby Smith's war letters from Mexico were published in Emma Jerome Blackwood, ed., *To Mexico with Scott: Letters of Captain E. Kirby Smith to His Wife* (Cambridge, Mass.: Harvard University Press, 1917).

[2] Also known as "horse" or "flying" artillery.

[3] Blackwood, ed., *Letters of Captain E. Kirby Smith,* p. 48.

[4] Ibid., p. 49.

[5] After a distinguished diplomatic career, Donelson was the 1856 vice presidential candidate for Millard Fillmore's unsuccessful second run at the White House as nominee of the American ("Know Nothing") Party.

[6] The solution was neither 54'40" nor a fight, but an extension of the 49th parallel to the Vancouver Strait, and enough ambiguity at that point to keep the issue alive for another thirty years.

[7] Blackwood, ed., *Letters of Captain E. Kirby Smith,* p. 18.

[8] George Gordon Meade, *The Life and Letters of George Gordon Meade* (New York: Charles Scribner's Sons, 1913), vol. 1, p. 39.

[9] Blackwood, ed., *Letters of Captain E. Kirby Smith,* p. 34.

[10] Major Brown's right leg was torn off by a Mexican shell fragment. When soldiers came to assist him, he said, "Men, go to your duties! Thank God! the country has not lost a younger man." *Harper's New Monthly Magazine,* July 1855, p. 172. The fort was at the site of present-day Brownsville.

[11] Zeb's academic records were among those lost in the fire of 1837.

[12] James Longstreet's memoir, *From Manassas to Appomattox* (Philadelphia: J. B. Lippincott & Co., 1896).

[13] In Joseph Pearson Farley, *West Point in the Early Sixties: With Incidents of the War* (Troy, N.Y.: Pafraets Book Co., 1902), pp. 77–78.

[14] See Taylor's official report of the battle, May 17, 1846, and the eyewitness reports reprinted in Theophilus F. Rodenbough, *From Everglade to Cañon with the Second Dragoons* (New York: Van Nostrand, 1875), pp. 514–16, as well as ch. 10, *passim*. See also Major Joseph I. Lambert, *One Hundred Years with the Second Cavalry* (Ft. Riley, Kans.: The Capper Printing Co., 1939), ch. 2; and *Niles Register,* May 30, 1846, 70.195.

[15] Frost, *Pictorial History of America,* p. 670.

[16] "Taylor's Battles in Mexico," *Harper's New Monthly Magazine,* July 1855, p. 175.

[17] Blackwood, ed., *Letters of Captain E. Kirby Smith,* p. 50.

[18] McCauley was riding master at USMA, 1840–41.

[19] See Rev. W. T. Hamilton, D.D., "Address Delivered at the Government Street Church, Mobile, Thursday Morning, Jan. 28, 1847, Over the Remains of Zebulon Montgomery Pike Inge" (Mobile: Dade & Thompson, 1847). Also personal conversations and correspondence between the author and Mr. Herndon Inge.

[20] Account in *Niles Register,* May 30, 1846, 70.195. Note that accounts from most infantrymen tended to underplay if not totally dismiss the impact of the cavalry charge.

[21] Longstreet, *From Manassas to Appomattox.*

[22] Blackwood, ed., *Letters of Captain E. Kirby Smith,* p. 51.

[23] See George A. McCall, *Letters from the Frontiers* (Philadelphia: J. B. Lippincott & Co., 1868), pp. 449–57, for a description of the two battles, particularly Palo Alto. The original copies of these letters are at the USMA Archives and are written on the personal stationery of General Arista.

[24] Six Goats participated in both of the opening battles: William W. Morris, 1820; Ephraim Kirby Smith, 1826; Nathaniel Wyche Hunter, 1833; Zebulon Montgomery Pike Inge, 1838 (KIA); Charles F. Morris, 1841 (WIA); and William Logan Crittenden, 1845.

[25] Quoted in Joseph Howard Parks, *General Edmund Kirby Smith* (Baton Rouge: Louisiana State University Press, 1954), p. 50.

Churubusco

[1] *American Whig Review,* December 1846, p. 173.

[2] Henry David Thoreau, "Civil Disobedience," in *Walden and Civil Disobedience,* ed. Owen Thomas (New York: W. W. Norton & Co., 1966), p. 224.

[3] Quoted in K. Jack Bauer, *The Mexican War 1846–1848* (New York: Macmillan, 1974), p. 69.

[4] Later in the war, Senator Daniel Webster remarked on Santa Anna's return, "the President must be gratified to know that in the subsequent battles, which have cost so much blood and treasure, the commanding general on both sides was of his own choosing." Philip Hone, *The Diary of Philip Hone, 1828–1851*, vol. 1 (New York: Dodd, Mead, 1889), October 8, 1847.

[5] George Gordon Meade, *The Life and Letters of George Gordon Meade* (New York: Charles Scribner's Sons, 1913), vol. 1, p. 76.

[6] Emma Jerome Blackwood, ed., *To Mexico with Scott: Letters of Captain E. Kirby Smith to His Wife* (Cambridge, Mass.: Harvard University Press, 1917), p. 53. See also John S. Jenkins, *History of the War Between the United States and Mexico, from the Commencement of Hostilities to the Ratification of the Treaty of Peace* (Auburn, N.Y.: Derby, Miller & Co., 1850), pp. 118–19: "The army had been looked upon by many as an unnecessary organization—the soldiers were said to be inefficient, and the officers better fitted to grace the salons of fashion and pleasure, than to meet the stern realities of the battle-field. The military school at West Point had also received its portion of censure, and there were those who termed it a nursery for carpet-knights, instead of warriors. But how soon were these errors dispelled when the day of trial came, and that little band on the Rio Grande were seen fighting their way, inch by inch, and step by step, over coming every obstacle, as if moved by one mind, and animated by one impulse!—how soon did the American people learn to respect and admire the genius and skill of the brave men who were instructed on the banks of the Hudson, and imbued with the revolutionary spirit still lingering around the scenes where they were nurtured!"

[7] *American Whig Review*, December 1846, p. 179.

[8] Meade, *The Life and Letters of George Gordon Meade*, p. 98.

[9] Letter from Pratt in his Cullum file.

[10] His obituary in the 1889 USMA Association of Graduates Reunion Book (pp. 59–60) noted that McClelland "never felt the sense of physical fear" and that "he was dogged, stubborn, and could not brook discipline or control." At USMA he was "very studious, but slow of comprehension." He died in 1888 at his home near Waterloo, Pennsylvania, age 69, while reading a book.

[11] It was a short time later in this battle that Taylor uttered his famous order, "A little more grape, Captain Bragg." See generally David Lavender, *Climax at Buena Vista* (New York: J. B. Lippincott & Co., 1966).

[12] Blackwood, ed., *Letters of Captain E. Kirby Smith,* p. 136.

[13] Ibid., pp. 146, 166.

[14] Ibid., p. 146.

[15] Ibid., p. 140.

[16] Ibid., pp. 142–43.

[17] Ibid., pp. 132, 155–56.

[18] Ibid., p. 94.

[19] Ibid., p. 96. Presumably either Martin Van Buren, or Kirby's classmate and presidential son Abraham Van Buren, who had retired from the Army.

[20] Ibid., p. 144.

[21] Ibid., p. 179.

[22] Richard McSherry, *El Puchero; or, A Mixed Dish from Mexico, Embracing General Scott's Campaign, with Sketches of Military Life, in Field and Camp, of the Character of the Country, Manners and Ways of the People, etc.* (Philadelphia: Lippincott, Grambo, 1850), p. 54.

[23] *Memoirs of Brigadier General William Montgomery Gardner,* edited and compiled by Elizabeth McKinne Gardner, Special Collections, USMA Archives, pp. 17–18.

[24] Blackwood, ed., *Letters of Captain E. Kirby Smith,* p. 192.

[25] Ibid., p. 178.

[26] Ibid., p. 200.

[27] Ibid., p. 201.

[28] Bomford was son of George Bomford, USMA 1805, and was 34th in a class of 45. Snelling was 24th in a class of 41.

[29] Blackwood, ed., *Letters of Captain E. Kirby Smith,* p. 204.

[30] Henry Howe, *Adventures and Achievements of Americans: A Series of Narratives Illustrating Their Heroism, Self-Reliance, Genius and Enterprise* (New York: G. F. Tuttle, 1859), p. 466. An ophicleide is a large brass instrument.

[31] Blackwood, ed., *Letters of Captain E. Kirby Smith,* p. 216.

[32] "Forlorn hope" was a traditional term for a storming party. It is derived from the Dutch *verloren hoop,* meaning lost company. The English version has a strongly ironic flavor.

[33] Blackwood, ed., *Letters of Captain E. Kirby Smith,* p. 217.

Chapultepec

[1] Mason graduated second in the Class of 1849.

[2] "The Battle of Molino Del Rey," *Southern Quarterly Review,* vol. 6, no. 12, pp. 281–315; and *Memoirs of Brigadier General William*

Montgomery Gardner, edited and compiled by Elizabeth McKinne Gardner, Special Collections, USMA Archives, p. 34.

3 Philip Hone noted in his diary on October 29: "Lieutenant Morris, the gallant son of Thomas Morris, and grandson of Robert Morris, the great financier of the Revolution, and friend of Washington, equally brave, was less fortunate than his young associates in arms. He, too, was wounded in the attack on 'Kings-Mill,' on the Eighth of September. He was shot in the leg, from which wound a hemorrhage ensued, and he died on the 17th, without entering 'the halls of Montezuma.' Alas, will his gallant deeds and death of glory assuage the grief of his parents, or dry the tears of his sisters? These are the trophies of West Point! Shall it not be supported?" *The Diary of Philip Hone, 1828–1851,* vol. 1 (New York: Dodd, Mead, 1889).

4 Richard McSherry, *El Puchero; or, A Mixed Dish from Mexico, Embracing General Scott's Campaign, with Sketches of Military Life, in Field and Camp, of the Character of the Country, Manners and Ways of the People, etc.* (Philadelphia: Lippincott, Grambo, 1850), pp. 107–8. McSherry was acting surgeon of Marines.

5 See Scott's report on the battle to William L. Marcy, Secretary of War, dated September 18, 1847, and other sources already noted. Some accounts credit Major Thomas H. Seymour with the flag raising, but this was probably at a different part of Chapultepec. Pickett said that he brought down the Mexican flag, not the legendary Mexican cadet, a claim substantiated by witnesses.

6 Quoted in K. Jack Bauer, *The Mexican War 1846–1848* (New York: Macmillan, 1974), p. 318. The flag raising was the signal for the execution of thirty of the San Patricio deserters, who were being held, heads in nooses, at the Plaza of Mixcoac two miles away. This was reportedly Colonel Harney's idea.

7 Quoted in ibid., p. 322.

8 *Diary of Philip Hone,* September 28, 1847.

9 *Memoirs of Brigadier General William Montgomery Gardner,* pp. 32–34.

10 See bio of Walker in *Confederate Veteran,* November 1899, p. 515.

11 James L. Morrison Jr., *The Memoirs of Henry Heth: The Young Cavalier,* Master's Thesis, The University of Virginia, 1960, p. 76.

12 Ibid., p. 81.

13 Ibid., p. 84.

14 Ibid., p. 84.

15 Ibid., p. 87.

16 Ibid., p. 91.

17 Ibid., p. 84.

James McNeill Whistler

1 George L. Hartsuff, letter of January 22, 1849, Cullum files.

2 Special Orders No. 119, January 1, 1849; USMA Post Orders, vol. 3, pp. 288–89.

3 USMA Staff Records, vol. 4.

4 See generally Douglas Southall Freeman, *R. E. Lee: A Biography* (New York: Charles Scribner's Sons, 1934), ch. 19.

5 *Ten Years in the Saddle: The Memoir of William Woods Averell,* ed. Edward K. Eckert and Nicholas J. Amato (San Rafael, Calif.: Presidio Press, 1978), p. 31.

6 Virginia Howell Davis, *Jefferson Davis: A Memoir* (New York: Belford Co. Publishers, 1890), v. 1, p. 412.

7 Stanley F. Horn, ed., *The Robert E. Lee Reader* (New York: Grosset & Dunlop, 1949), p. 74.

8 Ibid., p. 71.

9 *Ten Years in the Saddle,* p. 49.

10 Joseph Pearson Farley, *West Point in the Early Sixties: With Incidents of the War* (Troy, N.Y.: Pafraets Book Co., 1902), pp. 34–35.

11 Sylvanus Thayer, letter to George Cullum, December 18, 1855, Thayer Papers, USMA Archives.

12 "Gen. Jefferson Davis at West Point," *New York Times,* September 26, 1855; "Gen. Jefferson Davis at West Point," *New York Times,* October 10, 1855.

13 Quoted in Joseph Howard Parks, *General Edmund Kirby Smith* (Baton Rouge: Louisiana State University Press, 1954), p. 36.

14 Joseph was once saved from drowning by a private named Ryan, who went down with a ball in his shoulder by his father's side at Resaca de la Palma.

15 Cf. generally Gordon Fleming, *The Young Whistler* (London: George Allen & Unwin, 1978), ch. 5. Also Whistler's USMA Archives "X-file" folder.

16 Though a native New Englander who grew up in Russia, London and the northern United States, Whistler presented himself as a southern dandy.

17 See R. Ernest Dupuy, *Men of West Point* (New York: William Sloane Associates, 1951), pp. 33–35. Thompson S. Brown, USMA 1825, completed the St. Petersburg-Moscow railroad.

[18] *Ten Years in the Saddle,* p. 41.

[19] From *Military Reminiscences of Gen. Wm. R. Boggs, CSA* (Durham, N.C.: The Seeman Printery, 1913), p. xi. Boggs graduated second in the Class of 1852. See also "Whistler's First Drawings," *Century Magazine,* September 1910.

[20] It is unknown whether the instructor was his friend Professor Bailey, Captain Edward Boynton, or Lieutenant Caleb Huse.

[21] Lee to Totten, July 8, 1854. See Charles R. Bowery Jr. and Brian D. Hankinson, eds., *Daily Correspondence of Brevet Colonel Robert E Lee,* USMA Library Occasional Papers no. 5 (West Point, N.Y.: USMA Press, 2003), pp. 202–3.

[22] John Ross Key, "Recollections of Whistler While in the Office of the United States Coast Survey." The closest Whistler came to combat was in 1866 when he was in Chile during the Spanish blockade of the Chilean port of Valparaíso. He was on hand to witness the Spanish shelling the port. The scene of the blockading ships are the subject of his painting *Valparaíso.*

[23] See John C. Tidball, *Getting through West Point by One Who Did and for Those Who Want to Know,* unpublished ms., USMA Archives; W. Fletcher Johnson, *Life of Sitting Bull and History of the Indian War* (Philadelphia: Edgewood Pulishing Co., 1891), pp. 29–36; and USMA records.

[24] He was number 8 overall his plebe year, with 24 demerits; and number 13 his second year, with 29 demerits.

[25] One story has it that after graduation, McLean went to Buttermilk Falls and got into a fight in which sticks and stones were thrown. Many were hurt, including Bison. The fight was so unseemly that he was cashiered and his graduation revoked. The official records do not support this version of events, though the fight may have taken place at some other time.

[26] William H. Morris had accompanied Bison on some of these excursions and was also tried. He was found guilty and suspended for one year. Morris would later serve as a Union brigadier general, severely wounded at the Battle of Spottsylvania. After the war, he invented an automatic ejecting revolver.

[27] Johnson, *Life of Sitting Bull,* p. 34.

[28] The expedition was from June 1857 to June 1858.

[29] There are several problems with this story. Ives was admitted to the Academy on June 23, 1848, after Bison had left, so they would not have known each other well, though it is possible their paths crossed when Ives arrived at West Point but before he was officially admit-

ted. And Ives' detailed "Report Upon the Colorado River of the West," which is full of anecdotes from the trip, does not mention the incident, which surely it would have had it been true. Cf. House Exec. Doc. #90, 36th Cong. 1st Sess. This was a secondhand tale, like most Bison legends, with just enough factual grounding to make it seem plausible.

[30] Johnson, *Life of Sitting Bull,* p. 33.

[31] Ibid., pp. 35–36. Hall received the Medal of Honor for an engagement fought October 20, 1879, near White River, Colorado, where he single-handedly rescued a fellow officer surrounded by about 35 Indians. Cf. *Heitman's Historical Register,* p. 490.

William Logan Crittenden

[1] Turnley Diary, USMA Archives, p. 114. Sources, generally: Robert Granville Caldwell, *The Lopez Expeditions to Cuba, 1848–1851* (Princeton: Princeton University Press, 1915); Leonard J. Hill, *The Attitude of the United States Toward the Lopez Expeditions to Cuba, 1848–1851* (Pittsburg, Kans.: Kansas State Teachers College, May 1937); Thomas W. Wilson, *An Authentic Narrative of the Piratical Descents upon Cuba* (Havana, September 1851); H. M. Hardeman (Lucy Holcombe), *The Free Flag of Cuba, or, The Martyrdom of Lopez* (New York: I. DeWitt & Davenport Publishers, 1855); H. H. Crittenden, *The Crittenden Memoirs* (New York: G. P. Putnam's Sons, 1936); Louis Schlesinger, "The Personal Narrative of Louis Schlesinger, of Adventures in Cuba and Ceuta," *United States Democratic Review,* vol. 31, nos. 17–31 (September-November 1852).

[2] Hardeman, *Free Flag of Cuba,* p. 88.

[3] *Webster's Dictionary,* 1913 edition. The closest English equivalent is "freebooters." The expression "to filibuster," i.e., to take the Senate hostage through endless debate, entered the American political vocabulary in this era.

[4] Hardeman, *Free Flag of Cuba,* p. 89.

[5] The slave estimate is Caldwell's in *Lopez Expeditions to Cuba,* p. 19.

[6] 1851 census numbers cited in Hill, *Attitude of the United States,* p. 4.

[7] Quoted in ibid., p. 7.

[8] Caldwell, *Lopez Expeditions to Cuba,* pp. 32–33.

[9] Taylor, March 22, 1849, quoted in Hill, *Attitude of the United States,* p. 13.

[10] Davis, in Caldwell, *Lopez Expeditions to Cuba,* p. 49.

[11] The Spanish government monitored these developments from consulates in the U.S. and sent spies to infiltrate the movement. The

Spanish fomented a minor diplomatic crisis when they kidnapped a Cuban in America.

[12] See letter of Major William Hardy, Kentucky Regiment, *Tallahassee Sentinel,* June 7, 1850.

[13] One of the prosecutors was Judah P. Benjamin, later secretary of war and vice president of the Confederacy.

[14] Hill, *Attitude of the United States,* p. 27.

[15] Account of Charles N. Horwell in *New York Times,* October 4, 1851.

[16] Ibid.

[17] "Gen. Lopez-Van Vechten, &c," *New Orleans Delta,* October 23, 1851.

[18] Reprinted in *New York Times,* October 13, 1851.

[19] "Cuban Affairs," *New York Times,* October 11, 1851; also testimony of William May aboard the Saranac, in a letter to his brother Dr. Frederick May of Washington, quoted in Caldwell, *Lopez Expeditions to Cuba,* pp. 102–3, n. 7. Charles May of the Second Dragoons was William's nephew.

[20] *New York Times,* October 27, 1851.

[21] Letter of Thomas J. Herndon, Cincinnati Company of Volunteers, August 22, 1851.

[22] Wilson, *Authentic Narrative,* p. 17.

[23] Ibid., p. 23.

The Battle of Blue Waters

[1] After the riot, the New York Police were issued their first billy clubs, to be used for self-defense.

[2] James L. Morrison Jr., *The Memoirs of Henry Heth: The Young Cavalier,* Master's Thesis, The University of Virginia, 1960, p. 115.

[3] Ibid., p. 119.

[4] Cf. Leo E. Oliva, "Fort Atkinson on the Santa Fe Trail, 1850–1854," *Kansas Historical Quarterly,* Summer 1974, pp. 212–33.

[5] Two years later, the mice were gone but the cats were infested with fleas. Ibid.

[6] *Memoirs of Henry Heth,* p. 133.

[7] Ibid., p. 209.

[8] Ibid., p. 134.

[9] Ibid., p. 147.

[10] Ibid., p. 204.

[11] Translation courtesy of Dr. Alice Anderton, Ph.D. in linguistics, and the executive director of the Intertribal Wordpath Society.

[12] *Memoirs of Henry Heth,* p. 160.

13 Ibid., p. 162.

14 Buckner graduated eleventh in his class. He was a noted hero of the Mexican War. He left the service in 1855, served as a Confederate officer, and was elected governor of Kentucky in 1887.

15 *Memoirs of Henry Heth*, p. 173.

16 Ibid., p. 309.

17 *New York Times*, September 18, 1854.

18 *New York Times*, November 23, 1854.

19 *New York Times*, April 18, 1855.

20 *New York Times*, January 28, 1856.

21 Logan U. Reavis, *The Life and Military Service of Gen. William Selby Harney* (St. Louis: Bryan, Brand & Co.), p. 248.

22 Quoted in *New York Times*, July 17, 1855.

23 *Memoirs of Henry Heth*, p. 197.

24 Harney would admit to only one man in the Army being his better at swearing—his brother. Ibid.

25 John C. Symmes, first in the class, was offered but declined the same commission.

26 *The Papers of Jefferson Davis*, ed. Haskell M. Monroe Jr. and James T. McIntosh (Baton Rouge: Louisiana State University Press, 1971), vol. 5, p. 419. Cf. generally Harney's after-action report (AAR), September 1855, and Cooke's AAR, September 5, 1855.

27 *New York Times*, November 1, 1855.

28 See generally, Alban W. Hoopes, "Thomas S. Twiss, Indian Agent on the Upper Platte, 1855–1861," *Mississippi Valley Historical Review*, December 1933, pp. 353–64.

29 *New York Times*, September 4, 1855.

30 On November 14, 1855, Cooke's eldest daughter, Flora, married J. E. B. Stuart.

31 *Memoirs of Henry Heth*, pp. 197–98.

32 *New York Times*, October 6, 1855.

33 Warren made an effort to save as many of the artifacts as he could. When he returned from the West in 1858, he donated them to the Smithsonian Institution. Today it is the largest and most complete collection of pre–Civil War Teton Sioux relics in the world.

34 *Memoirs of Henry Heth*, p. 199.

35 "Howe was very generally disliked by his Army associates," Heth opined. Ibid.

36 *New York Times*, October 27, 1855.

37 *New York Times*, November 2, 1855.

38 *New York Times*, January 28, 1856.

[39] Quoted in *New York Times*, September 28, 1855.

[40] *New York Times*, March 24, 1856.

[41] *New York Times*, October 6, 1855.

[42] *New York Times*, October 12, 1855.

[43] *Memoirs of Henry Heth*, p. 200.

Solomon's Fork

[1] James L. Morrison Jr., *The Memoirs of Henry Heth: The Young Cavalier*, Master's Thesis, The University of Virginia, 1960, pp. 43–44.

[2] Lieutenant G. K. Warren, *Preliminary Report of Explorations in Nebraska and Dakota in the Years 1855–56–57* (Washington: Government Printing Office, 1875), p. 52. Warren's lengthy and detailed report is an important resource in the study of the geography of the plains of those days and of the Indians who dwelled there.

[3] Cf. William Y. Chalfant, *Cheyennes and Horse Soldiers* (Norman: University of Oklahoma Press, 1989), the definitive account of the battle; *The Letters of Major General James E. B. Stuart*, ed. Adele H. Mitchell (Stuart-Mosby Historical Society, 1990); H. B. McClellan, *I Rode with Jeb Stuart* (Bloomington: Indiana University Press, 1958), ch. 3.

[4] Sturgis graduated no. 32 in his class. In 1869 he became colonel of the Seventh Cavalry, with Custer as his lieutenant colonel. He was on a recruiting mission when the Little Bighorn expedition left, and was not present at the battle. His son James G. Sturgis, USMA 1875, no. 29, was killed with Custer.

[5] David S. Stanley, *Personal Memoirs of Major-General D. S. Stanley, USA* (Cambridge, Mass.: Harvard University Press, 1917), p. 42.

[6] Stuart's account is in his letters; Lomax was in *New York Times*, September 5, 1857; Stanley, *Personal Memoirs*, pp. 45–46.

[7] Stuart's diary from this period is reprinted in McClellan, *I Rode with Jeb Stuart*.

[8] Stanley, *Personal Memoirs*, pp. 46–47.

[9] *New York Times*, September 11, 1857, quoting a report from the *St. Louis Independence Messenger*. The *Times* discredited the report.

[10] Quoted in *New York Times*, September 19, 1857.

[11] *New York Times*, August 20, 1857.

[12] General Persifor Smith died suddenly in May 1858, and Sumner was one of his pallbearers, along with Colonel Charles May.

[13] *New York Times*, October 16, 1857.

[14] *New York Times*, March 13, 1858.

[15] *New York Times*, August 29, 1858.

[16] *New York Times,* March 16, 1858.
[17] *New York Times,* February 25, 1858.

The Pig War

[1] Cf. Tracy Elmer Strevey, *Pickett on Puget Sound,* Thesis, University of Washington, 1925; David Richardson, *Pig War Islands* (Eastsound, Wash.: Orcas Publishing Co., 1971); Colonel Ernest J. Whitaker (USMA 1941), "George Edward Pickett: Defender of the San Juans," in *West Pointers and Early Washington,* ed. Major General John A. Hemphill and Robert C. Cumbow (Seattle: The West Point Society of Puget Sound, 1992).

[2] Stevens was a Mexican War veteran, having fought in all of the major battles after the landing at Vera Cruz. He was brevetted for bravery at Churubusco and Chapultepec. He served in the Civil War as a Union brigadier general, and was killed in action at Chantilly after Second Bull Run (Manassas), September 1, 1862. Stevens was leading a charge of the 79th New York Highlanders, bearing the colors. His last words, directed to his men, were, "Highlanders! Follow your General!" The charge carried the day. He was posthumously promoted to major general.

[3] Forsyth later served on staffs of McClellan and Sheridan. He fought mostly in the West, but came east in spring 1864. He commanded troops at the Union victory at Five Forks, April 1, 1865, and was brevetted colonel. Pickett was the Rebel commander in that battle. On the ninth he was brevetted brigadier general. Forsyth was later in command at Wounded Knee, December 29, 1890.

[4] Martha Boltz writes, "Tribal custom ceremonies as late as the early 1900s seemed to involve an exchange of goods as well as obligations. It is possible that Pickett used the gloves in lieu of exchanging wedding rings, or it may have been a carry-over of an old West Point tradition. The gloves obviously held some deep meaning for him, since they were packed in the little red chest Morning Mist had brought with her." The gloves are now in the Washington Capitol Museum, Olympia, Washington. See "The General's Second Family: The One That History Forgot," *Washington Times,* December 1, 2001.

[5] Note that an 1879 decision by the Washington Territorial Supreme Court gave tribal marriages the same legal standing as any other marriages.

[6] The house still stands at 910 Bancroft Street, Bellingham, Washington.

[7] *New York Times,* September 9, 1859.

[8] Note that Harney's orders were written by the acting assistant adjutant general of the Department of Oregon, Lt. Alfred Pleasanton,

USMA 1844, graduated seventh. He was a cavalry corps commander at Gettysburg, fighting all three days and being brevetted for bravery. He was replaced in command by Phil Sheridan in March 1864, to his dismay.

[9] Richardson, *Pig War Islands,* p. 57.

[10] He remained in command August 1 to October 18, 1859. During the Civil War his only combat action was as a division commander in the Battle of Seven Pines in the Peninsular Campaign, May 31, 1862. His division was whipped by a brigade commanded by George Pickett.

[11] "The Little War Cloud in the West," *New York Times,* September 7, 1859.

[12] The American delegation was headed at the time by Archie Campbell.

[13] *New York Times,* September 29, 1859.

[14] *New York Times,* September 21, 1859.

[15] Pickett Cullum file.

[16] Quoted in *New York Times,* July 10, 1860.

[17] Quoted in *New York Times,* July 21, 1860.

[18] The previous commander, Harney's foe Sumner, took over the Department of California.

[19] Haller had been recommended for admission to West Point, but lost the slot to William B. Franklin, who graduated first in the Class of 1843. Haller was directly commissioned.

[20] Quoted in Whitaker, "George Edward Pickett: Defender of the San Juans," p. 196.

George Armstrong Custer

[1] George C. Strong, *Cadet Life at West Point* (Boston: T.O.H.P. Burnham, 1962), p. 289.

[2] Ibid.

[3] Ibid., p. 290.

[4] "Return of the Furlough Class of 1850," in Oliver E. Wood, *The West Point Scrap Book* (New York: D. Van Nostrand, 1871), p. 116.

[5] Cf. John Montgomery Wright, "West Point Before the War," *Southern Bivouac,* June 1885, p. 13. Wright was born in 1839 in Madison Barracks, New York. His father was General George Wright, USMA 1822, who led the forlorn hope and was wounded at Molino del Rey, was Pickett's commander on San Juan Island, and died in a shipwreck July 30, 1865, while traveling to take command of the Department of Columbia. John M. Wright was a leading member of the Class of 1863 who resigned in 1861 after the outbreak of the Civil War to join in the fight. He rose to the rank of major during the war, served as adjutant gen-

eral of Kentucky, 1875–79, and was chief marshal of the U.S. Supreme Court, 1888–1915. He died January 2, 1915. Custer is one of the most written-about figures in American history, and with considerable redundancy. Among the sources consulted generally for this section are the Custer, McCrea and other cadet files in the USMA Special Collections, with many letters and primary source material; Marguerite Merington, ed., *The Custer Story: The Life and Intimate Letters of General George A. Custer and His Wife Elizabeth* (New York: Devin-Adair, 1950); Frederic F. Van de Water, *Glory-Hunter: A Life of General Custer* (New York: Bobbs-Merrill, 1934); D. A. Kinsley, *Favor the Bold* (New York: Holt, Rinehart & Winston, 1967–68); Jay Monaghan, *Custer: The Life of General George Armstrong Custer* (Boston: Little, Brown, 1959); Stephen E. Ambrose, *Crazy Horse and Custer: The Parallel Lives of Two American Warriors* (Garden City, N.Y.: Doubleday, 1975); and Louise K Barnett, *Touched by Fire: The Life, Death, and Mythic Afterlife of George Armstrong Custer* (New York: Henry Holt, 1996).

[6] Morris Schaff, *The Spirit of Old West Point, 1858–1862* (New York: Houghton, Mifflin & Co., 1907), p. 194. Schaff knew Custer well at West Point and afterwards, and his memoir of his cadet days is an important source on West Point in the years before and during the Civil War.

[7] Schaff, *Spirit of Old West Point*, p. 86.

[8] The Land Ordinance of 1785 and the Northwest Ordinance of 1787 had provided for creating a public school system in Ohio.

[9] Quoted in Barnett, *Touched by Fire*, ch. 1.

[10] Ibid.

[11] "Custer As a Boy," *New York Times*, July 29, 1876, p. 2.

[12] Ibid.

[13] Bingham served eight nonconsecutive terms in Congress. He was a special judge advocate during the trial of the Lincoln conspirators, helped manage the impeachment of Andrew Johnson, and was U.S. minister to Japan, 1873–85.

[14] Custer letter, August 7, 1857.

[15] Strong, *Cadet Life at West Point*, p. 122.

[16] Farley, *West Point in the Early Sixties*, p. 78.

[17] Custer letter, June 30, 1858, at the start of his yearling year.

[18] Custer, "War Memoirs," *The Galaxy*, April 1876, p. 448.

[19] McCrea letter, January 19, 1861.

[20] Edward C. Boynton, *History of West Point: and its military importance during the American revolution: and the origin and progress of the United States Military Academy* (New York: D. Van Nostrand, 1863), p. 281.

[21] Ibid., p. 250.

[22] Stephen C. Lynford, Class of June 1861, April 4, 1859.

[23] Also Andrew A. Humphreys, who would serve as Meade's chief of staff at Gettysburg, and Major Robert Anderson, who would command at Fort Sumter.

[24] Custer, "War Memoirs," p. 450.

[25] Custer letter, August 7, 1857.

[26] Quoted in *"Skinned": The Delinquency Record of Cadet George Armstrong Custer, U.S.M.A. Class of June 1861*, ed. W. Donald Horn, with a foreword by Blaine L. Beal (Short Hills, N.J.: W. D. Horn, 1980), p. iii.

[27] Boynton, *History of West Point,* p. 279. Some have said that the demerits Custer was forgiven at the end of his first year were "Custer's luck," but in fact all cadets in his class were given the one-third reduction.

[28] Custer, "War Memoirs," p. 454.

[29] McCrea letter, September 23, 1860.

[30] Custer had no demerits April through June 1860, and was given a day of extended limits as a reward. But after July 4 he began accumulating skins again, and was at 95 by December.

[31] McCrea letter, December 22, 1858.

[32] "Ode to C.M.W." in Wood, *The West Point Scrap Book*, p. 137.

[33] Custer letter, August 7, 1857.

[34] Custer, "War Memoirs," p. 454.

[35] Strong, *Cadet Life at West Point,* p. 301.

[36] Ibid.

[37] *Ten Years in the Saddle: The Memoir of William Wood Averell,* ed. Edward K. Eckert and Nicholas J. Amato (San Rafael, Calif.: Presidio Press, 1978), p. 38.

[38] Custer letter, December 13, 1859.

[39] Custer West Point–era letter, date uncertain.

[40] Merington, *The Custer Story,* p. 8.

[41] Wright, "West Point Before the War," p. 18.

[42] McCrea letter, February 10, 1861, USMA Archives. Cf. McCrea's edited letters in *Dear Belle,* ed. Catherine S. Crary (Middletown, Conn.: Wesleyan University Press, 1965). Buck Buchanan ultimately did not graduate.

[43] McCrea letter, January 19, 1861. McCrea offered helpfully that a better idea would have been to take the whole notebook and replace it later by bribing an employee at the hotel.

[44] McCrea letter, February 10, 1861.

Absent Friends

[1] George C. Strong, *Cadet Life at West Point* (Boston: T.O.H.P. Burnham, 1962), pp. 73 74.

[2] Quoted in ibid., p. 297.

[3] Cf. Elizabeth Dey Jenkinson Waugh, *West Point* (New York: Macmillan Press, 1944), ch. 9.

[4] Hartsuff letter, January 22, 1849, USMA Archives.

[5] "Sectionalism in Our Army," *New York Times*, June 19, 1855, p. 4.

[6] "Southerners in the Army," *New York Times*, June 22, 1855, p. 4.

[7] "Sectionalism in Our Army," *New York Times*, June 21, 1855, p. 2.

[8] Charles W. Loring, "A Trip to Antietam," *Continental Monthly*, February 1863, p. 154.

[9] *The Papers of Jefferson Davis*, ed. Haskell M. Monroe Jr. and James T. McIntosh (Baton Rouge: Louisiana State University Press, 1971), vol. 5, p. 270.

[10] Cf. Waugh, *West Point*, pp. 115–16.

[11] Custer, "War Memoirs," *The Galaxy*, April 1876, p. 449.

[12] Morris Schaff, *The Spirit of Old West Point, 1858–1862* (New York: Houghton, Mifflin & Co., 1907), p. 145.

[13] Ibid., p. 147. Rodgers was an artillery officer during the first years of the Civil War and taught mathematics at West Point, 1864–65. He was a brigadier general and chief of artillery during the Spanish-American War.

[14] Ibid., p. 144.

[15] Ibid., p. 83.

[16] Lane resigned February 16, 1861, and became a Confederate artilleryman. He was in all the major battles in the East, serving under Pendleton at Gettysburg in the Sumter Artillery, Hill's corps, Anderson's division. He was probably at Appomattox as a lieutenant colonel.

[17] Schaff, *Spirit of Old West Point*, p. 165. Lincoln was elected with just under 40 percent of the popular vote.

[18] Ibid., p. 165.

[19] McCrea letter, November 10, 1860.

[20] Quoted in Peter S. Michie, *The Life and Letters of Emory Upton, Colonel of the Fourth Regiment of Artillery, and Brevet Major-General, U.S. Army* (New York: D. Appleton & Co., 1885), p. 28.

[21] Edward C. Boynton, *History of West Point: and its military importance during the American revolution: and the origin and progress of the United States Military Academy* (New York: D. Van Nostrand, 1863), p. 252. Among them was George L. Gillespie Jr. of Tennessee, who graduated second in the Class of 1862, joined the Union army

and received the Medal of Honor for actions at Cold Harbor. He was briefly acting secretary of war in 1901.

[22] Brigadier General Ellison Capers, *Confederate Military History*, vol. 5, *South Carolina* (Atlanta: Confederate Publishing Co., 1899). This citation courtesy of Joe Long, Curator of History, South Carolina Confederate Relic Room and Museum, Columbia, S.C.

[23] Custer, "War Memoirs," p. 453.

[24] Seymour was an artillery officer in many of the big eastern battles (but not Gettysburg). He was at Appomattox, and had been in the Five Forks battle as a brevet major general. He later made a career as a noted water-color painter and settled in Florence, Italy. Seven of the nine officers at Fort Sumter were West Point graduates. One of them, Richard Kidder Meade Jr. of Virginia, second in the Class of 1857, later joined the Confederacy when his state seceded.

[25] Custer, "War Memoirs," p. 452.

[26] Presidential order quoted in Schaff, *Spirit of Old West Point*, pp. 201–2.

[27] John F. Reynolds graduated 26th in the Class of 1841. He was brevetted twice for bravery in Mexico. On July 1, 1863, Major General Reynolds was urging his men forward on Seminary Ridge at Gettysburg when he was killed by a sharpshooter. A marker stands at the spot where he fell.

[28] Quoted in Schaff, *Spirit of Old West Point*, p. 204.

[29] Boynton, *History of West Point*, p. 261.

[30] Schaff, *Spirit of Old West Point*, p. 208.

[31] Ibid., p. 247.

[32] Joseph Pearson Farley, *West Point in the Early Sixties: With Incidents of the War* (Troy, N.Y.: Pafraets Book Co., 1902), p. 72.

[33] The oath of allegiance was first given on April 13, 1861, as the guns at Fort Sumter fired. But because several southern cadets who had graduated May 6, 1861 resigned immediately, the oath was readministered May 13. Two cadets declined and were dismissed. After graduation, three more of the Class of June 1861 resigned. In August 1861 the oath was amended to make it clear that it superseded any prior allegiance to any state or other country.

[34] McCrea letter, May 11, 1861.

[35] "Detention of West Point Cadets in Philadelphia," *New York Times*, May 9, 1861. See also letter by Lt. William Anthony Elderkin (USMA May 1861), May 8, 1861, USMA Archives.

[36] *New York Times*, June 22, 1861. The Class of 1862 almost graduated early as well, but it was felt that there was nothing to be gained by putting officers in the field who were little better trained than the

militia officers already being commissioned in large numbers, balanced against such a severe disruption of the Academy system.

[37] Custer, "War Memoirs," p. 454.

[38] Two of them, Frank A. Reynolds and George Owen Watts, graduated and then resigned. Clarence Derrick, who graduated fourth in the class, also resigned after graduation.

[39] Cf. Register of Officers and Cadets for May and June 1861, p. 11.

[40] Parker had in fact graduated number 28, seven places above Custer. The finding against him was retroactive. Custer met Parker in Washington briefly en route to Bull Run. By that time, Parker had resigned, and his name was removed from the original graduation list.

[41] Custer, "War Memoirs," p. 455.

[42] Ibid.

[43] William B. Hazen was an Immortal of the Class of 1855, graduating sixth from the foot. Before the Civil War, he served as a scout in the Southwest and was brevetted for gallantry. During the war he served in the western theater, fighting in many battles and rising to the rank of brevet major general. After the war he went on many foreign observation missions, and when he died in 1887 he was the chief signal officer of the Army. William E. Merrill was first in the Class of 1859, mentioned earlier. He was the son of Moses E. Merrill, who died at Molino del Rey with Ephraim Kirby Smith. He served as an engineer in the Civil War, was briefly a POW and wounded at Yorktown. He rose to the rank of brevet colonel. After the war he worked on many public works projects. He died on active duty in 1891.

[44] Stephen Vincent Benét graduated third in the Class of 1849. He spent the Civil War at West Point, as an instructor and testing experimental ordnance. In 1874 he became the chief of ordnance of the U.S. Army.

[45] Custer, "War Memoirs," p. 455.

[46] Ibid., p. 456.

[47] Special Orders No. 187, July 15, 1861, pp. 8–9. It is hard to understand Hazen's assessment of Custer's conduct, since he had been given 52 demerits in the 23 days between the end of term and the incident in question. It may have been a case of one Immortal looking out for another.

[48] Custer letter, May 31, 1861.

James McQueen McIntosh

[1] Most of the following data from Cullum, vol. 1. See also generally Ellsworth Eliot Jr., *West Point in the Confederacy* (New York: G. A. Baker & Co., 1941).

[2] This count from the 1948 Register of Graduates, pp. 167, 171.

[3] David S. Stanley, *Personal Memoirs of Major-General D. S. Stanley, USA* (Cambridge, Mass.: Harvard University Press, 1917), pp. 112–13. Stanley graduated ninth in the Class of 1852.

[4] After the Civil War, a debate arose over who could rightly claim the name "Kirby Smith." During the war, Edmund had become widely known simply as Kirby Smith. Ephraim's wife claimed that the name devolved from her husband to his son. Some of Joseph Lee Kirby Smith's friends claimed that he had been angry with his uncle for taking up the Rebel cause, and accused him of stealing Ehpraim's name. Edmund denied any bad blood in the family, and said that his nephew had written him friendly letters during the opening years of the war, before he was killed. He also claimed to have been called "Kirby" at West Point, but the only written evidence is that others called him "Seminole." Edmund, Ephraim's younger brother and JLK's uncle, went on to fame as a Confederate general, and was the last of the full generals to surrender his command, as well as the last to die. See Joseph Howard Parks, *General Edmund Kirby Smith* (Baton Rouge: Louisiana State University Press, 1954), pp. 118, 124–25.

[5] In the Alexander D. Bache (USMA 1825) papers, USMA Archives.

[6] The monument has never been found and that part of the story may be apocryphal, though Terrill senior probably made the statement. The two brothers are definitely not buried together—William is interred at West Point and James was buried on the battlefield. A third brother, Phillip M. Terrill, CSA, was killed at Winchester in November 1864.

[7] Cf. Paul N. Spellman, *A Forgotten Texas Leader* (College Station: Texas A&M University Press, 1999).

[8] Pratt letter in Cullum file, dated March 25, 1860.

[9] Morris Schaff, *The Spirit of Old West Point, 1858–1862* (New York: Houghton, Mifflin & Co., 1907), pp. 122–23.

[10] Borland was later captured and exchanged for Major William H. Forbes of Boston.

[11] AOG, June 12, 1922.

[12] W. E. Woodruff, *With the Light Guns in '61–'65: Reminiscences of Eleven Arkansas, Missouri and Texas Light Batteries in the Civil War* (Little Rock: Central Printing Co., 1903), pp. 14–15.

[13] Sources include: After-Action Reports of the various actions mentioned; Harvey S. Ford, "Van Dorn and the Pea Ridge Campaign," *Journal of the American Military Institute,* Winter 1939, pp. 222–36; Christine Schultz White and Benton R. White, *Now the Wolf Has*

Come: The Creek Nation in the Civil War (College Station: Texas A&M University Press, 1996); John Bartlett Meserve, "Chief Opothleya-hola," *Chronicles of Oklahoma,* December 1931, pp. 439–53; John Bartlett Meserve, "The MacIntoshes," *Chronicles of Oklahoma,* September 1932, pp. 310–25; Dean Trickett, "The Civil War in the Indian Territory, 1861," *Chronicles of Oklahoma,* September 1940, pp. 266–80; William Garret Piston and Richard W. Hatcher, *Wilson's Creek: The Second Battle of the Civil War and the Men Who Fought It* (Chapel Hill: University of North Carolina Press, 2000); *Fighting with Ross' Texas Cavalry Brigade CSA: Diary of Lt. George L. Griscom, Adjutant, 9th Texas Cavalry Regiment,* ed. Homer L. Kerr (Hillsboro, Tex.: Hill Junior College Press, 1976); Thomas W. Cutrer, *Ben McCulloch and the Frontier Military Tradition* (Chapel Hill: University of North Carolina Press, 1993); William L. Shea, *War in the West: Pea Ridge and Prairie Grove* (Fort Worth: Ryan Place Publishers, 1996).

[14] Stanley, *Personal Memoirs,* p. 61. Stanley claims that some "foolish officers" believed that if they joined the Confederacy and they lost the war, "they would be entitled to resume their places in the Army." Ibid.

[15] John McIntosh fought in almost every cavalry action in the East, and lost his leg at the third battle of Winchester. By war's end he would be a major general.

[16] Also known as Oak Hills by the Confederates.

[17] Samuel B. Barron, *Lone Star Defenders* (New York: Neale Publishing Co., 1908), p. 49.

[18] Maury, quoted in Cutrer, *Ben McCulloch and the Frontier Tradition,* pp. 290–91.

[19] William Baxter, *Pea Ridge and Prairie Grove: Scenes and Incidents of the War in Arkansas* (Cincinnati: Poe & Hitchcock, 1864), p. 103.

[20] McCulloch was born in Tennessee and both Sam Houston and Davy Crockett were close family friends. McCulloch almost left with Crockett for the Alamo, but had gotten sick with measles and was unable to accompany him. He later joined Houston and fought at the pivotal Battle of San Jacinto, earning a battlefield commission. In the Mexican War he served as Zachary Taylor's chief of scouts, and in later life he was a Texas legislator, a duelist, a marshal, a Forty-Niner, and mayor of Sacramento, California. He joined the Confederacy when Texas seceded and led the bloodless seizure of the Alamo and the Federal properties in San Antonio. In May 1861 he was the first citizen-soldier to be appointed a Confederate general officer.

[21] *Confederate Military History,* ed. Clement A. Evans (Confederate Publishing Co., 1899), vol. 10, ch. 4.

[21] A. W. Sparks, *The War Between the States, As I Saw It* (Tyler, Lee & Burnett, Printers, 1901), pp. 151–52.

[23] Lester N. Fitzhugh, *Cannon Smoke: The Letters of Captain John J. Good, Good-Douglas Battery, CSA* (Hillsboro, Tex.: Hill Junior College Press, 1971), p. 71.

[24] Cooper was originally from New York, and was one of only sixteen officers from free states to join the Confederate cause.

[25] AOR, McIntosh to Cooper, December 15, 1861.

[26] When John Mohr McIntosh led the family to America in 1736, he was accompanied by his cousin, Captain John McIntosh. The two shared as grandfather the patriarch of the clan, Jacobite Brigadier William McIntosh. Captain John's son William McIntosh, who was a Tory in the Revolution, lived amongst the Creeks and married a Creek woman. Their son was Chief William McIntosh, the same Lower Creek leader that Opothleyahola had threatened and helped kill, and Chilly's father. So Chilly McIntosh was descended five generations from Brigadier William McIntosh, and James McQueen McIntosh was six, along a different line.

[27] There was also the First Seminole Cavalry Battalion, mustered into service in November 1861.

[28] Sparks, *The War Between the States,* p. 161.

[29] Victor M. Rose, *Ross' Texas Brigade* (Kennesaw, Ga.: Continental Books, 1960), p. 44.

[30] Opothleyahola's people found refuge in Kansas, and eventually ten thousand of them were camped in southern Kansas. The federal government gave them what help it could, but there were few supplies and they suffered greatly through the winter months. In the spring, Opothleyahola offered to lead a force back into Oklahoma, but he died before it could be organized, in the summer of 1862.

[31] Letter to General S. Cooper, Adjutant-General C. S. Army, Richmond, Va., January 4, 1862.

[32] Sparks, *The War Between the States,* p. 175.

[33] Report of Colonel B. W. Stone, March 14, 1862.

[34] Griscom diary, *Fighting with Ross' Texas Cavalry Brigade CSA,* p. 15.

[35] Quoted in Ford, "Van Dorn and the Pea Ridge Campaign," p. 223.

[36] Report of Sergeant W. Kinney, 3rd LA Infantry, March 16, 1862.

[37] Brigadier General Albert Pike's AAR, March 14, 1862. Word spread that the Indians had begun scalping the dead. Brigadier General Curtis later sent word to Van Dorn that "we find on the battle-field, con-

trary to civilized warfare, many of the Federal dead, who were tomahawked, scalped, and their bodies shamefully mangled, and expresses a hope that this important struggle may not degenerate to a savage warfare." (Curtis to Van Dorn, March 9, 1862.) Pike's investigation showed that only one scalp had been taken, but the tales became exaggerated in the northern press. Henry Heth's friend Dabney Maury, who was Van Dorn's adjutant general, responded to Curtis that he hoped the reports of scalping were mistaken, and that the tribes fighting for the Confederacy had long been considered civilized. Both sides should renounce such practices, which he termed "unnatural war." He added, while on the topic of barbarism, that "many of our men who surrendered themselves prisoners of war were reported . . . as having been murdered in cold blood by their captors, who were alleged to be Germans." (Maury to Curtis, March 14, 1862.)

[38] *Battlefield of Pea Ridge, Arkansas: Battlefield Folklore* (Fayetteville, Ark.: Washington County Historical Society, 1958), p. 8.

[39] Report of Colonel B. W. Stone, March 14, 1862. The battery was the First Flying Battery, commanded by Captain Elbert, these particular guns by Lts. Gassen and Schneider.

[40] Frank Crawford Armstrong was the stepson of General Persifor Smith. He fought as a Union officer at Bull Run, but resigned in August 1861, joining McIntosh's staff. He fought at Chustenahlah, December 26, 1861. At war's end he was a Confederate brigadier general.

[41] Quoted in Cutrer, *Ben McCulloch and the Frontier Military Tradition,* from Rose, *Ross' Texas Brigade.*

[42] Alexander Poe, a blacksmith who lived near the spot where McIntosh fell, was asked whether he was kin to Edgar Allan Poe. "I guess so," he replied, "us Poe's all like our liquor." *Battlefield of Pea Ridge, Arkansas,* p. 6.

[43] Baxter, *Pea Ridge and Prairie Grove,* p. 95.

[44] Sparks, *The War Between the States,* p. 175.

Charles Nelson Warner

[1] Charles N. Warner letter to his sister Emma, February 1, 1862. Warner letters, diary and other documents from the collection of the Susquehanna County Historical Society, Montrose, Pennsylvania.

[2] Warner letter, May 21, 1862.

[3] Warner letter, March 13, 1862.

[4] Warner letter, March 23, 1862.

[5] Ibid.

[6] They probably relieved Sedgwick's badly mauled division.
[7] Warner letter, September 22, 1862.
[8] Warner diary, September 28, 1862.
[9] Warner letter, December 9, 1862.
[10] December 2, 1862.
[11] October 21, 1862.
[12] April 11, 1863.
[13] April 27, 1863.
[14] April 30, 1863.
[15] General Orders No. 47, April 30, 1863.
[16] Warner letter, May 2, 1863.
[17] May 2, 1863.
[18] May 2, 1863.
[19] May 6, 1863.
[20] Warner diary, May 3, 1863.
[21] Warner letter, May 6, 1863.
[22] May 6, 1863.
[23] May 9, 1863.

Gettysburg

[1] Henry Heth letter in *Southern Historical Society Papers*, vol. 4, pp. 151–60. It is said that Gettysburg is the most written-about single event in American history. Sources *inter alia* include after-action reports; Glenn Tucker, *High Tide at Gettysburg* (Gettysburg, Pa.: Stan Clark Military Books, 1995); Jaquelin Marshall Meredith, "The First Day at Gettysburg," *Southern Historical Society Papers*, vol. 24, pp. 182–87; Harry W. Pfanz, *Gettysburg: The First Day* (Chapel Hill: University of North Carolina Press, 2001); and others cited below.

[2] James L. Morrison Jr., *The Memoirs of Henry Heth: The Young Cavalier*, Master's Thesis, The University of Virginia, 1960, p. 270.

[3] Ibid., p. xxxiv.

[4] Ibid., p. 246.

[5] Ibid.

[6] See *A Fire-Eater Remembers: The Confederate Memoir of Robert Barnwell Rhett*, ed. William C. Davis (Columbia: University of South Carolina Press, 2000), pp. 63–64.

[7] Davis to Confederate Rep. W. P. Harris, December 3, 1861.

[8] Stockton Heth, Harry's youngest brother, served as his aide.

[9] Heth met Hayes during his presidency and said that he had once called on the president but Hayes refused the meeting. Hayes noted that Heth had "sent some shells over where [he] was." "Yes," Heth

replied, "I sent you my cards." Hayes was wounded in the leg by a piece of shrapnel from Heth's guns. *Memoirs of Henry Heth*, p. 252. During the battle, Hayes had his headquarters in the town doctor's office, which he shared with Major William McKinley and Lieuenant James A. Garfield, all three of whom would one day serve as president, the latter two both assassinated.

[10] Quoted in *Memoirs of Henry Heth*, p. 256.

[11] Ibid., p. 259.

[12] Lee to Jackson, February 27, 1863.

[13] Jackson to Lee, February 28, 1863.

[14] Lee to Davis, May 20, 1863.

[15] *Memoirs of Henry Heth*, p. 269; Heth letter in *SHSP*.

[16] Heth, Letter, op. cit.; *Memoirs of Henry Heth*, p. 270.

[17] Letter from Major-General Henry Heth, of A. P. Hill's Corps, A. N. V., *Southern Historical Society Papers*, vol. 4, pp. 151–60.

[18] The lead brigade was commanded by Brigadier General James J. Archer, a graduate of Princeton who had been brevetted for gallantry at Chapultepec and had seen a great deal of fighting in the war thus far. Archer's lead regiment was the Thirteenth Alabama, led by Colonel Birkett Davenport Fry. Fry had attended but not graduated from VMI, and was a member of the USMA Class of 1846. He was found deficient in mathematics in his yearling year and left the Academy. He later served as a lieutenant in Mexico and was a filibuster in Nicaragua.

[19] After the war, Calef took part in seeing to it that a memorial was erected to Buford at Gettysburg. He was able to track down the cannon that fired the first shot, tube #233, and it and three other original cannon were incorporated into the Buford memorial in 1895. Calef remained in federal service until 1900, retiring as a lieutenant colonel. He died in 1912 and is buried in Arlington National Cemetery.

[20] Heth's After-Action Report.

[21] *Memoirs of Henry Heth*, p. 272. Total losses for his division over three days were 420 killed, 2,116 wounded, and 1,534 missing.

[22] Heth After-Action Report, September 13, 1863. Staff officer Captain William W. McCreery, eleventh in the Class of 1860, was one of over a dozen men who were shot down waving the regimental banner.

Pickett's Charge

[1] Arthur Crew Inman, ed., *Soldier of the South: General Pickett's War Letters to His Wife* (Boston: Houghton Mifflin, 1928), p. 47. Cf.

generally Jeffry D. Wert, *Gettysburg: Day Three* (New York: Simon & Schuster, 2001); Lesley J. Gordon, *General George E. Pickett in Life and Legend* (Chapel Hill: University of North Carolina Press, 1998); Walter Harrison, *Pickett's Men: A Fragment of War History* (New York: D. Van Nostrand, 1870); James Longstreet, memoir, *From Manassas to Appomattox* (Philadelphia: J. B. Lippincott & Co., 1896); George R. Stewart, *Pickett's Charge: A Microhistory of the Final Attack at Gettysburg, July 3, 1863* (Dayton, Ohio: Morningside House, 1983).

[2] Captain H. T. Owen, 18th Virginia, "Pickett at Gettysburg," *Philadelphia Times*, March 26, 1881.

[3] Ibid. One of the counterfactuals of Gettysburg is whether Pickett's men could have provided the extra push needed to win the battle on the second day. Pickett believed his men were too tired to attack after their march, but many Union regiments went straight into battle after similar marches that day.

[4] Inman, *Soldier of the South*, p. 53.

[5] Quoted in Gordon, *General George E. Pickett*, p. 64.

[6] Inman, *Soldier of the South*, p. 18. Pickett's letters must be used with great circumspection, since they were heavily edited by his wife after his death.

[7] Pickett letter to General Arnold Elzey, June 2, 1863.

[8] Inman, *Soldier of the South*, p, 31.

[9] General G. Moxley Sorrel, *At the Right Hand of Longstreet* (Lincoln: University of Nebraska Press, 1999), p. 54.

[10] Quoted in Gordon, *General George E. Pickett*, p. 106.

[11] Cf. Tracy Elmer Strevey, *Pickett on Puget Sound*, Thesis, University of Washington (1925), p. 62.

[12] Inman, *Soldier of the South*, p. 54.

[13] Quoted in Gordon, *General George E. Pickett*, p. 107.

[14] Quoted in ibid., p. 111.

[15] Cf. David Shultz and Richard Rollins, "Measuring Pickett's Charge," *Gettysburg Magazine*, July 1, 1997.

[16] Cf. E. P. Alexander, "Pickett's Charge and the Artillery Fighting at Gettysburg," *The Century*, January 1887, p. 467. Also E. P. Alexander, *Military Memoirs of a Confederate* (New York: Charles Scribner's Sons, 1907), ch. 18 *passim.*

[17] James Longstreet, "Lee's Invasion of Pennsylvania," *The Century*, February, 1887, p. 628.

[18] General D. B. Fry, "Pettigrew's Charge at Gettysburg," *Southern Historical Society Papers*, vol. 7, pp. 91–93.

[19] Captain Robert A. Bright in *Southern Historical Society Papers*, vol. 31, p. 229. There was a Captain George T. Gordon of HMS *Cormorant* in the Northwest before the time of the San Juan affair, but it is doubtful this was the same person. Captain Gordon joined the Royal Navy in 1818, was made captain in 1846, was flag captain of the Baltic in 1854 and admiral in 1877. Gordon of the 34th North Carolina could have been a relative; more likely Pickett was using the coincidence of names to make a joke.

[20] Longstreet, "Lee's Invasion of Pennsylvania," p. 635.

[21] Quoted in Wert, *Gettysburg Day Three*, p. 121.

[22] Cf. Alexander, "Pickett's Charge and the Artillery Fighting at Gettysburg," p. 467.

[23] Ibid., p. 468.

[24] John Gibbon, *Personal Recollections of the Civil War* (New York: G. P. Putnam's Sons, 1928), pp. 146–47.

[25] J. H. Moore, "Longstreet's Assault," *Philadelphia Times*, November 4, 1882.

[26] John T. James, letter of July 9, 1863, in Thomas D. Houston, "Storming Cemetery Hill," *Philadelphia Times*, October 21, 1882.

[27] Quoted in Col. Joseph C. Mayo, "Pickett's Charge at Gettysburg," *Richmond Times Dispatch*, May 6, 1906.

[28] Cf. "The Battle of Gettysburg," *Southern Historical Society Papers*, vol. 32, pp. 183–95.

[29] Quoted in Wert, *Gettysburg Day Three*, p. 181.

[30] Mayo, "Pickett's Charge at Gettysburg."

[31] Some accounts say the bombardment lasted two hours (e.g., A. P. Hill's AAR), but it was probably 45 minutes to an hour. Alexander, "Pickett's Charge and the Artillery Fighting at Gettysburg," p. 468.

[32] Quoted in Wert, *Gettysburg Day Three*, p. 186.

[33] Inman, *Soldier of the South*, p. 60.

[34] Longstreet, "Lee's Invasion of Pennsylvania," p. 630.

[35] Quoted in Gordon, *General George E. Pickett*, p. 113. Also Owen, "Pickett at Gettysburg."

[36] Captain Winfield Scott, "Pickett's Charge As Seen from the Front Line," a Paper Prepared and Read before the California Commandery of the Military Order of the Loyal Legion of the United States, February 8, 1888.

[37] Alexander, "Pickett's Charge and the Artillery Fighting at Gettysburg," p. 469.

[38] Ibid.

[39] Longstreet, "Lee's Invasion of Pennsylvania," p. 630.

[40] Scott, "Pickett's Charge As Seen from the Front Line."

[41] Cf. "The Battle of Gettysburg," *SHSP.*

[42] Brigadier General Joseph R. Davis was a nephew of Jefferson Davis.

[43] Owen, "Pickett at Gettysburg."

[44] Pickett could also have been as far south as the Wentz House, near the Peach Orchard. Cf. Kathleen Harrison, "Where Was Pickett during Pickett's Charge?" *Civil War Quarterly,* vol. 11.

[45] Bright in *SHSP;* Fremantle quoted in Sorrel, *At the Right Hand of Longstreet,* p. 313.

[46] Moore, "Longstreet's Assault."

[47] See Captain W. R. Bond, *Pickett or Pettigrew?* (Scotland Neck, N.C.: W. L. L. Hall, 1888), p. 67.

[48] McCrea, June 15, 1875. Cf. *Dear Belle,* ed. Catherine S. Crary (Middletown, Conn.: Wesleyan University Press, 1965), pp. 208–9.

[49] Mayo, "Pickett's Charge at Gettysburg"; and Lee A. Wallace Jr., *3rd Virginia Infantry* (Lynchburg, Va.: H. E. Howard, 1986), p. 38. Captain Lewis came out of the battle unscathed. He was captured at the Battle of Five Forks on April 1, 1865, and died April 21 in the Union prison on Johnson's Island.

[50] Later, part of Trimble's lower leg was amputated, and it being too dangerous to move, Trimble was captured and spent most of the rest of the war a POW.

[51] James L. Morrison Jr., *The Memoirs of Henry Heth: The Young Cavalier,* Master's Thesis, The University of Virginia, 1960, p. 82.

[52] Henry Heth letter in *Southern Historical Society Papers,* vol. 4, pp. 151–60. Heth misquotes General Pierre Bosquet, who watched the charge and remarked, *"C'est magnifique, mais ce n'est pas la guerre."*

[53] Alexander, "Pickett's Charge and the Artillery Fighting at Gettysburg," p. 469.

[54] Ralph Kirshner, *The Class of 1861: Custer, Ames, and Their Classmates after West Point* (Carbondale, Ill.: Southern Illinois University Press, 1999), p. 57.

[55] Moore, "Longstreet's Assault."

[56] Scott, "Pickett's Charge As Seen from the Front Line."

[57] Captain William M. Owen, *In Camp and Battle* (Boston: Ticknor & Co., 1885), p. 251.

[58] Colonel Joseph Mayo, "24th Virginia Infantry's Action at Gettysburg," *Richmond Times Dispatch,* December 13, 1914.

[59] Bright in *SHSP.*

[60] William Youngblood, "Unwritten History of the Gettysburg Campaign," *Southern Historical Society Papers,* vol. 38, pp. 312–18.

[61] H. T. Owen, "Pickett at Gettysburg."

[62] Inman, *Soldier of the South,* p. 64, July 6, 1863.

[63] These are the figures given in Wert, *Gettysburg Day Three,* p. 291.

[64] Kemper survived the battle, and was elected governor of Virginia after the war.

[65] Lee to Pickett, July 9, 1863.

[66] Heth letter in *SHSP.* See also *Memoirs of Henry Heth,* p. 281.

Laurence Simmons Baker

[1] Henry Heth letter in *Southern Historical Society Papers,* vol. 4, pp. 151–60. This statement has its critics, particularly among the cavalry. Cf. John S. Mosby, *Stuart's Cavalry in the Gettysburg Campaign* (New York: Moffat, Yard & Co., 1908). A less partial account is by Edward G. Longacre, *The Cavalry at Gettysburg* (London: Associated University Presses, 1986).

[2] Also present at the battle was Colonel Lunsford L. Lomax of the Eleventh Virginia Cavalry, the same Lomax whom Stuart risked his life saving at the Battle of Solomon's Fork against the Cheyenne. Lomax charged and captured an enemy battery and its crew and routed that section of the Union line. He would serve throughout the war, attaining the rank of major general.

[3] Thompson later commanded the Sixth at Brandy Station in October 1863. He was discharged June 1, 1864, because of wounds received in action. Thompson was made brevet colonel on March 13, 1865, for gallant and meritorious services during the war.

[4] Note that some sources place Custer leading the charge but others do not. The author thinks it would be uncharacteristic for Custer not to have helped lead the charge; he led every one he had the chance to, previously and afterwards.

[5] Quoted in D. A. Kinsley, *Favor the Bold* (New York: Holt, Rinehart & Winston, 1967–68), p. 138.

[6] Quoted in Marguerite Merington, ed., *The Custer Story: The Life and Intimate Letters of General George A. Custer and His Wife Elizabeth* (New York: Devin-Adair, 1950), p. 11.

[7] In ibid., p. 60.

[8] Quoted in Kinsley, *Favor the Bold,* p. 138.

[9] Quoted in ibid., p. 138.

[10] James H. Kidd, *Riding with Custer: Recollections of a Cavalryman in the Civil War* (Lincoln: University of Nebraska Press, 1997), pp. 129–30.

[11] Quoted in Kinsley, *Favor the Bold,* p. 139.

[12] James Henry Avery, *Under Custer's Command: The Civil War Journal of James Henry Avery,* ed. Eric J. Wittenberg (Washington, D.C.: Brassey's, 2000), p. 173.

[13] "Leaves from a Raider's Diary," *New York Times,* March 26, 1865, p. 2.

[14] George Brinton McClellan and William Cowper Prime, *McClellan's Own Story* (New York: Charles L. Webster & Co., 1887), p. 365.

[15] G. A. Custer, "War Memoirs," *The Galaxy,* June 1876, p. 813.

[16] G. A. Custer, "War Memoirs," *The Galaxy,* November 1876, pp. 685–86.

[17] Washington was sent to Fort Delaware in June 1862, and exchanged that September for First Lieutenant James S. Blair of the First Maryland Volunteers. He went back to Johnston's staff. Washington's mother later gave Custer a button made from a piece of conch shell, originally from one of George Washington's coats. Custer had the button mounted on gold and gave it to Libbie as a brooch.

[18] Custer letter of May 15, 1862, in Merington, *The Custer Story,* p. 30.

[19] Cf. Morris Schaff, *The Spirit of Old West Point, 1858–1862* (New York: Houghton, Mifflin & Co., 1907), pp. 179–82. Schaff incorrectly gives the family name as Durfee. Schaff suggested that Lea should be buried next to Custer at West Point, "in memory of the love of two cadets whose West Point friendship the bitterness of war could not destroy." Ibid., p. 183. Bassett Hall, the site of the wedding, is currently a museum at Colonial Williamsburg.

[20] Merington, *The Custer Story,* p. 35.

[21] D. H. Strother, "Personal Recollections of the War by a Virginian," *Harper's New Monthly Magazine,* April 1868, p. 577.

[22] Cf. Edward G. Longacre, *Custer and His Wolverines: The Michigan Cavalry Brigade, 1861–1865* (Conshohocken, Pa.: Combined Publishing, 1997).

[23] Quoted in Kinsley, *Favor the Bold,* p. 134.

[24] Quoted in Jeffry D. Wert, *Gettysburg: Day Three* (New York: Simon & Schuster, 2001), p. 263.

[25] Farnsworth was born in Michigan in 1837, and was one of the "boy generals" promoted by Pleasonton in June 1863. He was not a West Point graduate; he was expelled from the University of Michigan in 1857 after a student died during campus revelry in which he had participated. Before the charge that took his life, he told Kilpatrick he

thought it was suicidal, noting that his men were " 'too good men to kill.' Kilpatrick turned, greatly excited and said: 'Do you refuse to obey my orders? If you are afraid to lead the charge, I will lead it.' Farnsworth rose in his stirrups and leaned forward, with his sabre half-drawn; he looked magnificent in his passion and cried: 'Take that back!' Kilpatrick rose defiantly, but repentingly said: 'I did not mean it; forget it.' For a moment, nothing was said. (Then) Farnsworth spoke: 'General, if you order the charge I will lead it, but you must take the awful responsibility.' " Speech by Captain Henry C. Parsons, Company L, First Vermont Cavalry, July 3, 1913. Parsons had participated in the charge.

[26] Kidd, *Riding with Custer,* p. 145.

[27] Quoted in Kinsley, *Favor the Bold,* pp. 151–52.

[28] Quoted in Wert, *Gettysburg Day Three,* p. 267.

[29] Kidd, *Riding with Custer,* p. 153.

[30] Longacre, *Custer and His Wolverines,* p. 238.

[31] In ibid., p. 238.

[32] Note that a report of the battle said to be Custer's, which appears in Frederick Whittaker's *A Complete Life of General George A. Custer* (Lincoln: University of Nebraska Press, 1993), first published in 1876, says that the charge of the First Michigan Cavalry was led by Colonel Town, not Custer.

[33] Quoted in Jay Monaghan, *Custer: The Life of General George Armstrong Custer* (Boston: Little, Brown, 1959), p. 148; and Longacre, *Custer and His Wolverines,* p. 238.

[34] Wiley C. Howard, *Sketch of Cobb Legion Cavalry and Some Incidents and Scenes Remembered* (Atlanta: n.p., 1901), pp. 8–9.

[35] Kidd, *Riding with Custer,* p. 155.

[36] Quoted in Monaghan, *Custer,* p. 149. This is from a report that was not included in the official records when they were assembled after the war. The report is reprinted in Whittaker's *A Complete Life of General George A. Custer.*

Five Forks

[1] Warner to Emma, July 3, 1863.

[2] Warner rose to the rank of brevet brigadier general during the war. He served as an assistant professor of mathematics at USMA, September 1865 to July 1868. He retired in 1887 as a major.

[3] Quoted in Robert Stiles, *Four Years under Marse Robert* (Washington: The Neale Publishing Co., 1904), pp, 219–20.

[4] Warner to Emma, July 4, 1863.

[5] Cushing's chief NCO, Sergeant Frederick Fuger, was awarded the Medal of Honor for his actions in the Angle, and later transferred to Warner's battery.

[6] Only the 24th Michigan, engaged nearby, took higher.

[7] Stiles, *Four Years under Marse Robert*, p. 219.

[8] John D. Imboden, "The Confederate Retreat from Gettysburg," in *Battles and Leaders of the Civil War, being for the most part contributions by Union and Confederate officers*, ed. Robert Underwood Johnson and Clarence Clough Buel (New York: Century Co.), vol. 3, p. 421.

[9] The story is in *Histories of the Several Regiments and Battalions from North Carolina in the Great War 1861–'65*, ed. Walter Clark (Goldsboro, N.C.: Nash Brothers, 1901), vol. 2, pp. 388–89. Minton was killed bearing the colors in action at Burgess Mill, October 27, 1864.

[10] John Brown Gordon, *Reminiscences of the Civil War* (New York: Charles Scribner's Sons, 1904), p. 416; and James L. Morrison Jr., *The Memoirs of Henry Heth: The Young Cavalier*, Master's Thesis, The University of Virginia, 1960, p. 335.

[11] *Memoirs of Henry Heth*, p. 302.

[12] For general reference, cf. Chris M. Calkins, *The Appomattox Campaign, March 29–April 9, 1865* (Conshohocken, Pa.: Combined Books, 1997).

[13] George E. Pickett, *The Heart of a Soldier: As Revealed in the Intimate Letters of Genl. George E. Pickett, C.S.A.*, ed. LaSalle Corbell Pickett (New York: Seth Moyle, 1913), p. 171.

[14] For example, see Captain W. R. Bond, *Pickett or Pettigrew?* (Scotland Neck, N.C.: W. L. L. Hall, 1888). The full historiography of Pickett's Charge is in Carol Reardon, *Pickett's Charge in History and Memory* (Chapel Hill: University of North Carolina Press, 1997).

[15] Griffin to Pickett, December 19, 1863.

[16] Pickett, *The Heart of a Soldier*, p. 148. *Tyee* is a Chinook word for "chief." Lee was not well disposed to officers seeking comforts in the midst of war. When General Hunton made a similar request during the siege of Richmond, Lee replied, "The idea of talking about going to see wives; it is perfectly ridiculous, sir." Quoted in Douglas Southall Freeman, *R. E. Lee: A Biography* (New York: Charles Scribner's Sons, 1934), vol. 4, p. 35.

[17] This gesture was in the spirit of the West Point tradition of giving a silver cup to the parents of the first male child of the class.

[18] Quoted in Gordon, *Reminiscences*, p. 419.

[19] Pickett, *The Heart of a Soldier*, pp. 167–68. The letter is dated January 28, 1865, which could be an error, or an indication of Sallie's embellishments.

[20] Randolph Harrison McKim, *A Soldier's Recollections: Leaves from the Diary of a Young Confederate: With an Oration on the Motives and Aims of the Soldiers of the South* (New York: Longmans, Green & Co., 1910), pp. 41–42. One alert sentry grabbed and shook Steuart, not knowing who he was. He quickly apologized, but Steuart slapped him on the back and said, "Good soldier! Good soldier! I'll remember this."

[21] Statement of George W. Van Vlack, June 1905.

[22] Quoted in Richard Wheeler, *Witness to Gettysburg* (New York: Harper & Row, 1987), p. 75.

[23] Pickett, *The Heart of a Soldier,* p. 173. In this context it would mean good luck, Godspeed.

[24] Ibid., pp. 173–74.

[25] Details on the Warren incident are in Bruce Catton, "Sheridan at Five Forks," *Journal of Southern History,* August 1955, pp. 305–15.

[26] Stiles, *Four Years under Marse Robert,* pp. 326–27.

[27] Gordon, *Reminiscences,* pp. 423–24.

[28] Pickett, *The Heart of a Soldier,* p. 177.

[29] Quoted in Gordon, *Reminiscences,* p. 154.

Appomattox

[1] Robert Stiles, *Four Years under Marse Robert* (Washington: The Neale Publishing Co., 1904), p. 333.

[2] Walter Harrison, *Pickett's Men: A Fragment of War History* (New York: D. Van Nostrand, 1870), p. 157. Harrison added, "To follow them in their misfortunes, whether as prisoners of war, or to the surrender, at Appomattox Court-House, of the few remaining to witness that last humiliation, would be useless. Thousands have gone to their eternal home in imperishable glory. Others were spared to shed bitter tears over the loss of a sacred cause for which they had toiled, suffered privations, and poured out their blood, to return to the peaceful avocations of civilized life, after four years of excitement and strife."

[3] Kershaw in Marguerite Merington, ed., *The Custer Story: The Life and Intimate Letters of General George A. Custer and His Wife Elizabeth* (New York: Devin-Adair, 1950), p. 153.

[4] Custer in ibid., pp. 150–51.

[5] Quoted in Jay Monaghan, *Custer: The Life of General George Armstrong Custer* (Boston: Little, Brown, 1959), p. 238.

[6] Two sailors also were given this distinction, Coxswain John Cooper and Boatswain's Mate Patrick Mullen.

[7] Quoted in E. P. Alexander, "Lee at Appomattox," in *Battles and Leaders of the Civil War*, vol. 5, ed. Peter Cozzens (Champaign: University of Illinios Press, 2002), p. 641.

[8] James H. Kidd, *Riding with Custer: Recollections of a Cavalryman in the Civil War* (Lincoln: University of Nebraska Press, 1997), pp. 298–300.

[9] David S. Stanley, *Personal Memoirs of Major-General D. S. Stanley, USA* (Cambridge, Mass.: Harvard University Press, 1917), p. 18.

[10] Wharton J. Green, *Recollections and Reflections* (Raleigh, N.C.: Edwards & Broughton Printing Co., 1906), pp. 92–93. Green was X-1853. He had entered West Point motivated by enthusiasm following the war with Mexico, but resigned in his third year, not wishing to serve in a peacetime army.

[11] Philip Henry Sheridan, *Personal Memoirs of P. H. Sheridan* (New York: Charles L. Webster & Co., 1888).

[12] Slocum graduated seventh in the Class of 1852. In the Civil War he rose to the rank of major general.

[13] Sheridan, *Personal Memoirs.* "At the time I thought, of course, my suspension a very unfair punishment, that my conduct was justifiable and the authorities of the Academy all wrong, but riper experience has led me to a different conclusion, and as I look back, though the mortification I then endured was deep and trying, I am convinced that it was hardly as much as I deserved for such an outrageous breach of discipline."

[14] Arthur MacArthur had a distinguished career after the war and eventually rose to the rank of lieutenant general. He was the father of Douglas MacArthur.

[15] In *Camp-Fire Sketches and Battle-Field Echoes of 61–5*, ed. W. C. King and W. P. Derby (King, Richardson & Co., 1868), pp. 250, 408–9.

[16] Kidd, *Riding with Custer*, pp. 308–9.

[17] Ibid., pp. 211, 216.

[18] James Henry Avery, *Under Custer's Command: The Civil War Journal of James Henry Avery*, ed. Eric J. Wittenberg (Washington, D.C.: Brassey's, 2000), p. 114.

[19] Kidd, *Riding with Custer*, p. 131.

[20] Ibid., p. 200.

[21] "Sheridan's Victory," *New York Times*, October 27, 1864, p. 2.

[22] G. A. Custer, "War Memoirs," *The Galaxy*, June 1876, p. 813.

[23] "Sheridan's Victory," *New York Times*, October 27, 1864, p. 2.

[24] George A. Custer to Emanuel Custer, October 16, 1864.

[25] In Frederic F. Van de Water, *Glory-Hunter: A Life of General Custer* (New York: Bobbs-Merrill Co., 1934), p. 109.

[26] Philip H. Sheridan, "The Last Days of the Rebellion," *North American Review*, September 1888, p. 275.

[27] Alexander, "Lee at Appomattox," p. 641.

[28] Morris Schaff, *The Sunset of the Confederacy* (Boston: J. W. Luce & Co., 1912), p. 209. They were about 200 miles from Tennessee at the time.

[29] LaSalle Corbell Pickett, ed., *The Heart of a Soldier: As Revealed in the Intimate Letters of General George E. Pickett, C.S.A.* (New York: Seth Moyle, 1913), pp. 176–77, 179.

[30] Quoted in Schaff, *Sunset of the Confederacy*, p. 225.

[31] There are several versions of this encounter. Custer had played through similar scenes with Sims and Gordon immediately prior to Longstreet. Some say it was Custer's chief of staff, Colonel Edward Whitaker, who met with Longstreet, but Longstreet says otherwise. Cf. also John Brown Gordon, *Reminiscences of the Civil War* (New York: Charles Scribner's Sons, 1904); and the letter by E. G. Marsh, 15th N.Y. Cavalry, in *Soldiers' Letters, from Camps, Battle-field and Prison,* ed. Lydia Minturn Post (Washington, D.C.: U.S. Sanitary Commission, 1865).

[32] Quoted in Morris Schaff, *The Spirit of Old West Point, 1858–1862* (New York: Houghton, Mifflin & Co., 1907), pp. 169–71. With Babcock were Captain William McKee Dunn for the Union, Lieutenant Colonel Charles Marshal as aide to Lee, and Rebel Private Joshua O. Johns.

[33] After the war Young was a congressman, minister to Guatemala and consul-general to Russia.

[34] Schaff, *Spirit of Old West Point*, p. 149.

[35] In Custer, "War Memoirs," *The Galaxy,* April 1876, p. 451.

[36] Wiley C. Howard, *Sketch of Cobb Legion Cavalry and Some Incidents and Scenes Remembered* (Atlanta, Ga.: n.p., 1901), pp. 4–5.

[37] P. M. B. Young, "The West Point Boys: Another Interesting Paper about the Men at the Military School, and Something of Their Careers: General Young Tells More of the Boys of '61," *Atlanta Constitution,* March 19, 1893, p. 9.

[38] Kidd, *Riding with Custer,* pp. 316–17.

[39] Sheridan, *Personal Memoirs,* p. 56.

[40] *New York Times,* July 9, 1876, p. 1.

[41] Schaff, *Spirit of Old West Point*, op. cit., p. 56.

[42] Cf. Gary W. Gallagher, *Stephen Dodson Ramseur: Lee's Gallant General* (Chapel Hill: University of North Carolina Press, 1985).

[43] Schaff, *Spirit of Old West Point*, pp. 56–57. Also Gallagher, *Stephen Dodson Ramseur*, pp. 26–27.

[44] George A. Forsyth, *Thrilling Days in Army Life* (New York: Harper Bros., 1900), pp. 189–90.

[45] Quoted in Schaff, *Spirit of Old West Point*, pp. 169–71.

[46] Alexander, "Lee at Appomattox," p. 648.

[47] *New York Times*, April 20, 1865, p. 2. In fact the entire McLean House did eventually disappear. In 1891, M. T. Dunlap bought the house for $10,000 with a view towards putting it on display at the Chicago World's Fair or on the Mall in Washington. The house was disassembled and put into crates. But financing for the venture fell through, and over time the contents of the crates were taken by souvenir hunters. When the National Park Service acquired the property in 1948, only the foundations were left. See Dorothea Andrews, " 'Surrender House' Will Stand Again," *Washington Post*, January 4, 1948, p. M17.

[48] Richard Miller Devens, *The Pictorial Book of Anecdotes and Incidents of the War of the Rebellion* (Hartford, Conn.: Hartford Publishing Co., 1967), p. 348.

[49] Custer promised the flag to Libbie. "With the verdancy of youth," she later wrote, "I really expected to see a veritable flag, though I don't know that I went so far as to hint that gallant men carried one around ready for emergencies. When I found myself in possession of a large honey-comb towel the poetry departed out of my anticipations." "Surrender Relics," *Washington Post*, April 1, 1905, p. 14.

The Reunion

[1] J. B. Jones, *A Rebel War: Clerk's Diary at the Confederate State's Capital* (Philadelphia: J. B. Lippincott & Co., 1866), p. 474.

[2] Gideon Welles, *Diary of Gideon Welles* (New York: Houghton Mifflin & Co., 1911), p. 278.

[3] Mason Diaries, Library of Congress, manuscript collection.

[4] *Collected Works of Abraham Lincoln*, ed. Roy P. Basler (New Brunswick, N.J.: Rutgers University Press, 1953), vol. 8, p. 393.

[5] See Paul Dahlgren diary, USMA Archives. Cadet Dahlgren was the son of Rear Admiral John Dahlgren.

[6] E. P. Alexander, "Lee at Appomattox," in *Battles and Leaders of the Civil War*, vol. 5, ed. Peter Cozzens (Champaign: University of Illinois Press, 2002), p. 651.

[7] In *Histories of the Several Regiments and Battalions from North Carolina in the Great War 1861–'65*, ed. Walter Clark (Goldsboro, N.C.: Nash Brothers, 1901), vol. 2, p. 578.

[8] Joshua Chamberlain, *The Passing of the Armies: an account of the final campaign of the Army of the Potomac, based upon personal reminiscences of the Fifth army corps* (New York & London: G. P. Putnam's Sons, 1915), p. 250.

[9] Quoted in Richard Wheeler, *Witness to Appomattox* (New York: Harper & Row, 1989), p. 233.

[10] General Order No. 9, Army of Northern Virginia, April 10, 1865.

[11] John Gibbon, *Personal Recollections of the Civil War* (New York: G. P. Putnam's Sons, 1928), p. 327.

[12] Ibid., pp. 320–21.

[13] Morris Schaff, *The Spirit of Old West Point, 1858–1862* (New York: Houghton, Mifflin & Co., 1907), p. 293.

[14] Quoted in Morris Schaff, *The Sunset of the Confederacy* (Boston: J. W. Luce & Co., 1912), p. 292. See also a slightly different version in John Brown Gordon, *Reminiscences of the Civil War* (New York: Charles Scribner's Sons, 1904), pp. 443–44.

[15] Gibbon, *Personal Recollections*, p. 331.

[16] Brag is a card game similar to poker, but antedating it and played with three cards. Note that this is the same Holloway referred to earlier who was the first West Point graduate to die in the Civil War.

[17] James Longstreet in *New York Times*, July 24, 1885.

[18] James L. Morrison Jr., *The Memoirs of Henry Heth: The Young Cavalier*, Master's Thesis, The University of Virginia, 1960, p. 309. Heth later wrote to Grant objecting that a wagon that was his personal property had been appropriated by the Union forces. Seth Williams and Rufus Ingalls, both Heth's friends, allowed Heth to take a better wagon and four mules to "go home in style." Heth gave them to his father-in-law, "and it enabled him to make a crop that year." Ibid., p. 307.

[19] Brigadier General John Gibbon, graduation speech at USMA, June 12, 1886, pp. 15–16.

[20] Gibbon letter, USMA Archives.

[21] Quoted in Jay Monaghan, *Custer: The Life of General George Armstrong Custer* (Boston: Little, Brown, 1959), p. 247.

[22] *New York Times*, April 20, 1865, p. 2.

[23] Schaff, *Spirit of Old West Point*, pp. 251–52. Schaff believed that of all the services West Point has rendered the nation, this was its greatest achievement.

[24] James M. Mullen, "The Last 15 Days of Baker's Command at Weldon," in *Histories of the Several Regiments and Battalions,* ed. Clark, vol. 5, pp. 269–84.

[25] Ibid., p. 275.

[26] Ibid., p. 276.

[27] Ibid., p. 280.

[28] Sherman to Baker, April 19, 1865. Johnston surrendered formally on April 26.

[29] Mullen, "The Last 15 Days," p. 282. James M. Mullen later became a prominent lawyer, state senator, and judge of the City Court of Petersburg.

Charles Dempsey

[1] Quoted in George S. Pappas, *To the Point* (Westport, Conn.: Greenwood Publishing Group, 1992), p. 349.

[2] Quoted in ibid., pp. 346–47.

[3] Robert Fletcher diary, November 8, 1864.

[4] Ibid., November 16, 1864.

[5] Ibid., April 15, 1865.

[6] *New York Times,* June 18, 1865.

[7] Fletcher diary, June 8, 1865.

[8] *New York Times,* June 16, 1868.

[9] *New York Times,* June 14, 1868.

[10] Ibid.

[11] *New York Times,* June 12, 1873.

[12] *New York Times,* June 18, 1865.

[13] His son William W. Dempsey graduated in the Class of 1916, but passed away in 1922 from the effects of an injury sustained in the line of duty.

[14] Upton's critical insight, implemented in the summer of 1864 at Spottsylvania, was to attack in column rather than line formation.

[15] E. A. Garlington, "Scenes of Cadet Life," unpublished ms., USMA Archives, p. 15. For reasons unknown, Upton committed suicide March 15, 1881, at age 42 while in command of the Presidio. Cf. John M. Hyson Jr. et al., "The Suicide of General Emory Upton: A Case Report," *Military Medicine,* October, 1990, pp. 445–52.

[16] Details in *New York Times,* February 23 & 24, 1870.

[17] Garlington, "Scenes of Cadet Life," pp. 3–4.

[18] Smith to Cullum, November 13, 1865, VMI Archives.

[19] Cullum to Smith, November 14, 1865, VMI Archives.

[20] Smith to Cullum, November 16, 1865, VMI Archives.

[21] From F. H. Smith's 1879 AOG speech, "West Point Fifty Years Ago." Only two graduates were older than Davies: Samuel Cooper, the New Yorker who became the inspector general of the Confederacy, age 80; and Benjamin L. E. Bonneville, a western explorer whose exploits were memorialized by Washington Irving, age 82.

[22] *New York Times*, June 18, 1875.

[23] *New York Times*, June 19, 1875.

[24] He graduated 28th in his class. Swift died March 2, 1871 at the Hoffman House in New York City, of an apparent overdose of morphine.

[25] Fletcher diary, May 29, 1866.

[26] Fletcher diary, May 30, 1866.

[27] The Class of 1866 for its part appended yet another verse on "Benny Havens', Oh!"

> Another star has faded, we miss its brilliant glow,
> For the veteran Scott has ceased to be a soldier here below;
> And the country which he honored now feels a heartfelt woe,
> As we toast his name in reverence at Benny Havens', oh!

[28] Hugh Lenox Scott letter, September 17, 1871, USMA Archives. See also obituary in *New York Times*, September 17, 1871.

[29] Cf. *Washington Post*, June 13, 1890, p. 1, and June 14, 1890, p. 4.

[30] *Brooklyn Eagle*, June 4, 1877, p. 2.

[31] Cf. *West Point Tic Tacs: A Collection of Military Verse, together with a Special Poem, "Cadet Grey," by Bret Harte* (New York: H. Lee & Co., 1878), p. 103; and the *Washington Post*, December 4, 1900, p. 6.

John Jordan Crittenden

[1] *New York Times*, June 15, 1866.

[2] Charles W. Larned, September 2, 1866.

[3] Larned to his mother, December 13, 1866.

[4] Oliver E. Wood, *The West Point Scrap Book* (New York: D. Van Nostrand, 1871), pp. 210–11.

[5] The full story is in ibid., pp. 209–14.

[6] *New York Times*, June 7, 1871. Frederick Dent Grant was among them. (Erroneous French in the source.)

[7] E. A. Garlington, "Scenes of Cadet Life," unpublished ms., USMA Archives, p. 31.

[8] Ibid.

[9] Ibid., p. 30. Note that his promotion to first lieutenant was the result of the need to fill slots after the Custer massacre. He took the slot in Troop G that had been McIntosh's.

[10] Garlington wrote of his very frank West Point memoir, "After I got started, I decided to complete it along these lines for my grandsons— one of them may want to go to the Academy; this will show him what *not to do* if he should become a cadet." Ibid., p. 45.

[11] Fletcher diary, August 26, 1864.

[12] Ibid., August 29, 1864.

[13] E. A. Garlington, "Scenes of Cadet Life," p. 7.

[14] USMA Post Orders, vol. 6, p. 226.

[15] Fletcher diary, June 29, 1865.

[16] Ibid., December 18, 1865.

[17] *New York Times,* July 10, 1871.

[18] Ibid.

[19] *New York Times,* June 7, 1873.

[20] Garlington, "Scenes of Cadet Life," p. 10.

[21] Fletcher diary, August 14, 1867.

[22] Ibid.

[23] Larned, June 12, 1866.

[24] Larned, June 16, 1866.

[25] Larned, June 21, 1866.

[26] Grant was not the first such cadet; he followed in the tradition of Abraham Van Buren, son of President Martin Van Buren, and next-to-last graduate of the Class of 1827.

[27] *New York Times,* June 7, 1871.

[28] Fletcher diary, October 2, 1866.

[29] *New York Times,* February 15, 1871.

[30] U.S. Grant III graduated sixth in his class.

[31] In addition to other Crittenden family sources already cited, see Jerry Cecil, "Lt. Crittenden: Striving for the Soldier's Life," *Greasy Grass,* vol. 11, May 1995.

[32] James Parker, "My Experiences As a Cadet at West Point," unpublished ms., USMA Archives, pp. 6–7.

[33] David A. Lyle later invented the "Lyle Gun," a mortar that fired a projectile linked to a cable or other line, used to save boats or people in distress at sea.

[34] Cf. Major E. A. Garlington, "The Seventh Regiment of Cavalry: The Army of the United States," in *Historical Sketches of Staff and Line with Portraits of Generals-in-Chief,* ed. Theo F. Rodenbough and William L. Haskin (New York: Maynard, Merrill & Co., 1896), pp. 256–57.

[35] Braden became a private school teacher, teaching at West Point, and after 1889 a professor of military science at the New York Military academy in Cornwall, N.Y.

[36] Eckerson was transferred to Company D, 7th Cavalry, and promoted to first lieutenant to date from June 25, 1876, the date of Custer's massacre. He was tried by a general court martial and dismissed from service June 30, 1878. He died in 1885 from a gastrointestinal ailment.

Hurrah for Custer

[1] "Notes from the Capital," *New York Times,* April 7, 1876, p. 1.

[2] The Senate voted 35 to 25 to convict, failing to achieve the necessary two-thirds majority.

[3] "Custer Contradicted by Merrill," *New York Times,* April 5, 1876, p. 1. "Benzine Board" was a term used to describe the officer review boards of the period; benzene was a cleaning agent, and the implication was that the Army was being scrubbed clean.

[4] See generally, "Rascalities of the Army Traders," *New York Times,* March 30, 1876, p. 1.

[5] "A Report Which Gen. Custer Claims to Have Made Is Nowhere to Be Found," *New York Times,* April 19, 1876, p. 1.

[6] "Gen. Custer's Testimony," *New York Times,* May 5, 1876, p. 1.

[7] "Gen. Custer and Gen. Merrill," *New York Times,* April 19, 1876, p. 1.

[8] "Review of the Armies," *New York Times,* May 24, 1865, p. 1.

[9] Walt Whitman in *Specimen Days,* journal entry for May 21, 1865.

[10] "A Historic Promenade," *New York Times,* February 7, 1881, p. 1. Joshua Chamberlain's horse was also spooked by the same wreath presentation, but he managed to control his mount.

[11] "An Incident of the Great Review," *New York Times,* July 10, 1876, p. 2.

[12] Quoted in Jay Monaghan, *Custer: The Life of General George Armstrong Custer* (Boston: Little, Brown, 1959), p. 251.

[13] Data below are from Mark G. Grandstaff, "Preserving the 'Habits and Usages of War': William Tecumseh Sherman, Professional Reform, and the U.S. Army Officer Corps, 1865–1881, Revisited," *Journal of Military History,* July 1998, pp. 521–45.

[14] Marguerite Merington, ed., *The Custer Story: The Life and Intimate Letters of General George A. Custer and His Wife Elizabeth* (New York: Devin-Adair, 1950), p. 162.

[15] Elizabeth B. Custer, *Following the Guidon* (New York: Harper Brothers, 1890), p. 312.

[16] Cf. generally, Edward M. Coffman, "Army Life on the Frontier 1865–1898," *Military Affairs,* Winter 1956, pp. 193–201; Edward E. Hardin, "An Army Lieutenant in Montana, 1874–76," *Military Affairs,* Summer 1959, pp. 85–91.

[17] "Gen. George A. Custer," *New York Times*, December 31, 1867.

[18] Robert M. Utley, *Frontier Regulars* (New York: Macmillan, 1973), p. 23.

[19] "Soldiers have been sentenced to be branded, as well as marked, with D, both for desertion and for drunkenness. The mark has commonly been placed on the hip, but sentences to be branded on the check and on the forehead have been adjudged. Other markings imposed by our courts have been HD for habitual drunkard, M for mutineer, W for worthlessness, C for cowardice, I for insubordination, R for robbery, T for thief. Sometimes also entire words were required to be marked as 'Deserter,' 'Habitual Drunkard,' 'Mutineer,' or 'Swindler.' The branding was done with a hot iron; the marking with India ink or gunpowder, usually pricked into the skin or tattooed." Marking and branding were both outlawed in 1872. Cf. Colonel William Winthrop, *Military Law and Precedents*, 2nd ed. (Washington: Government Printing Office, 1920), ch. 20, section 6.

[20] Major E. A. Garlington, "The Seventh Regiment of Cavalry," in *Historical Sketches of Staff and Line with Portraits of Generals-in-Chief*, ed. Theo F. Rodenbough and William L. Haskin (New York: Maynard, Merrill & Co., 1896), pp. 251–52.

[21] Gibbon in Wayne Michael Sarf, *The Little Bighorn Campaign, March–September 1876* (Conshohocken, Pa.: Combined Books, 1993), p. 53.

[22] For this period generally, see Minnie Dubbs Millbrook, "The West Breaks in General Custer," *Kansas Historical Quarterly*, Summer 1970, pp. 113–48.

[23] Quoted in Stephen E. Ambrose, *Crazy Horse and Custer: The Parallel Lives of Two American Warriors* (Garden City, N.Y.: Doubleday, 1975), p. 251. For the regulations on flogging see Winthrop, *Military Law and Precedents*.

[24] "2nd Cavalry," in *A History of the Troops Furnished by the State of Iowa to the Volunteer Armies of the Union which Conquered the Great Southern Rebellion of 1861* (New York: J. B. Lippincott & Co., 1866).

[25] Quoted in Ambrose, *Crazy Horse and Custer*, p. 287.

[26] Elizabeth B. Custer, *Tenting on the Plains or General Custer in Kansas and Texas* (New York: Charles L. Webster & Co., 1887), pp. 699, 702.

[27] "The Defence of Gen. Custer," *New York Times*, December 28, 1867, p. 1.

[28] Cf. Minnie Dubbs Millbrook, "Rebecca Visits Kansas and the Custers: The Diary of Rebecca Richmond," *Kansas Historical Quarterly*, Winter 1976, pp. 366–402.

Washita

[1] Philip Henry Sheridan, *Personal Memoirs of P. H. Sheridan* (New York: Charles L. Webster & Co., 1888). vol. 2, p. 307.

[2] Quoted in R. G. Athearn, *William Tecumseh Sherman and the Settlement of the West* (Norman: University of Oklahoma Press, 1956), p. 227.

[3] Robert M. Utley, *Cavalier in Buckskin: George Armstrong Custer and the Western Military Frontier* (Norman: University of Oklahoma Press, 1988), p. 61.

[4] Custer AAR to Sheridan, November 28, 1868.

[5] *Kansas: a cyclopedia of state history, embracing events, institutions, industries, counties, cities, towns, prominent persons, etc.*, ed. Frank W. Blackmar (Chicago: Standard Pub. Co., 1912), vol. 2, p. 177.

[6] Elliott in Evan S. Connell, *Son of the Morning Star: Custer and the Little Bighorn* (San Francisco: North Point Press, 1984), p. 195.

[7] "Indian Relics," *New York Times*, June 13, 1869.

[8] Sheridan, *Personal Memoirs*, p. 318.

[9] "The End of the Indian War and 'Ring,'" *New York Times*, December 22, 1868, p. 6; and "Sheridan's Winter Campaign," *New York Times*, December 4, 1868, p. 4.

[10] "The Indians. Col. Wyncoop's Letter Resigning His Agency," *New York Times*, December 19, 1868, p. 3.

[11] Red Star in Wayne Michael Sarf, *The Little Bighorn Campaign, March–September 1876* (Conshohocken, Pa.: Combined Books, 1993), p. 183.

[12] George Armstrong Custer, *My Life on the Plains. Or, Personal Experiences with Indians* (New York: Sheldon & Co., 1874), pp. 12, 16.

[13] Ibid., p. 18.

[14] Alexis (1850–1908) was Tsar Alexander II's fourth son.

[15] Cf. for example "The Imperial Buffalo Hunter," *New York Herald*, January 16, 1872, p. 7.

[16] Quoted in Stephen E. Ambrose, *Crazy Horse and Custer: The Parallel Lives of Two American Warriors* (Garden City, N.Y.: Doubleday, 1975), p. 258. Leland once wrote, "I never enjoyed the mere living as regards all that constitutes ordinary respectable life so keenly as I did after some weeks of great hunger, exposure, and misery, in an artillery company in 1863, at the time of the battle of Gettysburg." In *Gypsy Sorcery and Fortune Telling* (London: T. Fisher Unwin, 1891), p. 205.

[17] This was the same Sturgis who saved Sedgwick's column from a buffalo stampede during the campaign against the Cheyenne in 1857.

[18] Larned quoted in George Frederick Howe, "Expedition to the Yellowstone River in 1873: Letters of a Young Cavalry Officer," *Mississippi Valley Historical Review,* December 1952, p. 523. Larned's description of Custer's orders is reminiscent of the reaction of officers and civilians at the Rumsfeld-era Pentagon to the ubiquitous directives known as "snowflakes."

[19] Larned in ibid., p. 524.

[20] Barnitz in Connell, *Son of the Morning Star,* p. 168.

[21] Quoted in Utley, *Cavalier in Buckskin,* p. 50.

[22] Interview with Sturgis, originally printed in the *Chicago Tribune,* reprinted in the *Army and Navy Journal,* July 29, 1876.

[23] Utley, *Cavalier in Buckskin,* p. 46.

[24] Benteen letter to Theodore W. Goldin.

[25] Larned in Howe, "Expedition to the Yellowstone River," p. 526.

[26] Letter of June 28, 1873, in David S. Stanley, *Personal Memoirs of Major-General D.S. Stanley, USA* (Cambridge, Mass.: Harvard University Press, 1917), p. 239.

[27] Quoted in Ambrose, *Crazy Horse and Custer,* p. 360.

[28] Charles Larned diary, June 29, 1873, USMA Archives.

[29] Ibid.

[30] Stanley, *Personal Memoirs,* p. 240.

[31] Ibid., p. 241.

[32] Custer AAR, August 15, 1873, reprinted in Elizabeth Bacon Custer, *Boots and Saddles, or, Life in Dakota with General Custer* (New York: Harper & Bros., 1885), p. 289.

[33] Larned in Howe, "Expedition to the Yellowstone River," p. 532.

[34] Cf. Custer's own account, "Battling with the Sioux on the Yellowstone," *The Galaxy,* July 1876, pp. 91–102.

The Boy President

[1] George Armstrong Custer, *My Life on the Plains. Or, Personal Experiences with Indians* (New York: Sheldon & Co., 1874), p. 114.

[2] "Maj-Gen Custer on the Punishment of the Rebel Leaders," *New York Times,* May 7, 1865, p. 2.

[3] See "The President's Tour," *New York Times,* September 14, 1866, p. 5.

[4] Cf. Timothy Rives, "Grant, Babcock and the Whiskey Ring," *Prologue,* Fall 2000.

[5] "Marriage of Lieut. Grant," *New York Times,* October 21, 1874, p. 8.

[6] *The Arikara Narrative of Custer's Campaign and the Battle of the Little Bighorn,* ed. Orin G. Libby (Norman: University of Oklahoma Press, 1998), pp. 58–59.

[7] Custer, *My Life on the Plains*, p. 114.

[8] For information and data on the elections cited, see *Congressional Quarterly's Guide to US Elections,* ed. Robert A. Diamond (Washington, D.C.: Congressional Quarterly Inc., 1975), *passim.* In 1872 the Democrats endorsed Horace Greeley, the candidate of the Liberal faction of the divided Republican Party. But even with his party split, Grant won reelection with 55.6 percent of the vote, a 3 percent increase over his 1868 total.

[9] See for example "Tilden Out of the Contest," *New York Times,* June 23, 1876, p. 1.

[10] For Hancock's political career, see generally David M. Jordan, *Winfield Scott Hancock: A Soldier's Life* (Bloomington: Indiana University Press, 1988), chs. 24 & 26.

[11] See for example "The St. Louis Convention," *New York Times,* June 24, 1876, p. 1. The day before the nomination Lee said, "We of the South have a deeper, a more intense interest in this struggle than you [of the North] possibly have, and we are assured beyond all doubt that only with Hancock can we carry this country against the Radical [Republican] candidate." "The Wrangling Factions," *New York Times,* June 28, 1876, p. S1.

[12] Cf. *The Campaign Text Book. Why the people want a change. The Republican party reviewed: its sins of commission and omission* (New York: Democratic Party National Committee, 1876), pp. 316–19. In the 1884 race, the Democrats presented Custer's father to a massive pre-election rally in Michigan to invoke the spirit and memory of the state's favorite son. *New York Times,* October 30, 1884, p. 2.

[13] Marguerite Merington, ed., *The Custer Story: The Life and Intimate Letters of General George A. Custer and His Wife Elizabeth* (New York: Devin-Adair, 1950), p. 289.

[14] Grant went through three secretaries of war after Belknap: George M. Robeson, who was secretary of the Navy, acted as war secretary *ad interim,* March 2–6, 1876; Alphonso Taft, March 8–May 22; and James D. Cameron after May 22.

[15] Robert M. Utley, *Cavalier in Buckskin: George Armstrong Custer and the Western Military Frontier* (Norman: University of Oklahoma Press, 1988), p. 162.

[16] *New York Times,* May 6, 1876, p. 5.

[17] Custer quoted in Wayne Michael Sarf, *The Little Bighorn Campaign, March–September 1876* (Conshohocken, Pa.: Combined Books, 1993), p. 65.

[18] Quoted in Utley, *Cavalier in Buckskin,* p. 163.

The Sioux Campaign

[1] The Army also agreed to close three forts along the Powder River, abandoning the Bozeman Trail. Cf. Charles Francis Roe, "Custer's Last Battle," a monograph published by the National Highways Association (New York City, 1927), p. 1. For information on the Sioux campaign generally, see Wayne Michael Sarf, *The Little Bighorn Campaign, March–September 1876* (Conshohocken, Pa.: Combined Books, 1993); Robert M. Utley, *Custer and the Great Controversy* (Lincoln: University of Nebraska Press, 1998); and other works cited below.

[2] Sheridan's letter was reprinted in "The Black Hills," *New York Times*, March 27, 1875, p. 2.

[3] "The Black Hills Country," *New York Times*, January 25, 1876, p. 1.

[4] Senate Executive Document No. 81, vol. 1664, July 13, 1876.

[5] Col. F. W. Benteen, "An Account of the Little Big Horn Campaign," typescript copy, USMA Archives, p. 11.

[6] It was a victory of sorts, but unexploited and indecisive, and Crook brought charges against his operations commander Joseph J. Reynolds (USMA 1843). Colonel John Gibbon also took to the field from Montana, but was delayed by weather and accomplished little. A third column was to have been led by Custer and departed in early April, but on March 15 he was summoned to Washington to testify.

[7] See for example "A Vain Search for Gold," *New York Times*, April 30, 1876, p. 10. The story called the notion of gold in the Black Hills "the champion swindle of the Centennial year."

[8] Quoted in Evan S. Connell, *Son of the Morning Star: Custer and the Little Bighorn* (San Francisco: North Point Press, 1984), p. 106.

[9] Dale E. Brown, "Sherman and the Reporter," *Parameters*, August 2004.

[10] Custer quoted in Sarf, *The Little Bighorn Campaign*, p. 135.

[11] The order in full reads:

H.Q. OF THE DEPARTMENT OF DACOTA (IN THE FIELD), MOUTH OF THE ROSEBUD RIVER, MONTANA. 22nd June, 1876.

COLONEL, The General commanding the Brigade directs that as soon as your regiment is ready to march you are to leave the Rosebud River and follow up the Indian trail discovered by Major Reynolds a few days ago. It is of course impossible to give you definite instructions as to your movements. Even were it otherwise, the Officer in Command has too much confidence in your zeal, energy and skill to give you directions which might hamper your freedom of action when you have got into touch with the enemy. He wishes nevertheless to inform you as to his views with regard to your movements and as to the manner in which he desires the latter to be executed, unless you see good reason to depart from his wishes. In his opinion you should follow up the Rosebud until the direction of the above-mentioned trail has been ascertained with certainty. If it leads towards the Little Big Horn (as there is every likelihood of its doing) you are nevertheless to continue your advance southwards, till you reach approximately the source of the Tongue River and only then proceed towards the Little Horn, reconnoitring continually to your left in the meantime in order to prevent any Indians who might be tempted to go round your left flank, from escaping in a southerly or south-easterly direction. Colonel Gibbons' detachment is now on the march towards the mouth of the Big Horn. Immediately upon his arrival there he will cross the Yellowstone River and advance at any rate as far as the confluence of the Big and Little Horn Rivers. His subsequent movements will naturally depend upon circumstances. It is hoped, however, that the Indians on the Little Horn will be surrounded by both detachments in such a manner as to render their escape impossible. The officer in command of the Department desires you to reconnoitre very carefully the upper part of Tullock Creek during your march along the Rosebud, and to get into touch with Colonel Gibbons' detachment by means of your scouts, and inform him of the results of your investigations. The lower portion of Tullock Creek will be reconnoitred by Colonel Gibbons' detachment. The auxiliary steamer will proceed up the Big Horn as far as the fork, if the river appears navigable. The officer in command of the Department (who is with Colonel Gibbons' detachment) desires to receive your report before the expiration of the period for which your troops have received supplies, unless in the meantime you receive orders to the contrary.

With great respect, Your obedient servant, ED. W. SMITH, Captain 18th Regiment of Infantry, A.A.A.G. To Colonel G. A. CUSTER, 7th Regiment of Cavalry.

Had Terry wanted Custer to stick to the plan, he should not have given him so many loopholes to exploit; Terry's temporizing language gave ample room for interpretation and adaptation to the Custer way of war.

[12] Letter to Libbie, June 22, 1876.

[13] Edward C. Bailly, "Echoes from Custer's Last Fight: Accounts by an Officer Survivor Never Before Published," *Military Affairs*, Winter 1953, p. 176.

[14] A. Ward, "The Little Bighorn," *American Heritage*, April 1992; Sarf, *The Little Bighorn Campaign*, p. 160; Benteen, "An Account of the Little Big Horn Campaign," p. 1.

Little Bighorn

[1] Godfrey quoted in Wayne Michael Sarf, *The Little Bighorn Campaign, March–September 1876* (Conshohocken, Pa.: Combined Books, 1993), p. 175.

[2] Diary of Trooper Pat Coleman, USMA Archives.

[3] Col. F. W. Benteen, "An Account of the Little Big Horn Campaign," typescript copy, USMA Archives, p. 9.

[4] Marguerite Merington, ed., *The Custer Story: The Life and Intimate Letters of General George A. Custer and His Wife Elizabeth* (New York: Devin-Adair, 1950), p. 315.

[5] Custer led C, E, F, I and L troops; Reno had A, G and M troops; Benteen led D, H and K troops; B troops guarded the mule train.

[6] Edgerly in Edward C. Bailly, "Echoes from Custer's Last Fight: Accounts by an Officer Survivor Never Before Published," *Military Affairs*, Winter 1953, p. 173.

[7] Letter to General Edward S. Godfrey, August 17, 1908, USMA Archives. O'Neill was Lt. McIntosh's cook; later he was a sergeant. He died in 1914 and is buried in Arlington National Cemetery. See also Robert M. Utley, *Cavalier in Buckskin: George Armstrong Custer and the Western Military Frontier* (Norman: University of Oklahoma Press, 1988), p. 183.

[8] Sergeant John M. Ryan, *Hardin Tribune*, June 22, 1923. Ryan was first sergeant for Company M.

[9] "Account of Battle at Little Bighorn, by Two Moon," History Resource Center, Farmington Hills, Mich.: Gale Group, Document No. BT2352000951.

[10] Charles Francis Roe, *Custer's Last Battle* (New York: National Highways Association, 1927), p. 9.

[11] Kanipe in Sarf, *The Little Bighorn Campaign*, p. 212.

[12] In ibid., pp. 213–14.

[13] Edgerly in ibid., p. 216.

[14] Benteen, "An Account of the Little Big Horn Campaign," p. 9.

[15] Probably the most thorough attempt at reconstruction is John S. Gray, *Custer's Last Campaign: Mitch Boyer and the Little Bighorn Reconsidered* (Lincoln: University of Nebraska Press, 1991).

[16] Cf. generally, *Lakota Recollections of the Custer Fight*, ed. Richard G. Hardorff (Lincoln: University of Nebraska Press, 1991).

[17] See for example the interview in "The Death of Gen. Custer: Sitting Bull Tells the Story of the Fight," *New York Times*, May 7, 1881, p. 3. In this version, Sitting Bull and Custer engaged in lengthy negotiations via letters exchanged in the days before the battle, and during

the fight, lightning struck down many of the soldiers and their horses, indicating that the Great Spirit was on the Indians' side.

[18] "The Custer Fight," *New York Times,* August 10, 1881, p. 2, from the Fort Yates correspondent of the *Cincinnati Commercial.*

[19] Ibid.

[20] "Account of Battle at Little Bighorn, by Two Moon."

[21] Cf. Richard Allan Fox Jr., *Archaeology, History, and Custer's Last Battle: The Little Big Horn Reexamined* (Norman: University of Oklahoma Press, 1993).

[22] E. J. McClernand, "The Fight on Custer Hill," in Roe, *Custer's Last Battle,* p. 38. McClernand received the Medal of Honor for bravery at Bear Paw Mountain during the Nez Perce War a year after the Custer battle.

[23] "A Talk with Sitting Bull," *New York Times,* August 7, 1881, p. 2.

[24] In W. A. Graham, *The Custer Myth: A Source Book of Custeriana* (Lincoln: University of Nebraska Press, 1986), p. 345.

[25] H. W. Longfellow, "The Revenge of Rain-in-the-Face," *West Point Tic Tacs: A Collection of Military Verse, together with a Special Poem, "Cadet Grey," by Bret Harte* (New York: H. Lee & Co., 1878), pp. 113–14.

[26] C.f. Robert M. Utley, *Custer and the Great Controversy* (Lincoln: University of Nebraska Press, 1998), pp. 125ff.

[27] "Gen. Custer's Murderer," *New York Times,* February 12, 1881, p. 1.

[28] "The Custer Fight," *New York Times,* August 10, 1881, p. 2, from the Fort Yates correspondent of the *Cincinnati Commercial.*

[29] Ibid.

[30] Ibid.

[31] Thomas B. Marquis, *Keep the Last Bullet for Yourself* (New York: Reference Publications Inc., 1976).

[32] "Another Story of Gen. Custer's Death," *New York Times,* January 7, 1883, p. 5, reprinted from the *Mile City* [Montana] *Journal.*

[33] Benteen quoted in Evan S. Connell, *Son of the Morning Star: Custer and the Little Bighorn* (San Francisco: North Point Press, 1984), p. 78.

My Every Thought Was Ambition

[1] "The Causes and Consequences," *New York Times,* July 7, 1876, p. 1.

[2] Canby was an Immortal of the Class of 1839, graduating next to last. He was a veteran of the Seminole, Mexican and Civil wars, and was the only Regular U.S. general to die in the Indian wars.

[3] "What Is Thought in Washington," *New York Times,* July 8, 1876, p. 1.

[4] "Politics Run Mad," *New York Times,* July 8, 1876, p. 4.

[5] Ibid.

[6] George McClellan, *McClellan's Own Story: the war for the union, the soldiers who fought it, the civilians who directed it, and his relations to them* (New York: Charles L. Webster & Co., 1886), p. 365.

[7] Godfrey to Roe, February 28, 1918, USMA Archives.

[8] Quoted in Charles Francis Roe, *Custer's Last Battle* (New York: National Highways Association, 1927), p. 34.

[9] Grant quoted in Robert M. Utley, *Custer and the Great Controversy* (Lincoln: University of Nebraska Press, 1998), p. 44.

[10] Crittenden letter quoted in James B. Fry, "Comments by General Fry on the Custer Battle," *The Century,* January 1892, p. 387, n. 2.

[11] Interview with Sturgis, originally printed in the *Chicago Tribune,* reprinted in the *Army and Navy Journal,* July 29, 1876. See also Sturgis in "Gen. Custer's Death," *New York Times,* July 17, 1876, p. 5; "Gen. Custer's Death," *New York Times,* July 18, 1876, p. 5; and "Sturgis on Custer," *New York Times,* July 21, 1876, p. 8.

[12] Terry's communiqués were reprinted in the *New York Times,* July 7, 1876, p. 1.

[13] In 1967, the Army Board of Corrections reversed the decision of the court martial, and Reno was reburied with honors at the Custer Battlefield National Cemetery.

[14] See John S. Gray, "Nightmares to Daydreams," *By Valor and Arms: Journal of American Military History,* vol. 1 (Summer 1975), pp. 30–39, for information on parties visiting the battlefield.

[15] "General Custer's Burial," *New York Times,* September 13, 1878. See also Douglas D. Scott, P. Willey and Melissa A. Connor, *They Died with Custer: Soldiers' Bones from the Battle of the Little Bighorn* (Norman: University of Oklahoma Press, 1999).

[16] "Officers Who Died with Custer," *New York Times,* August 4, 1877, p. 5.

[17] Quoted in *New York Times,* May 21, 1877, p. 1.

[18] Crittenden's isolated gravesite was not being properly cared for, though the family was at first told it was because of a plan to relocate a road.

[19] Cf. "Gen. Custer's Remains," *New York Times,* September 1, 1878.

[20] The spur is in the possession of the Virginia Historical Society.

The Immortals

[1] Poe, "The Assignation."

[2] In fact, 1880 was the first of ten straight "Solid South" elections for the Democrats.

[3] Obituary in the *Montrose Independent Republican*, September 17, 1920, USMA Archives.

[4] Buckner was governor of Kentucky, 1887–91, and Democratic vice presidential candidate in 1896.

[5] Morris Schaff, *The Spirit of Old West Point, 1858–1862* (New York: Houghton, Mifflin & Co., 1907), p. 174.

[6] Cf. Elizabeth D. Leonard, *Lincoln's Avengers: Justice, Revenge and Reunion after the Civil War* (New York: W. W. Norton & Co., 2004).

[7] The equivalent of over $1 million today.

[8] "Jeff Davis to a Classmate," *New York Times*, March 7, 1886.

[9] "Reinterment at Richmond," *New York Times*, June 1, 1893, p. 5.

[10] Baker was also the representative of the Southern Express Company.

[11] "A Quarrel and Its Ending," *New York Times*, June 4, 1893.

[12] Longstreet's wife Louise died in 1889, and in 1897 he married Helen Dortch, his daughter's roommate at Brenau College, a woman less than half his age. She died in 1962 at age 99.

[13] Pickett, *Soldier of the South*, pp. 152–53.

[14] See John S. Mosby, *The Memoirs of Colonel John S. Mosby*, ed. Charles Wells Russell (Boston: Little, Brown & Co.), pp. 381–82, and an exchange of letters in the *Richmond Times-Dispatch*, March 21, 25 and April 2, 1911 between, respectively, Mosby, Miss K. C. Stiles and Dr. M. G. Elzey.

[15] Quoted in John Brown Gordon, *Reminiscences of the Civil War* (New York: Charles Scribner's Sons, 1904), pp. 157, 162–63, 167.

[16] Note that Sallie Pickett was not allowed to be buried alongside George because of concerns that every Confederate widow would want the same consideration. Her remains were placed in a vault near Arlington National Cemetery, which over time became rundown and neglected. Sallie was finally allowed to join George at Hollywood Cemetery in 1998.

[17] James L. Morrison Jr., *The Memoirs of Henry Heth: The Young Cavalier*, Master's Thesis, The University of Virginia, 1960, p. 326.

[18] On Waterloo, see John Keegan, *The Face of Battle* (New York: Penguin Books, 1978), pp. 117–21. The Duke of Wellington was frustrated at the excessive emphasis placed on the battle, which he felt should be left "as it is." One example of the symbolic power of the battle was the fate of Captain Keogh's horse. Captain Miles W. Keogh was born in Ireland and saw action in Europe as a member of the Battalion of St. Patrick in the Papal Guard. He died at Little Bighorn, and his horse, Comanche, was severely wounded by bullets and arrows but survived. In 1878, Colonel Sturgis issued an order stating that

the kind treatment of the horse "should be a matter of pride and solic-
itude on the part of every member of the Seventh Cavalry....
Wounded and scarred as he is, his very existence speaks in terms more
eloquent than words of the desperate struggle against overwhelming
numbers of the hopeless conflict and of the heroic manner in which
all went down on that fateful day." He ordered that Comanche "will
not be ridden by any person whatever, under any circumstances, nor
will he be put to any kind of work." He was paraded draped in
mourning garb on all the regiment's ceremonial occasions. Blacksmith Gustave Korn, who had fought at Little Bighorn, helped care
for Comanche until he was killed at the Battle of Wounded Knee in
1890. Comanche then began to fail, and died November 6, 1891. The
body was preserved, and is still on display at the Natural History
Museum at the University of Kansas.

[19] "General George A. Custer," *The Galaxy,* September 1876, p. 363.

[20] Walt Whitman, "Custer's Last Rally," *Specimen Days.* See also Robert
Taft, "The Pictorial Record of the Old West. IV. Custer's Last Stand.
John Mulvany, Cassilly Adams and Otto Becker," *Kansas Historical
Quarterly,* November 1946, pp. 361–90.

[21] "In Memory of Custer," *New York Times,* August 31, 1879, p. 7.
McDonald's best-known work is probably his bust of Washington Irving in Prospect Park, Brooklyn, completed in 1871. He was chosen
as the sculptor in part because he offered to raise approximately one-
third of the funds, though he failed to meet that goal. On December
21, 1878, Congress authorized using twenty surplus bronze cannon
for the Custer memorial project. Mr. James Gordon Bennett, pub-
lisher of the *New York Herald,* organized a private donation drive.
Thurlow Weed was chairman of the statue fund. Winfield Scott Hancock was an associate member.

[22] "Ending the Cadet Year," *New York Times,* June 8, 1882, p. 5.

[23] "The Duchess Peace Society," *New York Times,* September 1, 1879,
p. 5.

[24] Letter by Elizabeth Bacon Custer to Representative Daggett of
Nevada, quoted in "West Point's Custer Statue," *New York Times,*
April 23, 1880, p. 5, and April 24, 1880.

[25] Elizabeth Custer to General William T. Sherman, January 1, 1882,
USMA Archives.

[26] Spurgin memo, December 31, 1898, USMA Archives.

[27] Cf. Charles C. Baldwin, *Stanford White* (New York: Da Capo Press,
1976), pp. 41, 321–22; and Suzannah Lessard, "Architect of Desire,"
Washington Monthly, December 1996, p. 42. The style that White

wished to bring to West Point is embodied in Roosevelt Hall, the home of the National War College, at Fort Lesley J. McNair in Washington, D.C.

Whither the Goat?

[1] Cf. James S. Robbins, "Powhatan Clarke, Gallant Goat of the Class of 1884," *Assembly,* March/April 2003.

[2] The feat was noted in "Duncan's Remarkable Run," *Washington Post,* November 19, 1893, p. 6.

[3] Press release, USMA Archives file "Goats."

[4] Final Report of the West Point Study Group, July 27, 1977, p. 65.

[5] Ibid., p. 65.

[6] Ibid., p. 90.

INDEX

481